MW00637064

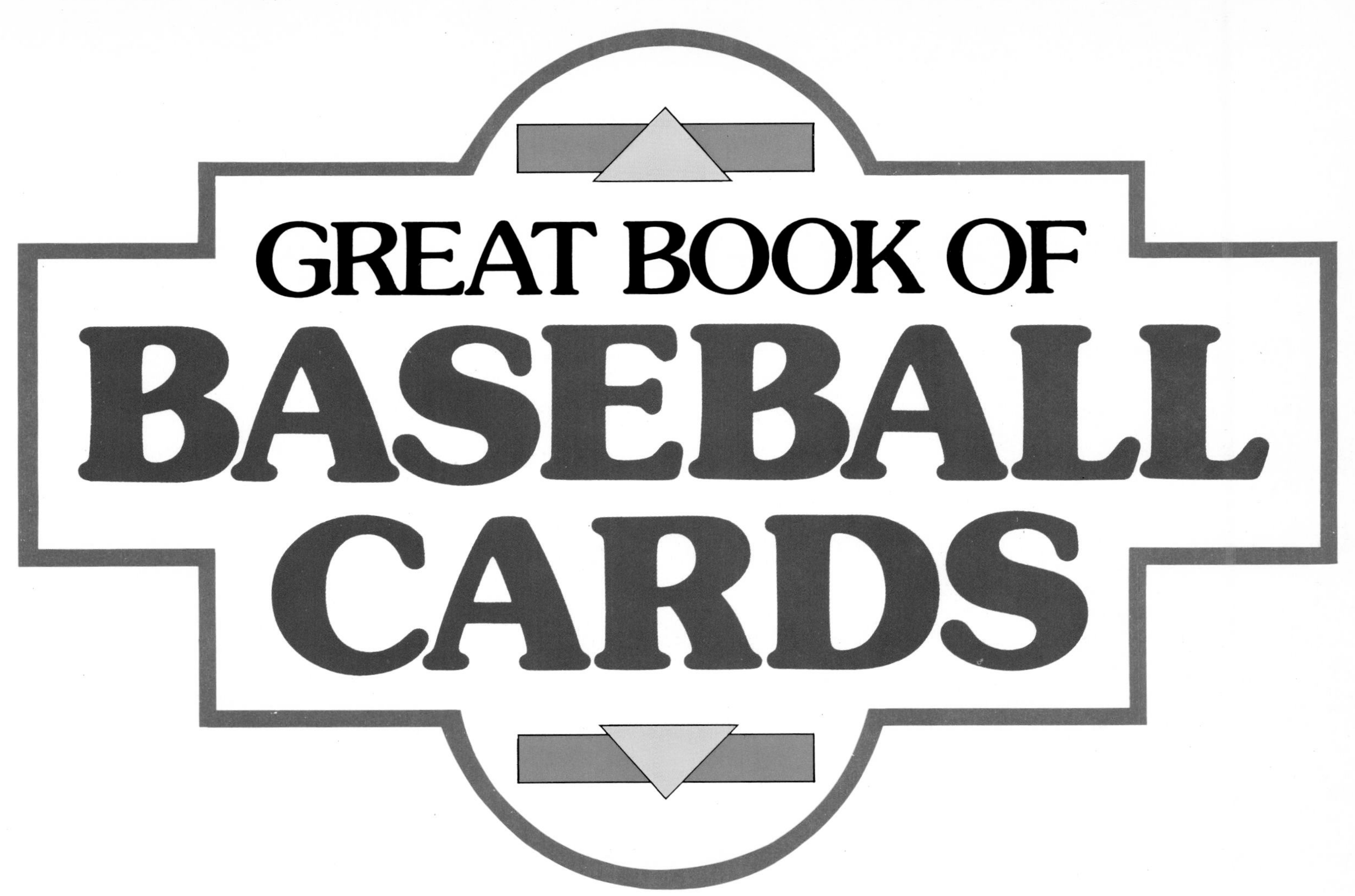

BEEKMAN HOUSE

Manufactured in Yugoslavia

h g f e d c b a

ISBN 0-517-68759-3

Library of Congress Catalog Card Number: 89-60925

This edition published by Beekman House,
Distributed by Crown Publishers, Inc.,
225 Park Avenue South,
New York, New York 10003

Contributing authors: Tom Owens, Steven Ellingboe, H.R. Ted Taylor, Robert Lemke
Photography: Sam Griffith Studios, Inc.
Special thanks to: AU Sports Memorabilia, Skokie, Illinois
Sports Collectors Store, La Grange, Illinois
Bill Mastro

CONTENTS

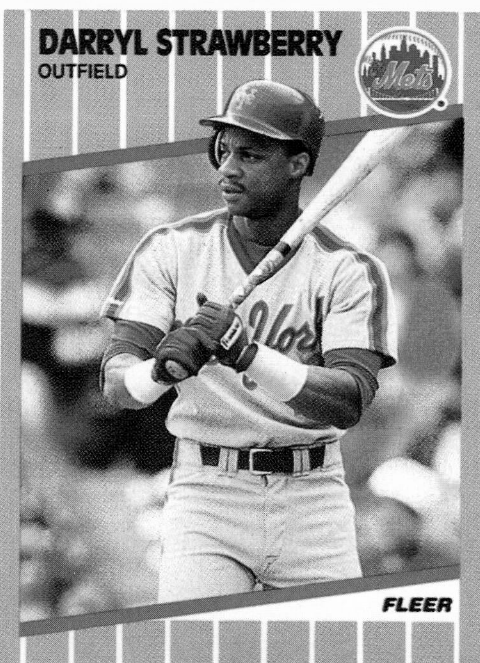

1989 Fleer, Darryl Strawberry

1989 to 1980

1985 Topps, Mark McGwire

CONTENTS

1984 Donruss, Don Mattingly

1981 Topps, George Brett

1979 to 1970

CONTENTS

1969 to 1960

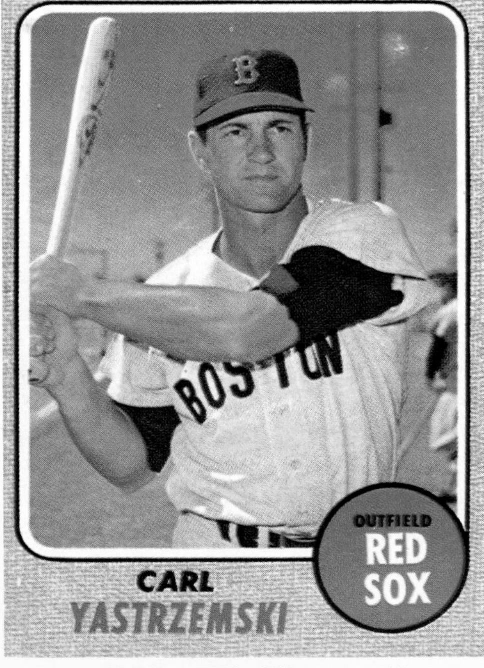

1968 Topps, Carl Yastrzemski

1959 Topps, Sandy Koufax

1959 to 1950

1954 Bowman, Jimmy Piersall

1949 to 1940

1949 Bowman, Satchel Paige

1939 Play Ball, Charlie Gehringer

1939 to 1930

1929 to 1920

1919 to 1910

1912 T-207 Brown Background, Zack Wheat

1909 to 1900

1909-1911 White Border, Tris Speaker

19th CENTURY

1888 Yum Yum, Jimmy Ryan

INTRODUCTION

Baseball cards have been around for more than 100 years—almost as long as the game itself—and right from the start people began collecting them. The earliest baseball cards were small local issues given out by the home-town heroes to promote the team—and the game. One of the first sets was produced by the N.L. pennant-winning Boston club and featured tiny $1 \times 2''$ photographs of the players. Baseball cards were to become a nationwide phenomenon during the 1880s, thanks to the tobacco industry. Machinery capable of mass-producing cigarettes had finally been invented, replacing the laborious hand-rolling process. For the first time, cigarettes could be made and sold cheaply. Virtually overnight, hundreds of small cigarette companies sprang up, and the competition was fierce. In order to entice smokers to buy their brand, tobacco companies began including a premium card in each pack of cigarettes. The small, colorful cards featured a wide range of subjects—movie stars, military uniforms, bathing beauties, animals, and even flags. The cards served a dual purpose: not only did they increase sales, they also helped stiffen the package, protecting the cigarettes.

In 1887 a Richmond, Virginia, cigarette company by the name of Allen & Ginter produced a set of 40 cards featuring the "Worlds Champions." Among the Oarsmen, Wrestlers, Pugilists, Rifle Shooters, Billiard Players, and Pool Players there were 10 baseball players included. These were the first nationally-distributed baseball cards ever produced. The idea caught on quickly, and by the following year, several other tobacco companies were using baseball cards to sell cigarettes. A uniquely American institution had been born.

Baseball cards were more than just a sales gimmick; they also played an important role in promoting the game. Before the days of television, the only contact most youngsters had with baseball was their local home-grown team. With baseball cards, kids could collect photos of big-name players they might never see in real life. Not surprisingly, as baseball grew in popularity, so did baseball card collecting.

The first phase of baseball card production came to an end in 1890, when most of the tobacco companies went out of business or merged. By the turn of the century, the powerful American Tobacco Company had swallowed up most of the competition and controlled virtually the entire cigarette market, there was little need for baseball cards to increase sales.

In the first decade of the twentieth century, there was a resurgence in baseball card production.

1888 Allen & Ginter, Jimmy Ryan

1888 Allen & Ginter, John Morrill

Baseball was now "the national pastime," and tobacco companies had a new gimmick to promote—the addition of Turkish tobacco to their cigarettes. Candy companies also jumped on the bandwagon and began including baseball cards in packages of caramels, mints, and chewing gum. A few years later, the start of World War I, a confusing proliferation of leagues, and the "Black Sox" scandal produced another lull. Caramel cards were big once again during the '20s, but then the Depression created another slump. Throughout the last 100 years, interest in baseball card collecting has waxed and waned but never died out completely, and now it's more popular than ever. Baseball cards have been used to promote every imaginable product; not just cigarettes and candy, but newspapers, bread, gasoline, clothes, cookies, hot dogs, potato chips, milk, soda pop, dog food, cereal, and gelatin desserts, just to name a few. When people realized that baseball cards were hot items all by themselves, the great card-producing companies like Goudey, Bowman, and Topps were born.

Today, baseball card collecting is incredibly popular. There are thousands of dealers and collectors nationwide, dozens of books, magazines and newsletters devoted to collecting, and card shows in every town. Baseball cards are now sought by investors as well as kids, for card prices can rise quickly, and even fairly recent sets can command hefty prices.

1933 Delong, Lefty Gomez

HOW TO COLLECT BASEBALL CARDS

One of the great things about baseball cards is that there is no right or wrong way to collect them. For those who are new to the hobby, however, a few words of advice might come in handy.

Perhaps the most important thing to do when you decide to start collecting baseball cards is to set goals. Nobody can collect everything; there are over a quarter of a million different baseball cards around. Choose your goals carefully. Decide what appeals to you, keeping an eye on your budget and the amount of time and energy you have to devote to collecting. Don't make your goals so easy that they're quickly attained or you'll soon lose interest. On the other hand, don't set your sights too high or you'll become discouraged.

The traditional approach has been to collect complete sets: one of each card issued by a particular company in a particular year. If you limit yourself to recent sets, this is usually a reasonable goal. As you get into some of the older sets, however, the price per card becomes too high for all but the wealthiest collectors. But don't worry: as more and more of the earlier baseball card sets have been priced out of the reach of full-set collectors, other modes of collecting have become just as popular.

Team collecting is a popular alternative to full-set collecting. You probably have one or two favorite teams, either from the past or present: why not specialize in the cards of those teams? You can collect cards from the team's entire history or from a particular era. Many team collectors begin at the point when they first became fans and collect from that point forward.

Superstar collecting is also quite popular. Again, each collector decides who is a superstar and who isn't. Your favorite player may be at the bottom of someone else's list, so there's plenty of room for everybody in this field. The great thing about superstar collecting is that your collection is almost never finished. To collect all of a player's cards, you will probably have to explore some unfamiliar territory: minor league sets, scarce regional issues, and other obscure sets. Some of these are likely to be expensive as well as hard to find. The bigger the star, the more cards he was pictured on, and the greater the challenge and expense of finding them all. Collectors of current superstars will find new issues each year to keep their collections alive.

An outgrowth of the superstar collecting craze is rookie card collecting. There's something special about a great player's first card, and it is usually the scarcest and most expensive of his cards. Rookie cards are popular with baseball card speculators. They buy up dozens of a player's first card, hoping he becomes a superstar. If he does, the cards can skyrocket in value, netting the speculator a nice profit. If you like a little action, rookie card speculation can liven things up.

Another specialty that is catching on is type collecting, where you try to collect just one card from each set. Again you should set limits: there are enough sets in existence to keep you busy and broke for the rest of your days. A reasonable goal might be to try to acquire one card from each set in this book. Or you could limit your collection to the post-World War II era, to tobacco cards, or to any type or era of baseball cards that appeals to you.

One final word about building a baseball card collection: condition. Of two identical baseball

1940 Play Ball, Honus Wagner

cards, the one in better condition is always worth more money. Most collectors want cards that are as close to original condition as possible. This means that if the cards were issued in panels on the back of cereal boxes, complete panels will be worth more than single cards, and entire boxes are worth the most. Cards that are in good shape will retain their value better and increase in value faster than cards in poor condition. Always try to collect the highest grade your budget allows.

Card grading is important because it helps buyers and sellers know what to expect, especially when dealing by mail. Unfortunately, unlike coins or diamonds, there is no single accepted grading system for baseball cards. There are standard terms, but some of them can be confusing (Near Mint and Excellent, for example). Each collector tends to grade cards his own way, so when bargaining with a dealer, ask what each term means. Some dealers and hobbyists don't pay much attention to grading, but always try to classify your cards when buying and selling. The following guide explains what to look for when grading your cards.

Mint (MT): A perfect card. Well-centered, with four sharp, square corners. No creases, edge dents, surface scratches, yellowing or fading, regardless of age. No printing imperfections (card out of register, badly cut). No stains from gum, wax, or other substances.

Excellent to Mint (EX-MT): A nearly perfect card. May have one or two corners that are not perfectly sharp. May have minor printing imperfections. No creases or scruffiness on surface. May show hint of paper or ink aging.

Excellent (EX): Corners and edges no longer sharp, though not markedly rounded or dented. Centering may be off, but all borders must show. No creases. Surfaces may show slight loss of original gloss.

Very Good (VG): Shows obvious handling. Corners are rounded and perhaps creased. One or two other minor creases may be visible. Surfaces exhibit some loss of luster, but all printing is intact. May show moderate gum, wax, or other stains. No major creases. No tape marks, markings, or writing. Exhibits no actual damage, just a lot of handling.

Good (G): Shows excessive wear or abuse. May have thumbtack holes in the margin, corners rounded into the design, or small tears. Has one or more major creases, breaking the paper, and several minor creases. May have some writing or stains. Back may have been taped or pasted, and small areas may be missing.

Fair (F): Has been tortured to death. Corners or other areas may be torn off. Card may have been trimmed or paper punched. Major portions of front or back printing may be missing. These cards are not considered collectible.

1953 Bowman Color, Stan Musial

1958 Topps, Mickey Mantle, Hank Aaron

HOW TO USE THIS BOOK

This book attempts to present the most information about baseball card collecting available between two covers, but it is not all-inclusive. There are just too many baseball card sets around for any book to cover them all. Besides, not all sets are considered truly collectible: many are too obscure, too rare, or just not popular with collectors. Therefore, we have chosen to concentrate only on those sets that are most popularly collected today.

The question of what constitutes a "real" baseball card must also be addressed. For the purposes of this book, a baseball card is defined as a picture of a contemporary baseball player on paper or cardboard in a size that can be held in the palm of the hand. With a few exceptions, we have excluded over-size cards, team-issued postcards, 5 × 7″ and 8 × 10″ photos, the small strip cards of the 1920s, and most of the various coins, discs, and other odd-size items that have appeared over the years.

If you are a novice collector, this book will help you focus on the most popular, collectible, and attainable sets. As you advance in the hobby, you may become interested in some of the rarer sets. If so, there are books with information and checklists on every obscure issue imaginable. But for the vast majority of hobbyists, this book should suffice: it covers enough interesting, collectible, and valuable baseball card sets to keep the average collector busy for years.

This book is arranged with the most recent sets first. It starts with 1989 and works backwards, with the oldest sets at the end of the book. Each listing is identified by the year of issue and the name of the company that produced it or the name by which it is known to collectors. Full-size color photographs of representative cards from each set are presented as an aid to identification.

Each listing includes six basic sections of information. The SPECIFICATIONS gives the card dimensions in inches, the basic layout of the card front and back, and the area and method of distribution. (The process of cutting the cards apart on the printing sheet was not always as accurate as it is today, and these sizes should be considered "ideal" and not exact. Excessive wear or actual trimming may also change the dimensions of a card.)

The HISTORY section tells the story behind each card set. You learn how it compared with other sets, and whether it was popular or panned by collectors. There is a detailed description of the card front and back, and any special subsets, rarities, or unusual features are also outlined. The good and bad points of each issue are then summarized in the FOR and AGAINST sections. The NOTEWORTHY CARDS describes any cards that are especially scarce, expensive, or unusual, including some of the more interesting error cards. Some sets also have a section called OUR FAVORITE CARD, where we reveal the fascinating stories behind some of the most unusual and interesting cards in the hobby.

Each listing ends with a VALUE section, which lists the price you can expect to pay for each set. Since there are entire books dedicated to listing the price of every card in every set, we have only listed the prices for complete sets, common cards, and any cards that command a premium. This should give you a pretty good idea of which sets are within your budget. We also give a 5-YEAR PROJECTION, which is an educated guess as to how well a set will appreciate over the long term compared with other sets: average, below average, above average, etc. For the purposes of this book, the "average" rate of appreciation is assumed to be about 10 percent per year. Remember this 5-year projection is only a rough estimate. Before investing or speculating in any baseball card, you should make your own appraisal of its potential as an investment. It is always a good idea to consult a reputable dealer when buying or selling baseball cards.

1985 Donruss, Kirby Puckett

1989 Fleer, Jose Canseco, Terry Steinbach, Mark McGwire

1989 TO 1980

1980 Topps, Mike Schmidt

1987 Fleer, Dwight Gooden

1986 Donruss The Rookies, Jose Canseco

1989 TOPPS

SPECIFICATIONS

SIZE: 2½ × 3½″. FRONT: Color photograph. BACK: Black and red printing on gray cardboard. DISTRIBUTION: Nationally, in 15-, 28-, or 54-card packages; complete sets sold through hobby dealers; factory-collated sets available through select retail chains.

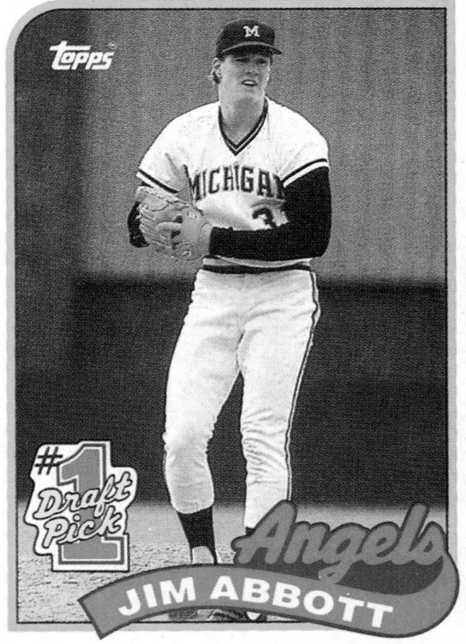

1989 Topps, Jim Abbott

1989 Topps, Tim Raines

1989 Topps, Gary Sheffield

HISTORY

Topps followed an impressive 1988 set with another sterling offering for the 1989 season. This 792-card set stuck with last year's white border. Few frills on each card front provide for a large, undisturbed photo (which includes rounded corners). The design of the 1989 Topps cards uses only a tiny company logo and cursive color team banner at the card bottom. The player's name is indicated in block letters, while the player position is omitted. Some card backs contain a new twist: a feature titled "1988 Monthly Scoreboard" shows how well a player produced in two offensive or pitching categories during each month of the 1988 season. Topps continues its devotion to detail by including minor league statistics on card backs. The 1989 set includes 700 individual player cards and several intriguing subsets. For the first time, ten "#1 Draft Pick" cards are included. These unique cards show promising rookies (most former Olympians) in their college uniforms, and gives their college stats and the major league teams that drafted them. Andy Benes, Jim Abbott, Steve Avery, Mark Lewis, Gregg Olson, Bill Bene, Robin Ventura, Ty Griffin, Willie Ansley, and Monty Fariss are highlighted in the set, representing baseball's first ten draft picks. Five rookies—Gregg Jefferies of the New York Mets, Steve Searcy of the Detroit Tigers, Mike Harkey of the Chicago Cubs, Sandy Alomar Jr. of the San Diego Padres, and Gary Sheffield of the Milwaukee Brewers—get specially marked "Future Star" cards. Topps, unlike other card companies, continues to recognize team managers with their own cards. Topps produced 22 All-Star cards that honor last year's participants (11 from each league). This gives superstar card collectors an extra challenge. Seven "Record Breakers" cards are available as well, making up the first seven cards in the set. George Bell, Wade Boggs, Gary Carter, Andre Dawson, Orel Hershiser, Doug Jones, and Kevin McReynolds are found on these cards. Topps salutes five bygone seasons with the "Turn Back the Clock" subset. Past Topps superstar cards are reprinted, and highlights from the 1964, 1969, 1974, 1979, and 1984 seasons are remembered. The 26 "Team Leaders" cards are horizontals, recalling Topps sets from the 1950s. The photos aren't identified on the Leaders cards, but many superstars (such as Darryl Strawberry, Mike Schmidt, Eric Davis, Tim Raines, and Bo Jackson) are shown in action in the subset. Because the photos of players aren't labeled, hobbyists have a chance to acquire shots of their favorite stars at lower prices. Incidentally, Topps bowed to Raines' wishes on card #560. They refer to the Expo star by his nickname "Rock" for the first time ever in the 1989 set.

FOR

Topps continued to be the biggest and the best. However, the 1989 set proved that Topps is willing to experiment with innovations while maintaining the quality collectors expect.

AGAINST

Few criticisms can be leveled against this outstanding set. Some investors may unfairly grumble that the 1989 Topps cards were too available, making them affordable to everyone.

NOTEWORTHY CARDS

As the largest set on the market, Topps provided the biggest variety of stars for collectors to choose from. The #1 Draft Pick subset was hotly pursued by many rookie card buffs. As usual, Don Mattingly, Jose Canseco, Roger Clemens, and Mark McGwire were popular cards, along with those of relative newcomers like Ricky Jordan, Chris Sabo, Sheffield, and Jefferies. Card #150 may be the only opportunity to see Fernando Valenzuela wearing a moustache.

VALUE

MINT CONDITION: Complete set, \$19; common card, 3¢–5¢; stars, rookies, 15¢–50¢; #1 Draft Picks, 50¢–\$1; superstars, hot rookies, 75¢–\$2. 5-YEAR PROJECTION: Well above average.

1989 FLEER

SPECIFICATIONS

SIZE: 2½ × 3½". FRONT: Color photograph. BACK: Black and yellow printing on gray cardboard. DISTRIBUTION: Nationally, in 15- or 54-card packages; complete sets sold through hobby dealers; factory-collated sets available through select retail chains.

1989 Fleer, Shane Rawley

1989 Fleer, Ken Griffey Jr.

1989 Fleer, Jose Canseco

HISTORY

The 1989 Fleer set has to be the most peculiar design the Philadelphia-based company has ever created for its regular issue. Creative, well-focused photos make up this set, but many of the photographs are blighted by the layout of the cards. Each photo rests on a gray background sliced up by white vertical stripes. Little space on the card is devoted to the player photo. The overly complicated design (which looks too much like one of Fleer's mass-produced 44-card boxed sets from 1988) gets more muddled when the player's head emerges from the background in an attempt to create a three-dimensional effect. The colored stripe bordering the top of each photo unpleasantly bisects the player's head. Also, some heads are poorly trimmed. The awkward card design forces shoddy cropping of several player photos. Card #341 of Ernest Riles misspells his first name on the front and back ("Earnest") and totally removes the bat from his hands; all the card shows is a player in a hitting crouch. Some hitters wind up swinging wooden fragments because the gray background blocks out most of the bat. Majestic swings are cut off by the cards' frills. Pitcher Shane Rawley (#579) was meant to be shown in his windup; however, it looks like he has no arms due to bad photo editing. Fleer made a futile attempt to remedy their stark card backs of the past. "Did you know?" is a space-filler inserted where players have few career statistics. The most interesting feature on Fleer backs is a chart detailing the player's performance before and after the All-Star game. Fleer continued with their "combo" cards in 1989, but little effort was put into these special cards. A card saluting Tom Browning's perfect game (#629) uses a hastily cropped group photo (a Reds teammate gets half his face in the shot). Other group photos aren't even posed. They rely on the coincidence of several notable players standing next to each other. Catchy titles like "Cannon Arms" and "Double Trouble" can only stretch so far. One of the most fascinating variations in collector history occurred in the 1989 Fleer set. Card #616 of Billy Ripken originally showed an obscenity written on his bat. Fleer immediately pulled the card, airbrushed the bat, and released a new version. Due to the unusual subject matter and scarcity, the first card may be quite rare in years to come. Rookie card fans get old-fashioned offerings from Fleer. Two rookies share the same card through duo portraits in this set, which is a mixed blessing. Having a flash-in-the-pan share a card with a budding superstar is disappointing; however, a Fleer rookie card that contains two successful rookies would be the ultimate triumph in first-year cards. The best 1989 Fleers are the 12 All-Star cards. Each shows an action pose of a player against a fading green backdrop, with a player portrait inset in the lower right of each card. Card backs contain a paragraph describing the star's accomplishments. Unfortunately, these cards are randomly inserted in wax packs, and are not considered a vital part of the complete set. Fleer once again produced a meaningless subset of team logo stickers. The stickers, which have seldom been viewed as legitimate collectibles, were inserted in wax packs and factory-collated complete sets.

FOR

The cards are numbered by team. Therefore, if you're looking for a member of a certain club, you have a good idea where to look. Also, what you can see of the 1989 Fleer photos looks good.

AGAINST

Besides the strange makeup of the cards, Fleer has failed to make a sufficient quantity of cards available to the hobby in recent years. This artificially escalates value, but limits the number of collectors who can enjoy the cards.

NOTEWORTHY CARDS

Look for the usual superstars. Cards numbered 628 to 639 are the "special" group cards, and cards numbered 640 through 652 are rookie cards. All will have a traditionally strong appeal to many hobbyists.

VALUE

MINT CONDITION: Complete set, $21; common card, 4¢; stars, superstars, 10¢–$1; special cards, 15¢–50¢; rookie cards, 15¢–$2. 5-YEAR PROJECTION: Average to above average, depending on eventual availability.

1989 DONRUSS

SPECIFICATIONS

SIZE: 2½ × 3½″. FRONT: Color photograph. BACK: Black and orange printing on white cardboard. DISTRIBUTION: Nationally, in 15- or 54-card packages with jigsaw puzzle pieces; complete sets sold through hobby dealers; factory-collated sets available through select retail chains.

1989 Donruss, Mark Grace

1989 Donruss, Melido Perez

1989 Donruss, Gary Sheffield

HISTORY

Donruss offered another trendy design in its 660-card set for 1989. Card tops and bottoms are rainbow-bordered in a variety of colors, from purple to orange to red. Black side borders are highlighted with special shellacked horizontal stripes for a "reflectorized" effect. The card fronts are cluttered with large, all-too-obvious team logos and the company's "Donruss 89" trademark, which sometimes obscures photos. Photo quality is just a notch above Score's efforts among 1989 sets. Like Score, many photos are dark and shadowy; some Donruss photos seem like nothing more than silhouettes. The Donruss card backs are the same standard format dished out every year. Statistics are only offered for the past five seasons, and rookies are simply written off without any stats (despite their minor league accomplishments). "No major league record" is the sole explanation Donruss offers on these cards. Card backs, with black print on a bright orange background, are easy to read and sort. Each card back contains the player's full name (not just his nickname). Donruss backs are the only ones that offer a detailed explanation of how each player joined his current team (via trade, free agency, etc.). Also, the highlights section on the card back has changed from a mere reiteration of past statistics to an informative profile of a player's career. Often, a Donruss card will mention a player's previous injuries, his starting status with the team, or any club records he may hold. Donruss maintained most of the standard features of past sets with the 1989 issue. For the eighth straight year, Donruss designated the first 26 cards in the set as "Diamond

Kings." One player from each team has his portrait painted by sports artist Dick Perez. Autograph collectors love to get the special cards signed, but many mainstream hobbyists have tired of the art work. Perez, however, has to be credited for producing some of his finest creations in several years. The "Rated Rookies" returned in 1989 as specially marked cards (#28-#47). From the moment they were printed, the cards of Gary Sheffield and Gregg Jefferies (who appears for the second straight year for Donruss) were the hottest sellers in this subset. Three perforated puzzle pieces are the premiums in wax packs of Donruss cards. Hall of Famer Warren Spahn is the eighth player to be featured on a Donruss puzzle, which can be acquired through pieces in wax pack purchases or by purchasing a complete set. The complete puzzle (painted by Perez) is shown on one card in the set. Two "special" cards were issued by Donruss. Card #643 salutes Jose Canseco for exceeding 40 homers and 40 stolen bases. Card #648 is entitled "Orel—59 and Counting," saluting Orel Hershiser for his record-setting scoreless-inning streak. The card is truly entertaining: A grinning Hershiser is captured juggling baseballs for the camera.

FOR

A wealth of first-time cards for rookies (more than 90) make the 1989 Donruss set unique.

AGAINST

The photos aren't very stimulating in the 1989 set. Also, sorting problems in wax packs created artificial shortages of certain cards.

NOTEWORTHY CARDS

Investors love speculating on the futures of the many rookie cards in the set. The 26 Bonus Cards (one star player from each team) were randomly distributed in wax packs. Although they shouldn't be considered a part of the full set, "complete set" collectors enjoy pursuing them.

VALUE

MINT CONDITION: Complete set, $20; common card, 3¢; stars, rookies, 10¢–50¢; Rated Rookies, 15¢–$2; Bonus Cards, 25¢–$1; superstars, hot rookies, 25¢–$2. 5-YEAR PROJECTION: Average.

1989 Score, Herm Winningham

1989 Score, Wrigley Field

1989 SCORE

SPECIFICATIONS

SIZE: 2½ × 3½". FRONT: Color photograph. BACK: Small color portrait with colored printing on white cardboard. DISTRIBUTION: Nationally, in 16- and 45-card packs; complete sets sold through hobby dealers; factory-collated sets available through select retail chains.

HISTORY

After seven years of collectors being content with Topps, Fleer, and Donruss sharing the baseball card market, Optigraphics and Major League Marketing got together to produce a 660-card set of "Score" cards in 1988. The set was a dazzling success, featuring cards with multicolored borders and action photography, and card backs with additional color portraits, statistics, and well-researched biographies. Suddenly, the "Big Three" card-makers had a competitor. However, Score's sophomore season proved to be a major disappointment. The company retained the major elements of its first set, but the 1989 set was marred by a weak card design and mediocre photography. Many photos are blurred or dark. A majority of the players are hard to identify. Hitters can't be seen because batting helmets hide their faces, and pitchers are obscured

1989 Score, Mike Harkey

by shadows. Due to Score's obsession with action photography, the poses quickly become boring. Almost invariably, players are shown at bat or pitchers are shown in their windups. Precious few cards in the set portray a player fielding or running the bases. Veteran collectors seemed more interested in the Score card backs. On the upper right of each card back is a color portrait of the featured player. A team logo, personal information, and even the player's uniform number is included. Below the major league career statistics, a paragraph summarizes the player's career. These paragraphs are the best part of the Score cards. Often, tribute quotes from other players will be included in the descriptive write-ups. Compared with the other major 1989 issues, the biggest blunder in this set was the failure to include current photos of several traded players. For instance, Bob Forsch is shown as a Cardinal, Jody Davis as a Cub, and Fred Lynn as an Oriole. Even though these players switched teams in mid-season, Score failed to find timely photos. The company was aware of the mistakes, because cards of these players contained complete 1988 statistics and a one-line mention of the trade on the card back. Score worked overtime to please rookie card collectors by designating 32 players (cards #620-#651) as Rookie Prospects, each receiving a specially marked card. However, the most popular 1989 Score cards may be the final nine cards of the set. Cards numbered 652 through 660 honor special achievements from the 1988 season, including Wrigley Field's first night game, Orel Hershiser's scoreless inning streak, and Wade Boggs' 200-plus hits for six straight seasons.

FOR

Score cards were as plentiful throughout 1989 as they were in 1988. Because some experienced collectors haven't accepted the new set yet, prices are still modest.

AGAINST

Disappointment in the overall quality of this second-year entry damaged the appeal of the 1989 Score cards.

NOTEWORTHY CARDS

The 32 specially designated Rookie Prospects cards are desirable, because not every company was as liberal in proclaiming rookie cards. Also, the usual array of current stars and superstars have some appeal.

VALUE

MINT CONDITION: Complete set, $17; common card, 3¢; stars, rookies, 10¢–50¢; Rookie Prospects, 25¢–$1.50. 5-YEAR PROJECTION: Below average.

1988 TOPPS

SPECIFICATIONS

SIZE: 2½ × 3½″. FRONT: Color photograph. BACK: Orange and black printing on gray cardboard. DISTRIBUTION: Nationally, in 15-, 28-, or 100-card packages with bubblegum; complete sets sold through hobby dealers; factory-collated sets sold through select retail chains.

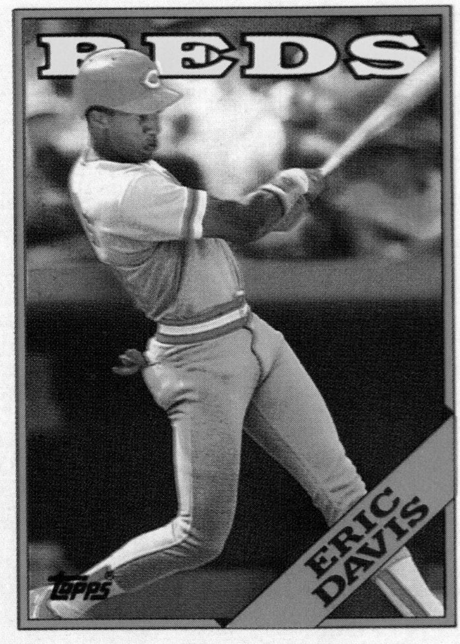

1988 Topps, Eric Davis

1988 Topps, Kevin Seitzer

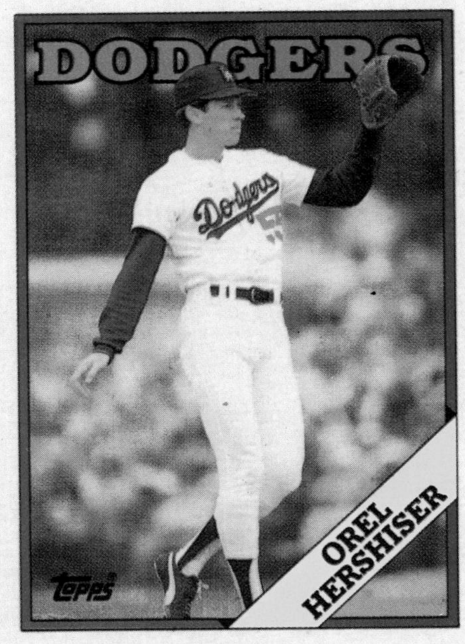

1988 Topps, Orel Hershiser

HISTORY

Topps, the granddaddy of them all, pulled out all their creative talents to produce a highly attractive and collectible set in 1988. With 792 cards—the same number as other recent Topps sets—the '88 edition put them in front of the pack as the company with the most players and the most variety. The card itself has been compared to a magazine cover; it features a white border around a sharp photo of the player, with his team's name in assorted colors blending into the background. The player's name is in a colorful band spanning the lower right of the card, and the Topps logo appears on the lower left on most cards. The '88 set features 22 All-Star cards: eight starters, two starting pitchers, and a reliever from each league. There are 26 manager cards, but because of Topps' penchant for printing early, two of them were not on the job in spring training of '88: Lou Piniella of the Yankees appears instead of Billy Martin, and Frank Lucchesi shows up as the Cubs skipper instead of Don Zimmer. The first seven cards in the set are record-breaker cards featuring Vince Coleman, Don Mattingly, Mark McGwire, Eddie Murray, the Niekro brothers, Nolan Ryan, and Benito Santiago. The Mattingly and McGwire cards are highly coveted, as is anything bearing their likeness. There are five cards carrying "Future Stars" designation, and the Kevin Elster and Joey Meyer cards were the hot items in this group. There are 10 cards of second-year players displaying the Topps All-Star rookie trophy under their name banner in the lower right. Tigers catcher Matt Nokes opened at $1 with that designation. Topps once again turned back the clock with card replicas from 1963, 1968, 1973, 1978, and 1983. There are also 26 team leader cards picturing various players on the front along with miscellaneous stats of interest. Some collectors turned the identification of the players pictured into a popular card-show pastime. Card backs keep the usual Topps horizontal format and are printed in orange and black with complete major league stats. A new feature for 1988 was a segment called "This Way to the Clubhouse," which tells how the player joined his current club—by trade, free agency, or draft. The specialty subsets stand apart from the regular cards in design and content. The first seven cards and the All-Star cards reminded veteran collectors of the 1958 Topps set, which was not exactly an artistic high point in baseball card history. The team leader cards retain the old-time format of a vignette photo, which, this year, might be confused with the Fleer set.

FOR

A fresh new design highlights this Topps issue.

AGAINST

Very little detracts from the positive impact this set made, and Topps made the backs even more readable.

NOTEWORTHY CARDS

The usual heavyweights—Mattingly, Roger Clemens, Wally Joyner, and Jose Canseco—joined new sensations McGwire, Nokes, Sam Horn, and Santiago, as the hot items. The mistakes in the set: The Padres name appears in white letters instead of blue on Keith Comstock's card, and Al Leiter's card is really Steve George. Both were sought after, commanding a premium.

VALUE

MINT CONDITION: Complete set, $23; common card, 4¢; stars, rookies, 15¢–35¢; superstars, hot rookies, 50¢–$1.50; Comstock error, $8. 5-YEAR PROJECTION: Well above average.

1988 TOPPS TRADED

SPECIFICATIONS

SIZE: 2½ × 3½". FRONT: Color photograph. BACK: Orange and black printing on gray cardboard. DISTRIBUTION: Nationally, complete boxed sets sold through hobby dealers.

1988 Topps Traded, Ty Griffin

1988 Topps Traded, Andy Benes

1988 Topps Traded, Mark Grace

HISTORY

Topps produced its eighth straight update set in 1988. The 132-card set, complete with its own collector's box, had its fall debut in 1981. The cards are identical to the company's 1988 regular 792-card set except they are numbered 1T through 132T. The 1988 Topps traded cards were incredibly popular due to the inclusion of 19 cards portraying members of the 1988 Gold Medal-winning U.S. Olympic baseball team. Jim Abbott, Robin Ventura, Ty Griffin, Ted Wood, Tino Martinez, and Andy Benes are the most famous of the group. As other members of the team start their pro baseball careers, the entire subset should soar in value. This idea originated in the 1985 Topps set, which included cards of 1984 Olympians Mark McGwire and Cory Snyder. Because Topps has the longest card-producing reputation, collectors look to them first for issues of new players. Cards of Walt Weiss, Chris Sabo, and Mark Grace make up the rookie contingent in the 1988 set. The regular 1988 Topps set was well received by collectors and because of the inclusion of the Olympic team cards, this traded set will be one of the most desirable subsets of the 1980s.

1988 TOPPS BOX BOTTOMS

FOR
Topps isn't known as "the real one" for nothing: This set is first-rate. For the first time, Topps gave their traded set a real purpose. The Olympic cards make the set truly memorable.

AGAINST
No faults can be found in this issue.

NOTEWORTHY CARDS
Any of the 19 Olympian cards will be worth keeping; plus, the cards of Sabo, Grace, and Weiss are the keys to the set.

VALUE
MINT CONDITION: Complete set, $15; common card, 8¢; rookies, 15¢–50¢; Olympian cards, 50¢–$2; Weiss, $1.50; Grace, Sabo, $2.50. 5-YEAR PROJECTION: Well above average.

SPECIFICATIONS
SIZE: Single card, 2½ × 3½"; panel, 5 × 7". FRONT: Color photograph. BACK: Orange and black printing on gray cardboard. DISTRIBUTION: Nationally, one of four 4-card panels printed on the bottom of Topps 36-count wax pack box.

HISTORY
Topps went back to the bottom panel idea in 1988 after experimenting with two-card side panels in 1987. Topps had "borrowed" the bottom panel idea in 1986 from Donruss (who then abandoned it in 1988). The 1988 box bottom cards salute players who broke major league records during '88. One panel features Bob Boone's 1,919th game as a catcher, Steve Bedrosian's 13 straight saves, Don Baylor's dubious honor of being hit with a pitch for

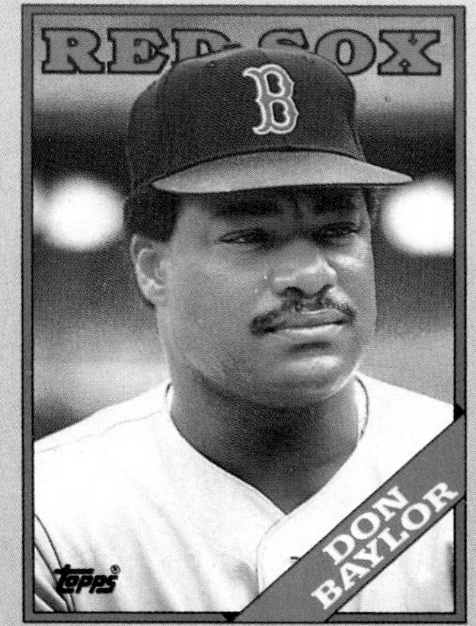

1988 Topps Box Bottoms

the 244th time in his career, and Juan Beniquez. Other panels feature Darrell Evans, Tony Gwynn, John Kruk, and Marvell Wynn; Joe Carter, Eric Davis, Howard Johnson, and Darryl Strawberry; and Rickey Henderson, Nolan Ryan, Mike Schmidt, and Kent Tekulve. There are 16 players in all, and the cards are labeled A through D. The card design resembles the regular 1988 set with the exception of a light blue border on the front instead of white. When the panels were cut apart, the cards fit right in with the regular issue; of course, purists say they should remain intact, and the entire box should be kept for maximum value. One other note: The box top contains a complete Don Mattingly card, identical to the regular issue except it is on slightly heavier stock and has nothing on the back. Years from now it may show up as a blank-backed regular issue, especially if it was carefully cut from the box.

FOR
It's another Topps product and that means collectors want it. It was scarce enough to be valuable down the road.

AGAINST
Box bottoms get scuffed on shelves, so Mint examples are virtually impossible to find.

NOTEWORTHY CARDS
Good assortment of superstars and future Hall of Famers like Schmidt and Ryan on the same panel.

VALUE
MINT CONDITION: Complete set of four panels, $10; single panel, $2; single card, 50¢. 5-YEAR PROJECTION: Well above average.

1988 TOPPS MAIL-IN GLOSSIES

SPECIFICATIONS
SIZE: 2½ × 3½″. FRONT: Color photograph. BACK: Red and blue printing on white cardboard. DISTRIBUTION: Nationally, in six 10-card sets available by mailing in premium cards found in Topps wax packs.

HISTORY
This was the fifth year Topps had offered mail-in glossy sets of "All Stars and Hot Prospects" in six series. Collectors could order one series for $1.25 plus six premium cards, or get the whole set for $7.50 and 18 premium cards. Confusion marked the 1988 edition early when anxious collectors started requesting the sets in late 1987 (when the '88 cards first appeared). Many got the 1987 set, which was nice, but not what they had ordered, or simply got their money back. The 1988 set looks no different from the first set issued in 1983. The cards have a glossy full-color photo in a chartreuse box surrounded by a white border. The player's name appears in microscopic type in the lower left. The backs don't include much information, just the name of the player, his team and position, a card number, and the line "Topps 1988 All-Star set, Collector's Edition." There's another collector's

1988 Topps Mail-In Glossies, Willie McGee

1988 Topps Mail-In Glossies, Tim Wallach

item attached to this set: the premium mail-in card, which includes instructions and Jack Clark's picture. Originally Topps said "card not included" next to Clark's photo, then they decided to include him anyway. (He's in subset five.) The line was covered with a black arrow in the early run and then struck altogether from the card later on. Cards with the line are truly rare, cards with the arrow are scarce, cards without the line or arrow are common. The inclusion of "hot rookies" in the set again this year made it a most collectible item. This set has gained stature over the years and is now considered an integral part of any Topps collection.

FOR

These are great-looking cards of popular rookies and stars.

AGAINST

No originality: the 1988 cards look like 1987's, which looked like those from the year before. At $7.50, plus the cost of 18 wax packs and postage, they were pretty expensive for a subset.

NOTEWORTHY CARDS

Rookie cards of Ellis Burks, Mike Greenwell, and Matt Nokes, along with the usual stars like Mattingly, Clemens, and Strawberry.

VALUE

MINT CONDITION: Complete set, $12; common card, 25¢; superstars, $1–$2. 5-YEAR PROJECTION: Average or a little above.

1988 Topps All-Stars, Rookies Glossies, Andre Dawson

1988 TOPPS ALL-STARS, ROOKIES GLOSSIES

SPECIFICATIONS

SIZE: 2½ × 3½". FRONT: Color photograph. BACK: Red and blue printing on white cardboard. DISTRIBUTION: Nationally, in rak-paks (All-Stars) and jumbo paks (Rookies).

1988 Topps All-Stars, Rookies Glossies, Rickey Henderson

HISTORY

All-Star glossies have been one of Topps' regular insert sets over the years and for the second year they added a glossy set of rookies. Since both were inserts in packages, the glossies are considered two 22-card series that make up one 44-card set. The design of both series is consistent with past issues. A 1988 All-Star glossy looks pretty much like a 1985 All-Star. A 1988 rookie glossy looks the same as in 1986. The All-Stars were inserts in the traditional rak-pak. The 22 cards represent the starters and managers of both leagues in the 1987 All-Star game in Oakland. This means you get stars like Don Mattingly, Wade Boggs, Eric Davis, and Mike Schmidt. A nice touch is the inclusion of the honorary captains, Billy Williams (N.L.) and Catfish Hunter (A.L.). The rookies came as inserts in Topps jumbo paks and represent 16 different teams. Players like Mark McGwire, Kevin Seitzer, Benny Santiago, and Ellis Burks started as collector's items. Because the cards could only be collected by buying the individual Topps packages, sets were difficult to complete. As a result, few collectors even bothered.

FOR

Nice cards of the game's superstars and leading rookies, especially if you collect "type" sets of individual players.

AGAINST

Format is unoriginal and information nil on the cards. They were abundant but difficult to collect, and were not taken seriously by many hobbyists.

NOTEWORTHY CARDS

They were all stars, at least for one season.

VALUE

MINT CONDITION: Complete set, $6 ($3 for each 22-card series); common card, 10¢–25¢; superstars, hot rookies, 40¢–75¢. 5-YEAR PROJECTION: Well below average.

1988 TOPPS K-MART

SPECIFICATIONS

SIZE: 2½ × 3½". FRONT: Color photograph. BACK: Red and blue printing on white cardboard. DISTRIBUTION: Nationally, through K-Mart stores and hobby dealers.

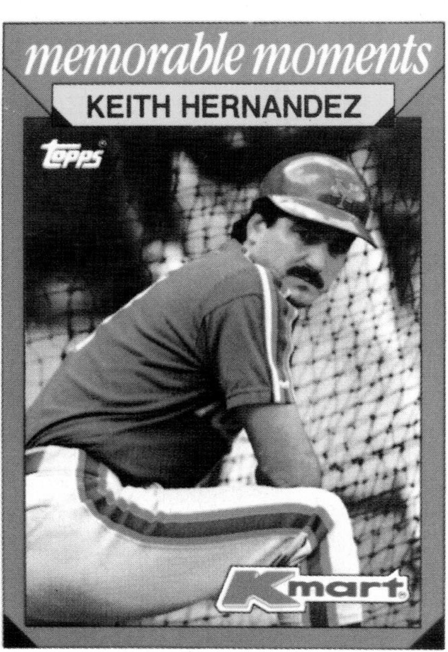

1988 Topps K-Mart, Keith Hernandez

HISTORY

One of the longest running boxed sets has been the Topps limited-edition "Memorable Moments" set for K-Mart. The tradition began badly in 1982 when Topps so overproduced the sets that K-Mart was literally giving them away just to get rid of them. This 33-card set was a close cousin to Topps' 1987 K-Mart effort. The cards are on thick, glossy stock with high-contrast photos. Unlike the store sets Fleer has produced, Topps put the K-Mart logo right on the card front for all to see. A brief write-up on the back describes something of note that the player accomplished. There is a checklist on the back of the box, which contains the cards and also one slab of bubblegum. While lots of the usual superstars appear, it is interesting to note that Pete Rose, who had retired as a player, shows up as card #22. Topps was the only major issuer to keep Rose's streak of baseball cards going for 25 years.

1988 Topps K-Mart, Pedro Guerrero

FOR

It's a Topps subset; consequently, many collectors will feel they must have it.

AGAINST

It has a track record of being the most plentiful of all boxed sets.

NOTEWORTHY CARDS

The Rose card is special, as are the usual Mike Schmidt, Don Mattingly, Jose Canseco, and Mark McGwire cards.

VALUE

MINT CONDITION: Complete set, $5; common card, 10¢; stars, 20¢–50¢; Mattingly, $1.50. 5-YEAR PROJECTION: Below average.

1988 FLEER

SPECIFICATIONS

SIZE: 2½ × 3½". FRONT: Color photograph. BACK: Red, white, and blue printing on white cardboard. DISTRIBUTION: Nationally, in 15-, 28-, or 54-card packages with team logo stickers; complete sets sold through hobby dealers; factory-collated sets available through select retail chains.

1988 Fleer, Mark Grace/Darrin Jackson

1988 Fleer, Orel Hershiser

1988 Fleer, Mark Grant

HISTORY

The 1988 Fleer set contains 660 cards, with a good assortment of posed and action photographs. A new design changed Fleer's traditionally conservative look: the cards feature a vignette photo which fades into white at the top of each card. This layout is comparable to the Team Leaders cards in the 1988 Topps set. A series of red and blue diagonal lines are printed on the card borders and continue behind the picture—another new design element for Fleer. The card backs include full career stats, plus a new feature entitled "At Their Best." An interesting graph shows how the player did during day games, night games, at home, and on the road—a lot of information in a tidy little package. Photos of every major league park appear on the back of the logo sticker cards, the premium that Fleer uses instead of bubblegum in each pack. The park collection makes an interesting, although unnumbered, subset. Also included are 19 specialty "Star Combo" cards, such as the Oakland A's young sluggers Jose Canseco and Mark McGwire in a pose entitled "Oakland's Power Team," and relievers John Franco and Steve Bedrosian in a "Game Closers" picture. Fleer has always shied away from individual cards of rookies, and this set includes more of their two-player "Major League Prospects" cards—including one with Mark Grace of the Cubs that began as a $1 item. They did go with some individual rookie cards however, and the Gregg Jefferies card was selling early on for as much as $5. Other newcomers included Shawn Abner, Melido Perez, Todd Frohwirth, Kevin Coffman, and Mark Carreon. As usual, Fleer produced some cards that got on the nerves of purists: Padres second baseman Tim Flannery is pictured holding a surfboard and Cardinals pitcher Ken Dayley is pictured wearing a glove on each hand. The 660-card vending set includes an additional 12-card World Series set that was not available in any other pack. Fleer's wax and cello packs included 12 All-Star cards in a

format that was a radical departure from the rest of the set. Fleer continued their tradition of numbering the set alphabetically by team. This is very helpful to collectors who build their sets by team. There was a distribution problem with this set: Collectors claimed they couldn't get the cards in stores and that dealers charged inflated prices. The good news is that, for those lucky enough to have latched on to a set or two, the investment potential is considerable.

FOR

New look, attractive format, a new feature called "At Their Best," and some daring player selections make Fleer's 1988 set truly collectible.

AGAINST

The main criticism against Fleer continued to be that the cards were difficult to obtain and that dealers inflated the prices accordingly.

NOTEWORTHY CARDS

Two-time minor league MVP Jefferies was a red-hot item when Fleer hit the shelves in late winter, along with first cards of Sam Horn, Grace, Jack McDowell, and Todd Benzinger.

VALUE

MINT CONDITION: Complete set, $29; common card, 6¢; stars, 15¢–30¢; hot rookies, superstars, 40¢–$3.50. 5-YEAR PROJECTION: Above average.

1988 FLEER UPDATE

SPECIFICATIONS

SIZE: 2½ × 3½". FRONT: Color photograph. BACK: Red and blue printing on white cardboard. DISTRIBUTION: Nationally, complete boxed sets sold through hobby dealers.

HISTORY

Fleer issued a 132-card "Update" set for the fifth straight year in 1988. While the set didn't get the acclaim that the Topps "Traded" set won (due to the inclusion of the 1988 Olympians), the Fleer issue is still admirable. Following tradition, the cards are patterned after the 660-card set issued earlier in the year. Alternating red and blue diagonal pinstripes make up a stunning background for each card. The player's name and position are listed in the upper left, while a team logo is found in the upper right. The background of the photo fades softly near the top, but the head of the player extends beyond, creating a three-dimensional effect. A small Fleer logo appears in the lower right below the photo. Card backs aren't very exciting.

1988 Fleer Update, Chris Sabo

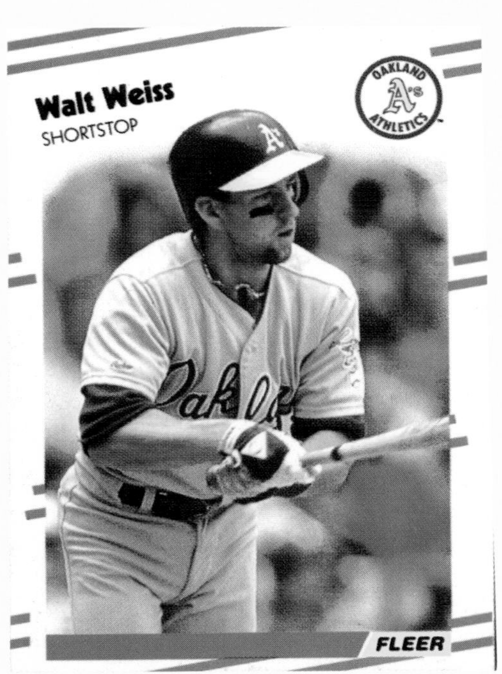

1988 Fleer Update, Walt Weiss

Even though the player's complete statistics are listed, many younger players have cards full of empty space. As always, the cards are numbered 1U through 132U, so as not to be confused with the 660-card set. Tommy Gregg's card mistakenly shows Pirate teammate Randy Milligan. Milligan also gets his own card. (This error is particularly noticeable since Gregg is white and Milligan is black.) The 660-card set contains a similar error: Bob Brower appeared on Jerry Browne's card.

1988 Fleer Update, Ricky Jordan

1988 Fleer Update, Randy Milligan

Fleer corrected the Brower-Browne mixup, but it seemed unlikely that a corrected version of the Gregg card would appear since only one print run of a season-ending subset is usually made. Another error in the update set was the misspelling of Mario Diaz's first name: the company wrongly called the Seattle Mariners shortstop "Marion." Fleer scooped Topps in three cases by picturing Mike Boddicker, Larry Parrish, and Brady Anderson with their correct clubs. Fleer also evened the score in this set by printing cards of several players who were included in Topps' 792-card set but were neglected in Fleer's larger set. The biggest post-season names of 1988 are included in the Update set: veterans like Dave Parker, Kirk Gibson, Lee Smith, and Jack Clark. Hot rookies include Chris Sabo, Walt Weiss, Mark Grace, and Ricky Jordan. The set comes in its own collector's box and contains 22 team logo stickers.

FOR

The cards look good, and the right players were included. Because the 1988 Fleer set was popular, the Update set became just as collectible.

AGAINST

All season-ending sets are more expensive to obtain. These were only available from hobby dealers.

NOTEWORTHY CARDS

If you can only get four cards from the set, get Sabo, Weiss, Grace, and Jordan.

VALUE

MINT CONDITION: Complete set, $11; common card, 5¢; rookies, 20¢; Weiss, Jordan, $1.50; Grace, $2; Sabo, $2.50. 5-YEAR PROJECTION: Below average.

1988 FLEER BOX BOTTOMS

SPECIFICATIONS

SIZE: Single card, 2½ × 3½"; panel 5 × 7". FRONT: Color photograph. BACK: Red and blue printing on brown cardboard. DISTRIBUTION: Nationally, on the bottom of wax-pack display boxes.

HISTORY

For the third year in a row, Fleer printed player and team logo cards on the bottom of their wax-pack display boxes. There were four different panels, including 12 players and four team logos. The format was the same in 1988 as it had been in 1986 and 1987. The cards are numbered C-1 through C-16 and include Dwight Evans, Andres Galarraga, Wally Joyner, Kirby Puckett, Shane Rawley, Ryne Sandberg, Mike Schmidt, Kevin Seitzer, Dave Stewart, Tim Wallach, and Todd Worrell. Team logos include the division champion Giants, Cardinals, Twins, and Tigers. An Andre Dawson card (minus any back information) was included on the box top; careful trimming could produce a single card of him. Given the fact that Fleer cards were hard to find, you can imagine how tough a box bottom was to locate, especially in Mint condition. Collectors are reminded, however, that the complete box is the most valuable, followed by the complete panel. Cards cut out individually are of less value.

FOR

These are nice cards of some of the better players.

AGAINST

There are no Don Mattingly or Mark McGwire cards. Who ever heard of such a thing in a 1988 set? Also, panels were marred by including only three players and one club logo.

NOTEWORTHY CARDS

The cards of Schmidt, Seitzer, and Joyner are well done.

VALUE

MINT CONDITION: Complete set of four panels, $8-$10; single panel, $2-$3; single card, 25¢. 5-YEAR PROJECTION: Average.

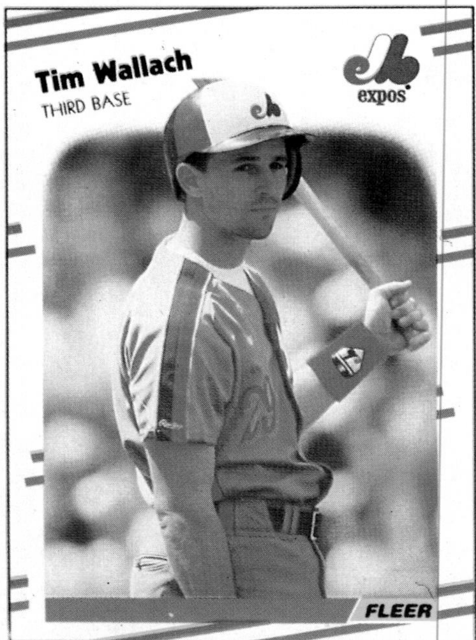

1988 Fleer Box Bottoms

1988 FLEER STAR STICKERS

SPECIFICATIONS

SIZE: 2½ × 3½". FRONT: Color photograph. BACK: Red and black printing on white cardboard. DISTRIBUTION: Nationally, in wax packs with logo stickers.

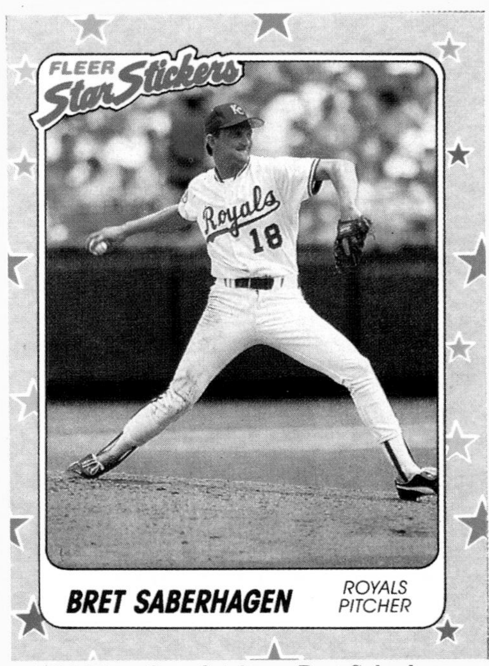

1988 Fleer Star Stickers, Bret Saberhagen

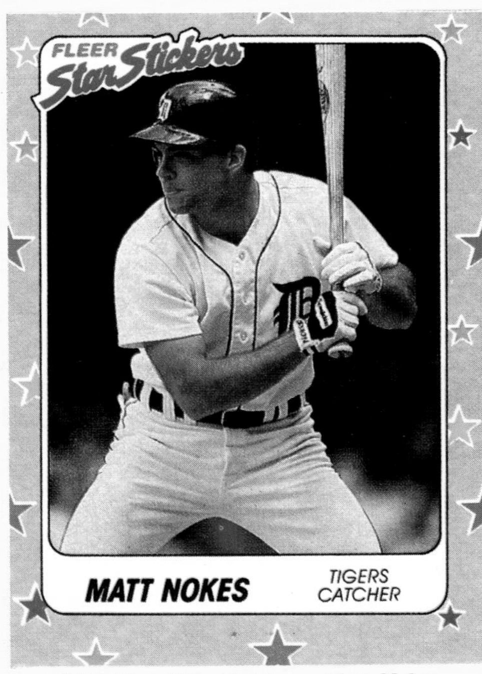

1988 Fleer Star Stickers, Matt Nokes

HISTORY

Fleer produced a set of 132 card-quality star stickers that are likely to end up in 9-pocket sheets with the regular issue. They were produced in wax packs with five player stickers and a logo card, with 36 packs to a box. The box also has three more cards and a logo card on the bottom. There are 131 player cards and a checklist card. Photos are different from the regular set and the quality is outstanding. The picture is enclosed by a white border inside a gray field with small red, blue, and yellow stars in it. At the upper left is "Fleer" in blue and the words "Star Stickers" in red. The backs are similar to the regular Fleer issue, including the "At Their Best" feature. Printing is in red and black on heavy white cardboard stock. Fleer must have expected that most sticker fronts would remain attached to their backs, otherwise they wouldn't have spent so much effort on a portion of the card that would normally be disposed of. Star stickers issued in the past (first in 1981) have been tough items to acquire because dealers tend to hoard them. Few ever made it to retail stores.

FOR

This was another attractive Fleer set, with most of baseball's top players.

AGAINST

As with other Fleer sets, the question of availability arises.

NOTEWORTHY CARDS

There are interesting cards of Mike Schmidt, Roger Clemens, and Andre Dawson, along with the usual "must include" stars.

VALUE

MINT CONDITION: Complete set, $22; common card, 5¢–10¢; stars, superstars, 25¢–$2. 5-YEAR PROJECTION: Average or slightly above.

1988 FLEER RECORD SETTERS (ECKERD)

SPECIFICATIONS

SIZE: 2½ × 3½". FRONT: Color photograph. BACK: Red and blue printing on white cardboard. DISTRIBUTION: Regionally, in Eckerd drugstores and through hobby dealers.

1988 Fleer Record Setters (Eckerd), Howard Johnson

1988 Fleer Record Setters (Eckerd), Wade Boggs

HISTORY

For the second straight year, Fleer released a 44-card boxed set distributed exclusively by Eckerd drugstores. The set is entitled "Record Setters," but for 1988, as in '87, the card contains no information as to what record the player had set. The card features a full-color photo with the words "1988 Fleer Record Setters" in a yellow band directly above the photo. There is no reference to Eckerd anywhere on the card. Above the yellow band are blue and red stripes. The player's name, team, and position appear in black on a white border below the photo. Under the border are two red and blue stripes. The backs contain the same data as a regular issue 1988 Fleer card; in fact, the format is strikingly similar. Although Fleer's regular cards are tough to acquire, the company has become "king of the boxed sets," and sets are both popular and plentiful. As in 1987, the player choices seem to be based on popularity and collectibility rather than actual records. George Bell, Wade Boggs, Dwight Gooden, Tony Gwynn, and Dale Murphy all appear in full, sharp color. Early on, dealer sets were often short one or two cards—usually Jimmy Key (#22) and Mike Scott (#36). As a result of the missing cards, sets were broken up and more individual cards than usual became available.

FOR

These cards feature great photography.

AGAINST

Because the same players appear on all of these special sets, they become tiresome.

NOTEWORTHY CARDS

Mark McGwire, Don Mattingly, and Roger Clemens are solid investments regardless of what set they appear in.

VALUE

MINT CONDITION: Complete set, $4; common card, 10¢; superstars, $1. 5-YEAR PROJECTION: Average.

1988 FLEER BASEBALL'S EXCITING STARS (CUMBERLAND)

SPECIFICATIONS

SIZE: 2½ × 3½". FRONT: Color photograph. BACK: Red and blue printing on white cardboard. DISTRIBUTION: Regionally, in Cumberland Farms stores in the Northeast and Florida.

HISTORY

For the second year running, Fleer created a 44-card boxed set for the Cumberland Farms stores. This set is called "Baseball's Exciting Stars" and is a rehash of the same old set of stars and superstars that appear in most regional Fleer offerings. These cards have a blue border with a red stripe in the middle. The player's name is in the upper left along with his team and position. At the bottom of the card is the set name with the year enclosed in a baseball. The card back is the normal 1988 Fleer back reprinted here with a different number. The pictures are original and of high quality. Dwight Gooden, for example, is shown autographing a baseball. The usual Don Mattingly, Tim Raines, Kevin Seitzer, and Ryne Sandberg cards are included. Logo stickers come with this set, as with all the Fleer sets, and you can work on your stadium collection by accumulating these extra cards. The box includes a complete checklist on the back.

FOR
This is an inexpensive way to acquire cards of current stars.

AGAINST
The same old Fleer set called something different in a different box: same players, same card backs.

NOTEWORTHY CARDS
The usual superstars appear in this set.

VALUE
MINT CONDITION: Complete set, \$4; common card, 10¢; stars, superstars, 35¢–50¢. 5-YEAR PROJECTION: Below average.

1988 Fleer League Leaders (Walgreens), Jose Canseco

1988 FLEER LEAGUE LEADERS (WALGREENS)

SPECIFICATIONS
SIZE: 2½ × 3½″. FRONT: Color photograph. BACK: Red and blue printing on white cardboard. DISTRIBUTION: Nationally, in boxed sets at Walgreens stores.

HISTORY
For the third straight year, Fleer produced an exclusive set for Walgreens stores. Like its two predecessors, this one is popular with collectors and dealers alike. The boxed set contains 44 cards and is entitled "League Leaders." Which category the player led the league in is not spelled out. Every player in the set is a star or superstar, with the usual compliment of Don Mattingly, Wally Joyner, Wade Boggs, and Mike Schmidt cards. The card features a full-color photo bordered in two shades of blue separated by a small strip of yellow. The card backs contain all the ingredients of other 1988 Fleer issues: complete stats, bio information, and "At Their Best." Included with the cards are the usual logo stickers, which this year included aerial photos of major league ballparks. There's nothing that sets this issue apart from other Fleer issues, except that Walgreens is a good-sized retail chain, making this set more readily available to the hobby's mainstream.

1988 Fleer League Leaders (Walgreens), Eric Davis

FOR
The photos are good and the quality is up to Fleer's usual high standards.

AGAINST
The same players appear in all these subsets and that lessens the value of any boxed set.

NOTEWORTHY CARDS
They are all stars or superstars.

VALUE
MINT CONDITION: Complete set $4; common card, 10¢; stars, 50¢; superstars, $1.50.
5-YEAR PROJECTION: Average or below.

1988 FLEER ALL-STARS (BEN FRANKLIN)

SPECIFICATIONS
SIZE: 2½ × 3½". FRONT: Color photograph. BACK: Red and blue printing on white cardboard. DISTRIBUTION: Regionally, through Ben Franklin stores.

1988 Fleer All-Stars (Ben Franklin), Matt Nokes

HISTORY
Fleer's 1988 All-Stars set was distributed exclusively by Ben Frankin dimestores. This was yet another of Fleer's 44-card boxed offerings. The cards have a border of blue and yellow vertical stripes with the player's name, team, and position in the upper left and the words "Fleer Baseball '88 All Stars" in a panel below the full-color photograph. As usual, the All-Stars set includes an

1988 Fleer All-Stars (Ben Franklin), Bobby Bonilla

impressive array of talent. Unlike Topps' and Donruss' 1988 issues, which concentrated on the '87 All-Star game, this set isn't of any particular team or game. All the popular names are here: Jose Canseco, Wade Boggs, George Bell, and Wally Joyner. Some unusual offerings also show up: Dave LaPoint, Bobby Bonilla, Charlie Hough, and Bruce Hurst. (At least they weren't boxed-set regulars in '88.) The logo stickers, along with the aerial photos of major league ballparks, are included in the box, and there is a checklist on the back. The best thing about the logo stickers is that they don't leave a gum stain on the cards.

FOR
Attractive, inexpensive star cards and the inclusion of Bonilla and Hurst make this Fleer set somewhat different from the rest.

AGAINST
Nothing innovative ever happens with these boxed sets. There's no such thing as a valuable boxed-set card.

NOTEWORTHY CARDS
The usual stars—Don Mattingly, Mark McGwire, and Bell—plus LaPoint, Bonilla, Hough, and Hurst.

VALUE
MINT CONDITION: Complete set, $4; common card, 10¢; stars, 50¢–$1. 5-YEAR PROJECTION: Below average.

1988 DONRUSS

SPECIFICATIONS

SIZE: 2½ × 3½″. FRONT: Color photograph. BACK: Blue and black printing on white cardboard. DISTRIBUTION: Nationally, in 15- or 54-card packages with jigsaw puzzle pieces; complete sets sold through hobby dealers.

1988 Donruss, Kevin Seitzer

1988 Donruss, Wade Boggs

1988 Donruss, Roberto Alomar

HISTORY

There isn't anything new or innovative about the 1988 Donruss set. A Donruss card always looks like a Donruss card. The borders are always wild and this year is no exception: light blue upper-left and lower-right corners, while the other two corners have alternating stripes of black and red with color fades. The colors work in some of the pictures but not in others, depending on the color of the player's uniform. Donruss also brought back another tradition: the "high number." Due to a printing problem (later corrected), Donruss cards numbered 600 and up (including the 26 "Bonus Cards" numbered BC-1 through BC- 26) were in short supply early in the year. Dealers immediately attached a premium to "high number" common cards, thus assuring that cards would be hoarded. The "Bonus Cards" are special inserts that portray stars like Eric Davis, Cal Ripken Jr., Darryl Strawberry, and Mike Schmidt. Collectors couldn't decide whether these cards made Donruss a 686-card set or if they should be treated as a subset to be collected separately. The jury is still out on where the cards belong. Since they are in the high numbers, their value has leaped past regular superstar cards. Donruss came back with two other old standbys: the "Diamond Kings" subset of painted player portraits (#1-#27) and "Rated Rookies" (#28-#47). Although the Diamond Kings idea is getting a bit tired, collectors still attach premium prices to star players. The best and most popular subset is the Rated Rookies, and hobby speculators load up on these cards because of Donruss' penchant for picking winners. The hottest

rated rookie was probably Cub Mark Grace, followed by Al Leiter (really him, not Steve George as on his 1988 Topps card), Roberto Alomar, and Gary Thurman. There probably isn't a gem like Jose Canseco (1986) or Mark McGwire (1987) in the 1988 set, however. This year's puzzle is Hall of Famer Stan Musial. One final thing that recommends the '88 Donruss set is the company's ongoing policy of speculating on young players rather than rehashing players who are on their way out. Such daring led them to issue a Gregg Jefferies card in 1988 (and not even as a Rated Rookie), which opened at around $3.50.

FOR

Donruss released more cards into the mainstream in 1988, which made collectors happy.

AGAINST

Dealers continued to charge high prices for brand-new cards, which turned off some collectors.

NOTEWORTHY CARDS

The Rated Rookies subset makes this set a speculator's dream. Superstar cards of Don Mattingly, Wade Boggs, McGwire, and Kevin Seitzer command top prices.

VALUE

MINT CONDITION: Complete set, $25; common card, 5¢; superstars, 35¢–$1.50; Jefferies, $5.
5-YEAR PROJECTION: Average or slightly above.

1988 DONRUSS THE ROOKIES

SPECIFICATIONS

SIZE: 2½ × 3½". FRONT: Color photograph. BACK: Aqua and black printing on white cardboard. DISTRIBUTION: Nationally, complete boxed sets sold through hobby dealers.

HISTORY

Donruss created "The Rookies" in 1986 to compete with the popular Topps Traded and Fleer Update sets. However, the Rookies set is smaller and has a more limited goal: only first-year players are included in this 56-card issue. The Donruss subset is always attractive. The cards are very similar to the 660-card set issued earlier in 1988. Full-color photos are set off by a small "The Rookies" logo in the lower right. The same black-and-red plaid borders are used, except that aqua is used instead of blue. The glossy cards have standard backs, except that green is again used instead of blue.

1988 Donruss The Rookies, Walt Weiss

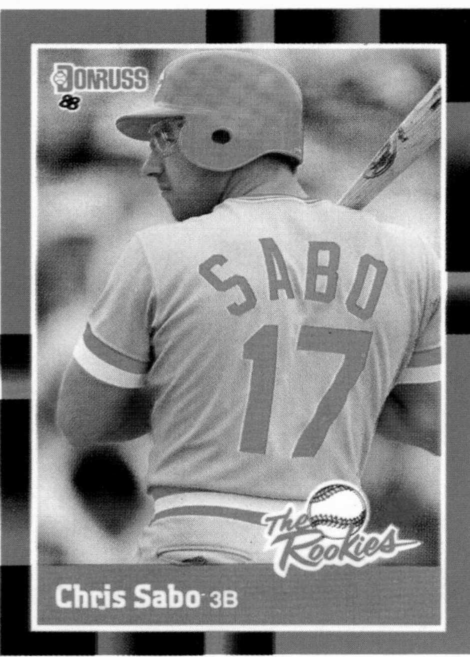

1988 Donruss The Rookies, Chris Sabo

True to Donruss tradition, the card back lists the player's contract status and how he was acquired by his current team. A total of 55 different rookies is included in the 1988 set along with an unnumbered checklist card. The Rookies set is issued in its own collector's box and was sold solely through hobby dealers. Because the set is small, its ultimate success depends on the future of players pictured on the cards. It was easy to forecast the success of the original 1986 set: Jose

Canseco, Wally Joyner, Barry Bonds, Kevin Mitchell, Pete Incaviglia, Will Clark, Bo Jackson, John Kruk, Danny Tartabull, and Ruben Sierra were the highlights of that issue. The rookie crop dwindled in 1987: Mark McGwire, Kevin Seitzer, Matt Nokes, Ellis Burks, and Bo Jackson were the biggest names in that set. Still fewer popular rookies were included in the 1988 set. Mark Grace, Chris Sabo, and Walt Weiss are the notable exceptions. Donruss also increased the availability of the 1988 Rookies set in response to the high demand for the previous two sets. These factors will benefit collectors who want to try investing in some inexpensive cards of rookie long shots but can't afford the Topps, Fleer, or Score issues.

FOR
The set is attractive and easy to find on the market.

AGAINST
It is half the size of the season-ending sets from Topps, Fleer, and Score, yet the price isn't that much lower. Also, there aren't many popular names in this set.

NOTEWORTHY CARDS
Grace, Sabo, and Weiss are the only noteworthy cards here.

VALUE
MINT CONDITION: Complete set, $9; common card, 7¢; Weiss, $1; Grace, Sabo, $2. 5-YEAR PROJECTION: Below average.

1988 Donruss All-Stars, Pop-Ups, Bret Saberhagen

1988 DONRUSS ALL-STARS, POP-UPS

SPECIFICATIONS
SIZE: 2½ × 3½″. FRONT: Color photograph. BACK: All-Stars: black printing on blue cardboard; pop-ups: red, blue, and black printing on white cardboard. DISTRIBUTION: Nationally, in wax packs, one pop-up card, one puzzle piece, and five cards; complete sets sold through hobby dealers.

1988 Donruss All-Stars, Pop-Ups, Wade Boggs

HISTORY
For the first time since 1983, the Donruss pop-up cards came in the same size as the All-Star cards; consequently, hobbyists have considered this to be one set of 64 baseball cards and 20 pop-ups. The 64 cards feature the members of the 1987 All-Star teams, the managers (John McNamara and Davey Johnson), and the Oakland Coliseum, where the game was played. The cards are similar to the regular 1988 Donruss issue, but instead of a team logo the cards carry either a National League or American League emblem. Card backs list All-Star stats for each player. The 20 pop-up cards are die-cut and can be punched out so the photo becomes a 3-D figure. Unfolded pop-ups are worth the same as cards; folded pop-ups are only worth about 25% as much. Each All-Star starter and both managers are featured on the pop-ups. Hobbyists warn not to punch out the pop-up cards because they are no longer Mint cards at that point. The smaller size (pop-ups used to be 3½ × 5″) made them adaptable to a standard plastic 9-pocket sheet and enhanced their long-term collectibility.

(pop-ups used to be 3½ × 5″) made them adaptable to a standard plastic 9-pocket sheet and enhanced their long-term collectibility.

FOR

The new size of the pop-up cards allows them to be combined with the 64 All-Star cards to make an attractive set.

AGAINST

The same stars as other subsets appear here, although this is not a serious problem since they were elected to the 1987 All-Star Game.

NOTEWORTHY CARDS

They are all stars, some brighter than others.

VALUE

MINT CONDITION: Complete set, $9–$10; common card, 25¢–75¢; stars 50¢–$1. 5-YEAR PROJECTION: Above average.

1988 DONRUSS DIAMOND KING SUPERS

SPECIFICATIONS

SIZE: 4¹⁵⁄₁₆ × 6¾″. FRONT: Color painting. BACK: Black and blue printing on white cardboard. DISTRIBUTION: Nationally, complete sets sold through hobby dealers and available through a mail-in offer.

HISTORY

For the fourth consecutive year, Donruss Diamond Kings were produced in a "super set" format. The cards are large-size replicas of the first 27 Donruss cards from 1988, featuring portraits by well-known sports artist Dick Perez. The Supers are almost twice the size of a regular card. The set includes such popular players as Mark McGwire, Jack Clark, and Cal Ripken Jr. The formula for inclusion is simple: one great player from each team. Sometimes the picked player gets traded, and Oakland had three Diamond Kings in 1988: McGwire, ex-Dodger Bob Welch, and ex-Brave Glenn Hubbard. The supers come with a complete 12-piece Stan Musial puzzle. The Diamond Kings subset has long been popular with autograph collectors. The Diamond Kings supers are not available from Donruss, but only through Perez's organization.

FOR

Attractive photos in a framable size, especially when autographed.

AGAINST

They are very expensive at $9.50 for 26 cards (the 27th is a checklist) and the format never changes. If you don't appreciate Perez's artwork, you'll like these jumbo cards even less.

NOTEWORTHY CARDS

McGwire's first Diamond King should be a valuable item down the road.

VALUE

MINT CONDITION: Complete set, $9.50; common card, 25¢. 5-YEAR PROJECTION: Below average.

1988 SCORE

SPECIFICATIONS

SIZE: 2½ × 3½″. FRONT: Color photograph. BACK: Color photograph with predominantly red, blue, and black printing on white cardboard. DISTRIBUTION: Nationally, in poly-wrapped packs of 17 cards; complete sets sold through hobby dealers.

1988 Score, Matt Nokes

1988 Score, Gregg Jefferies

1988 Score, Barry Bonds

HISTORY

Score became the fifth set of nationally distributed baseball cards and was the most eagerly anticipated set since Fleer started in 1981. Score is produced by the same company that produces Sportflics; however, this set immediately eclipsed Sportflics with a more conventional approach to the baseball card format. The set contains 716 cards but only 660 of them are really baseball cards; the other 56 are 2×2½″ "Great Moments in Baseball" trivia cards, Score's answer to puzzles, logo stickers, and bubblegum premiums. Score cards are distinguished by a sharp action photo on the front with a border in either blue, red, green, purple, gold, or orange. The player's name and position appear at the bottom. There is no team designation and the Score logo appears in the lower right. The set contains 110 cards in each of the six border colors. This may have been the first time collectors opted to display the back of the card instead of the front. The backs feature a full-color head shot of the player in the upper left, complete career stats, and a lengthy bio with career highlights. The backs are as colorful as the fronts. It has been years since a card set included so much information on the back. There are 25 Rookie Prospects cards, including Sam Horn, Billy Ripken, Gary Thurman, and Ellis Burks. Nine cards depict 1987 Major League highlights (much like the Topps '88 set) such as Don Mattingly's six grand slams, the hitting streaks of Paul Molitor and Benito Santiago, and the home run heroics of Mark McGwire. Taking another page from the Topps book, Score put together a five-card salute to Reggie Jackson. Each card features a nice photo of Mr. October and a lengthy write-up on his career. Like other first-time sets, the Score set had its share of mistakes. (They later issued some corrected versions.) Most of the problems involved misspelled names such as Terry Franconia (should be Francona), Robby Wine (should be Robbie), Dale Valle (instead of Dave), and six others. The hottest star card in the Score set in the early going was Red Sox second-year outfielder Burks. Mattingly (#1), Kevin Seitzer, Matt Nokes, McGwire, and Horn were also hot items. Score cards came wrapped in tamper-proof poly-bags, 17 to a pack. They were the last set out in 1988 due to problems with badly cut cards that showed up in earlier shipped packages. The card stock is superior to the traditional baseball card, which makes color reproduction second to none.

FOR

The 1988 Scores have the best-looking and most complete backs in baseball card history.

AGAINST

Action poses on card fronts often obscure the player's identity: many faces are lost in shadows or under hat brims.

NOTEWORTHY CARDS

The 25 Rookie Prospects cards showed some daring, and they could still produce some sleepers for investors. Mattingly's card is destined to be sought after in the coming years.

VALUE

MINT CONDITION: Complete set, $21; common card, 4¢; stars, 15¢–30¢; superstars, 35¢–$1; Burks, $1.50; Gregg Jefferies, $5. 5-YEAR PROJECTION: Above average.

1988 SCORE ROOKIE & TRADED

SPECIFICATIONS

SIZE: 2½ × 3½″. FRONT: Color photograph. BACK: Color photograph with predominantly red, blue, and black printing on white cardboard. DISTRIBUTION: Nationally, complete boxed sets sold through hobby dealers.

HISTORY

Just like the first Topps Traded set issued in 1981 and the first Fleer Update set issued in 1984, the first 110-card Score "Rookie & Traded" set was pursued for its historic value. It was Score's first fall subset, and it came out in Score's first year as a baseball card issuer. The updated Score cards follow the format of other season-ending sets. These cards are numbered 1T through 110T. Unlike other card companies, however, Score grouped all the first-time players in the last half of the set. Cards numbered 65T and above are rookies who were not included in Score's inaugural 660-card set, issued earlier in the season. The Score rookie and traded set maintains the outstanding photography and layout of the regular set, although the updated cards have orange borders. The vivid card backs retain the full-color player portraits, team logos, uniform numbers, personal information, major and minor league career statistics, and in-depth biographical information. The Score updates fill the traditional role of showing players pictured in the uniform of their current team. The 110-card set shows many traded players on their new teams. Some of the best-known relocated players include Kirk Gibson, Jay Howell, and Alfredo Griffin (Dodgers); Tom Brunansky (Cardinals); Goose Gossage (Cubs); Lee Smith (Red Sox); Chili Davis (Angels); John Candelaria (Yankees); and Dave Henderson, Don Baylor, and Dave Parker (Athletics). Most collectors buy fall update sets for the rookies they include. The Score update includes league Rookies of the Year Chris Sabo and Walt Weiss, along with Ricky Jordan, Tim Belcher, Mark Grace, Roberto Alomar, Brady Anderson, and Melido Perez. The complete set was sold in a collector's box manufactured by the company. There were 10 "Magic Motion" three-dimensional trivia cards included with each set, but these aren't viewed as collectibles yet. Since all major card companies release their season-ending cards in complete set form only, hobby dealers who offer individual cards acquired them by breaking up complete sets.

1988 Score Rookie & Traded, Damon Berryhill

1988 Score Rookie & Traded, Kirk Gibson

FOR

Score's 1988 debut set was a huge hit and the Rookie & Traded sets followed the same appealing format. First sets always capture the hobby's attention.

AGAINST
Many collectors scorn fall sets because they are only available through hobby dealers. Therefore, their collectibility is questioned. Also, some hobbyists believe the card companies hold out several cards from their main sets in order to make supplemental issues more appealing.

NOTEWORTHY CARDS
Four rookies—Weiss, Sabo, Grace, and Jordan—were the foundation of this set. These were some of the most popular cards of 1988.

VALUE
MINT CONDITION: Complete set, \$13; common card, 8¢; Weiss, \$1.50; Sabo, Jordan, Grace, \$2.50. 5-YEAR PROJECTION: Below average.

1988 SCORE BOX BOTTOMS

SPECIFICATIONS
SIZE: Single card, $2\frac{1}{2} \times 3\frac{1}{2}''$; panel, $5 \times 7''$. FRONT: Color photograph. BACK: Predominantly gold, blue, and red printing on white cardboard.

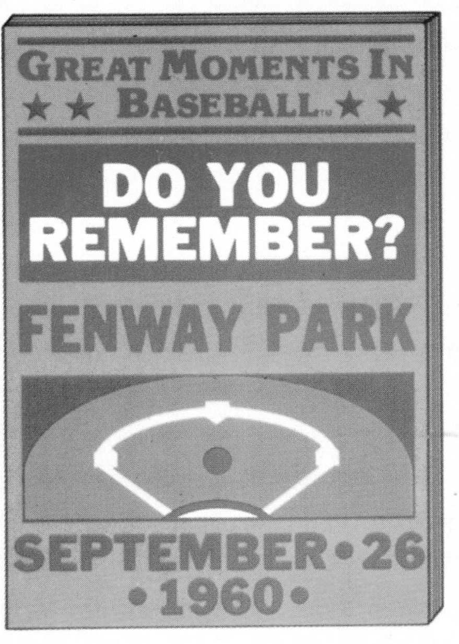

1988 Score Box Bottoms

DISTRIBUTION: Nationally, one of eight 4-card panels printed on the bottom of poly-wrapped pack display boxes.

HISTORY

They may have been the new kid on the block in 1988, but Score picked up on the box-bottom idea right away. They included three All-Star players and a question card on the bottom panel of their display boxes. The "Great Moments" trivia question is an adjunct to the 56 trivia cards included with their regular cards, while the All-Stars include 11 American League and 13 National League players on eight different box bottoms. Each card back, numbered 1 through 18, shows the player's name and position, and the appropriate league logo. Players include Jack Clark, Ryne Sandberg, Mike Schmidt, Ozzie Smith, Tim Raines, and Ozzie Virgil for the N.L.; while the junior circuit includes Terry Kennedy, Wade Boggs, Cal Ripken Jr., George Bell, Dave Winfield, Mark Langston, and Dwight Evans. Don Mattingly's regular Score card appears on the box top but is sufficiently over-printed to ensure no confusion about its origins. Like all box bottoms, these maintain their highest value when kept intact.

FOR

Collectors like them, which is why the companies keep this idea going.

AGAINST

Condition of box bottoms is usually poor because the boxes sit on the shelves and get scuffed.

NOTEWORTHY CARDS

The usual stars and superstars make up these panels.

VALUE

MINT CONDITION: Complete set of eight panels, $16; single panel, $2.50–$3; common card, 25¢.
5-YEAR PROJECTION: Above average.

1988 SPORTFLICS

SPECIFICATIONS

SIZE: 2½ × 3½". FRONT: Color photographs. BACK: Color photograph with predominantly red, blue, and black printing on white cardboard.
DISTRIBUTION: Nationally, in packages with baseball trivia cards; complete sets sold through hobby dealers.

1988 Sportflics, Don Sutton

1988 Sportflics, Dwight Evans

1988 Sportflics,
Jody Reed/Jeff Treadway/Keith Miller

HISTORY

Back for the third year (which some hobbyists didn't think would happen), Sportflics had a distinctive new look, a new border idea, and redesigned card backs that, like their baby brother Score, may be the best part of the card. Sportflics is a 225-card set with each card containing a red border featuring each player's name, position, and uniform number. The three-dimensional "magic motion" feature continued. The back has a color photo that takes up better than one-third of the card. The balance contains career stats and a complete bio. Three highlight cards are featured in the '88 set and the motion aspect allows three different highlights to be featured on each card. For example, card #180 includes Kirby Puckett's 10 consecutive hits, Juan Nieves' no-hitter, and Mike Schmidt's 500th homer. Card #222 features Steve Bedrosian's saves mark, Don Mattingly's eight homers in successive games, and Benito Santiago's 34-game hitting streak. Finally, card #221 highlights the achievements of Mark McGwire, Paul Molitor, and Vince Coleman. Three different cards also spotlight nine rookies, including Shawn Abner, Keith Miller, and Gary Thurman. Since the set is limited to 225 cards, most of the players portrayed are stars or at least solid regulars. The big-ticket cards such as Don Mattingly (#1), Matt Nokes, Wade Boggs, Ellis Burks, McGwire, and Eric Davis opened at $1 or more. The future of Sportflics is still a matter of speculation in the hobby, especially since Score cards moved into the number four slot in 1988. Over the years, 3-D cards have come and gone, however, none were as well-done as Sportflics.

FOR

Popular with kids and less-than-serious collectors, as well as people who appreciate novelties.

AGAINST

These are the most expensive of the five national sets, and by most accounts the fifth best, a bad combination.

NOTEWORTHY CARDS

The three rookie and three highlight cards top this set.

VALUE

MINT CONDITION: Complete set $30; common card, 10¢; superstars, 40¢–$1.50; Mattingly, $3.
5-YEAR PROJECTION: Below average.

1988 SCORE YOUNG SUPERSTARS

SPECIFICATIONS

SIZE: 2½ × 3½". FRONT: Color photograph. BACK: Color photograph with predominantly red, blue, and black printing on pink cardboard. DISTRIBUTION: Nationally, complete sets sold through hobby dealers and available through a mail-in offer.

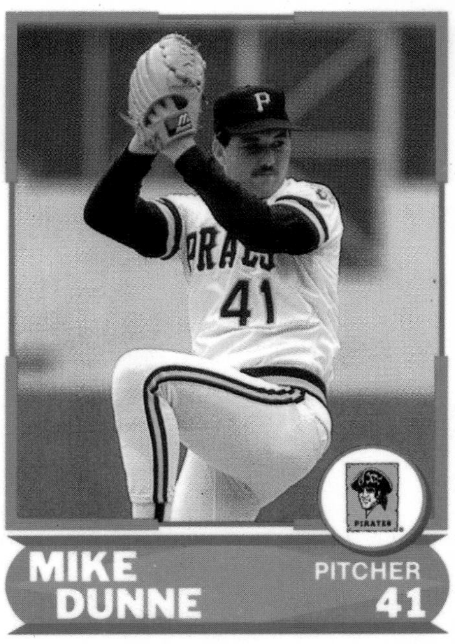

1988 Score Young Superstars, Mike Dunne

1988 Score Young Superstars, Ellis Burks

HISTORY

In an idea that had a familiar ring to it (Topps Kay-Bee Young Superstars), Score came up with a mail-in premium set that also borrowed from Topps' Glossy All-Stars and Hot Prospects. A 40-card set was available from Score by mailing in two wrappers and $1 for each one of five 8-card subsets. Just as the Kay-Bee set did in the past, Score featured cards of the top young players from 1986 and 1987. The card fronts show an action photo of the player inside a blue and green border. Team logos are printed on the lower right above the player's position and uniform number. (As a note, the 1988 Score regular cards have no team logos, and the only other '88 set to show a uniform number is Sportflics.) Card backs display a full-color portrait of the player (about one-third of the card) along with major league career totals. Score took a different approach by including a comment from a prominent baseball executive about the strengths of the young player. With a selection of players including Mark McGwire, Will Clark, John Kruk, Chris James, Ruben Sierra, and Ellis Burks, this set makes a solid addition to budding superstar collections. The series was so popular that another 40-card series came out later that year.

FOR

Good color, good player selection, and extensive information on baseball's budding superstars highlight this subset.

AGAINST

The second 40-card series received little publicity and was stockpiled by many hobbyists.

NOTEWORTHY CARDS

All 80 players have star potential. McGwire, Matt Nokes, Benito Santiago, Clark, and Burks have immediate collector appeal.

VALUE

MINT CONDITION: Complete set, $10; common card, 25¢–40¢; stars, 50¢–$1. 5-YEAR PROJECTION: Well above average.

1988 BASEBALL LEGENDS

SPECIFICATIONS

SIZE: 2½ × 3½". FRONT: Color photograph. BACK: Black, yellow, and gray printing on white cardboard. DISTRIBUTION: Nationally, in wax packs; complete sets sold through hobby dealers and Pacific Trading Cards.

1988 Baseball Legends, Luis Aparicio

1988 Baseball Legends, Willie Mays

1988 Baseball Legends, Roger Maris

HISTORY

This 110-card set of baseball's star players of the recent past was produced by Mike Cramer and his Pacific Trading Cards organization. It is considered a legitimate card issue because it was licensed by Major League Baseball and the Major League Baseball Alumni Association. It was marketed in wax packs in many retail chains such as Hook Drugs in Indiana and Dairy Mart in Ohio. It was also available in complete sets from many hobby dealers and from Pacific Trading Cards. The card quality is exceptionally high, with a full-color photo framed in red and enclosed in a silver border. The player's name and position appear in a colored banner beneath the photo. The card back contains a lengthy narrative of the player's career, and lists his best season and career records, where he currently resides, and when and for whom he played. Unlike past collector issues, this set includes several players still active in baseball such as Tigers manager Sparky Anderson, Twins coach Tony Oliva, Astros coach Yogi Berra, Yankees coach Clete Boyer, Rangers minor league coach Ferguson Jenkins, and Cardinals coach Red Schoendienst. The cards of Johnny Mize, Johnny Vander Meer, and Luke Appling are colorized black-and-white pictures. Most of the pictures in the Baseball Legends set are familiar to collectors, but the quality is exceptional.

FOR

Beautiful cards of many of the great names in recent baseball history highlight this set. Autograph collectors enjoy getting "old-timers" to sign their cards.

AGAINST

The familiar photographs give this set a "haven't I seen this before" look.

NOTEWORTHY CARDS

Joe DiMaggio, Mickey Mantle, Ted Williams, Willie Mays, and Al Kaline never looked better.

VALUE

MINT CONDITION: Complete set, $10; common card, 10¢; stars, 25¢–$1. 5-YEAR PROJECTION: Average.

1988 MOTHER'S COOKIES McGWIRE, CLARK

SPECIFICATIONS

SIZE: 2½ × 3½". FRONT: Color photograph. BACK: Red and purple printing on white cardboard. DISTRIBUTION: Northern California, in 18 oz. packages of Mother's Cookies.

1988 Mother's Cookies, Will Clark

1988 Mother's Cookies, Mark McGwire

HISTORY
One of the oldest regional producers of baseball cards, Mother's Cookies hit the market early in 1988 with two 4-card sets of two local fan favorites: first basemen Mark McGwire of the A's and Will Clark of the Giants. One cellophane-wrapped card of either player came in 18 oz. family-sized packages of cookies. The front of the package indicated whether the card inside was a Clark or a McGwire, but there was no way to tell which card was enclosed. The cards are the standard baseball-card size and have full-color, glossy photos. They have rounded corners and two-color backs. These cards are different from the regular Mother's Cookies Giants and A's cards given away at in-stadium events throughout the season. The Clark and McGwire cards were not supposed to be sold to hobby outlets or to the general public. Mother's Cookies stressed that the only way to get the cards was to buy the cookies. Nonetheless, dealers undoubtedly got them, and they became one of the most expensive regional card sets of 1988. By maintaining their tradition of not selling the cards outright, Mother's also ensured certain dealers would get top dollar for these sure-to-be-scarce cards.

FOR
Two of baseball's young superstars make any regional set collectible.

AGAINST
This will be a very difficult set to complete, especially if you don't live in the area of distribution.

NOTEWORTHY CARDS
Any and all of them are collector's items.

VALUE
MINT CONDITION: Complete set, $16–$20; single card, $2–$4. 5-YEAR PROJECTION: Well above average.

1988 MSA ICED TEA DISCS

SPECIFICATIONS
SIZE: 2¾″ diameter. FRONT: Color photograph. BACK: Red printing on white cardboard. DISTRIBUTION: Nationally, in canisters of iced tea and fruit drinks at various supermarket chains.

HISTORY
For the second straight year, Mike Schechter Associates produced a 20-player set of disc cards distributed in canisters of iced tea and fruit drinks. The discs came in panels of two and are approximately 2¾″ in diameter. Each disc shows a full-color head shot of the player in a baseball diamond in contrasting colors. The player's name is in the upper left, the words "Super Annual Collectors' Edition" are on the right side, and the

words "Super Stars" are centered beneath the picture. The cards show no major league team logos and all caps are airbrushed. The discs were distributed at Weis, Key Food, A&P, Lucky, Skaggs, Alpha Beta, Acme, King Kullen, Laneco, and Krasdale stores. In addition, Tetley Tea featured a set in major chains where their products were sold. These cards came in a tri-fold insert consisting of two player discs and a card that entitled the buyer to purchase either a facsimile-autographed baseball or a limited-edition printer's sheet of all the cards. The disc set included superstars and young players who have not yet made their marks. The former group includes Don Mattingly, Wade Boggs, Dwight Gooden, and Mike Schmidt; the latter includes Dave Magadan, Billy Ripken, and Ellis Burks.

FOR

An unusual presentation of current and potential stars.

AGAINST

Given all the store brands involved and the variations they will produce, collecting examples of each will be a nightmare. Also, purists hate airbrushed caps.

NOTEWORTHY CARDS

Why not a Ripken or Magadan card? Suppose they become big stars?

VALUE

MINT CONDITION: Complete set of 20 discs (from any store), $5; two-card disc, 25¢–50¢. 5-YEAR PROJECTION: Average.

1988 NESTLE DREAM TEAM

SPECIFICATIONS

SIZE: $2\frac{1}{2} \times 3\frac{1}{2}''$. FRONT: Color photograph. BACK: Blue and red printing on white cardboard. DISTRIBUTION: Nationally, in various chocolate products.

HISTORY

After an absence of three years, Nestle returned to baseball cards in 1988 with a 44-card set called "The Dream Team." The cards were distributed in various Nestle products. The yellow-bordered cards feature each player's name in a blue bar. Red stars frame the chocolate-brown line "1988 Nestle," and the picture is bordered in red. Produced by Mike Schechter Associates, this set was a very limited edition and had limited availability. The cards came in cello-wrapped packages of three along with a "header" or redemption card. The redemption offer allowed buyers to purchase a facsimile-autographed baseball or an uncut sheet of all 44 cards. Each league is represented by 22 players on the "Dream Team." Stars like Don Mattingly and Roger Clemens, who are usually found in such sets, are teamed up with less traditional picks such as Juan Samuel, Buddy Bell, and Frank White. Although the card backs display the Major League Baseball logo, all team logos on the caps have been airbrushed.

FOR

It is a limited-edition promotional issue that should be worth collecting. Includes impressive star players who don't usually show up in such sets.

AGAINST

A busy, somewhat garish design with colors all over the place and the lack of team logos hinder an otherwise nice set.

NOTEWORTHY CARDS

Kirby Puckett, Samuel, Bell, and White are different and interesting choices.

VALUE

MINT CONDITION: Complete set $12; common card, 25¢–35¢; superstars, 50¢–$1; uncut sheet, $10. 5-YEAR PROJECTION: Well above average.

1988 REVCO LEAGUE LEADERS

SPECIFICATIONS

SIZE: $2\frac{1}{2} \times 3\frac{1}{2}''$. FRONT: Color photograph. BACK: Red and black printing on white cardboard. DISTRIBUTION: Regionally, at Revco drugstores.

HISTORY

Topps began to make inroads against Fleer's retail-store boxed-set empire in 1988 by producing a 33-card boxed set for the Revco drugstore chain (which had issued a Fleer set, "Baseball's Hottest Stars," in 1987). Printed in Ireland, the new Topps entry has a glossy picture on the front (similar to other Topps subsets) and is printed in full color. The set includes a mixture of posed and action shots of the most popular players of the late 1980s, including emerging superstars like Kevin Seitzer and Danny Tartabull. Conspicuously absent from this set is Don Mattingly, but other fan favorites

1988 Revco League Leaders, Danny Tartabull

1988 Revco League Leaders, Juan Samuel

such as Wade Boggs and Mark McGwire are included. The card fronts have the Revco logo in the upper left and the Topps logo in smaller type along with the words "League Leaders" in the upper right. The player's picture is bordered in red with a black line. His name and team appear on a diagonal block in the lower right. Card backs are printed in red and black with 1987 season and combined career stats.

FOR

A nice new subset for that segment of the hobby that has to have everything that is produced.

AGAINST

Yet another subset in a series of subsets that threaten to overwhelm the hobby.

NOTEWORTHY CARDS

Emerging superstars such as Seitzer and Tartabull will dominate these subsets in the future, making this a good compilation of "League Leaders."

VALUE

MINT CONDITION: Complete set, \$3–\$4; common card, 10¢–15¢; superstars, 25¢–75¢. 5-YEAR PROJECTION: Average.

1987 TOPPS

SPECIFICATIONS

SIZE: 2½ × 3½″. FRONT: Color photograph. BACK: Yellow and blue printing on gray cardboard. DISTRIBUTION: Nationally, in 15-, 28-, or 54-card packages with bubblegum; complete sets sold through hobby dealers.

1987 Topps, Bo Jackson

1987 Topps, Don Mattingly

1987 Topps, Mike Greenwell

1987 Topps, Ruben Sierra

HISTORY

Topps dug into the card design archives for 1987, and the result was pleasing cards that won accolades from collectors. A full-color picture dominates the front in a simple wood-grain frame—no bells, no whistles, no funny borders. The cards include both action and posed player shots. The team logo is in the upper left, the player's name appears in a block in the lower right, and the Topps logo in the lower left. This was not the first time that a wood-grain finish had been successfully used. Topps used the idea in 1962, Hires Root Beer used it in 1958, and the last Bowman set used it (in both light and dark wood finishes) in 1955. Autograph collectors liked the card because there was ample room for that all-important signature. The card backs were a bit of a disappointment, however, with little information besides a few stats and a one- or two-line personal note. For example, "Dave (Righetti) grew up as a Giants and Athletics fan," or "Ricky (Wright) spends pleasurable time playing the guitar. He and his wife are parents of a daughter, Jenci." Rounding out the back is a section called "On This Date...," which highlights a date and a related baseball fact. For example, "April 17, 1969: Bill Stoneman pitched no-hitter for Expos vs. Phillies. Bill's 1969 Topps card was #67." Boring. Topps began the 792-card set with its usual Record Breaker cards. Also included were subsets of All-Stars and Team Leaders. Two quirks mark the All-Star set: the Dwight Gooden (#603) and Don Mattingly (#606) cards come with and without a trademark on the front. The ones with no trademark are more valuable. The hottest 1987 Topps card is of rookie phenom Mark McGwire, despite the fact that it wasn't really his first card. (McGwire was included in Topps' 1985 set as a member of the 1984 U.S. Olympic Team.) McGwire's card started the year as a 25¢ item and ended up at well over $3. A number of outstanding players appeared on their first Topps regular cards in 1987, including Wally Joyner,

Ruben Sierra, Mike Greenwell, and Barry Bonds. For the first time since 1972, Topps failed to list the player's position on the front of the card. However, they continued the tradition of including individual manager cards, earning the gratitude of team set collectors. The Team Leader cards, also with wood-grain borders, used a vignette photo of unidentified players. However, many collectors consider this subset a waste of 26 cards. The 1987 set restored Topps to its position as the number one baseball card producer.

FOR

These were the best-looking Topps cards of the 1980s to date.

AGAINST

Card backs are dull and inane. Topps didn't spend much time in that department.

NOTEWORTHY CARDS

The McGwire card is the cornerstone of this set. Other solid cards are Mattingly, Jose Canseco, and Eric Davis. Loads of strong first cards add to the strength of this set.

VALUE

MINT CONDITION: Complete set, \$25; common card, 5¢; stars, rookies, 20¢–50¢; Mattingly, \$2.50; McGwire, \$3.50. 5-YEAR PROJECTION: Well above average.

1987 Topps Traded, Dave Martinez

1987 Topps Traded, Matt Nokes

1987 TOPPS TRADED

SPECIFICATIONS

SIZE: 2½ × 3½″. FRONT: Color photograph. BACK: Yellow and black printing on white cardboard. DISTRIBUTION: Nationally, complete boxed sets sold through hobby dealers.

HISTORY

This was Topps' seventh annual Traded issue, and it continued the tradition of presenting cards of players traded during the season in updated uniforms. Topps also used this set as an opportunity to issue cards of new players who made an impact during the 1987 season. The Traded set contains 131 player cards and a checklist card. The wood-grain front is identical to the regular issue, as is the back, except the Traded set is printed on a better grade of cardboard. The cards are numbered 1T through 132T. Unlike past years, Topps did not test-market the Traded cards in wax packs, and distribution was limited to hobby dealers, who sold them as complete sets. The 1987 set marked the first appearance on a Topps card of Kevin McReynolds, who had appeared in past Fleer and Donruss sets but never in a Topps issue. His trade to the New York Mets made his inclusion in this issue a natural. The most sought-after card in the set, however, was Detroit catcher Matt Nokes, who had replaced long-time Tiger backstop Lance

Parrish. Other rookies included for the first time were Kevin Seitzer (also a red-hot item), John Smiley, Terry Steinbach, Benny Santiago, Chris James, and Casey Candaele. The Traded set also took note of managerial changes by including cards of Lee Elia, Larry Bowa, Tom Trebelhorn, Billy Gardner, and Cal Ripken Sr.

FOR

Because 1987 was another good year for rookies who made an impact on the game, this set should prove to be a good long-term investment.

AGAINST

It was still a limited-edition issue, despite the dealer distribution method. Many purists still refuse to recognize Topps Traded cards as legitimate issues.

NOTEWORTHY CARDS

Rookie cards of hot 1987 stars like Seitzer and Nokes, along with the first McReynolds Topps issue, make this traded set worthwhile.

VALUE

MINT CONDITION: Complete set, $10; common card, 6¢–10¢; stars, hot rookies, 20¢–80¢; Seitzer, Nokes, David Cone, $2. 5-YEAR PROJECTION: Above average.

1987 TOPPS MAIL-IN GLOSSIES

SPECIFICATIONS

SIZE: 2½ × 3½". FRONT: Color photograph. BACK: Red and blue printing on white cardboard. DISTRIBUTION: Nationally, six 10-card sets available by mailing in premium cards found in Topps wax packs.

HISTORY

For the fourth year in a row, Topps created a set of glossy cards available to collectors through a mail-in offer found in regular-issue wax packs. The standard-size cards are similar to previous mail-in sets, with a glossy full-color picture on the front framed by a thin orange border with the player's name in minute black type in the lower left. The backs are simple, containing only the player's name, team, position, and the words "Topps 1987 All-Star Set, Collector's Edition." Cards came in six series of ten each and could be purchased by series or as a complete set of 60. Topps often saves its best photography for the glossy sets, and the pictures of Roger Clemens, Reggie Jackson, Cal Ripken Jr., Robby Thompson, George Bell, Tim Raines, and Jose Canseco are truly outstanding. Though not a part of the mail-in set, Topps also issued a pair of 22-card insert sets. One was a rookie set that came as one-card inserts in "Jumbo Packs" (100-card offerings), and the other was an All-Star set included in rak-paks. The former included top newcomers for 1986; the latter included the starting players, pitchers, and managers from the 1986 mid-summer classic.

FOR

This set features outstanding photography with lots of big-name players. The cards are perfect for autographing.

AGAINST

The mail-in sets usually got banged up in shipment and Mint sets are hard to find. The mail-in set was very expensive for a new issue and it hasn't appreciated much in comparison to its original cost.

NOTEWORTHY CARDS

Clemens and Canseco were everyone's favorites in 1986, so their inclusion in this set was natural.

VALUE

MINT CONDITION: Complete set, $13; common card, 25¢; stars, superstars, $1–$2. 5-YEAR PROJECTION: Average.

1987 TOPPS K-MART

SPECIFICATIONS

SIZE: 2½ × 3½". FRONT: Color photograph. BACK: Red and blue printing on white cardboard. DISTRIBUTION: Nationally, boxed sets sold at K-Mart stores and through hobby dealers.

HISTORY

K-Mart celebrated their 25th anniversary by issuing a 33-card set entitled "Stars of the Decades" featuring reproductions of the cards of star players from the 1960s, 1970s, and 1980s. Card fronts feature a full-color photo set diagonally against a bright red background. The K-Mart logo is in the upper left, with "1962-1987" in the upper right. Centered below them is the legend "25th Anniversary" in black with a yellow stripe through

1987 Topps K-Mart, Tom Seaver

it. The player's name and position appear in black type under the photo. Card backs contain extensive player information, career highlights, and lifetime stats. A number is printed in white on a blue star in the upper left. The stars of the '60s include Mickey Mantle, Willie Mays, Hank Aaron, Bob Gibson, and Frank Robinson. Stars of the '70s include Pete Rose, Jim Palmer, Steve Carlton, Johnny Bench, and Reggie Jackson. Players from the '80s include Don Mattingly, Mike Schmidt, Dale Murphy, Rickey Henderson, and Dwight Gooden. The set was packaged in a special box with a stick of gum. This was the second Topps K-Mart set. The first was in 1982 in celebration of the store's 20th anniversary.

FOR

The set was an inexpensive way for collectors to get three decades of superstars.

AGAINST

It's a boxed set and the value will appreciate accordingly. In other words, it will never be all that valuable.

NOTEWORTHY CARDS

Great photos of Roberto Clemente in the '60s, Tom Seaver in the '70s, and Schmidt in the '80s.

VALUE

MINT CONDITION: Complete set, \$5; stars 15¢–50¢; Mantle, Mays, Mattingly, Aaron \$1. 5-YEAR PROJECTION: Average.

1987 TOPPS BOARDWALK AND BASEBALL

SPECIFICATIONS

SIZE: 2½ × 3½″. FRONT: Color photograph. BACK: Black and pink printing on white cardboard. DISTRIBUTION: Nationally, complete sets sold through hobby dealers and at the theme park in Orlando, Florida.

1987 Topps Boardwalk and Baseball, Pedro Guerrero

1987 Topps Boardwalk and Baseball, George Brett

HISTORY

Topps produced a special 33-card boxed set for the Florida theme park "Boardwalk and Baseball" early in 1987. The set is called "Top Run Makers," and features 33 of the top run producers of the 1980s. To come up with the top 33 players, Topps devised a stat called "Runs Produced Average," which is simply the hitter's runs scored plus RBIs, divided by the number of games played. The card features a glossy full-color photo along with the Boardwalk and Baseball trademark on the front. The player's name is in a yellow box in the lower left. The back lists the player's stats, team, position, and complete major league batting record for the 1980s. Packaged in a blue collector's box with a checklist on the back, the card set was a major marketing tool for the park in 1987. The 135-acre park, which became the Kansas City Royals' spring training home in 1988, includes a regulation ballpark and an amusement park.

FOR

It is an attractive collection of some of baseball's top offensive performers of the decade.

AGAINST

It is basically a rehash of other similar boxed sets.

NOTEWORTHY CARDS

Because of his Kansas City affiliation, George Brett will be called on to autograph more of these cards than anyone else. The Pedro Guerrero card is particularly attractive.

VALUE

MINT CONDITION: Complete set, $5; stars, 25¢–75¢; superstars, $1. 5-YEAR PROJECTION: Average.

1987 FLEER

SPECIFICATIONS

SIZE: 2½ × 3½". FRONT: Color photograph. BACK: Red and blue printing on white cardboard. DISTRIBUTION: Nationally, in 15-, 28-, or 54-card packages with team logo stickers; complete sets sold through hobby dealers.

HISTORY

Often criticized for being too conservative, Fleer unveiled a 660-card set for 1987 with an innovative front design and a new statistical feature on the back. The most striking feature of the '87 Fleer card is the frame. A light blue border fades to white down the sides as it approaches a solid blue bottom border. The player's name and position are in the top left; the team logo is in the lower right.

1987 Fleer, Pete Rose

1987 Fleer, Dwight Gooden/Roger Clemens

1987 Fleer, Don Mattingly

The Fleer logo appears at the bottom of the card in a thin band that matches the uniform colors of the team. For example, Expos cards have a blue band and the Pirates have a yellow one. Since the cards are organized by team (with the players in alphabetical order), the color bands help with rapid identification of the card. The card backs are attractive, with the player's club, position, and personal info printed in white on a blue background. Career totals are in blue on a white or pink background. A new feature found at the bottom is a scouting report. A rather complicated graph shows how a hitter does against various kinds of pitching. A similar graph shows how a pitcher does in related situations. (A company called Mountain Lion, Inc. provided these stats.) The 1987 Fleer set included what is probably its last Pete Rose card (#213), since they only include active players in their annual issue. Rose of course, did not play that season, but is listed as both a player and manager on his card. Fleer included its usual "Major League Prospects" rookie series—two to a card. Collectors who held on to #652 hit the jackpot with Kevin Seitzer's first card. No other cards in this subset showcase anyone who upset the balance of power that season, although the Devon White and Dave Magadan cards generated some interest. Fleer also continued with their dual-player specialty cards, and collectors took to three of them. One features Dwight Gooden and Roger Clemens and is called "Dr. K. and Super K." Another features Wally Joyner and Jose Canseco and is called "Rookie All-Stars." The third pictures Don Mattingly and Darryl Strawberry and is called "Sluggers from the Left Side." The usual logo sticker cards were included with the Fleer packs but are not considered an integral part of the series. A set of 12 special All-Star cards (#1-#12) was included with the regular set. Since The New York Mets cards were also numbered starting at #1, there was confusion as to where these cards fit into the set. Included in the 12 All-Star cards were Mattingly, Tim Raines, George Bell, and Kirby Puckett. Fleer angered a segment of the hobby with a small run of glossy tin-boxed sets.

FOR

Good photos, an attractive design, and innovative card backs marked the 1987 set.

AGAINST

Short-supply tactics caused prices to escalate beyond the resources of many hobbyists. Some gave up on Fleer in frustration at not being able to build sets.

NOTEWORTHY CARDS

Seitzer's rookie card, the last Fleer Rose card, and interesting specialty cards make this a landmark set.

VALUE

MINT CONDITION: Complete set, $40; common card, 5¢–10¢; stars, rookies, 25¢–$1; superstars, $1.25–$3; Canseco, $6; Seitzer, $8. 5-YEAR PROJECTION: Above average.

1987 FLEER UPDATE

SPECIFICATIONS

SIZE: 2½ × 3½″. FRONT: Color photograph. BACK: Red and blue printing on white cardboard. DISTRIBUTION: Nationally, complete boxed sets sold through hobby dealers.

HISTORY

Following a tradition that began in 1984, Fleer issued an Update set of 132 cards in 1987. The set includes 131 player cards and a checklist card. They are numbered U-1 through U-132 and are in alphabetical order. The cards retain the regular '87 issue format and were available solely through hobby dealers. The cards were packaged in a special collector's box. In a departure from previous issues, Fleer produced both a glossy "Tin Set" and a regular issue. Collectors—already annoyed with Fleer's regular-season glossy tin set—virtually ignored the high-priced Update edition. Fleer has always had a reputation for conservative player selection and it took them until their '87 Update set to include a card of Mark McGwire. Consequently, the McGwire card became

1987 Fleer Update, Kevin Seitzer

1987 Fleer Update, Mark McGwire

the hot item in the set. A total of 44 cards are included in the Fleer Update set that were not a part of the Topps Traded set; assuring that interest would be high for both companies. Fleer didn't issue manager cards, which gave them additional room to include some marginal players. It is unlikely that this set's value will ever approach that of Fleer's 1984 Update set (now valued at more than $200), but with the inclusion of potential superstars such as McGwire, Kevin Seitzer, and Matt Nokes, there is potential.

FOR
It is a limited edition and includes several major league stars of the future.

AGAINST
The set was scarce and unrealistically priced by dealers from the day it was released.

NOTEWORTHY CARDS
McGwire makes his Fleer debut and Nokes, Seitzer, Ellis Burks, and B.J. Surhoff add to the value of this set.

VALUE
MINT CONDITION: Complete set, $12; common card, 10¢–15¢; stars, potentially hot rookies, 40¢–$1; Seitzer, $2.25; Nokes, $2.50; Mike Greenwell, $3; McGwire, $3.75. 5-YEAR PROJECTION: Above average.

1987 FLEER BOX BOTTOMS

SPECIFICATIONS
SIZE: Single card, 2 × 3½"; panel, 5¼ × 7½". FRONT: Color photograph. BACK: Red and blue printing on gray cardboard. DISTRIBUTION: Nationally, one 4-card panel on the bottom of Fleer wax-pack boxes.

HISTORY
For the second consecutive year, Fleer included four-card panels on the bottom of their wax-pack boxes. The 1987 issue included 16 different cards in four 4-card panels. Each panel includes three player cards and a team logo card. The logo cards feature the 1986 playoff teams: the Mets, Red Sox, Angels, and Astros. Cards in the set carry the same design as those in the regular 1987 issue; only the photos and the numbering sequence are different. Cards are numbered C-1 through C-16. Logo cards have the team emblem set against a light blue and white background with the words "Limited Edition Logo" underneath. The Fleer logo appears in the upper right and the Major League Baseball logo is in the lower left. The 12 players included are all stars and superstars, and the cards of Mike Schmidt and George Brett are particularly attractive. Since the '87 Fleer set was so scarce, you can imagine how difficult complete sets of the 4-card panels were to acquire, especially in Mint condition. As with all box-bottom issues, the complete box is the most valuable. Full panels are next in value, followed by neatly cut individual cards.

FOR

The attractive, limited-edition cards of some of the top players of the day make these box bottoms worthwhile.

AGAINST

They are extremely scarce.

NOTEWORTHY CARDS

Schmidt and Brett—two "old-guard" superstars of the late 1980s—have very nice cards.

VALUE

MINT CONDITION: Complete set of four panels, \$15; single panel, \$3–\$4; single card, 50¢–\$1.
5-YEAR PROJECTION: Above average.

1987 Fleer Box Bottoms

1987 FLEER CLASSIC MINIATURES

SPECIFICATIONS

SIZE: 1 13/16 × 2 9/16″. FRONT: Color photograph. BACK: Red and blue printing on white cardboard. DISTRIBUTION: Nationally, complete boxed sets sold through hobby dealers.

1987 Fleer Classic Miniatures, Tony Gwynn

1987 Fleer Classic Miniatures, Kirby Puckett

HISTORY

In 1987 Fleer produced its second consecutive set of miniature baseball cards. Called "Classic Miniatures," the set contains 120 player cards (sized roughly between a 1950 and 1951 Bowman). The design is the same as the regular 1987 set, which is one of Fleer's most original, except they are high-gloss and the photos are different. Card backs are identical to the regular set, and provide a wealth of statistical information in an attractive format. The usual compliment of stars were included, but not players who had changed teams via trades or free agency. Consequently, N.L. MVP Andre Dawson, Reggie Jackson, Lance Parrish, and other popular players were simply omitted from the set. Collectors often have difficultly accepting smaller versions of popular sets and have seldom placed a premium on them. (The exception being Topps' 1975 smaller version.) Another drawback is that the set is generally available only within the hobby, giving it a collector-issue stigma. Finally, the cards don't fit into the normal 9-pocket plastic sheets, forcing collectors to search out smaller sheets if they care to display these cards.

FOR

Many of 1987's top players appear in an attractive, miniature format.

AGAINST

A lot of people don't like smaller-sized sets.

NOTEWORTHY CARDS

The cards of Wade Boggs, Pete Incaviglia, Wally Joyner, and Tim Raines have very nice portraits. The Don Mattingly card is a good action photo.

VALUE

MINT CONDITION: Complete set, \$6; common card, 10¢; stars, 25¢–75¢. 5-YEAR PROJECTION: Below average.

1987 FLEER GAME WINNERS

SPECIFICATIONS

SIZE: 2½ × 3½″. FRONT: Color photograph. BACK: Red and blue printing on white cardboard. DISTRIBUTION: Nationally, sold through hobby dealers; regionally, at Pay'n Save, Motts, M.E. Moses, Bi-Mart, and Winn's stores.

HISTORY

The undisputed boxed-set champion, Fleer in 1987 produced "Baseball's Game Winners," an interesting 44-card limited-edition set. The cards were created specifically for distribution at various stores. As usual, the cards did not carry the store name, only the Fleer logo. The full-color, standard-sized card has a light blue border with the name of the set at the bottom in yellow, red, and black type. Players were picked for their game-winning RBIs or runs scored in 1986. Pitchers were chosen on the basis of games won or saved. The reason for selection was listed at the top of the card along with the player's name. The card back has the usual Fleer look for 1987. Printed in red and blue, it features the player's lifetime career stats and

1987 Fleer Game Winners, Roger Clemens

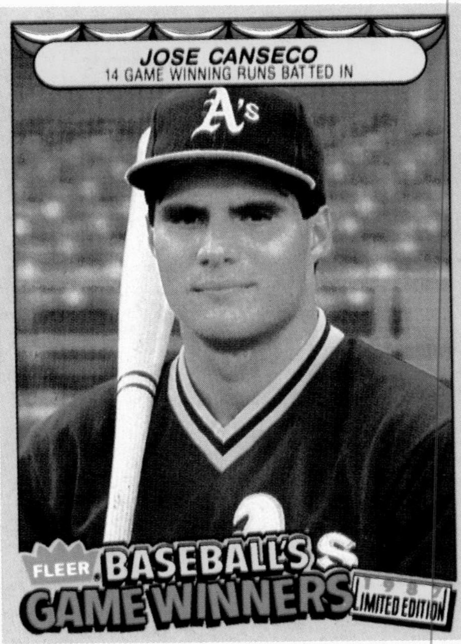

1987 Fleer Game Winners, Jose Canseco

personal information. Although this set was based on statistical performance, it yielded pretty much the same familiar cast of characters. Don Mattingly is there, based on his 15 game-winning RBIs in 1986, as are Eric Davis, Jose Canseco, Dwight Gooden, and Mike Schmidt.

FOR

An attractive set with a realistic theme for selecting players that is unique in limited-edition issues.

AGAINST

This is basically a rehash of the same players that almost always show up in special sets. Being a regional issue, it was somewhat scarce.

NOTEWORTHY CARDS

Red-hot 1986 stars Canseco and Roger Clemens make the set more attractive.

VALUE

MINT CONDITION: Complete set, $6; common card, 15¢; stars, 25¢–$1. 5-YEAR PROJECTION: Average.

1987 DONRUSS

SPECIFICATIONS

SIZE: 2½ × 3½". FRONT: Color photograph. BACK: Yellow and black printing on white cardboard. DISTRIBUTION: Nationally, in 15- or 54-card packages with jigsaw puzzle pieces; complete sets sold through hobby dealers.

HISTORY

Donruss always goes for wild borders and the 1987 660-card issue is no exception. The player photo is reproduced in brilliant color inside a rounded rectangle with a white border. All this is enclosed in a black frame interrupted on the sides by a gray

1987 Donruss, Jose Canseco

1987 Donruss, Eric Davis

1987 Donruss, Roger Clemens

band with little baseballs in it, set off by two yellow lines. The Donruss logo appears in the upper left and the team logo is in the lower right. The immediate problem with black borders is that they scuff easily and as time goes by it becomes harder to find Mint cards. (Collectors had the same problem with the 1971 Topps set.) The player's name and position appear in a solid color border at the bottom. Card backs are unexciting and similar to past Donruss offerings. You get up to five years of minimal personal stats and a few lines of career highlights. The first 27 cards are Diamond Kings, featuring the artwork of Dick Perez. Young stars Wally Joyner, Roger Clemens, Jose Canseco, Eric Davis, and Kevin McReynolds are the high-demand items in that subset. Three D-K cards were printed with the words "Donruss Diamond Kings" in a white band on the back instead of yellow. The Davis card was the only one corrected. The next 20 cards (#28-#47) are "Rated Rookies," the most popular Donruss subset among many collectors. Hot items in this category include Benito Santiago, B. J. Surhoff, Bo Jackson, Devon White, Chris James, and the hottest: Mark McGwire. Donruss also included an outstanding array of rookies that were not featured on the "Rated Rookies" cards. This gave them a chance to be the first company to issue cards of several potential stars. Highly prized '87 Donruss cards include Don Mattingly, Will Clark, Joyner, Pete Incaviglia, Clemens, and Ruben Sierra. The traditional Donruss puzzle portrait (another Perez offering) is a salute to Roberto Clemente. Card #612 in the set is the Clemente picture completed. As had become an annoying trend, Donruss cards were in short supply in 1987, especially at the beginning of the year. This drove prices and tempers through the roof. It was next to impossible to find a pack of Donruss cards on a store shelf, and some collectors went through the entire season without so much as a sample for their type book.

FOR

Scarce cards make good investments. The high number of rookies included makes the set desirable to true fans.

AGAINST

Scarce cards turn collectors off; if you can't get a card you usually get mad at the company that created the problem.

NOTEWORTHY CARDS

The McGwire card, because it was included in a scarce set, is the most valuable card in the set. The Clemens and Canseco "Diamond Kings" are attractive salutes to two exciting players from the previous season.

VALUE

MINT CONDITION: Complete set, $37; common card, 5¢–10¢; stars, rookies, 50¢–$2; McGwire $7.
5-YEAR PROJECTION: Above average.

1987 DONRUSS THE ROOKIES

SPECIFICATIONS

SIZE: 2½ × 3½″. FRONT: Color photograph. BACK: Black and yellow printing on white cardboard. DISTRIBUTION: Nationally, complete sets sold through hobby dealers.

1987 Donruss The Rookies, Mark McGwire

1987 Donruss The Rookies, Ellis Burks

HISTORY

For the second year in a row, Donruss issued "The Rookies," a 56-card boxed set featuring the top first-year performers of the 1987 season. The set contains 55 player cards and a checklist card issued in a colorful collector's box. Like all other Donruss issues of 1987, a Roberto Clemente puzzle was included, this one in miniature. Never one to miss out on a good bet, the Donruss '87 rookie set includes one player from the Donruss '86 rookie set—Bo Jackson of the Kansas City Royals. And although they had previously issued a 1987 Mark McGwire card, that didn't stop them from packaging him in this one too. The cards look just like the regular-season edition except for the borders, which are dark green instead of black. The card backs are identical except for the obvious numbering changes. There is no "R" designation by the number because Donruss assumed the different border colors would differentiate the two sets. Many valuable cards appear in the set—McGwire, Ellis Burks, Matt Nokes, Jackson, Mike Greenwell, Todd Benzinger—but the most noteworthy inclusion is the first Fleer card of Royals' star Kevin Seitzer. Donruss is recognized as the most daring of the four major card producers because they include many more first-year players in their regular issue. However, this makes it difficult for them to do anything different in the way of a postseason set that includes attractive first-year performers.

FOR

The set features attractive cards of 55 potentially hot big league players.

AGAINST

The scarcity of the cards and the inflated prices dealers charge for them is a turn-off.

NOTEWORTHY CARDS

Seitzer's first Donruss card and McGwire's second Donruss card of 1987 are the top picks in this set.

VALUE

MINT CONDITION: Complete set, $11; common card, 10¢; hot rookies, 40¢–65¢; McGwire, $2.25; Seitzer, $3. 5-YEAR PROJECTION: Above average.

1987 DONRUSS OPENING DAY

SPECIFICATIONS

SIZE: 2½ × 3½″. FRONT: Color photograph. BACK: Yellow and black printing on white cardboard. DISTRIBUTION: Nationally, complete sets sold through hobby dealers.

1987 Donruss Opening Day, Dale Murphy

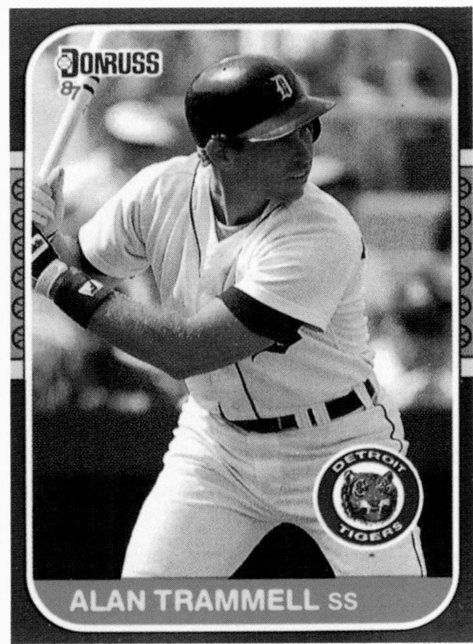

1987 Donruss Opening Day, Alan Trammell

HISTORY

Donruss surprised the hobby in 1987 by issuing a 272-card set of players who were in the opening-day starting lineup for each of the 26 Major League clubs. There are nine players from each of the 12 National League teams and ten (starters plus DH) from each of the 14 American League teams. Completing the set were 24 checklist cards (one for each team, with the Mets and Yankees sharing a card as well as the Cubs and White Sox). Donruss issued the set in an attractive collector's box with pieces of the full-size Roberto Clemente puzzle from their regular issue included for good measure. The design of the Opening Day set is identical to the regular set except for a maroon border instead of black. The card back resembles the regular issue in color, but includes a brief write-up on the player, personal information, and a one-line lifetime stats box. The cards are numbered in the upper left. A couple of things were working against the set from day one. Several top stars of 1987 were not in their team's opening-day lineup. As a result, the set was missing Mark McGwire, Tim Raines, Dwight Gooden, and Roger Clemens, to name a few. Collectors reacted unpredictably to the set. Dealers assumed it would be scarce and charged top dollar. Some collectors, angry with Donruss because of what many considered to be contrived shortages in the regular issue, stayed away from the set. Also, an error crept into the set: the photo of Pirate Bobby Bonds was actually Johnny Ray. Donruss caught the error early and few incorrect Bonds cards got into the hobby (Donruss estimated it was about 1 in 200).

FOR

It was a unique set that commemorated the 26-team opening-day lineups.

AGAINST

Many of 1987's top players were not in their teams' opening-day lineup, so the set is missing some of the brightest stars.

NOTEWORTHY CARDS

Reggie Jackson's first card upon his return to the Oakland A's in his final season is a nice memento of a great career.

VALUE

MINT CONDITION: Complete set, \$15–\$20; common card, 5¢–10¢; stars, hot rookies, 25¢–\$1; Bonds error, \$75. 5-YEAR PROJECTION: Below average.

1987 DONRUSS HIGHLIGHTS

SPECIFICATIONS

SIZE: $2\frac{1}{2} \times 3\frac{1}{2}$". FRONT: Color photograph. BACK: Tan and black printing on white cardboard. DISTRIBUTION: Nationally, complete sets sold through hobby dealers.

1987 Donruss Highlights, Darryl Strawberry

1987 Donruss Highlights, Benito Santiago

HISTORY

Donruss issued a 56-card "Highlights" boxed set for the third year in a row. The set features the players and pitchers of the week and of the month, for each week and month in the big leagues. Also included are cards highlighting special baseball events and milestones of the 1987 season. Donruss continued the tradition of making the set available only through hobby dealers toward the end of the year. Mark McGwire, the most visible newcomer to baseball in '87, is featured on three different cards. One salutes him as the "Rookie of the Year," another spotlights his rookie home run record, and a third celebrates his breaking Reggie Jackson's single-season Oakland home run record. For good measure, Donruss also includes McGwire on a card with teammate Jose Canseco that commemorates their Oakland RBI records. The cards look like the regular '87s except they come on glossy stock and have a light blue border instead of black. The same little baseballs show up in the middle of the card borders. Donruss includes 1987 Hall of Fame inductees Catfish Hunter, Billy Williams, and Ray Dandridge in the set. It was the first-ever baseball card of Dandridge, who spent his entire career in the Negro leagues. Since no color photo of Dandridge was available, they colorized a black-and-white one, and for consistency did likewise with the Hunter and Williams photos. It was the same process they used with Hall of Famers in the 1986 set.

FOR

The cards are a nice historical wrap-up of the season, and they appeal to collectors of baseball history.

AGAINST

Many collectors see it as a weak excuse to rerun star and superstar cards, and hobby enthusiasm for the set has waned since 1985.

NOTEWORTHY CARDS

The only Dandridge card issued by a major card producer is a nice addition to anyone's collection.

VALUE

MINT CONDITION: Complete set, \$9; common card, 10¢–20¢; stars, 50¢–\$1. 5-YEAR PROJECTION: Below average.

1987 SPORTFLICS

SPECIFICATIONS

SIZE: $2\frac{1}{2} \times 3\frac{1}{2}$". FRONT: Color photographs. BACK: Color photograph; red, blue, and black printing on white cardboard. DISTRIBUTION: Nationally, in three-card packages with team logo cards; complete sets sold through hobby dealers.

HISTORY

Amurol Products Co. returned for a second year in 1987 with a 200-card Sportflics set. Each "Magic Motion Baseball" package contained three baseball cards with three player photos per card, and two team logo trivia cards with facts about different

1987 Sportflics, Kent Hrbek

1987 Sportflics, Ryne Sandberg

1987 Sportflics, Bob Horner

teams. The front of the 1987 card is reminiscent of the 1986 edition. Through the wonders of modern technology, the cards show three different shots of the same player in 3-D action (a novel idea when Kellogg's introduced it years ago, and one that Amurol improved upon). Darrell Evans (#132) is observed swinging through a pitch in three stages. (Whether Evans really hit the ball is a mystery, because it's never seen on the card.) Ditto random batting shots of players such as Andre Dawson and Brian Downing. Sportflics also included a subset of the best players at each position in both leagues (three to a card) and another subset of "Hot Rookie Prospects." To cap it off, they produced a card called "The Best of the Best" (#197) that features six players in each phase of the magic motion. Sportflics introduced a full-color back photograph in this set. The company has built a reputation for having the best card backs in recent baseball card history. A nice full-color head shot of the featured player fills the upper left of the card, flanked by his name and number in white inside a blue box. Below the box are personal stats and major league lifetime record. As if that wasn't enough, Sportflics added a thorough biography of each player. Some collectors actually bought Sportflics for their backs and displayed them that way. They got one back photo wrong: Pat Tabler shows up on Cory Snyder's card (#24). They corrected the error, although three variations of the card surfaced before they got it right. The set never gained enough momentum to threaten any of the "Big Three" card manufacturers, and after two years Amurol produced a more competitive card, Score. In the first two editions of Sportflics (1986 and 1987), the player's position was absent from the front of the card.

FOR

The 1987 Sportflics set was readily available in stores and that helped it gain favor with collectors.

AGAINST

It was the highest priced of all the sets that year, and the novelty of the set had worn off.

NOTEWORTHY CARDS

The "Hot Rookie Prospects" card including Kevin Seitzer and five other lesser lights is a saver. Don Mattingly (#1) is the highest priced card in the set; Jose Canseco is a close second.

VALUE

MINT CONDITION: Complete set $32; common card, 10¢; superstars 30¢–$1; Seitzer, $2.50; Canseco, $2.50–$3; Mattingly, $3. 5-YEAR PROJECTION: Well below average.

1987 SPORTFLICS ROOKIES

SPECIFICATIONS

SIZE: 2½ × 3½″. FRONT: Color photographs. BACK: Color photograph; red, blue, and black printing on white cardboard. DISTRIBUTION: Nationally, two 25-card series sold through hobby dealers.

HISTORY

Sportflics continued with their "Rookies" set, but in 1987 they produced it in two installments. The first series of 25 player cards and 17 trivia cards was released in mid-summer; the second series came out in late fall. The cards are in the same style as the regular 1987 Sportflics edition and use the "Magic Motion" printing process that provides a 3-D look. In addition to the pictures on the front of the card, a full-color photo of the player appears on the back and takes up a third of it. The rest of the back includes a career record and extensive bio of the player. The individual write-ups and the amount of information make these card backs the best in the hobby. The set includes hot rookies of 1987 such as Mark McGwire, B.J. Surhoff, Kevin Seitzer, and Joe Magrane. Hobbyists did not exactly knock themselves out to acquire this set because all the featured players appeared in postseason sets issued by other companies. The novelty of a 3-D rookie set did not prove successful.

FOR

A nice 3-D collection highlighting the top young stars of 1987 with extensive player information.

AGAINST

Few people wanted a 3-D collection of the top young stars of 1987.

NOTEWORTHY CARDS

There are no cards worth gushing about.

VALUE

MINT CONDITION: Complete set, $13; common card, 25¢; stars 50¢–$1. 5-YEAR PROJECTION: Well below average.

1987 BURGER KING ALL-PRO

SPECIFICATIONS

SIZE. 2½ × 3½″. FRONT: Color photograph. BACK: Black printing on white cardboard. DISTRIBUTION: Pennsylvania, New Jersey, one 2-card panel with food purchase at Burger King restaurants.

1987 Burger King All-Pro, Wally Joyner

1987 CARD COLLECTOR'S COMPANY

SPECIFICATIONS

SIZE: 2⅛ × 3¼". FRONT: Color portrait. BACK: Red and blue printing on white cardboard. DISTRIBUTION: Nationally, complete sets sold through hobby dealers.

1987 Burger King All-Pro, Wade Boggs

HISTORY

Burger King issued its second edition of "All-Pro" cards in 1987. The 20-card set features many of the game's top stars (including the inevitable Don Mattingly) in the traditional baseball card size. The card fronts and backs are cluttered with stars at the top and bottom. The Burger King logo is prominent in the upper left, and the words "All-Pro 2nd Edition" tell collectors this is a continuation of the Mike Schechter-produced 1986 Burger King set. The player's name appears in yellow type below the photo along with his team and position in black type on a red band. Caps are airbrushed. The card back is printed in simple but striking black and white and includes a detailed narrative write-up of the player's career, along with '86 season and career stats.

FOR

Burger King continued their hobby involvement with this scarce local issue.

AGAINST

Airbrushed photos offend the sensibilities of collectors.

NOTEWORTHY CARDS

All 20 cards picture stars or superstars.

VALUE

MINT CONDITION: Complete set of panels, $10; single card, 50¢; stars, $1–$2. 5-YEAR PROJECTION: Average.

1987 Card Collector's Company, Jim Konstanty

HISTORY

In 1987 the New York-based Card Collector's Co. issued a complete 324-card reprint of the landmark 1951 Bowman set. The boxed set was marketed nationally, with an extensive advertising campaign. Considered by many to be the most attractive of the post-World War II sets, the '51 Bowman edition contains two of the most coveted of all rookie cards: Mickey Mantle and Willie Mays. The reprints could not be confused with the originals because they were done in a glossy finish on a totally different stock. The back of each card also carries the line "Reprint 1987 C.C.C." Card Collector's is headed by Richard Gelman, whose father, Woody, was a noted hobby pioneer. Gelman announced a total press run of 15,000 sets for the 1951 Bowman reprint. Much of the same criticism leveled at Topps when they reprinted their 1952 set in 1983 was hurled at Gelman; most notably, the color reproduction of the reprint was inferior to the original. (Although this is to be expected in a second-generation reproduction.) On the plus side, original Mint sets of the 1951 set are virtually impossible to acquire, and the Gelman issue gives hobbyists an opportunity to enjoy a historically significant set without needing a second mortgage. Later in 1987, Gelman's company issued a second reprint set, Bowman's 1952 baseball edition, also in a special collector's box.

FOR

Many collectors liked this landmark hobby set: it gave them a chance to obtain rookie cards of Mantle and Mays at an affordable price.

AGAINST

Purists don't like reprints.

NOTEWORTHY CARDS

Mays, Mantle, and many of the big stars of the early '50s—Robin Roberts, Bob Feller, Ted Williams—appear in this set.

VALUE

MINT CONDITION: Complete set, $25; common card, 10¢; stars, 50¢–$1. Team set, $4; Giants, $7; Yankees, Dodgers, $10. 5-YEAR PROJECTION: Below average.

1987 Coca-Cola White Sox, Bobby Thigpen

1987 COCA-COLA WHITE SOX

SPECIFICATIONS

SIZE: $2\frac{5}{8} \times 4''$. FRONT: Color photograph. BACK: Black printing on white cardboard. DISTRIBUTION: Team-issued, complete sets available through fan club.

HISTORY

The Chicago White Sox again issued a 30-card team set in collaboration with Coca-Cola in 1987. The set features the 1987 team, the team mascots, the club's organist, and even Minnie Minoso—a long-time ChiSox star and front office staff member. The cards are larger than the traditional size (the same as previous Coke sets). They are bordered in blue with a thin red frame. Player cards are identified with the uniform number, name, and position. (The organist, mascot, and Minoso have no numbers on their cards.) Backs contain year-by-year stats, the Coca-Cola logo, and the copyright line of the White Sox. The back of organist Nancy Faust's card also contains a mail-in offer for a record of the songs she regularly played at sporting events. The set was only available to members of the White Sox fan club, which made it a tough-to-complete, expensive regional issue.

FOR

It's a scarce team issue—the kind that collectors really like to acquire.

1987 Coca-Cola White Sox, Carlton Fisk

AGAINST

Because you had to join the White Sox fan club (at $10) to get one, it was a rather expensive set.

NOTEWORTHY CARDS

Rookie reliever Bobby Thigpen is included, as well as budding star Ozzie Guillen and possible future Hall of Famer Carlton Fisk.

VALUE

MINT CONDITION: Complete set, $12; common card, 15¢–25¢; stars, 50¢–$1. 5-YEAR PROJECTION: Average.

1987 DRAKE'S

SPECIFICATIONS

SIZE: 2½ × 3½″. FRONT: Color photograph. BACK: Black printing on gray cardboard. DISTRIBUTION: East Coast, on the bottom of boxes of Drake's products.

HISTORY

For the seventh straight year, Drake's issued a regional card set that collectors could put together by purchasing their products. The 33 cards were printed in panels on boxes of cakes, pies, and donuts. Each panel contained either two, three, or four cards depending on the product. One box had "Big Hitters" Mike Schmidt, Eddie Murray, and Steve Sax; another had cards of Ron Darling, Fernando Valenzuela, and John Tudor. The full-color cards are framed in yellow, with a Drake's logo in the upper left and the words "Super Pitcher" or "Big Hitter" in the upper right. The backs are simple and virtually unchanged from 1986. Complete career stats and the player's personal data are included, along with logos for assorted Drake's products. As with all box bottoms, the complete box is the most valuable. Neatly cut panels are next in value and are easier for collectors to display. Individually cut cards have the least value.

FOR

It's a nice set featuring many of the premier players in baseball.

AGAINST

As with most box-bottom sets, this one is difficult to complete and even harder to find in Mint condition.

NOTEWORTHY CARDS

They are all leading players. The Dwight Gooden and Don Mattingly cards are exceptionally nice.

VALUE

MINT CONDITION: Complete set of panels, $30–$40; single panel, 35¢–75¢; single card, 25¢; superstar panel, $1–$3. 5-YEAR PROJECTION: Above average.

1987 M&M's

SPECIFICATIONS

SIZE: Single card, 2½ × 3½″; panel, 5 × 3½″. FRONT: Color photograph. BACK: Red printing on white cardboard. DISTRIBUTION: Nationally, one 2-card panel in large-size packages of candy.

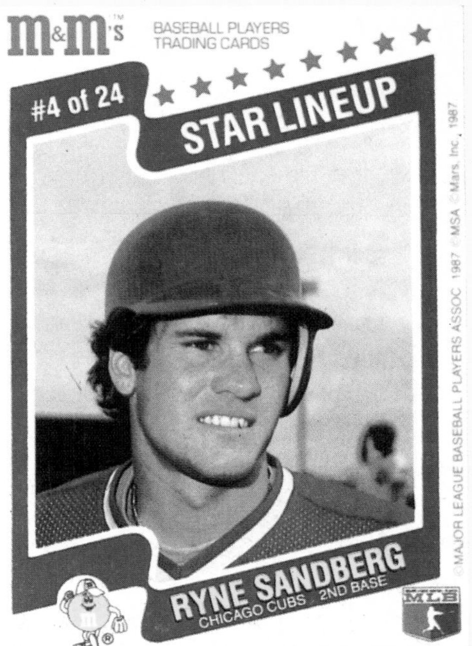

1987 M&Ms, Ryne Sandberg

1987 M&Ms, Wally Joyner

HISTORY

M&M's was the latest candy company to turn to baseball cards as a sales promotion. They hit the market in 1987 with a 24-card set called "Star Lineup" produced by the multifaceted Mike Schechter Associates. The cards were available in large-size packages of M&M's candy in 2-card strips, one strip to a package. The player photo is framed with a blue border that gives the appearance of a diagonal picture. The M&M's logo and the line "Baseball Player Trading Cards" appear in red printing in the upper left. A green M&M wearing a baseball uniform appears in the lower left, while the Major League Baseball logo appears in the lower right. Card backs have player stats since 1980 and brief career highlights. As with nearly all Schechter-made sets, players' caps were airbrushed. The players include Wally Joyner, Mike Schmidt, Roger Clemens, and Don Mattingly. The dilemma of the 2-card panel is whether to separate the cards or keep them intact. The best advice is to keep the cards together, though this makes displaying them in plastic sheets a challenge.

FOR

They are all stars and superstars, and that suits star-card collectors just fine. Also it's the first set to carry the M&M's banner.

AGAINST

Another set with airbrushed photos combined with a rehash of a superstar card format grows tiring. If you don't eat M&M's you may have never seen these cards.

NOTEWORTHY CARDS

They are all stars and superstars.

VALUE

MINT CONDITION: Complete set of panels $13; complete set of single cards, $6; single card, 10¢–25¢; stars, 50¢–$1. 5-YEAR PROJECTION: Average.

1987 Mother's Cookies, Chili Davis

1987 Mother's Cookies, Chris Brown

1987 MOTHER'S COOKIES

SPECIFICATIONS

SIZE: 2½ × 3½". FRONT: Color photograph. BACK: Red and purple printing on white cardboard. DISTRIBUTION: In-park promotion at six major league stadiums; promotion at 1987 National Sports Collectors Convention in San Francisco; eight cards available by mailing in premium coupon.

HISTORY

One of the most popular regional sets, Mother's Cookies again issued a set in 1987 (a 28-card set for each of six teams). It was also one of the toughest to complete. The 1987 issue includes the first-ever Mother's Cookies sets for the Texas Rangers and Los Angeles Dodgers, as well as a promotional tie-in with Bob Lee's National Sports Collectors Convention held that summer. In July and August of 1987, 20-card "starter packs" were given out as in-stadium promotions in Oakland, Seattle, Houston, San Francisco, Texas (Rangers), and Los Angeles. The starter packs included a coupon that could be mailed in for eight additional cards. The problem was that there was no guarantee they would be the eight cards needed to complete the set. Mother's Cookies believes in putting the "trading" back into trading cards. Unfortunately, this also put money into the pockets of dealers fortunate enough to corral large quantities of the cards. Four Mark McGwire cards were selling for well over $20 one year after they were issued. The cards have the usual Mother's high-gloss finish. Every set but the Oakland A's features current players. The A's set highlights every A's player to be selected to the A.L. All-Star team since the franchise moved to Oakland in 1968. Popular Oakland stars such as Reggie Jackson, Catfish Hunter, Rollie Fingers, and Jose Canseco, and skippers Billy Martin and Dick Williams, populate the set. As usual, the simple card backs include the Mother's logo, the player's name and number, how he was acquired (or his career All-Star stats in the A's set), and a line for an autograph.

FOR

Outstanding photography and a simple, elegant format are the highlights of this set.

AGAINST

It is an almost impossible set to complete, and Mother's lack of interest in selling directly to the collector makes the cost prohibitive.

NOTEWORTHY CARDS

There is a great market for the McGwire subset. Cards of other stars such as Will Clark, Canseco, and Fernando Valenzuela are sure to appreciate over the years.

VALUE

MINT CONDITION: Complete set of one team, $10–$12; McGwire subset, $17; common card, 25¢; stars, 50¢–$2; single McGwire cards, $4. 5-YEAR PROJECTION: Average.

1987 Ralston Purina, Roger Clemens

1987 Ralston Purina, Gary Carter

1987 RALSTON PURINA

SPECIFICATIONS

SIZE: 2½ × 3½". FRONT: Color photograph. BACK: Red printing on gray cardboard. DISTRIBUTION: Nationally, in boxes of cereal; complete sets available through a mail-in offer.

HISTORY

Ralston Purina returned to the baseball card market in 1987 with a 15-card set found in boxes of cereal. The cards were produced by Mike Schechter Associates. The standard-size cards have a rather garish front with full-color photos framed by a thin red border. The company logo appears in the upper left and the words "1987 Collector's Edition" are in the upper right. Between them are two crossed bats that take up nearly a third of the card. At the center of the bats is a star with the player's uniform number. The team logos on the players' caps are airbrushed, but the player's team affiliation along with his name and position appear in white type in a light blue box centered below the picture. Card backs include the player's lifetime major league stats and personal information. A card number appears in a little box in the lower left. The cards were packaged three to a box along with a game card that offered an uncut sheet of the set as well as other prizes. If you didn't win the uncut sheet, you could mail $1 and two game cards for a complete set. All the popular stars of the game appeared in this set but, like all such issues, collector interest was less than frantic.

FOR

Everybody's a star in this set, so it's just the ticket for people who covet such cards.

AGAINST

The airbrushed caps are a major turn-off.

NOTEWORTHY CARDS

Dave Parker didn't wear a hat, hence no airbrush. Mike Schmidt and Ryne Sandberg appear in batting helmets—maybe their team logos fell off.

VALUE

MINT CONDITION: Complete set, $12; common card, 20¢; stars, 25¢–75¢; uncut sheet of 15 cards, $9. 5-YEAR PROJECTION: Average.

1986 Topps, Pete Rose

1986 TOPPS

SPECIFICATIONS

SIZE: $2\frac{1}{2} \times 3\frac{1}{2}$". FRONT: Color photograph. BACK: Red and black printing on gray cardboard. DISTRIBUTION: Nationally, in 15-, 28-, or 54-card packages with bubblegum; complete sets sold through hobby dealers.

HISTORY

After several years of relatively staid designs, Topps surprised collectors with its 1986 set. Instead of the traditional white frame around the photo, there is a white border at the bottom and up three-quarters of the sides, and a broad black band across the top. The team name appears in huge letters in the top band. A color-coordinated circle at the lower left gives the player's position. Many collectors felt Topps gave too much prominence to the team name on its card fronts from '84 to '86 but dealers liked the 1986 design because it made the cards easier to sort into team sets. The player's name is in black across the bottom white border and the Topps logo is in the upper right. (The Topps logo was inadvertently left off the Ryne Sandberg card, but since the error was not corrected, it adds no value to the card.) Card backs feature complete major and/or minor league stats, along with biographical dates and figures. Some backs list career highlights or the player's first

1986 Topps, Vince Coleman

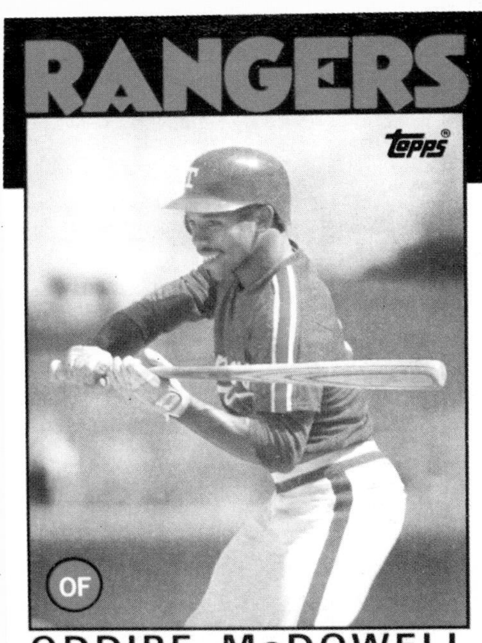

1986 Topps, Oddibe McDowell

Topps card appearance, and some include a "Talkin' Baseball" historical fact. At 792 cards, Topps was by far the largest of the nationally distributed card sets, leaving a lot of room for special cards. Following closely on the heels of Pete Rose's achievement of the all-time hit record, Topps opened its 1986 set with a Pete Rose card. There is also a 6-card set of special Rose cards. Each card features four miniature reproductions of Rose's earlier Topps cards, while the back details the milestones along his chase for the record. Topps reproduced a subset from an earlier issue on a group of "Turn Back the Clock" cards, which give capsule summaries of baseball history 5, 10, 15, 20, and 25 years ago and picture a Topps card of that year. A new Topps subset for 1986 was a series of Team Leaders cards, each depicting the player with the longest tenure on a particular team. The design of these cards was different from anything Topps had done before. The player photo fades into a white background with no defining line or border. The player is not identified on the front of the card. The card back lists the team's batting and pitching leaders in various statistical categories. Neither the design nor the concept proved popular with collectors. Other subsets picked up from previous years included a set of cards highlighting record-breaking performances of the previous season; cards for each team manager (with a team checklist on the back); and cards for each fan-elected starter in the 1985 All-Star Game, plus a lefthanded, righthanded, and relief pitcher for each squad.

FOR

An innovative design improves this issue.

AGAINST

Colors on the card backs make them hard to read and sort. Few of the year's promising rookies were included. (Topps might have elected to save them for its end-of-the-year "Traded" set at a much higher cost per card.)

NOTEWORTHY CARDS

A couple of numbering errors will cause confusion among collectors for a long time to come: The cards of Mariners manager Chuck Cottier and Expos manager Bob Rodgers both carry #141 on the back. (Rodgers was supposed to be #171.) Astros second baseman Bill Doran and Braves manager Bobby Wine are both #57. (Wine should have been #51.)

OUR FAVORITE CARD

One of the "Turn Back the Clock" cards depicts Fernando Valenzuela—the rookie sensation of the 1981 season—on the front of an '81-style card. At first glance, it appears to be a reproduction of Valenzuela's 1981 Topps "Traded" card. (Valenzuela's card in the regular set that year showed him with two other Dodgers "Future Stars.") A closer look, though, clearly shows that the photo is entirely new.

VALUE

MINT CONDITION: Complete set, $28; common card, 5¢; stars, rookies, 15¢–65¢; superstars, hot rookies, $1–$3. 5-YEAR PROJECTION: Above average.

1986 TOPPS TRADED

SPECIFICATIONS

SIZE: 2½ × 3½". FRONT: Color photograph. BACK: Red and black printing on white cardboard. DISTRIBUTION: Nationally, complete sets sold through hobby dealers.

HISTORY

Topps had the first, and most successful, postseason Traded set. The 1986 Topps Traded set marked the sixth annual issue. Traded sets were originally designed to update the regular set by offering cards of players who had been traded. A second, more popular, purpose is to present premier cards of new players. These hot rookie cards induce collectors to invest in the Topps Traded sets. As in past years, the 1986 Traded series was sold only as a complete set—and generally with a large mark up—through hobby

1986 Topps Traded, Wally Joyner

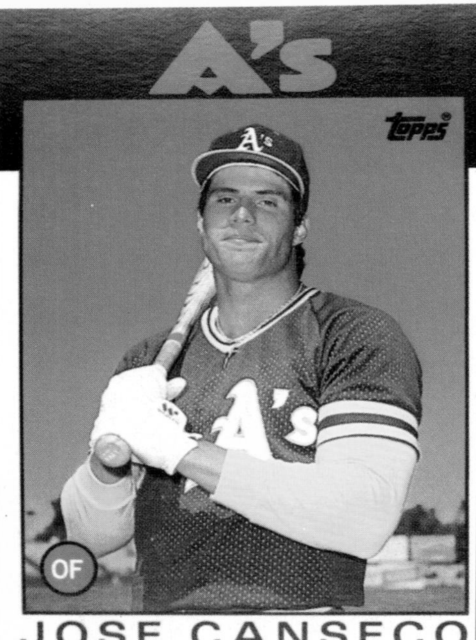

1986 Topps Traded, Jose Canseco

dealers. It came in a bright red box containing 131 player and manager cards and a checklist card. The format is identical to the '86 regular issue except the backs are much more readable because they are printed on white cardboard.

FOR

More potentially great players made their major league debuts in 1986 than in any year in recent history, thus a great many cards of new players are in high demand. Naturally, many will not pan out, but the cards of those who do will become more valuable with each passing year.

AGAINST

While collector resentment against postseason sets has virtually vanished in the face of their rising value, some still can't forgive Topps for not including most of the new players in their regular set at 2¢ per card, instead of in the Traded set at 6¢ to 8¢. Because Topps doesn't have a blanket contract to picture all players on its cards, and some players hold out from signing individual contracts on the advice of the union, the Topps Traded set did not include several potentially hot rookies like Ruben Sierra and Ed Correa.

NOTEWORTHY CARDS

The set includes rookie cards of hot 1986 stars such as Wally Joyner, Jose Canseco, Bo Jackson, Bobby Witt, Charlie Kerfeld, Kurt Stillwell, Mark Eichhorn, Danny Tartabull, Barry Bonds, John Kruk, Andres Galarraga, Pete Incaviglia, and Will Clark. There is also a card of Tom Seaver as a member of the Boston Red Sox.

VALUE

MINT CONDITION: Complete set, $14; common card, 6¢–15¢; stars, hot rookies, $1–$2; Jackson, $2.50; Clark, $3; Joyner, $4; Canseco, $5. 5-YEAR PROJECTION: Above average.

1986 TOPPS BOX BOTTOMS

SPECIFICATIONS

SIZE: Single card, 2½ × 3½"; single panel, 5 × 7". FRONT: Color photograph. BACK: Red and black printing on gray cardboard. DISTRIBUTION: Nationally, one of four 4-card panels printed on the bottom of Topps wax pack boxes.

HISTORY

Never one to let a good baseball card idea go by—even if it was "borrowed" from a competitor—Topps copied Donruss' idea from the previous year by printing four different 4-card panels on the bottom of its wax pack boxes. The theory was that kids and collectors would buy the last few packs in order to get the empty box. Many store owners and dealers, however, simply stacked the packs outside the boxes and sold the panels separately. The 16 cards that make up the box-bottom set are almost identical to the regular Topps cards for the year.

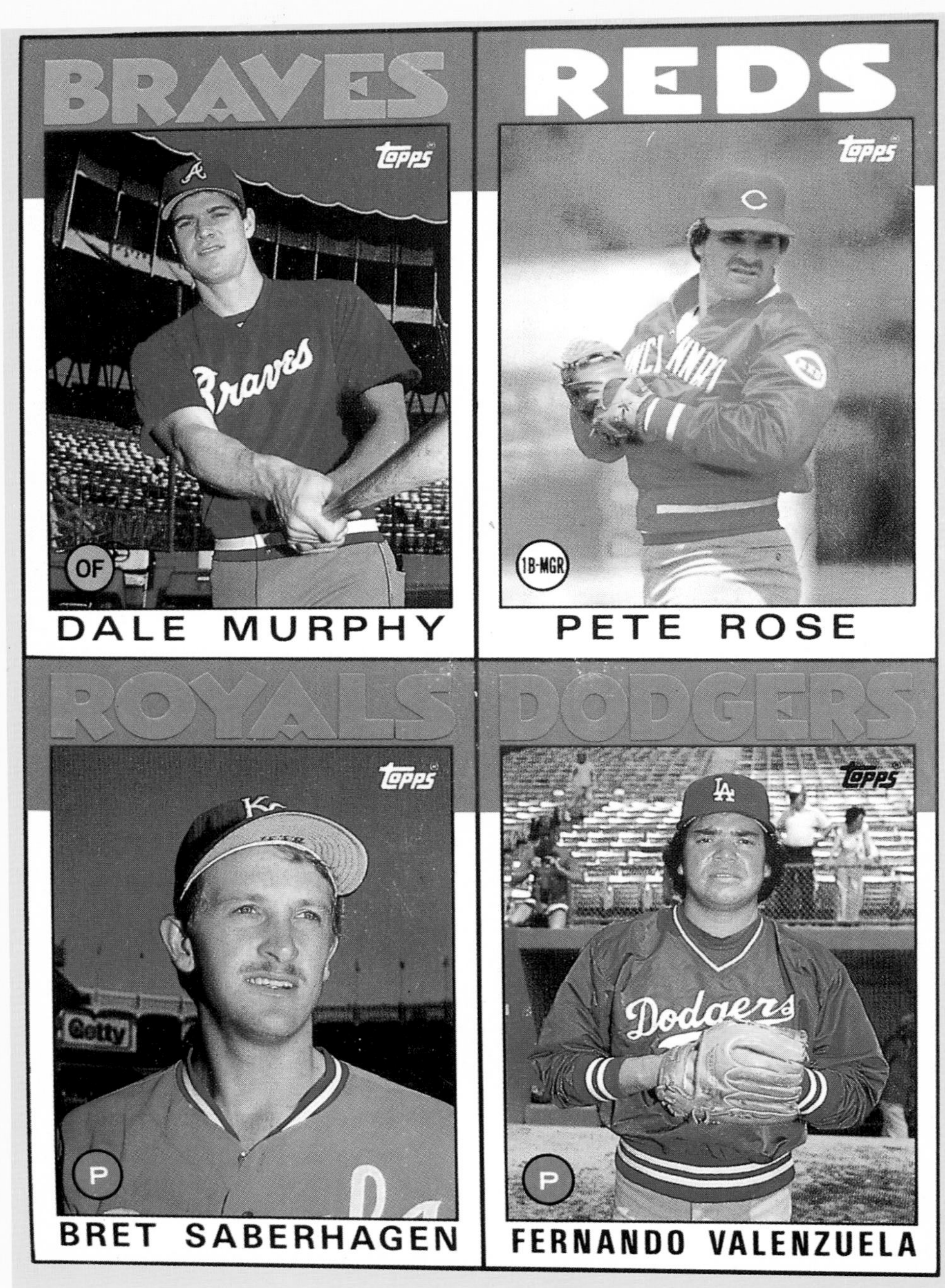

1986 Topps Box Bottoms

One difference is that the band across the top containing the team name is red instead of black. Also, the photos are different from those found on the regular issue. Card backs are nearly identical to regular '86 Topps, but the cards are lettered A through P instead of numbered. As with all box-bottom cards, the complete box is worth more than the panel itself, which is worth more than the individual cards.

FOR

The red band makes the box-bottom cards "the same, but different" from regular 1986 Topps cards—an idea that collectors seem to like. The cards are scarce for a relatively new set (especially cards in Mint condition).

AGAINST

It's hard to find these cards in Mint condition. The corners on the edge of the panel tend to crease and the card faces often got scuffed.

NOTEWORTHY CARDS

The set has rookie cards of Oddibe McDowell and Vince Coleman; cards of currently hot Dwight Gooden, Wade Boggs, and Don Mattingly; and cards of future Hall of Famers Pete Rose, Reggie Jackson, and Dale Murphy.

VALUE

MINT CONDITION: Complete set of four panels, \$12; single panel, \$3; single card, 50¢–\$2.50. 5-YEAR PROJECTION: Above average.

1986 TOPPS MAIL-IN GLOSSIES

SPECIFICATIONS

SIZE: 2½ × 3½". FRONT: Color photograph. BACK: Red and blue printing on white cardboard. DISTRIBUTION: Nationally, six 10-card sets available by mailing in premium cards found in Topps wax packs.

HISTORY

In its third year of offering mail-in glossy sets of "All-Star Collectors' Edition" cards, Topps changed the rules slightly but not the cards. As in the previous two years, the cards featured an ultra-simple front design: a large color photograph bordered by a colored frame with the player's name in tiny letters in the lower left. Card backs identify the player by name, team, and position, and have a card number and Topps logo. There are no player stats or biographical information. The only way to obtain the cards was to collect the "Spring Fever Baseball" sweepstakes cards in Topps wax or cello packs. For six cards and \$1 the collector could choose one of six 10-card sets. The 60-card set was an increase from the 40-card sets of 1984 and 1985. Besides established superstars, the 1986 issue contained many of the year's hottest rookies. A high-gloss finish on the front of the card makes it an attractive collectible.

1986 Topps Mail-In Glossies, Gary Carter

1986 Topps Mail-In Glossies, George Brett

FOR

Lots of big-name stars and hot rookies appear on cards that are relatively scarce compared with Topps' regular issue cards.

AGAINST

It was hard to get Mint cards through the mail; many were damaged en route, which forced collectors to buy from dealers. Also, the minimum cost of obtaining a 60-card set totaled nearly \$23 (36 sweepstakes cards taken from 35¢ wax packs, \$1 for each card subset, and 39¢ for postage). That's more than 30¢ a card—too high for a new issue. Also, the design is identical to the previous two issues.

NOTEWORTHY CARDS

Rookie cards of Oddibe McDowell, Dan Pasqua, Vince Coleman, and Ozzie Guillen are included, along with all the popular established stars.

VALUE
MINT CONDITION: Complete set, \$14; common card, 13¢; superstars, \$1–\$2. 5-YEAR PROJECTION: Below average.

1986 Topps All-Star Glossies, Reggie Jackson

1986 TOPPS ALL-STAR GLOSSIES

SPECIFICATIONS
SIZE: 2½ × 3½″. FRONT: Color photograph. BACK: Red and blue printing on white cardboard. DISTRIBUTION: Nationally, one card in 54-card rak-paks.

HISTORY
As in previous years, Topps created a 22-card All-Star Glossy set for inclusion as a bonus card in its 54-card rak-pak. As before, the set features the nine starters from the National and American League All-Star teams of 1985, along with managers Sparky Anderson and Dick Williams. The 1986 edition also includes a team card depicting the entire All-Star squad for each league. The design is virtually identical to previous years, with a player photo, an "All-Star" banner at the top with the year 1985 above it, and the player's name and position in a yellow box at the bottom. There is a high-gloss coating on the front of the card. Backs contain little more than a shield proclaiming "1985 All-Star Game Commemorative Set," the player's name and position, and a card number.

1986 Topps All-Star Glossies, Darryl Strawberry

FOR
They are an inexpensive way to get contemporary cards of the game's best players. Collectors can avoid paying dealers' high prices for these sets by waiting until next year's set is issued, when the price usually drops.

AGAINST
The design is too similar in format to previous years' issues. The set is quite abundant since most rak-paks end up in dealers' hands rather than store shelves.

NOTEWORTHY CARDS
They were all All-Stars, at least for one season.

VALUE
MINT CONDITION: Complete set, \$4; common card, 10¢–20¢; superstars, 40¢–50¢. 5-YEAR PROJECTION: Average, perhaps below.

1986 TOPPS MINIS

SPECIFICATIONS

SIZE: 2½ × 2⅞″. FRONT: Color photograph. BACK: Red and blue printing on white cardboard. DISTRIBUTION: Nationally, in wax packs and through dealers in vendor cases.

1986 Topps Minis, Brett Butler

1986 Topps Minis, Don Mattingly

HISTORY

The 1986 Topps minis came as a surprise to the hobby early in the year. Perhaps, like their 1975 mini set, it was a test to determine the small-size-card market (smaller cards would save enormously on printing costs). Some dealers believed Topps' statement that the set was only going to be offered regionally. They bought up store stocks at high prices, only to have the value of the set fall quickly when Topps made the minis available in vendor cases to dealers nationwide. The premise of this "Major League Leaders" set (as the issue was officially known) was to depict the leaders (the top five in some cases) in various 1985 statistical categories. The result was cards of all the popular stars and a few top rookies. There are 65 player cards in the set, along with a checklist. Topps picked up the design used in its special League Leaders cards in the regular 1986 set. The front of the card has a high-gloss finish. The player photograph fades into a white border with no frame or lines. A Topps logo at the upper left and the player name at the bottom are the only other design elements. Card backs feature a team logo, 1985 and career stats, and a brief run-down on why he qualified as a league leader.

FOR

The minis offered a rare chance for collectors to buy a Topps specialty issue in gum packs. It includes a good group of 1986's top stars. They are currently inexpensive and collectors like the small size.

AGAINST

The design of the card has not proved popular with collectors.

NOTEWORTHY CARDS

All the familiar stars and top rookies of other 1986 specialty sets are featured, but none are especially significant.

VALUE

MINT CONDITION: Complete set, $5.50; common card, 5¢; stars, 25¢; superstars, 50¢–$1.
5-YEAR PROJECTION: Average, or somewhat below.

1986 FLEER

SPECIFICATIONS

SIZE: 2½ × 3½″. FRONT: Color photograph. BACK: Black and yellow printing on white cardboard. DISTRIBUTION: Nationally, in 15-, 28-, or 54-card packages with team logo stickers; complete sets sold through hobby dealers.

HISTORY

It's surprising how closely the major card companies sometimes parallel one another's issues. In 1986 Donruss produced cards with a dark blue border and thin black stripes, and strangely enough, the 1986 Fleer cards also had a dark blue border. Fleer is known for having excellent quality

1986 Fleer, Teddy Higuera

1986 Fleer, Willie Wilson

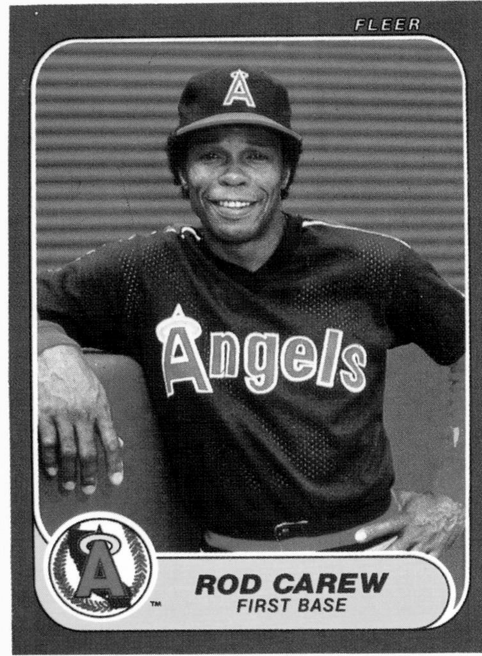

1986 Fleer, Rod Carew

photos, and the '86 cards were neatly complemented by the border, with a full-color team logo at the lower left, and a team-color coded "lozenge" at the bottom containing the player's name and position. The rounded corners of the photos are a nice contrast to the hard, square edges of the cards. For the first time in several years, card backs did not include a player photo and collectors didn't seem to miss the bug-size portraits. The popular and more readable vertical format was retained for 1986. Included are the basic statistics (the only complete minor and major league stats on a major card company issue in 1986) and, in most cases, a "Did You Know?" box of facts about the player's career. Fleer continued its sensible method of arranging cards alphabetically within teams. The 1985 World Champion Royals are pictured on the first 25 cards in the set, while the N.L. pennant-winning Cardinals follow. The rest of the teams appear on the basis of their 1985 won-loss percentage. With only 660 cards in its regular set, Fleer couldn't include many subsets beyond the checklists and a group of multiplayer feature cards. There are "In Action" cards of Dwight Gooden and Don Mattingly, and a handful of career milestone and record performance cards. Popular with collectors is a run of ten "Major League Prospects" cards, on which two potential rookie sensations (usually teammates) share a card front. This doesn't prevent Fleer from issuing single-player cards of them in the "Update" set at the end of the year. Fleer pulled a major marketing coup in 1986 by including a couple of specialty sets in their retail packs (they were not available in the vendor cases sold to dealers). One set was a 12-card "Fleer All Star Team" series; the other was a 6-card "Future Hall of Famer" group. The All Star Team cards are reminiscent of the 1958 Topps design and feature a photo of the player set against a borderless red or blue background with three yellow stars. A National or American League logo appears in black and white in the lower left, while the player's name, team, and position appear in yellow on a blue or red band at the bottom. Backs have a career summary. The Future Hall of Famer cards are similar in design, with light blue horizontal stripes in the background instead of stars. The player's name, team, and position are shown in a yellow panel at the bottom and to the left is an identifying logo. Again, the backs have a written career summary. Since these cards were not available in vendor cases, collectors had to assemble these specialty sets by buying individual card packs and trading. This has made these cards relatively expensive.

FOR

The presence of the All Star and Future HOFer cards made packs of '86 Fleer cards scarce compared with previous years.

AGAINST

There is not much to criticize in the 1986 Fleer set. Okay, maybe the All Star and Future Hall of Famer cards are too expensive.

NOTEWORTHY CARDS

Hot rookie cards of Jose Canseco, Cory Snyder, Kal Daniels, Benito Santiago, and Andres Galarraga (among the Major League Prospects two-player cards) make this set attractive.

VALUE

MINT CONDITION: Complete set, $70; common card, 4¢; stars, 10¢–30¢; superstars, hot rookies, 50¢–$8; All Stars and Future HOFers, $1–$2.50; Santiago, $5; Canseco, $33–$35. 5-YEAR PROJECTION: Above average.

1986 Fleer Update, Wally Joyner

1986 Fleer Update, Jose Canseco

1986 FLEER UPDATE

SPECIFICATIONS

SIZE: 2½ × 3½". FRONT: Color photograph. BACK: Black and yellow printing on white cardboard. DISTRIBUTION: Nationally, complete sets sold through hobby dealers.

HISTORY

In its third consecutive year of production, the 1986 Fleer "Update" set followed the successful formula of including as many rookie cards as possible among the 131 players. A checklist card completes the set. Unlike Topps and Donruss, the 1986 Fleer Update set missed one of the year's biggest rookies, Bo Jackson. The set does have a handful of cards that Topps lacks, including Ruben Sierra and Ed Correa. Other than the "U-" prefix of the card numbers on back, the design is the same as the regular 1986 Fleer cards. Like past issues, the '86 Updates were sold only through dealers in complete boxed sets. Many dealers broke up the sets into single-player lots from 1 to 100 cards to satisfy collectors, so single cards are relatively easy to obtain.

FOR

Lots of potential big-name rookie cards appear in an attractive, relatively limited-edition set.

AGAINST

The high cost of the set (it sold for $6 to dealers, but was marked up immediately to about twice that price) makes it less desirable.

NOTEWORTHY CARDS

The set has all the year's top rookies: Wally Joyner, Jose Canseco, and the rest—with the notable exception of Bo Jackson.

VALUE

MINT CONDITION: Complete set, $17; common card, 6¢–25¢; stars, hot rookies, 50¢–$1; Sierra, $2.50; Will Clark, $3; Joyner, $4; Canseco, $5. 5-YEAR PROJECTION: Above average.

1986 FLEER BOX BOTTOMS

SPECIFICATIONS

SIZE: Single card, 2½ × 3½"; panel, 5 × 7". FRONT: Color photograph. BACK: Black and yellow printing

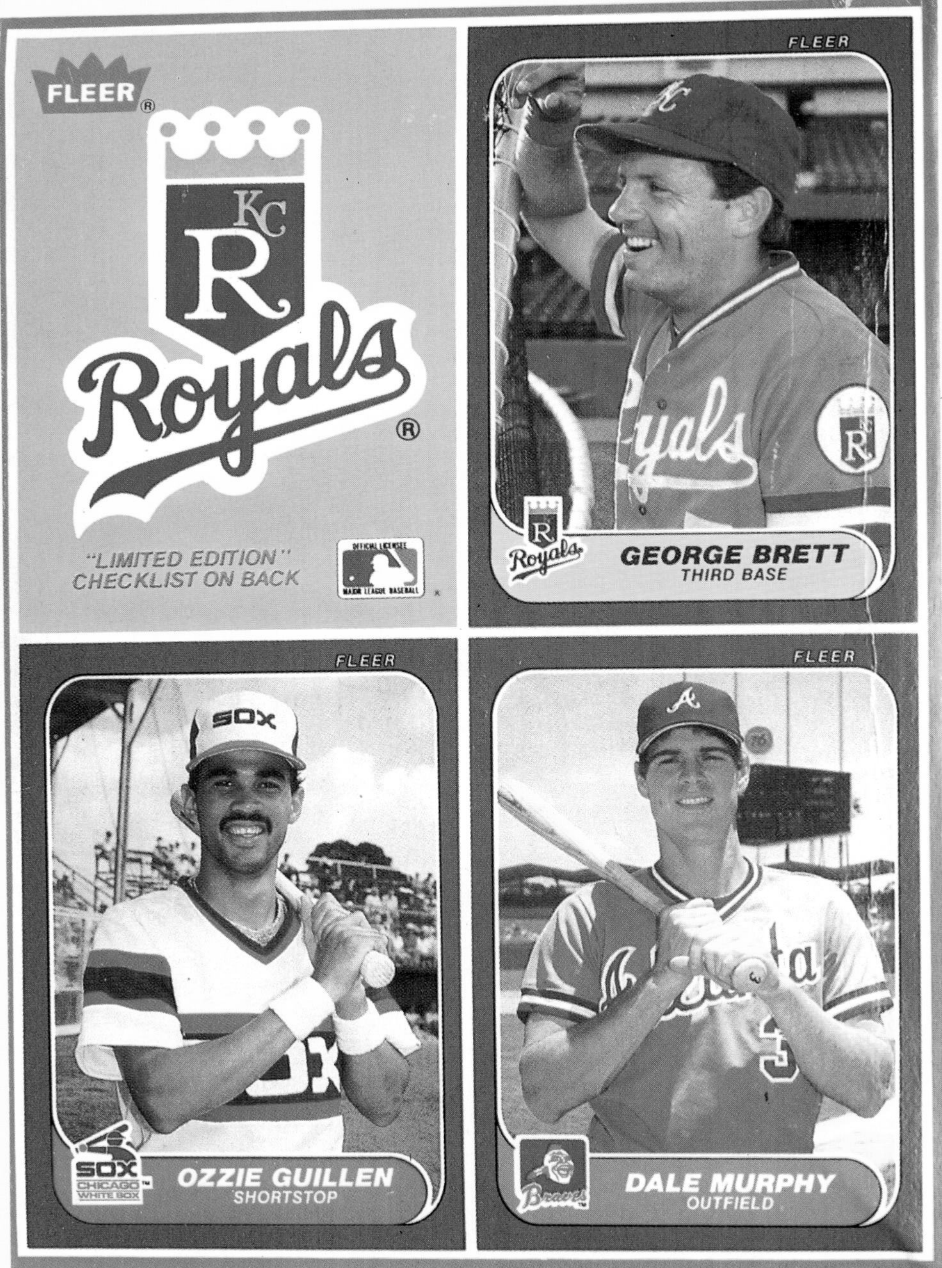

1986 Fleer Box Bottoms

on white cardboard. DISTRIBUTION: Nationally, one 4-card panel on the bottom of Fleer wax-pack boxes.

HISTORY

Like Topps, Fleer was at first hesitant to steal Donruss' idea of printing baseball cards on the bottom of its wax pack boxes to boost sales. Fleer produced two different panels featuring a total of six players and the team logos of the World Series competitors, St. Louis Cardinals and K.C. Royals. Fleer retained the same basic design as the year's regular-issue cards, with new photos and a different numbering system, C-1 through C-8. Like other box bottoms, the Fleer set can be hard to find in Mint condition because the edges and corners of the box tend to become creased and scuffed. Because Fleer wax packs were quickly grabbed up in search of All Star and Future Hall of Famer cards, the box bottoms are not easy to find. As always, value is greatest when the boxes are left intact.

FOR

They are limited-edition cards of some of the game's most popular players.

AGAINST

Should we really be patronizing Fleer for borrowing one of Donruss' better ideas?

NOTEWORTHY CARDS

What the heck, there are only six in the set: George Brett, Ozzie Guillen, Dale Murphy, Tom Browning, Gary Carter, and Carlton Fisk.

VALUE

MINT CONDITION: Complete set of two panels, $2; single panel, $1–$1.50; common card, 50¢–$1. 5-YEAR PROJECTION: Above average.

1986 FLEER MINIS

SPECIFICATIONS

SIZE: 1 13/16 × 2 9/16". FRONT: Color photograph. BACK: Black and yellow printing on white cardboard. DISTRIBUTION: Nationally, complete sets sold through hobby dealers.

HISTORY

It's amazing, but after more than ten years since one of the major card manufacturers produced a mini-size card set, two of the "Big 3" came out with minis in 1986. The Fleer issue seems to have won the collector vote for the best mini set of 1986, largely because they patterned their minis on the regular-issue cards for the year. (Topps used a different design for its set). Except for a new photograph on the front, a glossy finish, and a different card number on the back, the Fleer minis were no different from the standard-size cards. They feature a dark blue border, with a team logo and information panel in matching colors at the bottom. The 120 players in the set are divided roughly among the 26 major league teams.

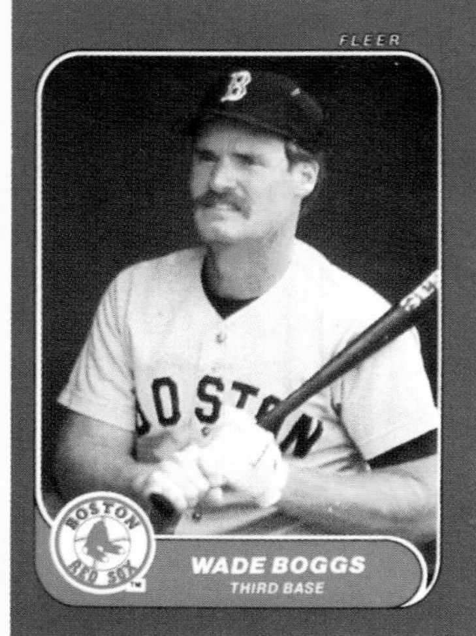

1986 Fleer Minis, Wade Boggs

1986 Fleer Minis, Kirby Puckett

FOR

Collectors seem to like mini cards, especially when they repeat the format of a normal-size issue.

AGAINST

It was fairly high priced because of relatively limited production.

NOTEWORTHY CARDS

The set includes a Jose Canseco rookie card plus an excellent selection of 1986's most popular players.

VALUE

MINT CONDITION: Complete set, $11; common card, 5¢; stars, 20¢–$1.25; Canseco, $1.50; Mattingly, $2. 5-YEAR PROJECTION: Average.

1986 FLEER LIMITED EDITION

SPECIFICATIONS

SIZE: 2½ × 3½″. FRONT: Color photograph. BACK: Black and red printing on white cardboard. DISTRIBUTION: Regionally, complete sets sold at various department stores and dimestores.

HISTORY

For the second straight year, Fleer produced a boxed set of 44 cards for distribution by the McCrory's department store chain. The set was also sold at McClennan, Britt's, and Green stores, and at independent dimestores served by McCrory's. As with most issues intended for sale over the counter to the public, dealers quickly moved in and snapped up most of them. The set, which was supposed to sell for about $2, quickly shot up to $5 in the hobby market. The cards feature a color photo (different from the regular-issue Fleer card) bordered at the top and bottom in bright green and on the sides by yellow. A yellow banner at the top proclaims "Fleer Limited Edition 1986" in red letters. The player's name, team, and position are printed in yellow at the bottom. No store names appear on the cards or on the box. A checklist is on the back of the box. Card backs have full career and biographical statistics along with a team logo and card number. Six team logo stickers, like those found in Fleer's wax packs, were included with each boxed set.

1986 Fleer Limited Edition, LaMarr Hoyt

1986 Fleer Limited Edition, Rich Gedman

FOR

This colorful set includes all of the expected superstars and some rookies. The photo quality is good.

AGAINST

Collectors were turned off by having to pay more than retail price to dealers who had gobbled up the available stock. Prices have retreated from one-time highs.

NOTEWORTHY CARDS

Many of the same superstars who appeared in other 1986 "special" card sets will be found here. The rookie cards of Oddibe McDowell and Vince Coleman are notable.

VALUE
MINT CONDITION: Complete set, $4.50; common card, 10¢; stars, hot rookies, 50¢–80¢. 5-YEAR PROJECTION: Average.

1986 FLEER STAR STICKERS

SPECIFICATIONS
SIZE: 2½ × 3½″. FRONT: Color photograph. BACK: Blue and black printing on white cardboard. DISTRIBUTION: Nationally, in wax packs with logo stickers.

1986 Fleer Star Stickers, Steve Carlton

HISTORY
Fleer repeated its 1981 idea of marketing baseball-card-size stickers in 1986. The results were the same: instead of reaching store shelves to be bought by youngsters, virtually the entire issue wound up in dealer's hands, resulting in an immediate price increase. The Star Stickers of 1986 feature a color photo (different from the regular Fleer cards) framed by a yellow ribbon with a dark maroon outer border. The player's name, team, and position appear in red below the photo. The front of the card can be peeled away from the back and used as a sticker, but naturally any sticker used this way becomes worthless to a collector. There are 131 individual player stickers in the set. A special sticker of Dwight Gooden and Dale Murphy has the set checklist on the back. Backs are nearly identical to the regular 1986 Fleer cards and feature complete major and minor league stats, biographical figures, and a card number.

FOR
For superstar or team collectors, the set offers more cards of the game's most popular players.

AGAINST
Collectors resent paying more than retail price for a new set that was supposed to be available to them over the counter. They generally panned the color scheme.

NOTEWORTHY CARDS
The 1986 Fleer Star Stickers contained one of the first Jose Canseco cards available to collectors, making unopened boxes and wax packs a popular item with "treasure hunters."

VALUE
MINT CONDITION: Complete set, $25; common card, 5¢; superstars, 35¢–$3; Canseco, $3–$4. 5-YEAR PROJECTION: Slightly above average.

1986 DONRUSS

SPECIFICATIONS
SIZE: 2½ × 3½″. FRONT: Color photograph. BACK: Blue and black printing on white cardboard. DISTRIBUTION: Nationally, in 15- or 54-card packages with jigsaw puzzle pieces; complete sets sold through hobby dealers.

HISTORY
Donruss deviated little in 1986 from its successful formula of the recent past. As in 1984 and 1985, Donruss deliberately printed fewer of its cards than collector demand might warrant. The result was an immediate shortage and correspondingly high prices. It was virtually impossible to find packs of cards on store shelves. The 660-card set featured an innovative design: player photos were in the shape of a parallelogram instead of a square. And rather than the usual black or white border, Donruss opted for a dark blue border with thin black horizontal stripes. A red and white "Donruss '86" logo appears in the upper left and a team logo or "Rated Rookie" logo appears in the lower left. The player's name and position appear in a strip in team colors beneath the photo. Backs are a virtual clone from previous seasons. A white box at the center features statistics of "Recent Major League Performance." Career highlights, brief vitals, and

1986 Donruss, Chili Davis

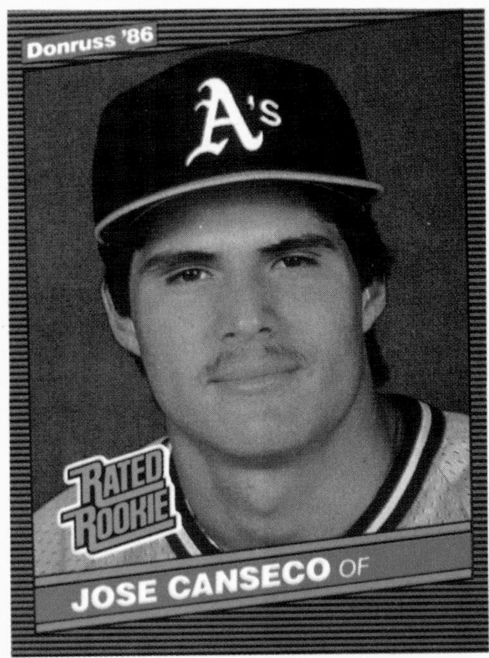

1986 Donruss, Jose Canseco

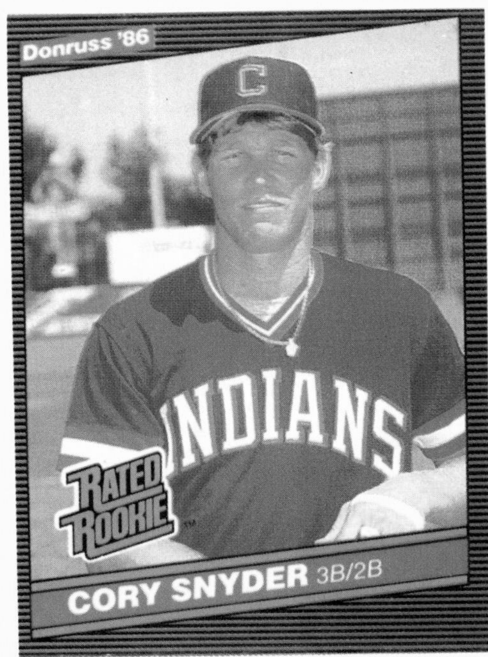

1986 Donruss, Cory Snyder

the status of the player's contract are in black on a light blue background. As in every year since 1982, the set opens with a 26-card run of "Diamond King" cards, one for each team. A player is featured in a painted portrait rather than a photo (none are repeated from previous years). A special "King of Kings" card featuring Pete Rose is the final card in the 1986 set. Following the Diamond Kings are the popular Rated Rookies cards featuring the year's fastest-rising stars. Other than Jose Canseco, Cory Snyder, Danny Tartabull (featured on a 1985 Rated Rookie card), and Andres Galarraga, the 1986 picks weren't looking like baseball's next generation of superstars by the close of the season. Donruss included few multiplayer cards in the 1986 set: a card showing Pete Rose's big hits to tie and break the all-time record, one featuring "Knuckle Brothers" Phil and Joe Niekro as Yankee teammates, and a card depicting the Cardinals' base-stealing duo Vince Coleman and Willie McGee.

FOR

The instant scarcity of the set made them a "must-have" for many collectors, even at high prices. It was a great investment for those who could lay hands on them early in the year.

AGAINST

The high cost of brand-new cards turned many collectors away from the set.

NOTEWORTHY CARDS

A few errors crept into this set in 1986. Most notable are two cards with the wrong position on the front: David Palmer was labeled as second baseman instead of pitcher; and Joel Youngblood was listed as pitcher instead of infielder. The errors were later corrected. Tom Seaver's card had to be corrected to get the right color-coordination in the bottom stripe with his name on it. The checklist initially listed card #45 as Billy Beane, but the card was issued as John Habyan. This, too, was later corrected. There were a handful of other variations, but none have generated much interest.

VALUE

MINT CONDITION: Complete set, $95; common card, 4¢–10¢; stars, rookies, 50¢–$2.50; Canseco, $40–$50. 5-YEAR PROJECTION: Above average.

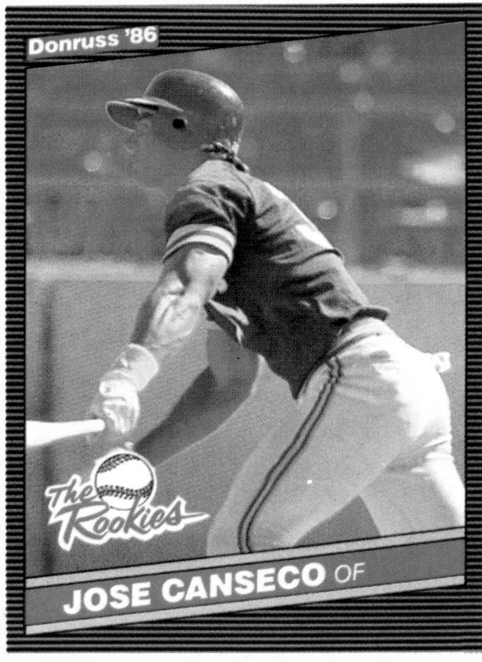

1986 Donruss The Rookies, Jose Canseco

1986 DONRUSS THE ROOKIES

SPECIFICATIONS

SIZE: 2½ × 3½″. FRONT: Color photograph. BACK: Black and green printing on white cardboard. DISTRIBUTION: Nationally, complete sets sold through hobby dealers.

1986 Donruss The Rookies, Wally Joyner

1986 Donruss The Rookies, Ruben Sierra

HISTORY

Donruss created the instant collectible of 1986 with its limited-production "The Rookies" 56-card boxed set. Dealers were notified of the availability of this first-time effort from Donruss, but by the time most of them got their checks to the company, the issue had been sold out. Dealers lucky enough to obtain quantities of the cards at the $3.90 issue price were able to turn around and get $15 to $25 for them immediately. The main attraction, besides the limited number printed, was the theme of the set. Rather than including traded ballplayers in its postseason set like Topps had done since 1981, and Fleer since 1984, Donruss composed this set entirely of new (or nearly new) ballplayers. Many of them had not yet played a game in the major leagues when their cards appeared. Donruss closely followed the design of its regular 1986 set, except The Rookies cards had a dark green border with black stripes instead of a blue border, and the backs were printed in green and black rather than blue. Donruss mistakenly labelled its statistics box on the card back "Major/Recent Minor League Performance" instead of "Recent Major/Minor League Performance." The error appears on all cards. The high-gloss finish on the front of the cards was a nice touch. Even at the high prices charged to collectors, the set may prove a good investment as more of the players become established stars.

FOR
Lots of potentially great players receive attractive cards in a limited edition.

AGAINST
Extremely high prices to collectors, with high mark-ups by dealers, turned a large segment of the hobby against the issue.

NOTEWORTHY CARDS
The set consists of the big-name rookies of 1986: Jose Canseco, Wally Joyner, Bo Jackson, Tracy Jones, Cory Snyder, Todd Worrell, Pete Incaviglia, and Ruben Sierra.

VALUE
MINT CONDITION: Complete set, $20; common card, 10¢–35¢; hot rookies, 75¢–$2; Clark, Jackson, Sierra, $3–$4; Joyner, $5; Canseco, $7. 5-YEAR PROJECTION: Average.

1986 DONRUSS BOX BOTTOMS

SPECIFICATIONS
SIZE: Single card, 2½ × 3½″; panel, 5 × 7″. FRONT: Color photograph. BACK: Black and blue printing on white cardboard. DISTRIBUTION: Nationally, one 4-card panel on the bottom of All-Star and wax pack boxes.

HISTORY
Although its competitors had stolen the idea, Donruss returned in 1986 with two special baseball card panels printed on the bottom of its regular-issue and All-Star pack boxes. Each panel included three player cards (featuring a different photo from the regular issue) and a picture of the Hank Aaron jigsaw puzzle that accompanied all 1986 Donruss issues. The idea, of course, was to encourage people to buy more packs so they could get the last one and claim the empty box. In reality, few boxes made it to store shelves for 1986; most were snapped up by dealers at the wholesale level.

FOR
It's still a good idea, even if it has been copied.

AGAINST
Donruss' choice of players wasn't too hot. It's hard to find cards in Mint condition because box bottoms tend to get creased and scuffed.

NOTEWORTHY CARDS
Here's the complete checklist: Kirk Gibson, Willie Hernandez, and Doug DeCinces from the regular wax pack box; Wade Boggs, Cecil Cooper, and Lee Smith from the All-Star box.

VALUE
MINT CONDITION: Single panel, $2–$3; single card, 15¢–35¢; Boggs, $1–$2. 5-YEAR PROJECTION: Below average.

1986 DONRUSS ALL-STARS

SPECIFICATIONS
SIZE: 3½ × 5″. FRONT: Color photograph. BACK: Black and yellow printing on white cardboard. DISTRIBUTION: Nationally, in cello packs with jigsaw puzzle pieces.

HISTORY
In its fifth year of oversize card issue, Donruss chose to go with an All-Star format. The 60 cards in the set represent the complete American and National League squads from the 1985 All-Star Game in Minneapolis, along with the managers, a card of the Metrodome, and a checklist. Like earlier large-size Donruss sets, the basic design of the regular issue was repeated, with vertical black stripes on a dark blue background (stripes were horizontal on the regular issue). Instead of team logos, each All-Star card shows a large (perhaps

1986 Donruss All Stars, Minneapolis Metrodome

too large) National or American League insignia in the lower left. Backs feature a team logo, personal data, career highlights, and 1985 and lifetime All-Star Game performance stats.

FOR
Good photos of lots of 1986's big stars and hot rookies appeal to autograph collectors.

AGAINST
Collectors don't generally like large cards.

NOTEWORTHY CARDS
They're virtually all big-name stars.

VALUE
MINT CONDITION: Complete set, \$6; common card, 7¢; stars, 25¢–90¢; Mattingly, \$1.50. 5-YEAR PROJECTION: Below average.

1986 DONRUSS POP-UPS

SPECIFICATIONS
SIZE: 2½ × 5″. FRONT: Color photograph. BACK: Red, black, and blue printing on white cardboard. DISTRIBUTION: Nationally, in packs of Donruss All-Star cards.

1986 Donruss Pop-Ups, Ryne Sandberg

1986 Donruss Pop-Ups, Roger Clemens

HISTORY

Really a separate issue from the Donruss All-Stars, the 18 Pop-Ups were inserted—one card to a pack—into All-Star cello packages. The 18 players in the Pop-Ups represent the nine starting players for the National and American Leagues in the 1985 All-Star Game in Minneapolis. The card front consists of a player photo against the background of the Metrodome. The area around the card is die-cut around the player to allow the background to be folded back. Card backs have the player's name, team, and position, a large All-Star Game logo, and instructions for folding the player figure. Naturally, cards that have not been folded are worth the most.

FOR

This innovative issue should be of interest to the superstar and team collector.

AGAINST

The set received little publicity.

NOTEWORTHY CARDS

Every player was an All-Star performer.

VALUE

MINT CONDITION: Complete set (unfolded), $5; common card, 15¢; stars, 50¢–75¢. 5-YEAR PROJECTION: Average or below.

1986 SPORTFLICS

SPECIFICATIONS

SIZE: 2½ × 3½". FRONT: Color photographs. BACK: Black, red, and blue printing on white cardboard. DISTRIBUTION: Nationally, in packs with baseball trivia cards; complete sets sold through hobby dealers.

HISTORY

A fourth major company entered the baseball card market in 1986 when Amurol Products Co. began marketing a 200-card Sportflics set. Since Topps had the exclusive right to sell its cards with gum, Amurol packaged a pair of baseball trivia cards in each 3-card pack of its new issue. Sportflics cards have a 3-D action effect, with between 3 and 12 different pictures on the front of each card. The cards give the illusion of watching a player swing or a pitcher throw the ball. The card of George Brett, for instance, shows a portrait of the Royals slugger when held at one angle, but when tilted up

1986 Sportflics, George Brett

1986 Sportflics, Carlton Fisk

or down, two other pictures appear, showing Brett at different stages in his swing. The photos are framed by a white border with no other design elements on the card front. While attempts to create 3-D baseball cards had been made as far back as the late 1960s, none had ever before captured the feeling of motion. Other cards in the set feature portraits of three different players, visible in turn as the angle of viewing changes. Triple-player cards were grouped under such headings as Strikeout Kings, Base Stealers, and Home Run Champs. Other cards feature as many as 6 or 12 different players on a single card. Card backs in the Sportflics set may be the best in recent baseball card history. Each single-player card features complete major league stats, biographical details, a brief career summary, team name and logo, and—a first for any major baseball card issue—the player's uniform number. The only element missing is the player's position. The regular issue features multiplayer cards that also serve as single-player cards. Hobbyists who stay away from multiplayer cards probably will not like Sportflics; youngsters probably will.

FOR

For a first-year product, Sportflics did a good job of getting its cards into the hands of kids and collectors. Much more widely distributed at the retail level than either Fleer or Donruss, Sportflics also effectively served the hobby market by making cases of its product available to dealers. The "Magic Motion" effect is innovative and will be especially attractive to younger collectors.

AGAINST

The large segment of the hobby who don't like bells and whistles on their baseball cards won't like the Magic Motion feature. Collectors, especially youngsters, may have trouble with the high cost of the cards. At three cards per 59¢ retail pack, the cost per card is nearly 20¢. Complete sets purchased from dealers were generally in the $30 to $35 range—two to three times what the other, much larger, sets from Topps, Fleer, and Donruss cost when new. Also, it's virtually impossible to find hobby dealers who will sell single cards.

NOTEWORTHY CARDS

Jose Canseco appears as one of six rookie prospects on card #178 "Future Stars."

VALUE

MINT CONDITION: Complete set, $35; common card, 15¢; superstars, $1–$2.50; Canseco, $10.
5-YEAR PROJECTION: Below average.

1986 SPORTFLICS ROOKIES

SPECIFICATIONS

SIZE: $2\frac{1}{2} \times 3\frac{1}{2}$". FRONT: Color photographs. BACK: Color photograph and printing on white cardboard. DISTRIBUTION: Nationally, in boxed sets of 50 player cards and 34 "Rookies Trivia Quiz Cards" sold through hobby dealers.

1986 Sportflics Rookies, Mike Kingery

1986 Sportflics Rookies, Mark Eichhorn

HISTORY

Hoping to take a respectable share of the market from the "Big 3" baseball card producers, Sportflics jumped on the postseason bandwagon in its first year by issuing a set of cards for 1986's hottest new players. Besides the Magic Motion 3-D action effect, the Rookies set offered something new for collectors: a full-color player photo on the back of the card. Also on the back, though somewhat obscured by the abundant use of vivid red, yellow, and purple, are some of the finest player biographies to appear in any recent card set, along with complete major league stats. Like the regular Sportflics issue, the Rookies cards include the player's uniform number on the back as well as a card number. The card front is distinguished from regular 1986 Sportflics by a light blue frame around the player photo separating it from the white border. A few "Tri-Star" cards, featuring notable rookies of the past, are included in the set.

FOR

It's a pleasant collection of the year's hottest prospects. If you like the 3-D action effect, it's a plus, if you don't . . .

AGAINST

. . . it's a minus. Some collectors just don't like "gimmicks" on their baseball cards. Also, the issue price, about 25¢ a card, is pretty steep for a new issue.

NOTEWORTHY CARDS

The popular rookie stars of 1986—including Jose Canseco and Wally Joyner—are featured.

VALUE

MINT CONDITION: Complete set, $15; common card, 15¢–45¢; hot rookies, $1–$3. 5-YEAR PROJECTION: Below average.

1986 SPORTFLICS DECADE GREATS

SPECIFICATIONS

SIZE: 2½ × 3½″. FRONT: Black-and-white or color photographs. BACK: Full color on white cardboard. DISTRIBUTION: Nationally, complete sets sold through hobby dealers.

HISTORY

Late in the 1986 season, Sportflics produced a "Decade Greats" boxed set of 75 player cards and 51 baseball trivia cards. The set appears to be an effort to attract the older collector, as players from the 1930s through the 1980s were included. Like Sportflics' regular issue, the cards feature a "Magic Motion" effect on the front, displaying three different photos that come into view as the card is

1986 Sportflics Decade Greats, Charlie Gehringer

1986 Sportflics Decade Greats, Joe Cronin

tilted. Most cards feature three different photos of the same player—a portrait and two action shots—while other cards feature pictures of three different players, such as "Best Catchers of the '60s." Player photos from the '30s and '40s are black and white. The photos have only a simple white frame. Card backs feature great career write-ups, but only abbreviated stats from the decade that the player represents in the set. Back printing is colorful in hues of blue, red, green, and yellow.

FOR

It's interesting to see familiar faces from older baseball cards come to life through the Magic Motion feature.

AGAINST

Nobody sells single cards for superstar or team collectors, and the high production cost of these cards made them expensive—up to $20 a set when new.

NOTEWORTHY CARDS

They're all superstars.

VALUE

MINT CONDITION: Complete set, $13; stars, 35¢–50¢; superstars, $1–$2.50. 5-YEAR PROJECTION: Below average.

1986 TOPPS SUPERSTAR (WOOLWORTH)

SPECIFICATIONS

SIZE: 2½ × 3½". FRONT: Color photograph. BACK: Blue and green printing on white cardboard. DISTRIBUTION: Nationally, complete sets sold at Woolworth stores.

1986 Topps Superstar (Woolworth), Don Mattingly

1986 Topps Superstar (Woolworth), Keith Hernandez

HISTORY

Collectors who purchased one of these 33-card "Superstar" sets for $2 or so at a Woolworth's store were indeed fortunate. Like so many other sets in recent years, dealers and speculators snapped up virtually the entire issue—at retail price if they couldn't buy them at warehouse or wholesale price first. They knew collectors would double their investment for them. This was the second straight year Topps had produced a specialty set for Woolworth. The set came boxed with a checklist on back and featured current players who have held hitting, home run, or RBI titles. This left out pitchers entirely, and made the set one of 1986's few superstars collections that doesn't include Dwight Gooden. The Woolworth issue is one of the better-looking sets of the year. A quality photo (the lower right of which "rolls up" like the 1962 Topps cards) is surrounded by a bright yellow border with red stars and a blue "Superstar" logo. The player's name appears in small black print in the lower left. The card front has an attractive high-gloss finish. A red banner at the top proclaims the issue a "Topps Collectors' Series." The back features an attractive baseball diamond layout with a few vital player stats, lifetime major league batting record, and the years he led the league in hitting, homers, or RBIs.

FOR

This is a Topps-quality set of big-name players in a pleasant format.

AGAINST

Collectors had to pay a premium price to get a set that was supposed to sell for about $2. And it's the same old line-up of big names that appear in a dozen other sets for 1986.

NOTEWORTHY CARDS

They're all stars.

VALUE

MINT CONDITION: Complete set, $4–$5; common card, 6¢–10¢; superstars, 50¢–75¢. 5-YEAR PROJECTION: Below average.

1986 Fleer Baseball's Best, Julio Franco

1986 Fleer Baseball's Best, Pedro Guerrero

1986 FLEER BASEBALL'S BEST

SPECIFICATIONS

SIZE: 2½ × 3½". FRONT: Color photograph. BACK: Blue and red printing on white cardboard. DISTRIBUTION: Regionally, complete sets sold at dimestores.

HISTORY

Another special boxed set for 1986, this 44-card issue is also known as the "Sluggers vs. Pitchers" set. Such a theme allowed Fleer to include all of baseball's big names. The set was intended to be sold at chain outlets such as McCrory, McLellan, Green, Kreg, and TG&Y for about $2. As happened all too often, dealers managed to buy up most of the available stock before the cards ever reached store shelves. This initially resulted in high mark-ups, but the price fell somewhat after the first buying rush. The cards feature a large color photo with a bright yellow, jagged-edge band across the top with the date, Fleer logo, and the words "Baseball's Best." In the lower left is a box with either the word "Pitchers" or "Sluggers." The pitchers' cards have a blue panel beneath the photo with the player's name and a pertinent stat in white type. The sluggers' cards have the same information in a red panel. Card backs have a team logo, card number, brief player biographical data, and complete major and minor league stats.

FOR

A decent-looking set that includes lots of star players and has a somewhat novel theme.

AGAINST

Some collectors were turned off by having to pay a dealer $5 to $6 for a card set they should have been able to find on local store shelves for $2.

NOTEWORTHY CARDS

By fortuitous timing, this set was the first widely available issue to include a card of 1986 American League rookie of the year runner-up Wally Joyner. As such, it was extremely popular. Overlooked sometimes is the fact that the set also contains rookie cards of Bobby Witt, Will Clark, and Jose Canseco. Virtually every other card in the set is a past, current, or potential superstar.

VALUE

MINT CONDITION: Complete set, $5; common card, 10¢–25¢; superstars, hot rookies, $1–$1.50. 5-YEAR PROJECTION: Above average.

1986 FLEER LEAGUE LEADERS (WALGREENS)

SPECIFICATIONS

SIZE: 2½ × 3½". FRONT: Color photograph. BACK: Red and blue printing on white cardboard. DISTRIBUTION: Nationally, complete sets sold at Walgreens.

HISTORY

Walgreens commissioned Fleer to create a specialty card set for them in 1986. The 44-card set is entitled "League Leaders" and features a mix of established stars and rookies chosen more for their collector appeal than for their league-leading stats. The card front features a large color photo of the player with a red band at the top and a blue band at the bottom. The top band displays the Fleer logo, the date, and "League Leaders." The bottom has the player's name, team, and position printed in white. Around all this is a white border with light blue stripes similar to the pinstripes on a baseball uniform. It is not a particularly attractive format. Backs are similar to regular 1986 Fleer cards, with major and minor league stats presented vertically, along with a large team logo. The sets were intended to sell for about $2, but, as usual, dealers

1986 Fleer League Leaders (Walgreens), Oddibe McDowell

1986 Fleer League Leaders (Walgreens), George Brett

got to them first, making it virtually impossible to find them in Walgreens. The set comes in a box with a checklist on the back and contains a handful of team logo stickers.

FOR

The photos and print quality are good; the players are mostly bona fide stars.

AGAINST

Too many of the same players as in other special 1986 sets. The design is gaudy. Single cards are not usually available.

NOTEWORTHY CARDS

It was one of the first sets in 1986 to contain a Jose Canseco rookie card.

VALUE

MINT CONDITION: Complete set, $5; common card, 10¢–20¢; superstars, 50¢–$1. 5-YEAR PROJECTION: Below average.

1986 Burger King All-Pro, Don Mattingly

1986 BURGER KING ALL-PRO

SPECIFICATIONS

SIZE: 2½ × 3½". FRONT: Color photograph. BACK: Black printing on white cardboard. DISTRIBUTION: Pennsylvania, New Jersey, one 2-card panel with food purchase at Burger King restaurants.

1986 Burger King All-Pro, Mike Schmidt

HISTORY

Burger King, which issued a number of regional team sets from 1977 to 1980, but sporadically since, got back into baseball cards in 1986 with a 2-card folder-panel (a Mike Schechter concept also used by True Value and Meadow Gold). The panel comes folded and glued and has to be torn open, which often damages the cards. Collectors save the unopened panels rather than separating the cards, to assure Mint condition. One 2-player panel was given away with the purchase of a Whopper in restaurants in the Pennsylvania and New Jersey areas. Besides the two players, there was a food coupon in the middle. The set includes the same 20 players found in similar '86 issues, and as usual, the player photos are devoid of team logos. The card front has a dark blue border with rows of white stars at the top and bottom, and a Burger King logo. A card number appears at the top, and the player's name, team, and position are in the bottom panel. The card back has minimal biographical details, a short career summary, and 1985 and career stats.

FOR

This fairly scarce regional set continues a long tradition of baseball card issues.

AGAINST

The panel format is not proving popular with collectors.

NOTEWORTHY CARDS

All 20 players are stars or superstars.

VALUE

MINT CONDITION: Complete set of panels, $10; common card, 20¢; superstars, 60¢–$1. 5-YEAR PROJECTION: Average.

1986 COCA-COLA DODGERS

SPECIFICATIONS

SIZE: 3½ × 5½″. FRONT: Color photograph. BACK: Black and red printing on white cardboard. DISTRIBUTION: Nationally, cards obtained by writing to players.

HISTORY

Although few hobbyists collect player postcards, the 32-card 1986 Dodgers team set broke down some of the barriers; the sponsorship by Coca-Cola ("Official Soft Drink of Dodger Stadium") gave it the "legitimacy" of a commercial sponsor. Unlike most recent team baseball cards, the Coke Dodgers were not given away at a promotional game or sold at the team's souvenir stand. To get a card, collectors had to write to the player pictured on the card. This meant a shortage of complete sets, since some players won't bother with fan mail. Also, because the cards were issued fairly late in the season, some players wouldn't be back in Dodger Blue when the 1987 baseball season rolled around. The card front features a large color photo of the player framed in white, with his name and team copyright notices printed at the bottom. The back is a regular postcard back with a place for the address and a box for the stamp. The Coke logo appears in the lower right. At the left, over the player's facsimile signature, is a message offering the fan the player's best wishes and an invitation to attend games at Dodger Stadium.

FOR

An attractive, large-size card set that is challenging to complete. It is likely to be sought after by Coke memorabilia collectors as well as baseball card collectors.

AGAINST

It is difficult to complete a set.

NOTEWORTHY CARDS

The 1986 Dodgers had few real stars. Still, there are nice cards of Fernando Valenzuela, Steve Sax, Mike Marshall, Orel Hershiser, Greg Brock, Pedro Guerrero, and rookie Mariano Duncan.

VALUE

MINT CONDITION: Complete set, $17; common card, 50¢; stars, rookies, $1–$2; Valenzuela, $3. 5-YEAR PROJECTION: Average, or a little above.

1986 COCA-COLA WHITE SOX

SPECIFICATIONS

SIZE: 2⅝ × 4″. FRONT: Color photograph. BACK: Black printing on white cardboard. DISTRIBUTION: Team-issued, complete sets available through a fan club offer; two cards given away at each Tuesday night home game.

HISTORY

For the third year in a row, the White Sox used a baseball card promotion to help fill the stands on traditionally slow Tuesday night home games. This was the second year Coke sponsored the set. The 30-card set includes active players, the team's field manager, general manager, mascots, stadium organist, and old-time ChiSox favorite, Minnie

1986 Coca-Cola White Sox, Joel Davis

1986 Coca-Cola White Sox, Harold Baines

Minoso. The card front features a large color photograph that is borderless at the top and sides. In a white panel at the bottom is the player's name, position and uniform number, and a bat with the Sox logo on it. The card back repeats the player identification and features complete major and minor league stats, along with the Coke logo.

FOR

It is a relatively scarce team-issued set.

AGAINST

There are no real negative points.

NOTEWORTHY CARDS

There are rookie cards of John Cangelosi, Bobby Bonilla, Ozzie Guillen, and a few others; along with future Hall of Famers Tom Seaver and Carlton Fisk.

VALUE

MINT CONDITION: Complete set, $12; common card, 25¢–30¢; stars, $1. 5-YEAR PROJECTION: Average, or a little below.

1986 DORMAN'S CHEESE

SPECIFICATIONS

SIZE: 1½ × 2″. FRONT: Color photograph. BACK: Black printing on white cardboard. DISTRIBUTION: Northeast and Chicago, one 2-card panel in packages of cheese.

1986 Dorman's Cheese, Reggie Jackson

1986 Dorman's Cheese, Eddie Murray

HISTORY

Another first-time baseball card issuer, Dorman's cheese, produced a 20-card set of mini-cards, inserting one 2-card panel in packages of cheese slices. Because the promotion was not on a national scale and the cards were not available other than by buying cheese, the Dorman's set is one of the scarcer 1986 issues. Like a number of other issues that year, Dorman's cards do not include team logos on the player photos, which makes the cards less attractive to most collectors. Also, many of the same photos that appear in other sets (Burger King, True Value, Meadow Gold, etc.) are in this set. Only the unique size of the cards distinguishes the Dorman's cards from other sets. The two cards on each panel are perforated at their joined edges for ease of separation. The card front features a player photo, a yellow strip at the bottom with the player's name, team, and position, and a Dorman's logo in the lower right. The back has another logo, brief biographical and 1985 season data, and a Players' Association logo. There are no card numbers.

FOR

The size makes this set interesting.

AGAINST

The same old players and pictures are seen over and over again in 1986 specialty sets.

NOTEWORTHY CARDS

They're all superstars.

VALUE
MINT CONDITION: Complete set of panels, $25; single card, 80¢; superstars, $1–$3. 5-YEAR PROJECTION: Average.

1986 DRAKE'S

SPECIFICATIONS
SIZE: Single card, 2⁷⁄₁₆ × 3⅜″. FRONT: Color photograph. BACK: Black printing on gray cardboard. DISTRIBUTION: East Coast, two or three cards printed on the bottom of boxes of snack cakes.

HISTORY
After five years of including single Topps cards in boxes of snack cakes, Drake's turned to a new format in 1986: printing cards on the bottom panel of the box. Although not a new idea (it had been used by Hostess in the 1970s), it was greeted with enthusiasm by many collectors. The only way to get the cards was to buy the product. This made East Coast collectors happy; they could pick up the boxes with the players they needed to complete their sets in grocery stores. Collectors living outside the Maine-to-Washington D.C. area, however, had to buy or trade for the set from somebody who had paid a lot of money for it—after all, boxes of snack cakes don't come cheap, even if they are purchased in day-old outlet stores. Drake's retained the "Big Hitters" and "Super Pitchers" theme used for its 1985 set, which naturally concentrated on superstars. The photos are all action shots of the 37 players represented. Card backs, with a design virtually stolen from the 1985 Topps issue, contain complete major league stats, brief vitals on the player, and ads for Drake's snack cakes. To obtain a complete set, the collector had to sample the entire Drake's line, since certain cards could only be found on one or two different products. As with other box-bottom cards, complete unopened boxes are worth the most, followed by empty opened boxes, bottom panels cut off the boxes, and finally, single cards cut from the panels.

1986 Drake's, Gary Carter

1986 Drake's, Dwight Evans

FOR
Box-bottom cards encourage trading and cooperation among collectors—the way baseball cards used to be. This is an attractive set of cards from a company with six years of continuous issues—quite a tradition by modern standards.

AGAINST
It is very difficult and expensive to complete a set like this. Many cards were printed so close to the edge of the box that they were creased. Since some cards share a common border, it is hard to cut them apart into singles.

NOTEWORTHY CARDS
Nearly all of the players featured are stars.

VALUE

MINT CONDITION: Complete set of panels, $30–$45; single panel, $2–$5; common card, 30¢–50¢; superstars, $2–$3. 5-YEAR PROJECTION: Above average.

1986 GATORADE CUBS

SPECIFICATIONS

SIZE: 2⅞ × 4¼″. FRONT: Color photograph. BACK: Blue, orange, and green printing on white cardboard. DISTRIBUTION: Chicago, complete sets given away at a special "Baseball Card Day" promotional game.

HISTORY

For the fifth year in a row, the Chicago Cubs held a baseball card give-away day at Wrigley Field, distributing 28-card sets sponsored by Gatorade. The card front features a large color action photo framed in red. Above is a red and blue Cubs logo, and the player's name, position, and uniform number are printed in black at the bottom. That information is repeated on the back, along with an orange and green Gatorade logo and the player's complete major and minor league record. The 28 cards in the set include 26 player cards, a group card of the coaches, and a card for mid-season replacement manager Gene Michael.

1986 Gatorade Cubs, Dennis Eckersley

1986 Gatorade Cubs, Bob Dernier

FOR

While not hard to find, this attractive team-issued regional set is not overabundant in the market.

AGAINST

There isn't really anything bad to say about the issue.

NOTEWORTHY CARDS

Besides the established Cubs stars, there are rookie cards of pitcher Jamie Moyer and a reserve catcher with the unlikely name of Steve Christmas.

VALUE

MINT CONDITION: Complete set, $8; common card, 25¢; stars, rookies, 40¢–$1.50. 5-YEAR PROJECTION: Average.

1986 JIFFY POP

SPECIFICATIONS

SIZE: 2¾″ diameter. FRONT: Color photograph. BACK: Black printing on white cardboard. DISTRIBUTION: Nationally, one disc in packages of popcorn.

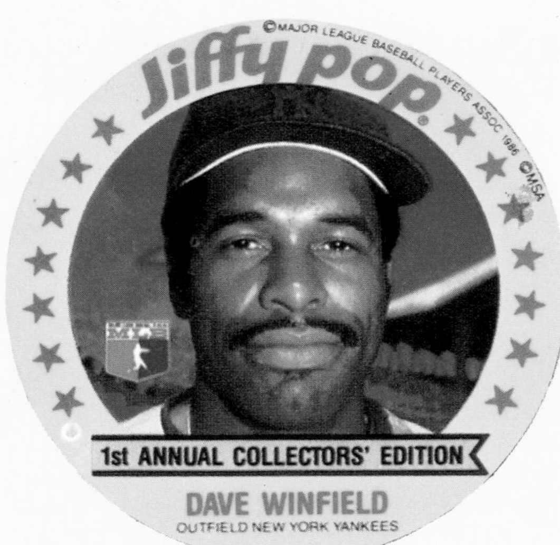

1986 Jiffy Pop, Dave Winfield

HISTORY

The 1986 season seemed to be the year for round baseball cards, with several companies issuing the "discs," as collectors call them. A blue banner beneath the player photo proclaims this 20-card superstar set to be a "1st Annual Collectors' Edition," but whether the promotion will be repeated remains to be seen. A round photo is surrounded by a yellow border with 14 stars and a Jiffy Pop logo. The player's name is printed in red with his position and team in black beneath. The back contains only rudimentary vital stats on the player along with his 1985 record. Produced by Mike Schechter Associates, the Jiffy Pop discs are similar to a dozen other '86 sets: they feature about the same 20 players, with no sign of team logos anywhere. Many collectors didn't get the cards by buying popcorn—they just waited for a dealer to get a quantity of cards.

FOR

The set is similar to other 1986 issues. There is nothing unique about it to recommend it to collectors.

AGAINST

Collectors don't like round cards and they don't like cards with the team logos removed. They especially don't like buying dozens of packages of a product to complete a set.

NOTEWORTHY CARDS

All the players are superstars.

VALUE

MINT CONDITION: Complete set, $35; common card, 75¢; superstars, $2–$4. 5-YEAR PROJECTION: Below average.

1986 KAY BEE YOUNG SUPERSTARS

SPECIFICATIONS

SIZE: 2½ × 3½″. FRONT: Color photograph. BACK: Red and black printing on white cardboard. DISTRIBUTION: Nationally, complete sets sold at Kay Bee toy stores.

1986 Kay Bee Young Superstars, Dan Pasqua

YOUNG SUPERSTARS OF BASEBALL
TOM BROWNING
KAY BEE

1986 Kay Bee Young Superstars, Tom Browning

HISTORY

Kay Bee, a mall-oriented toy store chain, commissioned Topps to produce a 33-card boxed set of baseball cards for 1986. It was one of the better issues of its type. The set had a specific theme ("Young Superstars of Baseball"), featured all new action photos, and included many hot rookies and rising stars of 1986. It was intended that complete boxed sets (with a checklist on the back) would sell for about $2 in the stores, but when the issue was released, many dealers rushed to their local mall and bought up the entire inventory, then marked it up from $4 to $6 and re-sold the sets to collectors. Kay Bee responded by putting more cards on the shelves, and the price dropped some. A large color action photo is framed in red with a white border, with the set title in white at the top. The Kay Bee logo is at the bottom. The player's name is printed in red on a yellow strip just above the photo. The card has a high-gloss finish. Card backs copy the interesting design Topps used in their 1971 issue. There is a black-and-white player photo in the upper left, biographical information and career summary at right, and 1985 and lifetime major league stats at the bottom.

FOR

A good choice of players and attractive cards make this set desirable.

AGAINST

It was too hard to find at the original issue price.

NOTEWORTHY CARDS

Lots of great young stars like Don Mattingly, Dwight Gooden, Tony Gwynn, Kirby Puckett, and Darryl Strawberry—plus plenty of potential greats like Mariano Duncan, Shawon Dunston, Jim Presley, Oddibe McDowell, and Dan Pasqua—make this one of the better boxed sets.

VALUE

MINT CONDITION: Complete set, $4.50; common card, 10¢–25¢; stars, hot rookies, 50¢–$1. 5-YEAR PROJECTION: Above average.

1986 LITE BEER ASTROS, RANGERS

SPECIFICATIONS

SIZE: Rangers, 4 × 6″; Astros, 4½ × 6¾″. FRONT: Color photograph. BACK: Black printing on white cardboard. DISTRIBUTION: Team-issued, at special baseball card promotional dates.

HISTORY

The two team sets are grouped together here because they are basically the same. These over-size cards were given away to fans attending late-season promotional games at Arlington Stadium and the Astrodome. The Astros cards feature a large color action photo (in some cases, the same photo was used on the team's police set) surrounded by a wide white border. The player's name appears above the photo, and his position is printed below. Rainbow bands of yellow, orange, red, and purple (it looks better than it sounds) run diagonally in the upper-right and lower-left corners of the card. A black-and-white Astros 25th Anniversary logo appears in the upper left and the Lite beer logo is in the lower right. The card back features detailed player personal data and career statistics. The 22 cards in the set are unnumbered and include 21 players and a card for manager Hal Lanier. The Lite beer Rangers set is slightly smaller and less gaudy. There is a large posed portrait photo with the player's name, position, and uniform number below. A red, white, and blue Texas Rangers logo is in the lower left and a blue Lite beer logo occupies the lower right. Like the Astros set, there is comprehensive player data on the back

#5 PETE INCAVIGLIA
Outfielder

1986 Lite Beer Rangers, Pete Incaviglia

of the card, a few vital statistics, complete major and minor league record, and details of the player's acquisition by the Rangers. There are 28 cards in this set, including individual cards for manager Bobby Valentine, the coaches, and Arlington Stadium.

FOR

The big size is a plus if you like larger cards. The sets feature up-and-coming teams with lots of rookies and stars.

AGAINST

Collectors don't seem to like over-size cards. The Astros photos were "recycled."

NOTEWORTHY CARDS

Some hot rookies were on the Rangers in 1986: Pete Incaviglia, Ed Correa, Bobby Witt. There are some good stars on the Astros, plus future Hall of Famer Nolan Ryan.

VALUE

MINT CONDITION: Complete set (either team), $55; common card, $1.25; stars, hot rookies, $2.50–$5; superstars, $5–$7. 5-YEAR PROJECTION: Average

1986 MEADOW GOLD

SPECIFICATIONS

SIZE: 2½ × 3½″. FRONT: Color photograph. BACK: Red printing on white cardboard. DISTRIBUTION: Regionally, one 2-card panel in specially marked boxes of dairy products.

1986 Meadow Gold, Bruce Sutter

HISTORY

Another company that made use of the 1986 folder-panel format was Meadow Gold Dairies. A 2-card folder featuring one of ten pairs of superstars could be found in specially marked boxes of the company's dairy treats. Slightly different variations of 18 of the cards were printed on the end flaps of ice-cream boxes. The panel consists of two player cards and a center card featuring a chance to "Win a day with a major league player" and special offers of baseball caps and autographed balls. Like the other folder-panel sets of 1986, these do not include team logos—either players were photographed without their caps or the logos were airbrushed. The player photo appears in a two-inch square box at the center of the card, framed in blue. At the top is a red Meadow Gold logo and the words "Super Stars Series" in blue. A red strip at the bottom has the Beatrice logo. The card back has a player biography, a "Did you know?" trivia question, 1985 and career stats, and brief vital data. A card number appears at the top along with another Meadow Gold logo. These folder-panels are one of the scarcer regional issues of 1986 and command a hefty premium.

FOR

They were worth good money for collectors lucky enough to obtain them. Other than that, there isn't anything positive you can say about them.

AGAINST

The same old superstars are included in this set as in many other 1986 specialty sets. Some cards even feature the same photos.

NOTEWORTHY CARDS

There are two uncorrected spelling errors: Rick Sutcliffe appears as "Sutcliff" and Cal Ripken is spelled "Ripkin."

VALUE

MINT CONDITION: Complete set of panels, $40; common card, 50¢; superstars, $2–$3. 5-YEAR PROJECTION: Below average.

1986 MOTHER'S COOKIES

SPECIFICATIONS

SIZE: 2½ × 3½″. FRONT: Color photograph (A's, Mariners, Giants); color painting (Astros). BACK: Red and purple printing on white cardboard. DISTRIBUTION: Houston, Seattle, Oakland, San Francisco, 20-card starter sets given out at baseball games; eight cards available through a mail-in offer.

1986 Mother's Cookies, Alvin Davis

1986 Mother's Cookies, Chuck Cottier

HISTORY

One of the most popular annual regional sets since distribution began in 1983, the Mother's Cookies 1986 issue featured four teams. At special baseball card day promotional games in July, 20-card starter sets of the home team were given out to the first 20,000 or 25,000 fans entering the stadium, along with coupons that could be sent in for eight more cards. The eight cards were not likely to be the same ones needed to complete a set, which promoted old-fashioned trading among collectors. (There was some dissatisfaction, however, when greedy dealers bought up thousands of half-price bleacher tickets and seized a large portion of the issue.) The A's, Giants, and Mariners were featured in a format similar to previous years: a borderless color photo with the player's name and team in white script lettering. The cards have a high-gloss finish with rounded corners. The Mariners and Giants sets include 26 players, the manager, and a group card of the coaches. The A's set has 24 single-player cards, plus the manager, and group cards of the coaches, the trainer, and equipment personnel. The Astros set is in a very different format from the other three teams. Instead of current players, the set features the 27 Houston players (Astros and Colt .45s) who have played in All-Star Games since the team was formed in 1962, plus a checklist. The set was part of the 1986 All-Star festivities hosted in the Astrodome that year. Instead of color photos, the Astros cards feature color paintings of the players. The card back contains a Mother's Cookies logo, a card number, the player's vital stats, and a line for obtaining an autograph.

FOR

This set has gorgeous photography and an innovative format.

AGAINST

Collectors were turned off by the artwork on the '86 Astros cards and the fact that "old-timers" were depicted instead of the current divisional championship team.

NOTEWORTHY CARDS

The hot stars on these teams include rookies Jose Canseco, Will Clark, and Rob Thompson.

VALUE

MINT CONDITION: Complete set: Astros, $8; Mariners, Giants, $9; A's, $25. Common card, 30¢; stars, rookies, 50¢–$1; Clark, $2.50; Canseco, $15. 5-YEAR PROJECTION: Above average.

1986 PERFORMANCE PRINTING RANGERS

SPECIFICATIONS

SIZE. $2\frac{3}{8} \times 3\frac{1}{2}''$. FRONT: Color photograph. BACK: Black printing on white cardboard. DISTRIBUTION: Arlington, Texas, complete sets given to fans attending a Texas Rangers game.

HISTORY

One of the later team-issued baseball card sets of 1986, the 28-card Texas Rangers set from Performance Printing had the advantage of including many of the team's promising young rookies who had been called up during the season. The same format used since 1983 was retained: a color player photo on the front, with a light blue box beneath containing the player's name, position, and team logo. The back features a portrait photo of the player in the upper left, along with brief biographical details, a line of major league career stats, and an ad for the set's sponsor. Cards are numbered by the player's uniform number.

FOR

A regional set in relatively limited supply, offering rookie cards of some potential stars on a good, young team. The current cost is fairly low.

AGAINST

The design is too similar to other years, and the cardboard is too thin.

NOTEWORTHY CARDS

A dream set for the rookie card speculator; it includes premier cards of Ruben Sierra, Pete Incaviglia, Bobby Witt, Ed Correa, Steve Buechele, Mike Loynd, Jose Guzman, and Mitch Williams.

VALUE

MINT CONDITION: Complete set, $7; common card, 10¢–15¢; stars, hot rookies, 25¢–50¢; Incaviglia, Sierra, $1–$2. 5-YEAR PROJECTION: Above average.

1986 Potato Chip Discs, Ozzie Guillen

1986 POTATO CHIP DISCS

SPECIFICATIONS

SIZE: 2¾″ diameter. FRONT: Color photograph. BACK: Black printing on white cardboard. DISTRIBUTION: Regionally, one card in boxes of potato chips.

1986 Potato Chip Discs, Paul Molitor

HISTORY

These round baseball cards (called discs by collectors) appeared in boxes of various brands of potato chips in 1986. All the sets were produced by Mike Schechter Associates, which handles many similar promotional issues. In the Detroit area, a 20-card set of Tigers players was issued in boxes of Cain's potato chips. In the Wisconsin-Illinois area, a 20-card set of the Chicago Cubs, White Sox, and Milwaukee Brewers was available in boxes of Jays potato chips. St. Louis Cardinal fans could find a 20-card set of the 1985 National League Champions in boxes of Kas chips. Collectors in the Kansas City area searched boxes of Kitty Clover chips for the 20 cards in that set. Three of the sets—Cardinals, Royals, and Tigers—featured the same basic design. A round photo is surrounded by a wide white border; beneath is a white strip with "1986 Annual Collectors' Edition" printed in blue. The player's name is in red below, and his team and position are in black at the bottom. The Royals discs have six red stars at the left and "1985 World Champions" at the right. The Cardinals discs say "1985 League Champions." Neither of the teams shows the logos—the players are either without caps, or the logo has been airbrushed. The Tigers cards feature the team logo, and have red stars on both sides. All three teams feature the potato chip brand logo in red at the top. The Cubs/White Sox/Brewers set differs from the others. The starred border surrounding the photo is in yellow, and "1986 Collectors' Edition" appears in red at the top along with a blue-and-white Jays logo at the upper left. The player's name is in red below the photo. All four sets feature the Players' Association logo on the front of the cards. Card backs are similar and feature brief vital data, abbreviated 1985 stats, and (on the Cain's, Kas, and Kitty Clover sets) a card number and the words "Snack Time." The Jays cards are not numbered. Each card was inserted into the box in a cellophane wrapper to protect it from grease and to protect the chips from ink.

FOR

These regional sets could only be acquired by buying the product, encouraging many collectors around the country to trade.

AGAINST

Collectors really don't like round cards. The photos were the same used on many other issues. There were no team logos on most cards.

NOTEWORTHY CARDS

Besides lots of established stars, the 1986 potato chip sets included rookie cards of Ozzie Guillen, Ernie Riles, Todd Worrell, and Vince Coleman. There are errors in the RBI figures on the Jays cards for Keith Moreland and Shawon Dunston.

VALUE

MINT CONDITION: Complete set: Kas, Kitty Clover, Cain's, $15; Jays, $20. Common card, 50¢; superstars, hot rookies, $2–$3. 5-YEAR PROJECTION: Below average.

1986 PROVIGO EXPOS

SPECIFICATIONS

SIZE: Single card, $2\frac{9}{16} \times 3\frac{5}{16}$". FRONT: Color photograph. BACK: Red and blue printing on white cardboard. DISTRIBUTION: Quebec, one 3-card panel with each $15 grocery purchase.

HISTORY

This 28-card set was released at the rate of one 2-player panel each week with a $15 purchase at Provigo groceries in Quebec. Large quantities of the cards also came into dealers' hands, making them available to collectors on both sides of the border. Each panel contains two Expos player cards and an advertising card featuring a grocery product on the front, and either a checklist or a mail-in offer for an album to house the cards on the back. Besides the 24 player cards, there are cards for the manager, two coaches, and mascot. The cards are perforated for ease of separation and must be separated to be mounted in the album. Naturally, most collectors prefer complete panels over single cards. The card front features an attractive color action photo, with a red and blue Expos logo and date above. A yellow band beneath the photo has the player's name and uniform number and a Provigo logo in red. Card backs repeat the front design, except for the photo. There are French and English vital stats and career highlights, along with a card number.

1986 Provigo Expos, Andre Dawson/Andres Galarraga

1986 Provigo Expos, Hubie Brooks/Dann Bilardello

FOR

Talented, up-and-coming players are featured on this Canadian set. American collectors appreciate the low price.

AGAINST

Collectors have nothing bad to say about this set.

NOTEWORTHY CARDS

Besides established stars like Tim Raines, Andre Dawson, and Hubie Brooks, all of the Expos highly rated '86 rookies appear here: Herm Winningham, Floyd Youmans, Mitch Webster, and Andres Galarraga.

VALUE

MINT CONDITION: Complete set of panels, $7; common card, 10¢; stars, rookies, 25¢–50¢; Dawson, Raines, $1–$1.50. 5-YEAR PROJECTION: Average.

1986 QUAKER

SPECIFICATIONS

SIZE: 2½ × 3½″. FRONT: Color photograph. BACK: Red and blue printing on gray cardboard. DISTRIBUTION: Nationally, one 3-card pack in boxes of Quaker Chewy granola bars; complete sets available through a mail-in offer.

HISTORY

One of many companies to use baseball cards to increase sales, the Quaker Oats company had Topps produce a 33-card superstar set for inclusion in 8-ounce boxes of its Chewy granola bars. Each box (at about $2) contained three cards along with a "header" card that offered a complete set of cards or a 1986 Topps baseball sticker starter kit for four proofs of purchase. The cards feature a head-and-shoulder player photo surrounded by a red frame. Naturally, with so many cards issued in

1986 Quaker, Wade Boggs

1986 Quaker, Don Mattingly

1986, a few of the photos in this set (Bret Saberhagen, Eddie Murray) were previously used by Topps. Blue "pillows" in the upper left and lower right contain the smiling Quaker man and Topps logo along with the card number. Yellow bars at the top and bottom show the product name, player's name, team, and position. Card backs proclaim the 1986 issue to be the "1st Annual Collectors' Edition" and give career and biographical information along with 1985 and lifetime stats.

FOR
This was one 1986 issue that didn't get into dealers' hands first. Collectors had to buy the product to get the cards. Quaker was one of the few companies who paid the teams to use their logos on the cards, making the set more attractive to collectors.

AGAINST
The same superstars are found in a dozen or more sets in 1986. It was relatively expensive to complete the set—about $8 plus postage.

NOTEWORTHY CARDS
With the exception of a rookie or two who might not make the grade and a few former stars who had lost their touch by 1986, the roster was made up of true stars and future Hall of Famers.

VALUE
MINT CONDITION: Complete set, $8; common card, 10¢–25¢; superstars, 75¢–$1. 5-YEAR PROJECTION: Average.

1986 TEXAS GOLD REDS

SPECIFICATIONS
SIZE: 2½ × 3½″. FRONT: Color photograph. BACK: Black and gold printing on white cardboard. DISTRIBUTION: Cincinnati, complete sets given away at a "Baseball Card Day" promotional game.

HISTORY
The 28-card Reds team set was sponsored by Texas Gold ice cream and given away at a promotional game at Riverfront Stadium in September. Card fronts are dominated by a color action photo surrounded by a bright red frame. A Reds logo appears in the lower left and the player's name, uniform number, and position are in black in the lower right. The card back has a Texas Gold logo and complete major and minor league statistics for

1986 Texas Gold Reds, Pete Rose

1986 Texas Gold Reds, Eric Davis

the player. There is no biographical data. There are 22 player cards, a coaches card, a team logo card, and three different cards for player-manager Pete Rose. One pictures him as a player, another as manager, and the third honors his 4,192nd big league hit.

FOR

An abundance of late-season hot rookies and three Pete Rose cards make this set enticing.

AGAINST

There are only positives with this issue.

NOTEWORTHY CARDS

Besides the trio of Rose cards, hot rookies appearing in this set include Kurt Stillwell, Tracy Jones, and Kal Daniels.

VALUE

MINT CONDITION: Complete set, $18; common card, 25¢; stars, hot rookies, 50¢–$2; Rose, $1–$2; Eric Davis, $3–$4. 5-YEAR PROJECTION: Above average.

1986 TRUE VALUE

SPECIFICATIONS

SIZE: 2⅝ × 3⅝″. FRONT: Color photograph. BACK: Black printing on white cardboard. DISTRIBUTION: Nationally, one 3-card folder-panel with each $5 purchase in hardware stores.

1986 True Value, Kent Hrbek

1986 True Value, Kirk Gibson

HISTORY

The True Value hardware store chain was one of several new national baseball card set sponsors in 1986. The company adopted an innovative format—issuing the cards in ten 3-card folder-panels. Actually, each folder contains four cards: three player cards and a sweepstakes card that also has an ad for an in-store special. The cards have perforated edges, top and bottom, so they can be removed from the folder. As usual, unopened folders are more valuable than individual cards. Although the cards are about eight percent larger than the current standard size, the player photo on the front is small and nearly lost amid the clutter of extraneous design elements. A red and blue True Value logo and the words "Super Stars Collector Series" in light blue and black appear above the photo. The photo is flanked by light blue bands inside a red frame with white stars. Beneath the photo is a pair of crossed bats and three baseballs. At the bottom is the player's name, team, position, and the Major League Baseball Players Association logo. Like many 1986 sets, the photos do not show team logos—either the players are shown without caps, or the team emblems have been airbrushed. Card backs repeat the information from the top of the front, along with brief biographical information and stats, a short career summary (on some cards), and a card number. One folder-panel was available with each $5 purchase at True Value stores. Since dealers were unable to acquire large quantities of cards, they have remained somewhat scarce.

FOR

The folder-panel concept is innovative.

AGAINST

There are no team emblems, and the perforated cards are hard to separate without damage.

NOTEWORTHY CARDS

The True Value cards use pretty much the same line-up of superstar players as a dozen other sets.

VALUE

MINT CONDITION: Complete set of panels, $9; complete set of single cards, $4; single card, 10¢; superstars, 50¢–75¢. 5-YEAR PROJECTION: Below average.

1986 ASTROS POLICE

SPECIFICATIONS

SIZE: 2⅝ × 4⅛″. FRONT: Color photograph. BACK: Blue and orange printing on white cardboard. DISTRIBUTION: Houston, 12-card starter sets given out at a promotional game; single cards given to youngsters by officers.

1986 Astros Police, Mike Scott

HISTORY

The Houston Astros picked a very good year to issue their first police safety set—the year they won the National League West. This made the set immediately popular with collectors, despite the fact that it was widely available through dealers with contacts in Houston. The set is sometimes advertised as the "Astros Kool-Aid" set because the company is shown on the back as the sponsor. Like most other police sets, the '86 Astros issue is slightly larger than the standard baseball card. It features a large color photo on the front framed with a dark blue line. The player's name, uniform number, team, and position appear at the bottom framed in an orange-ruled box. These colors are continued on the back of the card, which features a career summary and a concise safety message ("Tips From the Dugout") from the Houston police department. There is a Kool-Aid and team logo on the back along with a card number. The set contains 26 cards: one for each player on the 24-man roster, a card for N.L. Manager of the Year Hal Lanier, and a group coaches card. Unlike most other police sets, complete sets were not given out at the "Baseball Card Day" promotional game; only 12-card starter sets were distributed. To obtain the other cards, youngsters had to ask for them from police officers, the aim being to increase the rapport between youngsters and police.

FOR

It's a premier issue of a popular set by a popular team. Because they were not available as complete sets, they may become scarce.

AGAINST

There are no negatives here.

NOTEWORTHY CARDS

While the 1986 Astros were short of hot rookie players (aside from bullpen ace Charlie Kerfeld) there are many potential young stars in the set—Mike Scott, Kevin Bass, and Glenn Davis, to name a few. The issue also includes a card of future Hall of Famer Nolan Ryan.

VALUE

MINT CONDITION: Complete set, \$6; common card, 10¢–25¢; superstars, 50¢–\$1. 5-YEAR PROJECTION: Above average.

1986 BREWERS POLICE

SPECIFICATIONS

SIZE: 2¾ × 4″. FRONT: Color photograph. BACK: Blue printing on white cardboard. DISTRIBUTION: Wisconsin, complete sets given out at a "Baseball Card Day" promotional game; single cards given to youngsters by officers.

HISTORY

In its fifth straight year, the Milwaukee Brewers police set program was larger than ever. More than 65 local police agencies participated, each having their department name printed on the front of their cards. This makes it quite a challenge for collectors to complete the set: with 30 cards from 65 departments, that's 1,950 cards. The 1986 Brewers police set follows the same basic design as previous years: a color photo with the player's name, position, and uniform number below, and the message "The ___ Police Department/Kinney Shoes and WTMJ Radio/present the 1986/Milwaukee Brewers" at the bottom. The back of the card features the department badge along with a safety tip and a message from WTMJ for kids to listen to the station to hear which cards officers will be giving away that week. On the cards for other departments, the Milwaukee Brewers logo replaces the badge.

1986 Brewers Police, Paul Molitor

FOR

It is a good-looking, widely distributed set.

AGAINST

The police sets are always the same. It is impossible to "complete" a set.

NOTEWORTHY CARDS

Besides the last remnants of the Brewers' 1982 championship team, the '86 police set includes cards of the team's heralded rookie crop—Juan Nieves, Dan Plesac, and Rob Deer among others.

VALUE

MINT CONDITION: Complete set from one department, \$6; scarce department, up to \$20+; common card, 10¢–15¢; stars, rookies, 50¢–75¢. 5-YEAR PROJECTION: Average, or somewhat below.

1986 DODGERS POLICE

SPECIFICATIONS

SIZE: 2¾ × 4⅛″. FRONT: Color photograph. BACK: Blue printing on white cardboard. DISTRIBUTION: Los Angeles, complete sets given out at a "Baseball Card Day" promotional game; single cards given to youngsters by officers.

1986 Dodgers Police, Steve Sax

HISTORY

After a one-year layoff, the L.A. Dodgers sponsored a safety set in 1985. Complete sets were distributed at the May 18 "Baseball Card Day" game at Dodger Stadium. The 30-card set was the team's sixth police set since 1980, when they became the second major league team to sponsor such a set. The front of the large-size cards features a color photograph, the player's name and uniform number, and the Dodgers logo and date. The card back repeats the Dodgers logo, displays the Los Angeles Police Department badge, and has a safety tip for youngsters. A limited amount of player data is included as well.

FOR

This set marks a continuation of recent Dodgers' police sets.

AGAINST

All of these police sets have the same design.

NOTEWORTHY CARDS

Although 1986 was not a good year for the Dodgers, many of the players in this set are on the road to stardom.

VALUE

MINT CONDITION: Complete set, $5; common card, 15¢; stars, rookies, 50¢–75¢. 5-YEAR PROJECTION: Average.

1986 SMOKEY THE BEAR ANGELS

SPECIFICATIONS

SIZE: 4¼ × 6″. FRONT: Color photograph. BACK: Black printing on white cardboard. DISTRIBUTION: Team-issued, complete sets given away at a "Baseball Card Day" promotional game.

HISTORY

Another in the popular line of fire-prevention baseball cards featuring Smokey the Bear was issued in 1986 by the California Angels. Sets of 24 of the large-size cards were given away to fans at an August promotional game. Each card features a vignette photo in a round frame of red and blue. A team logo and a picture of Smokey appear in color at the upper corners, while a ribbon at the bottom heralds "Wildfire Prevention." The player's last name appears in a scroll at the top. There is limited player information on the card backs, plus a Smokey the Bear cartoon with a fire safety tip, along with the logos of the U.S. Forest Service, the U.S. Department of the Interior, and the California Department of Forestry. Cards are numbered 1 to 24 and include 23 player cards and one for manager Gene Mauch.

FOR

It was a popular theme for a set, and the Angels were divisional winners in 1986.

AGAINST

The photos are overwhelmed by the too-wide borders.

NOTEWORTHY CARDS

The set is notable for the rookie card of Wally Joyner, plus cards of future Hall of Famers Reggie Jackson and Don Sutton.

1986 Smokey the Bear Angels, Bobby Grich

VALUE

MINT CONDITION: Complete set, $7; common card, 20¢–30¢; stars, 50¢; Jackson, $1–$1.50; Joyner, $2. 5-YEAR PROJECTION: Average, or below.

1986 BLUE JAYS FIRE SAFETY

SPECIFICATIONS

SIZE: 2½ × 3½″. FRONT: Color photograph. BACK: Black printing on white cardboard. DISTRIBUTION: Ontario, single cards given to youngsters by firemen.

HISTORY

The third year of fire safety Blue Jays sets deviated little from the design used in earlier issues. A posed color photo of the player is surrounded by a bright blue border. Printed in black at the bottom are the player's name, position, and uniform number, along with a color team logo. Four sponsors' logos appear on the card back: The Ontario Association of Fire Chiefs, the province's Ministry of the Solicitor General, The *Toronto Star* newspaper, and Bubble Yum gum. The card back carries a fire safety message in baseball terminology, brief player biographical data, and 1985 and career stats. A statement in fine print at the bottom of the card says, "These trading cards are not to be sold for any purpose." There are 36 cards in the 1986 set,

1986 Blue Jays Fire Safety, Rick Leach

1985 Topps, Roger Clemens

including a team photo card, a Blue Jays Tenth Anniversary logo card, and individual cards for the manager and coaches.

FOR

A striking design highlights a good, young ball team.

AGAINST

The set is too similar in format to previous years.

NOTEWORTHY CARDS

A number of rookie cards, and all the established stars on this up-and-coming young team, make this set noteworthy.

VALUE

MINT CONDITION: Complete set, $10; common card, 25¢; stars, hot rookies, 50¢–$1. 5-YEAR PROJECTION: Above average.

1985 Topps, Alvin Davis

1985 TOPPS

SPECIFICATIONS

SIZE: 2½ × 3½″. FRONT: Color photograph. BACK: Red and green printing on gray cardboard. DISTRIBUTION: Nationally, in 15-, 28-, or 54-card packages with bubblegum; complete sets sold through hobby dealers.

1985 Topps, Don Mattingly

HISTORY

In its 35th consecutive year of baseball card production Topps did nothing extraordinary, relying on the company's tradition for quality to carry it in an increasingly competitive marketplace. Again producing a 792-card set, Topps chose an attractive, if not spectacular, format for 1985. Unlike the '83 and '84 cards, which had both a portrait and a full-length photo on the front, the '85 cards feature a single, large player photo, which somehow made the photos seem larger and more impressive. For the first time since 1965, Topps incorporated full-color team logos in the design, along with the team name, player name, and position in a color-coded panel at the bottom of the card. A white or black Topps logo appears at the top left. Backs were not designed to facilitate readability or card sorting, with red type on a light green background. Information on the backs is the usual blend of major and/or minor league stats, a better-than-average panel of player biographical data, and usually a baseball trivia question or line about career highlights at the bottom. Because Topps produces nearly 125 more cards in its annual set than the competition, they have more room for special subsets. In 1985, Topps opened with a run of ten "Record Breaker" cards featuring players who had set league marks during the 1984 season. Topps also revived an idea used in the 1970 Father-Son cards, with a set of horizontal format cards of currently playing sons of major league fathers, who were pictured on their own Topps cards in 1953 to 1967. A Topps innovation for 1985 was a group of cards depicting the "#1 Draft Pick" for each season since the draft was begun in 1968. The 12 cards in this subset included players whose major league careers had come and gone, as well as a few who had yet to play a game in the big leagues. How the hobby will react to a "rookie card" produced several years in advance of a player's actual debut is unknown, but if Shawn Abner lives up to his advance billing, collectors will be glad they saved his "pre-rookie" card from the 1985 set. In a similar vein, Topps devoted 15 cards to players on the 1984 U.S. Olympic baseball team. At the time the cards were produced, several had already begun minor league careers, but most were unknown. Today, however, the pre-rookie cards of players like Mark McGwire and Cory Snyder have become hot collector's items. Rounding out the 1985 Topps specialty cards were the traditional manager's cards and cards for the starters of the All-Star Game.

FOR

There are lots of interesting and potentially valuable cards in the innovative subsets.

AGAINST

Not much can be said against the 1985 Topps set.

NOTEWORTHY CARDS

Besides the pre-rookie cards in the draft pick and Olympic subsets, the big card in the 1985 Topps set was the first regular-issue appearance of Dwight Gooden. This was a card that could be literally picked out of a gum pack at 20¢ and sold for up to $4 by the end of the season.

VALUE

MINT CONDITION: Complete set, $90; common card, 5¢; stars, rookies, 25¢–$1; superstars, $1–$3; Gooden, $8; Don Mattingly, Roger Clemens, Kirby Puckett, $9; Eric Davis, $17; McGwire, $20. 5-YEAR PROJECTION: Above average.

1985 TOPPS TRADED

SPECIFICATIONS

SIZE: 2½ × 3½". FRONT: Color photograph. BACK: Red and green printing on white cardboard. DISTRIBUTION: Nationally, complete sets sold through hobby dealers; regionally, limited number of test packs sold with bubblegum.

1985 Topps Traded, Ozzie Guillen

1985 Topps Traded, Vance Law

HISTORY

About the only thing Topps changed in the fifth straight year of its "Traded" set was the color of the box—it was purple in 1985. Otherwise the format remained the same. This specially boxed edition included 131 cards of players (or managers) who were new to the major leagues or who had been traded since Topps printed its regular edition, along with a checklist. Actually, Topps also made a limited test run of wax packs, selling the 1985 Traded cards in gum packs—perhaps in response to collectors' charges that since Traded or Update sets are not available in retail stores, they are not a "legitimate" card issue. Compared with the 1984 Traded set that included Dwight Gooden—well, there is no comparison. The 1985 set has no instant rookie sensations. It's just a matter of waiting a few years to see who becomes a legitimate superstar to determine how valuable this set is going to be. Among the heralded names when the set was released in late 1985 were Vince Coleman, Ozzie Guillen, Mariano Duncan, Oddibe McDowell, Jim Presley, Tom Browning, Teddy Higuera, and Herm Winningham. None of them, however, had better than a good season in 1986, so it remains to be seen who will become the high-dollar item in this issue. As usual, the Traded set was a clone of the regular issue. The only difference is the white cardboard backs (as opposed to the gray of the regular issue), which makes the backs of the Traded cards much more readable.

FOR

Still reasonably priced compared with the 1983, '84, and '86 Traded sets, this set has exceptional potential.

AGAINST

Except for Coleman and Higuera, none of the rookies in this set are really big stars.

NOTEWORTHY CARDS

Don Sutton is one of the few sure Hall of Famers in the set. His card is one of the very few where he appears in the uniform of the Oakland A's.

VALUE

MINT CONDITION: Complete set, $14; common card, 6¢; stars, hot rookies, 50¢–$2; Higuera, $2–$3; Coleman, $4–$5. 5-YEAR PROJECTION: Above average.

1985 TOPPS MAIL-IN GLOSSIES

SPECIFICATIONS

SIZE: 2½ × 3½". FRONT: Color photograph. BACK: Red and blue printing on white cardboard. DISTRIBUTION: Nationally, five 8-card sets available by mailing in premium cards found in Topps wax packs.

HISTORY
Apparently pleased by collector response to its 1984 mail-in glossy set offer, Topps repeated the program in 1985. By saving and mailing in premium cards found in Topps wax packs (along with 75¢ postage for each five cards), collectors could choose any or all of five different 8-card sets of big-name players. Like the previous year, the 40-card issue contained 20 National Leaguers and 20 American Leaguers. Topps repeated the design of the 1984 set almost exactly, changing only the date on the back.

FOR
It's a semi-scarce set that features attractive, uncluttered photos of many of the most popular players of the 1985 season.

AGAINST
The unoriginal design and the high initial cost of cards (about 15¢ each when ordered from Topps) mar this set. Also, a large number of the cards sent by Topps to collectors were damaged in the mail, forcing collectors to buy from dealers or go through the hassle of trying to get replacements from Topps (and hoping they wouldn't be bent as well).

NOTEWORTHY CARDS
It appears that a large percentage of the 40 players in this set were "one-year wonders." Ten years from now collectors will be wondering why they were in a "Collector's Edition All-Star Set." The Dwight Gooden card qualifies as a rookie card. The Don Mattingly card was one of his first Topps special issues.

VALUE
MINT CONDITION: Complete set, $13; common card, 15¢; superstars, $1–$2.50. 5-YEAR PROJECTION: Below average.

1985 Topps Circle K, Lou Gehrig

1985 Topps Circle K, Willie Mays

1985 TOPPS CIRCLE K

SPECIFICATIONS
SIZE: 2½ × 3½″. FRONT: Black-and-white or color photograph. BACK: Red and blue printing on white cardboard. DISTRIBUTION: Southwestern U.S., complete sets sold for $2 at Circle K stores.

HISTORY
One of Topps' first ventures into producing a special card set for sale through a chain store was the "All Time Home Run Kings" issue of 1985. The set consists of cards of the 33 past and current players with the most career home runs. Unfortunately, Joe DiMaggio does not appear in the set; although he is checklisted as the 31st player on

the back of the box, the guy who had the 34th highest homer total, Lee May, made the set instead. The set is attractive, with very large photos in either black and white (players of the 1920s to 1950s) or color (players of the 1950s to 1980s), with an orange frame surrounded by a white border. The player's name appears in tiny letters at the lower left. Cards have a high-gloss finish. Card backs feature Topps and Circle K logos; personal data on the player; major league home run, RBI, and batting average figures, and a recap of major awards won by the player during his career. Card numbers are arranged by the player's ranking on the all-time home run list, with Hank Aaron as No. 1, Babe Ruth as No. 2, etc.

FOR
The issue has a concrete theme and includes lots of stars.

AGAINST
Collectors don't really like card sets that mix current and former players, even when they're all big names.

NOTEWORTHY CARDS
They've all achieved enough to make the list.

VALUE
MINT CONDITION: Complete set, $5; common card, 12¢; superstars, 25¢–70¢. 5-YEAR PROJECTION: Below average.

1985 TOPPS ALL-TIME RECORD HOLDER (WOOLWORTH)

SPECIFICATIONS
SIZE: 2½ × 3½″. FRONT: Black-and-white or color photograph. BACK: Blue and orange printing on white cardboard. DISTRIBUTION: Regionally, complete sets sold at Woolworth stores.

HISTORY
A second Topps special-edition boxed set for 1985 was the 44-card issue produced for Woolworth stores. For this set, Topps used the theme "All Time Record Holders," and the checklist on the back of the box lists a large number of current and future Hall of Famers along with some quite obscure players who still hold major league records. The cards feature a black-and-white or color photograph in a wood frame, with "Topps Collectors' Series" at the top, and "All-Time Record Holder" at the bottom. Beneath the frame is a simulated plaque with the player's name and the team he is most often associated with. Card backs have a card number set in a blue ribbon. There is a modest amount of personal data on the player, but most of the back is taken up with a description of the record or records held or shared by the player, along with other career highlights and a line of lifetime stats.

1985 Topps All-Time Record Holder (Woolworth), Dwight Gooden

1985 Topps All-Time Record Holder (Woolworth), Babe Ruth

FOR
The set's topic allows the inclusion of everybody from Babe Ruth to Henry Aaron to Dwight Gooden.

AGAINST

The design is not very appealing. Collectors don't like sets that mix players of different eras.

NOTEWORTHY CARDS

There are lots of past and present superstars.

VALUE

MINT CONDITION: Complete set, $4; common card, 15¢; superstars, 50¢. 5-YEAR PROJECTION: Below average.

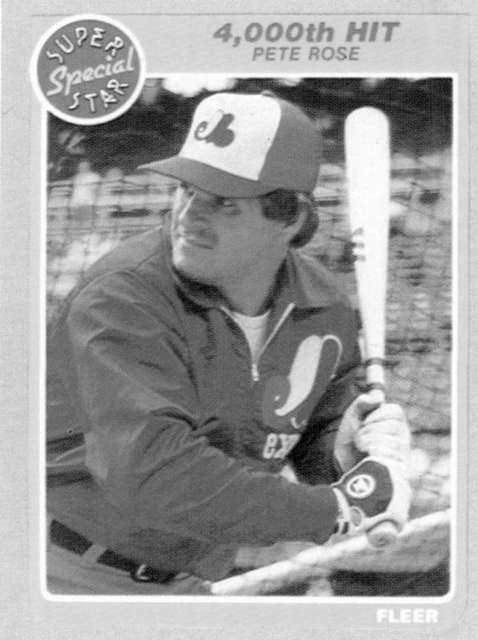

1985 Fleer, Pete Rose

1985 FLEER

SPECIFICATIONS

SIZE: 2½ × 3½″. FRONT: Color photograph. BACK: Red and black printing on white cardboard. DISTRIBUTION: Nationally, in packages with team logo stickers; complete sets sold through hobby dealers.

HISTORY

For the fifth consecutive year since returning to the "card wars" in 1981, Fleer retained its popular numbering system of arranging cards alphabetically within team, ranked by their 1984 season finish. Thus the Detroit Tigers were the first cards, followed by the San Diego Padres, and the rest of the teams on the basis of their winning percentage. The design of the 1985 Fleer set is fairly simple, but attractive. A large color photo of the player is framed by a shield in the team's colors. The player's name and position appear in black or white at the top of the shield, while a color team logo appears in the upper left. The whole card is surrounded by a gray border. For the third straight year, card backs incorporated a small black-and-white player portrait photo in the upper right. Complete major and/or minor league stats are

1985 Fleer, Dwight Gooden

1985 Fleer, Roger Clemens

provided, along with vital statistics and, in many cases, a "Did You Know?" trivia panel concerning the player's career. Except for the colors and updated stats, the backs were little changed from those of '83 and '84. Besides the normal player cards in the 660-card 1985 Fleer issue, there were a number of specialty cards known as "Super Star Specials." These included "In Action" cards, multiplayer feature cards, and career highlight cards. A first for Fleer in 1985 was a series of "Major League Prospects" cards, each featuring a pair of rookie players that Fleer felt were destined for stardom. Of the 20 players depicted on the ten cards, only a handful have shown any real potential: Danny Tartabull, Rob Deer, Shawon Dunston, and Glenn Davis.

FOR
This attractive, low-priced set has potentially valuable specialty cards.

AGAINST
The set doesn't seem to have gained the same respect valuewise as the other 1985 big sets.

NOTEWORTHY CARDS
There are none, except perhaps the Glenn Davis rookie card.

VALUE
MINT CONDITION: Complete set, $75; common card, 5¢; stars, 25¢–$2; superstars, hot rookies, $3–$7; Eric Davis, $18. 5-YEAR PROJECTION: Above average.

1985 Fleer Update, Teddy Higuera

1985 FLEER UPDATE

SPECIFICATIONS
SIZE: 2½ × 3½". FRONT: Color photograph. BACK: Red and black printing on white cardboard. DISTRIBUTION: Nationally, complete sets sold through hobby dealers.

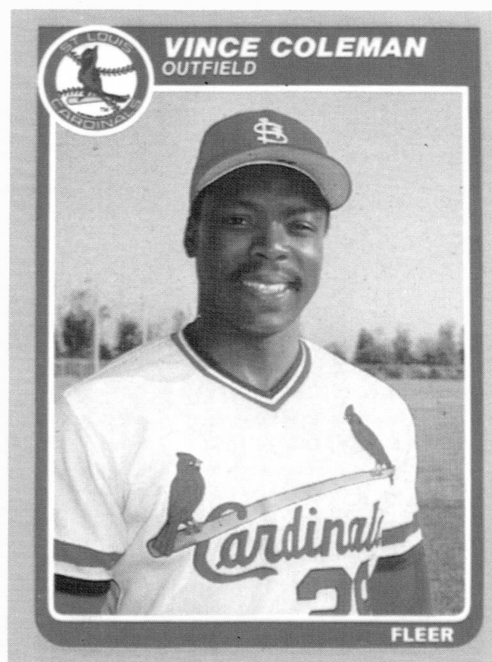

1985 Fleer Update, Vince Coleman

HISTORY
At the time the 1985 Fleer "Update" set of 132 cards was being released—near the close of the 1985 baseball season—the hobby was just beginning to realize how scarce the company's first issue was. As a result, many more sets were purchased than might otherwise have been the case. This, combined with a lack of really big-name players in 1985, has conspired to keep prices fairly low on the issue. Except for the "U-" prefix in front of the card number on back, there is nothing to distinguish the Updates from the regular 1985 Fleer cards. The same design and team color-coded scheme are used. Because Fleer has a blanket contract to print cards of all members of the Major League Players Association, whereas Topps signs individual players to contracts, the Fleer set has a handful of rookie cards that do not appear in Topps' Traded set for 1985. Whether any of them make it really big in the future will largely determine how valuable this set becomes.

FOR
There are no real strong points.

AGAINST
There are no real weak points.

NOTEWORTHY CARDS
Rookie cards of Mariano Duncan, Vince Coleman, Ozzie Guillen, Teddy Higuera, Oddibe and Roger McDowell, and Dan Pasqua, some of whom should eventually reach stardom, make this set collectible.

VALUE
MINT CONDITION: Complete set, $16; common card, 6¢; stars, hot rookies, 50¢–$4. 5-YEAR PROJECTION: Above average.

1985 FLEER LIMITED EDITION (McCRORY'S)

SPECIFICATIONS
SIZE: 2½ × 3½″. FRONT: Color photograph. BACK: Black and yellow printing on white cardboard. DISTRIBUTION: Regionally, complete sets sold in dime stores.

1985 Fleer Limited Edition (McCrory's), Reggie Jackson

HISTORY
The first Fleer special-issue cards for a retail store chain, the 1985 "Limited Edition" is sometimes known to collectors as the "McCrory's" set, although the McCrory's name doesn't appear anywhere on the cards, and the sets were also sold in McLellan, Kress, YDC, and Green stores. The 44-card set came packaged in its own box, with a checklist on the back. (Some collectors wonder why most of these specialty sets are issued in multiples of 11. The answer is that this allows several complete sets to be printed on a standard 132-card press sheet.) Like most boxed specialty sets, the 1985 Fleer Limited Edition emphasizes current favorites and superstars. Card fronts feature a color photo—which is different from the player's regular Fleer card—surrounded by a red-and-yellow frame. The words "Fleer Limited Edition 1985" appear in a yellow band at the top, while the player's name, team, and position appear in a red banner at the bottom. Card backs have a team logo, personal information, and stats for all seasons since 1973.

FOR
The set includes lots of stars and future Hall of Famers.

AGAINST
It is hard to come up with anything really wrong with this set.

NOTEWORTHY CARDS
The Robin Yount card indicates on the front that his position is "Shortshop"; however, since this error was not corrected, it adds no value to the card.

VALUE
MINT CONDITION: Complete set, $5; common card, 5¢–10¢; stars, $1–$2. 5-YEAR PROJECTION: Average.

1985 DONRUSS

SPECIFICATIONS
SIZE: 2½ × 3½″. FRONT: Color photograph. BACK: Yellow and black printing on white cardboard. DISTRIBUTION: Nationally, in wax packs with jigsaw puzzle pieces; complete sets sold through hobby dealers.

HISTORY
In 1985, for the second straight year, Donruss deliberately cut back its production of baseball cards to create a stronger-than-usual demand at the retail level. It worked. By mid-spring, wax packs were virtually impossible to find on store shelves, and dealers fortunate enough to have acquired some of the limited number of factory-collated sets

1985 Donruss, Danny Tartabull

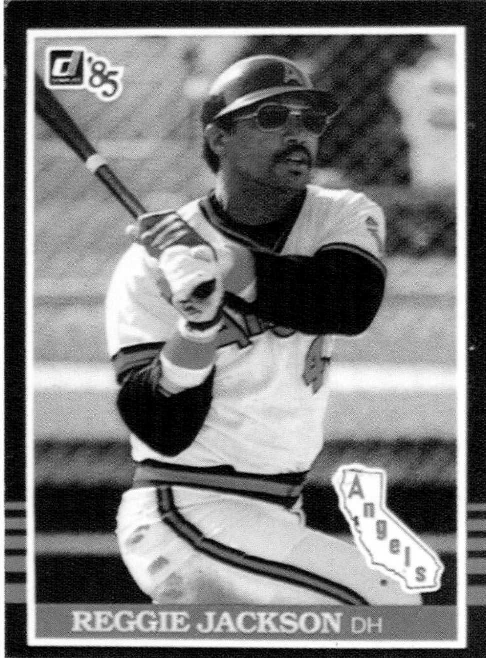

1985 Donruss, Reggie Jackson

1985 Donruss, Dwight Gooden

were able to charge exorbitant prices for them. The scarcity of the set combined with a very popular design made the issue especially attractive to collectors. For the first time on a major baseball card set since Topps' 1971 issue, a black border was used on the cards. A series of five horizontal red stripes toward the bottom on the borders sets off the stark blackness. Large color photos are undisturbed except for a Donruss logo in the upper left and a color team logo in the lower right. The player's name and position appear in a strip beneath the photo, color-coded by team. As had been the case since 1982, the Donruss set for '85 opened with a 26-card "Diamond Kings" series—one player from each major league team illustrated with a painting rather than a photo. In its fourth year, however, without repeating any players from previous years, the choice of "Kings" was not very impressive, and the paintings were not uniformly good. Next is the "Rated Rookies" subset featuring new players, most appearing for the first time on a major league baseball card, and many even before they'd appeared in a major league game. Of the 19 players thought to be primed for stardom, only a few—Shawon Dunston, Danny Tartabull, and Billy Hatcher—are still on track. Unlike previous years, Donruss only included one multiplayer feature card in the 1985 set, a "Two for the Title" card marking the race between Yankee teammates Don Mattingly and Dave Winfield for the American League batting crown.

FOR
These cards, which are relatively scarce, are rising fast in value.

AGAINST
It was difficult to find these cards in retail stores, which meant collectors had to buy from dealers at high mark-ups.

NOTEWORTHY CARDS
Among several noteworthy mistakes in the wax pack cards—which were collected by the time Donruss put together its full sets for dealer sales—was a wrong-photo card of Tom Seaver (#424). It was originally printed with a picture of Chicago White Sox teammate Floyd Bannister. Donruss should have gotten a clue from the fact that Bannister is shown pitching lefty on the card, while Seaver is a righty. Also, Terry Pendleton's name was incorrectly printed as "Jeff" on the front of his card; it was later corrected. In each case, the error cards are worth $1 or so, while the corrected Pendleton card is worth about $2 and the Seaver card about $5.

VALUE
MINT CONDITION: Complete set, $120; common card, 8¢; stars, 50¢–$3; superstars, hot rookies, $3–$8; Eric Davis, $16. 5-YEAR PROJECTION: Average.

1985 DONRUSS BOX BOTTOMS

SPECIFICATIONS
SIZE: Single card, 2½ × 3½". FRONT: Color photograph. BACK: Black and yellow printing on white cardboard. DISTRIBUTION: Nationally, one 4-card panel on the bottom of wax pack boxes.

HISTORY
Donruss created a sales gimmick in 1985 that was so successful it was immediately copied by both of its competitors. Donruss printed a special four-card panel on the bottom of its wax pack boxes. The intention was that the person who bought the last packs out of the box would get the bottom panel as a bonus. In practice, retailers often took the cards out of the original boxes and sold the panels by themselves. Donruss wasted one of the four cards by reproducing its Lou Gehrig jigsaw puzzle, combining it with cards of three players who seemed destined to be the hottest of 1985: Ryne Sandberg, Dwight Gooden, and Ron Kittle. All the photos are different from those used on the players' regular cards that year. Backs have slightly different career highlight write-ups. Cards are numbered PC-1 through PC-3 on the back and are not normally considered to be part of the complete 1985 Donruss set. In fact, the box-bottom cards are more common than the regular cards. However, since they pictured very popular players at the time, they remain in strong demand.

FOR
Donruss came up with an innovative sales gimmick.

AGAINST
The cards are somewhat hard to find in nice condition because the corners tend to become creased.

NOTEWORTHY CARDS
Gooden and Sandberg have winning cards.

VALUE
MINT CONDITION: Single panel $5; Kittle, 15¢; Sandberg, $1; Gooden, $3. 5-YEAR PROJECTION: Average.

1985 DONRUSS HIGHLIGHTS

SPECIFICATIONS
SIZE: 2½ × 3½". FRONT: Color photograph. BACK: Black and yellow printing on white cardboard. DISTRIBUTION: Nationally, complete sets available through hobby dealers.

1985 Donruss Highlights, Fernando Valenzuela

1985 Donruss Highlights, Eddie Murray

HISTORY

Donruss entered the lucrative postseason baseball card market in a big way with its 56-card "1985 Season Highlights" boxed set. The premise of the set was to cram as many currently hot names as possible into the issue by honoring important achievements and milestones of the season. This allowed Donruss to include a couple of cards of hot players Dwight Gooden and Don Mattingly. The real coup was Donruss' decision not to print very many of the sets, creating an instant scarcity that drove the retail price out of this world. Sold to dealers at $3 per set, the retail price had risen to $30 or more by the time most collectors were able to find them. The price has eased off somewhat since then. The Highlights cards followed the same basic format of the regular 1985 cards, using a black border with gold stripes (instead of red) toward the bottom. The front of the card is treated with a high-gloss finish. A red band beneath the player photo gives a capsule summary of the achievement being honored, while a more complete write-up is presented on the back. Besides the season highlights cards, the set contained cards for the player and pitcher of the month in each league, as well as Rookie of the Year cards for Vince Coleman and Ozzie Guillen.

FOR

It's an innovative idea with an attractive format.

AGAINST

A large number of collectors were turned off by the high profits made by some dealers. Many collectors feel they can live without the set, and prices have dropped considerably from their peak.

NOTEWORTHY CARDS

Most of the game's current big stars are represented by one, two, or three cards in this set.

VALUE

MINT CONDITION: Complete set, $22; common card, 10¢; stars, 50¢–$1.50; superstars, $2; Mattingly, $3. 5-YEAR PROJECTION: Below average.

1985 DONRUSS ACTION ALL-STARS

SPECIFICATIONS

SIZE: 3½ × 5″. FRONT: Color photograph. BACK: Blue and black printing on white cardboard. DISTRIBUTION: Nationally, in cello packs with jigsaw puzzle pieces.

HISTORY

For the third straight year, Donruss issued a super-size baseball card under the "Action All-Stars" label. Like the '83 and '84 issues, the fronts combine a large action photo with a smaller portrait. Unlike earlier issues, the backs no longer carry a player photo; they are more like the back design of the regular-issue cards for the year, combining career highlights, recent stats, and personal data. The fronts carried through with the basic color scheme of the 1985 Donruss cards, featuring a black border with intersecting horizontal and vertical white lines. The 60 cards in the set include the 59 players perceived to be the most popular, along with a checklist.

FOR

These are nice large-size cards with lots of superstars.

AGAINST

Collectors generally don't like large-size cards.

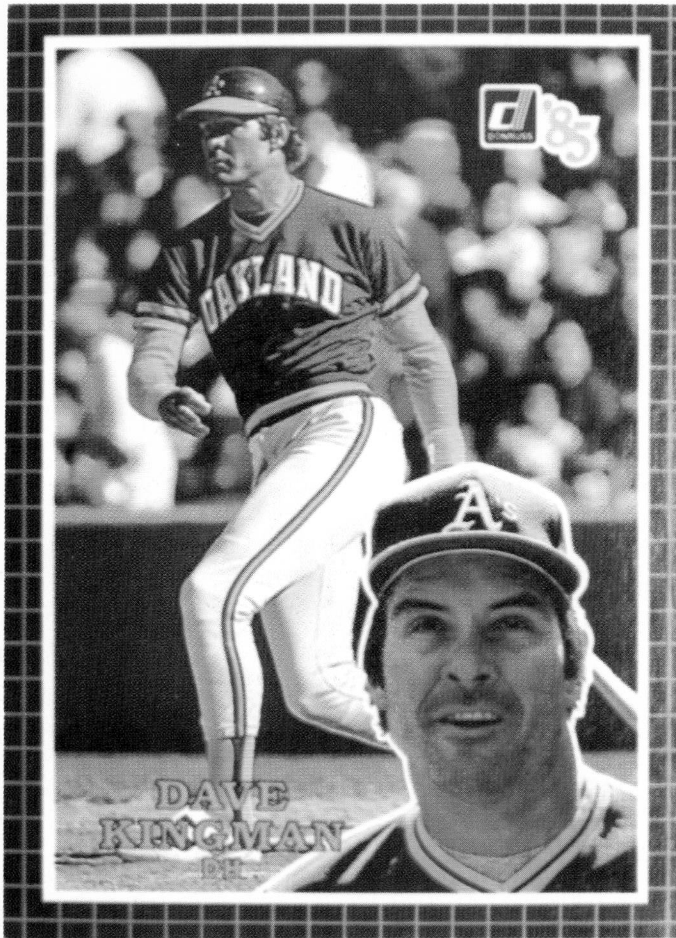

1985 Donruss Action All-Stars, Dave Kingman

NOTEWORTHY CARDS

You can obtain yet another Dwight Gooden rookie card.

VALUE

MINT CONDITION: Complete set, \$6; common card, 5¢–10¢; stars, 25¢–75¢; Mattingly, Gooden, \$1.
5-YEAR PROJECTION: Below average.

1985 DRAKE'S

SPECIFICATIONS

SIZE: 2½ × 3½". FRONT: Color photograph. BACK: Red and black printing on gray cardboard.
DISTRIBUTION: Mid-Atlantic states, one card in boxes of Drake's snack cakes and through a mail-in offer.

HISTORY

In its fifth year of baseball card production, Drake's changed the content of its set, adding 11 "Super Pitchers" cards to its traditional line-up of 33 "Big Hitters," for a 44-card set. While the batters' cards continued to be available in specially marked boxes of Drake's snack cakes, the pitchers' cards were available only by mailing in four proofs-of-purchase. This made the pitchers' cards somewhat scarcer than the hitters'. Actually, the entire 1985 Drake's issue is not easy to find compared with previous years. Again produced by Topps, the '85 Drake's featured no major change in design. A color game-action photo was sandwiched between a top panel proclaiming the issue to be the "5th Annual Collectors' Edition" and giving the card number, and a bottom panel containing the player's name, team, and position. A large, colorful Drake's logo appears in the lower left. Card backs were virtually identical to the regular-issue Topps backs for 1985, except for the color of the ink, a change of card number, and the addition of a Drake's logo.

1985 Drake's, Cal Ripken Jr.

1985 Drake's, Don Mattingly

FOR

The addition of a group of pitchers makes the set a more well-rounded superstar issue.

AGAINST

The design is too similar to previous years.

NOTEWORTHY CARDS

As with virtually every special set issued in 1985, there is a Dwight Gooden rookie card among the Super Pitchers. There are also loads of big-name players and many future Hall of Famers.

VALUE

MINT CONDITION: Complete set, $10; common card, 10¢; superstars, 50¢–$1; Mattingly, $2. 5-YEAR PROJECTION: Average.

1985 MOTHER'S COOKIES

SPECIFICATIONS

SIZE: 2½ × 3½″. FRONT: Color photograph. BACK: Red and purple printing on white cardboard. DISTRIBUTION: Houston, San Francisco, Oakland, Seattle, San Diego, 20-card starter sets given away at "Baseball Card Day" promotional games; eight additional cards available through a mail-in offer.

HISTORY

The 1985 Mother's Cookies issue—the bakery's third straight year of promotion—was also its largest, including five teams in the western U.S. As before, 20-card starter sets were given away at special promotional games, along with a coupon that could be redeemed for eight other cards by mail. It was then necessary to trade duplicates to obtain complete sets. Once again, the card front features a gorgeous color photo in a borderless, round-cornered format, highlighted by a high-gloss finish. Only the player's name and team appear on the front of the cards. Card backs are similar to previous years, with limited player data and stats, uniform and card numbers, a Mother's logo, and a line for obtaining an autograph.

1985 Mother's Cookies, Tony Gwynn

1985 Mother's Cookies, Steve Garvey

FOR

Among the most attractive baseball cards ever issued. A scarce regional set that was designed specifically to bring back the "good old days" of baseball card trading.

AGAINST

Maybe the teams weren't the most popular in baseball, but that is about all.

NOTEWORTHY CARDS

Good solid mix of rookies, established stars, and future Hall of Famers. Hot rookies included Rob Deer and Jim Presley.

VALUE

MINT CONDITION: Complete team set, $11; common card, 35¢; stars, rookies, 50¢–$2. 5-YEAR PROJECTION: Above average.

1985 SMOKEY THE BEAR ANGELS

SPECIFICATIONS

SIZE: 4¼ × 6″. FRONT: Color photograph. BACK: Black printing on white cardboard. DISTRIBUTION: Team-issued, complete sets given out at a "Baseball Card Day" promotional game.

HISTORY

After a successful premier issue in 1984, the California Angels teamed up with Smokey the Bear again in '85 to prevent forest fires. This time out, the cards were issued in a super-size format. A large color photo is framed by a wide white border. The player's last name is strung out the length of the top border on the photo. Beneath is the 25th Anniversary logo of the Angels, along with a color picture of Smokey, and the logos of the California Department of Forestry and the U.S. Forest Service. Card backs have a large cartoon of Smokey with a wildfire prevention tip. There is limited player personal data and a card number. Twenty-three players and manager Gene Mauch were included in the checklist.

1985 Smokey the Bear Angels, Tommy John

FOR
It has a popular theme.

AGAINST
The format is too unusual for most collectors' tastes.

NOTEWORTHY CARDS
Future Hall of Famers Reggie Jackson, Rod Carew, and Tommy John, plus hitting whiz Wally Joyner highlight the set.

VALUE
MINT CONDITION: Complete set, $7; common card, 25¢; stars, 50¢–$1; Joyner, $2. 5-YEAR PROJECTION: Below average.

1985 HOSTESS BRAVES

SPECIFICATIONS
SIZE: 2½ × 3½". FRONT: Color photograph. BACK: Blue and black printing on gray cardboard. DISTRIBUTION: Georgia, one 3-card package in boxes of Hostess products.

HISTORY
Having been out of the baseball card business since 1979, Hostess returned in '85 with an Atlanta Braves team set. Specially marked boxes of Hostess bakery products sold in Georgia carried a cellophane-wrapped package containing three Braves player cards and a contest card to win a Braves player for a day. The 22-card set included

1985 Hostess Braves, Gerald Perry

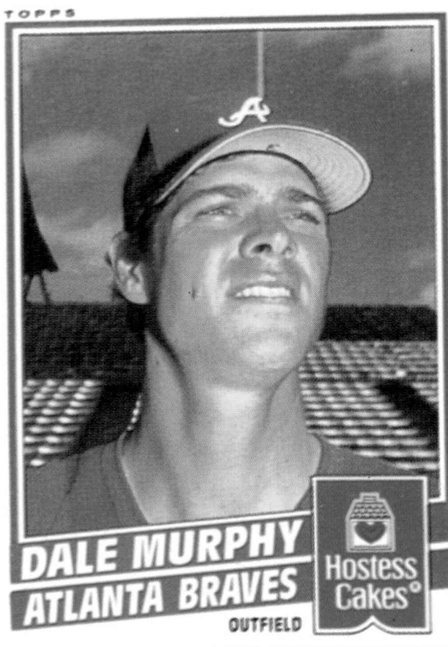

1985 Hostess Braves, Dale Murphy

manager Eddie Haas. Topps produced the cards for Hostess, and used the back design from its regular 1985 set, changing only the color of printing, card number, and adding a Hostess logo. Card fronts feature posed photos surrounded at the sides and top by a red frame. Two dark blue diagonal strips beneath the photo carry the player and team name. A large color Hostess logo appears in the lower right. The player's position is printed in black at bottom center, while the Topps name appears in black in the upper left.

FOR

Hostess issued a nice regional set that mixed veteran stars with some potentially great rookies.

AGAINST

There is nothing bad to say about it.

NOTEWORTHY CARDS

A first card of one-time relief ace Bruce Sutter in his new uniform. Also cards of potential Hall of Famer Dale Murphy, slugger Bob Horner, and rookies Brad Komminsk, Gerald Perry, and Albert Hall.

VALUE

MINT CONDITION: Complete set, $8; common card, 30¢; stars, 50¢–$1; Murphy, $3. 5-YEAR PROJECTION: Average.

1985 GARDNER'S BREWERS

SPECIFICATIONS

SIZE: 3½ × 2½″. FRONT: Color photograph. BACK: Blue and black printing on gray cardboard. DISTRIBUTION: Wisconsin, one card in packages of Gardner's products.

1985 Gardner's Brewers, George Bamberger

1985 Gardner's Brewers, Cecil Cooper

HISTORY

This was the third and final year Gardner's baking company of Madison issued a Topps-produced Milwaukee Brewers card set. As before, cards were packaged in loaves of bread and bags of buns, encouraging collectors to paw through entire store shelves looking for the players needed to complete a set. The design of the 1985 card was extremely innovative, beginning with the horizontal format. A square player photo on the left of the card is framed with blue and yellow rules, surrounded by a bright red border. To the right, a bakery logo, the player's name and position, and a team logo appear. Card backs are identical to the regular-issue Topps cards for 1985, but are printed in blue rather than red and green. Only the card number was changed. The 22-card set includes 21 players and manager George Bamberger. While it was rumored early in the year that a large quantity of the cards would become available through the hobby market, it never happened, and the set remains quite scarce.

FOR

It is a scarce regional set with an innovative design.

AGAINST

Perhaps the design is a bit too gaudy for some tastes.

NOTEWORTHY CARDS

The set contains the last of the Brewers' stars of the early 1980s and perhaps some future Hall of Famers: Robin Yount, Cecil Cooper, Paul Molitor, and Rollie Fingers.

VALUE

MINT CONDITION: Complete set, \$12; common card, 30¢; stars, \$1–\$2; Yount, \$2–\$3. 5-YEAR PROJECTION: Average.

1985 BREWERS POLICE

SPECIFICATIONS

SIZE: 2 13/16 × 4 1/8". FRONT: Color photograph. BACK: Blue printing on white cardboard. DISTRIBUTION: Wisconsin, complete sets given out at a promotional game; single cards given to youngsters by police officers.

1985 Brewers Police, Paul Molitor

HISTORY

The Milwaukee Brewers police set program was bigger than ever in its fourth year, with some 60 departments issuing 30-card sets of the hometown heroes emblazoned with the particular department's name. Card fronts follow the tried-and-true police set format: a color photograph surrounded by a wide white border. Beneath is the player's name, uniform number, and position, along with credit lines for the local police department and the *Milwaukee Journal*, the principal sponsor of the program. Complete sets were given to youngsters attending a special "Baseball Card Day" promotional game in May. As always, card backs carry a safety tip for youngsters, but are devoid of player data or statistics.

FOR

The attractive pictures were taken at spring training. The set has a good mix of young players and established stars.

AGAINST

The layout is too similar to that of previous years. The large number of departments issuing their own cards drives variety collectors crazy trying to complete a "set" of nearly 2,000 cards.

NOTEWORTHY CARDS

Besides the remnants of the Brewers 1982 A.L. Championship club, there were several potential stars among the rookies featured in the set, notably pitcher Ted Higuera. The set distributed by the Milwaukee Police Department is unique in that it includes a card for Jason Smith, a *Milwaukee Journal* paperboy. The back of the card extols the virtues of working as a paper carrier.

VALUE

MINT CONDITION: Complete set, $5; common card, 15¢; stars, 50¢–$1; Higuera, $1. 5-YEAR PROJECTION: Average.

1985 7-Up Cubs, Richie Hebner

1985 7-UP CUBS

SPECIFICATIONS

SIZE: $2\frac{1}{2} \times 3\frac{1}{2}$". FRONT: Color photograph. BACK: Black printing on white cardboard. DISTRIBUTION: Chicago, complete sets given out at a "Baseball Card Day" promotional game.

1985 7-Up Cubs, Lee Smith

HISTORY

The 1985 7-Up Cubs team set was the fourth straight year of promotional game premiums from the Cubs, and the second time in a row the set was sponsored by 7-Up. The 1985 set was the first time the cards were issued in the standard $2\frac{1}{2} \times 3\frac{1}{2}$" format. Color action photos of the team at Wrigley Field are surrounded by a dark blue frame and white border. A color team logo appears in the lower left, with the player's name, position, and uniform number at the bottom right. Card backs contain no player personal data, just complete major and minor league stats, a 7-Up logo and copyright notice. The 28-card set includes 26 player cards, a card for manager Jim Frey, and a group card of the coaches.

FOR

The standard format was a welcome break from earlier issues.

AGAINST

There are no negative comments.

NOTEWORTHY CARDS

While all the Cubs looked like stars the year before, when they won the National League East title, by the time these cards were issued the only player still playing like a champion was Ryne Sandberg.

VALUE

MINT CONDITION: Complete set, $7; common card, 15¢; Sandberg, $2. 5-YEAR PROJECTION: Below average.

1985 TIGERS, CARDINALS POTATO CHIP DISCS

SPECIFICATIONS

SIZE: 2¾" diameter. FRONT: Color photograph. BACK: Black printing on white cardboard. DISTRIBUTION: Michigan and Missouri, one card in packages of potato chips.

HISTORY

The reigning World Champion Detroit Tigers, and the team destined to win the 1985 National League title, the St. Louis Cardinals, were the subjects of team sets issued in their home states by the Cains and Kitty Clover potato chip brands. Single cards, packaged in cellophane, were in specially marked boxes of potato chips. The round cards feature a color photo on a white baseball diamond diagram set against yellow borders. Card backs, bearing the "Snack Time" logo, contain brief player vital stats and performance figures from the previous season. The 20 cards in each set were unnumbered. Single cards, packaged in cellophane, were in specially marked boxes of potato chips.

FOR

The cards had an innovative format which has often been copied since.

AGAINST

Collectors don't like round cards.

NOTEWORTHY CARDS

There are lots of stars, as might be expected from pennant-winning clubs.

VALUE

MINT CONDITION: Complete set: Tigers, $20; Cardinals, $15. Common card, 50¢–75¢. 5-YEAR PROJECTION: Below average.

1985 WENDY'S TIGERS

SPECIFICATIONS

SIZE: 2½ × 3½". FRONT: Color photograph. BACK: Red and black printing on white cardboard. DISTRIBUTION: Selected Michigan cities, one 3-card pack given away with purchase at Wendy's restaurants.

HISTORY

Everybody loves a winner, so naturally the 1984 World Champion Detroit Tigers inspired a number of baseball card sets the following year. Probably the nicest of them was the 22-card set produced by Topps for Wendy's in selected Michigan cities. Sponsored by Coca-Cola, one 3-card pack was given to patrons who ordered a Coke with their meal. The promotion lasted only through the month of April. The card front features an orange border surrounding a player photo. In the upper right is a

1985 Wendy's Tigers, Lance Parrish

1985 Wendy's Tigers, Alan Trammell

Coke logo, while a Wendy's logo appears in the lower left. The team name (printed in orange) and the player's name and position (printed in white) are in a blue box beneath the photo. As with most Topps-produced specialty sets of 1985, the card backs are virtual clones of the regular '85 Topps cards, except for the card number and the Wendy's logo. There are 21 player cards and a card for manager Sparky Anderson.

FOR

It is a nice-looking set of a World Championship team.

AGAINST

There is nothing bad to say about this one.

NOTEWORTHY CARDS

There is good Hall of Fame potential for a number of these players, not to mention the manager.

VALUE

MINT CONDITION: Complete set, $8; common card, 15¢; stars, 50¢–$1; Alan Trammell, $2. 5-YEAR PROJECTION: Average.

1985 TWINS FIRE SAFETY

SPECIFICATIONS

SIZE: 2½ × 3½". FRONT: Color photograph. BACK: Color printing on white cardboard. DISTRIBUTION: Minnesota, single cards given out at a promotional game; and also available at 7-11 stores.

HISTORY

The 7-11 convenience stores in Minnesota teamed up with the Twins in 1985 to produce a baseball card set aimed at increasing fire safety awareness among children. At a June promotional game, single cards and a large poster on which to mount the 12-card set were given to youngsters. The rest of the cards were available over the next eight weeks at local 7-11s. Card fronts feature an action photo of the player, a facsimile autograph, and a Twins logo. Card backs include color team and 7-11 logos, the player's name, position, uniform number, card number, personal data, and 1984 and lifetime stats. An orange box at the bottom highlights a fire prevention tip. It was reported that 20,000 of the sets were produced.

FOR

The standard card size is unusual in a safety set. The card fronts are clean-looking.

AGAINST

Only 12 players were available, which is not really a team set.

NOTEWORTHY CARDS

A rookie card of Minnesota slugging star Kirby Puckett appears.

VALUE

MINT CONDITION: Complete set, $6; common card, 25¢; stars, 75¢; Puckett, $2. 5-YEAR PROJECTION: Above average.

1984 TOPPS

SPECIFICATIONS

SIZE: 2½ × 3½". FRONT: Color photograph. BACK: Purple and red printing on gray cardboard. DISTRIBUTION: Nationally, in packages with bubblegum; complete sets sold through hobby dealers.

1984 Topps, Darryl Strawberry

1984 Topps, Steve Carlton

1984 Topps, Ted Simmons/Reggie Jackson/Graig Nettles

HISTORY

The 1984 Topps baseball card set was not viewed as one of the company's best efforts. While Topps retained the popular concept of combining a large action photo with a smaller portrait photo on the front of the card, the effect was spoiled by putting the team name in large block letters down the left side of the card, eating up too much space. The player's name and position are printed at the bottom of the card in the same color as the team name. A Topps logo is in the upper right of the photo. Instead of a natural background, as in '83, the portrait photos have a solid color background. The card backs feature unusual red and purple printing, and include complete major and minor league stats, personal data, and a few highlights from the previous season. A team logo appears in the upper right. The set once again contained 792 cards. The first six cards feature highlights of the previous season and include Steve Carlton winning his 300th game and becoming the all-time strikeout king; Dave Righetti, Bob Forsch, and Mike Warren pitching no-hitters; Rickey Henderson stealing 100 bases three seasons in a row; and Johnny Bench, Gaylord Perry, and Carl Yastrzemski retiring. Other specialty cards include Team Leader cards, which feature the top pitcher and batter of each club; All-Star cards for both leagues; and six numbered checklists. One interesting subset highlights active players who were leading their league in various career statistics. The N.L. RBI leaders were Tony Perez, Rusty Staub, and Al Oliver (#704); the A.L. hits leaders were Rod Carew, Bert Campaneris, and

Reggie Jackson (#712). Another subset includes the 1983 season leaders in major statistical categories. Included were batting leaders Bill Madlock and Wade Boggs (#131), victory leaders John Denny and LaMarr Hoyt (#135), and saves leaders Al Holland and Dan Quisenberry (#138). Missing from the 1984 set for the second year in a row were team rookie or "Future Stars" cards.

FOR

It is a typical Topps set.

AGAINST

Many collectors don't like the design.

NOTEWORTHY CARDS

All the regular stars are present, but few of the hot rookies of '84 made it into the set. (Topps may have been saving them for the Traded set to be released later in the year.) An exception is the premier card of Don Mattingly.

VALUE

MINT CONDITION: Complete set, $85; common card, 6¢; stars, 25¢–$1.50; Darryl Strawberry, $10; Mattingly, $35. 5-YEAR PROJECTION: Above average.

1984 Topps Traded, Yogi Berra

1984 TOPPS TRADED

SPECIFICATIONS

SIZE: $2\frac{1}{2} \times 3\frac{1}{2}$". FRONT: Color photograph. BACK: Blue and red printing on white cardboard. DISTRIBUTION: Nationally, complete sets sold through hobby dealers.

HISTORY

For the fourth year in a row, Topps produced a 132-card Traded set to supplement its regular baseball card issue. The Traded set features players who were traded, sold, or who otherwise changed teams after Topps released its regular 1984 issue. While most collectors appreciate the chance to get cards in the current year's design showing players in the "right" uniform, the principal attraction of the Traded set is the presence of rookie cards that were not included in the regular set. Also included in the issue are a sprinkling of cards of new managers. While most of the cards use new photos of the players, a few have had "new" uniforms created by an artist. The design of the Traded set is identical to the regular 1984 cards. The card back is easier to read because the cardboard is white instead of gray. The cards are numbered from 1-T to 132-T, the last card being a checklist. Like the 1981 to '83 Traded sets, the '84 issue was sold only through dealers in complete boxed sets.

1984 Topps Traded, Dwight Gooden

FOR

The set offers a chance for collectors to get updated cards of their favorite players. Also, it includes some hot rookies.

AGAINST
Because the cards are not sold to the general public, some collectors don't feel they are "real" baseball cards. The cost per card is relatively high.

NOTEWORTHY CARDS
The set includes manager cards such as Yogi Berra (a feature virtually overlooked by competitors in 1984). Future Hall of Famers Tom Seaver, Pete Rose, and Joe Morgan were also included. However, by the time the set was released in late September, Pete Rose was no longer an Expo, so his card was already outdated. All the big-name rookies of 1984 (notably Dwight Gooden) were part of the issue.

VALUE
MINT CONDITION: Complete set, $80; common card, 10¢–15¢; stars, $2+; Juan Samuel, Ron Darling, Bret Saberhagen, $5–$8; Rose, $9; Gooden, $40. 5-YEAR PROJECTION: Above average.

1984 TOPPS MAIL-IN GLOSSIES

SPECIFICATIONS
SIZE: 2½ × 3½". FRONT: Color photograph. BACK: Red and blue printing on white cardboard. DISTRIBUTION: Nationally, five 8-card sets available through a mail-in offer.

1984 Topps Mail-In Glossies, Andre Dawson

HISTORY
Seeking a competitive edge in the fourth year of its rivalry with Fleer and Donruss, Topps inserted a "Bonus Runs" game card into its 1983 wax packs. Prizes such as a trip to the World Series or baseball equipment could be won by having the right combination of "hits" hidden under scratch-off discs on the game card. Each card also had between one and eight "Bonus Runs" printed on it. In exchange for 25 bonus runs and a little cash, collectors could get one of five 8-card sets of special-edition superstar cards. The set contained the top 20 superstars from each league. Card fronts feature an attractive high-gloss finish that enhances the large color photo, which has a thin colored frame inside a white border. The player's name in small letters at the lower left is the only other design element. Card backs have no stats, just the player's name, team, position, a card number, and a "Topps 1984 All-Star Set Collector's Edition" designation.

FOR
A simple, attractive design highlights this semiscarce set of superstars.

AGAINST
Some collectors were turned off because most cards were damaged in the mail. If they wanted Mint cards, they had to buy them from dealers—at relatively high prices because dealers had the same problem. Also, at a cost of 30¢ for each bonus card plus postage, the per card price was high—around 15¢ or so.

NOTEWORTHY CARDS
While all players in the set are stars (or at least were in 1984), the best of the bunch is a Darryl Strawberry rookie card.

VALUE
MINT CONDITION: Complete set, $12; common card, 15¢–35¢; superstars, $1–$2. 5-YEAR PROJECTION: Average.

1984 TOPPS SUPERSTAR 5 × 7s

SPECIFICATIONS
SIZE: 4⅞ × 6⅞". FRONT: Color photograph. BACK: Red and purple printing on gray cardboard. DISTRIBUTION: Regionally, in cello packs.

1984 Topps Superstar 5x7s, Steve Garvey

HISTORY

A limited issue sold in certain areas of the country, the Topps 5 × 7 issue of 1984 was unusual in that the 30 cards were merely giant-size versions of the regular '84 Topps cards. Fronts and backs are exactly the same as the regular issue. All 30 players pictured in the set are stars from 1983, and include LaMarr Hoyt, Al Holland, John Denny, along with the usual Wade Boggs, Mike Schmidt, and Dale Murphy. Topps tested this issue for a few years before dropping it. There simply is no interest in modern cards that are not the standard 2½ × 3½". If anything, hobbyists prefer smaller cards.

FOR

It is something different for the superstar collector.

AGAINST

If you didn't like the design of the regular 1984 Topps cards, you'll hate them when they're twice as big.

NOTEWORTHY CARDS

They're all superstars.

VALUE
MINT CONDITION: Complete set, $9.50; common card, 20¢–35¢; superstars, $1–$2. 5-YEAR PROJECTION: Below average.

1984 TOPPS ALL-STAR GLOSSIES

SPECIFICATIONS
SIZE: 2½ × 3½″. FRONT: Color photograph. BACK: Red and blue printing on white cardboard. DISTRIBUTION: Nationally, in rak-paks; complete sets sold through hobby dealers.

HISTORY
Buoyed by collector response to its Glossies set of the previous year, Topps produced a similar issue in 1984 to honor the starting All-Stars of 1983. The 22-card set includes the starting nine players for the American and National Leagues, along with the managers and honorary team captains. Besides wholesaling the sets to dealers, Topps made single cards available by inserting them in rak-paks—cellophane-wrapped packages containing 36 regular cards and sold alongside the traditional wax packs with bubblegum. Card fronts feature a color photo with an All-Star banner at the top and a league emblem in the lower left. A glossy coating enhances the appearance of the card. Card backs have no stats or personal data on the player—only a name, team, position, card number, and a "1983 All-Star Game Commemorative Set" designation.

1984 Topps All-Star Glossies, Johnny Bench

1984 Topps All-Star Glossies, Gary Carter

FOR
It is an appealing set of 1983's All-Stars.

AGAINST
It was relatively expensive per card.

NOTEWORTHY CARDS
Most of the players are superstars.

VALUE
MINT CONDITION: Complete set, $5; common card, 15¢; stars, superstars, 50¢–$1. 5-YEAR PROJECTION: Average.

1984 FLEER

SPECIFICATIONS
SIZE: 2½ × 3½″. FRONT: Color photograph. BACK: Black and blue printing on white cardboard. DISTRIBUTION: Nationally, in packages with team logo and cap stickers.

1984 Fleer, Glenn Hubbard

1984 Fleer, Johnny Bench/Carl Yastrzemski

1984 Fleer, Jay Johnstone

HISTORY

If you want to get a feeling for what major league baseball was like in the early '80s, look at the 1984 Fleer set, which ranks as one of the finest major card sets of modern times. The design is clean and attractive. The photography was only occasionally short of perfect, and often inspired. Along with the usual mix of portraits and action poses are some unusual candid shots. Some collectors feel that a few of the pictures are not in keeping with the serious nature of baseball. Other collectors, however, feel that the candids show what the game and the players of the 1980s were really like. Some critics also contend that too many of the cards have "commercial messages" in the form of equipment brands, billboards, etc. Card fronts feature a large rectangular photo against a white border, framed at the top and bottom by a bright blue horizontal stripe. The top stripe contains only a white Fleer logo, while the bottom stripe has the player's name, also in white. The player's position is in small black letters at the bottom. A color team logo appears in the lower right. Card backs are almost exactly the same as in '83, with a black-and-white player photo in the upper right, a bio, major and minor league stats, and, space permitting, a trivia question about the player. The card number was moved to the upper left and the printing was mostly blue instead of brown. Once again, the 660 cards are arranged alphabetically by the player's name within each team, and the teams are arranged in order of their 1983 season finish. There are 14 checklist cards at the end of the set and a large group of "Super Star Special" cards—some featuring a single player, some featuring more than one. A group of four cards highlights the 1983 World Series. No major errors or variations occurred in the 1984 Fleer set.

FOR

This attractive set, perhaps destined to be a classic, is currently low priced.

AGAINST

Some collectors feel there are too many cards in the set that picture players in nontraditional poses.

NOTEWORTHY CARDS

You can't mention the '84 Fleer set without mentioning the Glenn Hubbard card (#182) on which the Braves second baseman is pictured with a big bearded smile—and a boa constrictor draped around his shoulders. On Jay Johnstone's card (#495), the Cubs outfielder is shown wearing a Budweiser umbrella-hat. Among the "Super Star Special" cards worth noting are six cards meant to be viewed side-by-side as pairs. One card in each pair has no left border, the other has no right border, so that they form a continuous picture when laid together. The pairs feature Wade Boggs and Rod Carew (1983's A.L. batting champ and runner-up); Expos teammates Tim Raines and Al Oliver; and the N.L. All-Star shortstop Dickie Thon. Rick Dempsey gets a card for winning the 1983 World Series MVP award. "Retiring Superstars" Johnny Bench and Carl Yastrzemski share a card. Gaylord Perry appears on two of the cards: one called "Going Out in Style," and the other showing him in the dugout pointing out how high George Brett is applying pine tar to a bat (titled "The Pine Tar Incident, 7/24/83"). Bench, Yaz, and Perry also appear on regular '84 Fleer cards, even though they all retired at the end of the 1983 season. The recent Hall of Fame election of Bench and Yaz will boost interest in these cards.

VALUE

MINT CONDITION: Complete set, $85; common card, 6¢; stars, 25¢–$1; Boggs, $7; Darryl Strawberry, $12; Don Mattingly, $35. 5-YEAR PROJECTION: Above average.

1984 FLEER UPDATE

SPECIFICATIONS

SIZE: 2½ × 3½". FRONT: Color photograph. BACK: Blue printing on white cardboard. DISTRIBUTION: Nationally, complete sets sold through hobby dealers.

HISTORY

Recognizing a good idea, Fleer introduced an updated version of their 1984 baseball card set in September. Using the same concept pioneered by Topps in 1981, Fleer issued cards of players who had been traded during the year and rookies who had been overlooked in the regular set. Like the Topps Traded set, the '84 Fleer Update issue was sold only through dealers as a complete set. It was not available over the counter at the stores that sold regular packs of Fleer cards. The 132-card set contains 131 player cards and a checklist card. It came boxed with an assortment of team logo and cap stickers. Other than the new pictures of the players, the only difference between the Update cards and the regular issue cards of 1984 is the U-1 through U-132 numbering system.

1984 Fleer Update, Kirby Puckett

1984 Fleer Update, Mike Vail

FOR

A well-done set with the same quality photography found in Fleer's regular 1984 edition. It gives collectors a chance to own '84 cards with players in their current team uniforms. The set also contains a lot of hot rookie cards.

AGAINST

Because the cards were only available through dealers, some collectors feel they are not "real" baseball cards.

NOTEWORTHY CARDS

Fleer did a good job of updating its 1984 set. Rick Sutcliffe and Ron Hassey (traded to the Cubs in June) are shown in their new uniforms. However, Mel Hall and Joe Carter (who went to the Indians in the same deal) are not included in the set. Pete Rose, who appears as a Phillie in the regular set, is pictured as an Expo in the updated issue; but by the time the cards had been issued, he was with the Reds. Rookie pitching sensations Dwight Gooden and Roger Clemens are two of the new players highlighted in the set.

VALUE

MINT CONDITION: Complete set, $225; common card, 20¢; stars, $2–$4; superstars, $4–$8; Kirby Puckett, $60; Gooden, $70; Clemens, $80. 5-YEAR PROJECTION: Above average.

1984 DONRUSS

SPECIFICATIONS

SIZE: 2½ × 3½". FRONT: Color photograph. BACK: Green and black printing on white cardboard. DISTRIBUTION: Nationally, in wax packs; complete sets sold through hobby dealers.

HISTORY

In its fourth year Donruss really hit its stride as a card producer. The company's 1984 set was acclaimed by most collectors as the best overall of the "Big 3." The set was not without controversy though. It seems there was some confusion as to what constituted a "complete" set. If you collected the set from wax packs, you could get 660 cards. If you bought a complete boxed set from a dealer, you got only 658 cards. The difference was a pair of special cards called "Living Legends" that were found only in wax packs. Both Living Legends cards featured a pair of superstars who had retired after the 1983 season; the cards were Donruss' way of saying farewell. However, Donruss jumped the gun by including Brewers reliever Rollie Fingers on one of the cards. Fingers came back from an '82 arm injury to make significant contributions in '84. Fingers shares his card with Gaylord Perry. The other card depicts Hall of Famers Carl Yastrzemski and Johnny Bench. These cards created a problem for dealers who had to sell sets that were "missing" two cards. Although the Living Legends cards were not numbered as part of the set (they were lettered

1984 Donruss, Don Mattingly

1984 Donruss, Ron Darling

*1984 Donruss,
Carl Yastrzemski/Johnny Bench*

"A" and "B"), collectors quickly decided they were necessary for a complete set. This created an instant demand for the cards pulled from wax packs, and the price jumped to a dollar apiece. Unlike the rest of the cards, the Living Legends are not very attractive: all that is pictured is a mug shot from the bill of the cap to the point of the chin. The design of the regular 1984 cards was the company's best up until that time. A sharp color photo fills virtually the entire card front. Toward the bottom, four curved yellow lines contain the team name and an '84 Donruss logo. Below the picture is a thin border with the player's name and position. A thin white border frames the whole card. Card backs are virtually identical to the previous two years. Year-by-year stats of the player's recent major league performance are in the white center section, and yellow bars at the top and bottom contain vital information and career highlights. Like the '82 and '83 sets, this set begins with a run of 26 Diamond Kings featuring a painted portrait of one player from each team. Donruss catered to the collector market with the next 20 cards in the set—the "Rated Rookies." These cards depict young players who Donruss felt might turn out to be the hot rookies of 1984. In all, more than 95 rookie cards are interspersed throughout the '84 set—a real bonanza for rookie card collectors. There was only one multiplayer card in this edition, called "Running Reds." The title is peculiar because the four players featured are St. Louis Cardinals. The mystery is cleared up on the back of the card where the full title, "Running Redbirds," appears. Besides the player cards, there are seven unnumbered checklists, a "Famous Chicken" card, and a card picturing the Duke Snider jigsaw puzzle, three pieces of which were inserted in each wax pack.

FOR

It is a good-looking recent set. The rookie cards give it special appeal for speculators. Printed in much more limited numbers than the company's '81 through '83 sets, it is quite scarce in comparison.

AGAINST

Donruss still had problems with color reproduction, resulting in "sunburned" white players and purple-hued black players. There were hard feelings regarding the missing Living Legends cards in the dealer sets.

NOTEWORTHY CARDS

Two major variations exist among the Rated Rookie cards: Mike Stenhouse (#29) and Ron Darling (#30) were originally printed in the wax-pack press run without their card numbers. This error was corrected in the printing for the dealer sets. On the backs of the Diamond Kings cards, the name of the art gallery that produces the player paintings (Perez-Steele Galleries) was misspelled "Perez-Steel." These cards were also corrected in the second printing. A number of cards that had incorrect first names, misspelled names, wrong teams, or wrong positions were not corrected.

VALUE
MINT CONDITION: Complete set, $200; common card, 10¢; stars, hot rookies, 50¢–$1; Bench-Yaz Legends, $5; Darryl Strawberry, $15; Don Mattingly, $75. 5-YEAR PROJECTION: Above average.

1984 DONRUSS ACTION ALL-STARS

SPECIFICATIONS
SIZE: 3½ × 5″. FRONT: Color photograph. BACK: Color photograph. DISTRIBUTION: Nationally, in cello packs with jigsaw puzzle pieces.

1984 Donruss Action All-Stars, Nolan Ryan

HISTORY
Following the success of its 1983 Action All-Stars set, Donruss issued a similar set in '84. Again in postcard-size format, the set is unique in that it was the first to feature color photos of the player on both front and back. The cards are in vertical format and feature a large color action photo, interrupted only by a small company logo in an upper corner. A thin stripe at the bottom contains the player's name and position. White and burgundy borders surround the photo. The card back has a color portrait photo of the player at the top with the team name printed as part of the gray background. Vital stats and career highlights are presented in red boxes below and are separated by a white band with yearly stats. Again in the '84 issue, there were 59 player cards and a checklist. The cards were sold in cello packs that contained six cards and three pieces of a 63-piece Ted Williams jigsaw puzzle.

FOR
This was an attractive follow-up of a very successful issue.

AGAINST
Some collectors don't like large-format cards.

NOTEWORTHY CARDS
Virtually all of the players in the set are stars.

VALUE
MINT CONDITION: Complete set, $6; common card, 7¢; superstars, 20¢–50¢; Wade Boggs, $1. 5-YEAR PROJECTION: Below average.

1984 DONRUSS CHAMPIONS

SPECIFICATIONS
SIZE: 3½ × 5″. FRONT: Color photograph. BACK: Black and brown printing on white cardboard. DISTRIBUTION: Nationally, in cello packs with jigsaw puzzle pieces.

HISTORY
Donruss had not yet given up on the idea of selling baseball cards of former players in 1984 when it issued a 60-card set of "Champions" (59 player cards and a checklist). The postcard-size cards combined Hall of Famers and current players arranged in statistical categories. The old-timers are depicted in Dick Perez paintings, while the

1984 Donruss Champions, Hank Aaron

current players have color photos. An "art deco" frame surrounds the photo and the card has a white border. There is brief career and biographical information on the back along with a photo of the Hall of Fame plaque of the stat leader in each category. The theme of the set is contrived, and collectors have generally not paid much attention to the issue other than to acquire single cards of their favorite players.

FOR

These are relatively inexpensive large-format cards of big-name past and current players.

AGAINST

The purpose of the set was unclear, and combining current and former players is not popular with collectors.

NOTEWORTHY CARDS

Nearly all of them are stars or superstars.

VALUE

MINT CONDITION: Complete set, $4; common card, 5¢; superstars, 25¢–75¢. 5-YEAR PROJECTION: Below average.

1984 MILTON BRADLEY

SPECIFICATIONS

SIZE: 2½ × 3½". FRONT: Color photograph. BACK: Black and red printing on gray cardboard. DISTRIBUTION: Nationally, in a board game.

HISTORY

Dice baseball games have always been popular with young fans, and the baseball cards they contain have often become collectible. Milton Bradley continued the tradition in 1984 with a new board game called "Championship Baseball," which simulates a game between American League and National League superstars. The 30 player cards

1984 Milton Bradley, Ron Kittle

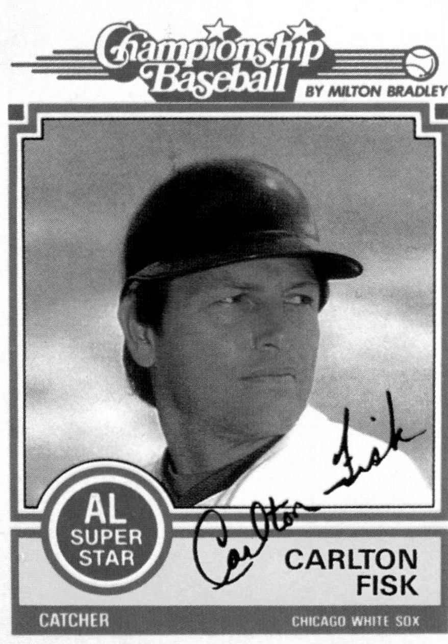

1984 Milton Bradley, Carlton Fisk

used were produced by Topps for Milton Bradley. A player photo appears on the front of the card and is surrounded by blue, red, and yellow lines, with a white border. Milton Bradley did not have permission to display team logos on the caps or uniforms, so these details have been airbrushed. Card backs give brief biographical details on the players. Pitchers' cards give career stats, which are used to play the game, and other players have dice charts on the back of their cards to indicate their play performance with each roll. Only nonpitcher cards give stats for the previous year. Milton Bradley had produced baseball games in 1969, '70, and '72, but they were not produced by Topps and were not in color.

FOR

All the cards feature superstars of 1984. They are produced by Topps.

AGAINST

The cards were only available with the game. The airbrushed caps and uniforms make the players look like softball players. Game cards are not generally as popular with collectors as regular cards.

NOTEWORTHY CARDS

Almost all are superstars, and the set includes the 1983 A.L. Rookie of the Year, Ron Kittle.

VALUE

MINT CONDITION: Complete set, $9; common card, 20¢–$1. 5-YEAR PROJECTION: Below average.

1984 NESTLE

SPECIFICATIONS

SIZE: 2½ × 3½". FRONT: Color photograph. BACK: Red and purple printing on gray cardboard. DISTRIBUTION: Nationally, in uncut sheets through a mail-in offer.

HISTORY

As an adjunct to its Dream Team baseball card issue, Nestle placed a special "header" card in Dream Team packages that offered one uncut sheet of 132 Topps cards for $4.75 plus five candy bar wrappers. A special offer that came with the first sheet allowed the collector to order the other five sheets necessary to make a complete set of 792 Nestle/Topps cards. The cards are identical to the regular 1984 Topps issue except the Nestle logo replaces the Topps logo on the front and back. Card numbers are the same on both issues.

FOR

This was the largest promotional baseball card set ever produced with Topps' cooperation. Although they are virtually identical to the regular Topps cards, they are much scarcer.

AGAINST

The set is too much like the regular 1984 Topps cards. Single cards are hard to find because of the problems involved in cutting the sheets into individual cards. At a total cost of $28.50 (not including the proofs of purchase from the candy bars), the set was quite expensive for a current issue. Beware of dealers who claim to have Nestle's proof cards, as some forgeries are sold to unsuspecting hobbyists. The fakes are black and white with blank backs.

NOTEWORTHY CARDS

Since the Nestle cards are the same as the regular Topps set for 1984, all the notable cards are the same.

VALUE

MINT CONDITION: Complete set, $400; common card, 25¢; stars, $7–$30; Don Mattingly, $150. 5-YEAR PROJECTION: Above average.

1984 NESTLE DREAM TEAM

SPECIFICATIONS

SIZE: 2½ × 3½". FRONT: Color photograph. BACK: Red and purple printing on gray cardboard. DISTRIBUTION: Nationally, in packages of candy bars.

1984 Nestle Dream Team, Eddie Murray

1984 Nestle Dream Team, Cal Ripken Jr.

1984 Nestle Dream Team, Andre Dawson

HISTORY

Nestle made its debut in the baseball card promotional market in a big way—with two separate collector issues produced by Topps. The Nestle Dream Team trading card issue was a 22-card set depicting an "All-Star" team from each league. Each league had eight starting fielders, plus a lefthanded and righthanded starting pitcher and a relief pitcher. All qualify as stars and there are a number of superstars in the lineups. The cards feature a color photo at center, surrounded by borders of white, orange, yellow, maroon, and white. A color team logo appears in a white circle in the lower left, and the Nestle logo is in the upper right. Card backs are almost identical to the regular issue Topps cards for 1984, except the logo over the card number is Nestle's and the card number has been changed. American League cards are numbered 1 to 11; National League cards are numbered 12 to 22.

FOR

This was a limited-edition issue. Unlike some promotional issues, the Nestle's cards show team logos.

AGAINST

The design is a bit gaudy; there's too much design, too little picture.

NOTEWORTHY CARDS

All are stars or superstars; none are worthy of special note.

VALUE
MINT CONDITION: Complete set, $17;* common card, 35¢–$2. 5-YEAR PROJECTION: Average.

1984 RALSTON PURINA

SPECIFICATIONS
SIZE: 2½ × 3½″. FRONT: Color photograph. BACK: Blue and red printing on white cardboard. DISTRIBUTION: Nationally, in boxes of cereal; complete sets available through a mail-in offer.

HISTORY
The 33-card set produced by Topps for Ralston Purina in 1984 was the cereal company's first baseball card issue. Like many other special-edition card sets of '84, it features only the top stars of the game. Also like many other issues, the set could be obtained from hobby dealers by the time specially marked boxes of cereal were put on store shelves. The front of the card features a close-up photo of the player with a blue banner at the top proclaiming "1st Annual Collectors' Edition" and a card number. The photo is bordered on the sides and bottom in red and yellow. The player's name appears in red at the bottom, along with his team and position in black. A Topps logo appears in the lower right and a Ralston Purina logo is in the upper left. Card backs are different from regular-issue Topps cards. At center is a red and white checkerboard. Printed over this in blue is the player's vital data, 1983 and lifetime stats, career highlights, and a few personal facts. For example, Gary Carter's card notes: "Wife: Sandy; two daughters. Hobbies include collecting baseball cards." Above the checkerboard design are red and blue banners identifying the issue, and the card number. At the bottom in a blue box is an advertising message. Four cards were included in each box of cereal and the complete set could be ordered for three proofs of purchase and 50¢.

1984 Ralston Purina, Ozzie Smith

1984 Ralston Purina, Wade Boggs

FOR
A distinctively different card issue for '84 with all the big-name stars.

AGAINST
Too many baseball card sets were produced in 1984 and most have the same superstars. The Ralston Purina set was much cheaper when bought from a dealer than when assembled from cereal boxes.

NOTEWORTHY CARDS
All of the cards feature star players; it is a bonanza for the superstar collector.

VALUE
MINT CONDITION: Complete set, $3.50; common card, 8¢; superstars, 25¢; Wade Boggs, 50¢. 5-YEAR PROJECTION: Average.

1984 DRAKE'S

SPECIFICATIONS

SIZE: 2½ × 3½". FRONT: Color photograph. BACK: Red and purple printing on gray cardboard. DISTRIBUTION: East Coast, in packages of bakery products; nationally, complete sets sold through hobby dealers.

1984 Drake's, Don Baylor

1984 Drake's, Steve Kemp

HISTORY

The 33-card "Drake's Big Hitters" set was produced by Topps, and like the previous three issues, it concentrated on baseball's current crop of sluggers. In keeping with this theme, every photo shows the player in a bat-swinging pose. There is a fancy red, blue, and yellow frame around the photo, with a Drake's logo in the lower left. The American League players' names appear in red and the National League players' names are in green in the lower right. There is a card number at the top, and a line proclaiming "4th Annual Collectors' Edition." A facsimile autograph across the front completes the design. Card backs are very similar to regular-issue 1984 Topps cards, except the Drake's logo appears in the upper left instead of the Topps logo.

FOR

Many of the game's most popular figures are included in this set, and it is generally inexpensive.

AGAINST

The cards are quite similar in design to those of previous years. Drake's has acquired a reputation for "dumping" its sets on the collector market after the product promotion is over.

NOTEWORTHY CARDS

Virtually all of the players are big-name stars. Two of special note are second-year cards of Darryl Strawberry and Ron Kittle.

VALUE

MINT CONDITION: Complete set, $5; common card, 5¢; superstars, 50¢–$1. 5-YEAR PROJECTION: Average.

1984 MOTHER'S COOKIES

SPECIFICATIONS

SIZE: 2½ × 3½". FRONT: Color photograph (current teams), color painting (San Francisco Giants All-Stars). BACK: Black (Mariners) or red and purple (Giants All-Stars, A's, Astros, Padres) printing on white cardboard. DISTRIBUTION: Home team cities, 20-card starter sets given out at a "Baseball Card Day" promotional game; additional cards available through a mail-in offer.

1984 Mother's Cookies, Nolan Ryan

1984 Mother's Cookies, Mike Scott

HISTORY

The West Coast Mother's Cookies company greatly expanded its baseball card issue in 1984 by producing five team sets. Four feature current teams, and one features the San Francisco Giants all-time All-Stars in commemoration of the 1984 All-Star Game held at Candlestick Park. There are a total of 140 cards—28 in each set. Partial sets of 20 cards were given away at a special "Baseball Card Day" promotional game for each home team. Certificates good for eight more cards were either distributed with the partial sets or made available in local advertising. The eight cards received would probably not be the same ones needed to complete a set, and Mother's Cookies hoped this would encourage card trading among collectors. As usual, complete sets were available from hobby dealers who had good connections. The four current-team sets feature 25 player cards, a card for the manager, and a group card of the coaches. The Mariners, A's, and Padres sets include a checklist card featuring the team's stadium. The Astros checklist card has a team logo on the front. The cards were printed on thin cardboard, and the front of the card has a glossy finish. Like previous Mother's Cookies sets, the 1984 cards have rounded corners. The card front features a borderless color photo—generally a three-quarter or full pose taken in the stadium. The photos are exceptionally sharp and colorful. The player's name and team appear in white type in an upper corner. Backs of the four current-team sets are virtually identical, except the Mariners are printed in black, while the A's, Astros, and Rangers are printed in red and purple. There is a Mother's Cookies logo in the upper right, with a year, team name, and card number below. At left are the player's name, position, uniform number, and vital data, including a "How Obtained" line. At the bottom there is a blank line for an autograph. The San Francisco Giants set includes both past and present Giants who have appeared in All-Star Games. The card fronts feature a color painting of the player which fades into a wide white border. The player's name and "Giants All-Star" appears in black at the bottom. Backs are similar to the current-team issues, with the logo, date, team, and card number at the right. At the left is the player's name, position, uniform number, personal info, and the years he appeared in the All-Star Game. There is a blank line below, but it does not have the "Autograph" notation.

FOR

The quality of the photography and production make the 1984 Mother's Cookies cards one of the most attractive of recent years. They are especially desirable to team collectors. The cards are fairly scarce regional issues that may be hard to come by in the future.

AGAINST

The method of distribution created many incomplete sets, while only a small number of complete sets were sold through hobby dealers. This made full sets difficult to assemble as demand picked up.

NOTEWORTHY CARDS

Many of the San Francisco Giants All-Star cards were superstars of their day: Mays, McCovey, Marichal, Cepeda. Lots of stars are in the other teams' sets: Nolan Ryan and Mike Scott of the Astros, Rickey Henderson and Joe Morgan of the A's, and Steve Garvey and Goose Gossage of the Padres. Also included were hot rookies Alvin Davis of the Mariners and Kevin McReynolds of the Padres. All of the Mariners' cards were posed in a studio instead of the traditional ballpark setting.

VALUE

MINT CONDITION: Complete set, $75; common card, 45¢; superstars, 50¢–$3. 5-YEAR PROJECTION: Above average.

1984 SMOKEY THE BEAR ANGELS

SPECIFICATIONS

SIZE: 2½ × 3¾". FRONT: Color photograph. BACK: Black printing on white cardboard. DISTRIBUTION: Anaheim, complete sets given away at a special "Baseball Card Day" promotional game.

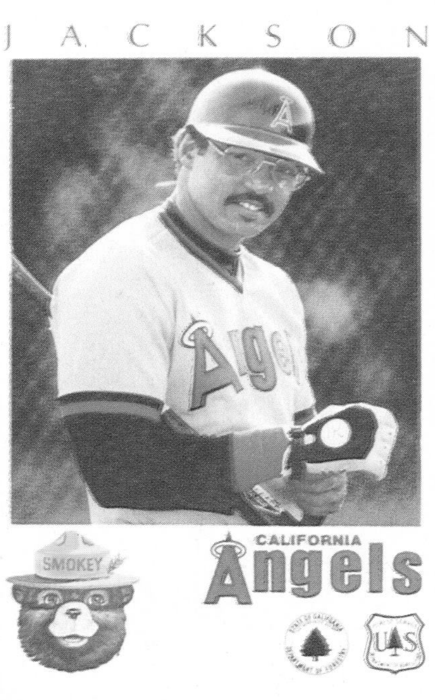

1985 Smokey the Bear Angels, Reggie Jackson

1985 Smokey the Bear Angels, Rod Carew

HISTORY

The California Angels were one of two major league teams to commemorate Smokey the Bear's 40th birthday by issuing special baseball card sets to fans attending a promotional game. Unlike the San Diego Padres set, the photos on the Angels cards do not include Smokey posing with the players. A color picture of the famous bear appears in the lower left of the card. A blue and red Angels logo appears at the right above the symbols of the U.S. Forest Service and the California State Department of Forestry. The player's last name appears above the picture on the front of the card. Most of the photos are game-action poses, although there are a few portraits. Card backs have a fire safety quote from the player, along with his 1983 stats and a few biographical details. The cards are not numbered. The 32-card set includes 29 player cards, a card for manager John McNamara, and two "header" cards. One header card has a color portrait of Smokey and a message explaining the set, while the other has the black-and-white logos of the state and U.S. forest services.

FOR

This safety set has a good theme: combining the popularity of Smokey the Bear with a baseball card issue.

AGAINST

The thin cardboard makes the cards susceptible to creasing.

NOTEWORTHY CARDS

The set displays a good combination of young and old stars from the '84 Angels: Dick Schofield and Gary Pettis, along with Reggie Jackson, Tommy John, Rod Carew, and Fred Lynn.

VALUE

MINT CONDITION: Complete set, $8.50; common card, 20¢; stars, 25¢–60¢; Jackson, $1.50. 5-YEAR PROJECTION: Above average.

1984 BLUE JAYS FIRE SAFETY

SPECIFICATIONS

SIZE: 2½ × 3½″. FRONT: Color photograph. BACK: Black printing on white cardboard. DISTRIBUTION: Ontario, five-card groups given away at fire stations and available through a mail-in offer.

HISTORY

The first safety set to feature the Toronto Blue Jays, this 35-card issue was co-sponsored by the *Toronto Sun* newspaper and the Ontario Association of Fire Chiefs. Groups of five cards were available every two weeks to children who stopped in at local fire stations. Cards could also be obtained by sending in a special coupon that appeared in the newspaper. Apparently recognizing the hobby demand for such cards, the makers added a note to the back of the cards that says, "These trading cards are not to be sold for any purpose." Unlike other recent police and fire sets, the Blue Jays cards are in the standard 2½ × 3½″ size (most safety sets have large-size cards). The front features a color action photo framed with a light blue border (rather than the customary wide white border) similar to the team's road jerseys. The player's name, position, and uniform number appear in black type at the bottom. A red, white, and blue team logo appears in the lower right. Backs have the logos of the co-sponsors, abbreviated biographical details of the player, and a fire safety tip. The card number (corresponding to the player's uniform number) appears on the back. The set includes cards of the entire Blue Jays staff, as well as cards for the coaches and manager.

1984 Blue Jays Fire Safety, Lloyd Moseby

1984 Blue Jays Fire Safety, Dave Stieb

FOR

One of the more attractive of the recent safety sets, and the first major regional issue of the team, making it popular with fans and collectors.

AGAINST

The method of distribution makes it hard for collectors outside the Toronto area to obtain a complete set.

NOTEWORTHY CARDS

Besides such well-known performers as Lloyd Moseby, Dave Stieb, Damaso Garcia, and Alfredo Griffin, the Blue Jays Fire Safety set was also the first to include team members Willie Aikens and Rick Leach in their new uniforms.

VALUE

MINT CONDITION: Complete set, $10–$12; common card, 25¢; stars, 50¢–$1. 5-YEAR PROJECTION: Above average.

1984 BRAVES POLICE

SPECIFICATIONS

SIZE: 2⅝ × 4⅛". FRONT: Color photograph. BACK: Red, blue, yellow, and black printing on white cardboard. DISTRIBUTION: Atlanta, single cards given out by local police officers.

1984 Braves Police, Dale Murphy

HISTORY

The Braves were one of the first baseball teams to issue a police safety set (in 1980), and the 30-card '84 issue marked the team's fifth consecutive issue. The format closely resembles the traditional police set format, with a slightly larger-than-standard card size. The 1984 Braves set features a color photo of the player on the front with a color team logo in the lower right. A Police Athletic League shield and an "A '84" appear in red in the wide white border at the top of the card. The player's name, position, and number appear in black in the lower left. Card backs are unusual in that they feature the logos of the sponsoring companies (Coca-Cola and Hostess) in full color. The rest of the card back contains a few biographical details and a safety message related in baseball terms, along with credit lines for the photographer and printer. The set contains the 25 Braves on the roster, and individual cards for the manager and coaches.

FOR

One of the easier police sets to obtain, perhaps because the Braves publicity director (a baseball card collector and well-known specialist in safety sets) has encouraged wide distribution.

AGAINST

Hobbyists get bored with the similarity in format to the previous four Braves police set issues.

NOTEWORTHY CARDS

Besides cards for popular Braves stars like Dale Murphy and Bob Horner, the manager and coaches cards are a veritable who's who of old-timers. All had significant major league playing experience—from manager Joe Torre to Hall of Fame coaches Bob Gibson and Luke Appling.

VALUE

MINT CONDITION: Complete set, $7; common card, 10¢; stars, $1; Murphy, $3. 5-YEAR PROJECTION: Average.

1984 GARDNER'S BREWERS

SPECIFICATIONS

SIZE: 2½ × 3½". FRONT: Color photograph. BACK: Red and purple printing on gray cardboard. DISTRIBUTION: Wisconsin, one card in packages of bakery products.

HISTORY

In 1984 the Gardner Baking Company of Madison repeated its successful baseball card issue of the previous year by inserting one of 22 different Milwaukee Brewers cards into loaves of bread and packages of buns. The cards, printed by Topps, used a completely different design and photos than their regular-issue cards of '84. Card fronts feature a color photo surrounded by a round-cornered pink and yellow frame with a blue border. The player's name, team, and position are designated in a red box below the photo. There is a Brewers logo in the lower left and a Gardner's logo at the top. A line at the bottom of the frame states "1984 Series

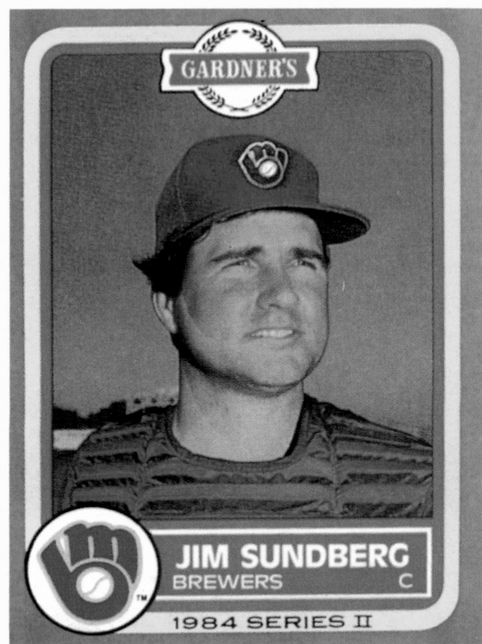

1984 Gardner's Brewers, Jim Sundberg

1984 Gardner's Brewers, Don Sutton

II." As in 1983, card backs are virtually identical to the regular Topps cards except for the card numbers. New manager Rene Lachemann is card #1, and the 21 player cards are numbered alphabetically. A blue Brewers logo appears in the upper right. As in '83, the Gardner's cards were not made available to dealers at the wholesale level, making it among the scarcest of the year's many regional issues. Because the cards were only distributed in the Wisconsin area, collectors around the country had to buy cards from dealers and collectors who had pulled them from the bakery products. At a cost of about 80¢ for a loaf of bread, the 1984 Gardner's Brewers cards were quite expensive per card.

FOR
A regional set of a popular team with lots of big-name stars makes for a popular issue.

AGAINST
The price was relatively high for an '84 set. Mint sets aren't easy to find because many cards were stained by the bread.

NOTEWORTHY CARDS
The regular 1984 Topps set did not have a card of manager Rene Lachemann, and it pictured new Brewers' additions Jim Sundberg and Bobby Clark with the Rangers and Angels, respectively. The Gardner's set offered these new Milwaukee favorites in their home team uniforms. All the other Brewers stars are present in the set.

VALUE
MINT CONDITION: Complete set, $18; common card, 30¢; Cooper, Simmons, $1; Fingers, Molitor, Sutton, $2; Yount, $3. 5-YEAR PROJECTION: Average.

1984
BREWERS POLICE

SPECIFICATIONS
SIZE: $2^{13}/_{16} \times 4^{1}/_{8}$". FRONT: Color photograph. BACK: Blue printing on white cardboard. DISTRIBUTION: Wisconsin, complete sets given out at a "Baseball Card Day" promotional game; individual cards given out by police officers.

HISTORY
If a collector were to try to assemble a "complete" set of 1984 Brewers police cards, he would need more than 1,500 different cards. At last count, at least 50 different law enforcement agencies around the state had become involved with the team's baseball card program. Each 30-card set was basically the same except for the department's name printed on the front. Reports are that some small communities had only 500 sets produced, while the Milwaukee Police Department had some 120,000. Besides the cards given out at the special promotional game, cards were supposed to be handed out (two per week) by officers to children encountered on the beat. This manner of

1984 Brewers Police, Robin Yount

distribution makes entire sets of some communities very difficult to assemble. In many cases, though, complete sets were slipped into the waiting hands of dealers and collectors. While it is likely that many of the varieties of this issue will be scarce in the future, the huge size of the issue makes it unlikely that the cards will actually be collected by town of issue; most collectors will be content with acquiring one of the more common sets. Like most recent police sets, the '84 Brewers cards are a bit larger than standard cards and feature a color photo surrounded by a wide white border. The front of the card lists the department of issue and includes the player's name, uniform number, and position. Card backs have the Brewers logo and a safety tip ostensibly from the player. The set includes 27 player cards, a team photo card, a card for manager Rene Lachemann, and a group coaches card.

FOR

One of the most common and inexpensive of recent police sets—as long as you stick to the common cities.

AGAINST

The many varieties from the different police departments makes it impossible to collect a complete set. Card photos are not of uniformly high quality.

NOTEWORTHY CARDS

All the popular Brewers stars are here including Robin Yount, Paul Molitor, and Rollie Fingers.

VALUE

MINT CONDITION: Complete set (any town), $5; common card, 15¢; stars, 50¢–$1. 5-YEAR PROJECTION: Average.

1984
7-UP CUBS

SPECIFICATIONS

SIZE: 2¼ × 3½″. FRONT: Color photograph. BACK: Black printing on white cardboard. DISTRIBUTION: Chicago, complete sets given away at a special "Baseball Card Day" promotional game.

HISTORY

For the third straight year, the Chicago Cubs held a special "Baseball Card Day" promotional game. For 1984, the sponsor was 7-Up. The 1984 Cubs set was quite similar to the '82 and '83 offerings. The cards feature a borderless color action photo, either vertical or horizontal. The only type on the front of the card is the player's uniform number, name, and position. Card backs feature complete

1984 7-Up Cubs, Larry Bowa

1984 7-Up Cubs, Dennis Eckersley

minor and major league stats, a copyright line, and a 7-Up logo. There are 26 player cards, a card for manager Jim Frey, and a group card of the coaches. Apparently because of a defect in the machinery that cut, sorted, and wrapped the cards many sets contained duplicates, resulting in incomplete sets.

FOR
It's a team-issued set of one of baseball's perennially popular teams, and one of 1984's hottest contenders.

AGAINST
The cards are not standard size and the format is almost identical to previous issues. On some cards, it's hard to pick the player out from the Wrigley Field background.

NOTEWORTHY CARDS
The 7-Up Cubs set is exceptional in that it includes most of the important players acquired in mid-season trades such as Dennis Eckersley and Rick Sutcliffe. The team's All-Star second baseman, Ryne Sandberg, is among the stars represented, along with old vets like Ron Cey and Larry Bowa.

VALUE
MINT CONDITION: Complete set, $12; common card, 40¢; stars, 50¢–75¢; Sandberg, $3. 5-YEAR PROJECTION: Average or above.

1984 DODGERS POLICE

SPECIFICATIONS
SIZE: 2⅞ × 4⅛″. FRONT: Color photograph. BACK: Blue printing on white cardboard. DISTRIBUTION: Los Angeles, single cards given to children by police officers; complete sets given away at a special "Baseball Card Day" promotional game.

HISTORY
For the fifth year in a row, the Los Angeles Dodgers and local police issued a baseball card set aimed at improving rapport between officers and youngsters. The theme of the safety messages printed on the backs of the '84 cards is DARE (Drug Abuse Resistance Education). The 30 cards in the set feature the roster players, manager Tommy Lasorda, and the coaches. Card fronts have a color photo of the player surrounded by the wide white border typically found on police sets. At the bottom is a blue and red Dodger logo, with the date, the player's name, and uniform number printed in black. Card backs have biographical data, stats, a drug abuse prevention message, and a small portrait photo of the player, all printed in blue. A total of five million cards was reported printed, enough for over 160,000 sets.

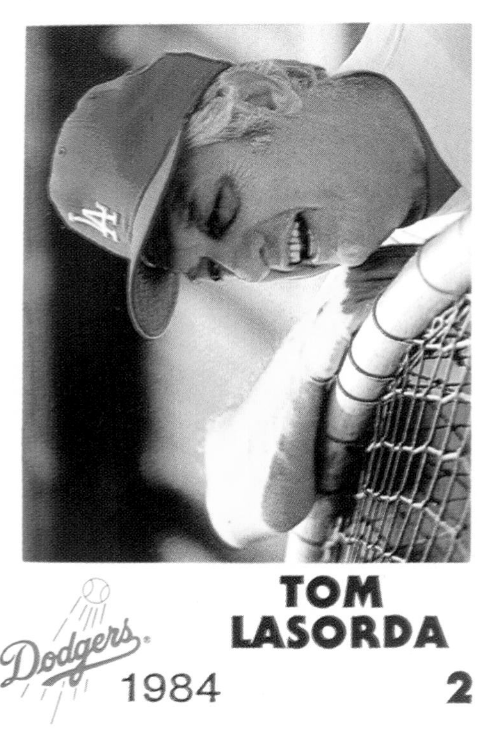

1984 Dodgers Police, Tommy Lasorda

FOR
The set is a continuation of the long-standing Dodgers police set tradition, and it has many new young players.

AGAINST
It is too similar to previous issues.

NOTEWORTHY CARDS

All the regular Dodgers stars are included.

VALUE

MINT CONDITION: Complete set, $6; common card, 20¢; stars, 25¢–75¢. 5-YEAR PROJECTION: Average or somewhat above.

1984 STUART EXPOS

SPECIFICATIONS

SIZE: 2½ × 3½″. FRONT: Color photograph. BACK: Blue printing on white cardboard. DISTRIBUTION: Canada, one card in boxes of Stuart Bakery products.

HISTORY

One of the largest single-team regional card sets in recent years, the 1984 Stuart Expos cards were released in two 20-card series over the course of the season. Similar in format to the company's premier set the previous year, the '84 card fronts feature a quality color photograph surrounded by a red border. A Stuart's logo and an Expos team logo appear in the lower corners, along with a graphic symbol for the year of issue. The player's name and uniform number are in black in the white border at bottom. Card backs feature the usual combination of player biographical and statistical information in both French and English, as is often seen on card sets originating in Quebec. Unlike many of its counterparts south of the border, the Stuart Expos cards were not generally made available in complete sets to dealers or collectors. The only way to get a complete set was to buy the company's products, which is the whole idea of a promotional baseball card issue. Besides the 25 roster players, the set includes cards for many of the team's young prospects, as well as the coaches, manager, and team mascot. The first 20 cards were among the earliest regionals of 1984, as they were distributed from May through July. The final 20 cards in the set were released in August.

FOR

It's a good-looking, scarce regional issue.

AGAINST

It is somewhat difficult and expensive to acquire a complete set; the issue of the set in two series over the course of the summer kept collectors guessing on the final choice of players.

NOTEWORTHY CARDS

The '84 Stuart Expos set was the first to contain a card of Pete Rose in the uniform of his new team, which made the set very popular with collectors. Besides established Expos stars like Andre Dawson, Tim Raines, and Gary Carter, the set also includes many rookie cards of young players who had spring or late-season trials with the team.

VALUE

MINT CONDITION: Complete set, $30–$35; common card, 30¢; stars, $1–$2; Rose, $2.50. 5-YEAR PROJECTION: Above average.

1984 WHEATIES INDIANS

SPECIFICATIONS

SIZE: 2¹³⁄₁₆ × 4⅛″. FRONT: Color photograph. BACK: Black printing on white cardboard. DISTRIBUTION: Cleveland, complete sets given out at a "Baseball Card Day" promotional game and sold at the Indians' gift shop.

1984 Wheaties Indians, Joe Carter

HISTORY

Wheaties cereal, which has been associated with various baseball card issues as far back as the 1930s, co-sponsored a set featuring the Cleveland Indians for the third year in a row. Complete 29-card sets were given away at a promotional game at Municipal Stadium. The remainder of the 15,000 sets printed were offered for sale at the Indians' gift shop. Once again choosing a format much like recent police sets, the 1984 Indians set features a full-color game-action photo of each player with a wide white border. The player's name and position appear in black at the bottom, while team and Wheaties logos appear in color at the left and right. Card backs have complete major league stats, along with a card number that corresponds to the player's uniform number. Besides the 26 player cards, there is a card for manager Pat Corrales and unnumbered cards for the coaches and team mascot.

FOR

Wheaties sponsorship gives the set a tie with many past baseball card issues and may make it more desirable to collectors in coming years as part of a long-running set.

AGAINST

The design is identical to previous years. The cardboard stock is very thin and easily damaged. Game-action photos are sometimes not the best way to showcase a player on a baseball card.

NOTEWORTHY CARDS

All of the Indians' crop of bright young stars are present in this set, including the players acquired in the mid-year trade with the Cubs—Mel Hall, Joe Carter, and Don Schulze.

VALUE

MINT CONDITION: Complete set, $6; common card, 15¢; Carter, $1. 5-YEAR PROJECTION: Average or a bit above.

1984 Smokey the Bear Padres, Tony Gwynn

1984 Smokey the Bear Padres, Kevin McReynolds

1984 SMOKEY THE BEAR PADRES

SPECIFICATIONS

SIZE: 2½ × 3¾″. FRONT: Color photograph. BACK: Black printing on white cardboard. DISTRIBUTION: San Diego, complete sets given out at a "Baseball Card Day" promotional game.

HISTORY

To commemorate Smokey the Bear's 40th anniversary with the U.S. Forest Service, the San Diego Padres joined the California Angels in issuing a promotional baseball card set. The 30-card set is one of the more innovative and entertaining baseball card issues ever produced. Each color photo shows the player with Smokey the Bear—some are shown giving or getting baseball tips, others are sitting on Smokey's lap, etc. All in all, it looks like the Padres had a good time posing for the photos. In addition to the photo, the front of the card has a color drawing of Smokey in the lower left, a brown and yellow Padres team identification, and the logos of the U.S. Forest Service and the California State Department of Forestry at right. The player's last name appears above the photo. Card backs are printed in black and have a brief player biography, '83 season record, and a fire safety message from the player. Cards are numbered by player uniform number. There are 18 player cards in the Padres/Smokey set, along with cards for manager Dick Williams and his four coaches. Former players Jerry Coleman and Dave Campbell are included in the set as members of the Padres broadcasting team, and there is a card for team Vice President Jack McKeon. Of special interest are cards of the famous San Diego mascot, the Chicken; and of umpire Doug Harvey, a San Diego resident. The Harvey card is significant in that it is the first baseball card of an umpire issued since the 1955 Bowman set. A "header" card picturing Smokey the Bear and explaining the issue rounds out the 30 cards in the set.

FOR

This is an imaginative, enjoyable set.

AGAINST

The set is a little short of players, basically featuring just the starters, and was produced too early in the year to include notable Padres trade acquisitions Goose Gossage, Graig Nettles, and Carmelo Martinez.

NOTEWORTHY CARDS

Young Padre batting stars Kevin McReynolds and Tony Gwynn, along with long-time Southern California favorite Steve Garvey, are among the stars in the set.

VALUE

MINT CONDITION: Complete set, $10; common card, 30¢; stars, 40¢–70¢; Gwynn, $2. 5-YEAR PROJECTION: Above average.

1984 TEXAS RANGERS

SPECIFICATIONS

SIZE: 2⅜ × 3½". FRONT: Color photograph. BACK: Black printing on white cardboard. DISTRIBUTION: Arlington, complete sets given away at "Baseball Card Night" promotional game.

1984 Texas Rangers, Danny Darwin

1984 Texas Rangers, Buddy Bell

HISTORY

A total of 10,000 sets of Texas Rangers cards were printed for distribution at a special promotional game. The 1984 Rangers 30-card set is virtually identical to the '83 issue and features a color-action photo of the player on the front. A blue panel below the photo has the player's name, team, and position. Card backs feature a black-and-white portrait photo of the player and are numbered according to uniform number. They also contain brief biographical and personal data and a line of major league stats. The bottom of the back includes an imprint from the set's sponsor, The Jarvis Press, Inc.

FOR

This team-issued set had a relatively small print run.

AGAINST

The cards are printed on stock that is quite thin. The lack of a format change from the previous year's issue lowers collector interest.

NOTEWORTHY CARDS

It's hard to find notable cards of a team that spent virtually the entire season in last place. However, some of the young players are now beginning to earn star status.

VALUE

MINT CONDITION: Complete set, $5; common card, 15¢–25¢; stars, 50¢–75¢. 5-YEAR PROJECTION: Below average.

1984 MINNESOTA TWINS

SPECIFICATIONS

SIZE: 2½ × 3½″. FRONT: Color photograph. BACK: Red and blue printing on white cardboard. DISTRIBUTION: Minneapolis, team issued, complete sets sold at the stadium and through a mail order.

HISTORY

For the second straight year, local collector Barry Fritz and Park Press created a Minnesota Twins card set for team issue. The 36-card set features all 25 of the roster players, the manager, coaches, and an aerial view of the Metrodome. There is also a Twins logo card and a special card honoring former Twins great Harmon Killebrew, who was elected to the Hall of Fame in 1984 (the first Twin to be so honored). The '84 cards feature a borderless posed color photo of the player taken at spring training. Card backs feature standard player biographical data along with complete major and minor league stats, a copyright line, and a card number, all printed in an attractive combination of blue and red. The baseball card set, along with a similar issue of postcards, was available for $5 at the stadium and through the mail.

1984 Minnesota Twins, Kent Hrbek

FOR

It's a reasonably priced team-issue card set, printed in relatively small numbers.

AGAINST

The format is virtually identical to the 1983 issue.

NOTEWORTHY CARDS

All of the rising young stars of the '84 Twins are included, plus all-time Twins favorite Harmon "The Killer" Killebrew.

VALUE

MINT CONDITION: Complete set, $6; common card, 15¢; stars, 25¢–75¢; Killebrew, $1. 5-YEAR PROJECTION: Below average.

1984 TRUE VALUE WHITE SOX

SPECIFICATIONS

SIZE: 2⅝ × 4⅛″. FRONT: Color photograph. BACK: Black printing on white cardboard. DISTRIBUTION: Chicago, two cards given out at selected Tuesday night games.

1983 True Value White Sox, Tom Seaver

HISTORY

For the second year in a row, the Chicago-based True Value hardware company sponsored a set of White Sox cards to be given out two at a time at selected Tuesday night home games at Comiskey Park. The 30-card set includes 25 players, a card for manager Tony LaRussa, a group card of the coaches, cards for past White Sox favorites Minnie Minoso and Luis Aparicio, and a card for stadium organist Nancy Faust (the first major league baseball card to feature a woman). The latter three cards were not distributed at the stadium, but were given out by the individuals themselves. Like the '83 cards, the 1984 True Value White Sox issue features a color photo of the player (most taken at spring training in Sarasota) surrounded by a wide white border. At the lower left is a red and blue "ChiSox" logo. At right, printed in black, are the player's name, position, and uniform number. Card backs, which are unnumbered, have the player's name and uniform number in the upper corners in a black band with a True Value logo between them. Complete major and minor league stats make up the rest of the card back. The coaches and Faust cards have blank backs. Because of the manner of distribution, complete sets of the 1984 True Value White Sox are rather difficult to acquire.

FOR

It is a great regional item for the team collector but is not widely distributed.

AGAINST

Complete sets are hard to find and somewhat costly. Not all cards were distributed in even numbers because of differing attendance at the various games.

NOTEWORTHY CARDS

Besides having the first card of a woman, the set features all of the White Sox stars of their division-winning 1983 team, and includes the first card of future Hall of Famer Tom Seaver as a White Sox pitcher.

VALUE

MINT CONDITION: Complete set, $24; common card, 35¢; Luzinski, Kittle, $1; Aparicio, Baines, Minoso, Seaver, $2. 5-YEAR PROJECTION: Average.

1983 TOPPS

SPECIFICATIONS

SIZE: 2½ × 3½″. FRONT: Color photograph. BACK: Orange and black printing on gray cardboard. DISTRIBUTION: Nationally, in packages with bubblegum.

1983 Topps, Reggie Jackson

1983 Topps, Ryne Sandberg

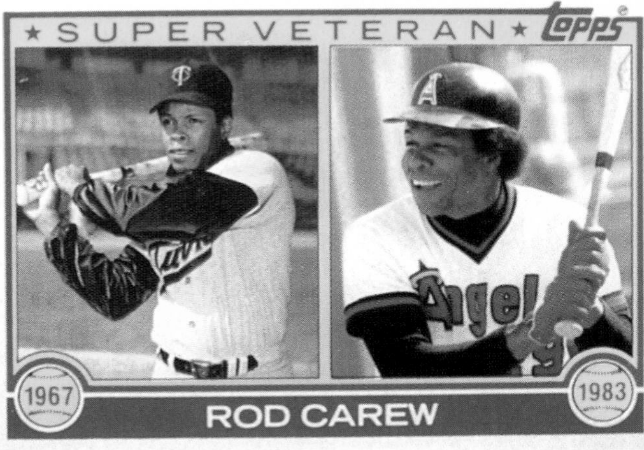

1983 Topps, Rod Carew

HISTORY

Topps reached back 20 years for the design for its 1983 set. Like the 1963 set, the '83 Topps cards feature a large color photograph of the player with a small round portrait photo inset in a lower corner. Unlike the '63 cards, the smaller photo is also in color. The top and bottom sections of the card are framed in team colors. A Topps logo intrudes into the photo at upper right. The player's name and position are in a white panel alongside the small portrait photo, and the team name appears in a colored band below. Card backs are horizontal in format and feature complete major and/or minor league stats, a few personal details, and 1982 season highlights if space was available. The '83 Topps design was popular with collectors, many of whom hailed it as one of the best in recent years. For the first time since 1962, the 792-card set did not feature any "Future Stars" or other special rookie cards, the company preferring to save these for its Traded set later in the year. A popular feature in the '83 set was a group of 34 "Super Veteran" cards, numbered in the set right after the player's regular card. The Super Veteran cards are in horizontal format and show the player in his first major league season on the left, and in a current photo on the right. There is a "Team Leaders" card for each club to honor the batting and pitching leaders. The back of each Team Leaders card has a team checklist. The first six cards in the set honor record-breaking performances of 1982. These include Lance Parrish, who threw out three runners in the 1982 All-Star Game. Other special cards include "League Leaders," "All-Stars," and six numbered checklists.

FOR

The 1983 set is an unusually popular recent Topps set; it has all of 1983's stars at a low price.

AGAINST

A lot of collectors felt that Topps' decision not to issue team rookie cards, as in past years, was intended to force collectors to buy the more expensive Traded set later in the year.

NOTEWORTHY CARDS

Pete Rose (#101), Rod Carew (#201), Reggie Jackson (#501), and Carl Yastrzemski (#551) have notable Super Veteran cards. Topps included rookie cards of Wade Boggs (which sold for $2.50 right out of the pack), Ryne Sandberg, and Tony Gwynn.

VALUE

MINT CONDITION: Complete set, $85; common card, 5¢; superstars, 50¢–$2; Sandberg, $7; Gwynn,$18; Boggs, $35. 5-YEAR PROJECTION: Above average.

1983 TOPPS TRADED

SPECIFICATIONS

SIZE: 2½ × 3½". FRONT: Color photograph. BACK: Black and red printing on white cardboard. DISTRIBUTION: Nationally, complete sets sold through hobby dealers.

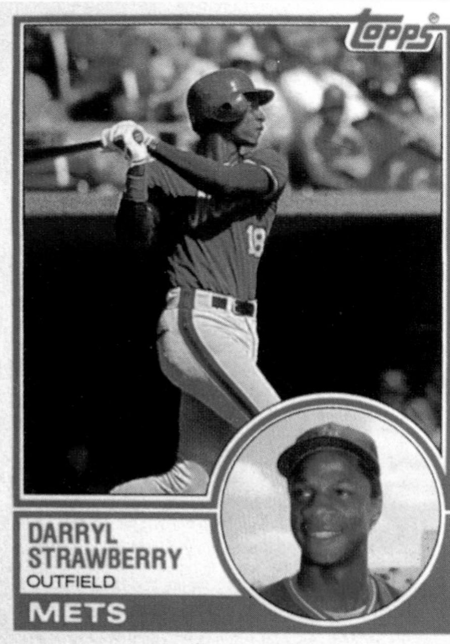

1983 Topps Traded, Darryl Strawberry

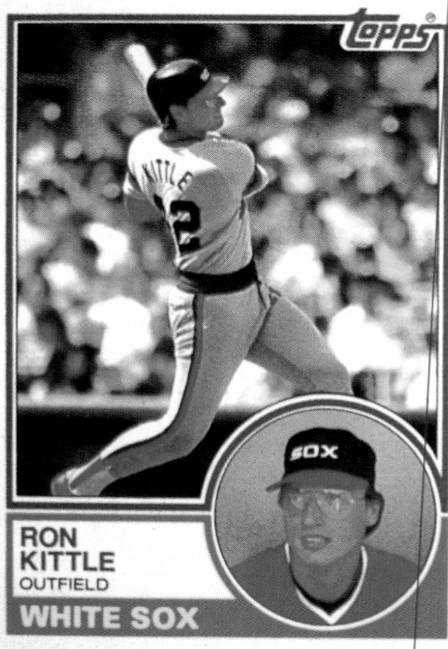

1983 Topps Traded, Ron Kittle

HISTORY

For the third straight year Topps produced a 132-card Traded set. The cards have the same design as the regular 1983 Topps issue, but the backs are a different color and the cards are numbered from 1T to 132T. The set includes players who had been traded since the regular 1983 Topps set was released, pictured in their new uniforms. The set also includes rookie cards of young players who did not appear in the regular set, and some of the new managers. As in previous years, the Traded cards were not sold in gum packs—only in complete boxed sets by dealers. Sets retailed for around $7, or about 5½¢ per card (compared with 2¢ per card for regular 1983 cards). The cards are numbered alphabetically by the player's last name, and the final card in the set is a checklist. Because the cards were sold only through hobby dealers, they were printed in far smaller quantities than the regular-issue Topps cards of the same year.

FOR

For collectors who favor Topps cards, the '83 Traded set was the only way to get cards of some players in their current uniforms; it was also the only way to get Topps cards of the hot new rookies.

AGAINST

Some collectors feel that because the cards are sold only as a complete set through dealers, they aren't "real" baseball cards, and the set is really a "collector's issue."

NOTEWORTHY CARDS

The high-demand cards in the Traded set each year are not the traded players, but the rookies. In the 1983 Traded set, big money was being paid for the Darryl Strawberry card. Topps was the only one of the "Big 3" card companies to have an 1983 card for the National League Rookie of the Year. There were also cards in the set for Ron Kittle (American League Rookie of the Year) and for high-demand rookies Julio Franco and Mel Hall.

VALUE

MINT CONDITION: Complete set, $70; common card, 10¢; superstars, 50¢–$2; Strawberry, $50. 5-YEAR PROJECTION: Above average.

1983 TOPPS GLOSSIES

SPECIFICATIONS

SIZE: 2½ × 3½″. FRONT: Color photograph. BACK: Red and blue printing on white cardboard. DISTRIBUTION: Nationally, complete sets as prizes in Topps contest and sold through dealers.

1983 Topps Glossies, Jim Palmer

1983 Topps Glossies, Lance Parrish

HISTORY

A scratch-off game card in packs of regular '83 Topps baseball cards offered a special set of 40 cards as a "consolation prize" for accumulated losing cards. Topps called this issue the "Collector's Edition All-Star Set," but collectors know it as "Glossies." With postage and handling fees, plus the cost of accumulating the game cards, the cost of collecting a set was more than $20. Luckily, Topps also wholesaled complete sets of the Glossies to dealers, and they were widely available in hobby channels for $8 or so (which was still not cheap). The Glossies got their nickname from the glossy coating on the front of the cards, which collectors find very appealing. The basic design of the set is simple: a large color photo of the player surrounded by a yellow border. The only printing on the front is the player's name in small type in the lower left. There are no stats or player data on the back of the card, just a Topps identification, the player's name, team, position, and the card number.

FOR

It is an extremely attractive and popular specialty set with lots of stars.

AGAINST

It was relatively expensive for a 1983 subset.

NOTEWORTHY CARDS

All of the cards in the '83 Glossies are stars.

VALUE

MINT CONDITION: Complete set, $11; common card, 15¢; superstars, 50¢–$1.50. 5-YEAR PROJECTION: Average.

1983 TOPPS FOLDOUTS

SPECIFICATIONS

SIZE: 3½ × 5⁵⁄₁₆″. FRONT: Color photograph. BACK: Color photograph. DISTRIBUTION: Regionally, in cello packs.

1983 Topps Foldouts, Gaylord Perry

HISTORY

Late in the 1983 baseball season, Topps introduced a test issue of "Baseball Foldouts." The Foldouts come in an accordion-style booklet (much like booklets of souvenir postcards) containing 9 cards. Each of the five different booklets (85 cards in all) features the current statistical leaders in one of five categories: pitching wins, home runs, batting average, saves in relief, or stolen bases. Only active players are featured, and some players appear in more than one booklet. The cards are unusual in that there is a player on each side of the card (except for the cover card, which has one player on the back), so each folder pictures 17 players. The cards feature a borderless color photo with a facsimile autograph. A black strip at the bottom gives the player's name, team, and career stats for the appropriate category. While some collectors will undoubtedly cut the individual cards out of the Foldouts, it appears that the set will retain its greatest value in complete, uncut form.

FOR

It is an innovative concept with nice large-size cards.

AGAINST

Team or superstar collectors can't display the cards they want without cutting the folder apart, which greatly reduces the value of the individual cards.

NOTEWORTHY CARDS

Since most of the career leaders in these categories are stars, most of the big-name players of 1983 are included.

VALUE

MINT CONDITION: Complete set of 5 booklets, $6; single folder, $1–$2. 5-YEAR PROJECTION: Below average.

1983 TOPPS '52 REPRINTS

SPECIFICATIONS

SIZE: 2½ × 3½″. FRONT: Color painting from photograph. BACK: Red and black printing on white cardboard. DISTRIBUTION: Nationally, complete sets sold through hobby dealers and through ads in sports magazines.

HISTORY

Rumors that Topps was planning to reprint at least one of its early baseball card sets were confirmed in early 1983 when the company announced a limited-edition (10,000 sets) reprint of its classic 1952 baseball card issue. Hobby purists were aghast, and dealers felt the availability of replica cards would lessen the demand for genuine '52 Topps cards and cause prices to plummet. Prior to the announcement of the reprint, a complete Mint-condition set of '52 Topps (if one could be found) cost $8,000. The Mantle card alone was selling for $1,000, and each of the commons in the 97-card high-number series was worth $35 in top grade. Even the most common card in the early series sold for $3. On the other hand, collectors who appreciated the beauty and history of the original '52 Topps set but could never afford it welcomed the reprints. Many modern collectors who don't know Johnny Sain from Ferris Fain simply had no interest in 30-year old baseball cards. For its part, Topps promised that nobody would ever confuse the reprints with the original cards; the reprints were smaller, printed on thinner white cardboard, and stated "TOPPS 1952 REPRINT SERIES" in bold red letters on the back. What Topps didn't publicize was that only 402 of the original 407 cards in the 1952 set were being reproduced. The company had gone to each player (or to the estate of deceased players) who had appeared in the 1952 set in an effort to obtain releases for the reissue. Five clearances could not be obtained, so the set was issued without cards of Dom DiMaggio, Saul Rogovin, Billy Loes, Solly Hemus, and Tommy Holmes. By the time the cards were actually released, the fuss had blown over. Topps priced many collectors right out of the market by setting the wholesale price so high that dealers had to charge $35 to $40 retail to make a profit. Additionally, many collectors decided not to buy after they actually saw the reprints; the quality of the printing and color reproduction was nowhere near that of the originals, and a lot of hobbyists felt they'd rather have no reprint than a bad one. When Topps saw that hobby demand for the set would not equal the supply, they began offering them to the general public (for $42 per set) through full-page ads in sports publications. Most collectors feel the experiment was a failure.

FOR

At about 10¢ a card, collectors who desire "the nearest thing" to rare old superstars of the 1950s may find the '52 reprints satisfactory.

AGAINST

There were numerous problems including poor quality, the failure to issue a complete reprint set, and the relatively high cost per card for a large 1983 issue.

VALUE

MINT CONDITION: Complete set, $55. 5-YEAR PROJECTION: Below average.

1983 FLEER

SPECIFICATIONS

SIZE: 2½ × 3½". FRONT: Color photograph. BACK: Brown and black printing on white cardboard. DISTRIBUTION: Nationally, in packages with team logo and cap stickers.

1983 Fleer, Ryne Sandberg

1983 Fleer, Reggie Jackson

1983 Fleer, Vida Blue

HISTORY

After the errors and variations that plagued Fleer's 1981 and '82 offerings, the company got back on the right track in 1983 with a near-perfect baseball card set. The 660-card issue is numbered alphabetically by player within each team. The 1982 World Champion St. Louis Cardinals opened the set, while the team with the worst won/loss record, the Minnesota Twins, came near the end. A set of 18 "Super Star Special" cards and 14 checklists are at the end of the set. There are also multiplayer cards and individual cards honoring players for important or unusual achievements. The design of the '83 Fleers is attractive and colorful. Round-cornered color photos are bordered by thin black and white lines inside a brownish-gray frame. A color team logo appears in a circle in the lower left, while a red Fleer logo is in the upper left. The player's name and position appear in black print below the photo. The card backs feature a small black-and-white photo of the player in the upper right—the first time a major card set had included a player photo on the back since the '71 Topps issue. In a vertical format, the backs contain the usual mix of vital data, complete major and minor league stats, and, space permitting, a "Did You Know?" trivia fact about the player. The 1983 cards were sold in packs with team logo and cap stickers. After all the problems of the previous years, this near-perfect set was welcomed by collectors.

FOR

The set has good potential for price appreciation.

AGAINST

Fleer vastly overestimated the collector demand for its 1983 card set. By the end of the year, dealers were able to purchase the overruns at huge markdowns: as low as $60 per case, or less than ½¢ per card. This will keep prices on the set quite low for the foreseeable future, though superstars and hot rookies will climb in value.

NOTEWORTHY CARDS

Fleer achieved a real coup by being the first major card company to have a Ron Kittle rookie card in its 1983 set. Donruss didn't have one at all that year, and Topps didn't until its Traded set was distributed in September—long after Kittle had sewn up American League Rookie of the Year honors. Until the Topps card hit the market, a Ron Kittle card could be pulled out of a 30¢ Fleer wax pack and sold for $2.50 or more. Like its two competitors, the '83 Fleer set also had a rookie card of Wade Boggs. Several of the "Super Star Special" cards are worth noting. Four of the cards were produced in pairs that form a single picture when laid side by side; one of the cards has no right border, the other card has no left border. One pair shows Kansas City Royals pitchers Bud Black and Vida Blue and is titled "Black & Blue." Another pair features Angels teammates Rickey Henderson and Reggie Jackson and is titled "Speed & Power." Fleer apparently felt the need to rectify their mistake of picturing Bo Diaz with Len Barker on a "Perfect Game" card in 1982; they issued a card showing Barker with Ron Hassey, who was the actual catcher in that 1981 game. The '83 card was titled "Last Perfect Game."

VALUE

MINT CONDITION: Complete set, $43; common card, 5¢; stars, 50¢–$2; Ryne Sandberg, $4; Tony Gwynn, $8; Boggs, $18. 5-YEAR PROJECTION: Average.

1983 DONRUSS

SPECIFICATIONS

SIZE: 2½ × 3½". FRONT: Color photograph. BACK: Yellow and black printing on white cardboard. DISTRIBUTION: Nationally, in packages with jigsaw puzzle pieces; complete sets sold through hobby dealers.

HISTORY

Donruss stood still in its third year of baseball card production. The 1983 set showed little innovation, and most collectors voiced disapproval. The cards again feature a large color photo surrounded by a

1983 Donruss, Ryne Sandberg

1983 Donruss, Cal Ripken Jr.

1983 Donruss, Pascual Perez

stripe that is color-coded by team. The Donruss logo and date were moved to the upper left. The photo is bordered at the bottom by a bat with the player's name, a baseball containing the position abbreviation, and a glove containing the team name. Card backs are virtually identical to the previous year, except the boxes highlighting the player's vital data and career summary are yellow instead of blue. Recent stats again appear in a wide white strip at center. As in the previous year, the 1983 Donruss set contains 660 cards, including seven unnumbered checklists. There are 26 artist-drawn Diamond Kings cards featuring one player from each team, a few multiplayer cards, and cards for the better-known coaches and managers. The final numbered card in the set is a picture of the Ty Cobb puzzle that was the 1983 premium. Collectors got three pieces (out of a total of 63) in each wax pack. Donruss made a major concession in 1983 by wholesaling complete, boxed, pre-sorted sets to dealers. The '83 Donruss set contained fewer errors and variations than the previous two sets.

FOR

Donruss improved the quality for its 1983 issue, making it an attractive major set with few errors or problems.

AGAINST

The design was too similar to the '82 issue to suit many collectors.

1983 DONRUSS ACTION ALL-STARS

SPECIFICATIONS

SIZE: 3½ × 5″. FRONT: Color photograph. BACK: Black and red printing on white cardboard. DISTRIBUTION: Nationally, in cello packs with jigsaw puzzle pieces.

HISTORY

In 1983, for the first time, Donruss introduced more than one yearly baseball card issue, and it met with critical success. The Action All-Stars are postcard-size cards that feature two color photos of the player on the card front—a large portrait at left, and a smaller action photo at right. The player's name and position are printed below the action photo, and the team name is incorporated into the gray background design. White and maroon borders surround the card. Unlike regular Donruss cards, the card backs present full major league stats for the player on a year-by-year basis, along with more detailed personal and career data. The stats are printed in white at the center, and red boxes at top and bottom contain personal and career data. The cards were sold in cello packs for 30¢ to 35¢, and each pack contained six cards and three pieces of a 63-piece Mickey Mantle jigsaw puzzle. The 60-card set contains 59 player cards and a checklist.

NOTEWORTHY CARDS

The set contains the rookie cards of Wade Boggs and Mel Hall. Two wrong-photo cards in the set were never corrected: the player on Dan Spillner's card is actually Ed Whitson, and the player on Joe Pittman's card is Padres teammate Juan Eichelberger. Two team-name errors were later corrected: Pascual Perez's card originally had a Twins designation on the card front, and Ron Jackson's card originally had an A's designation. Actually, there are two versions of the Jackson error card. Some cards got the team wrong, but got the frame color right—red, like the other Angels cards. "Double-error" cards have both the wrong team and the wrong frame color—green. Another error, later corrected, occurs on Bryn Smith's card (#88): on uncorrected cards his name is spelled "Byrn."

OUR FAVORITE CARD

Many collectors were surprised to see that on Mike Schmidt's card (#168), the famed Phillies third baseman was wearing uniform number 37, instead of his familiar number 20. According to Donruss, the photo was taken during 1982 spring training after Schmidt's jersey had been stolen.

VALUE

MINT CONDITION: Complete set, $45; common card, 6¢; stars, 50¢–$2; Sandberg, $4; Gwynn, $9; Boggs, $20. 5-YEAR PROJECTION: Above average.

1983 Donruss Action All-Stars, Reggie Jackson

FOR
The large format enhances an exceptionally popular design. All of the cards feature stars.

AGAINST
Some collectors don't like large-size cards.

NOTEWORTHY CARDS
A variation exists on the back of Reggie Jackson's card. On the more scarce version, the red printing from the lower data box extends into the last few lines of season stats. On later cards, the red was removed.

VALUE
MINT CONDITION: Complete set, $6; common card, 5¢; superstars, 25¢–50¢. 5-YEAR PROJECTION: Below average.

1983 Donruss Hall of Fame Heroes, Hank Aaron

1983 DONRUSS HALL OF FAME HEROES

SPECIFICATIONS
SIZE: 2½ × 3½". FRONT: Color painting. BACK: Red and blue printing on white cardboard. DISTRIBUTION: Nationally, in packages with jigsaw puzzle pieces.

1983 Donruss Hall of Fame Heroes, Ty Cobb

HISTORY
Although Donruss hit a home run with its Action All-Stars set, the company struck out with its second subsidiary issue, the Hall of Fame Heroes. The 44-card set features paintings by Dick Perez of 42 "old-timers" who have been enshrined in baseball's Hall of Fame. Unfortunately, the strain of producing so many paintings is evident in the quality of the artwork, which is not up to par for Perez. Card #43 is a picture of the Mickey Mantle jigsaw puzzle, three pieces of which were included in each wax pack of the Hall of Fame Heroes cards. Card #44 is a checklist. Vertical card backs are printed in colorful red, white, and blue, and feature a short biography of the player, along with pennants, bats, balls, and other baseball trappings. Donruss limited the set to better-known Hall of Famers of the 20th Century, with a heavy concentration of players from the '50s and '60s, but most collectors stayed away. Donruss learned that retrospective sets are not popular with the public.

FOR
The set includes inexpensive cards of famous players.

AGAINST
The artwork is generally unattractive.

NOTEWORTHY CARDS

They're all Hall of Famers.

VALUE

MINT CONDITION: Complete set, $4; common card, 5¢; superstars, 10¢–50¢. 5-YEAR PROJECTION: Below average.

1983 KELLOGG'S

SPECIFICATIONS

SIZE: 1⅞ × 3¼″. FRONT: Color photograph, 3-D effect. BACK: Black printing on white cardboard. DISTRIBUTION: Nationally, one card in boxes of cereal; complete sets available through a mail-in offer.

1983 Kellogg's, Pete Rose

HISTORY

The 1983 Kellogg's set of 60 cards was the 14th, and final, annual issue by the cereal company. (Kellogg's announced in 1984 that it would no longer produce card sets.) In the early years, Kellogg's had often been the only other major card producer besides Topps. However, by 1981 many companies were issuing baseball cards, and the value of using cards to sell cereal was questioned by Kellogg's officials. The '83 set was down-sized from the previous year, returning to the narrower 1⅞ × 3¼″ size. The set was also reduced in number from 64 to 60 cards. As had been the case for all but one year of Kellogg's sets, the cards had a three-dimensional look. The 3-D effect was created by laminating a thin piece of ribbed plastic to the front of the card. Behind the plastic, a sharp photo of the player is placed against a blurred stadium background, giving the card the illusion of depth. The effect is quite striking and made the cards very popular with collectors. The design of the '83 Kellogg's card was quite different from previous years. A frame consisting of two white stripes is set inside the picture area, with another white frame around the edge of the photo. As usual, a facsimile autograph is scrawled across the picture. Panels at top and bottom contain the name of the set, the Kellogg's logo, and the player's last name and position. The vertical card backs are also different from previous years, and feature career stats and a short player biography, along with a team logo and the logos of Major League Baseball and the Major League Baseball Players Association (which gave permission for the Kellogg's issues). In its final year, Kellogg's returned to the policy of placing individual cards in cereal boxes. Complete sets could be obtained by sending $3.95 and two box tops or proof-of-purchase seals to Kellogg's.

FOR

The final issue of Kellogg's cards has a lot going for it. The cards are attractive, there are a lot of superstars, and they were inexpensive, leaving a lot of room for price appreciation.

AGAINST

The narrow size makes the cards prone to curling and cracking as the plastic contracts with age. Cards with cracks in the plastic are worth much less than undamaged cards. It is difficult to buy single superstars since most '83s are dealt in complete sets; few collectors, it seems, were willing to buy cereal in order to hunt for superstars.

NOTEWORTHY CARDS

A majority of the cards in the 1983 Kellogg's set are legitimate stars or superstars. Quite a few great young players made their first and only appearances in the 1983 set, most notably Dale Murphy. There is an error on the front of Dan Quisenberry's card: his name is spelled "Quiesenberry." It is spelled correctly on the back.

VALUE

MINT CONDITION: Complete set, $12; common card, 10¢; stars, 25¢–75¢; Rose, Murphy, $1. 5-YEAR PROJECTION: Above average.

1983 DRAKE'S

SPECIFICATIONS

SIZE: 2½ × 3½″. FRONT: Color photograph. BACK: Black and orange printing on gray cardboard. DISTRIBUTION: Northeast, one card in packages of snack cakes; nationally, complete sets sold through hobby dealers.

1983 Drake's, Cal Ripken Jr.

1983 Drake's, Carl Yastrzemski

HISTORY

In 1983, Topps produced another 33-card set for Drake's bakeries. Single cards were inserted into family-size boxes of snack cakes. Drake's again wholesaled a large number of the cards to baseball card dealers, who made complete sets available to collectors at reasonable prices. The format of the card is similar to previous editions, with each photo showing the player in a game-action batting pose (in keeping with the "Big Hitters" theme of the set). All of the players are known for being power hitters or for compiling high batting averages. Like the previous two issues, the 1983 Drake's cards have a fancy frame around the photo, and a facsimile autograph. A banner at the top proclaims that this is the "3rd Annual Collectors' Edition." Backs are virtually identical to the corresponding Topps cards, except the cards are numbered alphabetically by player name and a Drake's logo and copyright line has been added.

FOR

The Drake's set contains inexpensive regional cards of big-name players.

AGAINST

Many collectors don't like the "busy" design of the '83 Drake's.

NOTEWORTHY CARDS

Most of the players in the set are stars or superstars. The 1983 set includes Cal Ripken Jr. for the first time.

VALUE

MINT CONDITION: Complete set, $6; common card, 7¢; superstars, 50¢–$1. 5-YEAR PROJECTION: Average.

1983 GRANNY GOOSE A'S

SPECIFICATIONS

SIZE: 2½ × 4¼″. FRONT: Color photograph. BACK: Black printing on white cardboard. DISTRIBUTION: Northern California, one card in bags of potato chips; complete sets given away at a promotional ball game.

1983 Granny Goose A's, Davey Lopes

HISTORY

For the third year in a row, Granny Goose Foods issued a 15-card regional set of Oakland A's baseball cards. The design of the cards is similar to previous issues. New for '83 was the inclusion of a tear-off coupon at the bottom of the card with a scratch-off "Instant Winner Game" box offering valuable prizes. If a prize was won, the coupon on the back of the tab could be mailed in to collect the prize. Cards with the tab intact and unscratched are worth twice as much as those without it. Also new in '83 was the inclusion of the date in the green and yellow A's logo on the front of the card. Otherwise, the format of the front was unchanged from earlier years. A color photo is surrounded by a white border, with a green box with yellow letters giving the player's name, uniform number, and position underneath. Card backs feature smaller type for the minimal player information, a smaller A's logo, and, for the first time, a Granny Goose logo. Single cards were distributed in large packages of potato chips, while complete sets (without tabs) were given away at a special game.

FOR

The Granny Goose issue is attractive for a regional set. It is also relatively inexpensive, which is great for team collectors.

AGAINST

The design is too similar to earlier issues.

NOTEWORTHY CARDS

Stars in the 1983 Granny Goose set include Rickey Henderson, Carney Lansford, and Dwayne Murphy.

VALUE

MINT CONDITION: Complete set (with tabs), \$13; common card, 40¢; stars, \$1; Henderson, \$6. 5-YEAR PROJECTION: Average.

1983 BRAVES POLICE

SPECIFICATIONS

SIZE: $2^5/_8 \times 4^1/_8$". FRONT: Color photograph. BACK: Color printing on white cardboard. DISTRIBUTION: Atlanta, single cards given out by police officers.

1983 Braves Police, Bob Horner

HISTORY

The 30-card 1983 Braves Police set is similar in design to the team's two previous sets. There is a notation in the upper right that they were the "1982 National League Western Division Champions." Otherwise, the cards are the same: a color photo with a white border, with Police Athletic League and team logos, and a player identification. The card number on the front corresponds to the player's uniform number. Backs feature the color logos of Coca-Cola and Hostess, along with a safety tip and a few lines about the player. Besides the player cards, there is a card for manager Joe Torre and for each coach.

FOR

The set is significant for Braves' team collectors because they won their division in 1982.

AGAINST

The cardboard is too thin. The design is too similar to previous years.

NOTEWORTHY CARDS

Atlanta stars include Dale Murphy, Bob Horner, Phil Niekro, and coach Bob Gibson.

VALUE

MINT CONDITION: Complete set, $14; common card, 40¢; stars, 50¢–$2; Murphy, $4. 5-YEAR PROJECTION: Average.

1983 Gardner's Brewers, Paul Molitor

1983 GARDNER'S BREWERS

SPECIFICATIONS

SIZE: 2½ × 3½". FRONT: Color photograph. BACK: Orange and black printing on gray cardboard. DISTRIBUTION: Wisconsin, one card in packages of bakery products.

1983 Gardner's Brewers, Robin Yount

HISTORY

One of 1983's scarcest regional sets was produced by the Gardner Baking Company. The 22-card set features the Milwaukee Brewers and consists of 21 player cards and a card for manager Harvey Kuenn. The cards were produced by Topps and inserted in specially marked packages of bread and hot dog and hamburger buns. Because sets were not available to dealers or collectors, the Gardner's set has retained its high value. Knowing that such sets are usually made available to dealers eventually, many collectors chose not to collect the cards out of bread products (at 75¢ or more per loaf), waiting instead for the sets to reach the wholesale market. When that didn't happen, there was a scramble to purchase sets that had been assembled from the loaves. Of course, collectors who lived outside of Wisconsin had no choice but to buy the cards in the aftermarket. (Gardner's "day-old" bakery outlets became a favorite hangout for collectors and dealers during this promotion, as a loaf of bread with a card could be bought for 25¢ or so, leaving a pretty good profit margin.) The cards feature a tombstone-shaped photo of the player, surrounded by a frame of pink, orange, and yellow, with a white border. There is a red and black Gardner's logo in the upper left and a yellow and blue Brewers logo in the lower right. Except for the card numbers (alphabetically by player name, with Kuenn as card #1), backs are identical to the regular-issue Topps cards of 1983; Gardner's logo doesn't appear on the back. Because the cards were inserted into packages of buns and bread, they absorbed grease from the products. There was concern at first that the cards would be permanently stained. In time, however, most stains disappeared.

FOR

It was a popular regional set of the reigning American League Champions. The issue is genuinely scarce and likely to hold its value well.

AGAINST

The design is a bit gaudy, but you can't really criticize a regional baseball card set that was actually distributed the way it was supposed to be.

NOTEWORTHY CARDS

All the stars from the A.L. pennant-winning 1982 Brewers are here: Robin Yount, Cecil Cooper, Paul Molitor, and Rollie Fingers.

VALUE

MINT CONDITION: Complete set, $24; common card, 50¢; Fingers, Molitor, $3.50; Yount, $6. 5-YEAR PROJECTION: Average.

1983 BREWERS POLICE

SPECIFICATIONS

SIZE: 2¹³⁄₁₆ × 4⅛". FRONT: Color photograph. BACK: Blue printing on white cardboard. DISTRIBUTION: Wisconsin, single cards given out by police officers; complete sets given away at a special promotional game.

HISTORY

A total of 28 police departments in the state of Wisconsin cooperated in the distribution of the 1983 Brewers Police set. Multiply that by the 30 cards in the set, and you get a whopping total of 840 varieties. Few collectors will attempt to assemble a "complete" set; most will be content to acquire one 30-card set, such as the one given away by the Milwaukee Police Department at a special promotional game. The other departments made the cards available to youngsters who asked police officers for them. All of the sets are basically the same except for the different police department names on the front of the card. Card backs have

1983 Brewers Police, Don Sutton

the Brewers logo, a police shield, and a safety, anti-crime, or personal development message from the player, stated in baseball terms. In addition to the player cards, there are four coach cards, a manager card, and a team photo card. Although it is conceivable that the various department sets could eventually take on individual identities and prices, most veteran collectors doubt it.

FOR

Police sets are great items for team collectors.

AGAINST

A "complete" set is impossible to obtain.

NOTEWORTHY CARDS

Robin Yount, Rollie Fingers, and all the other Brewers stars are featured.

VALUE

MINT CONDITION: Complete set, $7; common card, 20¢; stars, 50¢–$1. 5-YEAR PROJECTION: Average.

1983 THORN APPLE VALLEY CUBS

SPECIFICATIONS

SIZE: 2¼ × 3½″. FRONT: Color photograph. BACK: Black printing on white cardboard. DISTRIBUTION: Chicago, complete sets given away at a special promotional game.

1983 Thorn Apple Valley Cubs, Ryne Sandberg

1983 Thorn Apple Valley Cubs, Jody Davis

HISTORY

Similar to the Red Lobster set of 1982, this 27-card Cubs set was given away at a special promotional game co-sponsored by Thorn Apple Valley. The set consists of 25 player cards, a team card, and a card with the manager and coaches. As in '82, the set features borderless color photos—both action and posed—taken at Wrigley Field. A single line of type on the card has the player's name, uniform number (which is also the card number), and abbreviation for his position. Overall, the photo quality was improved from 1982; the players stand out from the background more sharply than in the previous set. Card backs again feature year-by-year major and minor league stats and statistical totals by league (where appropriate for players who were on A.L. clubs). There is a small ad for Thorn Apple Valley and a copyright line for the Cubs at the bottom of the card.

FOR

Cubs collectors will appreciate this scarce regional set.

AGAINST

The cards are not very professional in appearance, with most of the cards cut a fraction of an inch off the true dimensions.

NOTEWORTHY CARDS

The set contains rookie cards of Ryne Sandberg, Mel Hall, and Joe Carter.

VALUE

MINT CONDITION: Complete set, $9; common card, 25¢; stars, rookies, 50¢–$3. 5-YEAR PROJECTION: Average.

1983 DODGERS POLICE

SPECIFICATIONS

SIZE: 2$^{13}/_{16}$ × 4⅛″. FRONT: Color photograph. BACK: Blue printing on white cardboard. DISTRIBUTION: Los Angeles, single cards given out by police officers; complete sets given away at a promotional game.

HISTORY

The 1983 Dodgers Police set was basically the same as in previous years. The card front was simplified for '83: it features a color photo with only the player's name and uniform number, the date, and a Dodgers logo. Card backs feature a smaller photo of the player, his name, uniform number (also the card number), personal and career data, and an LAPD badge. There is no safety tip, just a note that the card is "from your friends at the LAPD." The 30-card set features 28 player cards, and cards for the manager and the coaching staff.

1983 Dodgers Police, Candy Maldonado

1983 Stuart Expos, Andre Dawson

1983 Stuart Expos, Gary Carter

FOR

Team collectors like police sets, especially when they continue from year to year.

AGAINST

The thin cardboard is too easily damaged.

NOTEWORTHY CARDS

The set contains the rookie cards of Greg Brock and Candy Maldonado.

VALUE

MINT CONDITION: Complete set, $6; common card, 25¢; stars, 50¢–$1. 5-YEAR PROJECTION: Average.

1983 STUART EXPOS

SPECIFICATIONS

SIZE: 2½ × 3½". FRONT: Color photograph. BACK: Red and blue printing on white cardboard. DISTRIBUTION: Quebec, one card in boxes of snack cakes; complete sets available through a mail-in offer.

HISTORY

One of the more elusive and expensive of the 1983 regional baseball card issues was the 30-card set of the Montreal Expos produced and distributed by Stuart's Baking. Single cards were inserted in the company's snack cake products during the baseball season; complete sets could be obtained through a mail-in offer at the end of the year. The cards feature the Expo players, manager, and coaches. Card fronts have a color photo with blue and red stripes beneath, surrounded by a wide white border. The player's uniform number and name appear at the bottom, with an Expos logo to the left, and a red Stuart's logo to the right. Like many Canadian baseball cards, the back is printed in both French and English, and contains little personal data and a short career summary. An Expos logo appears at the top and the card number is at the bottom. The year of issue is prominently displayed in a bar at the lower center. The theft of a large number of the '83 Stuart's cards made them more widely available than they might otherwise have been, and most collectors don't realize that the issue is actually rather scarce.

FOR
This good-looking, scarce regional issue features hot stars of the 1980s.

AGAINST
The set is still suffering from bad publicity connected with the theft of cards and their sale on the black market.

NOTEWORTHY CARDS
All of the Expos stars of 1983 are in the set: Gary Carter, Al Oliver, Tim Raines, and Andre Dawson.

VALUE
MINT CONDITION: Complete set, $10; common card, 25¢; stars, $1–$1.50. 5-YEAR PROJECTION: Average.

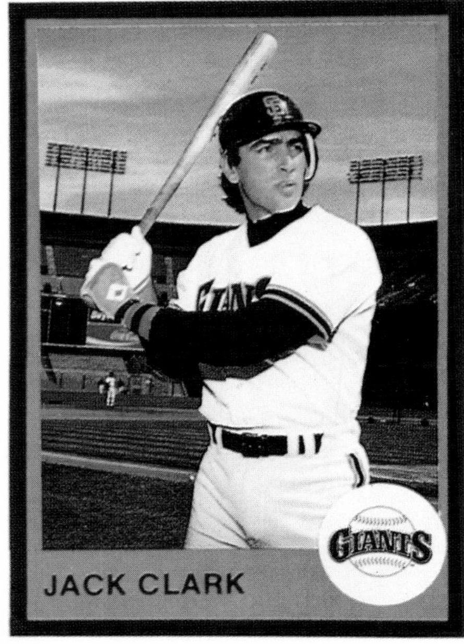

1983 Mother's Cookies Giants, Jack Clark

1983 MOTHER'S COOKIES GIANTS

SPECIFICATIONS
SIZE: 2½ × 3½". FRONT: Color photograph. BACK: Red and purple printing on white cardboard. DISTRIBUTION: San Francisco, 15-card starter sets given out at a promotional game; 5-card supplemental set through mail-in offer.

1983 Mother's Cookies Giants, Chili Davis

HISTORY
In 1983, for the first time in 30 years, Mother's Cookies sponsored a baseball card set. The 20-card set featured the San Francisco Giants (it was the first Mother's set to feature major league players). Fans attending a special promotional game were given a box containing 15 of the 20 cards and a coupon that could be sent to Mother's Cookies for five additional cards. The bakery did not guarantee that the five cards would be the same ones needed to complete the set. The idea was to encourage good old-fashioned baseball card trading. In reality, complete sets were readily available from dealers. The cards are attractive, but printed on rather thin cardboard. A sharp color photo of the player—generally a posed-action shot taken at Candlestick Park—is surrounded by a frame in the team's orange and black colors with a white border. The player's name appears in black in the orange part

of the frame, while a black and white team logo is in a circle at the lower right. Card backs have no stats, but include the player's name, position, uniform number, card number, personal data, and a line about how the Giants acquired him. There is a Mother's logo in the upper right and a space for the player's autograph at the bottom. The 20 cards in the set include 19 players and Hall of Fame manager Frank Robinson.

FOR
Mother's is a well-known name in baseball card history, having released minor league card sets in the '50s. The concept of issuing the cards and requiring trading to complete a set was good, even if it didn't work as well as planned.

AGAINST
It is relatively expensive for a recent issue. The card stock is too thin.

NOTEWORTHY CARDS
While Robinson is the biggest name on the 1983 Giants, there are also cards of Chili Davis and Jack Clark.

VALUE
MINT CONDITION: Complete set, \$15; common card, 50¢; stars, 75¢–\$1; Davis, Robinson, \$1.50; Clark, \$3. 5-YEAR PROJECTION: Average.

1983 WHEATIES INDIANS

SPECIFICATIONS
SIZE: $2^{13}/_{16} \times 4^{1}/_{8}$". FRONT: Color photograph. BACK: Blue printing on white cardboard. DISTRIBUTION: Cleveland, complete sets given out at a promotional game and sold in the Indians gift shop.

HISTORY
In 1983, for the second straight year, Wheaties cereal and the Cleveland Indians worked together to produce a baseball card set. The 32-card set includes 27 players, the manager, and four coaches. The cards retain the basic "police set" format: a color photo surrounded by a wide white border. Below the photo is an Indians logo, the player's name and position, and a Wheaties logo. Once again, the backs of the manager's and coaches' cards are blank except for a large Wheaties ad. The backs of the players' cards were changed in 1983 to feature complete major and minor league stats. In an interesting innovation, the stats are broken down in American League and National League totals where appropriate, and then major league totals are given. Complete sets were given away at a special promotional game at Municipal Stadium, and were subsequently on sale at the Indians gift shop.

JULIO
FRANCO
Infield

1983 Wheaties Indians, Julio Franco

FOR
The cards are appealing to team collectors.

AGAINST
The set is too similar in design to the 1982 issue.

NOTEWORTHY CARDS
Julio Franco's rookie card is in the set.

VALUE
MINT CONDITION: Complete set, \$7; common card, 15¢–25¢; stars, 25¢–75¢; Franco, \$1. 5-YEAR PROJECTION: Average.

1983 ROYALS POLICE

SPECIFICATIONS

SIZE: 2½ × 4⅛". FRONT: Color photograph. BACK: Blue printing on white cardboard. DISTRIBUTION: Fort Myers, Florida, single cards given out by police officers.

HISTORY

The ten cards in the 1983 Kansas City Royals Police set are virtually identical to the set issued in 1981 by the Ft. Myers Police Department. (Ft. Myers is the spring training base of the Royals.) The card front features a color photo, facsimile autograph and team logo, and the player's name, position, height, and weight. There is no card number. Backs feature logos for the sponsoring groups, a safety tip, and a short career summary. The easiest way to tell the 1983 Royals Police cards from the '81s is that the '83 cards do not have year-by-year stats.

FOR

An interesting team set in that it comes from the Royals spring training site.

AGAINST

There is no design change from the 1981 set except the loss of year-by-year stats, which is a minus.

NOTEWORTHY CARDS

George Brett, Dan Quisenberry, and Willie Wilson were stars on the 1983 Royals.

VALUE

MINT CONDITION: Complete set, $25; common card, $1.50; stars, $2–$3; Brett, $13. 5-YEAR PROJECTION: Average.

1983 MINNESOTA TWINS

SPECIFICATIONS

SIZE: 2½ × 3½". FRONT: Color photograph. BACK: Red and blue printing on white cardboard. DISTRIBUTION: Minneapolis, complete sets sold at souvenir stands and through a mail-in offer.

1983 Minnesota Twins, Kent Hrbek

HISTORY

One of the lesser-known and scarcer baseball card sets of 1983 was the 36-card Minnesota Twins team issue. Reportedly only 4,000 sets were produced, and they were quickly sold out at the Metrodome concession stands and through a mail-in offer. The cards feature attractive posed photos taken in spring training. The fronts have just the photo—no border or writing. Card backs feature full major and minor league statistics on an annual basis, personal data (including the player's nickname), and a card number. Besides the 25 regular player cards, there are 11 special cards. Each of the four coaches and manager Billy Gardner have their own cards, and they appear on a group card as well. Three multiplayer cards feature the Twins three-man catching corps, a trio of Minnesota-born Twins, and four big-hitting stars called "The Lumber Company." There is a team photo card and an aerial view of the Metrodome to round out the set.

FOR

The set is scarce enough to yield high dividends.

AGAINST

Most collectors have never heard of it, so demand is low.

NOTEWORTHY CARDS

Counting the team card, Twins star Kent Hrbek appears on four cards in the set. There are rookie cards of Gary Gaetti and Jim Eisenreich. For '50s collectors, the manager and coaches cards include former ballplayers Billy Gardner, Jim Lemon, and Johnny Podres.

VALUE

MINT CONDITION: Complete set, $10; common card, 40¢; stars, $1; Hrbek, $2. 5-YEAR PROJECTION: Below average.

1983 TRUE VALUE WHITE SOX

SPECIFICATIONS

SIZE: 2⅝ × 4⅛". FRONT: Color photograph. BACK: Black printing on white cardboard. DISTRIBUTION: Chicago, single cards given away at special Tuesday night games.

HISTORY

This 23-card set was co-sponsored by the Chicago White Sox and True Value Hardware stores. Partial sets were supposed to be given out at special Tuesday night games, but when a couple of the games were rained out, the cards were smuggled out to collectors and dealers instead. Because complete sets were not made available, the True Value White Sox cards of 1983 are a rather expensive regional set to assemble. The format of the cards is like a police set, with a large color photo and a wide white border. A red and blue Sox logo is in the lower left, while the player's name, position, and uniform number (also the card number) are in the lower right. Card backs feature year-by-year major and minor league statistics and a True Value ad.

FOR

These cards are great for team and superstar collectors, especially since the White Sox won the A.L. West in 1983.

AGAINST

Some collectors feel that the stigma of some of the cards winding up in dealers' hands taints the set.

1983 True Value White Sox, Harold Baines

NOTEWORTHY CARDS

The three cards not given out at games (Marc Hill, Harold Baines, and Salome Barojas) are scarcer than the rest of the set. The set includes the rookie card of Ron Kittle and Cy Young Award winner LaMarr Hoyt.

VALUE

MINT CONDITION: Complete set, $30; common card, 35¢; Kittle, $1; Barojas, Hill, $3; Baines, $7. 5-YEAR PROJECTION: Above average.

1982 TOPPS

SPECIFICATIONS

SIZE: 2½ × 3½". FRONT: Color photograph. BACK: Green and blue printing on gray cardboard. DISTRIBUTION: Nationally, in packages with bubblegum.

1982 Topps, Willie Stargell

1982 Topps, Dave Righetti

1982 Topps, Tim Raines

HISTORY

In 1982 Topps produced its biggest baseball card set ever—792 cards. The addition of 66 cards allowed Topps, for the first time since 1978, to eliminate "double prints" (cards printed more than once on a sheet and therefore twice as common as the others). While collectors applauded the increased number of cards, they were generally unenthusiastic about the design. The card front features a pair of color stripes which go down the left side and curve under the photo. They look like hockey sticks and draw attention away from the player photo. The card back is an incredibly hard-to-read combination of blue and green printing on gray cardboard. The first six cards in the '82 set highlight great performances of the 1981 season. Other special subsets include the American and National League All-Stars, 1981 statistical leaders from each league, and 40 "In Action" cards that depict players in action. The In Action cards are numbered in the set immediately after the regular card of that player. Each team manager is pictured on a card, along with the team's batting and pitching leaders. The popular "Future Stars" cards are also included, each card featuring three top prospects for a particular team. These cards have traditionally been some of the most valuable rookie cards in hobby history. The price for some cards has gone from 20¢ to $2 in a single season.

FOR

The first of the 792-card Topps sets includes no double-printed cards and has lots of potential for price appreciation.

AGAINST
Collectors overlook the set because of the unpopular design.

NOTEWORTHY CARDS
Because of a printing foul-up, some George Foster All-Star cards (#342) are found without the facsimile autograph on the front. A scarce variation card of Pascual Perez (#383) exists without his position "Pitcher" printed at lower left. Rookie cards include Von Hayes, Steve Bedrosian and Brett Butler, Dave Righetti, Kent Hrbek, Jesse Barfield, Jorge Bell, and Cal Ripken Jr.

VALUE
MINT CONDITION: Complete set, $75; common card, 5¢; superstars, 50¢–$2; Hrbek, $4; Barfield, $5; Bell, $10; Ripken, $13. 5-YEAR PROJECTION: Above average.

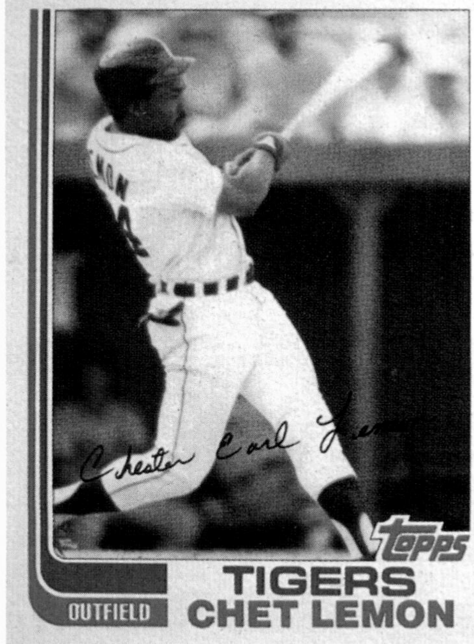

1982 Topps Traded, Chet Lemon

1982 TOPPS TRADED

SPECIFICATIONS
SIZE: 2½ × 3½". FRONT: Color photograph. BACK: Black and red printing on white cardboard. DISTRIBUTION: Nationally, complete sets sold through hobby dealers.

1982 Topps Traded, Reggie Jackson

HISTORY
For the second straight year, Topps produced a 132-card "Traded" set late in the season. The set, sold exclusively through dealers rather than in gum packs, offers cards of traded players in their new uniforms (some uniforms are created by airbrush artists), single cards of rookies who had previously appeared on "Future Stars" cards, and new cards of players who were missed by the regular 1982 Topps set. The Traded cards follow the design of the regular 1982 issue, but the photographs and print quality are not as good. Card backs are printed in red, rather than green; and the cards are numbered alphabetically from 1T to 132T, with the last card being the checklist.

FOR
The Traded set gives collectors a chance to see their favorite traded players in their new uniforms. It also provides hot rookies with a card of their own, whereas in the regular Topps set they had to share a card with two other prospects.

AGAINST
Because the Traded set is not available in retail stores, some purists feel it is not "legitimate." This has given rise to debates over which is a player's "real" rookie card. Despite this objection, most collectors feel that an '82 Topps set is incomplete without the Traded series.

NOTEWORTHY CARDS

The set has the first single-player cards of Jesse Barfield, Kent Hrbek, and Cal Ripken Jr. It includes the first cards of Reggie Jackson as a California Angel and Gaylord Perry as a Kansas City Royal.

VALUE

MINT CONDITION: Complete set, $21; common card, 9¢; superstars, 35¢–75¢; Jackson, $2.50; Barfield, Hrbek, $3.75; Ripken, $9. 5-YEAR PROJECTION: Above average.

1982 Fleer, Fernando Valenzuela

1982 FLEER

SPECIFICATIONS

SIZE: 2½ × 3½″. FRONT: Color photograph. BACK: Color printing on white cardboard. DISTRIBUTION: Nationally, in packages with team logo stickers.

HISTORY

After its acclaimed baseball card issue of 1981, Fleer really struck out in 1982. The biggest blow came when a federal court overturned Fleer's 1980 decision against Topps. The court reaffirmed that Topps had the exclusive right to market baseball cards with confectionery products such as bubblegum. Undaunted, Fleer simply sold its cards without the gum, putting team logo stickers in each pack of cards instead. That move has not gone unchallenged by Topps, who contends that the use of stickers is merely a ruse to facilitate the sale of baseball cards in illegal competition. The matter is likely to be in court for several years. Fleer also struck out with collectors. To some hobbyists, several errors and variations in the 660-card set seemed like an effort to stimulate the same type of demand that had been brought on by the "C" Nettles error card of the previous year. Many

1982 Fleer, Andre Dawson

1982 Fleer, Reggie Jackson/Dave Winfield

collectors boycotted the issue entirely. What really makes the set unpopular, however, is the poor quality of the photography: a majority of the photos are blurred or fuzzy, giving the cards an unprofessional look. The basic design of the cards isn't bad. A large photo is surrounded by a round-cornered frame in a different color for each team. A lozenge-shaped panel in the bottom of the frame contains the player's name, team, and position. The card back is similar to the previous year's issue. Complete major and minor league stats are presented, with the added touch of a color team logo in the upper right. The box containing the stats is yellow, while the overall design is in light blue. Fleer's best innovation in the 1982 set was a further refinement of its numbering scheme. Cards were still arranged in team order, with the World Champion Dodgers and the American League Champion Yankees as the first cards in the set, followed by the rest of the teams in order of winning percentage. Within each team, though, Fleer numbered the cards in alphabetical order—a simple, logical arrangement that had never before been used in a major set. Besides the individual player cards in the set, there are 19 special cards and multiplayer feature cards, along with 14 checklists.

FOR

Fleer had some good ideas for its 1982 card set; they just weren't properly executed.

AGAINST

Poor photography and the numerous error/variation cards make this a poor-quality set.

NOTEWORTHY CARDS

Of the many error/variation cards in the 1982 Fleer set, only one of them has any real potential for retaining its premium value. As with many Fleer and Donruss cards of 1981 and '82, there was a reversed negative card in the set where Padres pitcher John Littlefield looks as if he is pitching lefthanded. This card was corrected early in the print run and is quite scarce. Whether or not future collectors will feel it is necessary to have the card for a "complete" set will determine how well it holds its current value. Also corrected relatively early was a printing error on the back of Al Hrabosky's card (#438). This card, in fact, has three variations. On "double-error" cards, his first name is spelled "All" and his height is listed as 5′1″. On the first correction, the name was spelled right, but the height was still wrong. Finally, on the third try Fleer got the card right, giving his height as 5′10″. While the first version of this card is quite scarce, demand is limited and decreasing; it is not the type of error collectors will pay a great deal of attention to down the road. The specialty cards also contain a major mistake. Card #639 ("Perfect Game") pictures Indians Len Barker and Bo Diaz in honor of Barker's perfect game of May 15, 1981, when he retired all 27 Blue Jays without a baserunner. The only problem is that Diaz was not the Indians catcher in that perfect game; Ron Hassey was behind the plate. Another notable card pictures Pete Rose along with his son, Pete Jr., as a batboy and carries the title of "Pete and Re-Pete." Many collectors thought this was a bit too cute for a baseball card. Also, there is a Cal Ripken Jr. rookie card in the set.

VALUE

MINT CONDITION: Complete set (no variations), $25; common card, 3¢; stars, 25¢–75¢; Ripken, $7.50; "All" Hrabosky, $20; Littlefield "leftie," $75. 5-YEAR PROJECTION: Below average.

1982 DONRUSS

SPECIFICATIONS

SIZE: 2½ × 3½″. FRONT: Color photograph. BACK: Blue and black printing on white cardboard. DISTRIBUTION: Nationally, in packages with jigsaw puzzle pieces.

1982 Donruss, Kent Hrbek

1982 Donruss, Nolan Ryan

1982 Donruss, Keith Hernandez

HISTORY

When the federal court upheld Topps' exclusive right to market baseball cards with confectionery products like bubblegum, Donruss was undaunted. The Memphis card producer created a 63-piece Babe Ruth jigsaw puzzle and inserted three pieces into wax packs with its 1982 baseball cards. After all, kids and collectors buy packs of baseball cards for the cards themselves, not for the bubblegum. Donruss capitalized on the lessons learned in its premier issue, and the company's '82 product was considerably improved. The cardboard was beefed up to more closely resemble that used by Topps and Fleer, which better resists creasing. Far fewer errors occurred in the '82 set, creating fewer variations to vex collectors. Donruss increased the number of cards to 660, including seven unnumbered checklists. A specialty group entitled "Diamond Kings" was created to open the '82 set. One well-known player from each team was represented in a painted portrait created by baseball artist Dick Perez. These artistic cards proved to be instant collector favorites. The design of the '82 Donruss set was also widely acclaimed by collectors. A large color photo dominates the face of the card, framed with a border that is color-coded by team. A "Donruss '82" appears in the upper right, the team name appears in a baseball in the lower left, and the player's name and an abbreviation for his position appear in a bat that stretches across the bottom of the card. For the back, Donruss dropped the vertical format and went with a more traditional horizontal layout. A blue box at the top contains the player's vital data, while a similar blue box at the bottom features "Career Highlights." In between is a white band containing "Recent Major League Performance" stats. The small space allowed for these stats means that only a few years' worth are printed, along with career total figures. This innovation has not been widely accepted by collectors, many of whom like to see complete figures on their baseball cards. The '82 Donruss set expanded the use of multiplayer feature cards, but dropped the special cards for Cy Young winners that had been part of the 1981 set. Also in contrast to the previous issue, the '82 Donruss series offered one card per player, except for those who appeared in the Diamond Kings group. Donruss made points with many collectors by issuing cards for managers and for coaches who were well-known players at one time such as Johnny Podres and Harvey Haddix. A bit more controversial was the inclusion of the San Diego Chicken. Those collectors who enjoyed the Chicken's antics applauded the card; other collectors felt that mascots had no part being in a baseball card set. Nonetheless, the card has become fairly valuable. Most collectors feel that Donruss did an excellent job of improving its baseball card issue between 1981 and '82.

FOR

Donruss released a much improved set with lots of innovative cards and concepts.

AGAINST

Again, color reproduction was not as good as collectors expect from a major issue. There are still too many errors for most collectors.

NOTEWORTHY CARDS

Alan Trammell's regular and Diamond Kings cards had his name misspelled "Trammel" on the initial press run—later corrected in a second printing. Unnumbered Diamond Kings checklists will also be found with Trammell's name spelled both ways. Other errors which were later corrected include Shane Rawley's card, which shows Jim Anderson's photo; Juan Eichelberger's card, which has Gary Lucas' photo; Phil Garner's card, which has a reversed negative; and Randy Lerch's card listing his team as "Braves" instead of "Brewers." The set includes rookie cards of Cal Ripken Jr., Steve Sax, and Kent Hrbek.

VALUE

MINT CONDITION: Complete set, $27; common card, 3¢; stars, errors, 50¢–$2; Ripken, $8.
5-YEAR PROJECTION: Above average.

1982 CRACKER JACK

SPECIFICATIONS

SIZE: 2½ × 3½″. FRONT: Color photograph. BACK: Red, blue, and black printing on gray cardboard. DISTRIBUTION: Nationally, two 8-card sheets available through a mail-in offer.

HISTORY

In conjunction with its sponsorship of the first Old-Timers Classic game to benefit the former major league players' relief fund, Cracker Jack issued a 16-card set of "All-Time Baseball Greats" from the 1940s through the 1970s. There are two sheets with eight player cards each and a Cracker Jack advertising card at the center. There were eight National League players on one sheet, eight American Leaguers on the other. The cards were printed by Topps. A set of the Cracker Jack cards could be obtained by sending in box tops and 50¢. Some dealers were able to obtain quantities of the sheets as well. Most of the sheets ordered by collectors directly from Cracker Jack were creased in the mail; most collectors who desired Mint cards had to buy them from hobby dealers. The design of the Cracker Jack cards is interesting. The player's photo is set against a background of Cracker Jacks. A banner at the bottom of the card (red for American League, green for National League) has the player's name and position in white type. The name of the team that the player is most often associated with is printed in black script to the lower left of the photo, while the famous Cracker Jack logo appears to the right. Card backs have personal player information, a career summary, a lifetime batting or pitching record, and another Cracker Jack logo. The cards are separated on the sheets by dotted lines. They can be cut into individual cards, but few collectors do so and the value of the set is greatest in complete form. It is interesting to note that Topps generally chose photos or artwork of the players as they appeared later in their careers. Some of the pictures used on the '82 Cracker Jack cards appeared in earlier Topps issues. The paintings of Bob Feller and Ralph Kiner were used on 1953 Topps cards, while the photo of Brooks Robinson appeared—in black and white—on a 1969 Topps Deckle-Edge. Not all the players featured in the Cracker Jack set played in, or even made an appearance at, the old-timers' game.

FOR

The uncut mini-sheet is a different concept and the design is unique.

AGAINST

The sheet format makes it tough to get single cards of desired players.

NOTEWORTHY CARDS

Virtually everybody in the set is a Hall of Famer—or should be.

VALUE

MINT CONDITION: Complete set (uncut sheets), $9; common card, 25¢–50¢; Mickey Mantle, $1.
5-YEAR PROJECTION: Above average.

1982 DRAKE'S

SPECIFICATIONS

SIZE: 2½ × 3½″. FRONT: Color photograph. BACK: Blue and green printing on gray cardboard. DISTRIBUTION: Northeast, single cards in packages of snack cakes; nationally, complete sets sold through hobby dealers.

HISTORY

Most collectors learned a valuable lesson when Drake's wholesaled its 1981 card issue to dealers. In '82, collectors waited for the set to become available at a reasonable price from dealers, rather than trying to assemble it themselves by buying family-size packages of snack cakes. Once again, the theme of the issue was "Big Hitters" and it featured 33 cards of players known for their bat-handling. Again, although the cards were produced by Topps, the design of the front was completely different from the regular Topps issue. The

1982 Drake's Bill Buckner

1982 Drake's, Eddie Murray

1982 Drake's, Jack Clark

autographed player photos are larger than those used in '82, and are made to look like snapshots mounted at the corners in an album. The predominant color scheme of the National League cards is green; for the American League it is red. A banner at the top of the card heralds the set as "2nd Annual Collectors' Edition" and includes a card number. There is a Drake's logo at the bottom, along with the player's name, team, and position. The card back is quite similar to the '82 Topps and, surprisingly, does not feature a Drake's logo (there is a Drake's copyright line at the bottom, however). Also unlike the regular Topps set, the 33 cards are numbered alphabetically.

FOR

Drake's again came up with a good, inexpensive regional set with lots of stars in different poses.

AGAINST

The design is too busy for many collectors' tastes. Otherwise, you can't find much fault with the set.

NOTEWORTHY CARDS

Virtually everybody in the set is a star. Padres catcher Terry Kennedy's card uses the same photo as his regular 1982 Topps card.

VALUE

MINT CONDITION: Complete set, \$8; common card, 10¢; superstars, 50¢–75¢; Pete Rose, \$1.
5-YEAR PROJECTION: Average.

1982 TOPPS K-MART

SPECIFICATIONS

SIZE: 2½ × 3½″. FRONT: Color photograph. BACK: Red and blue printing on gray cardboard. DISTRIBUTION: Nationally, complete sets sold in K-Mart stores.

1982 Topps K-Mart, Pete Rose

1982 Topps K-Mart, Don Drysdale

HISTORY

This set is probably the least popular item in the great baseball card flood of 1982. Topps and K-Mart produced a 44-card set marking the 20th anniversary of the store chain. The "Limited Edition Collectors' Series" came in a cardboard box with a stick of bubblegum. The original price was $1.97, then $1, then two for $1, and finally, a dime apiece. The problem was simply overproduction (this may be the most plentiful set ever produced). Forty-one of the cards honor the American League and National League winners of the Most Valuable Player award from 1962 to 1981 (there's an odd number because Keith Hernandez and Willie Stargell shared the award in the National League in 1979). The card front depicts a color mini-version of the regular issue Topps baseball card from the year of the award. Backs recap the player's season performance that led to the MVP award. The three cards that round out the set are season highlight cards of Don Drysdale (1968, 58⅔ scoreless innings), Hank Aaron (1974, 715 career home runs), and Pete Rose (1981, 3,631 career hits). There is a glut of these sets on the market, and some dealers use them as giveaways.

FOR

For an incredibly low price there are a lot of superstars in the 44-card set. There's also a certain charm in seeing familiar cards reproduced in miniature form.

AGAINST

There's too much advertising on the cards. Demand for these cards will probably never catch up with supply.

NOTEWORTHY CARDS

There are two cards that don't depict actual Topps cards from the years those players received the MVP: the cards of Fred Lynn (A.L., 1975) and Maury Wills (N.L., 1962) are mock-ups of what the cards would have looked like if they had been issued. In Topps' regular 1975 set, Lynn was just one of four small pictures on a "Rookie Outfielders" card. Since it wouldn't do to reproduce a multiplayer card in the special K-Mart set, Topps artists gave Lynn his own 1975 rookie card after the fact. A similar situation arose with Wills, who didn't appear on a Topps baseball card until 1967. He was miffed that the company thought so little of his chances when he started out in the minor leagues, so he refused to allow the company to use his picture until he had been a major league star for eight years.

VALUE

MINT CONDITION: Complete set, $1; common card, 1¢. 5-YEAR PROJECTION: Above average.

1982 KELLOGG'S

SPECIFICATIONS

SIZE: 2⅛ × 3¼″. FRONT: Color photograph, 3-D effect. BACK: Black printing on white cardboard. DISTRIBUTION: Nationally, complete sets available through a mail-in offer.

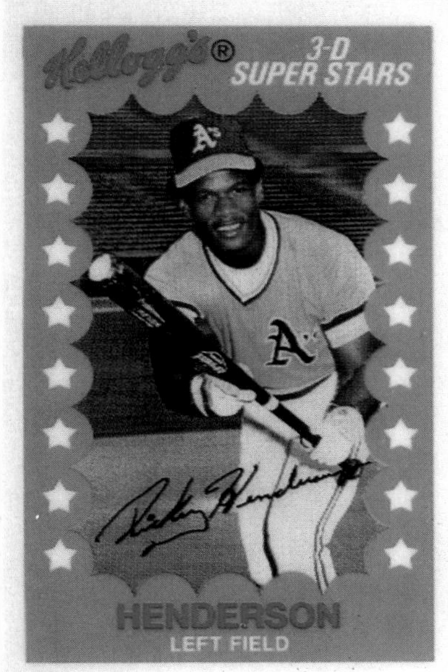

1982 Kellogg's, Rickey Henderson

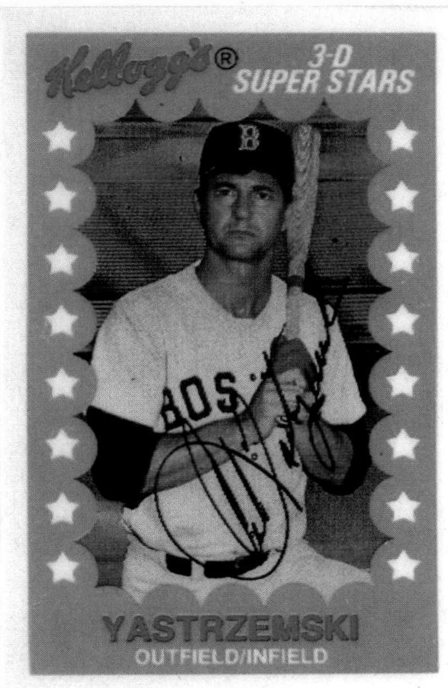

1982 Kellogg's, Carl Yastrzemski

HISTORY

The key word for the 1982 Kellogg's set was "smaller." The cards shrank in size from 2½ × 3½″ to 2⅛ × 3¼″ and the set was reduced from 66 to 64 cards. The card front features a color photo with a scalloped blue frame with white stars up and down the sides. A Kellogg's logo appears in red in the upper left, while the player's last name appears at the bottom in red, along with his position in white. The title "3-D Super Stars" is in white in the upper right. The 3-D look is produced by laminating a piece of ribbed plastic over the photo on front. On the card back is the usual combination of personal and career stats, and a short biography. There is no cartoon character on back, just the Kellogg's logo on a baseball, along with information on how the set could be obtained by sending in box tops from Kellogg's cereal along with $3.95. For the second straight year, individual cards were not packaged in cereal boxes. The narrower card size brought a return of the problem of curling and cracking, greatly reducing the value of the card.

FOR

Kellogg's offered an inexpensive set with lots of stars and lots of room to grow in value.

AGAINST

The problem with cracking and curling returned because of the smaller size. Single cards are hard to find because of a prevalence of complete sets on the market.

NOTEWORTHY CARDS

Many of the game's new young stars make their debut in the 1982 Kellogg's set, such as Fernando Valenzuela, Tim Raines, and Ozzie Smith.

VALUE

MINT CONDITION: Complete set, $12; common card, 6¢; stars, 20¢–25¢; Pete Rose, $1. 5-YEAR PROJECTION: Above average.

1982 SQUIRT

SPECIFICATIONS

SIZE: Single card, 2½ × 3½″; panel, 2½ × 9″. FRONT: Color photograph. BACK: Black and yellow printing on white cardboard. DISTRIBUTION: Nationally, one or two cards in cartons and six-packs of soft-drinks.

1982 Squirt, Reggie Jackson

1982 Squirt, Carlton Fisk

HISTORY

Buoyed by the success of their 1981 issue, Squirt returned in '82 with another Topps-produced baseball card issue. This time Squirt went overboard. The 22 cards in the set were distributed in different arrangements, but collectors didn't seem to care for any of them. As with the 1981 cards, virtually the entire issue immediately went into the hands of dealers. The cards feature an oblique color photo against a colorful red, yellow and green background. The Squirt logo is in red in the upper left. The player's name appears below the photo, and his team and position are in the lower right. The cards were issued in four ways: 1) one card on a ring-tab panel, with scratch-off contest; 2) two cards on a ring-tab panel, no contest; 3) one card on a can-hanger panel, with scratch-off contest; and 4) one card on a can-hanger panel, no contest. Most collectors are content to acquire any combination of panels that gives them a complete set of 22 cards. There are indications that some panels are scarcer than others, but nobody seems to know. Certainly they don't care enough to pay more money for one over another.

FOR

It's a nice group of recent superstar cards at a reasonable price. Someday somebody may sort out the variations and find out that some of these are really scarce. Whether collectors will care is another story. Demand may start to pick up on the better-known superstars.

AGAINST

The issue was so confusing it turned collectors off; besides, the cards are too fancy.

VALUE

MINT CONDITION: Complete set of panels, $6; common card, 9¢; stars, 75¢. 5-YEAR PROJECTION: Average.

1982 GRANNY GOOSE A's

SPECIFICATIONS

SIZE: 2½ × 3½″. FRONT: Color photograph. BACK: Black printing on white cardboard. DISTRIBUTION: Northern California, single cards in bags of potato chips; complete sets given out at a promotional game.

HISTORY

The 1982 Granny Goose Oakland A's set is not nearly as rare as the '81 issue. While the cards continued to be inserted in twin-bags of potato chips, complete 15-card sets were also given away on Fan Appreciation Day in Oakland. The '82 Granny Goose set is identical in design to the previous year's issue (you have to read the write-up on the back of the card to determine which is which). The card front features a color photo of the player surrounded by a white border. A green box at the bottom has the player's name, position, and uniform number. The A's team logo appears in the

1982 Granny Goose A's. Billy Martin

1982 Granny Goose A's, Rickey Henderson

lower left. The backs contain just a few personal stats along with an A's logo. The cards given away at the stadium were not in contact with potato chips, and collectors prefer them because they have no grease stains.

FOR

The uncluttered design features good photography.

AGAINST

The design is identical to the previous year, which can be confusing. The cardboard is too thin.

NOTEWORTHY CARDS

Besides manager Billy Martin, high-demand players in the set include Rickey Henderson, Tony Armas, and Dwayne Murphy.

VALUE

MINT CONDITION: Complete set, $12.50; common card, 40¢; stars, $2; Henderson, $7. 5-YEAR PROJECTION: Average.

1982 BRAVES POLICE

SPECIFICATIONS

SIZE: 2⅝ × 4⅛". FRONT: Color photograph. BACK: Color printing on white cardboard. DISTRIBUTION: Atlanta, single cards given away by police officers.

1982 Braves Police, Dale Murphy

HISTORY

In the same mold as the 1981 set, the '82 Atlanta Braves Police issue features cards of 24 players, five coaches, and manager Joe Torre. The card front has a color photo surrounded by a wide white border. In the upper left is the Police Athletic League logo, and at the upper right is a notation of the team's record-setting 13-game winning streak at the beginning of the season. The Braves logo is at the lower right and the player's name, position, and uniform number is at the lower left. The uniform number on front is also the card number. Card backs feature the Coca-Cola and Hostess logos, a write-up on the player, and a safety or anti-crime tip. Only about 8,000 of these sets were printed.

FOR
Since there were fewer sets produced, this issue is especially attractive to team collectors.

AGAINST
It is the same old design, and the cardboard is too thin.

NOTEWORTHY CARDS
The Bob Watson card is supposedly scarcer than the others in the set. Dale Murphy, Phil Niekro, and Bob Horner; rookies Brett Butler and Steve Bedrosian; and pitching coach Bob Gibson are the big names.

VALUE
MINT CONDITION: Complete set, \$17; common card, 35¢; stars, 50¢–\$2; Murphy, \$4. 5-YEAR PROJECTION: Above average.

1982 BREWERS POLICE

SPECIFICATIONS
SIZE: 2¹³⁄₁₆ × 4⅛". FRONT: Color photograph. BACK: Blue printing on white cardboard. DISTRIBUTION: Milwaukee, single cards given away by police officers; complete sets given out at a promotional game.

HISTORY
The 1982 Milwaukee Brewers Police set began a trend toward having different police jurisdictions hand out the same set of cards with the name of the police agency on the front of the card. The '82 Brewers Police cards can be found with either the Milwaukee, New Berlin, or State Fair Police department name printed as the third line of type on the front of the card. Like most other police sets, the cards were intended to build better rapport between the police department and local youngsters. The Brewers Police sets were also given away at a special promotional game at County Stadium to kids 14 and younger. The card front features the familiar color photo in a wide white frame, with the player's name, position, and uniform number. The uniform number is also the card number. Backs have a background badge, the Brewers logo, and a safety or anti-crime tip. There are 30 cards in the '82 Brewers set: 25 different player cards, a team card, and cards for manager Buck Rodgers, the coaches, and general manager Harry Dalton.

1982 Brewers Police, Robin Yount

FOR
Team collectors enjoy police sets, and Milwaukee had some good ballplayers in 1982.

AGAINST
The cardboard is extra thin, making the cards susceptible to damage.

NOTEWORTHY CARDS
Kevin Bass makes his only appearance in a Brewer Police set. Robin Yount and Rollie Fingers are the big names.

VALUE
MINT CONDITION: Complete set, \$10; common card, 20¢; stars, 50¢–\$1. 5-YEAR PROJECTION: Above average.

1982 RED LOBSTER CUBS

SPECIFICATIONS

SIZE: 2¼ × 3½″. FRONT: Color photograph. BACK: Black printing on white cardboard. DISTRIBUTION: Chicago, complete sets given out at a special promotional game.

1982 Red Lobster Cubs, Leon Durham

1982 Red Lobster Cubs, Lee Elia

HISTORY

Red Lobster seafood restaurants and the Chicago Cubs teamed up in 1982 to issue a special 28-card set given away at a promotional game. Each of the players on the 25-man roster is pictured in the set, along with a team photo card, a card for manager Lee Elia, and a group coaches card. Slightly narrower than the standard modern card width of 2½″, the card has a borderless color action photo (taken at Wrigley Field) with a facsimile autograph, and a single line of type with the player's name, uniform (and card) number, and abbreviation for his position at the bottom. The backs have complete major and minor league stats, playoff and World Series stats (when applicable), and an ad for Red Lobster. The cards were printed on relatively thin cardboard and were not cut evenly; most cards are a fraction of an inch off their true dimensions. The cards are not common and represent a true regional issue.

FOR

The borderless design was novel for a regional set.

AGAINST

The cards look unprofessional. Single cards are hard to find.

NOTEWORTHY CARDS

The set includes Ryne Sandberg's first card as a Cub.

VALUE

MINT CONDITION: Complete set, $10; common card, 25¢; stars, 50¢; Sandberg, $4. 5-YEAR PROJECTION: Above average.

1982 DODGERS POLICE

SPECIFICATIONS

SIZE: 2 13/16 × 4⅛″. FRONT: Color photograph. BACK: Blue printing on white cardboard. DISTRIBUTION: Los Angeles, individual cards given out by police officers; complete sets given away at a promotional game.

HISTORY

The 30-card 1982 Dodgers Police set features 25 individual players, along with special cards commemorating their Western Division, National League, and World Series victories; a trophy-checklist card; and a card for manager Tommy Lasorda. The card front follows the basic police set format: a color photo surrounded by a wide border

STEVE SAX
No. 52 – SECOND BASE
The Los Angeles Police Department
presents the World Champion

1982 Dodgers Police, Steve Sax

with a few lines of type below. The cards are arranged by uniform number on the front of the card. Backs have biographical and career information along with a safety tip.

FOR
Since the Dodgers won the World Series, team collectors really treasure this set.

AGAINST
As with most other police issues, the cardboard is too thin.

NOTEWORTHY CARDS
The set includes a rookie card of Steve Sax.

VALUE
MINT CONDITION: Complete set, $6; common card, 15¢; stars, 50¢–$1. 5-YEAR PROJECTION: Below average.

1982
HYGRADE EXPOS

SPECIFICATIONS
SIZE: 2 × 3″. FRONT: Color photograph. BACK: Black printing on white cardboard. DISTRIBUTION: Quebec, single cards in packages of meat products; complete sets available through a mail-in offer.

HISTORY
Collectors who are quick to jump on every new issue really got burned with the 1982 Hygrade set, which featured 24 Montreal Expos players. While single cards were issued in packages of the company's meat products, there was also a mail-in offer by which the complete set and a display album could be obtained for $3. Before most U.S. collectors had heard of the mail-in offer, the frenzy to obtain the newest regional set had driven prices to near $45, and Canadian dealers were selling all they could get. The cards, printed on very thin cardboard, are smaller than the current standard size and have rounded corners. The top half of the card front has a borderless color photo of the

André Dawson 10

1982 Hygrade Expos, Andre Dawson

Gary Carter 8

1982 Hygrade Expos, Gary Carter

player with the Hygrade logo in yellow and red in the corner. A white strip at the bottom of the card contains the player's name and uniform number. There is no card number other than the uniform number on the front. The card backs, printed entirely in French, contain an offer for the album to house the set.

FOR

This set is quite scarce, although not as rare as was first thought.

AGAINST

The fact that many collectors were burned on the price of the set turned off a lot of other hobbyists. Besides, the cards are too small and have rounded corners, neither of which is favored by most modern collectors. The thin stock is also a handicap since it makes the cards prone to damage.

NOTEWORTHY CARDS

All the Expos stars of 1982 are present: Gary Carter, Tim Raines, Andre Dawson, and Al Oliver.

VALUE

MINT CONDITION: Complete set, \$40–\$45; common card, \$1; stars, \$2–\$5; Raines, \$7.50. 5-YEAR PROJECTION: Average.

1982 ZELLERS EXPOS

SPECIFICATIONS

SIZE: Single card, 2½ × 3½″; panel, 3½ × 7½″. FRONT: Color photograph. BACK: Blue printing on white cardboard. DISTRIBUTION: Canada, 3-card panels available at Zellers department stores.

HISTORY

The 1982 Montreal Expos card set, produced and distributed by Zellers department stores in Canada, is one of the largest regional sets of modern times. The set consists of 60 individual cards in the form of 3-card panels. Each panel is numbered, and each card on the panel is lettered (for example, 1A, 1B, 1C). The cards feature baseball playing tips from 11 different players and coach Billy Demars. The front of the card has a circular photo of the player surrounded by red, white, and blue rings, on a yellow background. There is a red Zellers logo at top center, flanked by a pair of red circles announcing that the cards contain "Baseball Pro Tips" in English and French. The player's name and the name of the lesson appear below the photo. The playing tip is explained on the back, again in both languages, along with another Zellers logo and the player's name. The cards are most valuable as they were originally distributed—in 3-card panels.

1982 Zellers Expos, Gary Carter

FOR
The set features a novel format.

AGAINST
Collectors generally don't like cards that offer playing tips. They prefer a card that has a picture of the player and nothing more.

NOTEWORTHY CARDS
Star catcher Gary Carter is featured on 15 of the 60 cards. Other Expos stars like Tim Raines and Andre Dawson are also among the "instructors" in the set.

VALUE
MINT CONDITION: Complete 20-panel set, $14; single panel, 50¢–$1; common card, 25¢; star panel, $1–$2. 5-YEAR PROJECTION: Below average.

1982 WHEATIES INDIANS

SPECIFICATIONS
SIZE: 2 13/16 × 4 1/8". FRONT: Color photograph. BACK: Blue printing on white cardboard. DISTRIBUTION: Cleveland, partial sets given out at special games; complete sets sold at Indians gift shop.

1982 Wheaties Indians, Von Hayes

HISTORY
In 1982 Wheaties produced a baseball card set for the first time in 30 years. Unlike earlier issues, which featured players of many sports and teams, the '82 issue included only Cleveland Indians. The 30-card set includes 25 players, individual cards for the four coaches, and a card for the manager. The cards were given out ten at a time during three special promotional games, and the set was subsequently placed on sale at the team gift shop. In design the set closely resembles recent police sets. The card features a color photo (many are action photos) surrounded by a wide white border. The player's name and position appear below. There is a color Indians team logo in the lower left and a Wheaties logo in black at right. Card backs have only a Wheaties advertisement. The cards are unnumbered and printed on thin cardboard.

FOR
Wheaties returned to baseball cards with an attractive offering.

AGAINST
The biggest complaint is the lack of stats on the back. The fact that the set continued to be sold in the Indians gift shop after it was issued kept the price down.

NOTEWORTHY CARDS
The set includes the rookie card of Von Hayes.

VALUE
MINT CONDITION: Complete set, $7; common card, 15¢; Rick Sutcliffe, 75¢; Hayes, $1. 5-YEAR PROJECTION: Average.

1982 COKE-BRIGHAM'S RED SOX

SPECIFICATIONS
SIZE: 2½ × 3½". FRONT: Color photograph. BACK: Red and black printing on gray cardboard. DISTRIBUTION: Boston, three cards with soda and ice cream purchases; nationally, complete sets sold through hobby dealers.

HISTORY
Co-sponsored by Coca-Cola and Brigham's ice cream stores and produced by Topps, this 22-card issue of the Boston Red Sox was distributed at soda shops in 3-card cello packs with a purchase of Coke or ice cream. An advertising "header" card in

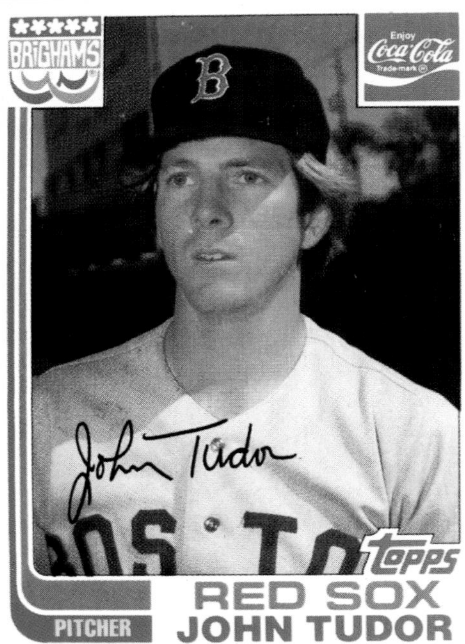

1982 Coke-Brigham's Red Sox, John Tudor

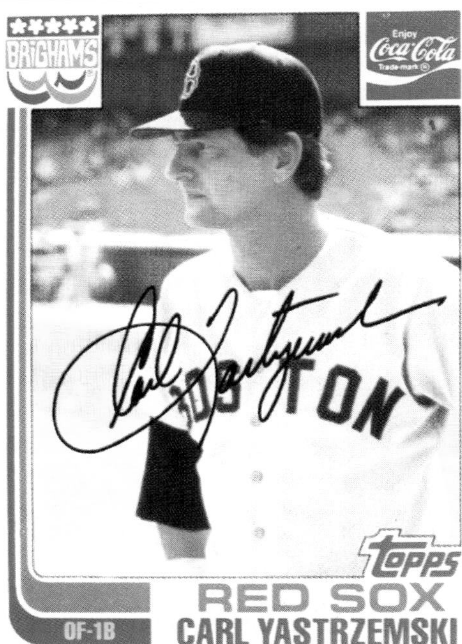

1982 Coke-Brigham's Red Sox, Carl Yastrzemski

each pack offered uncut sheets of 1982 Topps cards. It was another case where a large portion of what was supposed to be a regional issue was diverted to dealers. The set soon became widely available through hobby channels. The photos on the cards, as well as the basic design, are the same as the regular-issue 1982 Topps cards. On the front, a Brigham's logo in the upper left and a Coca-Cola logo in the upper right are the only discernible differences. (Some collectors, however, say the printing and color quality on these cards is superior to the regular '82 Topps cards.) On the back, the color scheme has been changed from green and blue to red and black. Card numbers were also changed, and are presented alphabetically. Brigham's and Coke logos also appear on the back.

FOR

The set offers variety for Red Sox collectors. Plus, the cards are from Topps.

AGAINST

They're not different enough to excite most collectors.

NOTEWORTHY CARDS

The big-name players are Jim Rice and Carl Yastrzemski.

VALUE

MINT CONDITION: Complete set, \$5; common card, 5¢; Rice, \$1; Yaz, \$2. 5-YEAR PROJECTION: Above average.

1982 COCA-COLA REDS

SPECIFICATIONS

SIZE: 2½ × 3½″. FRONT: Color photograph. BACK: Red and black printing on gray cardboard. DISTRIBUTION: Cincinnati, three cards in cartons of Coke.

1982 Coca-Cola Reds, Johnny Bench

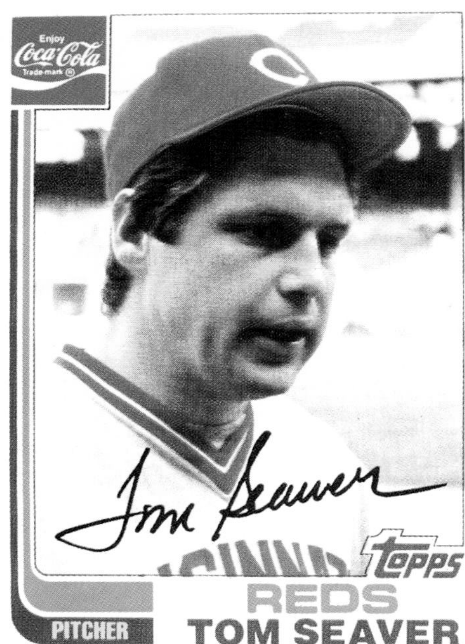

1982 Coca-Cola Reds, Tom Seaver

HISTORY

In contrast to the 1981 Coke cards, the '82 issue was a true regional set, produced by Topps for distribution in the Cincinnati area with soda purchases. The 22 player cards all feature Cincinnati Reds. A "header" advertising card, which was distributed with each cello pack of three player cards, offered uncut sheets of Topps cards. While the design of the 1982 Coke Reds is virtually identical to the regular '82 Topps set, seven of the cards feature different photos. Six of those players (including Cesar Cedeno) were traded to the Reds and appear in the regular '82 Topps set in different uniforms, while Paul Householder appeared in the 1982 Topps set on a "Reds Future Stars" card. Otherwise, the only difference on the card front is the addition of a Coke logo in the upper corner. On the back, rather than the green and blue of the regular Topps issue, the printing is in red and black. There is a Coke logo and trademark information on the back. The cards are numbered alphabetically.

FOR

Few collectors realize how scarce this regional set is. Once they do, expect prices to rise.

AGAINST

The design and most of the photos are too similar to the '82 Topps regular issue to attract most collectors.

NOTEWORTHY CARDS

The 1982 Coke Reds contain regional cards of Tom Seaver and Johnny Bench.

VALUE

MINT CONDITION: Complete set, $5; common card, 5¢; Seaver, Bench, $1.50. 5-YEAR PROJECTION: Above average.

1981 TOPPS

SPECIFICATIONS

SIZE: 2½ × 3½". FRONT: Color photograph. BACK: Red and black printing on gray cardboard. DISTRIBUTION: Nationally, in packages with bubblegum.

HISTORY

For the first time in years, Topps faced major competition in the baseball card market. The 1981 Topps set contained 726 cards and because the set was printed in six sheets of 132 cards each, there were again 66 double-printed cards. (Each sheet featured one row of 11 cards that was printed twice, making those cards twice as common as the others.) Among the double-printed cards are Mike Schmidt and the rookie card of Rich Dotson. Topps changed the design of the 1981 cards substantially from '80. The front of the card features a large photo of the player, surrounded by a thin border in team-coded colors. In the lower left is a large

1981 Topps, Mike Schmidt

1981 Topps, Tom Seaver

1981 Topps, 1980 Home Run Leaders

cartoon baseball cap in team colors containing the player's team and position. In the lower right is a small baseball bearing the Topps logo (which was not included in the 1980 card design). A white border surrounds the entire card. The card backs feature complete major and minor league year-by-year stats, along with a headline and/or cartoon panel highlighting some aspect of the player's career, if there was room. The first six cards in the set feature statistical leaders of the 1980 season. Record-breakers of the previous season are also highlighted in a special subset of cards, as are the 1980 playoffs and World Series. Team photo cards are included in the set for the last time, with the manager's photo in the upper right and a team checklist on the back. Once again, three "Future Stars" of each team share a card.

FOR

Topps used a simple and attractive design for their 1981 set.

AGAINST

After a year without featuring its logo on the front of the card—but faced with national competition for the first time since 1963—Topps once again added its name to the front. Most collectors feel these logos are an unnecessary design element that clutters the card. Because of competition from Fleer and Donruss, the 1981 Topps cards were issued earlier than ever before, making their appearance in some areas prior to the first of the year. This meant that few postseason trades were reflected in the issue, setting the stage for the first of the Topps' Traded sets.

NOTEWORTHY CARDS

There is a bonanza of rookie cards, including Fernando Valenzuela, Kirk Gibson, Leon Durham, Harold Baines, Mike Boddicker, Hubie Brooks and Mookie Wilson, Tim Raines, Tony Pena, and Lloyd Moseby.

VALUE

MINT CONDITION: Complete set, $80; common card, 5¢; superstars, 50¢–$2; Baines, Gibson, $4; Valenzuela, $8; Raines, $9. 5-YEAR PROJECTION: Above average.

1981 TOPPS TRADED

SPECIFICATIONS

SIZE: 2½ × 3½". FRONT: Color photograph. BACK: Red and black printing on gray cardboard. DISTRIBUTION: Nationally, complete sets sold through hobby dealers.

HISTORY

Faced with its first major competition since 1963, Topps scrambled for a competitive edge in 1981. They found it in their Traded set. Unlike subsequent years (when Traded sets had a "T" designation and featured different color printing on the back), the '81 Traded series was a real extension of the 726-card regular issue. The 132 cards in the Traded set are numbered from 727 to 858 and feature a back design identical to the rest of the 1981 issue. For this reason, many collectors think of these cards as the "high numbers" of the '81 set (the first high-number series since Topps began issuing its cards all at one time in 1973). Rather than packaging the cards in gum packs,

1981 Topps Traded, Rollie Fingers

1981 Topps Traded, Tim Raines

Topps boxed the 132-card set in a red carton and made it available only through baseball card dealers. This infuriated many collectors because the price was quite high in comparison to the regular 1981 cards. The regular cards could be bought for about 2¢ each in gum packs, while the 132-card Traded set was priced at around $9 (about 7¢ a card). Still, it was a good investment; two years later the set was selling in the $14 range, an increase of about 25 percent. Even though some collectors disliked the set, many praised it as being the only way that a player could be pictured in his current team's uniform after a mid-season trade. In addition, the Traded set gave the season's newest phenoms a card of their own to replace the "Future Stars" card they had earlier shared with two teammates.

FOR

As the years pass, collectors are going to forget that these cards were separately issued. They are, after all, in the same style as the rest of the '81 Topps set, and are consecutively numbered. Issued in far fewer numbers than the regular Topps cards of 1981, these cards will continue to be scarce and demand will increase as future collectors seek "complete" 1981 sets. The issue features a large number of stars and hot rookies.

AGAINST

Some collectors are never going to give the Traded set their stamp of approval. They feel that if a card set isn't available to the general public, it is only a "collector's issue," even if Topps' name is on it and the cards are consecutively numbered.

NOTEWORTHY CARDS

The single-player rookie cards of Danny Ainge (who opted for a pro basketball career), Fernando Valenzuela, Tim Raines, and Leon Durham are important in this set. So are cards of superstars in their "new" 1981 uniforms: Dave Winfield, Gaylord Perry, Rollie Fingers, Don Sutton, Ted Simmons, Fred Lynn, Greg Luzinski, Carlton Fisk, Bruce Sutter, and Joe Morgan.

VALUE

MINT CONDITION: Complete set, $24; common card, 10¢; hot rookies, 75¢–$1.25; Valenzuela, $5.50; Raines, $7. 5-YEAR PROJECTION: Above average.

1981 TOPPS 5 × 7s

SPECIFICATIONS

SIZE: 4⅞ × 6⅞". FRONT: Color photograph. BACK: Blue printing on white cardboard. DISTRIBUTION: Regionally, in cello packs; nationally, complete sets available through a mail-in offer.

HISTORY

For the second straight year, Topps test-marketed baseball cards in the 5 × 7" format, and again they found only limited success. Two different themes were attempted. The first consisted of 102 cards

1981 Topps 5x7s, Steve Carlton

offered as "Home Team Photos." These cards featured a large color photo on the front bordered in white, and a facsimile autograph. The backs had the player's name, team, and position; and at the bottom, a box with the checklist for the cards in that "home team" area. The cards were sold in the hometowns of the eleven teams included in the issue. In some cities, only one team was included: the Cincinnati Reds, Boston Red Sox, and Philadelphia Phillies sets included 12 cards each. In other areas, two teams were included in the "home team" set. In the New York area, the set contained 12 Yankees and six Mets; in Chicago, nine Cubs and nine White Sox; in Southern California, 12 Dodgers and six Angels; and in Texas, six Astros and six Rangers. A mail-in offer on the cellophane packaging offered complete team sets. The second oversize issue by Topps in '81 is known to collectors as the "National Photo Issue." The 15 cards in this group were sold in areas not served by the Home Team sets. The cards were essentially the same in format but did not have a checklist on the back. Ten of the cards in the "National" issue were the same photos found in the Home Team set, but there are five additional players in the national set: George Brett, Cecil Cooper, Jim Palmer, Dave Parker, and Ted Simmons. The issue was widely distributed among dealers and was not particularly scarce or in strong demand.

FOR
These large-format cards are appealing to superstar or team collectors.

AGAINST
Many collectors will not buy oversize cards.

NOTEWORTHY CARDS
Many of the cards in the issue are better-known stars and superstars.

VALUE
MINT CONDITION: Complete set of 117 cards, $42; common card, 20¢; superstars, 50¢–$2. 5-YEAR PROJECTION: Average.

1981 FLEER

SPECIFICATIONS
SIZE: 2½ × 3½″. FRONT: Color photograph. BACK: Yellow and black printing on white cardboard. DISTRIBUTION: Nationally, in packages with bubblegum.

HISTORY
Twenty years of court battles came to an end in 1980 when a Pennsylvania court ruled that Topps Gum Company did not have exclusive rights to market baseball cards with bubblegum. This ruling opened the door for the Fleer Company of Philadelphia to make its own contracts with major league baseball and the Players Association. In 1981, for the first time in 18 years, Fleer produced a set of baseball cards featuring current players. Throughout the '70s, Fleer had produced a number of baseball card sets, but they did not feature current players or photos of old-timers. They featured drawings by Robert Laughlin and were incorporated in such sets as "World Series Highlights" and "All-Star Games." They were sold

1981 Fleer, Mike Schmidt/Pete Rose/Larry Bowa

1981 Fleer, Ed Figueroa

1981 Fleer, Graig Nettles

with bubblegum, but were not popular with kids or collectors. The 1981 Fleer set, on the other hand, was a hit with both groups and Fleer has been a major force in the hobby ever since. Fleer's '81 set is widely known for the large number of errors and variations. Most collectors feel the set is complete at 660 cards, while others attempt to acquire each of the variations (an additional 40 cards) for a total of 700. The 1981 Fleer set was produced in three separate press runs. The first contains all of the error cards, while the second and third printings were undertaken to correct those errors. The range of Fleer error and variation cards in 1981 is too broad to describe here; a detailed checklist is necessary. For its first current-player set since 1963, Fleer came up with the reasonable idea of grouping the players by team and numbering them consecutively. The order of teams was determined by the team's winning percentage of the previous season. Thus, the first 27 cards in the set are of the 1980 World Champion Philadelphia Phillies. The next 23 cards are the American League pennant-winning Kansas City Royals. There are some exceptions, but by and large this system was followed closely. Besides the regular players' cards, there were a number of specialty cards in the set, most of them being second poses of superstars with titles like "Mr. Baseball" (Reggie Jackson) and "Home Run King" (Mike Schmidt). There are 15 numbered checklists in the series: 14 detail the listings of two teams each, and one lists the specialty cards. The set includes one multiplayer card (called "Triple Threat") featuring Mike Schmidt, Pete Rose, and Larry Bowa. The design is clean and attractive. The player photo on the front of the card has round corners and is surrounded by a colored stripe (generally the same color for each player on a given team). At the lower left the team name is printed in script inside a baseball. The player's name and position are printed in a yellow panel below the photo. A white border surrounds the whole card. The card back has a gray border, and a large white panel at center gives complete major and minor league stats on a year-by-year basis. This panel is surrounded by a round-cornered yellow frame with the title "Complete Major and Minor League Batting Record" (even on the pitchers' cards). This is one error in the Fleer set that was not corrected on any of the print runs. Below the stats are a few bits of the player's personal data. His name, team, and position appear in a black panel at the top of the card. To the left is the card number in a white circle, while a corresponding circle at the right has the player's cumulative major league batting average, or in the case of pitchers, earned run average. Despite the problems with errors and variations and the fact that the photography is not as good as Topps', the set has remained popular with collectors.

FOR

You've got to give Fleer credit for breaking Topps' virtual monopoly in the baseball card market. This set was a commendable effort. The error and variation cards are not expensive and they make an interesting challenge.

AGAINST

Most collectors are not interested in a lot of error cards, and such cards reflect poorly on the issuer. Overall, the photography on the '81 Fleer set is not as sharp as that of its principal competition.

NOTEWORTHY CARDS

The most notable card in the 1981 Fleer set is the first error card to be discovered and corrected, even before the first printing had been completed. Thus, it is also the scarcest and most expensive of the set. The error occurs on the back of Yankee third baseman Graig Nettles' card, which spells his name "Craig." The corrected version is far more common. Among the more than three dozen other variations in the set, those most likely to prove collectible down the road include the following: Kurt Bevacqua (#382), whose card shows a backward "P" on his Pirates cap due to a reversed negative (this was later corrected); on Tim Flannery's card (#493), a similar flopped negative shows him batting righthanded on the error card, lefthanded on the corrected version; the photo on card #514 is actually Billy Travers, though it is identified as Jerry Augustine (the card's front and back were corrected in the second printing); Pete Vuckovich's card (#547) actually shows Don Hood; and the Triple Threat card (#645) can be found both with and without the card number on the back.

VALUE

MINT CONDITION: Complete set (without variations), $24; common card, 3¢; stars, 25¢–$2; Valenzuela rookie card, $2; "C" Nettles, $12.
5-YEAR PROJECTION: Average.

1981 FLEER STAR STICKERS

SPECIFICATIONS

SIZE: 2½ × 3½". FRONT: Color photograph. BACK: Black and yellow printing on white cardboard. DISTRIBUTION: Nationally, in packages with bubblegum.

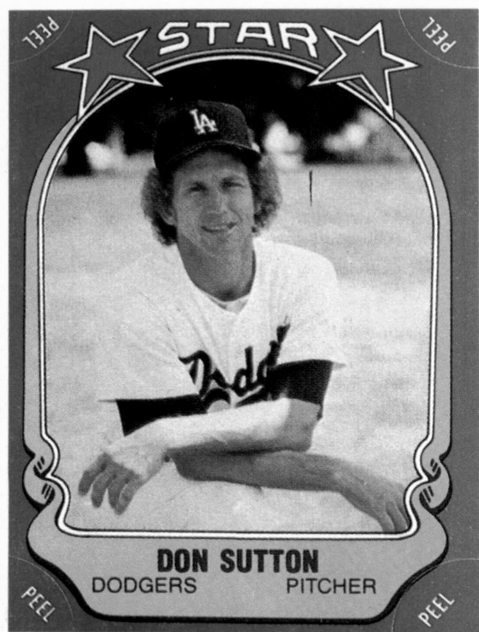

1981 Fleer Star Stickers, Don Sutton

1981 Fleer Star Stickers, Fred Lynn

HISTORY

Not content to publish only one baseball card set in 1981, Fleer came out with a subsidiary issue called "Star Stickers." Unlike other baseball stickers and stamps of the early '80s, the 1981 Fleer issue was in the standard 2½ × 3½″ format that card collectors have come to favor. There are 125 different player cards in the 128-sticker set. The three checklists that complete the set have sticker fronts of Reggie Jackson, Mike Schmidt, and George Brett. The photos and design of the Star Stickers are different from Fleer's regular '81 issue. The photo has an ornate yellow frame, surrounded by a deep blue border. Thumb notches at the corners (marked "Peel") facilitate stripping the sticky-backed picture from the cardboard. Stickers that have been separated are worth nothing to collectors. The card backs were identical to the backs of the regular Fleer set except for a change in card numbers.

FOR

These were produced in relatively limited quantities and are not that common today. If demand ever picks up, the value of the '81 Fleer stickers could rise rapidly, perhaps more rapidly than Fleer's regular 1981 issue.

AGAINST

Many hobbyists do not collect stickers and stamps. Most feel that "real" cards shouldn't do anything like stick to other objects.

NOTEWORTHY CARDS

Most of the 125 players in the '81 Fleer sticker set are stars (or at least minor stars). There is a "Triple Threat" sticker with Pete Rose, Mike Schmidt, and Larry Bowa.

VALUE

MINT CONDITION: Complete set, $45; common card, 20¢; stars 50¢–$3; Rose, $5. 5-YEAR PROJECTION: Average, perhaps a bit above.

1981 DONRUSS

SPECIFICATIONS

SIZE: 2½ × 3½″. FRONT: Color photograph. BACK: Black and red printing on white cardboard. DISTRIBUTION: Nationally, in packs with bubblegum.

HISTORY

Donruss immediately took advantage of Fleer's victory over Topps, which allowed competitors to market baseball cards with bubblegum. Donruss entered the 1981 "Card Wars" with a set of 605 cards. The effort was Donruss' first major sports card project, though the company had previously marketed nonsports cards with its bubblegum products and would continue to do so. The premier Donruss baseball card effort was not particularly well received by collectors. The cards were printed on very thin cardboard, making them susceptible to damage. The color reproduction was not the greatest; many white players looked like they were

1981 Donruss, Gaylord Perry

1981 Donruss, Joe Charboneau

1981 Donruss, Mike Schmidt

sunburnt, while many blacks had a purplish tint. Donruss also had difficulty sorting the cards in packs and boxes; collectors often complained of getting two or more of the same card in a single pack or handfuls of the same card in a single box. (Not bad if you're getting Pete Rose or the latest rookie phenom, but nobody wants to find two or more common cards in their wax pack.) More importantly, the 1981 Donruss set is noted for having more than three dozen variations. The Donruss cards exhibited virtually every kind of error to which baseball cards are prone. There were wrong photos, reversed negatives, misspelled names, incorrect statistics, rewritten biographies, etc. There are so many errors that collectors need a detailed checklist to keep track of them. In all, 38 player-card errors and four of the five unnumbered checklists were corrected in a second print run. While first run errors are generally the scarcest, few command any substantial premium. Some of them, like the wrong or reversed photos, will probably attain higher value in the future, but most will remain curiosities. Donruss did a few things right in 1981. They reintroduced the idea of multiplayer feature cards, which had last been seen in a Topps set in 1969. Card #537 ("Best Hitters") featured George Brett and Rod Carew. Donruss also featured more than one card for superstars like Pete Rose, Reggie Jackson, and Steve Garvey. There were special cards for 1980 MVPs George Brett and Mike Schmidt, and for Cy Young Award winners Steve Carlton and Steve Stone. Overall, the design of the 1981 Donruss cards was attractive. A large color photo dominates the card, surrounded by thin black-and-white lines and then a thick colored line, with a white border all around. A Donruss logo and the year '81 appear in the upper left, and the team name is in heavy shadowed type in the lower right. The player's name and position appear on a single line at the bottom. The back of the 1981 Donruss is a departure from what Topps had been doing. Vertical in format, it features previous season and lifetime stats. Most of the back is devoted to a "Career Highlights" section, presented chronologically. The usual personal data appears such as full name, birthplace, residence, height, and weight. Also included is a card number and a large design at the top incorporating another Donruss logo, bats, a ball, banners, and other elements, plus a line declaring "First Edition Collector Series." Many of the photos in the set were taken at Chicago's two major league parks, Wrigley Field and Comiskey Park.

FOR

Overall, it is an attractive premier effort for a new baseball card company.

AGAINST

The card stock is too thin, which makes the card easily damaged. Lots of error cards create confusion. The photo reproduction is not the best.

NOTEWORTHY CARDS

All the big stars are in the set, along with rookie cards of Cal Ripken Jr., Tim Raines, and Kirk Gibson.

VALUE

MINT CONDITION: Complete set (without variations), $25; common card, 3¢; stars, 25¢–$1; Rose, $1.50; Raines, $5; Ripken, $9. 5-YEAR PROJECTION: Average.

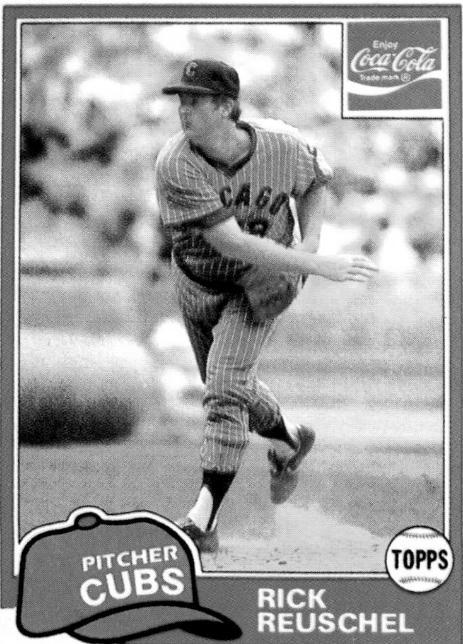

1981 Coca-Cola, Rick Reuschel

1981 Coca-Cola, Bill Buckner

1981 COCA-COLA

SPECIFICATIONS

SIZE: 2½×3½". FRONT: Color photograph. BACK: Black and red printing on gray cardboard. DISTRIBUTION: Regionally, in cartons of Coke; nationally, complete sets sold through hobby dealers.

HISTORY

Intended as a premium with the purchase of Coca-Cola, the 132 cards in the 1981 Coke set (produced by Topps) rarely reached the store shelves. Dealers and collectors bought up most of the supply from distributors and put them directly into hobby channels. Eleven teams are represented in the issue, and each team has 11 player cards and a "header" card. The back of the header card offered collectors a chance to buy uncut sheets of regular '81 Topps cards for $4. This was the first time uncut sheets of a major baseball card set were made available to collectors. The 11 teams represented in the '81 Coke issue are the Astros, Cardinals, Cubs, Mets, Phillies, Pirates, Reds, Red Sox, Royals, Tigers, and White Sox. The cards are virtually identical to the regular Topps cards of 1981. The principal difference on the front is the red and white Coke logo found in either the upper left or right. The card back is the same as the regular set except for the card number, a Coke logo instead of the Topps logo, and the Coca-Cola trademark information on the bottom of the card. Because so many of these cards were bought in cases by dealers, they are quite common for what would otherwise have been a regional issue. However, some teams are scarcer than others. The '81 Coke cards are usually sold in team sets, rather than as a complete set of 132.

FOR

These "regional" cards are scarcer variations of a major national issue.

AGAINST

The cards are too common to have much status as a real regional issue. The use of the same photos as on regular '81 Topps cards gives collectors little incentive to acquire them.

NOTEWORTHY CARDS

Because only 11 players per team were chosen, they are generally better-known players and stars.

VALUE

MINT CONDITION: Complete set, $17; common card, 5¢; superstars, 25¢–$2. 5-YEAR PROJECTION: Above average.

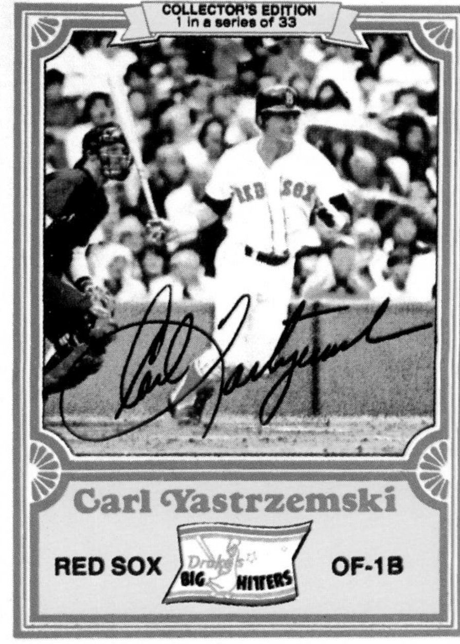

1981 Drake's, Carl Yastrzemski

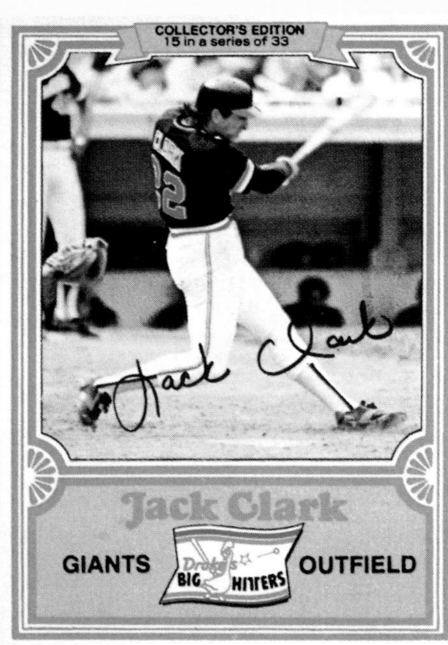

1981 Drake's, Jack Clark

1981 DRAKE'S

SPECIFICATIONS

SIZE: 2½ × 3½". FRONT: Color photograph. BACK: Black and red printing on gray cardboard. DISTRIBUTION: Northeastern U.S., in packages of bakery products; nationally, complete sets sold through hobby dealers.

HISTORY

A lot of collectors and dealers got stung with early purchases of Drake's 33-card "Big Hitters Collector's Edition." The cards (produced by Topps) were originally inserted in family-size boxes of snack cakes in the Northeast section of the country. Because 1981 was the first big year for regional card issues in a long time, most collectors and dealers assumed that the cards could only be obtained by buying the product. Then Drake's wholesaled huge quantities to dealers. Collectors who had been paying $8 for the set in early summer found the sets for $2 by late autumn. (Drake's continued the policy of wholesaling cards within the hobby in subsequent issues, but by then collectors knew better than to pay big money for sets that had been collected from bakery boxes.) The set is innovative and features well-known hitting stars (both for average and power). The card front features a game-action picture showing the player at bat. The photo has a facsimile autograph across it and is framed in a gaudy series of borders, panels, and banners. The predominant color scheme on the American League cards is red and yellow. On National League cards it is blue. A large panel below the photo has the player's name, team, and position, and a pennant with the Drake's logo. There is a card number at the top in a yellow banner. The card back is quite similar to the regular 1981 Topps cards except for the Drake's logo, a new card number, and a batting tip, "What Makes a Big Hitter," at the top of the card. The '81 Drake's set represented a return to the baseball card market for the bakery. The company had issued a 36-card set in 1950 that has become quite valuable.

FOR

The set features different poses of lots of stars on a set that is, at least nominally, a regional issue.

AGAINST

Drake's cards still suffer from the fact that many collectors paid too much in their haste to get them. The design is a bit too loud.

NOTEWORTHY CARDS

The 1980 A.L. Rookie of the Year, Joe Charboneau, is included.

VALUE

MINT CONDITION: Complete set, \$6; common card, 5¢; superstars, 50¢–75¢; Pete Rose, \$1.
5-YEAR PROJECTION: Average.

1981 KELLOGG'S

SPECIFICATIONS

SIZE: 2½ × 3½". FRONT: Color photograph, 3-D effect. BACK: Black printing on white cardboard. DISTRIBUTION: Nationally, complete sets available through a mail-in offer.

HISTORY

There were several significant changes in the Kellogg's baseball card set for 1981. For the first time, the cards were produced in the 2½ × 3½" format that has been the standard for baseball cards since 1957. Also for the first time, the cards were not packaged individually in boxes of cereal; collectors had to mail in two box tops and \$3.95 to receive the complete set. At 66 cards, it was the largest set since 1971. A color photo on the front is surrounded by a yellow frame with red stars. A white border frames the whole card. A sheet of finely ribbed plastic is used to create the three-dimensional effect. This effect is obtained by setting a sharp photo of the player against an indistinct stadium background. Kellogg's used the expanded size of the card to greatly increase the biographical and career data on the back of the card. There is a cartoon figure of Tony the Tiger, along with logos for the player's team, the Major League Baseball Players Association, and Major League Baseball. The change to a wider card seems to have solved the old problem of curling and cracking.

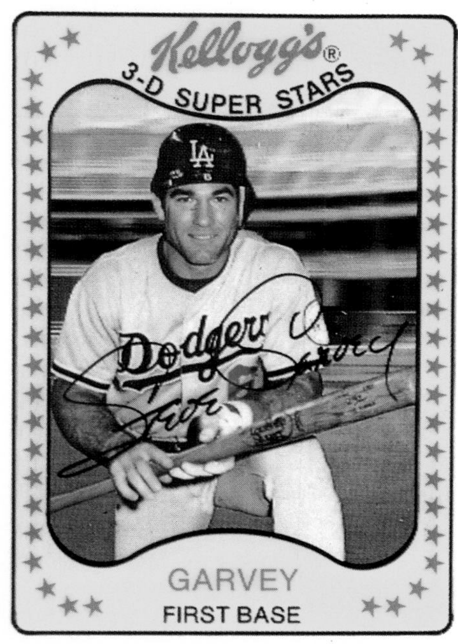

1981 Kellogg's, Steve Garvey

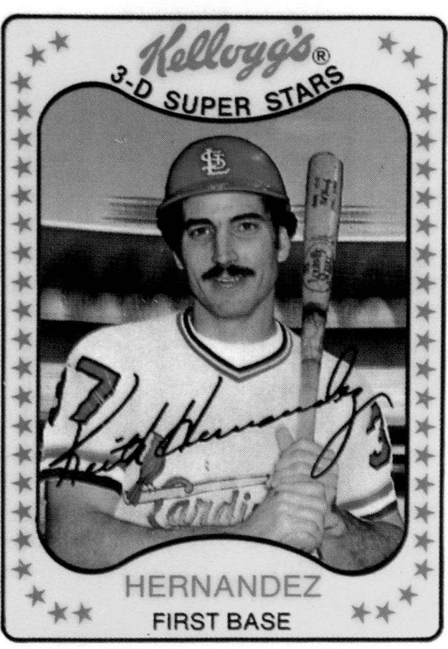

1981 Kellogg's, Keith Hernandez

1981 Kellogg's, George Brett

1981 Kellogg's, Rod Carew

FOR

The cards were finally issued in the standard size. There is no problem with curling or cracking cards.

AGAINST

Since the '81s were only available as complete sets, it is hard to buy single cards, as few dealers want to break up sets.

NOTEWORTHY CARDS

Most of the big names are here, along with a lot of regular stars.

VALUE

MINT CONDITION: Complete set, $9; common card, 6¢; stars, 25¢–90¢; Rose, $1. 5-YEAR PROJECTION: Average.

1981 SQUIRT

SPECIFICATIONS

SIZE: Single card, 2½ × 3½"; panel, 2½ × 10½". FRONT: Color photograph. BACK: Black and red printing on gray cardboard. DISTRIBUTION: Nationally, one 2-card panel in cartons of soda.

HISTORY

In 1981, Squirt soda joined more than a dozen other companies who had issued baseball cards in an attempt to boost sales. The soft-drink maker had the right idea—getting Topps to print the cards—but the whole program fell through on the retail level. One 2-card panel with a ring tab at top was supposed to be found hanging on six- and eight-packs of soda. However, the cards seldom found their way to the store shelves. Instead, soda distributors sold the cards to local dealers and collectors. If by chance the distributor didn't, the individual retailer did. The net result was that collectors saved a lot of money. Rather than having to buy 22 cartons of Squirt at $1.50 to $2 apiece, collectors could pick up the complete set from dealers for $6 to $8. The 1981 Squirt set consists of 33 different player cards, available in 22 different panel combinations. Cards #1-#11, generally the big-name stars, were each paired with two different cards. The cards were perforated for easy separation, but separating the cards lessened their value. Buyers seem to want the 1981 Squirt issue only as two-card panels.

FOR

They're cheap considering they're "real" Topps cards and virtually every player featured is a big name. They're not as common as you'd think.

AGAINST

They're too gaudy for most collectors. The way dealers acquired the cards left a bad impression on many hobbyists.

NOTEWORTHY CARDS

Virtually every player in the 1981 Squirt set is a star, or was in 1981. The set contains a card of Joe Charboneau, who was Rookie of the Year in the A.L. that year. He vanished from major league baseball two years later.

VALUE

MINT CONDITION: Complete set of panels, $15; complete set of single cards, $9; common card, 20¢. 5-YEAR PROJECTION: Average.

1981 GRANNY GOOSE A'S

SPECIFICATIONS

SIZE: 2½ × 3½". FRONT: Color photograph. BACK: Black printing on white cardboard. DISTRIBUTION: Northern California, single cards in packages of potato chips.

HISTORY

A classic example of a modern regional set, the 15-card Granny Goose Oakland A's issue was found in bags of potato chips, one card per bag. Cards were not available to dealers or collectors. Since the cards were included only in large-size bags of chips (at $1.20 a bag), it was an expensive set to collect. One dealer actually bought a truckload of chips, opened each bag to get the card, and then gave the chips away. It was not an unprofitable venture. He sold the common cards later at $5.75 apiece, and star cards for $8 to $12 each. The rare Dave Revering card sold for $79. The card front features a large color photo of the player surrounded by a white border. Below the photo is a green box containing the player's name, uniform number, and position in yellow letters. A green and yellow A's logo appears in the lower left. The card back has a short write-up of the player's 1980 season performance, a few vital stats, and another A's logo. The cards are numbered by the player's uniform number, which appears on the front and back. The Granny Goose cards are printed on thin cardboard and are easily damaged. Because they were packaged with potato chips, most of the cards picked up grease stains that detract from their appearance. Naturally, cards without stains are worth more.

1981 Granny Goose A's, Billy Martin

1981 Granny Goose A's, Jeff Newman

FOR

This is a truly scarce regional issue.

AGAINST

It is hard to find Mint cards. The scarcity of the cards makes it an expensive set.

NOTEWORTHY CARDS

Although Rickey Henderson and manager Billy Martin are the stars of the set, their cards are not the most valuable. That honor goes to the Dave Revering card. In true regional set fashion, the Revering card was withdrawn from distribution when he was traded to the Yankees in mid-May. His card is one of the rarest of the 1980s.

VALUE

MINT CONDITION: Complete set, $85; common card, $1; Martin, $8; Henderson, $20; Revering, $45. 5-YEAR PROJECTION: Below average.

1981 BRAVES POLICE

SPECIFICATIONS

SIZE: 2⅝ × 4⅛″. FRONT: Color photograph. BACK: Color printing on white cardboard. DISTRIBUTION: Atlanta, individual cards given out by police officers.

1981 Braves Police, Dale Murphy

HISTORY

The 27-card Atlanta Braves Police set of 1981 was co-sponsored by local Coca-Cola and Hostess distributors, whose color logos appear on the back of the cards. The card front features a color portrait photo of the player surrounded by a wide white border. An Atlanta Police Athletic League logo appears in the upper left and, for some reason, there is a green bow in the upper right. The Braves logo appears in the lower right, while the player's name, uniform number, position, height, and weight are printed in the lower left. The back features a sentence about the player and a safety or anti-crime tip. Like other police sets, the '81 Braves cards were intended to be given away to kids by police officers in the hope of better rapport.

FOR

The green bow makes this set the perfect Christmas gift.

AGAINST

For purposes other than gift-giving, the green bow is extraneous. The cardboard is too thin.

NOTEWORTHY CARDS

The Terry Harper card is the scarcest card in the set. Stars include Dale Murphy, Phil Niekro, Bob Horner, Gaylord Perry, and coach Hank Aaron.

VALUE

MINT CONDITION: Complete set, $12; common card, 3¢; stars, 50¢–$2.50; Murphy, $3. 5-YEAR PROJECTION: Above average.

1981 DODGERS POLICE

SPECIFICATIONS

SIZE: 2¹³⁄₁₆ × 4⅛″. FRONT: Color photograph. BACK: Blue printing on white cardboard. DISTRIBUTION: Los Angeles, individual cards given out by police officers; complete sets given out at a promotional game.

HISTORY

The 32-card Los Angeles Dodgers Police set used the same basic format introduced a year earlier. In addition to the individual players' cards, there is a card for manager Tommy Lasorda, a group coaches card, and one for the entire team. The card features a color photo on the front, surrounded by a wide

1981 Dodgers Police, Coaches

white border. The player's name, position, and uniform number (which is also the card number) appear under the photo, along with a dateline and a Dodgers logo. The card back contains a miniature LAPD badge at the bottom along with a safety tip ostensibly written by the player. These cards are quite common because complete sets were given away at a special promotional game in addition to being distributed by police officers.

FOR

Good photos mark this police set.

AGAINST

This issue is an odd size.

NOTEWORTHY CARDS

The cards of Ken Landreaux and Dave Stewart are somewhat scarcer than rest. The set includes the rookie card of Fernando Valenzuela.

VALUE

MINT CONDITION: Complete set, $10; common card, 25¢; stars, 50¢–$1.50; Valenzuela, $3. 5-YEAR PROJECTION: Average.

1981 MARINERS POLICE

SPECIFICATIONS

SIZE: 2⅝ × 4⅛″. FRONT: Color photograph. BACK: Red and blue printing on white cardboard. DISTRIBUTION: Seattle, individual cards given out by police officers.

1981 Mariners Police, Maury Wills

HISTORY

The only Seattle Mariners Police issue, this set contains 16 cards and was co-sponsored by local Kiwanis, the Washington State Crime Prevention Association, Coca-Cola, and Ernst Home Centers, all of whose logos appear on the back of the card. The back also has a card number and a safety or anti-crime message called "Tips From the Mariners." The front of the card uses the usual police set format: a large color photo with a wide white border. A colored border surrounding the photo reduces the white space somewhat. The player's name and position appear below the photo with a team logo at bottom.

FOR

Because it was a one-year set, it is more desirable to team collectors.

AGAINST
There are only 15 players represented, so it is not a true "team" set.

NOTEWORTHY CARDS
Manager Maury Wills is the biggest name in the group.

VALUE
MINT CONDITION: Complete set, $5; common card, 30¢; stars, 75¢. 5-YEAR PROJECTION: Average.

1981 ROYALS POLICE

SPECIFICATIONS
SIZE: 2½ × 4⅛". FRONT: Color photograph. BACK: Dark blue printing on white cardboard. DISTRIBUTION: Fort Myers, Florida, individual cards given out by police officers.

1981 Royals Police, George Brett

HISTORY
At only ten cards, this is the smallest modern major league police set. The Royals set was distributed by the Ft. Myers Police Department in conjunction with a local bank and a trucking company. (The Royals conduct spring training in the Ft. Myers area.) The card front follows the tried-and-true format of a color photo surrounded by a wide white border. There is a facsimile autograph on the face of the card, along with a team logo, and the player's name, position, and personal data. The cards are unnumbered. The card back is unusual in that it contains recent stats for the player, along with a safety message and sponsors' logos.

FOR
It is an unusual set for team collectors.

AGAINST
With only ten players, the set is too small to be a true "team" set.

NOTEWORTHY CARDS
The biggest names are George Brett and Willie Wilson.

VALUE
MINT CONDITION: Complete set, $28; common card, 75¢–$1; Wilson, $5; Brett, $13. 5-YEAR PROJECTION: Average.

1980 TOPPS

SPECIFICATIONS
SIZE: 2½ × 3½". FRONT: Color photograph. BACK: Black and blue printing on gray cardboard. DISTRIBUTION: Nationally, in packages with bubblegum.

1980 Topps, George Foster

1980 Topps, Don Sutton

1980 Topps, Dave Parker

HISTORY

Topps stuck with tradition in its last year of issuing a national card set unchallenged by competitors. The basic design is quite close to the 1974 issue. A round-cornered photo is surrounded by a colored border in a white frame. Colored pennants cover the upper-left and lower-right corners of the photo. The flag at the top carries the player's position with his name to the right in the white border. The pennant at the bottom contains the team name. Unlike every year since 1979, the Topps logo does not appear on the front of the card. There is a facsimile autograph across the face of the card. Card backs have the usual mix of major league stats, personal info, a few headlines about the player's best performances, and a cartoon of the player. The Topps set for 1980 again numbered 726 cards. Since Topps prints its cards on six sheets of 132 cards each, this meant that one row of 11 cards on each sheet was printed twice. Among the superstars who populate the '80 double-prints are Fred Lynn, Mike Schmidt, Rod Carew, and Carl Yastrzemski. The 1980 set includes a 7-card group of statistical leaders from the American and National Leagues in 1979. The most interesting card from this subset (#205) pictures brothers Joe and Phil Niekro, along with Mike Flanagan. Card #202 pictures league homer champs Dave Kingman and Gorman Thomas. Card #203 features league RBI leaders Dave Winfield and Don Baylor. The first subset features highlights of the previous season; for example, card #1 is of Lou Brock and Yaz entering the 3,000-hit club. Rookie "Future Stars" cards were in color this year and were again arranged by team, three players to a card.

FOR

The set represents a good value. The design is attractive, and it is a jumping off point for some collectors.

AGAINST

Not many negative comments can be made about this set; it's a typical Topps effort in the days before Fleer and Donruss became competitors.

NOTEWORTHY CARDS

Topps was known to use old photos on its team cards, but in the 1980 set they really reached for one, using a 1977 picture of the White Sox to represent the current year's team. The best rookie cards of 1980 weren't on the 3-player Future Stars cards; Rickey Henderson, Rick Sutcliffe, and Dave Stieb had their premier cards all to themselves. Among the team prospect cards, the big names are Mets Jesse Orosco and Mike Scott, Gary Ward of the Twins, Tom Herr of the Cardinals, Dickie Thon of the Astros, and Dan Quisenberry of the Royals.

VALUE

MINT CONDITION: Complete set, $140; common card, 9¢; superstars, $1–$5; Henderson, $30. 5-YEAR PROJECTION: Above average.

1980 TOPPS SUPERSTAR PHOTOS

SPECIFICATIONS

SIZE: 4⅞ × 6⅞″. FRONT: Color photograph. BACK: Black printing on gray or white cardboard. DISTRIBUTION: Regionally, test-marketed in different manners.

HISTORY

A recent example of how market hype can stimulate demand, the 1980 Topps "Superstar Photo" issue was apparently a test issue to determine the market for large-format cards. However, dealers quickly gobbled up available supplies and, as with many test issues, Topps never really had a chance to gauge demand in the youth market. The 60 cards (mostly stars and superstars) have an attractive white-bordered color photo on

1980 Topps Superstar Photos, Jim Rice

the front, with only a facsimile autograph in blue ink to identify the player. The card back has the player's name, team, position, and card number. The set was issued on two different cardboard stocks. The first issue is on thick white cardboard; the second is on thinner gray cardboard. The back of the latter version carries a large Topps logo at center. Six of the biggest names in the set were triple-printed, making them much more common than the remaining 54 cards, but no less valuable. There was an inclination in the hobby at the time of issue (and for a while thereafter) to price the supposedly scarcer "white backs" significantly higher than the "gray backs." This seems to have died down, and few collectors differentiate between the two versions or pay a large premium for either one of them.

FOR

Very attractive large-format photos of superstars at an extremely low price; cheaper by far than the regular issue Topps cards of the same year.

AGAINST

Dealers who are buried in these cards probably bought them at inflated prices and have been reluctant to sell at the prices collectors are willing to pay. This oversupply may persist for quite some time until the demand catches up with the supply.

VALUE

MINT CONDITION: Complete set, $6; common card, 7¢; stars, 35¢; superstars, 50¢–$1. 5-YEAR PROJECTION: Below average.

1980 Kellogg's, Johnny Bench

1980 Kellogg's, Rod Carew

1980 KELLOGG'S

SPECIFICATIONS

SIZE: 1⅞ × 3¼". FRONT: Color photograph, 3-D effect. BACK: Blue printing on white cardboard. DISTRIBUTION: Nationally, single cards in cereal boxes; complete sets through a mail-in offer.

HISTORY

The 1980 Kellogg's cards were a bit narrower than those of the previous year. A blue border with white enhancements surround the color photo on the front. A Kellogg's logo appears in red at the top, and the words "3-D Super Stars" is at the bottom. Diagonal yellow stripes at the upper left and lower right contain the player's position and last name. The 3-D effect is created by overlaying the photo with a piece of ribbed plastic. The card back contains personal and career stats, along with a team logo and the cartoon character from the cereal. The complete 60-card set could also be obtained by sending in box tops and cash.

FOR

The Kellogg's set is handsome and inexpensive, with room for value growth.

AGAINST

Most collectors don't like the narrow format. The plastic facing on the cards is prone to curling and cracking.

NOTEWORTHY CARDS

There is a high percentage of superstars and potential superstars in the set.

VALUE

MINT CONDITION: Complete set, $20; common card, 15¢; stars, $1–$3; Rose, $5. 5-YEAR PROJECTION: Above average.

1980 Burger King All-Stars, Rollie Fingers

1980 BURGER KING ALL-STARS

SPECIFICATIONS

SIZE: 2½ × 3½". FRONT: Color photograph. BACK: Blue and black printing on gray cardboard. DISTRIBUTION: Nationally, given away with food purchase at Burger King restaurants.

HISTORY

In 1980 Burger King and Topps finally produced a baseball card set that was available nationwide. It was known to many collectors as the "Pitch, Hit & Run" set, partly because of the Burger King advertising on the back of the cards. The set consists of 33 player cards and an unnumbered checklist card. There are three basic subsets of cards in this set: 11 each of well-known pitchers, hitters, and speedy runners and fielders. While the set is basically styled after the regular Topps issue of 1980, there are differences. The backs have a Burger King ad instead of a player cartoon, and the card numbers are different. On the card front the Burger King logo (for the first time ever) appears, along with the words "Collector's Series." Most of the photos used in the set are the same as those used in the 1980 Topps set, but a few have been changed. Since most of the players in this set are of All-Star caliber, the '80 Burger King Pitch, Hit & Run set is in demand by superstar collectors. The set is readily available due to stockpiling by collectors and dealers during the promotion.

1980 Burger King All-Stars, Joe Morgan

FOR

It's a real specialty set, with the Burger King logo to differentiate it from the regular Topps cards.

AGAINST

It's usually sold as a set and finding single cards of a particular player is difficult.

NOTEWORTHY CARDS

Almost all of the cards in the 1980 set are stars.

VALUE

MINT CONDITION: Complete set, $11; common card, 15¢; stars, 75¢–$2. 5-YEAR PROJECTION: Above average.

1980 BURGER KING PHILLIES

SPECIFICATIONS

SIZE: 2½ × 3½". FRONT: Color photograph. BACK: Blue and black printing on gray cardboard. DISTRIBUTION: Philadelphia, given away with food purchase at Burger King restaurants.

1980 Burger King Phillies, Dallas Green

HISTORY

The Phillies were the only team to have a special Burger King regional set produced by Topps in 1980 (although Burger King distributed an All-Star set nationally). This set has a Burger King logo on the back of the card to differentiate it from the regular 1980 Topps cards. Otherwise, except for the card numbers on back, the 23 Topps and Burger King cards were similar. Many sets were sold to hobby dealers, so they are plentiful, though certainly less numerous than their Topps counterparts.

FOR

The Burger King logo on back gives the cards a separate identity from the regular Topps issue.

AGAINST

There is nothing bad to say about the set.

NOTEWORTHY CARDS

Big-name Phillie stars of 1980 who appear in the Burger King team set are Pete Rose, Mike Schmidt, and Steve Carlton.

VALUE

MINT CONDITION: Complete set, $5.50; common card, 10¢–20¢; stars, 50¢–80¢; Carlton, $1.25; Schmidt, $2; Rose, $2.50. 5-YEAR PROJECTION: Average, or somewhat above.

1980 DODGERS POLICE

SPECIFICATIONS

SIZE: 2¹³⁄₁₆ × 4⅛". FRONT: Color photograph. BACK: Blue printing on white cardboard. DISTRIBUTION: Los Angeles, individual cards given out by police officers; complete sets given out at a special promotional game.

1980 Dodgers Police, Don Sutton

HISTORY

The 30-card 1980 Dodgers police set was the first set to be issued by the Los Angeles Police Department. The card features a color photo set in a wide white border. Below the photo are the player's name, uniform number (which is also the card number), and position. The front has a few vital stats, such as height and weight. The card back features the Dodgers logo, along with a baseball tip and a safety or anti-crime message. An LAPD badge appears in the background. Besides the individual players' cards in the set, there is a team photo card. The cards were intended to be given out by Los Angeles police to youngsters in order to establish better rapport.

FOR

This is the first issue in a long run of Dodger police sets.

AGAINST

The thin cardboard is prone to damage. Like most police-card sets, these are an odd size.

NOTEWORTHY CARDS

Dodger stars include Steve Garvey, Don Sutton, and Pedro Guerrero.

VALUE

MINT CONDITION: Complete set, $8; common card, 15¢–25¢; stars, 50¢–$1.50. 5-YEAR PROJECTION: Above average.

1980 GIANTS POLICE

SPECIFICATIONS

SIZE: 2⅝ × 4⅛″. FRONT: Color photograph. BACK: Orange and black printing on white cardboard. DISTRIBUTION: San Francisco, individual cards given out by police officers; complete sets given out at a special promotional game.

HISTORY

The 1980 Giants police set is very similar in design and format to the '79 set. The easiest way to tell the difference between the two is that the 1979 cards have a "#" symbol in front of the player's uniform number on the card front. Otherwise, the design is much the same. A color photo is surrounded by a wide white border. At the bottom left is the team logo. Under the photo is the player's name, uniform (and card) number, and position. A facsimile autograph appears on the photo. The back has a combination of advertising logos and safety and baseball tips. Like most police sets, the 31-card San Francisco Giants issue has found its way into the hobby in good numbers. Complete sets were given away at a promotional game at Candlestick Park.

FOR

This is the second (and last) police set from the team that came up with the idea.

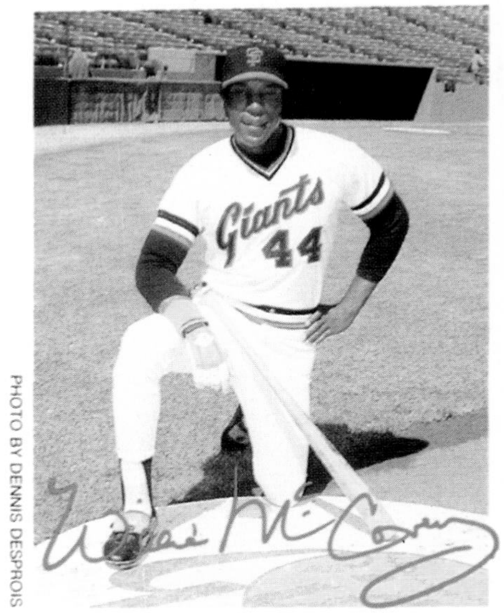

1980 Giants Police, Willie McCovey

AGAINST

Thin cardboard makes cards susceptible to damage.

NOTEWORTHY CARDS

The star cards are Willie McCovey and Jack Clark.

VALUE

MINT CONDITION: Complete set, $10; common card, 25¢; stars, 50¢–$1; McCovey, Clark, $2–$3. 5-YEAR PROJECTION: Above average.

1979 TO 1970

1972 Topps, Johnny Bench

1979 Topps, Reggie Jackson

1975 Topps, George Brett

1979 TOPPS

SPECIFICATIONS

SIZE: 2½ × 3½″. FRONT: Color photograph. BACK: Black and green printing on gray cardboard. DISTRIBUTION: Nationally, in packages with bubblegum.

1979 Topps, Johnny Bench

1979 Topps, Steve Garvey

1979 Topps, Tom Seaver

HISTORY

In 1979 Topps continued the success of the previous year's issue with a similar 726-card set. The card front features a large photo of the player with a thin white border. Underneath the photo is the player's name and position, and below that is a color banner with the team name. New for '79 was the Topps logo on the card front, an innovation most collectors disliked. Card backs are basically the same as in '78 and feature year-by-year major league and/or minor league stats, personal information, and a few lines of career highlights, space permitting. The panel at the right has a "Baseball Dates" quiz, with questions about famous events in baseball history. The double-printed cards in this set include a lot of superstars such as Joe Morgan, Steve Garvey, Tom Seaver, Johnny Bench, Jim Hunter, Buddy Bell, and Reggie Jackson. Several subsets feature record-setting performances of the previous season. Cards #1-#8 honor the league-leading performers in batting, home runs, RBIs, stolen bases, wins, strikeouts, ERA, and relief pitching. Other cards note major league records set during the season. One 8-card subset features career records, mostly by retired ballplayers. For the first time, rookie "Prospects" cards were arranged by team, each card featuring black-and-white photos of three promising young players.

FOR

Topps equaled the caliber of its '78 set.

AGAINST

Topps decided to put its logo on the front of the card.

NOTEWORTHY CARDS

One of the most collectible variation cards of recent years popped up in the 1979 Topps set. In the early print runs, Texas Rangers shortstop Bump Wills' team is identified as "Blue Jays," a team for which he had never played. The error was corrected in later press runs. It was once thought that the uncorrected version was the scarcer of the two, but most collectors now believe the corrected version is scarcer. Demand for the variation has cooled somewhat, but both cards command a premium. Notable rookies who made their baseball card debut in the 1979 Topps set include Ozzie Smith, Carney Lansford, Willie Wilson, Bob Horner, Pedro Guerrero, Kevin Bass, and Bob Welch.

VALUE

EX-MT CONDITION: Complete set, $135; common card, 10¢; superstars, $1–$5; Guerrero, $7; Smith, $12. 5-YEAR PROJECTION: Average, or a little above.

1979 Hostess, Terry Whitfield

1979 HOSTESS

SPECIFICATIONS

SIZE: Single card, 2¼ × 3¼"; panel, 7¼ × 3¼". FRONT: Color photograph. BACK: Black printing on white cardboard. DISTRIBUTION: Nationally, one 3-card panel on the bottom of snack cake boxes.

1979 Hostess, Dale Murphy

HISTORY

In 1979 Hostess produced the last of five consecutive baseball card issues: a 150-card set that came in 3-card panels printed on the bottom of family-size boxes of snack cakes. Hostess used much the same format as in previous years. The card front features a large color photo with a white panel containing the player's name, team, and position at the top. (In '78 the panel was at the bottom.) Card backs are virtually identical to the four previous years, with a large card number in a black circle in the upper left, and a few lines of biographical information, and career statistics. Although the cards were meant to be cut apart, many complete panels and entire boxes were saved by collectors. Entire boxes have traditionally been the most valuable, followed by complete 3-card panels. Individual cards are worth the least. (An entire box may be worth up to 33 percent more than the three individual cards.) To be considered top grade, an individual 1979 Hostess card should be neatly trimmed with even margins. Most collectors prefer the card to be cut right on the dotted line, rather than inside it. Certain cards—those which came on boxes of less-popular snack products or were distributed in areas with few collectors—are especially hard to find.

FOR

Because they are scarcer than Topps cards, Hostess common cards are worth two to three times as much. Stars and superstars, however, are usually priced lower than the corresponding Topps issue. These cards are a good bet for future increase in value. They are attractive, contain a high proportion of stars, and since they can seldom be bought as a complete set, they are a challenge to collect.

AGAINST

Because most of the cards were collected as uncut panels and boxes, individual superstar cards can be hard to find; the superstar collector often has to pay for two unwanted cards to get the card he wants.

NOTEWORTHY CARDS

Most of the year's big-name players are included in the 1979 Hostess set—a notable exception being Carl Yastrzemski. There is a card of Yankees catcher Thurman Munson, who died in a plane crash in August of that year.

VALUE

EX-MT CONDITION: Complete set of 3-card panels, $275; complete set of single cards, $160; single panel, $4; single card, 25¢–50¢; stars, $2–$5; Dale Murphy, $5; Pete Rose, $8. 5-YEAR PROJECTION: Above average.

1979 Kellogg's, Gaylord Perry

1979 KELLOGG'S

SPECIFICATIONS

SIZE: 1[15]/16 × 3¼". FRONT: Color photograph, 3-D effect. BACK: Blue printing on white cardboard. DISTRIBUTION: Nationally, single cards in cereal boxes; complete sets available through a mail-in offer.

1979 Kellogg's, Tom Seaver

HISTORY

In its tenth year of baseball card production, Kellogg's made the set bigger and the individual cards smaller. Three additional cards make it a 60-card set, while the cards are 3/16" narrower. Once again, the cards have a 3-D effect produced by placing a layer of ribbed plastic over the photo. The color photo is topped by a red and yellow panel with a big Kellogg's logo, while a smaller yellow panel at the bottom gives the player's last name and position. Blue stripes with white stars form a frame at the sides of the pictures. The whole design is surrounded by a white border. Card backs continue to offer a player biography and stats, along with a team logo and a picture of Tony the Tiger. To obtain a complete set of cards, collectors could either buy many boxes of cereal to get the individual cards packed inside or they could mail in box tops and cash.

FOR

The set has good growth potential.

AGAINST

Many collectors don't like the narrow format. 3-D cards tend to curl and crack.

NOTEWORTHY CARDS

A lot of the game's big stars make their first Kellogg's appearance in the '79 set: Ron Guidry, Paul Molitor, and Jason Thompson, to name a few. The set also includes stars who had been skipped for a year or two, such as Pete Rose and Carl Yastrzemski.

VALUE

EX-MT CONDITION: Complete set, $25; common card, 25¢; stars, $1–$4; Rose, $10–$12. 5-YEAR PROJECTION: Above average.

1979 BURGER KING

SPECIFICATIONS

SIZE: 2½ × 3½". FRONT: Color photograph. BACK: Black and green printing on gray cardboard. DISTRIBUTION: Philadelphia and New York, given away with food purchase at Burger King restaurants.

HISTORY

Only two Burger King team sets were produced by Topps for 1979—the Yankees and the Phillies. Each set features 22 player cards and an unnumbered checklist card. Although some players had different photos on the Burger King issue, the set was virtually identical to the regular '79 Topps cards, with the exception of card numbers on the backs. The cards were given away with purchases at Burger Kings in the New York and Philadelphia areas, and collectors and dealers managed to get their share. None of the '79 Burger King cards are scarce, though as a whole they are harder to find than their '79 Topps counterparts.

1979 Burger King, Pete Rose

1979 Burger King, Mike Schmidt

FOR

These are legitimate regional cards, making them a good item for team collectors.

AGAINST

Being nearly identical to the Topps cards, the set is confusing to collectors.

NOTEWORTHY CARDS

There are no hot rookie cards in this set, but a few notable superstars appear: Pete Rose, Mike Schmidt, Steve Carlton, Thurman Munson, Catfish Hunter, Ron Guidry, Tommy John, Rich Gossage, and Reggie Jackson.

VALUE

EX-MT CONDITION: Complete set (single team), $5–$7; common card, 10¢–20¢; superstars, $1–$2; Munson, Carlton, $1.50; Jackson, Schmidt, $2; Rose, $2.50. 5-YEAR PROJECTION: Above average.

1979 GIANTS POLICE

SPECIFICATIONS

SIZE: 2⅝ × 4⅛". FRONT: Color photograph. BACK: Orange and black printing on white cardboard. DISTRIBUTION: San Francisco, single cards given out by police officers; 15-card starter sets given out at a promotional game.

1979 Giants Police, Jack Clark

HISTORY

The 30-card 1979 San Francisco Giants Police set was the first such issue by a major league club since the little-known Baltimore Orioles set of 1972. Following the pattern set by the basketball card issue of the Portland Trailblazers in 1977 and '78, the Giants cards were meant to improve relations between local police and neighborhood children. Cards were given out one or two at a time to kids who walked up to the officer and asked for them. A starter set of 15 cards was also available at a special baseball card promotional game at Candlestick Park during the season. The San Francisco Giants police set follows what has become something of a standard design for police sets. A color photo of the player is set in a wide white frame. A facsimile autograph appears in blue on the face of the card. Uniform number, name, and position are printed below the photo, along with a color team logo. The back contains a logo for KNBR radio, a baseball tip, and a safety or anti-crime tip. The '79 Giants cards are numbered according to the player's uniform number. Like most later police sets, the 1979 Giants cards found their way into dealer and collector hands in large numbers.

FOR

This was the first of the modern major league baseball police sets, so it has historical significance.

AGAINST

Like later police sets, it was printed on thin cardboard, making it prone to damage.

NOTEWORTHY CARDS

All 25 roster players, the coaches, and manager are featured in the set; big names include Willie McCovey, Jack Clark, and Bill Madlock.

VALUE

EX-MT CONDITION: Complete set, $15; common card, 30¢; stars, 50¢–$2; McCovey, $3. 5-YEAR PROJECTION: Above average.

1978 TOPPS

SPECIFICATIONS

SIZE: 2½ × 3½". FRONT: Color photograph. BACK: Blue and orange printing on gray cardboard. DISTRIBUTION: Nationally, in packages with bubblegum.

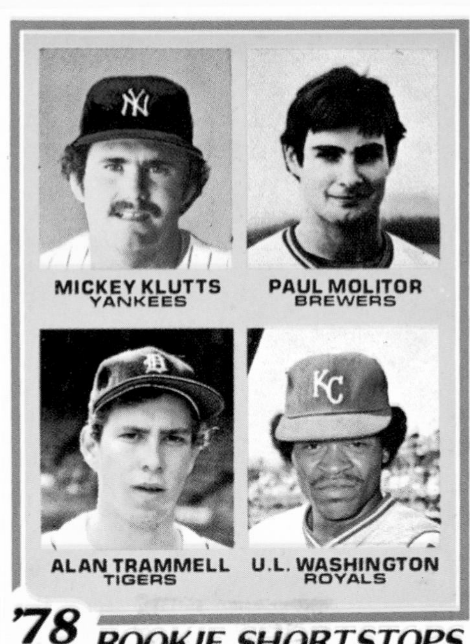

1978 Topps, Rookie Shortstops

1978 Topps, Eddie Murray

1978 Topps, Reggie Jackson

HISTORY

In 1978 Topps added 66 cards to its set, bringing the total to 726 cards—the biggest issue since '72. But since 66 cards take up only half a press sheet, Topps began double-printing certain cards. One row of 11 cards on each sheet was repeated, making those cards twice as common as the rest of the cards on the sheet. Many of the big names in the 1978 set were double-prints—Pete Rose, Tony Perez, Cecil Cooper, Ron Guidry, and Graig Nettles—but it hasn't kept their prices down. There were several subsets in the '78 Topps issue. The first seven cards honor baseball records set by Lou Brock, Sparky Lyle, Willie McCovey, Brooks Robinson, Pete Rose, Nolan Ryan, and Reggie Jackson. Statistical leaders in both leagues share a run of eight cards, and three cards highlight the league playoffs and World Series. The rookie cards, which appear toward the end of the set, again feature four players per card by position rather than team. The design of the 1978 Topps set is one of their finest of the decade. Maximum space is devoted to a large player photo with a thin white border. In the white border at the lower left, the team name appears in script, while the player's name is in small type at the right. A white baseball in an upper corner holds the abbreviation for the player's position. On cards of the previous season's starting All-Stars, the baseball is replaced with a red, white, and blue shield (except for Richie Zisk, the starting left fielder for the American League—they forgot his shield). Year-by-year career stats dominate the back of the cards, and in a box at the right is a baseball situation, which allows the cards to be used to play a game of baseball.

FOR

The 1978 Topps cards feature a superior design, a good bunch of rookie cards, and a decent value for the price.

AGAINST

Topps' decision to return to double-printing some cards was to plague collectors for the next four years. There's no card more abundant than a recent Topps double-print common.

NOTEWORTHY CARDS

You could assemble a virtual All-Star team of the rookies who made their first appearance in the 1978 Topps set. Principal collector interest is in the premier card of Eddie Murray, one of the most expensive single cards in the set. Other notable rookies include Mario Soto, Floyd Bannister, Ray Knight, Bob Knepper, Jack Morris, Lou Whitaker, Lance Parrish, and, sharing a "Rookie Shortstops" card, Alan Trammell and Paul Molitor. Though Dale Murphy appears on card #708 "Rookie Catchers" (with Parrish), it is not his rookie card. He appeared on a similar card in the 1977 set.

VALUE

EX-MT CONDITION: Complete set, $200; common card, 10¢; superstars, $3–$5; Trammell/Molitor, Murphy/Parrish, Murray, $35. 5-YEAR PROJECTION: Above average.

1978 HOSTESS

SPECIFICATIONS

SIZE: Single card, 2¼ × 3¼"; panel, 7¼ × 3¼". FRONT: Color photograph. BACK: Black printing on white cardboard. DISTRIBUTION: Nationally, one 3-card panel on the bottom of snack cake boxes.

1978 Hostess, George Brett

1978 Hostess, Johnny Bench

HISTORY

In its fourth year of issuing baseball cards Hostess continued to run with its successful format. Again in 1978, the company issued a 150-card set in the form of 3-card panels printed on the bottom of family-size packages of snack cakes. For 1978, the type in the white panel at the bottom of the card designating the player's team and position was made smaller, resulting in room for a larger photo. The cards are bordered by a dotted line, meant as a guide for separating the cards. The card backs contain player names and vital stats, card numbers, and year-by-year major league totals. Because the hobby was in full swing by '78, many collectors knew to not cut the cards off the boxes. Traditionally, box-bottom cards retain a premium value if left uncut. Complete boxes are worth more than the value of the three cards and 3-card panels also have an added value. As with the other Hostess issues, some panels are more difficult to find because they were distributed on less popular brands or in parts of the country where there are few collectors. Overall, the '78 Hostess set is a bit more challenging than the company's other issues.

FOR

This is a high-quality set picturing great players.

AGAINST

It is difficult, if not impossible, to find single cards of superstars in top condition.

NOTEWORTHY CARDS

Many of today's current superstars are present in the 1978 Hostess set, as well as a first-year card of Eddie Murray.

VALUE

EX-MT CONDITION: Complete set of panels, $260; complete set of single cards, $140; common card, 25¢–50¢; stars, $2–$5; Rose, $9; Murray, $10. 5-YEAR PROJECTION: Above average.

1978 KELLOGG'S

SPECIFICATIONS

SIZE: 2⅛ × 3¼". FRONT: Color photograph, 3-D effect. BACK: Blue printing on white cardboard. DISTRIBUTION: Nationally, single cards in cereal boxes; complete sets available through a mail-in offer.

1978 Kellogg's, Dave Winfield

1978 Kellogg's, George Foster

HISTORY

In its 1978 card set, Kellogg's gave itself plenty of advertising. The company name appears on the front in big script in the upper left, and a cartoon of Tony the Tiger appears on the back in the space usually reserved for a player photo. The photo on the front of the card is bordered at top and bottom by large red and yellow banners. The top one reads "Kellogg's 3-D Super Stars"; the bottom banner gives the player's last name and position. The photo is bordered on the sides by light and dark blue stripes in a neon effect. The '78 cards had Kellogg's characteristic 3-D look, achieved by laminating a piece of finely ribbed plastic over a sharp player photo against a fuzzy stadium background, giving the visual effect of depth. The set remained at 57 cards for 1978. Single cards came wrapped in envelopes in cereal boxes. Hobbyists could obtain a complete set by mailing in box tops and money. The set is fairly common.

FOR

Kellogg's continued its customary attractive format.

AGAINST

The 1978 Kellogg's cards are almost always sold as a complete set so it is difficult to acquire individual cards. The plastic coating on face of cards is prone to curling and cracking.

NOTEWORTHY CARDS

There are not a great number of superstars in the 1978 Kellogg's set, though there is a rookie card of Eddie Murray. Pete Rose is noticeably absent—the only year he doesn't appear in the Kellogg's set.

VALUE

EX-MT CONDITION: Complete set, $33; common card, 25¢; stars, $2–$4; Murray, $9. 5-YEAR PROJECTION: Above average.

1978 BURGER KING

SPECIFICATIONS

SIZE: 2½ × 3½". FRONT: Color photograph. BACK: Blue and orange printing on gray cardboard. DISTRIBUTION: Houston, Dallas, Detroit, and New York, given away with food purchase at Burger King restaurants.

HISTORY

Following the 1977 baseball card promotional giveaway in New York Burger Kings, the company expanded the program in '78 to include four teams: the Astros, Rangers, Tigers, and Yankees. A total of 92 player cards and four unnumbered checklists were issued—23 player cards and a checklist for each team. As with the 1977 cards, there is no Burger King advertising or logos. Some of the player photos are different from those found on the regular 1978 Topps cards. The only distinction from the Topps set on most of the cards is the card number on the back. Otherwise, the cards are identical. There are no rarities among the '78 Burger King cards to compare to the 1977 Lou Piniella card. All team sets are in decent supply since collectors and dealers were able to obtain quantities of them when they were issued.

1978 Burger King, Mark Fidrych

1978 Burger King, Reggie Jackson

FOR

These are regional cards that are scarcer than the regular Topps issue but not a great deal more expensive.

AGAINST

Their similarity to regular Topps cards of 1978 is confusing. Unless the card is one of the few with different pictures, even superstar collectors don't bother to acquire the Burger King cards.

NOTEWORTHY CARDS

High-demand cards found in the 1978 Burger King sets: Ferguson Jenkins (Rangers); Alan Trammell, Jack Morris, and Lou Whitaker (Tigers); Thurman Munson, Ron Guidry, Jim Hunter, and Reggie Jackson (Yankees).

OUR FAVORITE CARD

An excellent choice for collectors who like to dabble in "superstar futures" is the set of the Detroit Tigers. Two long-time infield stars in the A.L. have their own rookie cards—second baseman Lou Whitaker and shortstop Alan Trammell—along with pitcher Jack Morris. What makes these cards special is that all three had to share their regular '78 Topps cards with three other players. In the next few years, when collectors look back on the great Tiger teams of the '80s, these cards are going to be in big demand. Too bad the Burger King people missed another Tiger rookie phenom of '78, Lance Parrish.

VALUE

EX-MT CONDITION: Complete team set: Astros, Rangers, Yankees, $10; Tigers, $35; common card, 25¢–35¢; superstars, 75¢–$2; Whitaker, $6; Morris, $7; Trammell, $10. 5-YEAR PROJECTION: Average.

1977 TOPPS

SPECIFICATIONS

SIZE: 2½ × 3½″. FRONT: Color photograph. BACK: Green printing on gray cardboard. DISTRIBUTION: Nationally, in packages with bubblegum.

1977 Topps, Bruce Sutter

1977 Topps, Rookie Catchers

1977 Topps, Thurman Munson

HISTORY

The 1977 Topps issue continued the trend toward a cleaner, simpler design. The card front features a large color photo of the player with a facsimile autograph across it. A wide white border at the top contains the team name in color-coded type, with the player's name below and his position in a banner to the right. Card backs include personal and career stats, a baseball cartoon, and, space permitting, a few career highlights in headline style. (Nobody has ever figured out what the figures at the bottom of the card are; they look like fence posts overgrown with weeds.) For the fifth straight year, the set contained 660 cards. It opens with eight cards featuring the American and National League leaders in several statistical categories. There are cards honoring the record-setting 1976 performances of George Brett, Minnie Minoso, Jose Morales, and Nolan Ryan. A 5-card subset titled "Turn Back the Clock" recalls great baseball moments of the past. A 4-card novelty set called "Big League Brothers," depicts George and Ken Brett, Bob and Ken Forsch, Lee and Carlos May, and Paul and Rick Reuschel (the two Reuschels are wrongly identified on the card front). There are cards featuring a team photo and a picture of the manager. The cards for the Mariners and the Blue Jays (their first year of major league play) include the coaches as well. Once again, the multiplayer rookie cards group the players by position, rather than team.

FOR

Many of the photos were taken during the 1976 season, so collectors can see some of the special Bicentennial uniforms adopted by the teams.

AGAINST

This was the last year that Topps produced fewer than 700 cards.

NOTEWORTHY CARDS

The rookie cards are the hottest in the set. One of the most sought-after cards is #477, "Rookie Catchers," featuring Dale Murphy. Other in-demand rookie cards are Bruce Sutter, Denny Martinez, Andre Dawson, Jack Clark and Lee Mazzilli, and Steve Kemp and Tony Armas. Besides the misidentified Reuschels, there are two other wrong photos in the 1977 set: Dave Collins (#431) is actually Paul Splittorff; and Gil Patterson (#472) is really Sheldon Gill. Talk about luck: Patterson, 1-2 for the Yankees that year (his only season in the major leagues), never appeared on another baseball card. The same is true for Gill, who never played an inning of major league ball. Also notable is the last regular-issue card of Brooks Robinson; he retired in 1977.

VALUE

EX-MT CONDITION: Complete set, \$250; common card, 15¢; superstars, \$3–\$7; Dawson, \$25; Murphy, \$65. 5-YEAR PROJECTION: Average, or a little above.

1977 HOSTESS

SPECIFICATIONS

SIZE: Single card, 2¼ × 3¼"; panel, 7¼ × 3¼". FRONT: Color photograph. BACK: Black printing on white cardboard. DISTRIBUTION: Nationally, one 3-card panel on the bottom of boxes of snack cakes.

1977 Hostess, Steve Garvey

1977 Hostess, Keith Hernandez

HISTORY

In its third year of issuing baseball cards, Hostess again produced a 150-card set. The cards came in 3-card panels printed on the bottom of family-size boxes of snack cakes. The design of the cards was virtually unchanged. The card front features a color photo with a rounded bottom, on top of a white panel containing the name, team, and position of the player in red and blue letters. The card backs list the player's name and vital stats, a card number, and year-by-year major league totals. Many complete 3-card panels and even entire boxes were saved by collectors, and these are more valuable than the individual cards. If the cards have been separated, they must be neatly trimmed with even borders. Most collectors prefer cards cut on the dotted line, rather than inside it. Cards that came on boxes of less-popular items are now scarcer than the rest of the series.

FOR

This is an attractive, easy-to-collect set that has potential for price appreciation—especially the star cards.

AGAINST

Because of the prevalence of complete boxes and panels, it is sometimes hard to buy an individual superstar card; the collector must buy the whole panel to get the desired card.

NOTEWORTHY CARDS

All of the superstars of 1977 are in the set.

VALUE

EX-MT CONDITION: Complete set of panels, $275; complete set of single cards, $165; single card, 30¢–50¢; stars, $2–$6; Brett, $7; Rose, $9. 5-YEAR PROJECTION: Above average.

1977 KELLOGG'S

SPECIFICATIONS

SIZE: 2⅛ × 3¼". FRONT: Color photograph, 3-D effect. BACK: Blue printing on white cardboard. DISTRIBUTION: Nationally, one card in boxes of cereal; complete sets available through a mail-in offer.

HISTORY

The 1977 Kellogg's set is considered one of their most attractive. Once again the 57-card set features a 3-D effect, achieved by laminating a layer of ribbed plastic over a sharp player photo

1977 Kellogg's, Ferguson Jenkins

1977 Kellogg's, Greg Luzinski

superimposed on a fuzzy stadium background. For '77, the player photo has a bright red and gold oval frame with his name and position in an oval panel at the bottom. The card is surrounded by a wide white border. Card backs again feature a team logo, personal and career information, stats, and a small photo of the player. This was the last time the player photo appeared on the backs.

FOR

This set is regarded as one of Kellogg's finest.

AGAINST

Like all Kellogg's 3-D issues, the plastic on the front is prone to curling and cracking, which lowers the card value.

NOTEWORTHY CARDS

George Brett and Dave Winfield make their first appearance on a Kellogg's card in 1977. Some Lyman Bostock cards mistakenly picture Dock Ellis on the back. This was quickly corrected, and the error card is scarcer than the corrected version.

VALUE

EX-MT CONDITION: Complete set, $35; common card, 30¢–45¢; stars, $1–$4; Rose, $10. 5-YEAR PROJECTION: Above average.

1977 BURGER KING YANKEES

SPECIFICATIONS

SIZE: 2½ × 3½". FRONT: Color photograph. BACK: Green printing on gray cardboard. DISTRIBUTION: New York, with food purchase at Burger King restaurants.

1977 Burger King Yankees, Thurman Munson

1977 Burger King, Lou Piniella

HISTORY

The Topps Burger King Yankees set was one of very few regional sets produced in 1977. Because the cards carry absolutely no advertising for Burger King, they are sometimes confused with the regular Topps cards of '77. It's no wonder: the two sets are virtually identical and many of the player photos are the same. One notable exception is the Reggie Jackson card: the Burger King card pictures him in his Yankees uniform, while the regular Topps card shows him in an Orioles uniform painted by an artist to look like a Yankees uniform. The set contains 23 numbered player cards plus an unnumbered checklist. Although the '77 Burger King cards were a regional issue, they are widely available around the country. This is due to collectors and card dealers obtaining large quantities of the cards. With the exception of the Lou Piniella card, the set is not at all scarce.

FOR

It's a quality, regional team set. Some cards are desirable because the photos are different from the regular '77 Topps.

AGAINST

The lack of Burger King advertising creates confusion.

NOTEWORTHY CARDS

Many Yankee superstars appear in the set: Jackson, Thurman Munson, Jim Hunter, Graig Nettles, Piniella, and manager Billy Martin.

OUR FAVORITE CARD

The Lou Piniella card is one the most valuable cards of the '70s. It is also one of the few cards to be written up in baseball literature. In his book *The Bronx Zoo*, Yankees relief pitcher Sparky Lyle relates the story of the card. Originally, Piniella was not included in the set. Annoyed at being ignored, he went to see Yankee owner George Steinbrenner, who suggested to Burger King that they add Piniella to the set. Since the card was added so late, very few got into circulation. (This made the 1977 Burger King set the only one to have 23 player cards; subsequent sets have only 22 cards). This is one case where the confusion between the Topps and Burger King cards can work to the collector's advantage. Since the photo of Piniella is identical on both cards, a lucky collector going through a dealer's stack of '77 commons may be able to come away with the Burger King version (#23) rather than the Topps version (#96).

VALUE

EX-MT CONDITION: Complete set, $35; common card, 30¢–50¢; Munson, Jackson, $4; Piniella, $15–$20. 5-YEAR PROJECTION: Average.

1976 TOPPS

SPECIFICATIONS

SIZE: 2½ × 3½". FRONT: Color photograph. BACK: Black and green printing on gray cardboard. DISTRIBUTION: Nationally, in packages with bubblegum.

1976 Topps, Carl Yastrzemski

1976 Topps, Babe Ruth

1976 Topps, Hank Aaron

HISTORY

After several years of card designs in which the border practically overwhelmed the photo, Topps moved toward a simpler design in 1976. The card front is dominated by a large, clear player photo. The player's name and team are in a pair of colored strips at the bottom, and his position is shown by a small drawing in the lower left. All-Star cards have a star in the the lower left indicating the player's league and position. The card back design is one of Topps' best. A bat and ball appear at the left, with the card number inside the ball. Neatly arranged on the right are the player's name, position, personal stats, and complete major/minor league statistics. When space permitted, a few career highlights were included on the bottom. The 660-card set includes a number of special subsets. The most significant is the 44-card "Traded" set issued later in the season. These cards feature 43 players who were traded after the regular cards were printed, shown in their "new" uniforms (usually painted on by an artist). The Traded card fronts are similar to the regular '76 cards, except for a "Sports Extra" headline announcing the player's move to a new team and the date. The back continues the newspaper clipping format and presents details of the deal. The Traded cards carry the same number as the regular cards, except with a "T" suffix. There is a separate checklist for the Traded group. Opening the 1976 Topps issue is a 6-card subset recounting the record-setting performances of the previous season. A 15-card series features the statistical leaders of 1975—one card for each league in seven categories—the last card honoring the top relief pitchers in both leagues. The first 14 cards feature the league's three leaders in a certain category. There are two cards dedicated to the League Championship Series and the World Series. A 10-card series titled "The Sporting News All-Time All-Stars" features a lineup of baseball's greatest players, such as Babe Ruth, Ty Cobb, and Honus Wagner. The cards have black-and-white player photos on the front, and lifetime stats on the back. The most interesting subset for collectors is the "Father & Son" set, which pictures former major league players with their active major league player sons. The cards show miniature versions of the players' old baseball cards. The dad/lad combinations are Gus and Buddy Bell, Ray and Bob Boone, Joe Coleman Sr. and Jr., Jim and Mike Hegan, and Roy Smalley Sr. and Jr. Two versions of the team cards were issued in 1976: one came with the regular set on the same cardboard stock; the other was printed on much thinner, white cardboard available in uncut sheet form directly from Topps. Rookie cards feature four players to a card, grouped by position.

FOR

The set has a pleasing diversity, and the special cards are better-conceived than in the past. The set contains no outrageously expensive cards, though the value of the whole set is respectably high.

AGAINST

The worst thing you can say about the '76 Topps set is that there are no outstanding rookie cards.

NOTEWORTHY CARDS

Hank Aaron's final regular card as a player appears in the set. He is also honored on card #1 for establishing the career RBI mark of 2,262. One of the few notable rookies in the set is Ron Guidry.

VALUE

EX-MT CONDITION: Complete set, $245; Traded set, $8; common card, 16¢; superstars, $4–$10; Guidry, Mike Schmidt, George Brett, $12; Pete Rose, $15. 5-YEAR PROJECTION: Well above average.

1976 Hostess, Jon Matlack

1976 HOSTESS

SPECIFICATIONS

SIZE: Single card, 2¼ × 3¼″; panel, 7¼ × 3¼″. FRONT: Color photograph. BACK: Black printing on white cardboard. DISTRIBUTION: Nationally, one 3-card panel on the bottom of boxes of snack cakes.

HISTORY

The 1976 Hostess set was basically the same as the company's premier issue the year before. The 150-card set came in 3-card panels printed on the bottom of family-size boxes of snack cakes. Entire boxes are the most valuable, followed by complete panels, which are worth about 20 percent more than individual cards. Panels or cards cut from the box must be trimmed neatly with even margins to be considered top grade. The design for 1976 was almost unchanged from '75. In keeping with the Bicentennial theme of 1976, the bottom of the card has red, white, and blue stripes containing the player's name, team, and position. Card backs include brief biographical details and career stats. The 1976 Hostess cards are attractive and in fairly strong demand. While Hostess common cards are twice as expensive as the same '76 Topps cards, there are far fewer existing Hostess cards than Topps cards in any given year. Superstars, on the other hand, are a much better buy in the Hostess series than the Topps. As with the 1975 issue, 3-card panels found on boxes of less popular products were scarcer than the rest of the series.

1976 Hostess, Hank Aaron

FOR

The set has a reasonable amount of cards at a low price.

AGAINST

The 1976 cards are a quarter-inch smaller than the standard cards.

NOTEWORTHY CARDS

The set includes the first Hostess card picturing George Brett, as well as several Hall of Famers.

VALUE

EX-MT CONDITION: Complete set of panels, $300; complete set of single cards, $175; common card, 30¢–50¢; stars, $3–$7; Pete Rose, $19. 5-YEAR PROJECTION: Above average.

1976 KELLOGG'S

SPECIFICATIONS

SIZE: 2⅛ × 3¼". FRONT: Color photo, 3-D effect. BACK: Blue printing on white cardboard. DISTRIBUTION: Nationally, one card in boxes of cereal; complete sets available through a mail-in offer.

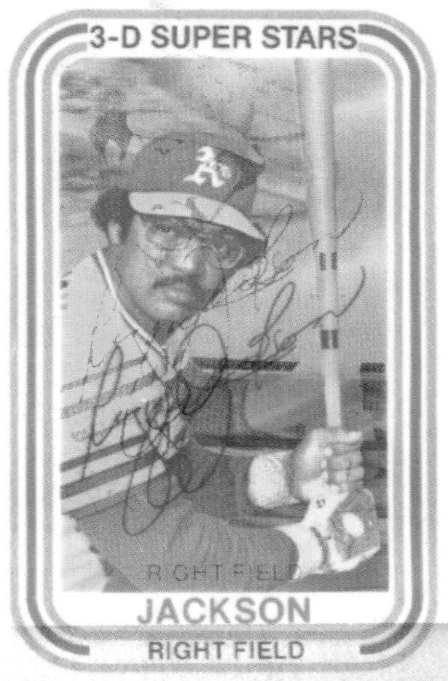

1976 Kellogg's, Reggie Jackson

1976 Kellogg's, Thurman Munson

HISTORY

While Kellogg's retained the 2⅛ × 3¼" format, 57-card set size, and 3-D look for 1976, the cards underwent a major design change for the first time in several years. Instead of blue and white borders, the '76 cards have alternating red and blue stripes around the photo, with a wide white border. The cards feature a 3-D effect created by laminating a piece of ribbed plastic over a sharp player photo superimposed on a fuzzy stadium background. Card backs include biographical details, major league career stats, another photo, and a team logo. The first three cards in the set are believed to have been printed separately from the other 54, and are somewhat scarcer. Collectors could either assemble a set by buying boxes of cereal to get the cards inside, or send in money and box tops for a complete set.

FOR

The cards are attractive, and so is the price.

AGAINST

The plastic lamination on these cards is prone to cracking and curling, resulting an unsightly and worthless card.

NOTEWORTHY CARDS

Thurman Munson makes his premier appearance for Kellogg's. The card of Clay Carroll comes in two variations, with a Red Sox or White Sox logo on the back.

VALUE

EX-MT CONDITION: Complete set, $55; common card, 50¢–75¢; stars, $2–$6; cards #1-#3, $7; Pete Rose, $10. 5-YEAR PROJECTION: Above average.

1975 TOPPS

SPECIFICATIONS

SIZE: Regular card, 2½ × 3½"; mini card, 2¼ × 3⅛". FRONT: Color photograph. BACK: Green and red printing on gray cardboard. DISTRIBUTION: Nationally, in packages with bubblegum.

HISTORY

In 1975 Topps produced two card sets identical in every way except for size. The mini-cards (about 20 percent smaller than the traditional size the company adopted in 1957) were test-marketed in the Midwest and on the West Coast. Collectors snapped up virtually the entire issue and prices on the 660 "minis" are generally double those of the

1975 Topps, Robin Yount

1975 Topps, Hank Aaron

1975 Topps, Harmon Killebrew

regular-size cards. In fact, the minis are the most popular Topps set of the 1970s. It's hard to say whether it's because of the card design or in spite of it. The 1975 design is a real eye-popper, and collectors either love it or hate it. A round-cornered color photo is framed with a distinctive two-tone border in mod colors. The team name is printed at the top in bold, colorful letters. The player's name is at the bottom, with his position abbreviated in a baseball at the lower right. The only word to describe the overall effect is "loud." The card backs are in vertical format—an unusual choice for Topps. Besides the usual personal info and career stats, there is a baseball trivia question. The '75 set opens with seven cards dedicated to notable or record-setting performances of the previous season. A large subset of 24 cards features the American League and National League MVPs since 1951, pictured in miniature versions of the Topps cards from their MVP season. The '74 season stat leaders in each league have a set of special cards, and there is an 8-card subset highlighting the League Championship Series and World Series. Rookie cards have four players to a card, grouped by position.

FOR

In terms of dollar value, this has been the fastest-rising baseball card set of the 1970s. It seems that each year one of the many rookies in the set reaches superstardom. Some people see the design of the set as a major point in its favor.

AGAINST

Some people see the design as the set's only major drawback.

NOTEWORTHY CARDS

There are two wrong-photo cards in the 1975 set: Steve Busby (#120) is really Fran Healy, and Larry Haney (#626) is really Dave Duncan. The last regular-issue card of Hall of Fame slugger Harmon Killebrew appears in the '75 set. The real high point of the 1975 Topps set, though, is the incredible number of big-demand rookie cards. You could make up an All-Star team from the players who made their initial baseball card appearance in 1975. These include Robin Yount, George Brett, Jim Rice, Gary Carter, Fred Lynn, and Keith Hernandez.

OUR FAVORITE CARDS

Topps cheated a bit on three of the cards in the MVP Award winners set. The set includes Roy Campanella cards for 1951 and 1955, and there is a Maury Wills card for 1962, but Topps never actually issued those cards. Campy was one of many stars of the early '50s who jumped between Topps and Bowman card sets in different years, sometimes appearing in both, sometimes in one or the other. Wills was miffed at Topps for not signing him to a baseball card contract when he was a minor leaguer, and he refused to appear on a Topps card until 1967.

VALUE

EX-MT CONDITION: Complete set, $490; common card, 25¢; superstars, $5–$8; Hank Aaron, $10; Pete Rose, $15; Mike Schmidt, $20; Hernandez, $25; Yount, $30; Carter, Rice, $35–$45; Brett, $55–$65. 5-YEAR PROJECTION: Above average.

1975 HOSTESS

SPECIFICATIONS

SIZE: Single card, 2¼ × 3¼"; panel, 7¼ × 3¼". FRONT: Color photograph. BACK: Black printing on white cardboard. DISTRIBUTION: Nationally, one 3-card panel on the bottom of boxes of snack cakes.

HISTORY

In 1975 Hostess issued the first of five consecutive annual baseball card sets. The 150 cards in the set included most of the big-name stars of that year. Like many other promotional issues, the '75 Hostess cards were printed right on the bottom of the box; but unlike other box-bottom cards, the Hostess cards had player statistics printed on the backs. (Printing on the back requires a second trip to the printing press—an expensive proposition—and most issuers elected to skip it.) Also unlike many box-bottom cards, the Hostess cards didn't share a common border, which made it easier to cut the cards apart evenly. Cards that have been cut off the box in a sloppy fashion have little collector value. All cards should have neat, even borders or be trimmed outside of the dotted line. As with all such cards, the entire box is the most valuable, followed by complete 3-card panels, with individual cards worth the least. (An entire box is worth perhaps 25 to 50 percent more than the three individual cards.) Because many entire boxes were saved, it is possible to build a complete collection

1975 Hostess, Ken Holtzman

1975 Hostess, Joe Morgan

in either form. The 1975 Hostess cards are appealing: maroon corners frame a color photo, the player's name and position are printed in blue in the white space below, and beneath that, the team name is printed in red. Panels that were printed on less popular products and sold in smaller quantities may be hard to find. Even so, these scarcer cards are not prohibitively expensive.

FOR

While the 1975 Hostess cards are scarcer than the regular Topps issue, they are much less expensive, especially for the stars. A '75 Topps Robin Yount rookie card, for example, is three to four times as expensive as the '75 Hostess card. For less than the cost of the Topps Yount card you can buy a complete 1975 Hostess set and get the Yount card plus the cards of Al Oliver and Andy Messersmith.

AGAINST

Many cards were sloppily cut, and Mint sets are hard to find.

NOTEWORTHY CARDS

Variations exist for several '75 Hostess cards. Burt Hooton's card can be found with his name spelled "Hooten"; Doug Rader's card can be found with his name spelled "Radar"; and Bill Madlock's card sometimes comes with the wrong position indicated, "Pitcher" instead of "Infield." There is also a wrong-photo card in the set—the picture on the Milt May card is Lee May. All of the variations have the same value.

VALUE

EX-MT CONDITION: Complete set of 3-card panels, $300; complete set of single cards, $135; common card, 30¢–50¢; stars, variations, $1–$2; Reggie Jackson, $6; Yount, $8; Hank Aaron, $9; Rose, $10.
5-YEAR PROJECTION: Above average.

1975 Kellogg's, Joe Morgan

1975 Kellogg's, Luis Tiant

1975 KELLOGG'S

SPECIFICATIONS

SIZE: 2⅛ × 3¼". FRONT: Color photograph, 3-D effect. BACK: Blue printing on white cardboard. DISTRIBUTION: Nationally, single cards in boxes of cereal; complete sets available through a mail-in offer.

HISTORY

The 1975 Kellogg's set was a lot like many of its predecessors. A sharp color photograph of the player is superimposed on a blurry stadium background, and a ribbed plastic sheet is laminated over the whole thing to give it a 3-D appearance. The effect is very pleasing, and the cards have been quite popular. The photo is framed by a blue border with white stars, which is surrounded by a thin white border. A red panel at the bottom of the photo contains the player's last name, and a smaller red panel at the upper right contains his position. The back of the card features a small photo of the player, a team logo, biographical information, and major league stats. The number of cards was increased in 1975 from 54 to 57 cards. Individual cards were found packaged in boxes of cereal, and the complete set could be ordered directly from the company by sending in cash and box tops.

FOR

These cards are attractive and inexpensive. The 3-D look is especially popular with superstar collectors, and these cards really jazz up a display of regular cards.

AGAINST

The plastic lamination is prone to cracking and curling with age, greatly lowering the value of a card. As with all the Kellogg's sets, it is difficult to find single cards since the cards are usually sold in complete sets.

NOTEWORTHY CARDS

Steve Garvey, Carl Yastrzemski, and Mike Schmidt make their first appearance in the Kellogg's series. The Jim Hunter card can be found with either the Yankees or A's logo on the back of the card. (He was acquired by New York prior to the opening of the 1975 season.) The Oakland version is scarcer.

VALUE

EX-MT CONDITION: Complete set, $110; common card, 60¢; stars, $1–$4; Schmidt, Reggie Jackson, Yastrzemski, $8–$12; Pete Rose, $16–$20.
5-YEAR PROJECTION: Average.

1975-1976 TWINKIES

SPECIFICATIONS

SIZE: $2\frac{1}{4} \times 3\frac{1}{4}''$. FRONT: Color photograph. BACK: Black printing on white cardboard. DISTRIBUTION: West Coast, one card on the bottom of boxes of snack cakes.

ROBIN YOUNT
INFIELD
Milwaukee BREWERS

1975-1976 Twinkies, Robin Yount

AL OLIVER
OUTFIELD
Pittsburgh PIRATES

1975-1976 Twinkies, Al Oliver

HISTORY

This was a test issue limited to the West Coast area. The cards were printed on the bottom of 25-cent Hostess Twinkies packages. Those who want to collect a full set of 60 cards will find the common cards somewhat more expensive and the star cards about the same price as the regular Hostess issue. Like all box-bottom baseball cards, the value is greatest if the cards are left on the original package. Those cards that have been cut from the package should be neatly trimmed. Each year, Twinkies cards have the same card numbers as the corresponding Hostess issue. The 1975 Twinkies series includes all of the first 36 of the Hostess cards, but is skip-numbered thereafter, from card #40 to #136. Steve Garvey, Robin Yount, and Hank Aaron are among the stars included in the last 24 cards of the Twinkies set for '75. The '76 Twinkies are the first 60 cards from the Hostess set of that year.

FOR

These cards are just as desirable as the Hostess sets.

AGAINST

There is no difference between these sets and the 1975 and '76 Hostess cards. However, because the Twinkie cards were used as cardboard liners for the cellophane packages, many were damaged by stains from the Twinkies.

VALUE

EX-MT CONDITION: Complete 1975 set, $80; common card, 60¢; Aaron, $7; Yount, $8; Pete Rose, $10. Complete 1976 set, $80; common card, 60¢; Brooks Robinson, Johnny Bench, Rod Carew, Garvey, $5. 5-YEAR PROJECTION: Average.

1974 Topps, Thurman Munson

1974 TOPPS

SPECIFICATIONS

SIZE: 2½ × 3½″. FRONT: Color photograph. BACK: Black and green printing on gray cardboard. DISTRIBUTION: Nationally, in packages with bubblegum.

HISTORY

In 1974, for the first time, Topps released all of its 660 cards at one time at the beginning of the year. This created a problem, however. Prior to the opening of the season there was a lot of talk that the San Diego Padres were going to be sold and moved to Washington, D.C. Everybody was so sure the deal would go through that Topps prepared most of the Padres cards with the team designation "Washington, Nat'l League" on the front. When the sale fell through, Topps went back to press to correct the cards, but the error version had already been issued in gum packs. The scarce Washington variations are priced several times as high as the San Diego cards. In all, 15 cards were affected by the error, including the team card and Dave

1974 Topps, Hank Aaron

1974 Topps, Harmon Killebrew

Freisleben's "Rookie Pitchers" card (#599). The Dave Winfield rookie card was not affected. As in 1973, the basic design of the card is good, but the set is marred by the use of action photos that depict the player as a small figure in a giant stadium or with too many other players. The 1974 issue featured a record number of subsets for Topps. Since Hank Aaron was just two home runs short of breaking Babe Ruth's career homer record, Aaron was featured on the first six cards in the set;

card #1 was a special career summary card, and cards #2-#6 picture miniature versions of Aaron's Topps cards from 1954 to 1973, four cards at a time. The backs of those cards have a running story of Aaron's distinguished career. Team managers again share a card with their coaches (except Tigers manager Ralph Houk, who has card #578 to himself). There are the usual subsets honoring the previous season's statistical leaders, league playoffs, and the World Series. The starting All-Star lineups appear on a 9-card subset, each card featuring the starters, by position, of both leagues. The rookie cards are arranged by position rather than team, with four players per card. As in 1973, Topps issued 24 unnumbered team checklist cards, with a team name and year at top, a panel of facsimile autographs below, and a team checklist on the back. The '74 team checklist cards are bordered in red. Later in the season Topps produced a 44-card "Traded" set, inserting the cards in regular gum packs. There are 43 player cards and a checklist. The cards are similar in format to the rest of the '74 cards except for a big panel below the player's photo that says "TRADED." Most of the uniforms shown on the traded cards are the work of Topps artists; rarely did Topps obtain actual photos of the players in their new uniforms. The backs of the Traded cards have a "Baseball News" feature that gives the details of the trade. Card numbers in the Traded set correspond to the regular set except for a "T" suffix after the number. The only really notable player in the Traded set for 1974 is Juan Marichal.

FOR
For the collector who likes recent cards but still wants a challenge, collecting this set with all its variations can be an interesting undertaking.

AGAINST
Busy photos and confusing variations mar the set.

NOTEWORTHY CARDS
There are two well-known error cards in the set. Jesus Alou (#654) was originally printed without his position designated in the upper right. The card without the word "OUTFIELD" is the more valuable version. Card #608, "Rookie Pitchers," can sometimes be found with Bob Apodaca's name spelled "Apodaco." Big-name rookie cards in '74 include Dave Parker, Frank White, Winfield, Ken Griffey, Bill Madlock, and Gorman Thomas.

VALUE
EX-MT CONDITION: Complete set, \$340; common card, 20¢–30¢; stars, \$4–\$8; Aaron specials, \$3; "Washington" players, \$3.50; Traded set, \$6.50; Alou error, \$7; Aaron #1, \$12; Parker, Pete Rose, Willie McCovey "Washington," \$20; Winfield, \$27; Mike Schmidt, \$37. 5-YEAR PROJECTION: Average.

1974 TOPPS DECKLE-EDGE

SPECIFICATIONS
SIZE: 2⅞ × 5″. FRONT: Black-and-white photograph. BACK: Black printing on gray cardboard. DISTRIBUTION: East Coast, test-marketed in packages with bubblegum.

1974 Topps Deckle-Edge, Willie Stargell

HISTORY

One of the more popular and scarce Topps test issues of the mid-1970s is the 72-card "Deckle-Edge" set. The cards feature a borderless black-and-white photo on the front with only a blue facsimile autograph at the bottom. The cards get their nickname from the unusual manner in which they were cut, giving the edges a scalloped appearance. The card backs have a mock newspaper clipping about some event in the player's career at the bottom. At the top, in script, are the player's name, team, and position, as well as the date and location of the picture—unusual on a baseball card. Many of the photos were taken at spring training the previous year. The '74 Deckle-Edges are a true test issue, having been sold only in limited areas on the East Coast. Like many Topps test issues, proof versions in uncut sheet form will sometimes be found, as will cards cut from those sheets with straight edges. (Such items were usually "rescued" from the garbage at Topps' printing plant.) The '74 Deckle-Edge cards are quite scarce, and the stars among them are in high demand.

FOR

One of the better-known test issues that makes an engaging addition to team or superstar collections.

AGAINST

The set is extremely scarce and expensive.

NOTEWORTHY CARDS

Hall of Fame players in the set include Bob Gibson, Jim "Catfish" Hunter, Lou Brock, Willie McCovey, Willie Stargell, Carl Yastrzemski, Hank Aaron, Brooks Robinson, Frank Robinson, and Johnny Bench.

VALUE

EX-MT CONDITION: Complete set, $1,200; common card, $10–$15; stars, $20–$40; superstars, $50–$150; Pete Rose, $240. 5-YEAR PROJECTION: Below average.

1974 KELLOGG'S

SPECIFICATIONS

SIZE: 2⅛ × 3¼". FRONT: Color photograph, 3-D effect. BACK: Blue printing on white cardboard. DISTRIBUTION: Nationally, single cards in boxes of cereal; complete sets available through a mail-in offer.

1974 Kellogg's, Dick Allen

HISTORY

After a one-year experiment with "regular" baseball cards, Kellogg's returned in 1974 to its successful and popular 3-D cards. The 3-D look was achieved by laminating a piece of ribbed plastic over the photograph on the front to create an illusion of depth. Kellogg's returned to the smaller card size used in 1972, while the set size remained at 54 cards. Blue and white borders surround the player photo on front. The player's last name appears in a yellow banner at the bottom, while his position is printed in a yellow shield at the top. Once again, card backs contain a typical arrangement of biography and stats, along with a small player photo. Complete sets could be obtained by sending in money and box tops. Individual cards could be found in boxes of Kellogg's cereal.

FOR

This set marked a return to the popular 3-D look.

AGAINST

The return to 3-D brought back the problem of the plastic lamination curling and cracking with age.

NOTEWORTHY CARDS

Johnny Bench returned to the 1974 Kellogg's set after a three-year absence.

VALUE

EX-MT CONDITION: Complete set, $40; common card, 30¢–60¢; stars, $1.50–$5; Pete Rose, $11. 5-YEAR PROJECTION: Average.

1973 TOPPS

SPECIFICATIONS

SIZE: 2½ × 3½″. FRONT: Color photograph. BACK: Black and yellow printing on gray cardboard. DISTRIBUTION: Nationally, in packages with bubblegum.

1973 Topps, Roberto Clemente

1973 Topps, Reggie Jackson

1973 Topps, Willie Mays

HISTORY

Having produced its largest set ever (787 cards) in 1972, Topps cut back to 660 cards in 1973, and this was to be the company's standard for the next five years. The '73 set was the last to be issued in different series. Starting in 1974, all Topps cards were released at one time early in the year (until 1981, when Topps began issuing Traded sets). This means the '73 set contains the last "high numbers" of the '70s. Cards #529-#660 (the high numbers) are considerably scarcer than the rest of the set. The cards are well designed: the front features a large, round-cornered photo bordered by a thin line, against a white border. The player's position is indicated by a small silhouette of a player in action, set in the lower right of the photo. The player's name and team appear in a white panel below the photo. For the first time since 1968, Topps used a vertical format for its regular-issue card backs. A player cartoon appears at the top, with personal info in a black panel at center, and a career summary and stats in a gold box below. The choice of photos for this set was one of Topps least successful efforts. Too often they opted for action photos showing a tiny, barely identifiable player against a huge stadium background. On other cards there are so many players pictured that it's hard to tell who is featured. Only a few photos are effective. There are several special subsets in the 1973 Topps set. Card #1 depicts Babe Ruth, Hank Aaron, and Willie Mays as all-time home run kings. An 8-card set honors the league leaders in various statistical categories, while a 10-card set highlights the League Championship Series and World Series.

There is a group of All-Time Leader cards and, for the second year in a row, pictures of current big leaguers when they were kids. The "Boyhood Photo" cards include Jim Palmer, Gaylord Perry, Chris Speier, Sam McDowell, Bobby Murcer, and Catfish Hunter. Rookie cards feature three players per card, grouped by position rather than team. Another interesting subset are the manager/coaches cards. These horizontal cards picture the manager in color at the left, with small black-and-white photos of the coaches at the right. The inclusion of the coaches (for the first time in many years) allows collectors to have '73 cards of such old-timers as Johnny Podres, Ernie Banks, Elston Howard, Lew Burdette, Ted Kluszewski, Larry Doby, Warren Spahn, Bill Mazeroski, Jim Gilliam, and Tommy Lasorda.

FOR

The design is good even though most of the photos aren't that great.

AGAINST

There are far too many bad photos. There are also too many "specialty" cards that collectors don't find special.

NOTEWORTHY CARDS

The only really "hot" card in the set is the rookie card of Mike Schmidt, one of three players featured on a high-numbered card (#615, "Rookie Third Basemen"). A few other rookie cards worth mentioning are Buddy Bell, Rich Gossage, Gary Matthews, and Dwight Evans. There are a couple of wrong photos in the '73 set: the photo on the Ellie Rodriguez card is John Felske, and the photo on the Joe Rudi card is Gene Tenace. The last regular-issue cards of Willie Mays and Roberto Clemente are found in this set. (Clemente was killed in a plane crash on December 31, 1972.) There is a little-known specialty series in the 1973 Topps set: a subset of unnumbered team checklist cards. The cards have the team name on the front at the top with facsimile autographs at the bottom in a white panel. There is a blue border around the front of the card. Card backs have a team checklist. These cards are not usually listed in the price guides, and few collectors have them in their "complete" '73 sets.

VALUE

EX-MT CONDITION: Complete set, $600; common card, #1-#528, 25¢–35¢; #529-#660, $1; team checklist card, $2–$3; stars, $5–$8; Clemente, Mays, Aaron, Jackson, Yastrzemski, $10–$12; Rose, $20; Schmidt, $175. 5-YEAR PROJECTION: Average.

1973 KELLOGG'S

SPECIFICATIONS

SIZE: 2¼ × 3½″. FRONT: Color photograph. BACK: Blue printing on white cardboard. DISTRIBUTION: Nationally, single cards in boxes of cereal; complete sets available through a mail-in offer.

1973 Kellogg's, Mickey Lolich

HISTORY

Some collectors call this "the 2-D set" because it was the only set Kellogg's produced without the 3-D effect. The 54-card set features a player photo in the shape of a shield, with a blue and white frame against a red background. The card has a white border with a row of nine blue stars at the top and bottom. The player's position is below the photo, with his last name in a yellow banner underneath. The backs feature a small photo of the player along with biographical information and career stats. The 1973 Kellogg's cards returned to the slightly larger 2¼ × 3½″ format. As usual, the cards were available in boxes of cereal, but in 1973 collectors could also get a complete set by sending in cash and box tops. The mail-in offer was continued in later sets, which made the Kellogg's cards fairly abundant from 1973 on.

FOR

Unlike the 3-D sets, the 1973 cards are not prone to curling and cracking.

AGAINST

Because it lacks the 3-D effect, the '73 set is sometimes spurned by collectors.

NOTEWORTHY CARDS
All the big names of 1973 are included, except for Hank Aaron, Carl Yastrzemski, and Frank Robinson.

VALUE
EX-MT CONDITION: Complete set, $40; common card, 40¢; stars, $2–$4; Pete Rose, $10. 5-YEAR PROJECTION: Below average.

1972 TOPPS

SPECIFICATIONS
SIZE: 2½ × 3½″. FRONT: Color photograph. BACK: Black and orange printing on gray cardboard. DISTRIBUTION: Nationally, in packages with bubblegum.

1972 Topps, Lou Brock

1972 Topps, Rod Carew

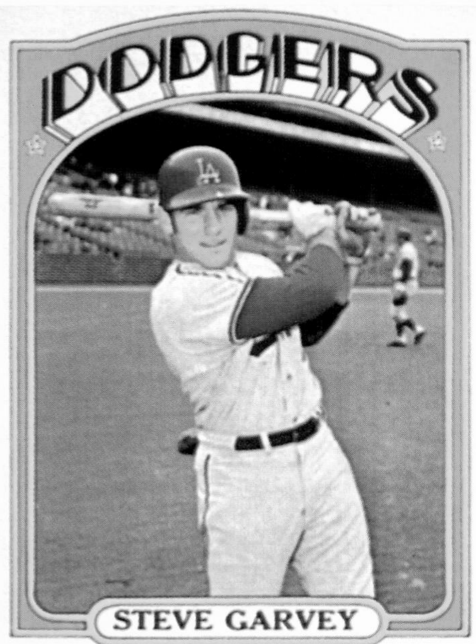

1972 Topps, Steve Garvey

HISTORY
In 1972 Topps issued its largest card set to date—787 cards. The '72 cards were also Topps' most flamboyant. "Psychedelic" is the word often used to describe them. A color photo shaped like a tombstone is surrounded by a multi-colored frame (sometimes the colors harmonize, sometimes they clash) with a white border. The team name is at the top of the card in colorful "superhero" type, and the player's name appears in a white panel below

the picture. Unusual for a Topps card is that the player's position is not indicated on the front. Card backs include the usual personal and career stats, along with a baseball trivia question. There are four levels of scarcity in the 1972 Topps set: #1-#394 are the most common, followed by #395-#525 and #526-#656, with the "high numbers" #657-#787 being the rarest. The high numbers are probably much scarcer than current price levels would indicate, but the lack of collector interest in completing full sets from 1972 keeps the prices low The high-number cards of superstars Rod Carew and Steve Garvey, and the Steve Carlton "Traded" card are priced more in line with their scarcity. Topps took advantage of the increased set size to include a record number of special subsets. One of the largest and most innovative was a set of more than six dozen "In Action" cards. This concept allowed Topps to include at least two cards of each current superstar. (The player's In Action card was numbered immediately after his regular card.) Topps used this theme again in later years, but many collectors don't like In Action cards, and they are almost always less valuable than the player's regular card. (An In Action superstar card is worth about half as much as the regular card of the same player.) A subset highlighting the statistical leaders of 1971 features photos of the top ranked player and the two runners-up (one from each league) on each card. A 10-card series highlights the 1971 League Championship Series and World Series. The World Champion Pirates were given the honor of having their team card as the #1 card. Topps may have gotten a bit too sentimental with its "Boyhood Photo" subset, depicting 16 current stars. Still, some collectors have always wondered what guys like Tom Seaver and Brooks Robinson looked like when they were younger. There is a short series of cards depicting various award winners of 1971. The final subset is a group of seven "Traded" cards. Unlike later Topps Traded cards, which were numbered outside the regular set, the '72 Traded cards are numbered as part of the regular issue (#751-#757). The cards are similar to the rest of the set, but feature a large stenciled "TRADED" across the front of the card, and details of the transaction on the back. Four big names are included in the Traded set: Steve Carlton, Frank Robinson, Denny McLain, and Joe Morgan. Rookie cards for 1972 have either three teammates per card or three players at the same position from different teams.

FOR

It is a large set, and for those who like subsets there are lots of specialty cards.

AGAINST

The design is too gaudy for most people.
The high numbers are a serious impediment to completing a set.

NOTEWORTHY CARDS

Two error cards appear in the '72 set, both on specialty cards. Jerry Bell and Darrell Porter's names are reversed on the Brewers Rookies card. On the National League ERA leaders card, the player identified as Dave Roberts (2.10 ERA in '71) is really Danny Coombs (6.21 ERA in '71). The best rookie card in the set is "Red Sox Rookies" (#71), with both Cecil Cooper and Carlton Fisk. Most other rookie cards feature lesser stars: Toby Harrah, Chris Chambliss, Ben Oglivie/Ron Cey, Dave Kingman, and George Hendrick.

OUR FAVORITE CARD

Many of the In Action cards provide real insight into the player's character. An example is Billy Martin's card (the only manager to have an In Action card), which shows the Tigers skipper in a characteristic pose—beefing with an umpire.

VALUE

EX-MT CONDITION: Complete set, $950; common card, #1-#525, 25¢; #526-#656, 60¢; #657-#787, $1.60; superstars, $5–$10; Willie Mays, Carl Yastrzemski, Hank Aaron, Steve Carlton, Reggie Jackson, Robinson Traded, Oglivie/Cey, $11–$12; Cooper/Fisk, Carew In Action, Pete Rose In Action, $20; Carlton Traded, $33; Rose, Carew, Garvey, $60–$65. 5-YEAR PROJECTION: Above average.

1972 KELLOGG'S

SPECIFICATIONS

SIZE: 2⅛ × 3¼". FRONT: Color photograph, 3-D effect. BACK: Blue printing on white cardboard. DISTRIBUTION: Nationally, in boxes of cereal.

HISTORY

There were some changes in the 1972 Kellogg's set: the cards were smaller, and the number of cards was reduced from 75 to 54. Once again the cards featured a 3-D effect, achieved by laminating a piece of ribbed plastic over a sharp player photo against a blurry stadium backdrop. The 1972 cards are readily identified by the diagonal red stripes across the upper-left and lower-right corners. The player's last name is in the upper-left stripe and his position is in the lower-right stripe. The photo is surrounded by a blue border with white embellishments. Card backs feature the usual small player photo and personal and career stats, with

1972 KELLOGG'S ALL-TIME GREATS

SPECIFICATIONS

SIZE: 2¼ × 3½". FRONT: Colorized photograph, 3-D effect. BACK: Blue printing on white cardboard. DISTRIBUTION: Nationally, one card in packages of toaster pastries.

1972 Kellogg's, Wilbur Wood

the addition of a short biography. In 1971, many collectors had ignored the cereal boxes and waited instead for surplus cards to become available at the end of the promotion. When this didn't happen, they were left out in the cold. So in '72, collectors rushed out and bought boxes of cereal to get the cards, but Kellogg's fooled them once again by making large quantities of the cards available to selected dealers. As a result, the '72 set is much easier and less expensive to complete than the '71 set.

FOR

Since the cards are readily available, they are reasonably priced.

AGAINST

There is a tendency for the plastic lamination to curl and crack with age and handling.

NOTEWORTHY CARDS

The smaller set size for '72 meant fewer superstars as well.

VALUE

EX-MT CONDITION: Complete set, $50; common card, 45¢; stars, $4–$8; Pete Rose, $13. 5-YEAR PROJECTION: Average, or slightly above.

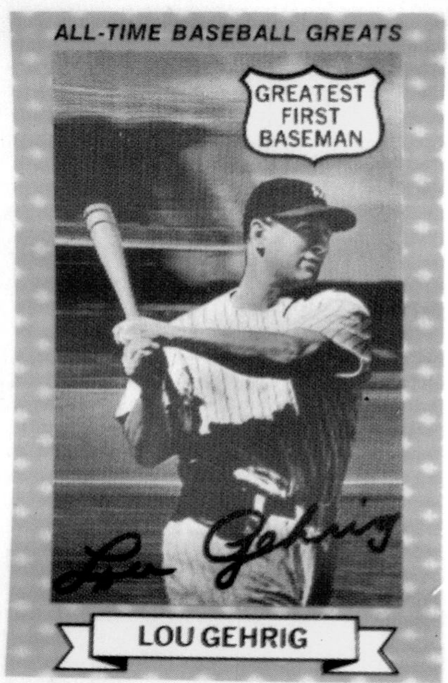

1972 Kellogg's All-Time Greats, Lou Gehrig

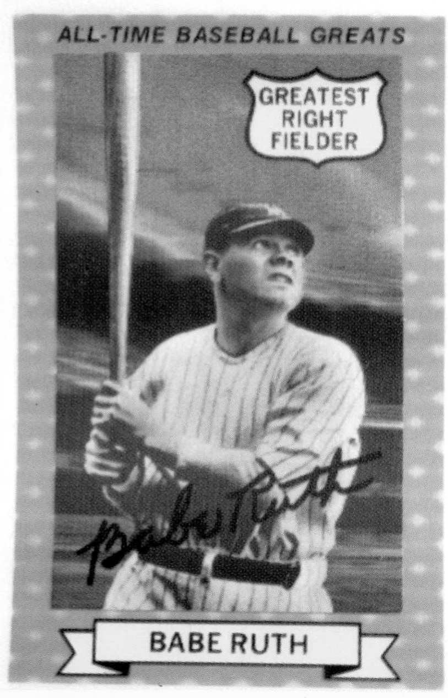

1972 Kellogg's All-Time Greats, Babe Ruth

HISTORY

The "1972 Kellogg's All-Time Greats" cards had been issued two years before in bags of pretzels. Only the copyright date was changed (to 1972) for the Kellogg's issue. Because there is no mention of the pretzel company (or the cereal company) on the cards, they are best known for having been inserted in packages of Kellogg's Danish-Go 'Rounds. The All-Time Greats cards are similar to Kellogg's 3-D cards, and are produced by the same company, Xograph. For this series, a sharp black-and-white player photo was colorized and placed on a blurry stadium background and then covered with a piece of ribbed plastic to give it a 3-D look. The player's name is in a yellow banner at the bottom, and his position ("Greatest" or "Finalist") is in a yellow shield at the top. Backs feature another photo of the player, a short biography, and a career summary with lifetime stats.

FOR

A unique set for All-Time Greats collectors. The cards are quite attractive and the 3-D effect makes the old-timers seem to come alive.

AGAINST

Most collectors don't like cards of players issued after their careers are over—they don't seem legitimate. Also, there is the problem of the plastic cracking and curling as a result of age and handling.

NOTEWORTHY CARDS

The 15-card "All-Time Baseball Greats" set features 14 Hall of Fame players (Babe Ruth has two cards in the set). All the big names like Lou Gehrig, Ty Cobb, Honus Wagner, and Walter Johnson, are included.

VALUE

EX-MT CONDITION: Complete set, \$12; common card, 40¢; Ruth, \$2–\$3. 5-YEAR PROJECTION: Below average.

1971 Topps, Willie Mays

1971 Topps, Steve Garvey

1971 TOPPS

SPECIFICATIONS

SIZE: $2\frac{1}{2} \times 3\frac{1}{2}$". FRONT: Color photograph. BACK: Green and black printing on gray cardboard. DISTRIBUTION: Nationally, in packages with bubblegum.

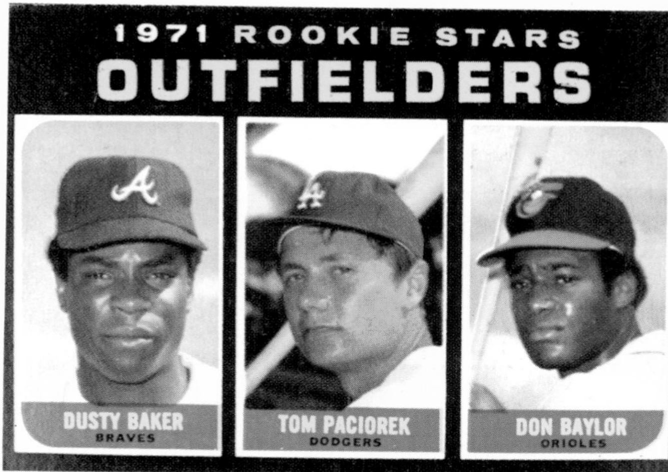

1971 Topps, Rookie Outfielders

HISTORY

The Topps 1971 set was the largest ever—792 cards. The design was one of their simplest and most attractive: the card front features a large color photo with a thin white border, surrounded by a black frame. The team name is in bright colors at the top of the card, with the player's name and position in lower-case letters underneath. A facsimile autograph across the photo completes the front design. The card back features an innovative small black-and-white "snapshot" of the player—making it the first baseball card to have a player photo on both front and back. The photo left little room for other info, so stats were limited to previous season and cumulative lifetime figures. Another interesting feature is a line giving the year of the player's first pro game and first major league game. In addition, there is a brief player biography and a few vital stats. Although the '71 Topps cards are extremely attractive in Mint condition, the black borders show wear easily. The ink tends to flake off the edges, making Mint cards hard to come by. (Some unscrupulous people touch up the edges with a black crayon to make a slightly worn card look better.) Compared to other '70s Topps sets there were few special subsets in the 1971 issue. The winners and runners-up in various statistical categories are featured by league on a 12-card set; an 8-card set highlights the American League and National League playoffs; and a 6-card set recounts the Orioles' victory over the Reds in the World Series. The many rookie cards include some individual player cards as well as cards with two or three players grouped either by team or by position. Because the cards were released in series as the baseball season progressed, some are scarcer than others. Cards #1-#523 are the most common, followed by #524-#643, with the "high numbers," #644-#752, being the most challenging.

FOR

It is one of Topps' most attractive sets. There are lots of superstars—as well as little-known players—much to the delight of team collectors.

AGAINST

It is extremely hard to find Mint cards due to the black borders, which quickly show signs of wear. Collectors like complete year-by-year stats on the back of their cards.

NOTEWORTHY CARDS

There are lots of good rookie cards in the '71 set, most notably Steve Garvey. Other rookie cards include Dave Concepcion, Ken Singleton, Ted Simmons, George Foster, Greg Luzinski, and (sharing a "Rookie Outfielders" card) Dusty Baker and Don Baylor.

OUR FAVORITE CARD

Pete Rose collectors can find a "hidden" Rose card in the '71 set. The Cincinnati Reds baserunner on second, behind Phillies pitcher Chris Short on Short's card (#511), is ol' Charlie Hustle himself.

VALUE

EX-MT CONDITION: Complete set, $1,000; common card #1-#523, 35¢; #524-#643, 75¢; #644-#752, $1.75; superstars, $5–$15; Baylor/Baker, $20; Roberto Clemente, Reggie Jackson, Willie Mays, Hank Aaron, Carl Yastrzemski, $22–$27; Rose, $50; Garvey, $60. 5-YEAR PROJECTION: Average, perhaps above.

1971 TOPPS SUPERS

SPECIFICATIONS

SIZE: 3⅛ × 5¼". FRONT: Color photograph. BACK: Green and black printing on gray cardboard. DISTRIBUTION: Nationally, in packages with bubblegum.

HISTORY

In 1971, for the second straight year, Topps produced a separate set of oversize cards called Supers. The cards feature a borderless, round-cornered photo, with only a facsimile autograph for identification. The round corners tend to hold up well to handling. The back is an enlarged version of the player's regular '71 card; only the card number is different. The Super set contains 63 cards—up

1971 Topps Supers, Bert Campaneris

from 42 the previous year. The larger set size eliminated the need for short-printed cards and so there are no real scarcities. Since most of the players in this special set are stars and the cards are much scarcer than the regular Topps cards, it is an expensive set to collect.

FOR

These cards are great for superstar collectors. Considering their scarcity, they are reasonably priced.

AGAINST

Many collectors don't like oversize cards or cards with rounded corners.

NOTEWORTHY CARDS

Virtually every Hall of Fame caliber player active in 1971 is present in the Supers set.

VALUE

EX-MT CONDITION: Complete set, \$165; common card, 75¢; stars, \$1–\$4; Roberto Clemente, Reggie Jackson, Hank Aaron, Tom Seaver, Willie Mays, Carl Yastrzemski, \$10–\$15; Pete Rose, \$25. 5-YEAR PROJECTION: Above average.

1971 TOPPS GREATEST MOMENTS

SPECIFICATIONS

SIZE: $2\frac{1}{2} \times 4\frac{3}{4}''$. FRONT: Color and black-and-white photographs. BACK: Black printing on white cardboard. DISTRIBUTION: Regionally, test-marketed in packages with bubblegum.

HISTORY

One of the scarcest and most popular Topps test issues, the 55-card "Greatest Moments" set is quite challenging for '70s card set collectors. Each of the horizontal-format cards depicts a career highlight of an active player. The front has a small color photo of the player at the left, and a larger black-and-white deckle-edge action "snapshot" at the right. There is a small caption in the white border of the photo. The whole design is set off by a black background, which presents the same problem of chipping and flaking as the regular '71 Topps issue. The card back is made to look like a real front page from the team's hometown newspaper, with a large headline and a story describing the "Great Moment" and picturing a detail from the front photo.

FOR

These unusual cards can spice up a superstar collection; virtually every player in the set is a star.

AGAINST

The cards are rare and very expensive.

NOTEWORTHY CARDS

Virtually everybody in the set is a star: when the commons include players like Jim Perry, Bill Freehan, Rico Petrocelli, and Jim Wynn, you know it's loaded with stars.

1971 Topps Greatest Moments, Ernie Banks

VALUE

EX-MT CONDITION: Complete set, $1,050; common card, $4; Hall of Famers, $20–$60; Pete Rose, Reggie Jackson, Johnny Bench, $100–$150. 5-YEAR PROJECTION: Average, perhaps a bit below.

1971 KELLOGG'S

SPECIFICATIONS

SIZE: 2¼ × 3½". FRONT: Color photograph, 3-D effect. BACK: Blue printing on white cardboard. DISTRIBUTION: Nationally, one card in boxes of cereal.

1971 Kellogg's, Pete Rose

HISTORY

Collectors had gotten burned in 1970: they bought the Kellogg's cards in cereal boxes, one at a time, only to find complete sets available later that year. In '71, many collectors ignored the cereal cards and waited for a complete-set offer at season's end. But Kellogg's outsmarted them again; the cards were never made available in complete sets. By the time collectors realized this, the specially marked cereal boxes were gone, resulting in a mad scramble to complete sets. The 1971 set is the most valuable and difficult to complete set of the 14 Kellogg's issues. Once again, the set contains 75 cards with a 3-D effect. A color photo is surrounded by a blue border with white highlights and a wide white frame (resulting in a much smaller picture area). The player's last name and position appear in a red star in an upper corner. On the card back, a small photo of the player appears in the upper left, along with an official team logo.

FOR

The set is genuinely challenging to complete, and it has good potential for price appreciation.

AGAINST

The plastic lamination on the card front has a tendency to crack and curl with age and handling.

NOTEWORTHY CARDS

There are fewer big names in the 1971 Kellogg's set than in previous sets. Notably absent in '71 were Hank Aaron, Brooks Robinson, Reggie Jackson, and Johnny Bench. There was still no Carl Yastrzemski card. Superstars who do appear in the set include Tom Seaver, Roberto Clemente, Frank Robinson, Willie Mays, and Pete Rose.

VALUE

EX-MT CONDITION: Complete set, $650; common card, $5; stars, $10–$30; Rose, $65. 5-YEAR PROJECTION: Above average.

1971 BAZOOKA

SPECIFICATIONS

SIZE: Single card, 2 × 2⅝″; panel, 5⁵⁄₁₆ × 2⅝″. FRONT: Color photograph. BACK: Blank. DISTRIBUTION: Nationally, one 3-card panel on each box of bubblegum.

1971 Bazooka, Hank Aaron

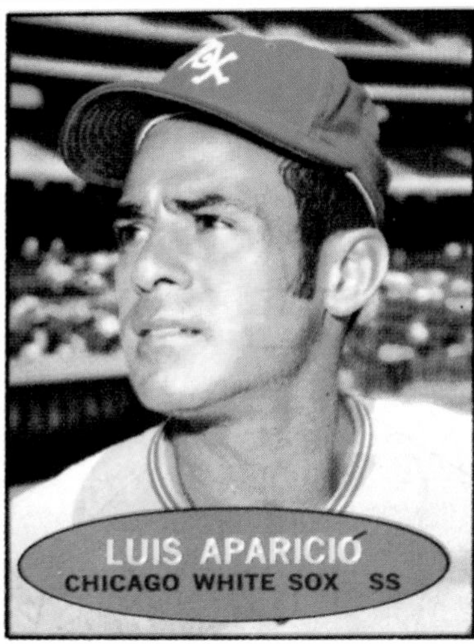

1971 Bazooka, Luis Aparicio

HISTORY

The final Bazooka bubblegum set was issued by Topps in 1971. It reverted to the same basic formula used since the second Bazooka set was issued in '60. A strip of three baseball cards was printed on the bottom of 25-piece boxes of Bazooka bubblegum (the box retailed for about 20¢ back then). In all, there were a dozen different panels in 1971, with 36 different cards. The cards were meant to be cut off the box along the dotted lines, but cards that were cut evenly are somewhat scarce. Collectors will generally pay 10 to 15 percent more for a 3-card panel than for the three individual cards, and entire boxes command a 25 to 50 percent premium. Like many earlier Bazooka sets, the 1971 issue contains a high percentage of Hall of Famers. The format of the cards is little changed from early years: a color photo of the player is surrounded by a white border. The player's name, team, and position are printed in a red oval at the bottom of the card. The '71 Bazookas are unnumbered.

FOR

The 1971 set returned to featuring individual cards of current players. There are lots of stars, and the cards are scarcer than regular Topps cards of the same year.

AGAINST

The cards are too small to suit most collectors, who prefer the standard 2½ × 3½″.

NOTEWORTHY CARDS

Fan favorites Willie Mays, Hank Aaron, Reggie Jackson, Pete Rose, and Carl Yastrzemski grace the set.

VALUE

EX-MT CONDITION: Complete set of single cards, $140; single card, $2; Hall of Famers, $5–$7; Aaron, Mays, Yastrzemski, Jackson, $15–$20; Rose, $25. 5-YEAR PROJECTION: Average.

1971 MILK DUDS

SPECIFICATIONS

SIZE: 1¹³⁄₁₆ × 2⅝″. FRONT: Sepia-tone photograph on light tan cardboard. BACK: Blank. DISTRIBUTION: Nationally, on the back of boxes of Milk Duds.

1971 Milk Duds, Reggie Smith

1971 Milk Duds, Ray Fosse

HISTORY
Perhaps one of the more underrated baseball card sets of the early 1970s, the Milk Duds issue of '71 contains a high percentage of superstar players among its 69 cards. Surprisingly, the Milk Duds cards are seldom found cut off the original box. It's a good thing, too, because there is no identification on the card, just the player's picture, his name, and a short line about his 1970 performance. Empty boxes are most common (they apparently made their way into hobby channels directly from the printer or the candy company) and there is no premium attached to a box still full of candy. Cards cut from the box are worth about half as much as a complete box.

FOR
The set offers good value; the cards are priced only a little higher than the same 1971 Topps cards but they are much less common. Complete boxes make a nice shelf display.

AGAINST
The cards are too small and are not in full color. Storing the flattened boxes takes up a lot of space.

NOTEWORTHY CARDS
Hall of Famers include Luis Aparicio, Harmon Killebrew, Hank Aaron, Roberto Clemente, and Willie Mays, among others. Thurman Munson is pictured at the beginning of his short career.

VALUE
EX-MT CONDITION: Complete set of boxes, $950; single box, $2; Hall of Famers, $25; Aaron, Clemente, $40; Rose, $80. 5-YEAR PROJECTION: Above average.

1970 TOPPS

SPECIFICATIONS
SIZE: 2½ × 3½". FRONT: Color photograph. BACK: Blue and yellow printing on white cardboard. DISTRIBUTION: Nationally, in packages with bubblegum.

1970 Topps, Hank Aaron

1970 Topps, Willie Mays

1970 Topps, Tom Seaver

HISTORY

Because it was issued at the beginning of the decade, the 1970 Topps set is a popular starting point for modern baseball card collectors. At 720 cards, it was the largest issue produced by Topps up to that point. The design is simple and attractive. A color photo is surrounded by a thin white frame inside a gray border. The team name is printed in an upper corner of the photo in colorful block letters. The player's name is in script at the lower left, and his position is in the lower right. The gray border is not as susceptible to wear and tear as the black border that Topps used in 1971. The card backs are bright and easy to read, featuring a cartoon, a short career summary, personal data, and year-by-year major and/or minor league stats. The '70 cards were issued one series at a time as the year progressed, and the later a series was released, the scarcer it became. Cards #1-#459 are the most common, followed by #460-#546 and #547-#633, with #634-#720 being the hardest to find. The most expensive card in the set is Johnny Bench, who appears in the high numbers along with Nolan Ryan, Frank Robinson, and Al Kaline. Topps began a three-year tradition in 1970 by making the team card of the World Series winner (the Amazin' Mets that year) card #1 in the set. The Mets also figure prominently in two special subsets: an 8-card run recapping the 1969 American League and National League playoffs, and a 6-card set highlighting the World Series. There were also special cards for 1969's statistical leaders in major categories. The winner in each league shares a card with the two runners-up, creating some three- and four-player cards with a lot of superstars. Topps also ended a three-year tradition in 1970 by issuing the last separate set of The Sporting News All-Star cards. (The cards, which had also been issued in 1958-1962, were started again in 1982.) Like most of its predecessors, the 1970 All-Star cards were different from the rest of the set. They feature a color portrait of the player "tearing through" a front page from *The Sporting News* with a January 24, 1970, dateline. (Curiously, the newspaper features headlines about the Sharks, a forfeit, and the Caribbean Series.) All-Star card backs feature a large cartoon portrait of the player. As with most subset cards, an All-Star card is worth less than the regular card for the same player (except for rare high-number cards). The '70 All-Stars contains 20 cards: eight starting fielders for each league, and both lefthanded and righthanded pitchers. The rookies are arranged by team, featuring either two or three players.

FOR

A good place to start a modern collection. The 1970 set has many of the best features of the '60s without the gimmick cards that would be seen later in the '70s. There are many older Hall of Famers still playing or managing, as well as some of the better-known veterans of the game today. Considering its age and the scarcity of high-number cards, the price is reasonable.

AGAINST

There are no real faults, but eagle-eyed error hunters will have a field day with card backs and some "strange" photos.

NOTEWORTHY CARDS

Topps sometimes cheated on the photos for their playoff and World Series subsets by using game-action photos from other games. Probably Topps' worst year in this respect was '70, when three of the eight league playoff cards had wrong photos. Cards #195 and #196, purporting to show Games 1 and 2 of the National League pennant series from Atlanta, are actually from Game 3, at New York. The giveaway is that the Mets are wearing home uniforms. On card #201, which claims to show the deciding game of the Orioles-Twins playoffs, Baltimore catcher Andy Etchebarren is pictured, but he only played in the first and second games of that series. The 1970 set also contains a number of "equipment errors." Grant Jackson (#6) is shown pitching while wearing a batting glove, and Steve Huntz (#282) is shown throwing the ball with a batting glove. Outfielder Bob Watson posed with a catcher's mitt (#407), and Cardinals shortstop Dal Maxvill (#503) is shown in a fielding pose wearing a batting helmet. The hot rookie card of 1970 is Thurman Munson. Others of note are Vida Blue, Gene Tenace, Jerry Reuss, and Bill Buckner.

OUR FAVORITE CARD

How can you choose between these two? Dick Ellsworth's card (#59) shows the Cleveland Indians pitcher in a Cubs uniform. Ellsworth last played for the Cubs in 1966, and in between had been with the Phillies and the Red Sox. The "Angels Rookies" card (#74) features pitcher Wally Wolf. That's actually Wolf's second "rookie card." He appeared on the 1963 Topps "Rookie Stars" card (#208) seven years earlier. Actually, Wolf's '63 debut card was a bit premature, because he didn't appear in the major leagues until 1969.

VALUE

EX-MT CONDITION: Complete set, $950; common card, #1-#459, 30¢; #460-#546, 40¢; #547-#633, 50¢; #634-#720, $1.25; superstars, $6–$18; Hank Aaron, Al Kaline, Carl Yastrzemski, Willie Mays, Roberto Clemente, Tom Seaver, $20–$25; Nolan Ryan, Munson, Reggie Jackson, $30–$40; Rose, $70; Bench, $75. 5-YEAR PROJECTION: Average or above.

1970 TOPPS SUPERS

SPECIFICATIONS

SIZE: 3⅛ × 5¼". FRONT: Color photograph. BACK: Blue and yellow printing on yellow cardboard. DISTRIBUTION: Nationally, in packages with bubblegum.

1970 Topps Supers, Bob Gibson

HISTORY

Unlike the 1969 Topps "Super" cards, which were about the same size as regular baseball cards, the 1970 Supers were postcard-size. The cards were printed on heavy, white glossy stock and then trimmed to give them rounded corners. Card fronts have borderless color photos with a facsimile autograph. The card back is an enlarged version of the player's regular '70 Topps card back. There were 42 cards in the set, and it is believed that this resulted in three "short-printed" cards, which are scarcer than the rest. Cards of Ollie Brown and Frank Robinson (#36 and #37) are somewhat scarcer than the others, and Boog Powell's card (#38) is the scarcest of all. Overall, the '70 Supers were distributed in larger quantities than the '69s, making them less expensive.

FOR

They make a nice addition to superstar or team collections.

AGAINST

Some collectors don't like oversize cards or round corners.

NOTEWORTHY CARDS

Proportionately, there are a lot of stars and hometown favorites in the '70 Supers.

VALUE

EX-MT CONDITION: Complete set, $175; common card, 75¢; stars, $3–$6; superstars, $8–$15; Tom Seaver, Carl Yastrzemski, Reggie Jackson, Frank Robinson, $15–$20; Pete Rose, $25; Powell, $45. 5-YEAR PROJECTION: Above average.

1970 KELLOGG'S

SPECIFICATIONS

SIZE: 2¼ × 3½". FRONT: Color photograph, 3-D effect. BACK: Blue printing on white cardboard. DISTRIBUTION: Nationally, one card in boxes of cereal; complete sets sold by hobby dealers at the end of the season.

1970 Kellogg's, Bert Campaneris

HISTORY

In 1970 Kellogg's began a 14-year series of baseball card issues. The Kellogg's cards are significant because for many years they were the only nationally distributed issue besides Topps. The cards feature a sharp color photo of the player set against a blurred stadium background, surrounded by a blue border. A layer of ribbed plastic laminated over the picture gives a 3-D effect. Card backs include a few biographical and career details along with major league stats, all printed in blue. This was the first widespread baseball card issue to utilize the 3-D look, which Topps had tried on a test basis in 1968. (The cards were produced by Xograph Co.) One "3-D Super Star" card was packaged in each box of Kellogg's cereal. A lot of collectors consumed a great deal of corn flakes trying to find all 75 cards—at a total cost of $50 or more. Kellogg's had a surprise in store at the end of the season, and many hobbyists were shocked to learn that the company had sold its leftovers to selected dealers and toy stores. The price of the set plummeted to $5, though it has since regained its market value.

FOR

These are attractive cards at a reasonable price.

AGAINST

The cards tend to crack and curl because of the plastic lamination, greatly reducing their value.

NOTEWORTHY CARDS

About every third card in the 1970 Kellogg's set is a star of Hall of Fame proportions. All the names you'd expect are present, with the exception of Hank Aaron and Carl Yastrzemski.

VALUE

EX-MT CONDITION: Complete set, $85; common card, 60¢–75¢; stars, $2–$4; Willie Mays, Roberto Clemente, Reggie Jackson, $3–$5; Pete Rose, $7–$9. 5-YEAR PROJECTION: Above average.

1970 TRANSOGRAM

SPECIFICATIONS

SIZE: 2⁹⁄₁₆ × 3½". FRONT: Color photograph. BACK: Blank. DISTRIBUTION: Nationally, on the bottom of boxes of toy baseball player statues.

HISTORY

The 1970 Transogram cards were produced in two series. There was a 45-card group of players from all teams, and a special 15-card series honoring "The Amazin' Mets," the 1969 World Champions. While the cards themselves were little changed for '70 (they were narrower in 1969), they were issued differently. Instead of one card per box with one toy player figure inside, the 1970 boxes contained three figures and had three cards printed on the

1970 Transogram, Boog Powell

1970 Transogram, Harmon Killebrew

bottom. The cards (bordered by a dotted line) feature a color portrait photo with a white frame and yellow border. Player names appear in red below the picture, with team, position, and a few biographical details in black. There are no card numbers, and the backs are blank. All of the cards in the '69 and '70 Transogram sets feature the same photos, with the exception of Joe Torre and Johnny Callison (whose reversed photo from '69 was corrected in '70). The 1970 Transogram cards are most valuable when still attached to the box with the statues inside. Entire boxes are worth twice as much as the three single cards, while cards in panels of three are worth about 50 percent more.

FOR

Another issue for the superstar collector. The Mets cards are especially nice for the team collector.

AGAINST

They are hard to find in top condition. The cards are really not that attractive.

NOTEWORTHY CARDS

There are several stars and Hall of Famers, plus Mets such as Jerry Grote, Bud Harrelson, and Tug McGraw.

VALUE

EX-MT CONDITION: Complete set of single cards, $300; single card, $1; stars, $5–$10; Willie Mays, Tom Seaver, Hank Aaron, Roberto Clemente, Reggie Jackson, Carl Yastrzemski, Nolan Ryan, $25–$40; Pete Rose, $40–$50. 5-YEAR PROJECTION: Average.

1969 TO 1960

1969 Topps, Rod Carew

1967 Topps, Hank Aaron

1966 Bazooka, Pete Rose

1969 TOPPS

SPECIFICATIONS

SIZE: 2½ × 3½″. FRONT: Color photograph. BACK: Black and pink printing on white cardboard. DISTRIBUTION: Nationally, in packages with bubblegum.

1969 Topps, Reggie Jackson

1969 Topps, Mickey Mantle

1969 Topps, Boog Powell

HISTORY

The 1969 Topps set is unusual in several ways, all of which make it popular and collectible. For one thing, Topps again set a record for the number of cards issued, with 664. Distribution of the series was also unusual. There are four levels of scarcity in the '69 set, but the "high numbers" (cards #514-#664) are not considered the scarcest; that distinction goes to cards #219-#327. Cards #1-#218 and #328-#512 are considered the most common. There are enough collectible (and valuable) variations in the 1969 set to keep a collector busy for some time assembling a complete set. The '69 set features the last Topps multiplayer feature cards. It bypasses the team cards that had been a staple since 1956. The three special subsets of the previous year returned in 1969: a 12-card rundown of the statistical leaders in each league; a group of eight World Series cards detailing the Tigers' win over the Cardinals; and a *Sporting News* All-Star group of 20. Rookies were grouped two or three to a card, by team or league. he design of the 1969 set is somewhat similar to he '67 set. A large color photo bordered in white occupies most of the card front. The team name is printed in colored block letters at the bottom. The player's name and position are contained in a circle in one of the upper corners. Card backs returned to a horizontal format in '69, again combining complete major and/or minor league stats, a cartoon, and a short biography.

FOR

In its basic form, the 1969 set is inexpensive and relatively easy to collect.

AGAINST

If a collector desires a complete set of 1969 Topps, he or she must do some studying to learn what actually constitutes a complete set. Variation cards in this set are sometimes hard to locate, and are quite often very expensive.

NOTEWORTHY CARDS

Reggie Jackson has his own rookie card in 1969 and it's the hottest novice card in the set. The other big-name rookies in the set are Amos Otis, Al Oliver, Graig Nettles, and Rollie Fingers. The largest and most expensive group of variation cards in this set are the so-called "white letter" cards. There are many cards in the set with the player name or team name in white letters, but 23 cards (in the #440-#511 range) appear with these elements in either yellow (common) or white (scarce). Among common players in this group, the white-letter varieties are worth 20 to 30 times more than the yellow-letter cards. There are three superstars in the group: Willie McCovey (#440), Gaylord Perry (#485), and Mickey Mantle (#500). This is also the last regular-issue Mickey Mantle card of his career; he had retired at the end of the previous season. There are a pair of team/pose variations: Clay Dalrymple (#151) and Donn Clendenon (#208). The Dalrymple card can be found with a portrait and the team name "Orioles," or with the player in a catching position and the team "Phillies." Clendenon is seen with either "Houston" on the front or "Expos." There is a wrong-name variation on the "Royals Rookies" card (#49): on the common card, Ellie Rodriguez's name is spelled correctly; the scarcer version has the name spelled "Roriquez." Paul Popovich (#47) and Ron Perranoski (#77) can be found with and without a team logo (the logo was airbrushed to reflect a trade). Checklist 2 (#107) lists either "Jim Purdin" or "John Purdin" (correct) as card #161. There is a flopped negative of Larry Haney (#209). There is a "hidden ball trick" (#465) where Tommy John is shown following through on his pitching motion with the ball still in his glove. There are three let's-fool-the-photographer cards: on two of those, Gary Geiger (#278) and Mack Jones (#625) are shown batting from the other side; the third is one of the classic baseball cards of all time (#653), purporting to be the rookie card of Aurelio Rodriguez but actually picturing the Angels' batboy.

OUR FAVORITE CARDS

While on the subject of rookies, there is a Lou Piniella rookie card in the '69 Topps set (#394, "Pilots Rookies"). Actually, Piniella never played for Seattle; he was traded to Kansas City before the beginning of the season. Also, it isn't even Piniella's "real" rookie card; he appears in the '68 set (#16, "Indians Rookies"). But that's not his true rookie card either. The "real" Lou Piniella rookie card is in the 1964 Topps set (#167, "Senators Rookies"). If you think three rookie cards is some kind of record, you're wrong. The real record for rookie-card appearances is in the '69 Topps set where Bill Davis appears on his fifth rookie card in as many years. Davis had an Indians rookie card in 1965 through 1968, and a Padres Rookies card in 1969. Davis never appeared on a regular Topps card. In parts of three major league seasons (33 games with the '65 and '66 Indians 31 games with the '69 Padres), Davis amassed a .181 batting average, striking out 28 times in 105 at-bats.

VALUE

EX-MT CONDITION: Complete set, $1,500; common card, 20¢–60¢; superstars, $1–$4; Johnny Bench, Pete Rose, Tom Seaver, Nolan Ryan, $35–$45; Perry (white letters), $50; McCovey (white letters), $65; Mantle (yellow letters), $75; Jackson, $275; Mantle (white letters), $450. 5-YEAR PROJECTION: Above average.

1969 TOPPS SUPERS

SPECIFICATIONS

SIZE: 2¼ × 3¼″. FRONT: Color photograph. BACK: Black printing on white cardboard. DISTRIBUTION: Nationally, in wax packs.

1969 Topps Supers, Tony Oliva

HISTORY

Topps called them "Super Baseball Cards" on the back, a name that stuck with collectors and is also applied to the similar postcard-size issues of 1970 and '71. The 1969 Topps Supers, though, weren't bigger than the regular-issue cards of that year. What was super about the cards was the high-gloss finish that really enhanced the color photo on the front of the card. The only other design element on the front is a facsimile autograph. Card backs contain only a rectangular box at the bottom with the player's name, team, and position, a copyright line, and a card number. The cards have rounded corners. Superstars abound in the '69 Super set, and even the common cards are relatively scarce. The set was distributed in very limited numbers and is expensive and challenging for the collector today. Because of the high quality of the cards and the attractive photos, these cards are the highlight of many superstar collections.

FOR

These cards are extremely attractive, scarce, and valuable; the set contains a generous number of superstars.

AGAINST

The high dollar value of even common cards and the high demand for stars make it difficult to complete.

NOTEWORTHY CARDS

Most of the big-name stars of 1969 are in the Super set. There is a "last" card of Mickey Mantle and a rookie card of Reggie Jackson.

VALUE

EX-MT CONDITION: Complete set, \$3,100; common card, \$9; stars, \$10–\$20; superstars, \$50–\$90; Brooks Robinson, Roberto Clemente, Frank Robinson, Tom Seaver, \$150–\$200; Hank Aaron, Willie Mays, Jackson, Carl Yastrzemski, \$250–\$300; Pete Rose, \$500; Mantle, \$650. 5-YEAR PROJECTION: Average.

1969 Topps Deckle-Edge, Pete Rose

1969 Topps Deckle-Edge, Carl Yastrzemski

1969 TOPPS DECKLE-EDGE

SPECIFICATIONS

SIZE: 2¼ × 3¼". FRONT: Black-and-white photograph. BACK: Blue printing on white cardboard. DISTRIBUTION: Nationally, in packages with regular '69 Topps cards.

HISTORY

Designed to resemble the popular wallet-size photos of movie stars of the 1950s, the Topps Deckle-Edge set of '69 takes its name from the scalloped effect on the white border of the cards. Photos are black and white, and the only other feature on the front of the card is a light-blue facsimile autograph. The same blue ink is seen on the back, where the player's name and card number are shown in a small rectangular box at the bottom of the card. Although the back of the card says there are 33 photos in the set, there are actually 35; card #11 can be found as either Jim Wynn (scarce) or Hoyt Wilhelm (common), and card #22 can be found as either Joe Foy (scarce) or Rusty Staub (common). The Deckle-Edge cards were inserted in regular packs of '69 Topps cards, and are not especially rare today; all the same, collecting a complete set is still a challenge.

FOR

These are unusual cards for a superstar collection.

AGAINST

They're black and white with a "funny" edge.

NOTEWORTHY CARDS

Most of the 35 players in the set are stars or minor stars of the era. The big-name players include Brooks Robinson, Carl Yastrzemski, Roberto Clemente, Pete Rose, and Willie Mays.

VALUE

EX-MT CONDITION: Complete set, $40; common card, 25¢–40¢; stars, $3.50–$5; Wynn, Foy, $6; Rose, $8. 5-YEAR PROJECTION: Below average.

1969 KAHN'S

SPECIFICATIONS

SIZE: 2¹³⁄₁₆ × 3¼″ or 2¹³⁄₁₆ × 3¹⁵⁄₁₆″. FRONT: Color photograph. BACK: Blank. DISTRIBUTION: Chicago, Ohio, Pittsburgh, and St. Louis, single cards in packages of meat products; complete sets sold through the company.

1969 Kahn's, Bill Mazeroski

1969 Kahn's, Bob Veale

HISTORY

A 15-year history of baseball card issues came to an end for the Kahn's meat company in 1969. While late '60s Kahn's sets certainly have their fans, the issues are too similar and too confusing to many collectors who would otherwise be attracted to these scarce regional issues. Individual cards were inserted in packages of the company's meat products. They could be also be purchased as a complete set directly from the company. The cards were coated to protect the meat from absorbing card ink. A total of 22 players (drawn from six teams) make up the final Kahn's card issue. Teams represented include the Cubs, White Sox, Reds, Indians, Pirates, and Cardinals. As in the previous year, Kahn's '69 cards came in two sizes; the smaller cards measure 2¹³⁄₁₆ × 3¼″ with the advertising tab and 2¹³⁄₁₆ × 1⅞″ without the tab. The larger cards measure 2¹³⁄₁₆ × 3¹⁵⁄₁₆″with the tab and 2¹³⁄₁₆ × 2¹³⁄₁₆″without the tab. The two sizes were apparently issued for insertion in different sized packages of meat. Only three players—Hank Aaron, Jim Maloney, and Tony Perez—appear in the smaller format for 1969. The cards keep the same basic design used by Kahn's since 1966. The upper portion of the card is an advertising tab with a red Kahn's logo, separated from the actual baseball card by a dotted line. While collectors prefer cards with the tab, the cards are more often found without it. Values quoted below are for cards without tabs. Cards with the tab are worth some 15 to 20 percent more. The card features a color photo set against a border of alternating colored stripes. The player's name is printed at the top and a facsimile autograph appears across the front. Card backs are blank and—like all Kahn's cards—unnumbered. Because the same players appeared in some or all of the identical 1966 to '69 cards, a detailed checklist is necessary to positively identify any particular player's card that appeared in more than one year.

FOR

These are great regional cards with lots of appeal for team or star collectors.

AGAINST

The set is too similar to the previous three years, making them confusing.

NOTEWORTHY CARDS

The biggest name in the set is Aaron.

VALUE

EX-MT CONDITION: Complete set, $275; common card, $5–$6; stars, $9–$12; Aaron, $60–$70. 5-YEAR PROJECTION: Average, or a bit below.

1969 NABISCO TEAM FLAKES

SPECIFICATIONS

SIZE: $1\frac{3}{4} \times 3''$. FRONT: Color photograph. BACK: Blank. DISTRIBUTION: Nationally, on the back of cereal boxes.

1969 Nabisco Team Flakes, Bob Gibson

1969 Nabisco Team Flakes, Frank Robinson

HISTORY

Taking a cue from the Post cereal cards of the early '60s, Nabisco produced a 24-card set in 1969. The cards were printed on the back of cereal boxes, eight to a box. Three different panels were produced. The cards—especially uncut panels of cards—are not common. (Complete panels are worth some 50 percent more than the total value of the individual cards.) The color photos on the cards do not feature any team logos, a sure sign that Nabisco did not pay royalties to Major League Baseball. Most of the players are stars. The photos are bordered in black, with the player's name, team, and position appearing at the bottom. Between the black frame of the photo and the cutting line is a yellow outer border that varies in width, causing some cards to be slightly larger than others. The cards have blank backs and are unnumbered.

FOR

One of the scarcer national issues of the late '60s, with lots of stars.

AGAINST

The lack of team logos diminishes the cards' popularity, and they are smaller than standard size.

NOTEWORTHY CARDS

The Nabisco Team set is loaded with stars of the day.

VALUE

EX-MT CONDITION: Complete set (neatly cut from box), $300; common card, $4; stars, $10–$25; Hank Aaron, Tom Seaver, Willie Mays, Roberto Clemente, $30–$40; Pete Rose, $60. 5-YEAR PROJECTION: Average.

1969 TRANSOGRAM

SPECIFICATIONS

SIZE: 2½ × 3½″. FRONT: Color photograph. BACK: Blank. DISTRIBUTION: Nationally, on the bottom of boxes containing toy baseball player statues.

1969 Transogram, Billy Williams

HISTORY

The Transogram toy company produced a 60-card set in conjunction with its line of toy baseball player statues in 1969. The cards were printed on the bottoms of the boxes. While the players shown on the cards were stars of the day, the statues inside were generic and not really identifiable as any specific player. Decals were included to make the uniform look like the player on the box. The cards feature a color photo surrounded by a white, round-cornered border. The player's name appears below the photo in red, with the team name and a few personal details in black. There is no card number. All of this is on a yellow background separated from the rest of the box by a black dotted line (meant as a guide for cutting the card off the box). Collectors prefer the cards still attached to the box, or the complete box with the toy inside. Complete boxes with the toy inside are worth double the values listed below. The '69 Transogram cards are not extremely popular with collectors, so even though they are quite scarce, the price is not particularly high.

FOR

For superstar and team collectors, the cards offer something different.

AGAINST

As with all cut-out cards, the original trimming is important in determining the value of the card. Too often they are poorly cut.

NOTEWORTHY CARDS

The Johnny Callison card features a reversed negative.

VALUE

EX-MT CONDITION: Complete set (neatly cut from box), $400; common card, $3; stars, $10–$35; Tom Seaver, Willie Mays, Hank Aaron, Roberto Clemente, $50–$60; Pete Rose, Carl Yastrzemski, $75; Mickey Mantle, $130. 5-YEAR PROJECTION: Below average.

1969-1970 BAZOOKA ALL-TIME GREATS

SPECIFICATIONS

SIZE: Side-panel card, 1¼ × 3⅛″; bottom-panel card, 3 × 6¼″; complete box, 5½ × 6¼″. FRONT: Black-and-white photograph. BACK: Blank. DISTRIBUTION: Nationally, one 5-card panel on each box of bubblegum.

HISTORY

In producing its second "All-Time Greats" set for Bazooka, Topps adopted a style similar to that used the previous year. The bottom of the box was taken up with a large "Baseball Extra" card, made to resemble a newspaper account of a famous baseball accomplishment. A contemporary photo of the player involved is used. Each side of the box features a pair of tall, narrow cards of Hall of Famers. As with the '63 set, the photos are generally those taken later in the players' lives, so the athletes tend to look old. Many of the same photos from the 1963 All-Time Greats set were recycled in the '69-'70 effort. While collectors prefer this set in 12 complete boxes, the better-known

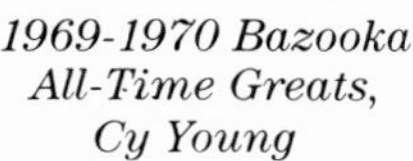
1969-1970 Bazooka All-Time Greats, Cy Young

1969-1970 Bazooka All-Time Greats, Babe Ruth

players are also avidly collected in the small side-panel cards and large Baseball Extra bottom panels. Add about 25 percent to card-price totals for a complete box. Although a full set of 12 bottom panels will contain 48 side-panel cards, there are only 30 different All-Time Great cards. Several of the cards appear with two different bottom panels.

FOR

These are inexpensive cards of some of baseball's greatest players.

AGAINST

The cards are either too large (bottom panel) or too small (side panel). All-Time Greats cards are not particularly popular with collectors, who prefer cards actually issued during the career of the player. If a card is issued later, it should at least have a picture of the player as he looked during his heyday.

NOTEWORTHY CARDS

Such expected big names as Babe Ruth, Ty Cobb, and Lou Gehrig are in the set.

VALUE

EX-MT CONDITION: Complete set (neatly cut from box), \$100. Bottom-panel cards: common card, \$3–\$5; Cobb, Gehrig, \$7–\$10; Ruth, \$12. Side-panel cards: common card, 50¢–75¢; stars, \$2–\$4; Cobb, Gehrig, \$6; Ruth, \$8.50. 5-YEAR PROJECTION: Below average.

1968 TOPPS

SPECIFICATIONS

SIZE: 2½ × 3½″. FRONT: Color photograph. BACK: Black and yellow printing on white cardboard. DISTRIBUTION: Nationally, in packages with bubblegum.

1968 Topps, Vada Pinson

1968 Topps, Roger Maris

1968 Topps, Maury Wills

HISTORY

There's no telling how popular the 1968 Topps set would be if the design weren't so unusual. The best way to describe it is to say that it looks as though a color photo had been laid on top of a burlap sack. The player's name is printed below the photo on the brown-mesh background, while a colored circle at the lower right contains the player's team and position. The design is not really unattractive, it's just...different. The card backs retain the vertical format of the previous year, but the elements are rearranged so that the cartoon appears at the bottom and the stats in the middle. After the 1967 high of 609 cards, the '68 set returned to the 598 cards that had been the norm in '65 and '66. Besides the N.L. and A.L. statistical leader cards (the first 12 in the set) and the World Series specials (eight cards on the Cardinals' win over the Red Sox), the 1968 set marks the return of an All-Star subseries—20 players chosen by *The Sporting News.* Other than a few multiplayer feature cards and the usual checklists and rookie cards, these were the only special cards in the set. While the last several series in '68 (#534-#598) are nominally considered high numbers, they are not really much more rare or expensive than the first 533 cards.

FOR

It is one of the easier late '60s sets to assemble (owing to the lack of rare high numbers). There are some good rookie cards.

AGAINST

Some people don't like the "burlap" look of the set.

NOTEWORTHY CARDS

The '68 set has rookie cards of Nolan Ryan and Jerry Koosman (on the same card) and Johnny Bench. The last cards of Roger Maris and Eddie Mathews are included. Casey Cox (#66) can be found with his team name in white or yellow letters. Pitcher Steve Hamilton (#496) is shown wearing a first baseman's glove.

VALUE

EX-MT CONDITION: Complete set, \$1,450; common card, #1-#533, 35¢; #534-#598, 75¢; stars, \$4-\$6; superstars, \$10-\$20; Willie Mays, Hank Aaron, Steve Carlton, Carl Yastrzemski, \$20-\$25; Cox (yellow letters), \$40; Pete Rose, Tom Seaver, \$45-\$50; Bench, Ryan/Koosman, Mickey Mantle, \$135-\$150. 5-YEAR PROJECTION: Above average.

1968 TOPPS GAME

SPECIFICATIONS

SIZE: $2\frac{1}{4} \times 3\frac{1}{4}''$. FRONT: Color photograph. BACK: Blue printing on white cardboard. DISTRIBUTION: Nationally, in packages with '68 Topps baseball cards and in boxed sets.

1968 Topps Game, Mickey Mantle

1968 TOPPS 3-D

SPECIFICATIONS

SIZE: 2¼ × 3½". FRONT: Color photograph, 3-D effect. BACK: Blank. DISTRIBUTION: Regionally, in wax packs.

1968 Topps Game, Pete Rose

HISTORY

The idea of issuing baseball cards that could be used to play a game was not new for Topps; they had done the same thing with their Red Backs and Blue Backs sets of 1951. The '68 game cards follow the same concept. Besides a color head-and-shoulders portrait of the player and a facsimile autograph at the bottom, each of the 33 cards has a baseball term: "line out," "error," "single," etc. The backs of the round-cornered cards feature a baseball motif. The set is not very popular with collectors, who don't normally like baseball cards that are intended for any other purpose than to be looked at. Because of the lack of demand, it is relatively difficult (though inexpensive) to assemble a complete set.

FOR

The big names in the set make cheap additions to a superstar collection.

AGAINST

They're too small, they have rounded corners, and they were intended to be used as a game—three strikes against them.

NOTEWORTHY CARDS

A large percentage of the 33 game cards in this set are stars, or at least were considered stars in 1968.

VALUE

EX-MT CONDITION: Complete set, $40; common card, 30¢; stars, $2–$5; Pete Rose, Mickey Mantle, $10. 5-YEAR PROJECTION: Below average.

1968 Topps 3-D, Bill Robinson

1968 Topps 3-D, Willie Davis

1968 Bazooka, Curt Flood

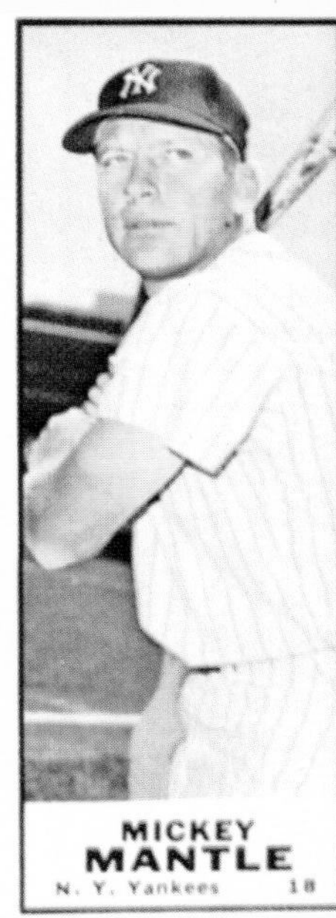

1968 Bazooka, Mickey Mantle

HISTORY

Two years before Kellogg's began its lengthy run of 3-D baseball cards, Topps experimented with a similar issue. The cards were given a 3-D look by placing a sharp color photo of the player over a fuzzy stadium background. A layer of plastic was laminated over this, giving the illusion of depth when the card was tilted or moved. The card front contains the player's name and, in a circle in the upper left, his position and team. Topps produced just 12 cards in this limited-edition test set. The cards are unnumbered and have a blank back. They were sold in a generic wrapper with a color sticker identifying the issue. Because of extremely limited printing quantities and distribution, these cards are very rare today and command a high price. The Topps 3-D cards represent the most expensive baseball card for every player in the set.

FOR

They are extremely rare and very valuable if you happen to find one in a shoe box or at a yard sale.

AGAINST

The extreme rarity and high dollar value make them impractical for most collectors.

NOTEWORTHY CARDS

The only Hall of Famer in the 3-D Topps test set is Roberto Clemente. Three others of special note are Rusty Staub, Tony Perez, and Boog Powell.

VALUE

EX-MT CONDITION: Complete set, $5,500; common card, $350; Staub, Powell, $500; Perez, $650; Clemente, $1,400. 5-YEAR PROJECTION: Below average.

1968 BAZOOKA

SPECIFICATIONS

SIZE: Side-panel card, 1¼ × 3⅛″, bottom-panel card, 3 × 6¼″, complete box, 5½ × 6¼″. FRONT: Color photograph. BACK: Blank. DISTRIBUTION: Nationally, one 5-card panel on each box of bubblegum.

HISTORY

Topps radically changed the nature of Bazooka baseball cards in their tenth year of issue. The 1968 Bazooka set consists of 15 numbered boxes. The bottom of each box has a player photo and a series of baseball instruction drawings called "Tipps from the Topps." Each box side contains two tall, narrow cards. Since four of the side-panel cards were repeated (Tommy Agee, Pete Rose, Ron Santo, and Don Drysdale are found on the sides of box #6 and box #15), there are 71 different cards in the 1968 Bazooka set: 15 bottom-panel cards and 56 side-panel cards. Cards are worth 25 to 50 percent more when boxes are left intact.

FOR

The set is something different for the superstar collector.

AGAINST

The unusual format and card size make the set unpopular. Except for the superstars, there is little demand for '68 Bazookas, especially the "Tipps" cards, as collectors have traditionally shunned this type of card.

NOTEWORTHY CARDS

Al Kaline, Frank Robinson, Juan Marichal, Bob Gibson, Harmon Killebrew, Roberto Clemente, and Brooks Robinson are among the stars in the set.

VALUE

EX-MT CONDITION: Complete set (neatly cut from box), $650; common card, $3; stars, $15-$25; Willie Mays, Hank Aaron, Carl Yastrzemski, $45; Rose, $70; Mickey Mantle, $100. 5-YEAR PROJECTION: Below average.

1968 KAHN'S

SPECIFICATIONS

SIZE: 2$2\frac{13}{16} \times 3\frac{1}{4}$" or $2\frac{13}{16} \times 3\frac{7}{8}$". FRONT: Color photograph. BACK: Blank. DISTRIBUTION: Regional home-team area, single cards in packages of meat products; complete sets available by mail.

1968 Kahn's, Johnny Bench

1968 Kahn's, Billy Williams

HISTORY

Things really get confusing with the 1968 Kahn's set. The cards are in the same basic format as '66 and '67. This can cause confusion when trying to figure out the correct year a player's card was issued since some players appeared in two or three of those years. In addition, there are two different sizes of cards in the 1968 set and a number of variations within each group. A record number of teams is represented in the '68 issue: the Cubs, White Sox, Braves, Reds, Pirates, Indians, Tigers, and Mets. Perhaps the easiest way to describe the set is to say that there is a total of 50 cards of 38 different players. The two sizes of cards were designed to fit into different size packages of meat. The smaller size set contains 12 cards; the larger size has the same 12 cards plus 26 others. Like the Kahn's sets of '66 and '67, the format is a two-part card separated by a dotted line. Naturally, collectors prefer cards with both halves intact. The values quoted below are for cards without the tab. Cards with the tab are worth about 35 percent more. The lower portion of the two-part card is a player photo bordered by alternating stripes of different colors. The player's name is printed in the upper border, and a facsimile autograph appears across the front of the card. The top portion of the card continues the striped format and has a red Kahn's logo. With the advertising tab, the smaller cards measure $2\frac{13}{16} \times 3\frac{1}{4}$"; without the tab they are $2\frac{13}{16} \times 1\frac{7}{8}$". The larger cards measure $2\frac{13}{16} \times 3\frac{7}{8}$" with the ad tab; $2\frac{13}{16} \times 2\frac{11}{16}$" without the tab. Again, to distinguish between the large-size 1968 cards and the same cards that may appear in the previous two sets requires a detailed checklist. Besides the size differences, the colors of the background stripes vary. Because of all this confusion, the later Kahn's cards are not as popular with collectors as they might otherwise be.

FOR

These are reasonably priced regional cards, especially considering how scarce they are.

AGAINST

It's all too confusing for the average collector.

NOTEWORTHY CARDS

Johnny Bench makes a rookie card appearance in the '68 set. Henry Aaron and Billy Williams are the other superstars represented.

VALUE

EX-MT CONDITION: Complete set, $500; common card, $4-$6; stars, $8-$10; Aaron, $60-$70; Bench, $200. 5-YEAR PROJECTION: Average, or a bit below.

1967 TOPPS

SPECIFICATIONS

SIZE: 2½ × 3½". FRONT: Color photograph. BACK: Green and black printing on white cardboard. DISTRIBUTION: Nationally, in packages with bubblegum.

1967 Topps, Steve Carlton

1967 Topps, Brooks Robinson

1967 Topps, Maury Wills

HISTORY

One of the most popular sets of the '60s, Topps' 1967 effort combines attractive cards with the real challenge of assembling a set that contains some very rare cards. More so than in most years, the high numbers in the '67 set (cards #534-#609) are considerably scarcer than the other series. Part of the scarcity in the '67 highs comes from the fact that some of the cards in that group are double-printed, but collectors can't agree on which ones. Since a Hall of Famer (Brooks Robinson), several superstars (Tommy John, Rocky Colavito, Maury Wills, Jim Bunning), and the rookie cards of two future Hall of Famers (Rod Carew and Tom Seaver) appear in the high-numbered series, the value of these cards, and of the set as a whole, is considerable. At 609 cards, this was Topps' largest to date. The design of the cards is simple but effective. A large color photo of the player is bordered in white. Within the area of the photo, the player's name and position are printed in small letters at the top, while the team name is printed in color block letters at the bottom. There is a facsimile autograph on the photo (except for Milt Pappas, #254). The 1967 issue was the first where Topps adopted a vertical format for card backs; however, all the old familiar elements are there: a cartoon, year-by-year stats, a few lines about the player, biographical details, and a card number. After a year's absence, the subset devoted to the previous year's World Series returned in 1967 and recounted the Orioles' four-game sweep of the

Dodgers. League leaders in the various major stat categories were another subset in the issue. Rookie cards were printed in a horizontal format with two players per card on a team or league basis.

FOR

The set features a popular design. There are some scarce cards and a few varieties to keep things interesting.

AGAINST

The set is relatively expensive for cards that aren't very old.

NOTEWORTHY CARDS

The Seaver and Carew rookie cards are the only premier cards worthy of special note. Whitey Ford makes his final appearance in a regular baseball card set that year. Two of the 1967 cards, Bob Priddy (#26) and Mike McCormick (#86), will be found with or without information on the back indicating trades to other teams. As in 1959, the cards without the traded line are most valuable. Checklist 3 (#191) will be found with card #214 listed as Tom Kelley (incorrect) or Dick Kelley (correct). The set contains Topps' first card of Maury Wills. The bubblegum company apparently snubbed Wills when handing out baseball card contracts to minor leaguers in the mid-'50s, and Wills held a grudge against them until he was traded to the Pirates in '67. The Wills card appears in the high-number series.

OUR FAVORITE CARDS

The Tigers rookie cards are really messed up. Card #72 purports to show John Matchick and George Korince. Actually, it shows Matchick (who played under the name "Tommy" but who was born John Thomas Matchick) with Ike Brown, who didn't get his own rookie card until 1970. (Matchick, interestingly, turned an unassisted triple-play with Syracuse of the International League in 1966.) To make up for the mistake, Topps gave Korince another chance, and pictured him on card #526 (where he is paired with Pat Dobson). Korince ended up with three rookie cards. His only other baseball card is in the '68 Topps set (#447, "Tigers Rookies"). Not bad for a guy with a lifetime pitching record of 1-0 and a 4.24 ERA.

VALUE

EX-MT CONDITION: Complete set, $2,700; common card, #1-#457, 45¢; #458-#533, $1.50; #534-#609, $4.50; stars, $2–$4; superstars, $25–$35; Steve Carlton, Carl Yastrzemski, Tommy John, $45–$55; Pete Rose, Wills, $70; Carew, Brooks Robinson, Mickey Mantle, $125–$160; Seaver, $450. 5-YEAR PROJECTION: Above average.

1967 BAZOOKA

SPECIFICATIONS

SIZE: Single card, 1⁹⁄₁₆ × 2½″, panel, 4¹¹⁄₁₆ × 2½″. FRONT: Color photograph. BACK: Blank. DISTRIBUTION: Nationally, one 3-card panel on the bottom of each box of bubblegum.

1967 Bazooka, Frank Howard

1967 Bazooka, Tommy Agee

HISTORY

In 1967—its ninth year of issuing baseball cards as part of Bazooka gum boxes—Topps got a little lazy. Besides recycling the format and design of the four previous years, a total of 38 of 48 cards in the '67 set were exactly the same cards issued the previous year—same picture, same card number. As might be expected, collectors need to have an original, complete gum box to figure out whether one of these 38 cards is a '66 or '67. Complete boxes are scarce and are worth 25 to 50 percent more than the total value of the three cards. There is also a premium (10 to 15 percent) attached to uncut 3-card panels. In all cases, the condition of the cards depends primarily on how well they were originally cut from the box.

FOR

The photo quality is good.

AGAINST

Since Topps used the same photos, there is confusion between the '66 and '67 issues. The cards are in a nonstandard size.

NOTEWORTHY CARDS

Mickey Mantle, Willie Mays, Hank Aaron, and a few other superstars are all back from earlier years; the best-known players among the ten new cards are Jim Kaat and Denny McLain.

VALUE

EX-MT CONDITION: Complete set (neatly cut from box), $500; common card, $5; stars, $15–$35; Aaron, Mays, Carl Yastrzemski, $45–$50; Pete Rose, $75; Mantle, $100. 5-YEAR PROJECTION: Average.

1967 KAHN'S

SPECIFICATIONS

SIZE: 2¹³⁄₁₆ × 4″. FRONT: Color photograph. BACK: Blank. DISTRIBUTION: Georgia, New York, Ohio, and Pittsburgh, in packages with meat products; complete sets available through the mail.

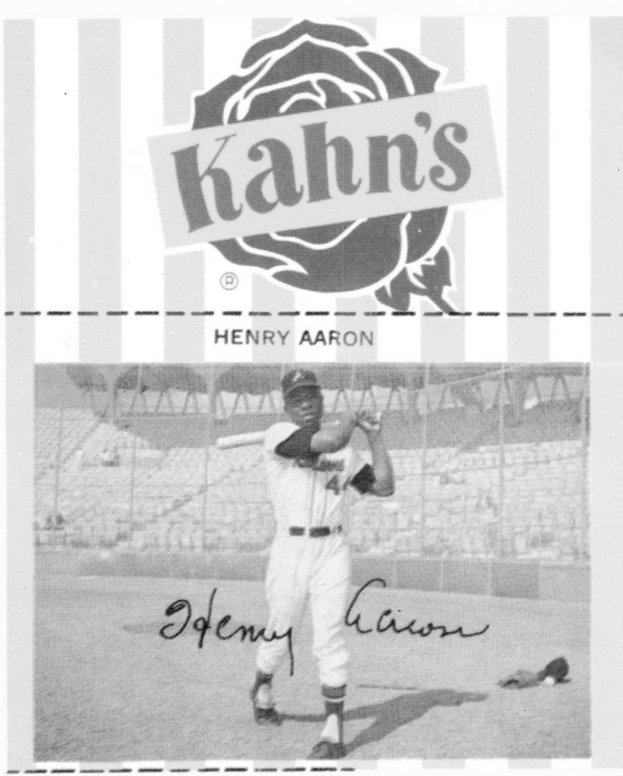

1967 Kahn's, Hank Aaron

HISTORY

The 1967 Kahn's set is almost identical to the '66 set, and causes identification problems among the cards of players who appear in both. The cards were issued in the same two-part format, a 2¹³⁄₁₆ × 2¹¹⁄₁₆″ player card at the bottom with a 2¹³⁄₁₆ × 1⁵⁄₁₆″ advertising tab at top. The two are separated by a dotted line. Cards with the Kahn's tabs are worth up to 50 percent more than those without the tabs. Like the '66 set, the 1967 cards feature a color photo with a facsimile autograph across the front, and the player's name printed in the top border. Also like the 1966 cards, the '67s feature a border design of alternating color stripes. Several different color pairs were used in 1967 in addition to the yellow and white stripes found in 1966. Cards with stripes other than yellow or white are easily identified as '67s, but when a card is found with yellow and white stripes it takes a detailed checklist by photo pose to differentiate the two years. The card backs are blank and the cards are unnumbered. The 41 cards in the 1967 set are made up of players from the Reds, Indians, Pirates, Braves, and, for the first time, the New York Mets.

FOR

The cards are a good value for the price.

AGAINST

Since the 1966 and '67 cards are similar, there is confusion over which cards are which.

NOTEWORTHY CARDS

Hank Aaron, Pete Rose, and Willie Stargell are featured, along with many minor stars of the era.

VALUE

EX-MT CONDITION: Complete set (with tabs), $400; common card, $4–$5; stars, $8–$10; Stargell, $40; Aaron, $65; Rose, $100. 5-YEAR PROJECTION: Average, or a bit below.

1966 TOPPS

SPECIFICATIONS

SIZE: 2½ × 3½″. FRONT: Color photograph. BACK: Black and orange printing on white cardboard. DISTRIBUTION: Nationally, in packages with bubblegum.

HISTORY

One of the more underrated Topps sets of the '60s, the 598-card issue of 1966 is a much more challenging set than most collectors realize. The high numbers (#523-#598) are considerably scarcer than the preceding several series, and the

1966 Topps, Joe Morgan

1966 Topps, Luis Tiant

1966 Topps, Jim Hunter

"semi-highs" (#447-#522) are a lot harder to find than their price tags would indicate. The first 110 cards in the set are the most common, followed by cards #111-#446, which are just a bit more difficult. While there is nothing spectacular about the design of the 1966 set, the cards are attractive. A large color photo dominates the front of the card. In the upper left a diagonal stripe carries the team name, while a band of the same color at bottom has the player's name and position. The backs are not much different from the previous year, combining year-by-year major and/or minor league stats, a short career summary, a cartoon, and the usual biographical stats. There are a handful of multiplayer feature cards included in the set, after having been suspended the previous year. A 12-card special subset honors the league leaders in various major statistical categories for 1965. Each of the cards pictures the winner and two runners-up. Most of the team managers had their own cards in '66; the Houston Astros had two—Lum Harris and Grady Hatton. Rookie cards were generally arranged by team, with two or three players per card.

FOR

It's an attractive, challenging set that is still reasonably priced because it lacks hot rookie cards.

AGAINST

There are no apparent negative aspects to collecting the 1966 set.

NOTEWORTHY CARDS

The mix of cards in the 1966 Topps set is a fascinating blend of old-time baseball history, baseball as it was in the '60s, and baseball as it is today. Manager cards offer such stars of the '40s and '50s as Hank Bauer, Eddie Stanky, Harry Walker, Red Schoendienst, and Gil Hodges. Superstars still active in 1966 include Mickey Mantle, Willie Mays, and Hank Aaron. Finally, the set includes rookie cards of Jim Palmer, Don Sutton, and Ferguson Jenkins. Like the '59 set, this set offers some cards that can be found both with and without notice of sale or trade to another team. Like 1959, the cards without the added lines are more valuable. The four cards with the variations are Merritt Ranew (#62), Bob Uecker (#91), Dick Groat (#103), and Alex Johnson (#104). In addition to several minor varieties (which few collectors bother with) among the checklist cards, the second checklist card (#101) can be found with either Bill Henry (correct) or Warren Spahn listed as card #115. Because of the configuration of cards on press sheets of the high-number series, it is assumed that some cards were double-printed. This has affected the prices of the presumably single-printed Willie McCovey and Gaylord Perry cards. Chicago Cubs second baseman Ken Hubbs (killed when his light plane crashed in February 1964) appears in the 1966 Topps set. Hubbs' photo appears on Dick Ellsworth's card (#447).

1966 Bazooka, Pete Rose

1966 Bazooka, Ron Santo

VALUE

EX-MT CONDITION: Complete set, $2,800; common card, #1-#446, 50¢; #447-#522, $2; #523-#598, $7; stars $20–$35; Aaron, Carl Yastrzemski, Sutton, $50; Uecker (no traded line), Palmer, $50–$55; Pete Rose, McCovey, $60–$65; Mays, $120; Perry, $150; Mantle, $175. 5-YEAR PROJECTION: Average.

1966 BAZOOKA

SPECIFICATIONS

SIZE: Single card, 1⁹⁄₁₆ × 2½″, panel, 4¹¹⁄₁₆ × 2½″. FRONT: Color photograph. BACK: Blank. DISTRIBUTION: Nationally, one 3-card panel on the bottom of each box of bubblegum.

HISTORY

In 1966 Topps did something different, so collectors today can tell that year's cards from those with the identical design (and sometimes even identical card numbers) issued from '63 to '65: they increased the size of the set from 36 to 48 cards. The small line of type in the white border at the bottom now reads: "NO. xx OF 48 CARDS." There was still a problem: 38 of the 48 cards in the 1966 Bazooka set also appear in the '67 set, with the very same card number and photo. You have to have complete 3-card panels or boxes to tell the difference between most '66 and '67 Bazookas. Because many collectors desire original packaging when accumulating this type of card, a premium of 25 to 50 percent is attached to a complete box above the values of the three individual cards. Complete 3-card panels are worth 10 to 15 percent more than single cards. Poorly cut cards are quite common and in little demand; collectors want cards to be neatly cut with even borders.

FOR

The Bazooka sets have good photos and many star players.

AGAINST

The difficulty of assembling them into a complete set makes it too challenging a project for most collectors. The cards are not a popular size.

NOTEWORTHY CARDS

The set contains the first Bazooka card for Pete Rose. Carl Yastrzemski is back after a year's absence from the Bazooka series.

VALUE

EX-MT CONDITION: Complete set (neatly cut from box), $450; common card, $4–$5; superstars, $15–$35; Hank Aaron, Willie Mays, Yastrzemski, $40–$55; Rose, $75; Mickey Mantle, $100. 5-YEAR PROJECTION: Average.

1966 KAHN'S

SPECIFICATIONS

SIZE: 2¹³⁄₁₆ × 4″. FRONT: Color photograph. BACK: Blank. DISTRIBUTION: Ohio, Pittsburgh, Atlanta, single cards in packages of meat products; complete sets available through a mail-in offer.

1966 Kahn's, Pete Rose

HISTORY

With the 1966 set, things begin to get a bit confusing among the Kahn's cards. The issue includes 32 players from the Reds, Pirates, Indians, and Braves in their first year in Georgia. There was a radical format change in the '66 set: the cards now came in two parts. The basic card, 2¹³⁄₁₆ × 2¹¹⁄₁₆″, is separated by a dotted line from a 2¹³⁄₁₆ × 1⁵⁄₁₆″ advertising tab at the top. A color photograph of the player dominates the card, flanked and bordered at the bottom by yellow stripes. At the top are alternating yellow and white stripes, which continue on to the ad tab where they are joined by a red Kahn's logo. Cards with the advertising tab still attached are more desirable than those without it and command up to 35 percent more. The card portion features a facsimile autograph across the front with the player's name printed at the top. Backs are blank and the cards are unnumbered. As in many previous years, single cards could be found in meat packages, or the set could be obtained through a mail-in offer. Because the '66 Kahn's cards are so similar to the 1967 issue, collectors will need a checklist detailing each year's cards to differentiate the two.

FOR

These are scarce regional cards at a good price for the team or star collector.

AGAINST

The distracting circus-stripe design and the lack of dating on cards make the set less desirable.

NOTEWORTHY CARDS

Roberto Clemente rejoined the Kahn's lineup in 1966, but Frank Robinson was gone (traded to the Baltimore Orioles). Still around are Hank Aaron, Pete Rose, and Willie Stargell.

VALUE

EX-MT CONDITION: Complete set, $550; common card, $5.50; stars, $6–$9; Stargell, $45; Clemente, Aaron, $60; Rose, $100. 5-YEAR PROJECTION: Average, perhaps a bit below.

1966 PEPSI TULSA OILERS

SPECIFICATIONS

SIZE: Single card, 2½ × 3¼″; panel, 5½ × 6¾″. FRONT: Sepia-tone photograph. BACK: Black printing on white cardboard. DISTRIBUTION: Oklahoma, one 2-card panel on cartons of soda.

HISTORY

The last of three Pepsi-Cola issues for the Tulsa Oilers, the 1966 set again featured the farmhands of the Cardinals. By '66, however, the Tulsa team had moved up a class to Triple-A ball as a member of the expanded Pacific Coast League. The 24 cards in the set were not evenly printed on the 2-card panels in which they were issued; eight cards were

1966 Pepsi Tulsa Oilers, Walt Williams

1966 Pepsi Tulsa Oilers, Bob Pfeil

double prints and can be found with either of two partners on panels. The card backs have the usual mix of stats and biographical data, and the detachable part of the panel at top gave details on how card owners could redeem them (along with bottle caps) for a $24 bounty or tickets to Tulsa ball games. Like all cards issued in panels, the cards are worth more intact than separated.

FOR

Since this is a high minor league set, more of the players are recognizable than would be the case with most minor league teams. The issue is relatively common in collector circles, but not as common as its currently low price would indicate.

AGAINST

There is limited demand for minor league sets that don't contain any superstars.

NOTEWORTHY CARDS

The 1966 Oilers had many players who appeared in the major leagues, including Alex Johnson, Coco Laboy, Charlie Metro, Ted Savage, Robert Tolan, and Walt "No Neck" Williams.

VALUE

EX-MT CONDITION: Complete set, $45; common card, $2; major leaguers, $3. 5-YEAR PROJECTION: Below average.

1965 TOPPS

SPECIFICATIONS

SIZE: 2½ × 3½". FRONT: Color photograph. BACK: Black and blue printing on white cardboard. DISTRIBUTION: Nationally, in packages with bubblegum.

1965 Topps, Roberto Clemente

1965 Topps, Luis Tiant

1965 Topps, Jim Kaat

HISTORY

A relatively straightforward Topps set from the mid-'60s, the issue returned to the set size of 598 cards, tying a Topps record from 1962. The extra 11 cards in the '65 set were additional player cards, not specialty subsets. For the first time since 1957, there were no multiplayer feature cards. The first 12 cards represent American League and National League statistical leaders for the 1964 season, and an 8-card group highlights the 1964 World Series victory of the Cardinals over the Yankees. Rookie cards in '65 were shared by between two and four players, generally arranged by team, but also included a pair of "Rookie Stars" cards for the N.L. and the A.L. Team cards and numbered checklists are part of the set. The design of the 1965 Topps cards features a large color photo surrounded by a colored, round-cornered frame and a white border. The frame widens at the bottom of the card to carry the player's name and position at the lower right. At the lower left is a pennant with a color team logo and the team name. The card backs feature annual major and/or minor league stats and, space permitting, a cartoon and headline about the player. The usual biographical details are there as well. While cards #523-#598 are considered high numbers, they are not much more scarce than the rest of the issue.

FOR

It's a high-quality Topps set without a great deal of challenge or anything spectacular about it—just simple, attractive cards.

AGAINST

While there is nothing spectacular in favor of the '65 set, there are no glaring problems either.

NOTEWORTHY CARDS

There are a good number of rookie cards in the 1965 set that feature players who have long-term potential, including Joe Morgan, Catfish Hunter, Tug McGraw, Tony Perez, and Steve Carlton. Other notable rookie cards that year are Luis Tiant and Denny McLain. The Jim Kaat card (#62) misspells his name on front as "Katt." The Lew Krausse card (#462) has a photo of Pete Lovrich.

OUR FAVORITE CARD

The 1965 set contains another example of a player having a joke at the expense of the Topps photographer. Noted baseball funnyman Bob Uecker is pictured batting lefthanded (#519). Since he only managed to compile a lifetime .200 batting average hitting righthanded, it's unlikely he was experimenting in front of the camera. Besides, the grin on his face shows he's enjoying the ruse.

VALUE

EX-MT CONDITION: Complete set, $2,000; common card, #1-#446, 35¢–55¢; #447-#522, $1.10; #523-#598, $2; stars, $5–$10; Morgan, Roberto Clemente, Hunter, Lou Brock, Uecker, Perez, $25–$40; Hank Aaron, Willie Mays, Carl Yastrzemski, $40–$50; Carlton, $90–$100; Pete Rose, $150; Mickey Mantle, $335. 5-YEAR PROJECTION: Average.

1965 TOPPS EMBOSSED

SPECIFICATIONS

SIZE: 2⅛ × 3½". FRONT: Gold-foil embossment. BACK: Black printing on white cardboard. DISTRIBUTION: Nationally, in packages of regular Topps cards with bubblegum.

1965 Topps Embossed, Ernie Banks

1965 Topps Embossed, Frank Robinson

HISTORY

The 72 cards of the 1965 Topps Embossed set were inserted individually in packs of the regular '65 Topps baseball cards. The cards are unique in the history of the hobby because they feature an embossed profile of the player on gold foil-like cardboard. There are 36 cards for each league: the embossments on the American League cards are framed in blue, and the National League cards are surrounded in red. There is a gold border on the edge of the card. The player's name appears in white below the picture, with his team and position at the bottom. Card backs are blank except for a decorative rectangle at the bottom with the card number and copyright line. These cards are not particularly popular, which in some ways is good because they are extremely hard to find in Mint condition. The high-relief areas of the embossed portraits tend to lose their gold ink when rubbed, leaving white spots.

FOR

A real challenge for the condition-conscious collector who doesn't want to spend a lot of money.

AGAINST

The pictures don't look anything like the players they are supposed to represent.

NOTEWORTHY CARDS

Virtually all of the players are stars, or at least were considered above-average in 1965.

VALUE

EX-MT CONDITION: Complete set, $50; common card, 40¢; superstars, $2–$4; Mantle, $10. 5-YEAR PROJECTION: Below average.

1965 BAZOOKA

SPECIFICATIONS

SIZE: Single card, 1⁹⁄₁₆ × 2½"; panel, 4¹¹⁄₁₆ × 2½". FRONT: Color photograph. BACK: Blank. DISTRIBUTION: Nationally, one 3-card panel on the bottom of each box of bubblegum.

HISTORY

Topps really created problems for collectors with its 1965 issue of Bazooka cards. Besides using the same design as in '63 and '64, half of the 36 cards carry the same card numbers as they did in 1964. The pictures are different, but you have to compare original 3-card panels and checklists to find out what year's cards you have. As you approach the higher numbers in the set, the situation gets worse;

1965 Bazooka, Bob Aspromonte

1965 Bazooka, Jim Fregosi

the last two panels—Frank Robinson, Sandy Koufax, and Rocky Colavito (#31, #32, and #33) and Al Kaline, Ken Boyer, and Tommy Davis (#34, #35, and #36)—are the same players and numbers as in the previous year. If you have any of these cards from '64 or '65, you'll need complete original boxes to tell which year is which. The confusion has kept the Bazooka issues from becoming popular. Because the cards were issued as part of the package, they are often found poorly cut. Original 3-card panels are worth perhaps 10 percent more than the individual cards; a complete box is worth about 25 to 50 percent more than the individual cards.

FOR

There are lots of big-name players in the set, and collectors find the photos attractive.

AGAINST

The confusion over the same card numbers makes the set too hard to figure out for all but the devoted specialist. The cards are too small to be really popular; most collectors aren't attracted to cards that aren't the standard 2½ × 3½″.

NOTEWORTHY CARDS

Lots of Hall of Famers are back from previous years, along with some new stars—Boog Powell, Bob Gibson, and Juan Marichal.

VALUE

EX-MT CONDITION: Complete set (neatly cut from box), $375; common card, $5; stars, $15–$25; Hank Aaron, Willie Mays, Roberto Clemente, $35–$45; Mickey Mantle, $100. 5-YEAR PROJECTION: Average.

1965 KAHN'S

SPECIFICATIONS

SIZE: 3 × 3½″. FRONT: Color photograph. BACK: Black printing on white cardboard. DISTRIBUTION: Upper Midwest, individual cards in packages of meat products; complete sets available through a mail-in offer.

1965 Kahn's, Joe Torre

1965 Kahn's, Ralph Terry

HISTORY

The 1965 Kahn's set features the largest number of players of the entire 15-year series. Forty-five cards are included in the set, representing players from the Reds, Indians, Pirates, and Milwaukee Braves (the Tribe's last year in the beer city). The format for the '65 set remained the same as that used the previous year. The entire front of the card is a borderless color photo, with only a facsimile autograph added. The card back features brief career information and annual stats through the 1964 season. The cards are unnumbered. Like other later Kahn's sets, the 1965 issue was available in two ways. Single cards could be collected in packages of Kahn's meat products, or the complete set could be ordered through the mail. The addition of the Milwaukee Braves helps make the '65 issue one of Kahn's more popular sets.

FOR

There are numerous good players and great teams for the regional and team collector. The 1965 Kahn's are attractive cards at attractive prices.

AGAINST

It's hard to say anything bad about the '65 Kahn's.

NOTEWORTHY CARDS

Joining the all-star lineup of Frank Robinson and Pete Rose in the '65 set is Henry Aaron. Roberto Clemente is curiously absent. Willie Stargell and Joe Torre also appear for the first time in 1965.

VALUE

EX-MT CONDITION: Complete set, $650; common card, $8; stars, $10–$15; Robinson, $45; Stargell, $75; Aaron, $110; Rose, $225. 5-YEAR PROJECTION: Above average.

1964 TOPPS

SPECIFICATIONS

SIZE: 2½ × 3½". FRONT: Color photograph. BACK: Orange printing on white cardboard. DISTRIBUTION: Nationally, in packages with bubblegum.

1964 Topps, Mickey Mantle

1964 Topps, Sandy Koufax

1964 Topps, Hank Aaron

HISTORY

Hot on the heels of their attractive 1963 card design, Topps came up with another winner in '64. A large color photo at the center of the card bleeds into a white top panel that contains the team name in large, colored block letters. A panel at the bottom of the card contains the player's name and position. The layout is clean, simple, and attractive. The card back features an innovative "hidden" baseball quiz question. When a white panel at the bottom of the card was rubbed with a coin, the answer to a trivia question appeared. The remainder of the card back is mostly devoted to yearly major and/or minor league career statistics, with minimal biographical details at top. Also unusual for the back design is that it is printed entirely in orange, rather than in two colors as had been done in most years. While the traditional high-number cards of 1964 (#523-#587) are scarcer than the rest of the set, they are generally regarded as common. Cards #371-#522 are just a bit harder to find than the first 370 cards in the set. Topps continued to downplay specialty subsets in '64, following the '63 pattern. There is a 12-card group of 1963's statistical leaders and a 5-card run detailing the Dodgers' four-game sweep of the Yankees in the 1963 World Series. Rookie cards are generally arranged by team, two players per card. The set contains several multiplayer cards featuring star players.

FOR

The set exhibits an attractive design at a reasonable cost. There are numerous stars without many gimmicky specialty cards.

AGAINST

The high price of the Pete Rose card may be discouraging to collectors.

NOTEWORTHY CARDS

Rose got his own card in the 1964 Topps set. The photo on the '64 Rose card is an enlarged version of the same photo used on his rookie card. Still, the card is more attractive than the one issued in 1963 (his head appeared with three other heads, all were postage-stamp size). Rose's 1964 card is currently valued at 25 to 30 percent of his '63 rookie card. Card #550 is an "In Memoriam" card of Cubs second baseman Ken Hubbs, who died in a plane crash on February 13, 1964. Significant rookie cards in '64 include Lou Piniella, Tommy John, and Phil Niekro. The photo on Bud Bloomfield's card (#532) is actually Jay Ward, who also appears on card #116. Unfortunately for Bloomfield, he never did appear as a major leaguer on a baseball card. One of the funniest writing errors occurs on the card back of Phillies rookie (#561) Dave Bennett: "The 19-year-old righthanded curveballer is just 18 years old. . . ."

OUR FAVORITE CARD

You'd think that after Topps had been taken in by Lew Burdette pretending to be a lefthanded pitcher on his '59 card, they'd be more careful. But not only is Joe Koppe (#279) pictured in the '64 set with a glove on the wrong hand, but Burdette is shown pitching leftie once again.

VALUE

EX-MT CONDITION: Complete set, $1,800; common card, #1-#522, 50¢–80¢; #523-#587, $2; stars, $5–$10; superstars, $20–$30; Hank Aaron, Willie Mays, Carl Yastrzemski, Sandy Koufax, $35–$50; Rose, $125–$135; Mickey Mantle, $175. 5-YEAR PROJECTION: Average.

1964 TOPPS STAND-UPS

SPECIFICATIONS

SIZE: 2½ × 3½″. FRONT: Color photograph. BACK: Blank. DISTRIBUTION: Nationally, in packages with bubblegum.

1964 Topps Stand-Ups, Roberto Clemente

1964 Topps Stand-Ups, Dick Groat

HISTORY

For several years beginning in 1960, Topps test-marketed a variety of baseball player novelties in addition to its regular annual card set—such things as tattoos, rub-offs, stick-ons, and coins. In '64, two separate sets of baseball cards were added to the regular set. Each was packaged and sold separately. The scarcest of these is the 77-card "Stand-Up" set. The first die-cut cards produced on a widespread basis by Topps since its All-Stars of 1951, the Stand-Up set features a full-length color photo of the player at the center of the card. There is a yellow background on the top half of the card and a green background on the bottom half. A yellow rectangle at the bottom center, on which the player stands, contains his name, team, and position. Directions for punching out the player and folding down the yellow background to make the card stand are printed on the left. When folded, only the player's picture and the green background are visible. There is a black facsimile autograph across the front. The cards are unnumbered. Collectors prefer these cards unpunched and unfolded. Cards that have been folded are worth about 50 percent less. There were 55 double-printed cards in the set. Hall of Famers Warren Spahn, Eddie Mathews, Billy Williams, Juan Marichal, Don Drysdale, Willie McCovey, and Carl Yastrzemski are among the 22 players single-printed in the set. The set is somewhat popular, but if it became a high-demand item, collectors would quickly find out how scarce and underpriced the cards are.

FOR

This scarce, interesting Topps set was issued in the standard size; it is a challenge to collect.

AGAINST

Some collectors don't like cards that are designed to be folded, spindled, or mutilated.

NOTEWORTHY CARDS

Star-quality players in the Stand-Up set include Hank Aaron, Ernie Banks, Roberto Clemente, Al Kaline, Mickey Mantle, Willie Mays, and Frank Robinson.

VALUE

EX-MT CONDITION: Complete set, $1,250; common card, $3; single-printed card, $15; stars, $20–$50; Aaron, Marichal, Mathews, Drysdale, Mays, McCovey, Spahn, $60; Yastrzemski, Mantle, $200.
5-YEAR PROJECTION: Above average.

1964 TOPPS GIANTS

SPECIFICATIONS
SIZE: 3⅛ × 5¼″. FRONT: Color photograph. BACK: Black printing on white cardboard. DISTRIBUTION: Nationally, in packages with bubblegum.

1964 Topps Giants, Ron Santo

HISTORY
The third Topps baseball card issue for 1964 (in addition to its regular card set and the Stand-Ups), the Topps Giants set was the company's first issue in postcard-size format. The 60 cards in the set feature large color photos surrounded by a white border. The only other design element on the front of the card is a white baseball in a lower corner with the player's name at center, position at top, and team at bottom. Card backs contain a second photo of the player at the center, surrounded by a newspaper-style write-up of a high point in his career. The '64 Giants are the "Rodney Dangerfield" of early '60s Topps cards: they "don't get no respect." Although they were distributed in huge quantities, these supplies have been virtually absorbed in the past couple of years. Though the hobby generally doesn't flock to buy cards in postcard-size, the superstars in this set are favorite and inexpensive targets for collectors.

FOR
These large-format cards are available at a low price.

AGAINST
The cards are oversized, and they are generally perceived as being too plentiful.

NOTEWORTHY CARDS
There are lots of Hall of Famers, future Hall of Famers, and players who probably deserve to be Hall of Famers.

VALUE
EX-MT CONDITION: Complete set, $55; common card, 15¢; stars, $1–$4; Mickey Mantle, $7; Sandy Koufax, $10; Willie Mays, $11. 5-YEAR PROJECTION: Above average.

1964 BAZOOKA

SPECIFICATIONS
SIZE: Single card, 1$\frac{9}{16}$ × 2½″; panel, 4$\frac{11}{16}$ × 2½″. FRONT: Color photograph. BACK: Blank. DISTRIBUTION: Nationally, one 3-card panel on the bottom of each box of bubblegum.

1964 Bazooka, Mickey Mantle

1964 Bazooka, Dick Groat

HISTORY

The problem of differentiating between the various Bazooka issues returned with the 1964 cards. The '64 Bazookas used the exact same design and format as the 1963 cards. To make matters worse, 19 of the 36 cards have the same card numbers as the previous year (some even carried the number again in 1965). Luckily the pictures are different. If you really want to know what year card you have, you have to have it in the original 3-card panel and compare the other cards on it to a checklist for each year. Because the cards were issued on the bottom of gum boxes, they are often found roughly cut. Cards in the original panel are worth 10 to 15 percent more than individual cards; complete boxes are worth 25 to 50 percent more. Cards that are poorly cut (especially when cut into the picture) can be considered in Very Good condition, at best.

FOR

The photo quality is outstanding.

AGAINST

The cards are too small, plus you have the aggravation of trying to figure out what year the cards were issued.

NOTEWORTHY CARDS

Lots of the big names from earlier years are back in '64; Willie McCovey makes his first appearance on a Bazooka card.

VALUE

EX-MT CONDITION: Complete set (neatly cut from box), $475; common card, $5; stars, $18–$25; Roberto Clemente, Hank Aaron, Willie Mays, Carl Yastrzemski, $45; Mickey Mantle, $100. 5-YEAR PROJECTION: Average.

1964 KAHN'S

SPECIFICATIONS

SIZE: 3 × 3½″. FRONT: Color photograph. BACK: Black printing on white cardboard. DISTRIBUTION: Ohio, Western Pennsylvania, in packages of meat products; complete sets available through a mail-in offer.

1964 Kahn's, Bill Virdon

1964 Kahn's, Pedro Ramos

HISTORY

In 1964 Kahn's finally made a major change in the format of its baseball card set. Smaller in size than in the previous nine years, the '64s feature a borderless color photo on the front of the card. The only other design element is a black facsimile autograph. The familiar ad message, "Compliments of Kahn's 'The Wiener the World Awaited,'" appears on the back of the card at the bottom. The card backs also contain brief biographical information and career stats. The 31 cards in the set are unnumbered. Three teams—the Reds, Indians, and Pirates—are represented.

FOR

The new format is an improvement.

AGAINST

There is nothing negative to note.

NOTEWORTHY CARDS

Pete Rose makes his debut on a Kahn's card in the 1964 set, and joins Roberto Clemente and Frank Robinson in the superstar ranks.

VALUE

EX-MT CONDITION: Complete set, $650; common card, $8; Robinson, $60; Clemente, $150; Rose, $300. 5-YEAR PROJECTION: Average.

1963 Topps, Stan Musial

1963 TOPPS

SPECIFICATIONS

SIZE: 2½ × 3½". FRONT: Color photograph. BACK: Black and yellow printing on yellow cardboard. DISTRIBUTION: Nationally, in packages with bubblegum.

HISTORY

This was probably the first large modern baseball card set where a single card has accounted for the set's rise in stature. The set price of the 576-card Topps set of '63 was largely determined by the fortunes of one card (#537 "Rookie Stars"). And the value of that card was largely determined by the on-field performance of one of the four players whose postage-stamp-size photos appear on the card—the kid in the lower left, Pete Rose. The 1963 Topps Pete Rose rookie card has overshadowed the rest of what is really an excellent and highly collectible set. For '63, Topps dropped the number of cards in the issue to 576 (22 less than the previous year). One of Topps' most highly acclaimed designs, the 1963 cards feature a large color photo, with a smaller black-and-white picture in a colored circle at the bottom right of the card.

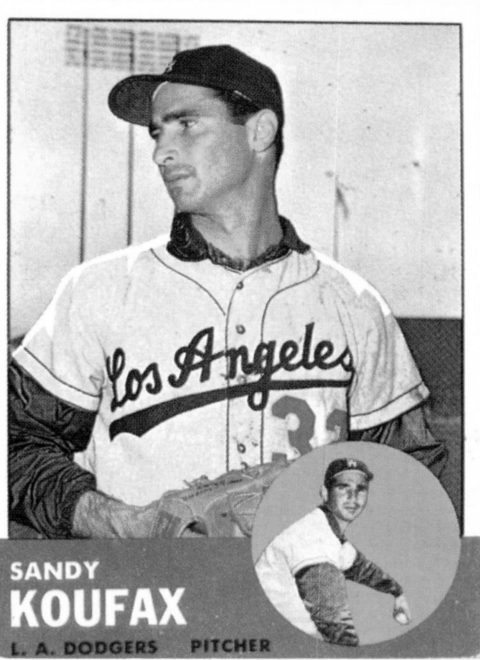

1963 Topps, Sandy Koufax

1963 Topps, Rookie Stars

In a wide band of color below the picture the player's name, team, and position are listed. Card backs once again featured year-by-year major and/or minor league stats. These are combined with a cartoon, a career summary, and short biographical details. Like all Topps sets between '52 and '73, the 1963 set was issued in series. The first few series (cards #1-#288) were released in early spring, when interest in baseball and baseball cards was at its peak. As the year progressed, fewer and fewer cards were sold, resulting in smaller quantities of cards #289-#446, and even fewer "semi-high" cards (#447-#506) and "high numbers" (#507-#576). As high numbers go, the '63 cards are really quite scarce. While this has contributed to the huge price tag on the Rose card in their midst, it is really the demand for that particular card that supports the price. Some fans of the '63 set, and dealers who handle a lot of cards, contend that it is really the semi-highs in the set that are the scarcest. One of the reasons the set is so popular is that there are far fewer specialty cards. The first ten cards in the set honor the A.L. and N.L. statistical leaders of 1962, with the winner in each league sharing a card with the four runners-up. Another 7-card subset recounts the 1962 World Series. The Rookie Stars cards are unusual in that they are not arranged by team or position.

FOR

The set is one of the most attractive and challenging of all the Topps issues. The lack of gimmicky specialty cards is a big plus.

AGAINST

The extremely high price for the Rose rookie card makes building a complete set an expensive project.

NOTEWORTHY CARDS

Collectors should be aware that the Rose card was counterfeited in 1982. The counterfeit is relatively easy to spot: if held up to a strong light it will appear somewhat transparent, and you can see the shadow of your fingers behind it. This resulted from printing the card on thinner cardboard than the original. If a genuine '63 card is held to the strongest light, no light penetrates. Two of the other Rookie Stars cards in 1963 contain the only significant variations in the set. The common versions of cards #29 and #54 have the date "1963" in yellow at the top, while the scarcer variety have the date "1962" in white. All seven of the checklist cards exist with subtle variations, but few collectors bother with them. Besides Rose, two other significant rookie cards appear in the 1963 set: Rusty Staub and Willie Stargell. Though Gaylord Perry appears on a Rookie Stars card, it is not his rookie card; he appeared on his own card in the '62 set. Some photo errors in the 1963 set are worth mentioning. Don Landrum's card (#113) has two photos of Ron Santo. Eli Grba's card (#231) pictures Ryne Duren. Ray Herbert's card (#8) has the picture reversed. The 1963 Topps set features the last contemporary baseball card of Stan Musial.

VALUE

EX-MT CONDITION: Complete set, $2,850; common card #1-#196, 60¢; #197-#446, $1.50; #447-#506, $7; #507-#576, $3.75; stars, $5–$15; superstars, $20–$35; Sandy Koufax, Musial, Duke Snider, Carl Yastrzemski, Willie McCovey, $45–$60; Willie Mays, Hank Aaron, Lou Brock, $65–$80; Roberto Clemente, $120; Stargell, $135; Mickey Mantle, $275; Rose, $560. 5-YEAR PROJECTION: Average.

1963 FLEER

SPECIFICATIONS

SIZE: 2½ × 3½". FRONT: Color photograph. BACK: Black and yellow/green printing on white cardboard. DISTRIBUTION: Nationally, in packages with a cookie.

HISTORY

The 1963 Fleer 66-card set was another round in the early battles of the "Card Wars." In '59 Fleer issued its Ted Williams set; in '60 and '61 Fleer issued sets of old-timers. By 1963, Fleer apparently felt ready to take on Topps in the market for

1963 Fleer, Ken Boyer

1963 Fleer, Don Drysdale

1963 Fleer, Tommy Davis

current players' cards. To avoid Topps' monopoly on issuing baseball cards with "confectionery" products, Fleer packaged its '63 cards in a waxed wrapper with a cookie. Topps' lawyers contested this approach in court and won. It is not known whether Fleer had intended to issue more than the 66 cards that year. Regardless, the court order kept Fleer out of the market for current players' cards for another 18 years. The 1963 Fleer cards are not unlike the '63 Topps in design. The card is dominated by a large color photo of the player, either a portrait or posed action shot. In the lower left, where Topps had a black-and-white photo of the player, Fleer had a line drawing of a player representing the position of the player on a diamond-shaped background. The name, team, and position were to the right in the wide white bottom border. The backs of the '63 Fleers are vertical in format and feature a short write-up on the player plus 1962 and lifetime stats. The card number is in a circle at the lower center in front of a pair of crossed bats. Cards in the '63 Fleer set are generally numbered by team, though a few players at the end of the set do not follow this sequence. The cards were widely distributed before the court order stopped the circulation, and surviving cards are not particularly scarce, with two exceptions—Joe Adcock (#46) and an unnumbered checklist. In terms of sheer numbers of each card issued, the '63 Fleers are not in the same league with Topps, but current prices do not really reflect this overall difference in scarcity. The Fleer set has developed new followers though, and it is expected to be one of the better performers in price for several years.

FOR
An important set in terms of baseball card history. It is small enough to complete easily and there are many stars. The card quality is decent.

AGAINST
You can't say much against the '63 Fleers; they were in there pitching to break up Topps' corner on the baseball card market.

NOTEWORTHY CARDS
Fleer had an ace card or two up their sleeve in the 1963 set. Most important, the first nationally distributed baseball card of Maury Wills appeared in this set. That was quite a coup for Fleer, because Wills had been named the N.L. MVP in 1962, an award that is noted on the front of his card. Because Topps had overlooked Wills when handing out baseball card contracts to minor leaguers in the early '50s, Wills refused to appear on a Topps card until 1967. Other major stars in the set include Willie Mays, Carl Yastrzemski, Brooks Robinson, Sandy Koufax, Warren Spahn, Bob Gibson, and Roberto Clemente. The most valuable cards, though, are Joe Adcock (#46) and the unnumbered checklist. It is believed that somewhere toward the end of the printing run the Adcock card was replaced on the press sheet with the checklist card, making both of them scarce today.

VALUE
EX-MT CONDITION: Complete set, $450; common card, $1.50; superstars, $12–$25; Adcock, $60; unnumbered checklist, $90. 5-YEAR PROJECTION: Way above average.

1963 Bazooka, Willie Mays

1963 Bazooka, Harmon Killebrew

1963 BAZOOKA

SPECIFICATIONS
SIZE: Single card, $1\frac{9}{16} \times 2\frac{1}{2}$"; panel, $4\frac{11}{16} \times 2\frac{1}{2}$". FRONT: Color photograph. BACK: Blank. DISTRIBUTION: Nationally, one 3-card panel on the bottom of each box of bubblegum.

HISTORY
After three years of nearly identical card issues, Topps changed the format and design slightly for its 1963 Bazooka series. The company also returned to a 36-card set, as opposed to the 45-card set issued in '62. The cards were still distributed as a 3-card panel on the bottom of 20-piece boxes of bubblegum. They were meant to be cut off the box and cut into individual cards. Complete panels are worth about 10 percent more, and entire boxes are worth 25 to 50 percent more. As with all baseball cards meant to be cut off a box, top grade Bazooka cards are somewhat hard to find. For 1963, the Bazooka cards were a quarter-inch smaller all around, and the colored rectangular strips that had carried the player information in the '59 to '62 issues were replaced with white ovals at the bottom of the cards. Within the oval, the player's name appears in red; his team name and position are in black. Card numbers returned to the '63 Bazookas in small black type in the white border below the picture. Unlike some other Bazooka card issues, there are no known scarcities among particular panels in this set.

FOR
The set has loads of big-name players.

AGAINST
The size is unpopular. The cards are difficult to find in top condition.

NOTEWORTHY CARDS

There is a fairly high proportion of star players in the 1963 Bazooka offering. Hall of Famers Stan Musial (in his last season), Carl Yastrzemski, and Brooks Robinson appear on a Bazooka card for the first time.

VALUE

EX-MT CONDITION: Complete set (neatly cut from box), $500; common card, $4.50–$5.50; stars, $20–$30; Roberto Clemente, Musial, $35; Willie Mays, Hank Aaron, Yastrzemski, $45; Mickey Mantle, $100. 5-YEAR PROJECTION: Above average.

1963 BAZOOKA ALL-TIME GREATS

SPECIFICATIONS

SIZE: 1⁹⁄₁₆ × 2½". FRONT: Black-and-white bust photograph in gold "frame," white border. BACK: Black printing on yellow background. DISTRIBUTION: Nationally, in boxes of bubblegum.

HISTORY

When you bought your 20-piece box of Bazooka bubblegum in 1963, you got a lot of baseball cards along with the thick chunk of gum. Besides the three cards of current players on the bottom of the box, there were five "Golden Edition" baseball cards inside. Sets that featured old-time stars were a popular gimmick for baseball card issuers in the early '60s (and have been, off and on, since then). The "All-Time Greats" seem to have been a response to similar issues by Fleer in '60 and '61. The Bazooka set numbered 41 cards, all Hall of Famers. They were the same size as the cards on the bottom of the box, but did not have to be cut from anything or cut apart. The cards were not particularly popular with youngsters. Other than Babe Ruth, Ty Cobb, Lou Gehrig, and a few others, most of the players in the set were unknown to youngsters in 1963. Because many of the photos used on these cards were taken long after the player's career was over, a lot of baseball's great stars of the early years just look like old men in this issue.

1963 Bazooka All-Time Greats, Cy Young

1963 Bazooka All-Time Greats, Christy Mathewson

FOR

These cards offer a look at yesterday's stars at a reasonable price.

AGAINST

They share the same unpopular size as the other Bazooka cards of the '60s. Collectors have never been particularly attracted to cards of baseball players issued after their playing days; many hobbyists don't consider them legitimate. The All-Time Greats are also a fairly difficult set to collect because they were not saved in great numbers. Even so, they remain inexpensive.

NOTEWORTHY CARDS

They're all Hall of Famers.

VALUE

EX-MT CONDITION: Complete set, $190; common card, $3; Gehrig, Cobb, $20; Ruth, $25. 5-YEAR PROJECTION: Average.

1963 KAHN'S

SPECIFICATIONS

SIZE: 3¼ × 4″. FRONT: Black-and-white photograph. BACK: Black printing on white cardboard. DISTRIBUTION: East Coast, Midwest, in packages of meat products; complete sets available through a mail-in offer.

1963 Kahn's, Roberto Clemente

HISTORY

After eight years with the same design, Kahn's changed the format of its baseball card issue for 1963—but only a little. The black-and-white photo that occupies most of the front of the card now has a white border all around. The facsimile autograph and the advertising strip at the bottom remain. Card backs once again feature year-by-year stats and career information. There were five teams in the '63 Kahn's lineup: the Reds, Pirates, Indians, Cardinals, and, for the first time, Yankees. A total of 30 cards were issued with no variations. The cards are not numbered. As in the previous few years, cards were available individually in packages of meat products, or in a complete set through a mail-in offer.

FOR

Adding the Yankees expanded the roster of teams.

AGAINST

Kahn's didn't change the design enough to make the cards really different from previous years. Also, the cards are not really attractive compared to contemporary issues.

NOTEWORTHY CARDS

The addition of Yankee players in the '63 set gives Kahn's collectors such well-known players as Bobby Richardson, Tony Kubek, and Elston Howard, along with familiar big-name stars Frank Robinson and Roberto Clemente.

VALUE

EX-MT CONDITION: Complete set, $475; common card, $8; stars, $10–$15; Robinson, $50; Clemente, $110. 5-YEAR PROJECTION: Average.

1963 POST

SPECIFICATIONS

SIZE: 3½ × 2½″. FRONT: Color photograph. BACK: Blank. DISTRIBUTION: Nationally, on backs of cereal boxes.

HISTORY

The 200-card set issued with Post cereals in 1963 is one of the most challenging baseball card sets of the '60s. The method of distribution, printing cards as part of the cereal box, produced some very scarce cards to challenge today's collectors. Many cards were printed on only one or two different brands or sizes of cereal. If those brands were not very popular, the cards on those boxes were not widely distributed. Consequently, they are rare and expensive today. Besides the basic 200 cards in the set there are also numerous variations (the most frequent variation was in the color of the photo background). Some collectors specialize in these variations. A detailed checklist will be necessary

★ ★ ★ No. 101 ★ ★ ★

Orlando Cepeda

SAN FRANCISCO GIANTS — FIRST BASE

Ht. 6'1"; Wt. 200; Bats Right; Throws Right; Born Sept. 17, 1937; Home: Bayamon, P. R.

1962 proved to be a great season for Orlando. In 5 big league years, he hit over .300 - 4 times (.297 in 1960); 24 or more HRs 5 times; 100 or more RBIs 3 times (twice with 96). The Sporting News chose him as NL Rookie of the Year in 1958; led in doubles (38) in 1958 and in HRs (46) and RBIs (142) in 1961. Orlando started his pro career in 1955, led his league in batting twice, and has played in 7 All-Star Games.

★ ★ ★ MAJOR LEAGUE BATTING RECORD ★ ★ ★

	Games	At Bat	Runs	Hits	2B	3B	HR	RBI	Avg.
1962	162	625	105	191	26	1	35	114	.306
LIFE	764	2987	471	922	163	16	157	553	.308

1963 Post, Orlando Cepeda

	Games	At Bat	Runs	Hits	2B	3B	HR	RBI	Avg.
1962	160	612	96	164	21	5	37	107	.268
LIFE	493	1513	233	411	55	10	87	254	.278

1963 Post, Leon Wagner

for the collector to determine what he wants to collect and how much he can afford to collect. The cards were printed with thin black lines separating them on the package, making it difficult to neatly cut the cards off the box. Well-trimmed cards, therefore, are especially desirable among collectors, and the accuracy of the trim must be taken into consideration when grading the card. While they are not common, complete panels (the entire back of the box) or even complete cereal boxes are not all that unusual. Such premium items have a value 150 to 200 percent more than the total value of the individual cards. The cards have a color photo of the player at the left end of the card, and a biography on the right. A pale yellow panel at the bottom of the card carries the player's 1962 and career stats. The backs are blank. The 200 cards are numbered by team; the first 11 cards belong to the Minnesota Twins, the next 12 cards to the New York Yankees, etc. The 1963 Post cereal cards were reproduced in a slightly smaller size for boxes of Jell-O.

FOR

This is an extremely challenging modern set. Old accumulations of these sets can often yield cards worth lots of money.

AGAINST

The rarity of some cards makes this an extremely difficult set to complete. It's hard to find cards in top condition.

NOTEWORTHY CARDS

Virtually all of the big stars of 1963 are present in this set except Stan Musial, then in the final year of his career. The photos of Los Angeles Angels teammates George Thomas and Lee Thomas are reversed. Some common cards are worth a lot of money because of their scarcity. The most valuable cards are listed below.

VALUE

EX-MT CONDITION: Complete set (neatly cut from box), $2,600; common card, $1.25; stars, scarce commons, $15–$30; Lee Thomas, Floyd Robinson, Jim Bunning, Jerry Lumpe, Manny Jimenez, Tom Haller, Hank Aaron, Curt Flood, $50–$80; Billy Williams, Willie Davis, Roger Maris, Jerry Adair, Eddie Kasko, Frank Thomas, $90–$125; Mickey Mantle, Carl Yastrzemski, Bob Aspromonte, $225–$250. 5-YEAR PROJECTION: Average.

1963 JELL-O

SPECIFICATIONS

SIZE: 3¼ × 2½". FRONT: Color photograph. BACK: Blank. DISTRIBUTION: Upper Midwest, one card on the back of each 3-oz. or 6-oz. box of Jell-O.

★ ★ ★ No. 51 ★ ★ ★

Al Kaline

DETROIT TIGERS — OUTFIELDER

Ht. 6'2"; Wt. 180; Bats Right; Throws Right; Born Dec. 19, 1934; Home: Birmingham, Mich.

Despite a broken collarbone suffered by Al on May 26, 1962, that kept him out of action almost 2 months, he hit more HRs in 1962 than in any previous season (29). Youngest player (by 1 day) to ever lead AL in batting, .340 in 1955. Hit 3 HRs (2 in 1 inning) in game, April 17, 1955. Named AL player of the year by Sporting News, 1955. Hit .385 in 10 All-Star Games.

★ ★ ★ MAJOR LEAGUE BATTING RECORD ★ ★ ★

	Games	At Bat	Runs	Hits	2B	3B	HR	RBI	Avg.
1962	100	398	78	121	16	6	29	94	.304
LIFE	1304	4903	792	1511	242	51	188	788	.308

1963 Jell-O, Al Kaline

★ ★ ★ No. 19 ★ ★ ★

Whitey Ford

NEW YORK YANKEES — PITCHER

Ht. 5'10"; Wt. 184; Bats Left; Throws Left; Born Oct. 21, 1928; Home: Lake Success, N. Y.

The 1961 season was Whitey's best with 25 wins and only 4 losses topped off by 2 shutout wins in the World Series. That season credited him with the Sport Magazine Award (a Corvette) as MVP in the World Series and the Cy Young Award as Pitcher of the Year. He holds the World Series record of most consecutive scoreless innings (33⅔), and most games won (10) plus many other records. He pitched in 6 All-Star Games.

★ ★ ★ MAJOR LEAGUE PITCHING RECORD ★ ★ ★

	Games	IP	Won	Lost	Pcts.	Hits	Runs	ER	SO	Walks	ERA
1962	38	258	17	8	.680	243	90	83	160	69	2.90
LIFE	355	2296	175	71	.711	1954	805	711	1369	890	2.83

1963 Jell-O, Whitey Ford

HISTORY

The 200 cards in the 1963 Jell-O set are nearly identical to those issued by Post cereals. The only difference between the two issues is that the Jell-O cards are a quarter-inch narrower than their Post counterparts. Type size on the Jell-O cards is also a bit smaller, but a card would have to be examined side by side with a Post card to tell the difference by type size alone. The cards were printed on the back of packages of Jell-O. A solid black line around the card was to be used as a guide in cutting it from the box. Whether or not a card has been neatly trimmed from the box is a major factor in its grading. Some collectors prefer cards that have been trimmed outside the black guide line; some prefer the lines to have been cut off. While they are not common, it's possible to find some uncut boxes and some complete boxes still filled with Jell-O. These items command prices two to three times more than an individual card. The Jell-O set was numbered consecutively within team groupings. While the usual demand for superstars is an important factor in pricing these cards, there is also a scarcity factor to be considered. Because some of the cards were printed on the backs of the less popular 6-ounce size, or on less popular flavors of Jell-O, they were not sold in the same quantities as cards on the 3-ounce boxes of popular flavors. Consequently, fewer have survived, and they are often more valuable as a result. A detailed checklist is necessary to determine which cards are scarce. This factor makes the set a challenge to collect, though it is not nearly as demanding as the 1963 Post issue. There are many color variations in the set, usually associated with the background behind the player's picture. They have little effect on price, and most collectors do not concern themselves with these variations.

FOR

A challenging, but by no means impossible, set to collect.

AGAINST

It is easily confused with the '63 Post issue. Because of sloppy cutting work, it is sometimes hard to find cards in top condition. It is expensive for an early 1960s set.

NOTEWORTHY CARDS

The photos of Los Angeles Angels teammates George Thomas and Lee Thomas are reversed. All the big-name stars of 1963 are in the set, except for Stan Musial.

VALUE

EX-MT CONDITION: Complete set (neatly cut from box), $2,100; common card, $1.50; scarce card, $15–$40; Yastrzemski, Mays, Gibson, Aaron, $60; McCovey, $100; Mantle, $175. 5-YEAR PROJECTION: Below average.

1963 SUGARDALE

SPECIFICATIONS

SIZE: $5\frac{1}{8} \times 3\frac{3}{4}$". FRONT: Black-and-white photograph. BACK: Black and red printing on white cardboard. DISTRIBUTION: Cleveland, Pittsburgh, in packages of hot dogs.

1963 Sugardale, Victor Davalillo

HISTORY

The second and final year of baseball card production by the makers of Sugardale hot dogs consisted of a 31-card set virtually identical in format to the previous year's issue. The 25 Cleveland Indians players in the set are skip-numbered between 1 and 28, while the six Pirate players are lettered A to E. Like the '62 Sugardales, the '63 issue has a player photo on the front of the card, along with a biography. A facsimile autograph appears above the bio. Ads for the company and the team appear at the bottom of the horizontal-format cards. The backs contain a line drawing and a baseball playing tip from the player pictured on the front. A Sugardale logo appears at the bottom. The cards have rounded corners. To differentiate the '63 cards from the earlier issue, it is necessary to read the biography on the front for mention of the 1962 season.

FOR

It is an important issue for team and regional collectors.

AGAINST

The cards are too large to suit most collectors. The set is not particularly attractive and is quite expensive. If it was at all popular, there's no telling how much it would cost.

NOTEWORTHY CARDS

There are no big stars in the set. The cards of Jim Perry and Bob Skinner are scarcer than the others because they were withdrawn from distribution when those players were traded in mid-season.

VALUE

EX-MT CONDITION: Complete set, $1,200; common card, $40–$50; Perry, Skinner, $150. 5-YEAR PROJECTION: Average.

1963 PEPSI COLT .45s

SPECIFICATIONS

SIZE: Single card, 2⅜ × 3¾"; panel, 2⅜ × 9⅛". FRONT: Black-and-white photograph. BACK: Black printing on white cardboard. DISTRIBUTION: Houston, one panel in each carton of soda.

HISTORY

The value of the 1963 Colt .45s is being held artificially low by the rarity of a couple of cards. Since few collectors can hope to complete the set, they're unwilling to start. The cards' distribution varied widely when they were placed on store shelves in cartons of Pepsi. It appears that the card of John Bateman was never publicly distributed. A similar situation seems to have occurred with Carl Warwick's card, but some made their way into the hobby's commercial channels. The cards themselves are perforated at the top and bottom

1963 Pepsi Colt .45s, Carl Warwick

1963 Pepsi Colt .45s, J.C. Hartman

and could be detached from a long strip that offered a Colt .45s schedule for the '63 season. Complete panels are worth about twice as much as individual cards. On the back of the card is a typical biographical and statistical summary of the pictured player.

FOR

This truly scarce regional major league issue of a popular expansion team is a must for Astros team collectors.

AGAINST

It's almost impossible to complete a set without a large outlay of cash for the rare Bateman card.

NOTEWORTHY CARDS

A rookie card of Rusty Staub is included in this set; it also includes manager Bob Lillis in his playing days.

OUR FAVORITE CARD

For whatever reason, the Bateman card was never distributed and is extremely rare today. A collector desiring an example could search the hobby publications and every card show within driving distance for a year without ever seeing one for sale. It ranks as one of the legitimate great rarities in the hobby, but has yet to be priced as such. Still, it is out of reach for most collectors.

VALUE

EX-MT CONDITION: Complete set (in panels without Bateman), $150; common card, $3.50; Staub, $15–$20; Warwick, $50; Bateman, $400.
5-YEAR PROJECTION: Above average.

1963 Pepsi Tulsa Oilers, Pepper Martin

1963 Pepsi Tulsa Oilers, Roy Majtyka

1963 PEPSI TULSA OILERS

SPECIFICATIONS

SIZE: Single card, 2½ × 3½"; panel, 5 × 7". FRONT: Sepia-tone photograph. BACK: Black printing on white cardboard. DISTRIBUTION: Tulsa, one 2-card panel with cartons of soda; complete sets available through a mail-in offer.

HISTORY

For the second straight year, Pepsi in 1963 sponsored a set for the Cardinals' Texas League team. Two-card panels, perforated for easy separation, were attached by means of a ring tab to one of the bottles in each carton of Pepsi. The detachable tab challenged collectors to assemble a complete set of 24 cards and match the names with those found under the cork liners of bottle caps. A complete matched set of cards and bottle caps could be sent to the bottling plant for a $24 reward—and you got the cards back. Any ten of the Pepsi Oilers cards shown at the gate were good for free admission on certain Pepsi Nights at the ballpark.

FOR

The set is relatively inexpensive, indicating that collectors obtained large quantities of the uncut panels during or after the promotion.

AGAINST

There is little demand for minor league sets unless they include a superstar.

NOTEWORTHY CARDS

The '63 Pepsi Tulsa Oilers set contains the last contemporary card of '30s Cardinals shortstop Pepper Martin, who was managing the Tulsa team.

VALUE

EX-MT CONDITION: Complete set, $35; common card, $1.50; Martin $5. 5-YEAR PROJECTION: Below average.

1962 TOPPS

SPECIFICATIONS

SIZE: 2½ × 3½". FRONT: Color photograph. BACK: Black and red printing on gray cardboard. DISTRIBUTION: Nationally, in packages with bubblegum.

1962 Topps, Babe Ruth

1962 Topps, Lou Brock

1962 Topps, Gaylord Perry

HISTORY

Although the Topps set for 1962 is numbered through card #598, a number of significant photo variations push the total for a complete set to more than 600 cards. Even at 598 cards, this issue was Topps' biggest ever to date. The design of the '62s is one of those Topps creations that a collector either loves or hates. The photo on the front of the card is set against a wood-grain background. The lower right of the picture has been airbrushed to make it look as if it is curling away from the wood background. In that exposed corner, the player's last name is printed in white capital letters. The player's first name, team, and position are indicated in black lettering. Card backs feature a return to abbreviated statistics, giving only the previous season's performance and the cumulative career record. There is a short paragraph about the player's career, a pertinent cartoon, and the usual biographical details. In the year after his historic record-breaking 61 home runs, Roger Maris' card (#1) opens the set. Virtually all of the specialty series within the 1962 set are copies of those done the previous year. There are subsets for league statistical leaders of 1961 (four per card), a number of multiplayer feature cards, a series detailing the Yankees' victory over the Reds in the '61 World Series, and the usual checklist and team photo cards. All-Star cards, which had traditionally been issued toward the end of the set, are in the middle of the 1962 issue. The most significant new series in this set is the first of the multiplayer rookie cards. Topps utilized the concept of grouping five player photos by position, regardless of team, on each of eight "Rookie Parade" cards, the last eight cards of the set. Nine of the stars of 1962 are featured on second cards within the set, usually in a sequence of photos showing action on the field. These are the predecessors of the "In Action" cards that would come in later years. There are ten "Babe Ruth Special" cards tracing his baseball career. As with most specialty cards in recent sets that depict old-time players, demand for the Ruth specialty cards is much less than expected. The 1962 set can be divided into three degrees of scarcity. Cards #1-#370 are the most common; cards #371-#522 are somewhat scarce; and the high numbers, #523-#598, are scarcer still. Because 1962 was the first year for the New York Mets and the Houston Colt .45s, most of their players are shown without caps and in uniforms of their previous teams, sometimes airbrushed to hide details.

FOR

The unusual design of the '62 set is quite popular with some collectors. There are enough variation cards, major and minor, to keep the avid collector busy for years—and more probably will be discovered.

AGAINST

If you don't like the '62 design, you probably hate it enough to keep you from collecting the cards. The varieties, some of them very minor in nature, can drive a collector crazy.

NOTEWORTHY CARDS

There are several major variations in the 1962 set, disregarding the numerous color-tint differences that some collectors cherish. All of the popularly collected variations occur between #129 and #190, and all involve pose or card-number variations. Lee Walls (#129) will be found facing either right or left. The Angels team card (#132) can be found with or without two small portraits in the upper corners. Billy Hoeft's card (#134) can be found facing slightly right or facing straight out. Card #139 can be found three ways: as "Babe Hits 60," with Hal Reniff's portrait, or with Reniff in a pitching pose. Bill Kunkel's card (#147) can also be found in portrait or pitching variations. Carl Willey (#174) is seen with and without a cap. And, finally, Eddie Yost (#176) and Wally Moon (#190) can be found in portrait or batting poses. Two other variations that are a bit less popular are Bob Buhl's card (#458) and Willie Tasby's card (#462). In the more common version, they are shown with Braves and Senators caps. In the scarcer type of cards, the logos have been airbrushed from the caps, reflecting trades. Notable rookie cards in the '62 set include Gaylord Perry and Lou Brock on individual cards; and Sam McDowell, Jim Bouton, Joe Pepitone, and Bob Uecker, who appear on multiplayer rookie cards. Some 1962 Topps cards have backs printed in Spanish. These cards were originally issued in Venezuela.

OUR FAVORITE CARD

In terms of number of stars gathered on a single baseball card, it would be hard to beat the "Manager's Dream" card (#18). The card features Mickey Mantle and Willie Mays facing the camera and smiling. However, if you look in the background, you'll see another group of players posing for a different photographer. In that group are Elston Howard, Hank Aaron, and George Altman. The photo is one of many taken at All-Star Games that appear on Topps multiplayer feature cards.

VALUE

EX-MT CONDITION: Complete set, $3,400; common card, #1-#522, $1.50; #523-#598, $5–$8; Bouton, Pepitone, McDowell, $25; stars, Reniff (pitching), $30–$40; Perry, Willie Mays, Hank Aaron, Mickey Mantle (All-Star), $45–$60; Brock, Bob Gibson, Willie McCovey, $60–$75; Uecker, $90; Maris, $100; Carl Yastrzemski, $125; Mantle, $300. 5-YEAR PROJECTION: Average.

1962 BAZOOKA

SPECIFICATIONS

SIZE: Single card, $1\frac{13}{16} \times 2\frac{3}{4}''$; panel, $5\frac{1}{2} \times 2\frac{3}{4}''$. FRONT: Color photograph. BACK: Blank. DISTRIBUTION: Nationally, one 3-card panel on the bottom of each box of bubblegum.

1962 Bazooka, Willie Mays

1962 Bazooka, Luis Aparicio

HISTORY

Not one to tamper with success—even to the point of being stationary—Topps left the design of the 1962 Bazooka cards unchanged from that of '60 and '61. The bottom of each 20-piece box of bubblegum again features a 3-card panel. Many of these Bazooka cards are found poorly trimmed, a condition that reduces their value considerably. Cards still attached to the complete gum box are worth 25 to 50 percent more than individual cards. Three-card panels cut from the boxes but not separated are also worth about 10 percent over the total value of the three individual cards. While at first glance the 1962 cards seem exactly like the previous two years, there is an important difference: the '62 cards are not numbered. Some 1962 Bazookas have surfaced with card numbers. These may be printer's proofs, rather than actual cards, but the question is still unresolved. Numbered 1962 Bazookas sell for several times the value of the unnumbered versions, but that situation may change. The other big change in '62 was the expansion of the set from 12 panels (36 cards) to 15 panels (45 cards). This seems to have been done as a result of National League expansion that season; the set features players of the newly formed Houston Colt .45s and New York Mets. Distribution of three of the 15 panels seems to have been somewhat uneven and they are quite scarce—Ed Mathews, Vada Pinson, Ernie Banks, and Harmon Killebrew are the stars featured on those panels.

FOR

The set is not too expensive and has a few scarce cards to keep it challenging. The new Mets and Colts cards are great for team collectors.

AGAINST

The cards are too small to be attractive to most collectors, who prefer the standard $2\frac{1}{2} \times 3\frac{1}{2}''$ size.

NOTEWORTHY CARDS

Hank Aaron is back in '62, and two other Hall of Famers—Sandy Koufax and Whitey Ford—make their first Bazooka appearance in this set.

VALUE

EX-MT CONDITION: Complete set (neatly cut from box), $1,300; common card, $7–$8; stars, $25–$40; Aaron, Willie Mays, Roberto Clemente, Roger Maris, $50–$60; Mathews, Mickey Mantle, Banks, Killebrew, $150–$200. 5-YEAR PROJECTION: Average.

1962 POST

SPECIFICATIONS

SIZE: $3\frac{1}{2} \times 2\frac{1}{2}''$. FRONT: Color photograph. BACK: Blank. DISTRIBUTION: Nationally, on the back of cereal boxes.

HISTORY

The most attractive and easiest to complete set of the 1960 to '63 Post cereal issues is the 200-card 1962 set. Unlike the '61 set, which could be obtained directly from the company through a mail-in offer, the 1962 cards were only available on the backs of cereal boxes. Single cards were printed on the backs of the small serving-size cereal boxes, while panels of eight cards made up the back of family size boxes of most Post brands. Because black lines dividing the cards were shared by two cards, it is difficult to find '62 Posts with a

1962 Post, Willie Mays

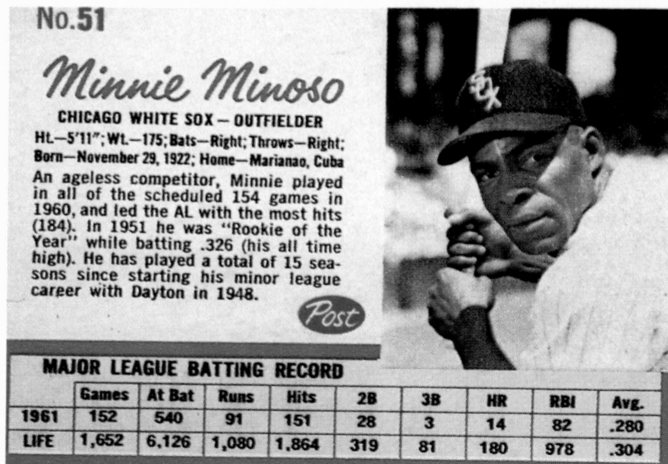

1962 Post, Minnie Minoso

complete black border, though some collectors try. Most will settle for a card that is neatly trimmed inside the black line, with straight edges. Cards that have ragged edges, or that have been cut into the photo or colored part of the design, are worth much less than neatly cut cards. Complete panels are worth two to three times more than the total value of the individual cards on the panel. Once again, the Post set was numbered by teams, with the American League preceding the National League. There are far fewer error and variation cards in the 1962 set, many of them being color variations of little interest to most collectors. The design of the '62 set is similar, though more attractive, than the 1961 cards. The color photo of the player appears on the right of the card. The card number is printed in red in the upper left, while the player's name is in blue script. There are some personal figures and a career summary printed in a yellow panel to the left of the photo, and a red and white Post logo appears in the lower right of that panel. The player's 1961 and lifetime stats are printed in a white box at the bottom of the card. This box is surrounded by a heavy red border on the N.L. cards and a blue border on the A.L. cards. The backs are blank. A virtually identical set of 200 cards was printed and distributed in Canada on Post cereals. The photos on these cards are slightly smaller to accommodate the French and English text. All card numbers and photos are the same but the layout has been slightly rearranged. The '62 issue is the only Post set to have a Canadian version, which is worth about twice as much as its U.S. counterpart.

FOR

It is an attractive, relatively inexpensive national set of the early 1960s.

AGAINST

It is hard to find an Excellent or Mint set.

NOTEWORTHY CARDS

Mickey Mantle and Roger Maris' cards were printed on thin cardboard with an advertising back and inserted into early spring issues of several national magazines to promote the set. They are valued about the same as the regular card, though the complete ad insert or magazine is a highly prized item. Two of the most popularly collected variations in the set are the Joe Adcock (#145) and Jim Gentile (#27) cards. The former can be found with the script-lettered name spelled correctly, which is more common, or incorrectly as "Adock." On the Gentile card, the more common variation lists his home as Baltimore, Maryland, while the scarcer type gives his home as San Lorenzo, California. The Post set also features a handful of scarce cards that were distributed on the backs of less popular cereals, and they are much in demand today. They are Early Wynn (#55), Marty Keough (#69), Norm Sebern (#92), Gil Hodges (#101), Norm Larker (#113), Gordy Coleman (#116), Jim Brosnan (#125), Jerry Lynch (#127), Willie McCovey (#131), Juan Marichal (#140), and Bill White (#158).

VALUE

EX-MT CONDITION: Complete set, $950; common card, 60¢–80¢; stars, scarce commons, $10–$20; superstars, scarce stars, $25–$40; Coleman, McCovey, Marichal, Mantle, $50. 5-YEAR PROJECTION: Average, or a bit above.

1962 JELL-O

SPECIFICATIONS

SIZE: 3½ × 2½". FRONT: Color photograph. BACK: Blank. DISTRIBUTION: Upper Midwest, one card on the back of each Jell-O box.

No. 5

Mickey Mantle

NEW YORK YANKEES – OUTFIELDER

Ht.—6'; Wt.—200; Switch-Hitter; Throws—Right; Born—October 20, 1931; Home—Dallas. Texas

The AL's home-run king for the 4th time in 1960 (40), he also finished 2nd for the MVP Award. Mickey won the MVP title in 1956, with a BA of .353, and again in 1957 with a BA of .365 (his all-time high). He has hit 14 World Series HR's—one behind Ruth's record of 15. He ranks 6th in lifetime HR's with 374. All-Star Games (1953-1961).

MAJOR LEAGUE BATTING RECORD

	Games	At Bat	Runs	Hits	2B	3B	HR	RBI	Avg.
1961	153	514	131	163	16	6	54	128	.317
LIFE	1,552	5,519	1,244	1,700	241	66	374	1,063	.308

1962 Jell-O, Mickey Mantle

No. 55

Early Wynn

CHICAGO WHITE SOX – PITCHER

Ht.—6'; Wt.—200; Switch-Hitter; Throws—Right; Born — January 6, 1920; Home — Venice, Florida

Seeking the charmed circle of 300 major league victories (a figure reached by only 12 pitchers in the history of baseball), Early developed a sore arm upon reaching his 292nd win. The 1962 season should see him clinch No. 300. His '61 season mark was 8-2 marking another fine year in his 24 years of professional ball playing.

MAJOR LEAGUE PITCHING RECORD

	Games	IP	Won	Lost	Pct	Hits	Runs	ER	SO	Walks	ERA
1961	17	110	8	2	.800	88	50	45	64	47	3.52
LIFE	644	4,343	292	227	.563	4,070	1,940	1,701	2,214	1,704	3.52

1962 Jell-O, Early Wynn

HISTORY

The 1962 Jell-O set is a direct spin-off of the 1962 Post cereal set, and it was originally intended to feature the same 200 cards. The Jell-O version contains only 197 cards. Brooks Robinson (#29), Ted Kluszewski (#82), and Smoky Burgess (#176) were not issued in the Jell-O set. Also, card #19 in the Jell-O set is Ken Aspromonte; card #19 in the Post set is Rocky Colavito. The Jell-O cards were only issued in the Upper Midwest, one card on the back of each box of Jell-O. Because each card was printed only on certain sizes and flavors of the gelatin dessert, the cards that appeared on the 6-ounce size or on the less popular flavors are today scarcer than other cards in the set. A detailed checklist is necessary to sort them out. Overall, the '62 Jell-O cards are much scarcer than their Post counterparts. The Jell-O cards are virtually identical in design to the Posts, except for three elements: the red Post logo is missing to the left of the photo on the Jell-O version; the red or blue color stripes that surround the stat box at the bottom of the card do not appear on the Jell-O set; and the stats are printed in a yellow box, rather than white. Like the Post cards, the backs of the Jell-O cards are blank. Because the Jell-O cards were printed one to a box, it is not too difficult to find them bordered by a complete black line, and cards are generally worth more that way. Complete boxes are worth three to five times more than the value of the individual card.

FOR

This regionally issued version of a popular set is scarce.

AGAINST

The cards are not as attractive as their Post counterparts, are much harder to assemble into a complete set, and are much more expensive.

NOTEWORTHY CARDS

The set features the same stars and superstars as the Post issue.

VALUE

EX-MT CONDITION: Complete set (neatly cut from box), $3,100; common card, $3–$4; stars, $20–$100; scarce cards, $25–$70; Carl Yastrzemski, $200; Mickey Mantle, $400. 5-YEAR PROJECTION: Below average.

1962 KAHN'S

SPECIFICATIONS

SIZE: $3\frac{1}{4} \times 4''$. FRONT: Black-and-white photograph. BACK: Black printing on white cardboard. DISTRIBUTION: Upper Midwest, individual cards in packages of Kahn's meat products; complete sets available through a mail-in offer.

HISTORY

The Minnesota Twins joined the Kahn's lineup in 1962. With representatives from the Pirates, Reds, and Indians, a total of 38 players are included in the set. Three of the players have two variation cards apiece. The tried and true design that Kahn's had used since 1955 was retained for '62. The card front is dominated by a borderless black-and-white photo, on which was printed a facsimile autograph. Under the photo is a half-inch white strip bearing a Kahn's advertisement. The back of the unnumbered card offers career information about the player. Like other Kahn's issues, the 1962 cards had a protective wax coating to prevent damage to either the cards or the meat products in which they were packaged. Besides the single cards in meat packages, the company also made complete sets available through a mail-in offer. This has helped keep the price of 1962 Kahn's reasonable.

1962 Kahn's, Gary Bell

FOR
These regional cards are relatively inexpensive considering that they aren't all that common.

AGAINST
The design remained unchanged from eight years earlier.

NOTEWORTHY CARDS
Three of the 1962 Kahn's cards exist with variations. The card of Gus Bell comes with and without what collectors call "the fat man" included in the photo. Bob Purkey's card can be found missing the facsimile signature. Vic Power is seen in the set as a member of the Twins or Indians. Roberto Clemente and Frank Robinson are the only Hall of Fame players represented in the set.

VALUE
EX-MT CONDITION: Complete set, $860; common card, $6–$8; stars, $15; common variations, $25; Robinson, $55; Power (Twins), Bell (with fat man), Purkey (without autograph), $90; Clemente, $135. 5-YEAR PROJECTION: Average.

1962 SUGARDALE

SPECIFICATIONS
SIZE: 5⅛ × 3¾". FRONT: Black-and-white photograph. BACK: Black and red printing on white cardboard. DISTRIBUTION: Cleveland, Pittsburgh, in packages of hot dogs.

HISTORY
This large-format set contains 22 cards showing the Cleveland Indians and Pittsburgh Pirates. The Indians cards are numbered 1 to 19, though no card #6 was issued; the Pirates cards are designated by the letters A to D. Horizontal in format and with rounded corners, the Sugardale card front features a black-and-white photo of the player with biographical data below. At the right is a short career summary with a facsimile autograph above. The bottom of the card carries advertisements for Sugardale and the team. Card backs feature baseball tips (ostensibly written by the player depicted on the front) along with a line drawing demonstrating the principle. Another Sugardale ad is at the bottom. The cards are quite scarce, but because they are not popularly collected, their value is not as high as it might otherwise be, though the cards are plenty expensive as it is.

FOR
They are scarce regional cards for team or single-player collectors—much rarer than their current price tag would indicate.

AGAINST
The cards are too large to please most collectors. They are also rather unattractive. Their scarcity makes completion of a full set a real tax on the patience and pocketbook.

NOTEWORTHY CARDS
Bob Nieman's card (#10) was only recently discovered, and is currently priced quite high. The only superstar in the set is Roberto Clemente.

VALUE
EX-MT CONDITION: Complete set, $1,000; common card, $40; Nieman, $200; Clemente, $450. 5-YEAR PROJECTION: Average.

1962 BELL BRAND DODGERS

SPECIFICATIONS

SIZE: 2 7/16 × 3½″. FRONT: Color photograph. BACK: Black printing on white cardboard. DISTRIBUTION: Southern California, individual cards inserted into packages of snack chips.

1962 Bell Brand Dodgers, Don Drysdale

1962 Bell Brand Dodgers, Lee Walls

HISTORY

While the design of the fourth and final Bell Brand chips issue was identical to the 1960 and '61 sets, the cards were printed on thicker cardboard stock with a glossy surface, giving the cards a better overall appearance. There were again 20 cards in the set, all Los Angeles Dodgers. On the front of the card a color player photo with a facsimile autograph is surrounded by a white border. At the bottom, the player's name, team, and position are printed. The card backs are similar to the previous design; they combine a statistical review of the player's 1961 performance, along with the Dodgers home schedule and a Bell advertisement. Cards were numbered according to the player's uniform number. There are no especially scarce cards in the 1962 Bell set.

FOR

It is the least expensive of the Bell sets, making it a good item for regional collectors and Dodgers fans.

AGAINST

The design is the same as the previous two years, which creates confusion among collectors.

NOTEWORTHY CARDS

Hall of Famers include Duke Snider, Walt Alston, Sandy Koufax, and, for the first time since the 1958 premier set, Don Drysdale.

VALUE

EX-MT CONDITION: Complete set, $300; common card, $8–$10; Alston, Maury Wills, $20; Drysdale, $30; Snider, Koufax, $40. 5-YEAR PROJECTION: Average.

1962 KAHN'S ATLANTA CRACKERS

SPECIFICATIONS

SIZE: 3¼ × 4″. FRONT: Black-and-white photograph. BACK: Black printing on white cardboard. DISTRIBUTION: Atlanta, in packages of Kahn's meat products.

HISTORY

A separate issue for Kahn's in 1962 was a 24-card set of the Double-A Atlanta Crackers, a Cardinals farm team. This was Kahn's only minor league set, and though the cards are really quite scarce, there is less demand for them than for Kahn's major league card sets. The Atlanta Crackers cards follow the standard Kahn's format: a large black-and-white

1962 Kahn's Atlanta Crackers, Tim McCarver

photo with a white strip along the bottom carrying a Kahn's advertising message. There is no facsimile autograph on the cards. The card backs carry an abbreviated career summary of the player and an offer for free Atlanta tickets. The cards are unnumbered.

FOR

The set is of interest to minor league collectors and St. Louis Cardinals fans.

AGAINST

It's a minor league set in a not particularly attractive format.

NOTEWORTHY CARDS

There are a few former major leaguers as well as a young Tim McCarver on his way up.

VALUE

EX-MT CONDITION: Complete set, \$250; common card, \$8–\$10; McCarver, \$25. 5-YEAR PROJECTION: Below average.

1962 PEPSI TULSA OILERS

SPECIFICATIONS

SIZE: Single card, 2½ × 3½″; panel, 5½ × 7″. FRONT: Black-and-white photograph. BACK: Black printing on white cardboard. DISTRIBUTION: Oklahoma, one 2-card panel in cartons of soda.

1962 Pepsi Tulsa Oilers, Jeoff Long

1962 Pepsi Tulsa Oilers, Pepper Martin

HISTORY

These 24 cards were originally issued in 2-card panels. A ring tab at the top of the panel allowed it to be placed over the neck of a soda bottle. The cards were perforated and could be detached from the panel. Cards are more valuable when still attached as a pair to the original ring tab. The Tulsa Oilers were a Double-A club of the Cardinals. Quite similar in appearance to subsequent 1963 and '66 issues, the premier 1962 set can be differentiated by the angled bottle cap to the right of the player's name and the words "Pepsi-Cola" in script.

FOR

The set is readily available today, apparently because collectors were able to secure undistributed quantities during or after the local promotion.

AGAINST

There is virtually a complete lack of name players in this set. Most of the cards would not be recognized by anybody but the most fervent Cardinals fan.

NOTEWORTHY CARDS

The best card in the set is that of manager Pepper Martin, famed sparkplug of the Cardinals "Gashouse Gang" of the late '30s. Also included in the set is former major league (1962 to 1975) shortstop Dal Maxvill, now general manager for the St. Louis Cardinals.

VALUE

EX-MT CONDITION: Complete set, $35; common card, $1.50; Martin, $5. 5-YEAR PROJECTION: Below average.

1961 TOPPS

SPECIFICATIONS

SIZE: 2½ × 3½". FRONT: Color photograph. BACK: Black and green-gold printing on gray cardboard. DISTRIBUTION: Nationally, in packages with bubblegum.

HISTORY

After producing 572-card sets for two years, Topps increased the size in 1961 to 589 cards. Actually, only 587 cards were issued, with 586 numbers. Card #426, which was checklisted as the Braves team card, was not issued at all. Instead, Topps put out a Braves team card and a player card of Jack Fisher (both #463). Cards #587 and #588, which were supposed to be All-Star cards, were also never issued. There is, however, a full complement of ten All-Star player cards and a manager card for each

1961 Topps, Jackie Jensen

1961 Topps, Roger Maris

1961 Topps, Dick Groat

league. The design of the 1961 cards is simple. A large color photo dominates the card, with two rectangular, colored boxes underneath. The player's name and position are in the left box and the team name is in the right box. The card backs have a black band at the top containing biographical information, and complete major and/or minor league statistics are given below. Where space permits, there is a cartoon highlighting some part of the player's career. For the first time, checklists were issued as numbered cards within the Topps set. Also new for 1961 was the concept of issuing cards for various statistical leaders of the previous season. Each league's statistical winner shares a card with three runners-up in the categories of batting average, home runs, ERA, winning percentage, and strikeouts. Multiplayer cards were continued in 1961, as was a subset recounting the previous season's World Series—8 cards detailing the Pirates' win over the Yankees in seven games. There is a 10-card set of "Baseball Thrills" cards, recounting dramatic games, plays, and individual records in a newspaper format. Another innovation was a 16-card series honoring the players in each league who won the MVP award every year since 1951. Finally, the set closes with a 22-card group of *The Sporting News* All-Star selections. These cards feature a player photo "bursting out" of a front page from the paper. There are really only two levels of scarcity in the 1961 set: #1-#522 are the common cards, while #523-#589 are among the scarcest high numbers ever produced by Topps. (In 1973 Topps began issuing all its cards at one time.) The only superstars in the '61 highs are the All-Star cards, and they are usually in less demand than the regular cards of the same players. Three other high-number cards command a premium: the team cards of the expansion Minnesota Twins and the Pittsburgh Pirates, and the card of Hall of Famer Hoyt Wilhelm.

FOR

The 1961 set is popular, good-looking, and—with the scarce high-number series—as challenging as any regular Topps set of the '60s.

AGAINST

The scarcity of the high numbers makes the set too formidable for some collectors, as well as too expensive.

NOTEWORTHY CARDS

There are few good rookie cards; Billy Williams and Juan Marichal are the only premier cards worth noting. There are two wrong-photo cards in the set. The Sherman Jones card actually pictures Eddie Fisher. The Dutch Dotterer card is also wrong, but it's all in the family; the player pictured is Dutch's brother, Tommy. It was a good deal for Tommy; he never made the major leagues or had a card of his own, while Dutch had three other cards.

OUR FAVORITE CARD

One of baseball's better-known umpires, Bill Kunkel, used to be a major league pitcher—though not a great one. Kunkel lost the only two games he started (with Kansas City in 1961), but brought his lifetime record up to 6-6 in 1962 and 1963 as a relief pitcher for the A's and Yankees, adding four saves to his credit. His 4.29 ERA is nothing to brag about. Kunkel's rookie card as a player appears in the 1961 Topps set, with a heavily retouched photo taken in a minor league park supposedly showing him in the Kansas City A's uniform.

VALUE

EX-MT CONDITION: Complete set, $3,900; common card #1-#522, 80¢–$1.25; #523-#589, $15; stars, Williams, $25–$45; Willie Mays, Hank Aaron, Marichal, Wilhelm, Brooks Robinson All-Star, Ernie Banks AS, Roger Maris AS, Al Kaline AS, Frank Robinson AS, Whitey Ford AS, Warren Spahn AS, $50–$75; Carl Yastrzemski, $90; Aaron AS, Mays AS, $100; Mickey Mantle, $225; Mantle AS, $250.
5-YEAR PROJECTION: Average.

1961 BAZOOKA

SPECIFICATIONS

SIZE: Single card, 1 13/16 × 2 3/4"; panel, 5 1/2 × 2 3/4". FRONT: Color photograph. BACK: Blank. DISTRIBUTION: Nationally, one 3-card panel on boxes of bubblegum.

1961 Bazooka, Mickey Mantle

1961 Bazooka, Roger Maris

HISTORY

You'd need checklists to tell the 1961 Bazooka baseball cards from the '60s; the cards are identical in size and design. Although the player photos are different each year, many players appear in both sets. Luckily, the card numbers are different for each year. Once again, there is a small line of type at the bottom of the card that states: "NO. xx OF 36 CARDS." The 1961 Bazookas were printed on 3-card panels on the bottom of 20-piece boxes of Topps bubblegum sold under the Bazooka name. Although the panels were designed to be cut apart, complete panels are worth slightly more than the individual cards, while an entire box is worth 25 to 50 percent more. Cut cards must be neatly trimmed to command top value.

FOR

It's a handsome set with lots of big-name players.

AGAINST

The cards are too small to be popular. It is difficult to find a Mint set.

NOTEWORTHY CARDS

There are fewer Hall of Famers and superstars in the 1961 issue (even Hank Aaron is absent) and a lot more players today's fans may not recognize (Chuck Estrada, Ernie Broglio, and Frank Herrera). The Roger Maris card is noteworthy since it was the year he hit 61 home runs to break Babe Ruth's long-standing record.

VALUE

EX-MT CONDITION: Complete set, $750; common card, $6–$8; superstars, $25–$35; Maris, $50; Willie Mays, $65; Mickey Mantle, $125. 5-YEAR PROJECTION: Average.

1961 POST

SPECIFICATIONS

SIZE: 3 1/2 × 2 1/2". FRONT: Color photograph. BACK: Blank. DISTRIBUTION: Nationally, on the back of cereal boxes and through a mail-in offer.

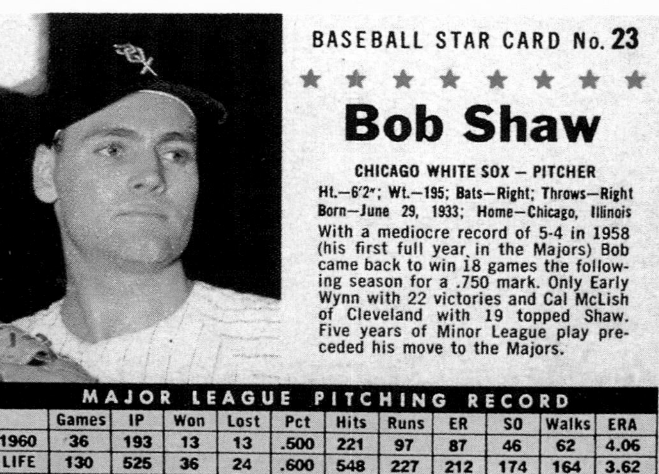

1961 Post, Bob Shaw

1961 Post, Tito Francona

HISTORY

In its second year of baseball card production, Post cereal adopted the method of distribution it would use until 1963. Cards were printed on the backs of boxes of cereal (one card on a single-serving box and seven cards on a family-size box). In addition, a 10-card sheet featuring one team (printed on slightly thinner cardboard) could be obtained from the company through a mail-in offer. To obtain a complete 200-card set, cards from the mail-in offer are necessary, as some of them were never printed on the cereal boxes. The sheets were perforated for easy separation, while the cereal box cards had to be cut apart along black lines. Since two cards often shared the same dividing line, it took careful cutting to separate the cards neatly. Some collectors prefer cards with the black lines showing, others prefer cards without any trace of the line. Either way, the cards must be cut straight, with no part of the photo or statistical box trimmed away. Entire boxes are worth more than three times the value of the individual cards, while complete panels and sheets are worth about twice as much as the single cards. The cards feature a color portrait of the player at the left, with a white panel to the right containing the card number, a row of eight red stars, the player's name, team, position, personal data, and a career summary. At the bottom of the card is a panel of stats from the 1960 season and the player's cumulative major league record. The card backs are blank. The cards are numbered by team starting with the American League. Two cards are out of sequence for no apparent reason: Paul Foytack (#62) of the Detroit Tigers is numbered with the Cleveland Indians; Mel Roach (#163) of the Milwaukee Braves is numbered with the Los Angeles Dodgers. There are a lot of variation cards in the 1961 Post set. Some have different team names, caps, or uniforms; others have lines indicating sales or trades to different teams. Few occur on both the company-mailed sheets and the cereal-box cards; usually they are on one or the other. Few command any sort of premium, and most collectors consider their set complete at 200 cards, regardless of variation. Serious collectors will need a checklist.

FOR

An exciting, endlessly challenging baseball card set of the '60s. Condition-conscious collectors will enjoy the challenge of assembling a high-grade set, and there are plenty of variations for variety collectors.

AGAINST

The variations confuse many collectors. The cards are more bland than the '62 and '63 Post sets. It's hard to find cards in Mint condition.

NOTEWORTHY CARDS

At least nine of the 1961 Post cereal cards are scarcer and more valuable than the others. These cards either had a smaller print run or they were printed on the single-serving boxes or on a less popular brand of cereal. The scarce '61s are Gil McDougald (#10), Bob Shaw (#23), Gene Woodling (#70), Chuck Estrada (#73), Chuck Stobbs (#94), Chuck Cottier (#113), Bill Virdon (#135), Mel Roach (#163), and Roy McMillan (#183).

VALUE

EX-MT CONDITION: Complete set, $1,000; common card, $1; stars, $3–$15; scarce cards, $25–$65; Mickey Mantle, $75. 5-YEAR PROJECTION: Average, perhaps below.

1961 FLEER

SPECIFICATIONS

SIZE: 2½ × 3½". FRONT: Color or colorized photograph. BACK: Red and black printing on white cardboard. DISTRIBUTION: Nationally, in packages with bubblegum.

HISTORY

Although Fleer had only limited success with its old-timers set in 1960, they were undaunted and issued another "Baseball Greats" set the next year. They even expanded the set to 154 cards. The set is divided into two series: #1-#88 is the more common, while the #89-#154 series is scarcer and about twice as expensive per card. The first card in each series is a checklist: card #1 features a group photo of Frank Baker, Ty Cobb, and Zack Wheat; card #89 has George Sisler and Pie Traynor on the front. The cards are numbered alphabetically. Most card fronts feature photos of the players as they

1961 Fleer, Babe Ruth

1961 Fleer, Edd Roush

1961 Fleer, Honus Wagner

appeared after their careers were over. Some photos are in color, but most are black-and-white photos that have been colorized. The photo is surrounded by a white border with five blue stars on each side near the top. The player's name appears in a blue pennant below the photo, superimposed on four red and white stripes. Backs are horizontal, with a red box at the top containing the player's name, birth date, and where applicable, date of death. The card number appears in a trophy at the upper left. At the bottom of the card, a career summary appears on the left, and a lifetime major league record is on the right. Some collectors recall that the 1961 Fleer old-timers set was issued well into '62, and in fact the company did not produce another issue until its current-players set in 1963. Perhaps this is why there are two distinct series.

FOR

More old-timers appear in this set on relatively inexpensive cards.

AGAINST

Collectors don't like cards that are issued after the player's career is over.

NOTEWORTHY CARDS

Because Ted Williams was under contract to Fleer, he appears in the 1961 old-timers set even though he was still playing (it was his last season in the majors). It may be one of the most underrated cards of the '60s.

VALUE
EX-MT CONDITION: Complete set, $350; common card #1-#88, $1; #89-#154, $2; superstars, $3–$5; Cobb, Lou Gehrig, Honus Wagner, checklists, $6–$9; Babe Ruth, Williams, $15. 5-YEAR PROJECTION: Average.

1961 KAHN'S

SPECIFICATIONS
SIZE: 3¼ × 4″. FRONT: Black-and-white photograph. BACK: Black printing on white cardboard. DISTRIBUTION: Ohio, Western Pennsylvania, single cards in packages of Kahn's meat products; nationally, complete sets available through a mail-in offer.

Compliments of Kahn's
"THE WIENER THE WORLD AWAITED"

1961 Kahn's, Frank Robinson

HISTORY
For the first time, Kahn's made complete sets of cards available through a mail-in offer in 1961. Individual cards continued to be packaged with meat products. The '61 set contained 43 cards (one more than in 1960), but included only three teams instead of six: the Pirates, Reds, and Indians. Once again, the card fronts closely resemble the first Kahn's issue back in 1955. The cards have a borderless black-and-white photo with a facsimile autograph across it. On the bottom is a white strip bearing a Kahn's ad. The backs of the unnumbered cards feature vital player data as well as major league stats. Because of the availability of complete sets, the 1961 issue is the first Kahn's set to be relatively inexpensive.

FOR
These are great cards for team collectors.

AGAINST
After seven years, the design was predictable.

NOTEWORTHY CARDS
Hall of Famers Roberto Clemente and Frank Robinson are the big names in the set, but fans who followed these teams in the '60s will find lots of familiar faces.

VALUE
EX-MT CONDITION: Complete set, $500; common card, $9–$11; stars, $15–$20; Robinson, $60–$65; Clemente, $90. 5-YEAR PROJECTION: Average or below.

1961 NU-CARD BASEBALL SCOOPS

SPECIFICATIONS
SIZE: 2½ × 3½″. FRONT: Black-and-white photograph. BACK: Red and black printing on white cardboard. DISTRIBUTION: Nationally.

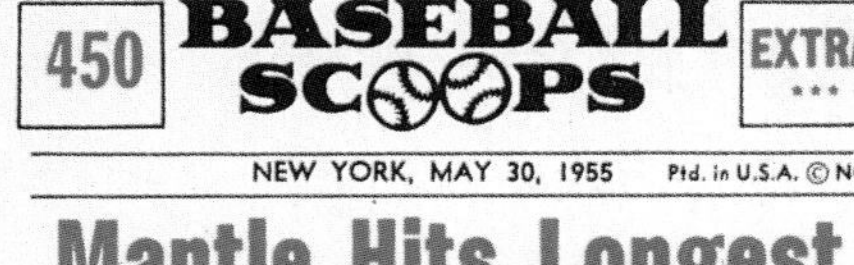

Mantle Hits Longest Homer at Stadium

1961 Nu-Card Baseball Scoops, Mickey Mantle

462 BASEBALL SCOOPS EXTRA
MILWAUKEE, OCT. 10, 1957 Ptd. in U.S.A. ©NCI
AARON'S BAT BEATS YANKEES IN SERIES

1961 Nu-Card Baseball Scoops, Hank Aaron

HISTORY
For its second "great moments" set, Nu-Card sensibly chose to go with the 2½ × 3½" size preferred by collectors. Otherwise, the set is unchanged from the year before, and even includes many of the same "great moments." There are 80 cards in the 1961 Scoops set (#401-#480). The card front is a simulated newspaper front page. There is a large black-and-white photo, a headline, and a line that gives the date and location of the great moment. The card number appears in the upper left. Card backs also give the card number, along with a newspaper-style write-up of the event. This issue concentrates on the period from 1950 to 1961, which makes the set more popular with collectors. The set was reprinted years later, but the photos on the reprints were not as clear as the originals.

FOR
It is a novel format with good cards for superstar collectors.

AGAINST
Some collectors don't like in-action cards, especially ones that reach back into baseball history. The Nu-Card sets are generally considered collector issues.

NOTEWORTHY CARDS
Most of the great moments in the Nu-Card set involve big-name players.

VALUE
EX-MT CONDITION: Complete set, $75; common card, 35¢–45¢; superstars, $5–$7.50. 5-YEAR PROJECTION: Average.

1961 GOLDEN PRESS HALL OF FAME

SPECIFICATIONS
SIZE: 2½ × 3½". FRONT: Color painting or colorized photograph. BACK: Black printing on white cardboard. DISTRIBUTION: Nationally, in booklets of 33 cards.

HISTORY
Another retrospective Hall of Famers set from the early 1960s was the Golden Press issue. The 33 cards came in a booklet and were perforated so they could be punched out. Each card depicts a Hall of Famer, and the set includes a good selection of the best-known players. The card fronts feature attractive paintings or colorized photos, with the player's name and position in a white panel at the bottom. The card backs recap the player's career and include a line of lifetime stats and the date of his induction into the Hall of Fame. The original booklets still exist in sufficient numbers for the collector who is willing to do a little digging.

1961 Golden Press Hall of Fame, Lou Gehrig

1961 Golden Press Hall of Fame, Rogers Hornsby

1961 Bell Brand Dodgers, Sandy Koufax

FOR
These are attractive, inexpensive cards of baseball's greatest players of the first half of the 20th century—great for the superstar collector.

AGAINST
Most collectors don't like cards issued after a player's career is over.

NOTEWORTHY CARDS
All the expected players are here including Babe Ruth, Ty Cobb, Lou Gehrig, and Joe DiMaggio.

VALUE
EX-MT CONDITION: Complete booklet, $65; complete set of single cards, $45; common card, 50¢; Dizzy Dean, $4; Gehrig, DiMaggio, Cobb, $6; Ruth, $10. 5-YEAR PROJECTION: Average.

1961 BELL BRAND DODGERS

SPECIFICATIONS
SIZE: 2 7/16 × 3½″. FRONT: Color photograph. BACK: Black printing on white cardboard. DISTRIBUTION: Southern California, in packages of snack chips.

HISTORY
The Bell Brand snack chip company made few changes in its third consecutive Los Angeles Dodgers baseball card set. Once again, the set contained 20 cards, and the design was virtually identical to the previous year. A color photo of the player appears on the front, surrounded by a wide white border. There is a facsimile autograph across the photo, and the player's name, team, and position appear at the bottom. While the cards are one-sixteenth inch narrower than the 1960 version, most collectors hardly notice the difference. To tell the two years apart, the back of the card must be consulted. 1961 card backs have 1960 season stats, a Dodgers home schedule, a Bell ad, and the card number. Unlike the 1960 cards, the '61s are skip-numbered by the player's uniform number, from #3 (Willie Davis) to #51 (Larry Sherry). There are no known scarcities in the 1961 Bell set.

FOR
It's a good-looking Dodgers team set, and a good value among early '60s regional sets.

AGAINST
The similarity to the 1960 set is confusing to most collectors.

VALUE
EX-MT CONDITION: Complete set, $300; common card, $8–$10; stars, $18–$20; Duke Snider, Sandy Koufax, $25–$35. 5-YEAR PROJECTION: Average.

1961 MORRELL DODGERS

SPECIFICATIONS

SIZE: 2¼ × 3¼". FRONT: Color photograph. BACK: Brown printing on white cardboard. DISTRIBUTION: Southern California, one card in packages of Morrell meat products.

1961 Morrell Dodgers, Sandy Koufax

1961 Morrell Dodgers, Tommy Davis

HISTORY

Only six cards were issued in the third and final year of Morrell's Los Angeles Dodgers issue. The cards are slightly smaller in size than the previous two years' offerings, but the basic format remained unchanged from 1960. A color posed-action photo appears on front; player stats and a small ad on back. Only two players appear in both the '60 and '61 sets: the Dodgers' ace pitching pair, Don Drysdale and Sandy Koufax. The inclusion of only four new player cards—Frank Howard, Tommy Davis, Norm Larker, and Maury Wills—has led some to speculate that remainders of the 1960 issue may have been stuffed in meat packages alongside the six new 1961 cards. In any event, the 1961 Morrells are not particularly scarce, but since five of the six players are stars, they are expensive.

FOR

This is a regional issue with beautiful photography and players from a popular team.

AGAINST

At six cards, it is not a complete team issue.

VALUE

EX-MT CONDITION: Complete set, $175; Larker, $15; Davis, Howard, $25; Wills, $35; Drysdale, $45; Koufax, $80. 5-YEAR PROJECTION: Above average.

1961 PETERS' MEATS TWINS

SPECIFICATIONS

SIZE: 4⅝ × 3½". FRONT: Colorized photograph. BACK: Blank. DISTRIBUTION: Minneapolis, as the bottom of packages of hot dogs.

HISTORY

The Peters' meat products company welcomed the Minnesota Twins to Minneapolis with a 26-card issue in 1961. The set features most of the Twins roster, along with managers Cookie Lavagetto and Sam Mele. The cards were printed on heavily waxed cardboard as part of the company's packaging. The cards have a photo of the player at the right end of the card. In the upper left is a card number in a white panel; below is the player's name, flanked by Peters and Twins logos. A

\#18 (COLLECT ALL 26) MINN.

HARMON
"Killer"
KILLEBREW

TWINS

First bonus player in Twins history. Signed in 1954. Star quarterback in high school. Had many college scholarship offers. Started career as third baseman, switched to first base. Cookie Lavagetto, the manager, says he will be a natural. In 1959 he tied for most home runs in the American League with Rocky Colivito with 42. Came back in 1960 with 31 in spite of missing about a third of games. Hit 27 home runs during last half of season. Bats and throws right handed.

Age 25 — Height 6' — Weight 185

1961 Peters' Meats Twins, Harmon Killebrew

biography takes up most of the space, and the player's age, height, and weight appear at the bottom. Like all baseball cards that had to be cut off a package, many Peters cards are found poorly trimmed, and value is greatly reduced when the photo or information panels are cut into. Uncut cards from the hot dog packages are worth 25 to 50 percent more than individual cards. Card backs are blank and were protected from grease stains (and from getting ink on the hot dogs) by a heavy coating of wax.

FOR

A great first-year regional issue for collectors of Minnesota Twins cards. Also, the cards are quite scarce.

AGAINST

The cards are not standard size.

NOTEWORTHY CARDS

Hall of Famer Harmon Killebrew is the big star in the set; also appearing is long-time major league pitcher Jim Kaat.

VALUE

EX-MT CONDITION: Complete set, $575; common card, $15; Kaat, $45; Killebrew, $150. 5-YEAR PROJECTION: Average.

1961 UNION OIL

SPECIFICATIONS

SIZE: 3 × 4". FRONT: Sepia-tone photograph. BACK: Blue printing on white cardboard. DISTRIBUTION: West Coast, given away with purchase at gas stations.

HISTORY

The 67-card set of Pacific Coast League players issued by Union Oil in 1961 was the largest of the company's three sets. Previous issues featured players from a single team (Sacramento in 1958 and Seattle in 1960); the '61 set represented players and managers from six teams. The card front features a borderless sepia-tone photograph—generally a posed-action shot. On the back is a short biography of the player, along with ads for a local radio station and Union 76. The cards are not numbered. Cards from each team's hometown were distributed at gas stations in that area. The six teams represented in the set include Hawaii, Portland, San Diego, Sacramento, Spokane, and Tacoma. The Spokane set and, to a lesser degree, the Hawaii set are considered scarcer than the others.

1961 Union Oil, Gaylord Perry

FOR

This regional issue includes many former and future major leaguers.

AGAINST

The set is generally hard to find outside the original distribution areas.

NOTEWORTHY CARDS

The 1961 Union Oil set contains a number of former and future major league players, including managers. The most notable former player in the set is Herb Score, who appears on a San Diego card. The best-known of the soon-to-be major leaguers who appeared in the set is Gaylord Perry, who was then pitching for Tacoma. Two cards in the set, Preston Gomez (Spokane) and George Prescott (Hawaii), were withdrawn from distribution early and are scarcer than the rest. The card of Norman Hershberger (San Diego) sometimes pictures Bobby Knoop.

VALUE

EX-MT CONDITION: Complete set, $375; common card, $3–$10; Score, $20; Prescott, Gomez, $30–$35; Perry, $60. 5-YEAR PROJECTION: Above average.

1960 TOPPS

SPECIFICATIONS

SIZE: 2½ × 3½". FRONT: Color photograph. BACK: Black and gold printing on gray or white cardboard. DISTRIBUTION: Nationally, in packages with bubblegum.

1960 Topps, Carl Yastrzemski

1960 Topps, Mickey Mantle/Ken Boyer

HISTORY

Holding the line at 572 cards for the second year in a row, the 1960 Topps set is a collector favorite. There are enough specialty cards to make them distinctive without being gimmicky, and the format is unusual. Also, there are lots of good rookie cards and big-name stars. As the first set of the decade, it is a popular starting point for some collectors of Topps cards. The most notable feature is the horizontal format; in fact, they are the only horizontal standard-size Topps cards. A portrait photo occupies the right two-thirds of the card, with a smaller black-and-white action pose to the left. A solid-color band below the photo contains the player's name, team, and position, and a color team logo. The names are printed in two colors, alternating with each letter. Card backs in '60 give only the previous season and lifetime totals. There is a cartoon and a short career summary or, on some cards, previous season highlights written as a diary entry. Once again the set features multiplayer cards and team cards with series checklists on back. A new 7-card subset (which would be included off and on for many years in Topps sets) recounted the 1959 World Series victory of the Dodgers over the White Sox. Team managers and coaches were featured on vertical-format cards. Each manager has his own card, while the coaches share a card (three "head" shots per card) on an orange background. Many Hall of Famers appear among these manager and coaches cards. There are two subsets of rookie cards in the 1960 set. Cards #117-#148 are the *Sport* magazine "1960 Rookie Star" cards. These cards have an orange background with red and black lettering, and a red, white, and blue diagonal ribbon containing a round color photo of the player. One of the hobby's hottest cards—the premier card of Carl Yastrzemski—is in this subset, along with rookie cards of Jim Kaat and Frank Howard. The second rookie subset is a 10-card run titled "Topps All-Star Rookie," which features a team of rookies "Selected by the Youth of America." On these cards the player photo appears at the left and there is a picture of the Topps rookie trophy at the right. Most of the players in this group had appeared on baseball cards previously, but the Willie McCovey card is his first appearance. The backs of the rookie cards are quite similar to the rest of the set. Again in 1960, the set closes with a series of 20 All-Star cards. On these cards the player's picture is placed in front of a large number "60" on a white background. This set has three levels of scarcity: cards #1-#440 are common, #441-#506 are semi-high, and #507-#572 are high-number cards. Because of the many stars in the 1960 set, especially the high-demand Yastrzemski card, the price has risen steadily in the last several years.

FOR

It's a challenging but collectible set, with an original design and a lot of good rookie and specialty cards.

AGAINST

The horizontal format does not allow for the best presentation of the player photos.

NOTEWORTHY CARDS

The important rookie cards in the '60 Topps set are Yastrzemski, McCovey, Kaat, and Howard. A photo mix-up reversed the portraits of White Sox pitchers Gary Peters and J.C. Martin, though the small black-and-white photos to the left are correct.

OUR FAVORITE CARD

Topps really dug into the archives for Cubs manager Charlie Grimm's card; it uses a colorized picture of "Jolly Cholly" from the 1948 Cubs yearbook.

VALUE

EX-MT CONDITION: Complete set, $2,800; common card #1-#440, $1; #441-#506, $1.25–$1.75; #507-#572, $6; stars, $20–$45; Willie Mays, Hank Aaron, Mays All-Star, Aaron AS, $40–$50; McCovey, $90; Mickey Mantle AS, $135; Yastrzemski, $175; Mantle, $250. 5-YEAR PROJECTION: Average.

1960 BAZOOKA

SPECIFICATIONS

SIZE: Single card, 1¹³⁄₁₆ × 2¾"; panel, 5½ × 2¾". FRONT: Color photograph. BACK: Blank. DISTRIBUTION: Nationally, one 3-card panel on the bottom of boxes of bubblegum.

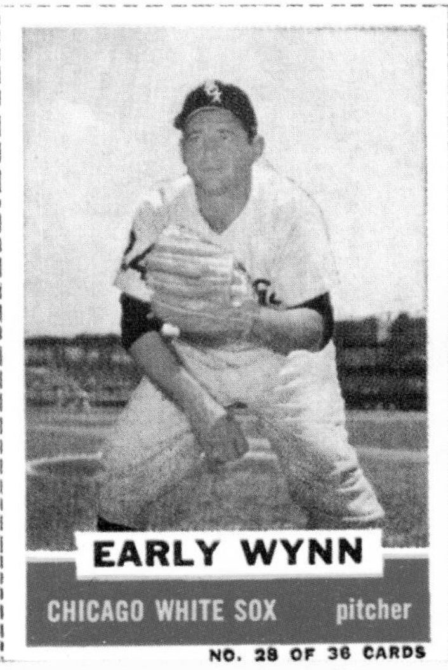

1960 Bazooka, Early Wynn

HISTORY

Hoping that three smaller cards would offer more incentive to buy than last year's single large-format card, Topps made the cards smaller for 1960, increased the set size to 36 cards, and issued them on 3-card panels on the bottom of each box of Bazooka bubblegum. The '60 set kept the same basic design: a color photo with multicolored stripes at the bottom containing the player's name, team, and position. Below that, in tiny type, is a card number and notation that the set contains 36 cards. All 12 of the 1960 Bazooka panels seem to have received equal distribution. Complete boxes are quite scarce and worth 25 to 50 percent more than the individual cards. Three-card panels, however, are remarkably common and command only a small premium. Cards and panels cut from the boxes are worth top money only if they are neatly cut or cut close to the dotted lines. Topps did a great job of mixing superstars, stars, and lesser-known players on the panels; only two of the 12 panels do not depict a Hall of Famer.

FOR
It's not a difficult or expensive set to complete.

AGAINST
Most collectors don't like cards that are not the standard 2½ × 3½″ size. Also, cards that have to be cut from a box get a lot of abuse in the process and are hard to find in top condition.

NOTEWORTHY CARDS
There are too many superstars to name; the 36 cards include 13 Hall of Famers and another six or eight potential Hall of Famers.

VALUE
EX-MT CONDITION: Complete set (neatly cut from box), $600; common card, $7–$9; stars, $30–$45; Hank Aaron, Willie Mays, Roberto Clemente, $60; Mickey Mantle, $135. 5-YEAR PROJECTION: Average.

1960 LEAF

SPECIFICATIONS
SIZE: 2½ × 3½″. FRONT: Black-and-white photograph. BACK: Black printing on white cardboard. DISTRIBUTION: Nationally, in wax packs with a marble.

HISTORY
Since Topps had a lock on the bubblegum card market, the Leaf gum company of Chicago issued its 144-card set in wax packs with a marble (making the packs hard to store and easily damaged). The 1960 set was Leaf's second and last baseball card issue, their only other set was a 98-card effort in 1948-49. The '60 Leaf cards were widely distributed, but in much smaller numbers than the Topps cards of the same year. The card features a black-and-white studio portrait of the player surrounded by a white border. The player's name, team, and position appear in black type beneath the photo. Card backs have a number in a baseball at the upper left, along with the player's vital data, a brief career summary, and previous season and lifetime stats. Like the 1948-49 issue, the 1960 set is divided into two equal series:

1960 Leaf, Duke Snider

cards #1-#72 are fairly common, while #73-#144 are considerably harder to find. Although the '60 Leafs are much scarcer than their Topps counterparts, they are not nearly as popular, possibly because black-and-white cards seemed outdated by 1960.

FOR
The scarce high-number cards make this set challenging to collect.

AGAINST
The high numbers can be hard to find and nearly ten times as expensive as the low numbers, making it costly to assemble a full set.

NOTEWORTHY CARDS
Chuck Tanner's card (#115) actually pictures Ken Kuhn—a mistake that was never corrected. A wrong photo that was later corrected (creating a collectible variation) was Jim Grant's card (#25), which originally showed Brooks Lawrence. The corrected version shows a dark cap with a light "C" (for Cleveland); the error card has a white pinstriped cap with a dark "C" (for Cincinnati). The few superstars in the '60 Leaf set include Luis Aparicio, Brooks Robinson, and Duke Snider.

VALUE
EX-MT CONDITION: Complete set, $950; common card #1-#72, $1; #73-#144, $10; stars, $4–$7; Aparicio, $5; Snider, Robinson, $12-$15. 5-YEAR PROJECTION: Average, or a bit below.

1960 POST

SPECIFICATIONS

SIZE: 7 × 8¾". FRONT: Color photograph. BACK: Blank. DISTRIBUTION: Nationally, on the back of cereal boxes.

HISTORY

The 1960 set was the first of four annual baseball card issues by Post cereal. Although it is the rarest of the sets and the smallest (only nine cards), it has the largest cards (the giant cards took up most of the back of the cereal box). The set includes two

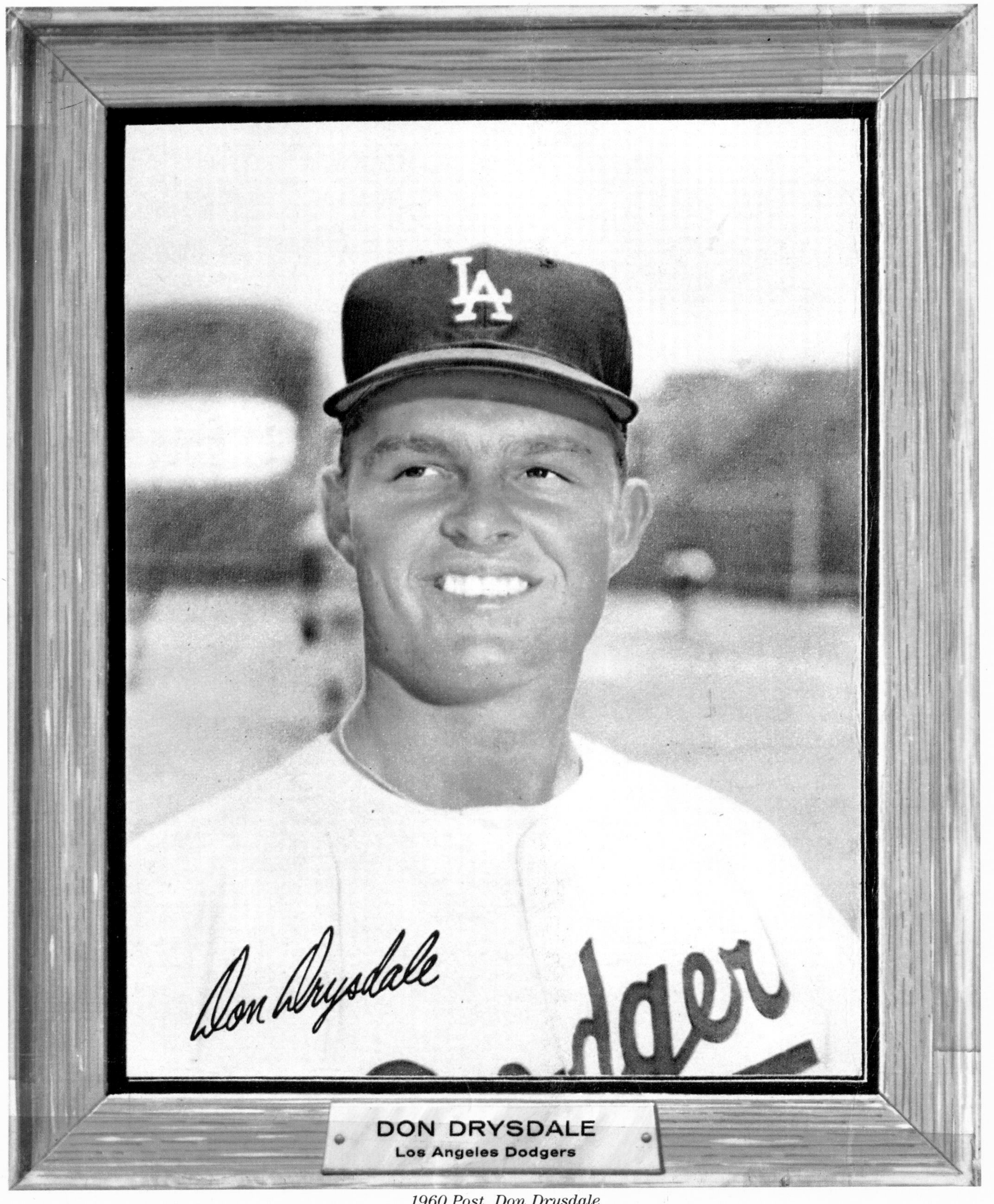

1960 Post, Don Drysdale

basketball and two football stars along with the five baseball players. The cards feature a large color photo of the player against a solid background, surrounded by a wood-grain frame. A brass plate printed on the bottom of the frame contains the player's name and team, and a facsimile autograph is scrawled across the photo. The cards are unnumbered and the back is blank. The 1960 Post cards are quite rare and very valuable. The baseball player cards are the most expensive of the group, followed by the football players and then the basketball players. Although the cards were meant to be cut from the box, a surprising number are found with portions of the box still intact. On cards that have been removed from the box, a neat trimming job is essential for maximum value. Cards that have been cut inside the wooden frame are worth considerably less, and cards with the frame cut off are least valuable.

FOR

This historical first set from Post is a collector favorite today. Oversize cards make attractive additions to superstar collections.

AGAINST

Large-size cards don't fit easily into a standard collection. The cards are also very rare and expensive.

NOTEWORTHY CARDS

The entire set consists of superstars. Included are baseball legends Don Drysdale, Al Kaline, Harmon Killebrew, Ed Mathews, and Mickey Mantle; football greats Frank Gifford and John Unitas; and basketball stars Bob Cousy and Bob Pettit.

VALUE

EX-MT CONDITION: Complete set of five baseball players (neatly cut from box), $1,900; Cousy, Pettit, $90; Drysdale, Killebrew, Mathews, Gifford, Unitas, $200; Kaline, $250; Mantle, $1,000. 5-YEAR PROJECTION: Below average.

1960 Fleer, Babe Ruth

1960 Fleer, Ted Williams

1960 FLEER

SPECIFICATIONS

SIZE: 2½ × 3½″. FRONT: Color or colorized photograph. BACK: Red and blue printing on white cardboard. DISTRIBUTION: Nationally, in packages with bubblegum.

HISTORY

Effectively blocked out of the market by Topps' exclusive contracts to produce cards of current players, Fleer tried a different approach in 1960. The Philadelphia company's '59 Ted Williams set had only limited success, since only Ted's fans were likely to buy the cards. The '60 Fleer set was another old-timer issue called "Baseball Greats." At the time it was a novel idea, but it would be widely copied in the following years. Unfortunately, the set was not a raging success, and Fleer found that kids who bought bubblegum cards wanted current players, not past heroes. Since Fleer still had Ted Williams under contract they included him in the set, but it wasn't enough to make a dent in Topps' popularity. Part of the problem was that most of the photos are of old men: instead of using a photo from the player's active years, he was usually depicted as a manager or coach, or as a participant in an old-timers game. Some players were pictured in street clothes. The cards feature an octagonal photo—color or tinted black-and-white—framed with four brightly colored corners. The player's name appears in white at the bottom of the card, and there is a white border around the whole design. Card backs are horizontal, with a card number in a Fleer crown at the upper left. On the right are the player's name, nickname, date of birth (and death when applicable), and positions played. There is a short career summary, and lifetime and World Series stats. A copyright line and photo credit are at the bottom. The 1960 Fleer old-timers set is complete at 79 cards. Apparently Fleer intended to issue a card for Pepper Martin (#80), and collectors occasionally come across a Martin card back with Joe Tinker or Lefty Grove on the front.

FOR
These are inexpensive cards of baseball's greats: from Cap Anson to Ted Williams.

AGAINST
There is little demand for old-timer cards and these are not especially attractive.

NOTEWORTHY CARDS
Along with the usual big names of baseball's past, the Ted Williams card stands out as the only card of an active player. This card may be vastly underrated as a collectible. The last Topps-issued card of Williams, in 1958, is worth about 20 times as much as his 1960 Fleer card.

VALUE
EX-MT CONDITION: Complete set, $150; common card, $1–$1.25; superstars, $2–$3; Nap Lajoie, $6; Williams, Lou Gehrig, Ty Cobb, $8–$10; Babe Ruth, $15. 5-YEAR PROJECTION: Below average.

1960 KAHN'S

SPECIFICATIONS
SIZE: 3¼ × 4". FRONT: Black-and-white photograph. BACK: Black printing on white cardboard. DISTRIBUTION: Regionally, in packages of Kahn's meat products.

HISTORY
Kahn's increased the scope of their baseball card issue in 1960 to 42 players from six teams. In addition to the teams included in last year's set (the Reds, Pirates, and Indians), the 1960 issue

1960 Kahn's, Jim Perry

added both Chicago teams and the St. Louis Cardinals. The card front followed the format established in 1955: a borderless black-and-white photo with a facsimile autograph across it, and a Kahn's ad in a strip underneath. Instead of the player stories featured on the backs in '58 and '59, the 1960 set contains player career stats and biographical details. Once again, the cards were packaged with Kahn's meat products and have a wax coating on them. The cards of each team were sold in that team's hometown area.

FOR
The 1960 Kahn's cards are an interesting variation for team collectors. They are less expensive per card than earlier issues.

AGAINST
It's the same old format.

NOTEWORTHY CARDS
Pitcher Ron Kline can be found either as a Pirate or a Cardinal. There is also a scarce blank-back version of Harvey Kuenn's card. Hall of Famers include Frank Robinson and Roberto Clemente.

VALUE
EX-MT CONDITION: Complete set, $1,350; common card, $17; stars, $30–$40; Robinson, $100; Clemente, Kuenn (blank back), $225. 5-YEAR PROJECTION: Average.

1960 NU-CARD BASEBALL HI-LITES

SPECIFICATIONS

SIZE: 3¼ × 5⅜". FRONT: Black-and-white photograph. BACK: Red and black printing on white cardboard. DISTRIBUTION: Nationally.

1 BASEBALL HI-LITES EXTRA ...

ST. LOUIS, WEDNESDAY, OCTOBER 6, 1926 Printed in U.S.A. ©CVC

BABE HITS 3 HOMERS IN A SERIES GAME

His 3 Breaks Record in Series Game

St. Louis, Oct. 6, 1926.—Babe Ruth broke the world's record by hitting 3 home runs in today's fourth game of the Yankee-Cardinal World Series. In the first inning, Flint Rhem, Card pitcher, fanned Earl Combs and Mark Koenig on 7 pitched balls. Ruth, then connected with the first pitch for a 400 ft. homer over the right field fence.

In the third inning, with 2 outs, Rhem tried to fool Ruth with a slow floater. The startled St. Louis crowd watched the ball sail over the right field wall again. In the fourth, relief twirler Reinhart, taking no chances, walked the Babe.

When Ruth stepped into the batter's box in the sixth, there were two men on base, so Reinhart elected to pitch to him. With the count at 3 and 2, Reinhart tried a fast one over the inside corner. Babe swung and the ball soared to the center field seats—a 450 ft. homer.

The St. Louis Cardinals crowd, which sat silent on his first 2 drives, stood up and cheered. They had just seen World Series history made—a new record.

1960 Nu-Card Baseball Hi-Lites, Babe Ruth

HISTORY

This novelty issue contains 72 cards depicting great moments in baseball history. The cards use a black-and-white photo on a simulated newspaper front page to tell the story. The front is printed in red and black, with a card number in the upper left, and a line at the top giving the date and place of the feat. The featured bits run the gamut from the game's early days through 1959 and are written up in some detail at the bottom of the card. Card backs have a baseball trivia question concerning another card in the set. While the set is not widely collected, those who specialize in superstar players like to obtain cards from this set to add to their collection. The set was later reprinted, and photos on the reproductions are darker than on the originals.

FOR

This set offers more baseball history than most cards.

AGAINST

Collectors don't like large-size cards or retrospective issues.

NOTEWORTHY CARDS

Since most of the great moments recounted in the set feature great players, it is full of big-name stars.

VALUE

EX-MT CONDITION: Complete set, $125; common card, 75¢–$1; superstars, $7–$9. 5-YEAR PROJECTION: Below average.

1960 LAKE TO LAKE BRAVES

SPECIFICATIONS

SIZE: 2½ × 3¼". FRONT: Blue and white photograph. BACK: Red printing on white cardboard. DISTRIBUTION: Northeastern Wisconsin, single cards stapled on cartons of milk.

1960 Lake to Lake Braves, Lew Burdette

HISTORY

The 1960 Lake to Lake Milwaukee Braves set is one of the more challenging sets to collect in top condition. The cards contained an offer on the back whereby kids could get a Braves premium prize by saving the cards and redeeming them at the local dairy office. The cards were then punch-canceled in the lower right and returned to the owner along with the prize. (For 20 cards the collector could get a Braves' pen-and-pencil set; for 100 cards, a pair of tickets to a Braves game.) The cards usually have holes in the upper right where they were stapled to the carton of milk. Ideally, the cards should be unstapled and unpunched; however, since uncirculated cards are quite difficult to find, most collectors will accept cards with staple holes. Few collectors want cards that have been punch-canceled. The card fronts have a square blue and white photo of the player that is borderless on the top and left. The bottom and right edges are bordered in blue. The player's name and position appear in the bottom border, with a Braves logo to the left. The unnumbered 28-card set features the 1960 Braves roster, along with cards for the manager and coaches.

FOR

It is a scarce regional set of a popular team.

AGAINST

It's almost impossible to find in top condition.

NOTEWORTHY CARDS

The Billy Bruton card is unaccountably scarce. While Bruton was traded to the Tigers early in the season, it does not seem likely that his card was withdrawn for that reason. Six other Braves who appear in the set were traded before Bruton, and their cards are not scarce. Ray Boone's card is also somewhat hard to find. Two of the three Braves Hall of Famers from that era (Hank Aaron and Warren Spahn) are part of the set, but Ed Mathews does not appear.

VALUE

EX-MT CONDITION: Complete set (with staple holes only), $450; common card, $5; stars, $8–$10; Spahn, $25; Boone, $55, Aaron, Bruton, $150.
5-YEAR PROJECTION: Below average.

1960 BELL BRAND DODGERS

SPECIFICATIONS

SIZE: 2½ × 3½". FRONT: Color photograph. BACK: Black printing on white cardboard. DISTRIBUTION: Southern California, single cards in packages of snack chips.

1960 Bell Brand Dodgers, Walt Alston

HISTORY

After a one-year layoff, Bell Brand snacks came out with a 20-card Los Angeles Dodgers set in 1960. Single cards were inserted in packages of potato chips and corn chips. The design of the '60 set is quite different from the company's earlier effort, and the size was changed to the now-standard 2½ × 3½" size. The card front features a color photo of the player surrounded by a white border. The player's name, team, and position appear at the bottom of the card, and there is a facsimile autograph across the photo. Half the card back is a 1960 Dodgers home game schedule; the other half is taken up with a recap of the player's 1959 season performance, a Bell logo, and a card number. Distribution was better than in 1958, and there are no confirmed scarcities, though the Clem Labine, Walter Alston, Johnny Klippstein, and Sandy Koufax cards may be somewhat harder to find. Because the cards were packaged with chips, some may have grease stains, which makes them less valuable.

FOR

This is a superb regional set that is not too expensive.

AGAINST

There is really nothing to be said against the set.

NOTEWORTHY CARDS

The set includes many popular Dodgers stars of the early '60s like Koufax, Duke Snider, and Alston, and the rookie card of Maury Wills. Unfortunately, there is no Don Drysdale or Gil Hodges card in the 1960 set.

VALUE

EX-MT CONDITION: Complete set, $420; common card, $12–$15; Wills, $30; Koufax, Snider, $45–$50; Labine, Klippstein, Alston, $75–$90. 5-YEAR PROJECTION: Average.

1960 MORRELL DODGERS

SPECIFICATIONS

SIZE: 2½ × 3½″. FRONT: Color photograph. BACK: Black and red printing on white cardboard. DISTRIBUTION: Southern California, single cards in packages of Morrell meat products.

1960 Morrell Dodgers, Duke Snider

HISTORY

In 1960 Morrell Meats produced the second of three Los Angeles Dodgers sets containing 12 unnumbered cards. The card front was basically unchanged, consisting of a color photo with no borders or writing whatsoever. On the card back, the advertising portion was greatly reduced and player stats for previous seasons were added. While there are no error cards in the 1960 set, three cards are scarcer than the rest: Carl Furillo, Gil Hodges, and Duke Snider. The Furillo card was probably withdrawn early in the season when "Skoonj" surrendered the right fielder job to Frank Howard.

FOR

The common cards are reasonably priced, and the three scarce cards are challenging.

AGAINST

Morrell should have issued rookie cards of Frank Howard and Tommy Davis.

NOTEWORTHY CARDS

Walt Alston, Don Drysdale, Sandy Koufax, and Duke Snider are the Hall of Famers in the set.

VALUE

EX-MT CONDITION: Complete set, $500; common card, $12–$15; Alston, $25; Drysdale, $40; Koufax, Furillo, $75; Hodges, Snider, $150. 5-YEAR PROJECTION: Average.

1960 DARIGOLD FARMS SPOKANE INDIANS

SPECIFICATIONS

SIZE: 2⅜ × 2⁹⁄₁₆″. FRONT: Black-and-white photograph. BACK: Black printing on white cardboard. DISTRIBUTION: Spokane, single cards with cartons of milk.

1960 Darigold Farms Spokane Indians, Willie Davis

HISTORY

In 1960 Darigold Farms produced a 24-card set of the Triple-A Spokane Indians (the Los Angeles Dodgers' farm club), which was distributed with cartons of milk. The design was changed somewhat from the previous year. The card fronts again featured a black-and-white photo of the player against a solid background, but with the addition of a white border around the card and a facsimile autograph across the photo. An ad appears in the bottom border. The card backs have an Indians logo in the upper left with personal data on the player to the right. Career highlights and 1959 season performance are at the bottom, along with a card number. The set features cards of major league players who don't appear on any other issue, making it popular with team collectors who want as many cards as possible of those who played with the Dodgers in the early '60s.

FOR

This is a scarce regional issue of a top minor league team.

AGAINST

Minor league cards are generally less popular with collectors.

NOTEWORTHY CARDS

Three stalwarts of the 1960s make their card debuts in this set: Frank Howard, Willie Davis, and Ron Fairly.

VALUE

EX-MT CONDITION: Complete set, $375; common card, $20; Howard, Davis, Fairly, $25–$30. 5-YEAR PROJECTION: Below average.

1960 UNION OIL

SPECIFICATIONS

SIZE: 3⅛ × 4″. FRONT: Color photograph. BACK: Black printing on white cardboard. DISTRIBUTION: Seattle, cards given away with purchase at gas stations.

HISTORY

The 1960 Union Oil set features nine members of the Seattle Rainiers of the Pacific Coast League. The cards were distributed at Seattle-area gas stations. Unlike most one-team minor league sets of this era, these cards are in color. The card front features a borderless, posed action photo of the player. The card backs offer personal data, a uniform number, and a "Thumb-Nail Sketch" biography, along with a Union 76 ad and photo credit.

1960 Union Oil, Ray Ripplemeyer

FOR

This is a scarce regional set.

AGAINST

The cards are oversized and have no major leaguers of special interest.

NOTEWORTHY CARDS

The Ray Ripplemeyer card was withdrawn early in the promotion and is rarer than the rest. The most notable player is Gordy Coleman, who went on to a nine-year career with the Indians and the Reds.

VALUE

EX-MT CONDITION: Complete set, $75; common card, $3–$4; Coleman, $5; Ripplemeyer, $45. 5-YEAR PROJECTION: Below average.

1959 TO 1950

1959 Topps, Mickey Mantle

1954 Topps, Jackie Robinson

1955 Topps, Willie Mays

1959 TOPPS

SPECIFICATIONS

SIZE: 2½ × 3½". FRONT: Color photograph. BACK: Red and green (low numbers) or black and red (high numbers) printing on gray or white cardboard. DISTRIBUTION: Nationally, in packages with bubblegum.

1959 Topps, Mickey Mantle

1959 Topps, Roy Campanella

1959 Topps, Stan Musial

HISTORY

In expanding its 1959 set to 572 cards (the largest ever to that date), Topps added a number of specialty subsets to the regular player cards. The cards in this set feature a nearly round color photo with a solid-color background at top and bottom and a white border all around. A facsimile autograph appears across the photo. The player's name is printed in lowercase letters at the top of the card on an angle. There is a color team logo in the lower left and two lines of type at the lower right with the player's team and position. Card backs have year-by-year major and/or minor league stats, a cartoon, and a short write-up on the player, plus the usual biographical details. On the low-number cards (#1-#506), this information is printed in red and green ink, with the card number in white in the upper left in a green box. On the high number cards (#507-#572), the printing is in black and red, with the card number in a black box. There were several multiplayer cards, sometimes from the same team, sometimes from opposing teams. Checklists were again printed on the backs of team cards. One specialty group new to the 1959 set was a 10-card run of highlights from the previous season, mostly featuring big-name players. Another 31-card specialty group that debuted in 1959 was the "Rookie Stars" series chosen by the editors of *The Sporting News*. The cards (numbered alphabetically from #116-#146) feature a radically different design from the regular '59 cards. The players are pictured against a background of red, white, and blue stripes on a black shield. The lettering is in yellow and white, and there is a white border. The backs are similar to the regular cards in the set. The first rookie card—Bob Allison—was an excellent choice, because he went on to win the A.L. Rookie of the Year award with the Washington Senators. Most of the other 30 rookies, however, never really made it big in the major leagues, and several never played an inning of big league ball. The final 22 cards of the 1959 set are *The Sporting News* "All-Star Selection" players. Players on these cards are pictured in a shield-shaped photo at the center of the card. There is an eagle above the shield on a blue (American League) or red (National League) background. Interestingly, the shields and eagles are designed differently on the A.L. and N.L. cards. Though the '59 Topps set was released in several series over the summer, only the final 66 cards, the high numbers, are more scarce than the rest. Besides the All-Star cards, these high numbers include a unique Roy Campanella card and the rookie cards of Bob Gibson and Harmon Killebrew.

FOR

This interesting and varied set has many historic innovations that would shape Topps cards for years to come. The set is challenging to complete.

AGAINST

Few collectors dislike the 1959 set.

NOTEWORTHY CARDS

The first card in the set is the only time Topps pictured a baseball commissioner (Ford C. Frick). Roy Campanella (#550, "Symbol of Courage") is pictured in a wheelchair; a tragic December 1957 accident left the former Brooklyn Dodgers catcher permanently crippled. The card back features an inspirational message from N.L. president Warren Giles, who tells of Campy's fight to overcome the effects of the accident and his return to baseball as a coach for the Los Angeles Dodgers. There is a wrong-photo card in the '59 set: Camilo Pascual is pictured on Ralph Lumenti's card. Pascual has his own card as well, but the name is misspelled "Camillo" on the front. Despite the wrong photo, the Lumenti card can be quite valuable—if it doesn't have the small line that was added to the back indicating Lumenti was sent down to the minor leagues in mid-season. Five '59 Topps cards are known to exist with and without the lines indicating trades or options. (These variations were produced in mid-season press runs when the lines were added to the card backs.) The five cards are: Lumenti (#316), Bob Giallombardo (#321), Harry Hanebrink (#322), Billy Loes (#336), and Dolan Nichols (#362). Stan Musial, whose only previous Topps card was in the 1958 All-Star series, appears on a regular Topps card for the first time in 1959.

OUR FAVORITE CARD

The earliest known example of a ballplayer fooling the Topps photographer appears in the '59 set on Lew Burdette's card (#440). When the photographer showed up, Burdette grabbed a lefthander's glove and posed in the wind-up. Burdette was a righthander.

VALUE

EX-MT CONDITION: Complete set, $2,900; common card, #1-#506, $2; #507-#572, $6–$8; stars, $45–$60; Campanella, Willie Mays, Hank Aaron, $70–$85; Mickey Mantle All-Star, Gibson, $150–$200; Mantle, $250–$300. 5-YEAR PROJECTION: Above average.

1959 BAZOOKA

SPECIFICATIONS

SIZE: 2¾ × 5″. FRONT: Color photograph. BACK: Blank. DISTRIBUTION: Nationally, one card on the bottom of each box of bubblegum.

1959 Bazooka, Willie Mays

HISTORY

Topps sold bubblegum without baseball cards for a number of years under the Bazooka brand name. The gum was sold in a small, thick square, wrapped in wax paper with a cartoon insert. Topps began using baseball cards as box bottoms in 1959 to sell their gum. The 23 cards in this issue were printed (one per box) as the bottom panel. A large color photo with a facsimile autograph makes up the majority of the card front. At the bottom is the player's name, position, and team in color strips; a team logo is included in the lower left. A white border surrounds the entire card. The card backs are blank and unnumbered. The cards could be separated from the boxes, though like all baseball cards issued as part of a package, complete boxes are worth more than neatly trimmed cards. There are two levels of scarcity among the '59 Bazookas. Initially, nine cards were released and they are more common than the group of 14 that was issued later. The 14 are considered scarce by hobbyists. It's especially hard to find them neatly trimmed.

FOR

Assembling a complete set is a most challenging project for the hobbyist who specializes in 1950s and '60s cards.

AGAINST

The cards are hard to find in Mint condition.

NOTEWORTHY CARDS

Virtually all of the players on the '59 Bazookas are stars, or at least they were when the cards were issued. There are some color variations in the strips at the card bottom.

VALUE

EX-MT CONDITION: Complete set of single cards (neatly cut from box), $3,000; common card, $30–$40; scarce card, $100–$125; Hank Aaron, Ernie Banks, Willie Mays, Duke Snider, $250–$300; Mickey Mantle, $650. 5-YEAR PROJECTION: Average.

1959 FLEER TED WILLIAMS

SPECIFICATIONS

SIZE: 2½ × 3½″. FRONT: Color or colorized photograph. BACK: Red and blue printing on gray cardboard. DISTRIBUTION: Nationally, in packages with bubblegum.

1959 Fleer Ted Williams

HISTORY

Effectively shut out of the market by Topps' monopoly on player contracts, Fleer tried a bold new idea in 1959: an entire baseball card set featuring one player—the immortal Ted Williams. The 80 cards in the set trace his life and baseball career to the point of "The Splendid Splinter." Color photos appear in the set along with black-and-white photos that have been colorized. There is a bat and ball that contains Williams' name in either the bottom left or bottom right, and a caption in the white border below the photo. Problems with printing or distribution of the set created a scarcity of the card titled "Ted Signs for 1959" (#68). Some years ago, a counterfeit card was produced. It can usually be detected by the "pinkish" tint of the photo, and the screen-like pattern over the face of the card which results from making printing plates from an existing photo instead of a new negative. Many of these counterfeits have now been stamped "Reproduction" on the back and are sold to collectors for a couple of dollars as fillers until they can buy the authentic cards.

FOR

If you're a Ted Williams fan, you'll love this set.

AGAINST

The quality is not great. Many of the cards are nonbaseball in nature, like those featuring his military career. The real "Ted Signs for 1959" card makes collecting a complete set difficult.

NOTEWORTHY CARDS

There is extra demand for the second card in the set ("Ted's Idol—Babe Ruth"): it pictures Ruth and Williams together.

VALUE

EX-MT CONDITION: Complete set, $250; common card, $1.25; "Ted's Idol," $4; "Early Years," $6; "Ted Signs for 1959," $150. 5-YEAR PROJECTION: Below average.

1959 KAHN'S

SPECIFICATIONS

SIZE: 3¼ × 4". FRONT: Black-and-white photograph. BACK: Black printing on white cardboard. DISTRIBUTION: Ohio, Western Pennsylvania, in packages of meat products.

1959 Kahn's, Vada Pinson

HISTORY

For 1959, the Kahn's set featured three teams. Joining the Pirates and Reds in the 38-card set were the Cleveland Indians. The card front was little changed from previous years. The dominant feature was a black-and-white borderless photo with a facsimile autograph. Below the picture was a white strip with a Kahn's ad. The card backs again contained a short story ostensibly written by the player. The paragraphs were titled "The Toughest Play I Had to Make" or (for pitchers) "The Toughest Batter I Have to Face." The cards are not numbered.

FOR

The set includes some big-name stars.

AGAINST

The format is virtually unchanged from five years earlier. The cards are quite expensive on a per-card basis.

NOTEWORTHY CARDS

Dick Brodowski's card is in short supply as—to a lesser degree—are the cards of Harvey Haddix, Woodie Held, and Cal McLish. Frank Robinson and Roberto Clemente are the biggest names. Billy Martin is pictured in the set—a memento of his only year with the Indians.

VALUE

EX-MT CONDITION: Complete set, $2,750; common card, $25–$30; stars, $50–$60; Rocky Colavito, Martin, $70; Robinson, $125; Haddix, Held, McLish, $250; Clemente, $325; Brodowski, $350. 5-YEAR PROJECTION: Average.

1959 MORRELL DODGERS

SPECIFICATIONS

SIZE: 2½ × 3½". FRONT: Color photograph. BACK: Black printing on white cardboard. DISTRIBUTION: Southern California, one card in packages of meat products.

1959 Morrell Dodgers, Gil Hodges

HISTORY

One of several companies to welcome the Dodgers to Los Angeles in their early years, Morrell Meats issued the first of three consecutive baseball card sets in 1959—the year the Dodgers were World Champs. In the popular 2½ × 3½″ size, the card front features a gorgeous, borderless color photo of one of 12 Dodgers pictured in the Coliseum. The card back is mainly advertising for the company's "Wieners, Smokees, Cheesefurters, and Polish Sausages." The player information was limited to the name, and date and place of birth. The "Mirro-Krome" cards were produced for Morrell by H.S. Crocker & Co. The 1959 Dodgers set was not actually Morrell's first baseball card issue: John Morrell & Company also issued the 1954 Red Heart dog food cards, which are still being collected today.

FOR

These are beautiful regional cards of a popular team with lots of stars.

AGAINST

They're fairly expensive for 1959-vintage cards. Two player identification errors detract from the quality of the set.

NOTEWORTHY CARDS

Stars in the '59 Morrell Dodgers set include Don Drysdale, Gil Hodges, Sandy Koufax, and Duke Snider. The error cards in the set: Stan Williams is identified as Clem Labine on the card back, and Joe Pignatano is identified as Norm Larker on the card back.

VALUE

EX-MT CONDITION: Complete set, $800; common card, $50; Drysdale, Koufax, Snider, $125–$150. 5-YEAR PROJECTION: Average.

1959 DARIGOLD FARMS SPOKANE INDIANS

SPECIFICATIONS

SIZE: 2½ × 2⅜″. FRONT: Black-and-white photograph. BACK: Black printing on white cardboard. DISTRIBUTION: Spokane, single cards on cartons of milk.

1959 Darigold Farms Spokane Indians, Tommy Davis

HISTORY

The 22 cards in the 1959 Darigold Spokane set were issued with cartons of milk. The card front features a black-and-white photo of the player set against a solid-color background. A white strip beneath the photo has the player's name and position, while a dark colored strip carries an ad. The unnumbered card back features a team logo in the upper left. In the right is the player's personal data, nickname, marital status, and children's names. Toward the bottom are career highlights, lifetime major and/or minor league stats, and an abbreviated record for the previous season. One reason this set is popular is that Spokane was the Dodgers top farm club in 1959. Another reason is that the set is a genuinely scarce, regional issue.

FOR

It is an attractive, though hard-to-find, regional set.

AGAINST

Many collectors aren't interested in minor league sets.

NOTEWORTHY CARDS

There are several players in the set who never appeared on a major league baseball card. This makes their minor league cards popular with team collectors. Tommy Davis (who was spending his last full season in the minors before heading up to an 18-year major league career) is included.

VALUE

EX-MT CONDITION: Complete set, $375; common card, $15; major leaguers, $25; Davis, $35. 5-YEAR PROJECTION: Below average.

1958 TOPPS

SPECIFICATIONS

SIZE: 2½ × 3½". FRONT: Color photograph. BACK: Red and black printing on gray cardboard. DISTRIBUTION: Nationally, in packages with bubblegum.

1958 Topps, Mickey Mantle

1958 Topps, Roger Maris

HISTORY

The 1958 Topps set is popular and can be quite challenging, depending on how it is collected. Topps once again increased the number of cards in the set—to 494. The set is actually numbered to 495, but card #145 was not issued. Early series checklists show that card was to have been Phillies first baseman Ed Bouchee. The card was pulled from distribution, though, after Bouchee was suspended from baseball early in the season for off-field misconduct. Later checklists show a blank after card #145. There are two types of checklists in the 1958 set. Rather than issuing checklists as separate, unnumbered cards like those of '56 and '57, Topps used the backs of team cards as checklists. While most of the checklists were by number and series, the backs of some Braves, Tigers, Orioles, and Redlegs team cards will be found with checklists arranged in alphabetical order. Most collectors either love or hate the design of the '58 Topps set. The card front features a portrait or posed-action photo of the player set against a plain, brightly colored background. A color team logo is in a lower corner and there is a contrasting color strip at the bottom with the player's position and name. One of the most interesting oddities of the 1958 Topps set is the "yellow-letter variations" on 33 cards between #2 and #108. These variations apparently happened midway through the printing of the first series: either the player's name or the team name are in yellow rather than white. Many other cards in the set have yellow lettering in these places, but the 33 cards in the first series are found with both yellow and white letters. Topps greatly increased the number of multiplayer feature cards in the set. These usually feature the players photographed in a stadium setting. An innovation was the inclusion of 20 All-Star cards selected by *Sport* magazine. These cards feature photos of the chosen players set against a star-studded blue (N.L.) or red (A.L.) background. A 21st All-Star card shows 1957 World Series managers Casey Stengel and Fred Haney together. Card backs are quite similar to '56 and present cartoon-style highlights from the player's career, along with the usual bio and stats. Topps dropped the season-by-season stats and returned to "Year" and "Life" figures as had been used from '52 to '56.

FOR

Since there are no scarce '58 Topps cards, a collector can assemble a complete 494-card set rather easily. Those collectors who desire a challenge, however, can delve into the yellow-letter and checklist variations. The 1958 Topps set is one of the better bargains in the hobby today (if it can be purchased in Mint or Excellent condition).

AGAINST

The variations can become maddening, although most collectors don't bother. Even though this set was generally regarded as being attractive, a lot of collectors don't like it.

NOTEWORTHY CARDS

Besides all the usual superstars, Stan Musial makes his first Topps appearance on one of the All-Star cards. Ted Williams (#1) makes his last Topps appearance. Notable rookie cards include Roger Maris, Orlando Cepeda, Vada Pinson, and Curt Flood. Luis Aparicio, Early Wynn, Bob Lemon, Al Kaline, Roberto Clemente, and Hank Aaron have yellow-letter variation cards. Because of the construction of printing plates for the later series, four of the high-numbered cards are quite a bit scarcer than other high numbers: Billy Harrell, Carroll Hardy, Preston Ward, and Gary Geiger. There are a couple of wrong-photo cards: the picture on Mike McCormick's card is Ray Monzant, and the photo on Milt Bolling's card is really Lou Berberet. The cards that can be found with yellow and white letters are #2, #8, #11, #13, #20, #23, #24, #30, #32, #33, #35, #46, #50, #52, #53, #57, #58, #60, #61, #65, #70, #76, #77, #78, #79, #81, #85, #92, #97, #98, #100, #101, and #108.

OUR FAVORITE CARD

While there had been multiplayer feature cards before, none have ever featured players from different teams on the same card until 1958. In that set, Topps photographers took advantage of the opportunity at the World Series and All-Star Game to picture rival players on the same card. Certainly the best in this set is the card titled "World Series Batting Foes" (#418) featuring Mickey Mantle and Hank Aaron posing in their slugging stances. In a set where single-player cards of Mantle and Aaron command exorbitant prices, surely the combination of the two on the same card is going to be worth far more someday than its current price.

VALUE

EX-MT CONDITION: Complete set, $3,100; common card, $2–$3; Clemente, $60; Clemente yellow-letters, Aaron, $100; Mays, $110; Aaron yellow-letters, $175; Maris, $225; Williams, $250; Mantle, $400. 5-YEAR PROJECTION: Average.

1958 HIRES ROOT BEER

SPECIFICATIONS

SIZE: Card with tab, 2⁵⁄₁₆ × 7″; card without tab, 2⁵⁄₁₆ × 3½″. FRONT: Color photograph. BACK: Black printing on gray cardboard. DISTRIBUTION: Nationally, one card in cartons of soda.

1958 Hires Root Beer, Larry Doby

HISTORY

The Hires root beer set is one of the more interesting and unusual baseball card issues of the late 1950s. A long tab attached to a baseball card at a perforation line was designed to hold the card in a carton of root beer. The tab carried an offer (for a dime and two bottle caps) for membership in the Hires Baseball Club, which included a book of major league baseball tips and a "valuable membership card." Cards with the tab still attached are more scarce and are worth about 33 percent more than an individual card. The design of the card itself is novel and features a photograph of the player as if viewed through a knothole in a fence. The color photos are heavily retouched. A black strip at the bottom contains the player's name, team, and position. Card backs feature a Hires root beer bottle at left and a bottle cap with the card number in the upper right. A player biography appears in the center, and a box to the right contains personal data. The Hires set is peculiarly numbered from #10-#76. Since card #69 was not issued, the complete set consists of 66 cards.

FOR
Though it was a nationally distributed set, the 1958 Hires cards were produced in limited numbers, making it a popular and challenging set. The design is innovative and attractive.

AGAINST
The cards are hard to find with tabs.

NOTEWORTHY CARDS
Though there are only a handful of superstars—Duke Snider, Pee Wee Reese, Don Drysdale, Willie Mays, and Hank Aaron—in the Hires set, many of the popular home-team players of the era are represented.

VALUE
EX-MT CONDITION: Complete set (without tabs), $1,300; common card, $8–$10; stars, $10–$25; Reese, Drysdale, $35–$50; Snider, $100; Mays, Aaron, $150–$175. 5-YEAR PROJECTION: Average.

1958 HIRES ROOT BEER TEST SET

SPECIFICATIONS
SIZE: Card with tab, 2 5⁄16 × 7″; card without tab, 25⁄16 × 3½″. FRONT: Sepia-tone photograph. BACK: Black printing on gray cardboard. DISTRIBUTION: Nationally, one card in cartons of soda.

HISTORY
The 8-card Hires test set was released only in selected cities (corresponding to the team of the players pictured). The test set has the same physical characteristics as the regular 66-card 1958 Hires set and was distributed the same way—in soda cartons. The cards were issued with a long tab at the bottom, which was separated from the card by a perforation. The tab was designed to be stuck into a soda carton. The tab carried an offer to join the Hires Baseball Club. Cards with the tab intact are quite scarce and are worth 50 percent more than the individual cards. In general, this set is much more scarce than its regular-issue counterpart. Card fronts feature a sepia-tone photograph of the player set against a solid yellow or orange background. The player's name appears in brown script at the top of the card, while the team and position are printed below the photo. Card backs contain a box of personal data on the right and a player biography on the left. The cards are unnumbered and there are no Hires logos. The Hires name appears only on the detachable tab.

FOR
It's a rare, nationally issued test set.

AGAINST
These test issue cards are even harder to find with the tabs intact than the regular Hires set.

NOTEWORTHY CARDS
There is only one really big name in this issue—Willie Mays. The other players in the set are Johnny Antonelli, Jim Busby, Chico Fernandez, Bob Friend, Vernon Law, Stan Lopata, and Al Pilarcik.

VALUE
EX-MT CONDITION: Complete set (without tabs), $875, common card, $65–$75; Mays, $325–$350. 5-YEAR PROJECTION: Below average.

1958 KAHN'S

SPECIFICATIONS
SIZE: 3¼ × 4″. FRONT: Black-and-white photograph. BACK: Black printing on white cardboard. DISTRIBUTION: Ohio, Western Pennsylvania, in packages of meat products.

1958 Kahn's, Ed Bailey

HISTORY

A third team was added to the Kahn's lineup in 1958 when the Phillies joined the Pirates and Reds in a 29-card issue. The card front was virtually identical to those of the previous years: a borderless black-and-white photograph with a facsimile autograph above a white strip with a Kahn's ad. The card back had printing on it for the first time—a few short paragraphs titled "My Greatest Thrill in Baseball." Once again, the cards are unnumbered. Like other Kahn's issues, cards have a wax coating to protect them from the meat (and to protect the meat from the card ink). The cards were inserted in packages of Kahn's meat products.

FOR

Team collectors like scarce regional cards.

AGAINST

The design lacks originality.

NOTEWORTHY CARDS

Three of the '58 Kahn's cards are scarcer than the rest: Wally Post, Charlie Rabe, and Frank Thomas. Hall of Famers Roberto Clemente and Frank Robinson are part of the set.

VALUE

EX-MT CONDITION: Complete set, \$2,200; common card, \$25–\$30; minor star, \$35–\$75; Robinson, \$150–\$175; Post, Rabe, Thomas, \$225–\$250; Clemente, \$375. 5-YEAR PROJECTION: Above average.

1958 BELL BRAND DODGERS

SPECIFICATIONS

SIZE: 3 × 4″. FRONT: Sepia-tone photograph. BACK: Black printing on white cardboard. DISTRIBUTION: Southern California, inserted in packages of Bell Brand snack chips.

HISTORY

The 10-card Bell Brand set of 1958 is the rarest of the four baseball card issues by the snack chip company. The set was just one of several regional issues that welcomed the Dodgers and the Giants to major league baseball in California in 1958. All of the players featured are Los Angeles Dodgers, including Roy Campanella, who was injured in an off-season auto accident in 1957 and never played for the team in California. Distribution of the cards was erratic and several of them are scarce. Because they feature members of one of baseball's most

1958 Bell Brand Dodgers, Roy Campanella

popular teams of the '50s, all of the cards are popular. The design is interesting and somewhat unusual for a baseball card. A sepia-tone photograph of the player is in a green wood-grain frame. A facsimile autograph, also in green, is printed across the photo. The player's name appears in brown in a white plate at the bottom of the frame. Card backs feature a traditional mix of player personal information, year-by-year major league stats, and a short career summary. A Bell logo appears at the bottom of the card. The cards are unnumbered.

FOR

Since the Bell Brand cards were issued when the Dodgers moved to Los Angeles, many team collectors use them as a starting point.

AGAINST

The cards are quite expensive and elusive. The odd size is a problem.

NOTEWORTHY CARDS

Virtually all ten of the '58 Bell Dodgers cards feature star players. Value, though, is based more on scarcity. Distribution of the cards was not even, and some are scarcer than others. At the top of the hard-to-find list is Gino Cimoli, who was traded to the Cardinals in mid-1958. As was often the case with single-team regional cards, the Cimoli card was pulled from circulation when he was traded, thus creating an instant rarity. The Johnny Podres and Duke Snider cards are also considered quite scarce.

VALUE

EX-MT CONDITION: Complete set, $800; common card, $30; Sandy Koufax, $85; Campanella, Cimoli, Podres, $100–$150; Snider, $125–$150. 5-YEAR PROJECTION: Average.

1958 SAN FRANCISCO CALL-BULLETIN GIANTS

SPECIFICATIONS

SIZE: 2 × 4″. FRONT: Black and orange photograph. BACK: Black printing on orange cardboard. DISTRIBUTION: San Francisco, in the daily newspaper.

1958 San Francisco Call Bulletin Giants, Ray Crone

HISTORY

The *San Francisco Call-Bulletin*, a daily newspaper, issued a 25-card set welcoming the Giants to San Francisco after their move from New York in 1958. The cards were inserted in the paper early in the spring. Printed on thin orange cardboard, the card front features a black and orange photograph of the player, with his name and position in a black strip on the bottom. The lower third of the card is a detachable numbered stub used in playing a lottery-type giveaway game sponsored by the newspaper. (Cards with the tab attached are worth about 35 percent more.) Card backs feature a Giants' home schedule. Stub backs carry advertisements for the giveaway game and a local radio station.

FOR

It's a rather scarce regional issue popular with team collectors.

AGAINST

The cards are quite unattractive and somewhat expensive.

NOTEWORTHY CARDS

There are cards for rookie Orlando Cepeda as well as Giant superstar Willie Mays, but the real rarity in the set is Tom Bowers' card. Bowers was a hot preseason pitching prospect for the Giants, but he spent the 1958 season in the minor leagues. In fact, Bowers never pitched an inning of major league baseball and this is the only baseball card he appears on. Some collectors believe the Bowers card was never actually issued and the surviving examples came from sources at the paper. Bobby Thomson appears in the set even though he spent the '58 season with the Chicago Cubs.

VALUE

EX-MT CONDITION: Complete set, $750; common card $10–$12; Cepeda, $50–$60; Bowers, $200; Mays, $225–$250. 5-YEAR PROJECTION: Below average.

1958 BOND BREAD BUFFALO BISONS

SPECIFICATIONS

SIZE: 2½ × 3½″. FRONT: Black-and-white photograph. BACK: Black printing on white cardboard. DISTRIBUTION: Buffalo, New York, cards inserted in packages of bakery products.

HISTORY

The 9-card Bond Bread set features players of the Triple-A Buffalo Bisons; all of the players in the set made the big leagues. The cards are interesting because an ad for the TV series *Casey Jones*

1958 Bond Bread Buffalo Bisons, Luke Easter

appears in the bottom margin on the front. Each card features a black-and-white photo of the player with his name and position in the top margin. Card backs carry an ad for Bond Bakery and show a loaf of bread and a box of pastry on the bottom half. The top half has the player's vital stats and an extremely personal write-up of the player—including his home address and the names and ages of his children.

FOR

The cards are relatively inexpensive, if you can find them.

AGAINST

It's in black-and-white at a time when most cards were in color.

NOTEWORTHY CARDS

The best-known player in the set is Luke Easter, a former Negro League standout who played six seasons with the Cleveland Indians in the '40s and '50s and then played another several seasons of minor league ball. Most collectors feel the 1958 Bond card of Easter was not distributed in as large numbers as the other cards in the set. Also in the set is manager Phil Cavarretta, whose major league playing career stretched from 1934 through 1955.

VALUE

EX-MT CONDITION: Complete set, $90; common card, $5–$7; Cavarretta, $12; Easter, $35. 5-YEAR PROJECTION: Below average.

1958 UNION OIL

SPECIFICATIONS

SIZE: 2½ × 3½". FRONT: Black-and-white photograph. BACK: Black printing on white cardboard. DISTRIBUTION: Sacramento, cards given away at service stations.

1958 Union Oil, Jim Greengrass

HISTORY

The Union Oil Company (through its Union 76 service stations) has a long history of baseball-related giveaways. The company's first baseball card issue was a 10-card set featuring the Triple-A Sacramento Solons. The cards feature a borderless, black-and-white posed-action photo with the player's name, team, and position in a white strip at the bottom of the card. The card backs repeat the name and position, and include age, height, and weight, along with abbreviated stats of the previous season, a "Union 76 Sports Club" pennant ad, and a notice that the card is good for admission to a Solons game on a specified date. The unnumbered cards are quite scarce, but not costly.

FOR

The set contains many former major leaguers.

AGAINST

Minor league cards are not very popular with collectors.

NOTEWORTHY CARDS

Most of the players in the set were major leaguers—Dick Cole, Jim Greengrass, Nippy Jones, Carlos Paula, Kal Segrist, Sibby Sisti, Marshall Bridges, Al Heist, and Joe Stanka. Only one—Bud Watkins—never played baseball in the major leagues.

VALUE

EX-MT CONDITION: Complete set, $120; common card, $12–$15. 5-YEAR PROJECTION: Below average.

1957 Topps, Brooks Robinson

1957 TOPPS

SPECIFICATIONS

SIZE: 2½ × 3½″. FRONT: Color photograph. BACK: Blue and red printing on gray cardboard. DISTRIBUTION: Nationally, in packages with bubblegum.

HISTORY

What has become today's standard size for baseball cards—2½ × 3½″—was adopted by Topps for its 1957 set. Though the cards were reduced in size by about 11 percent from the Topps issues of '52 to '56, the set size increased from 340 to 407 cards. The '57 set also marked the first appearance of color photos on Topps cards rather than the colorized photos used previously. The set contains a pleasing mix of portrait and posed-action player shots in various stadiums. The set has no fancy features, just big sharp photos with the player's name, team, and position printed at the bottom in various combinations of yellow, white, red, and blue. All of this was framed in a white border. Card backs were greatly improved for 1957: for the first time, Topps included complete major league (or minor league, in the case of rookies) stats on a year-by-year basis rather than just for the previous season, along with cumulative lifetime figures. Space permitting, there was also a baseball quiz cartoon on card backs. The rest of the back has biographical details of the player, a short career sketch, and the familiar baseball with the card number inside. There are three levels of scarcity in the 1957 Topps set: cards #265-#352 (the fourth series) are scarcer than cards #1-#264 (the first three series) and #353-#407 (the fifth series). Consequently, they are worth about five times more than the cards in the other series. Again in 1957, Topps produced team cards. This year they used a bigger photo set in a gold frame with the team name in a "plaque" at the bottom. A color team logo appears in the lower right. Identification of the players in the photo is on the card back. For the second straight year, A.L. and N.L. presidents William Harridge and Warren Giles appear in the '57 Topps set, though this year they are together on a single card. Topps produced four unnumbered checklist cards for its '57 set, and today they are among the most sought-after cards of the '50s (but generally in unmarked condition only). The first checklist covers Series 1-2, the next covers Series 2-3, etc. Each is successively scarcer than the one before it. An unmarked Series 4-5 checklist in Excellent to Mint condition is one of the most valuable cards in the set.

1957 Topps, Sandy Koufax

FOR

The 1957 Topps set features a clean design with big, clear photos. The challenge of completing a set that includes 88 scarce cards has made the '57 Topps set a great collector favorite. As the first of the now-standard-size cards, it is a popular starting point for collectors of modern card sets.

AGAINST

From a collector's standpoint, the set is perfect.

NOTEWORTHY CARDS

Again in 1957 (with Topps having a virtual monopoly in the baseball card field), all of the game's big stars were present except Stan Musial. Hall of Famers Brooks Robinson, Frank Robinson, and Don Drysdale had their rookie cards in the set, as did stars Jim Bunning, Bill Mazeroski, Rocky Colavito, and Tony Kubek. The scarce fourth series contains high-demand cards of Brooks Robinson and Sandy Koufax, along with the popular New York Giants and Brooklyn Dodgers team cards in their last years in New York. Hank Aaron's card (#20) has a reversed negative, which makes it look like he is batting lefthanded. If you look at the famous number 44 on his uniform, you can see "Hammerin' Hank" wasn't trying to fool the photographer: the numbers are backward. A different type of variation appears on Mickey Mantle's card (#95). When Mantle's photo was taken, there was a man in sport shirt and slacks standing behind him, and the end of Mantle's bat appears at about the man's belt line. In order not to distract from Mantle, Topps airbrushed the man out of the picture by blending him into the background. The effort wasn't as effective as hoped for, however, and Topps went back to the airbrush again. Today, '57 Topps Mantle cards can be found with and without the man in the background. There is also a wrong-photo card: the picture on Jerry Snyder's card (#22) is actually teammate Ed Fitz Gerald. Fitz Gerald also appears on his own card (#367).

OUR FAVORITE CARD

It's a tie between the two multiplayer feature cards that Topps returned to for the first time since 1954. "Dodger Sluggers" portrays an awesome array of batting power: Carl Furillo, Gil Hodges, Roy Campanella, and Duke Snider. The quartet was photographed kneeling and leaning on their bats before the familiar fences of Ebbets Field. "Yankees' Power Hitters" gives us a glimpse into the Yankee dugout, where Mickey Mantle and Yogi Berra are standing on the steps, bats on their shoulders. These two cards were extremely popular with youngsters in '57 and remain popular with collectors today.

VALUE

EX-MT CONDITION: Complete set, $5,500; common card, $3.50; #265-#352, $13; Willie Mays, Drysdale, Aaron, Frank Robinson, Roberto Clemente, Checklist 2-3, $75–$100; Checklist 3-4, $150; Koufax, Brooks Robinson, Checklist 4-5, $250; Ted Williams, $300; Mantle, $550–$600. 5-YEAR PROJECTION: Average.

1957 KAHN'S

SPECIFICATIONS

SIZE: 3¼ × 4". FRONT: Black-and-white photograph. BACK: Blank. DISTRIBUTION: Cincinnati, Pittsburgh, in packages of meat products.

1957 Kahn's, Ted Kluszewski

HISTORY

The Kahn's baseball card set was expanded to 29 cards in 1957 when the Pittsburgh Pirates joined the Cincinnati Reds in the set. The format is identical to the previous year. The card front features a black-and-white photo with a facsimile autograph and a Kahn's ad at the bottom in a white strip. You need a checklist to differentiate the '57 and '56 Reds cards. Once again, card backs are blank. The unnumbered cards were inserted in packages of Kahn's meat products.

FOR
This is an early regional set that is especially popular with team collectors.

AGAINST
The relatively high cost per card is a deterent to all but the most serious collector.

NOTEWORTHY CARDS
Pirates star Roberto Clemente appears in this set along with rookie Bill Mazeroski. The Dick Groat card can be found with a facsimile autograph "Richard Groat" or with the name "Dick Groat" printed.

VALUE
EX-MT CONDITION: Complete set, $1,700; common card, $40; stars, $75–$95; "Richard" Groat, Frank Robinson, $200; Clemente, $350. 5-YEAR PROJECTION: Above average.

1956 TOPPS

SPECIFICATIONS
SIZE: 2⅝ × 3¾". FRONT: Colorized photograph. BACK: Red, black, and green printing on white or gray cardboard. DISTRIBUTION: Nationally, in packages with bubblegum.

HISTORY
For the second year in a row, Topps produced a horizontal-format card set. Somewhat similar in design to the '55s, the 1956 set combines a portrait photo of the player with an action shot in the background. Unlike the 1955 issue, however, the '56 cards feature a stadium setting as the background (sometimes cleverly faked by using two different photos). A white outline around the portrait separates the player from the background. The two photos used on each card have been colorized. The smaller action photos make an interesting study as some of them were used on more than one card. Yogi Berra's card (#110) depicts the Yankees catcher at home plate, waiting for a throw, while a Cleveland Indian slides in safely. On Gene Woodling's card (#163), there is a closer view of the sliding Indian—Woodling—from the same photo, but Berra has been airbrushed. Some of the larger player portraits are repeated from the 1955 cards, and in some cases from the 1954 issue. A two-color rectangular panel in either of the upper corners displays the player's name, team, and position. The card backs feature a three-panel cartoon detailing the player's career. Biographical data appears above the cartoon with 1955 and career stats below. Cards #1-#180 can be found with either white or gray backs, but few collectors differentiate between the two in terms of value or collectibility. Cards #181-#260 are considered somewhat scarce and are a bit more valuable than the rest of the set. This was Topps' first year of producing baseball cards without competition from Bowman or any other national issuer, but they were not resting on their laurels. They increased the number of cards from 206 the previous year to 340 in 1956.

1956 Topps, Mickey Mantle

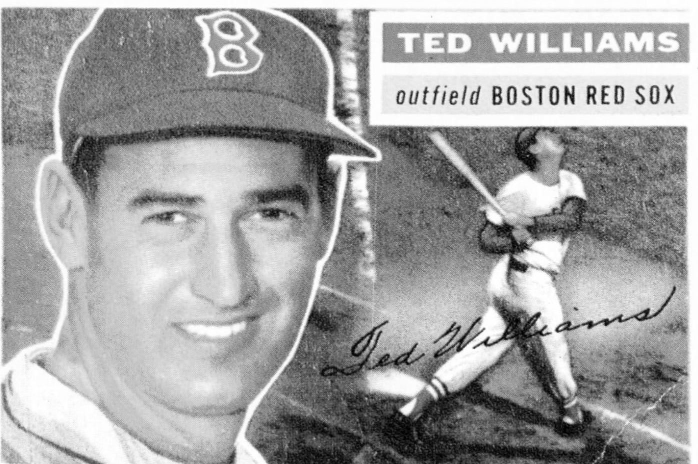

1956 Topps, Ted Williams

FOR
The cards are attractive and not excessively scarce or expensive. Few collectors have anything bad to say about the '56 Topps set. It almost always appears in collectors' top-ten lists of all-time favorite issues.

AGAINST

The cards have a tendency to lose their gloss rather easily, and condition-conscious collectors may find it challenging to complete a set without scuffed cards.

NOTEWORTHY CARDS

Because there was no major competition in 1956, Topps had almost all the superstars to itself—with the exception of Stan Musial, who does not appear in the set. Mickey Mantle is included for the first time since 1953. Topps added three new types of cards to their set for 1956. The most significant of these were team cards. Sure, the pictures were so small you couldn't identify anybody, but Topps did list the players at the bottom of the card. Six of the team cards can be found in three collectible variations: 1) with the team name centered in the black band in the middle of the card, 2) with the team name to the left in the black band, and 3) with the date 1955 included in the black band. The six teams found this way are the Braves, Cubs, Phillies, Orioles, Indians, and Redlegs. Another innovation was the issue of two unnumbered checklists. For the first time, collectors knew the total number of cards in the set and which players they were missing. Unfortunately for today's collectors, the checklists weren't that important in 1956. You only needed two of them, and they were used to keep track of the cards you had. After you got both of them, you threw additional ones away because they were no good for trading. Today the checklists are the scarcest of the 1956 Topps cards and are in demand, especially in unmarked form. Cards of A.L. and N.L. presidents William Harridge and Warren Giles (#1 and #2) were unpopular in 1956 and are still unpopular today. These cards tended to be the first inserted in the spokes of bicycles.

OUR FAVORITE CARD

The card of Hank Aaron pictures two superstars on one card. The portrait photo is the same picture Topps used on Aaron's '54 and '55 cards, but the small action photo is actually Willie Mays. In colorizing the photo, the Topps artist merely painted a Braves uniform on Mays (shown as he prepares to slide into home plate). The photo is a well-known picture of Mays and had been used by Dell in its 1955 *Who's Who in Baseball.*

VALUE

EX-MT CONDITION: Complete set, $4,500; common card, $5–$8; team card (no date), $6; team card (with date), $25; superstars, $60–$90; Aaron, Mays, Ted Williams, Roberto Clemente, Sandy Koufax, checklists, $140–$175; Mantle, $500–$600. 5-YEAR PROJECTION: Above average.

1956 KAHN'S

SPECIFICATIONS

SIZE: 3¼ × 4″. FRONT: Black-and-white photograph. BACK: Blank. DISTRIBUTION: Cincinnati, in packages of Kahn's meat products.

1956 Kahn's, Roy McMillan

HISTORY

In its second season of issuing baseball cards, Kahn's adopted the format and distribution that it would follow into the late '60s. The 15-card set features a black-and-white photo of the player in a posed-action shot. A small white band below the photo contains a Kahn's ad. A facsimile autograph on the front of the card is the only identification. The backs are blank and unnumbered. As in 1955, only Cincinnati Redlegs players were included. The '56 Kahn's cards were inserted into packages of meat products. They are not nearly as scarce as the previous issue, but are a challenging set nonetheless.

FOR

This scarce and valuable regional set is of special interest to Reds team collectors.

AGAINST

The high cost per card makes completing a set expensive.

NOTEWORTHY CARDS
The '56 Kahn's set has the true rookie card of Frank Robinson. Robinson won the N.L. Rookie of the Year award in 1956 but didn't debut on a Topps card until 1957. All the other well-known Reds of the mid-1950s are represented.

VALUE
EX-MT CONDITION: Complete set, $1,000; common card, $50; stars, $60–$70; Ted Kluszewski, $100; Robinson, $200. 5-YEAR PROJECTION: Above average.

1956 RODEO MEATS A'S

SPECIFICATIONS
SIZE: 2½ × 3½″. FRONT: Color photograph. BACK: Black printing on gray cardboard. DISTRIBUTION: Kansas City, in packages of hot dogs.

1956 Rodeo Meats A's, Enos Slaughter

HISTORY
For the second and final year, the Rodeo Meats company of Kansas City, Missouri, issued a baseball card set of the Kansas City A's. Unlike the 38-card 1955 issue, the '56 set is limited to 13 players. All of the players on these cards appeared in the previous set. Since neither set is numbered, card backs must be examined to determine the year of issue. Both years' cards are virtually identical except the '56 card back does not have an ad for a card album. Card fronts feature a heavily retouched player photo surrounded by a narrow white border. There is a white strip with the player's name printed below the photo. At the left is a blue-and-white Rodeo logo. The cards contain no player data or stats.

FOR
There are no confusing variations in this set and team collectors like it.

AGAINST
The design is too similar to the 1955 set. Also, with only 13 players, it's not an entire team set.

NOTEWORTHY CARDS
Even though they trimmed it to 13 cards, Rodeo kept most of the team's better-known stars: manager Lou Boudreau and local favorites Enos Slaughter, Vic Power, Bobby Shantz, and Gus Zernial.

VALUE
EX-MT CONDITION: Complete set, $750; common card, $50; Boudreau, $100; Slaughter, $150. 5-YEAR PROJECTION: Below average.

1955 TOPPS

SPECIFICATIONS
SIZE: 3¾ × 2⅝″. FRONT: Colorized photograph. BACK: Black, red, and green printing on white cardboard. DISTRIBUTION: Nationally, in packages with bubblegum.

1955 Topps, Roberto Clemente

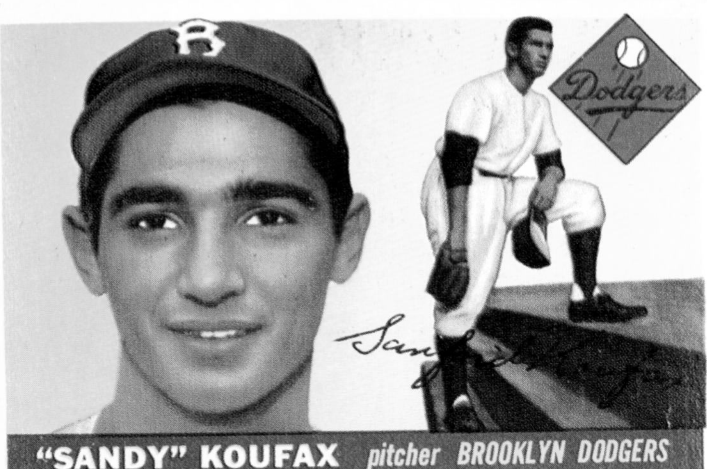

1955 Topps, Sandy Koufax

HISTORY
The smallest regular-issue Topps set was the 1955 offering, which had only 206 cards. It was originally supposed to have 210, but four cards (#175, #186, #203, and #209) were never issued. Ongoing litigation between Topps and Bowman over certain players' contracts accounts for the missing four cards (they probably were players whom the courts awarded to Bowman on an exclusive basis). Since this was the year before Topps introduced its first checklists, collectors went crazy looking for the quartet of cards that could never be found. It is not known whether Topps limited its regular '55 set to 210 cards because they were simultaneously issuing the 66-card (132-player) "Double Header" set, or whether the set was prematurely cut off by Topps' "Card Wars" victory over Bowman that year. Topps' subsequent purchase of Bowman eliminated the only major competition Topps had (at least for awhile). The card fronts were designed horizontally for the first time in Topps' history and feature two color photos of the player—a head shot on one side of the card and an action shot on the other side. A facsimile autograph appears over the action picture. The player's name, position, and team appear in a strip at the bottom. The team logo is in either the upper left or upper right. Card backs have minimal player information—previous year and lifetime stats, vital data, a short career write-up, and a baseball question and answer. The '55 set is believed to contain two levels of scarcity—cards #1-#160 are common, and high-numbered cards (#161-#210) are scarce. Superstar collectors will find many high-demand cards in the high-number series, including superstars Roberto Clemente, Willie Mays, Yogi Berra, Duke Snider, Phil Rizzuto, and Gil Hodges. Snider's card (#210) is hard to find in good condition because, being the last card in the set, it was often damaged when cards were rubber-banded in stacks.

FOR
Topps' first horizontal card was a popular design that was essentially a rearrangement of the successful 1954 design. The different levels of scarcity make it a challenging set for collectors to complete, though none of the cards is so scarce as to make the set unattainable.

AGAINST
Topps recycled many of the portraits and action photos from its '54 issue in creating this set. In addition, many of the portraits (such as Henry Aaron) were used three years in a row.

NOTEWORTHY CARDS
The set contains the rookie cards of Sandy Koufax (#123), Harmon Killebrew (#124), and Clemente (#164). The only baseball card ever issued of college football star Harry Agganis (#152) appears in the set. The "Golden Greek" was a 1951 All-American quarterback at Boston University. He opted for a career in professional baseball upon graduation and signed with the Boston Red Sox in 1953. He became the starting first baseman for the Sox in 1954, his second year in pro ball. His career ended on June 27, 1955, when he died of pneumonia at age 25.

OUR FAVORITE CARD
Although he appeared in both Topps' regular-issue and Double Header sets in '55, Jack Parks (#23) never played an inning of major league baseball. A perpetual back-up to Milwaukee Braves catcher Del Crandall, Parks was never able to crack the lineup. Dozens of examples of players appearing on baseball cards without ever making the major leagues can be found in Topps sets from the early '50s through the early '70s.

VALUE
EX-MT CONDITION: Complete set, $3,600; common card, #1-#160, $5; #161-#210, $11; Killebrew, $150; Koufax, Snider, Mays, $300–$350; Clemente, $500.
5-YEAR PROJECTION: Above average.

1955 TOPPS DOUBLE HEADERS

SPECIFICATIONS
SIZE: $2\frac{1}{16} \times 4\frac{7}{8}$". FRONT: Color painting. BACK: Black, red, and blue printing on white cardboard. DISTRIBUTION: Nationally, in packages with bubblegum.

1955 Topps Double Headers, Jackie Robinson

HISTORY

Always willing to borrow a good baseball card idea from the past, Topps issued a second set of cards in 1955 called "Double Headers." The concept was first used in the Mecca cigarette set of 1911. The 66-card Topps set consists of 132 players, all of whom appeared in the regular '55 Topps set. The cards are perforated one third of the way up, which allows them to be folded over (as they were when they were inserted into packs of bubblegum). When the card is open to its full size, there is a color painting of the player set against a stadium background. When the top of the card is folded down over the painting, the upper body of a second player appears over the lower legs and feet of the first player, but with a different stadium background. In both configurations, a white rectangular panel in the upper left contains the player's name in black and his position and team in red. The card back gives short career summaries for both players, along with '54 and lifetime stats. When individual cards are placed side by side in reverse numerical order, the stadium backgrounds form a continuous scene, which makes it appear as if the players are all on the same baseball diamond. The stadium background bears a strong resemblance to Brooklyn's old Ebbets Field. While the Double Headers are significantly more scarce than the regular-issue cards, they do not command as high a premium as might be expected. The cards are not that popular.

FOR

Even though the cards are a real challenge to collect today, they can sometimes be found in complete sets of unperforated cards.

AGAINST

The paintings are not very flattering, and the necessity of two players sharing feet and legs sometimes results in pictures that are out of perspective. The perforations are easily torn, resulting in a lack of high-grade cards.

NOTEWORTHY CARDS

Hall of Famers Jackie Robinson, Ernie Banks, Warren Spahn, Henry Aaron, Monte Irvin, Ted Williams, Harmon Killebrew, and Al Kaline are in the set. Since the Double Headers contain only players who appear in the low-number series of regular-issue '55 Topps, such superstars as Willie Mays, Roberto Clemente, and Yogi Berra are not included.

OUR FAVORITE CARD

Because of the predominance of righthanded hitters in baseball, a lefthanded catcher is a rarity—his throwing arm would often be blocked by the batter when he attempted to pick off a base stealer. Nevertheless, there is a lefthanded catcher pictured on a Double Header—Dale Long of the Pittsburgh Pirates. Long is best remembered for his major league record of hitting home runs in eight consecutive games in '56. The short write-up on back of the card reads, "They were thinking of making a catcher out of lefthanded Dale—thus this rare picture of him. He's a top prospect for the Buc First Base job this year." Even though he is pictured as a catcher on the Double Header card, his position is given as "1st base." Eventually, Long did catch two games for the Chicago Cubs in 1958.

VALUE

EX-MT CONDITION: Complete set, $1,800; common card, $18; Irvin, $25; Banks, Kaline, Killebrew, Spahn, $75–$90; Williams, Robinson, $100–$150; Aaron, $175. 5-YEAR PROJECTION: Below average.

1955 BOWMAN

SPECIFICATIONS

SIZE: 3¾ × 2½″. FRONT: Color photograph. BACK: Red and black printing on gray cardboard. DISTRIBUTION: Nationally, in packages with bubblegum.

1955 Bowman, Hank Aaron

HISTORY

The '55 Bowman set is judged solely on the basis of its design—collectors either love it or they hate it. Bowman's final (and only horizontal-format) set features a gorgeous color photo of the player in a simulated television screen border. A plate at the bottom of the screen says "Color TV." This was Bowman's attempt to tie televised baseball and color television together because of the rise in popularity of both in the mid-1950s. Many collectors fail to notice that the idea of using a TV set in a baseball card design was not a new idea: Drake's bakery used the concept in its 1950 regionally issued, black-and-white set. (Topps resurrected the idea for its 1966 football card issue.) The only other design element on the front is a white strip that contains the player's last name in black type. There are two distinctive "wood finishes" on the TV cabinets that form the card's border. The wood is much lighter on cards #1-#64 than on cards #65-#320. The photos are sharp and the color reproduction was as good as any that would come along for years, even though this was only the second major set to use actual color photos. All of the pictures in the '55 Bowman set were shot in Philadelphia's Shibe Park (Philadelphia was Bowman's home base). The card backs are also horizontal and feature the card number in a baseball glove in the upper left. To the right in a black box are the player's name (in script), position, and team. At the right in a gray-pink panel is the player's vital data. A red box at the lower right has—on most cards—previous season and lifetime stats. On other cards—the managers, coaches, umpires, and rookies—the box contains a baseball trivia question and answer. The large gray panel on the left contains either a short baseball biography or a short essay by the player in categories such as "My Biggest Thrill in Baseball," "My Advice to Youngsters," or "The Best Hitter (Pitcher, Fielding Play, etc.) I've Ever Seen." Some of these are quite interesting. There are two degrees of scarcity in the set: cards #1-#224 are relatively common, and cards #225-#320 are considerably scarce. It is within those high numbers that one of the '55 Bowmans' most controversial features appears—umpire cards. This was the first time in the 20th century that umpires were pictured in a card set. It was unusual for two reasons: most collectors don't like umpire cards, and umpires have been forbidden in their contracts from accepting money or other considerations for commercial endorsements. The 31 umpire cards in the set contain one Hall of Famer (Jocko Conlan) and several former players. Bowman again used an innovative numbering system: the cards are numbered in pairs by team—cards #1 and #2 feature New York Giants, cards #3 and #4 picture Baltimore Orioles, etc. This system was followed throughout the low numbers, although there were exceptions. Before Bowman could produce a 1956 set, Topps bought them out and began their virtual baseball card monopoly. The '55 Bowman set remains quite popular today.

FOR

Collectors who don't mind a television set used as a border really like the set. It is well done and not too hard to complete.

AGAINST

Some collectors don't like the format. By 1955, Bowman had lost a large number of the game's stars to Topps' exclusive baseball card contracts, and they did not feature the hot rookies that Topps did in '55.

NOTEWORTHY CARDS

The biggest name Bowman had on an exclusive basis was Mickey Mantle. Other Hall of Famers they had to themselves were Bob Lemon, Ralph Kiner, George Kell, Robin Roberts, Bob Feller, Whitey Ford, Pee Wee Reese, Early Wynn, and Roy Campanella. There are a number of collectible variations in the set. Cards of the Bolling brothers, Milt (Red Sox) and Frank (Tigers), can be found with their numbers interchanged. Using Bowman's numbering system, the correct versions are Milt Bolling (#48) and Frank Bolling (#204). A similar situation exists for Don Johnson and Ernie Johnson (they are not related). Card backs of #101 have Orioles pitcher Don Johnson's write-up, though some card fronts picture Ernie Johnson. Card backs of #157 always have an Ernie Johnson write-up, but the fronts can sometimes be found with Don Johnson's picture. Erv Palica's card (#195) can be found with (scarce) or without (common) a final line in the biography on back that reads, "Sent to Baltimore when Preacher Roe retired." Harvey Kuenn's card (#132) can be found with his name spelled correctly on the back (scarce), or incorrectly (common) as "Kueen."

OUR FAVORITE CARD

You've got to love the write-up on Eddie Waitkus' card back (#4). In his essay, "My Biggest Thrill in Baseball," the Baltimore Orioles first baseman begins, "In 1949 I was shot by a deranged girl. . . ." Naturally, being shot was not Waitkus' biggest thrill—he goes on to say how he won the "Comeback Player of the Year" award.

VALUE

EX-MT CONDITION: Complete set, $3,500; common card #1-#224, $4; #225-#320, $9; umpire, $9; stars, $8–$15; Hall of Famers, $30–$40; Campanella, Yogi Berra, Hoyt Wilhelm, Al Kaline, $45–$65; Willie Mays, Hank Aaron, $90–$100; Ernie Banks, $200; Mantle, $325. 5-YEAR PROJECTION: Average.

1955 RED MAN

SPECIFICATIONS

SIZE: 3½ × 4". FRONT: Color painting. BACK: Red printing on gray cardboard. DISTRIBUTION: Nationally, one card in each box of Red Man chewing tobacco.

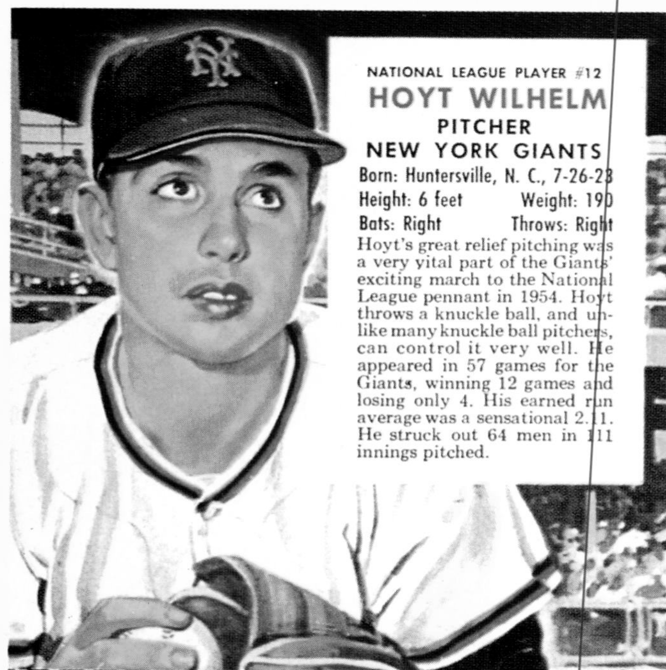

1955 Red Man, Hoyt Wilhelm

HISTORY

Red Man failed to make any big changes in its fourth and final year of baseball card production. The '55 Red Man set was the last set issued in conjunction with a tobacco product: the '55 Red Mans marked the end of an era that began when the first baseball cards were inserted into cigarette packs in 1886. The real popularity of Red Man cards, though, is that they are a rather scarce national issue of the '50s featuring plenty of stars and superstars. Though they are more scarce than the 1955 Topps and Bowman cards, the superstars in this set are priced much lower. Although the commons are priced higher, fewer of them are needed to complete a set. The 50-card 1955 set has no variations. J. Taylor Spink, editor of *The Sporting News*, selected 25 players from each of the major leagues to compose the "All-Star Series." Because of conflicting contracts with Bowman and Topps, there are fewer big-name stars in the '55 set than before. The card front features a borderless color painting—sometimes the same painting used in previous years' cards. In such cases, the background color was changed, or a stadium scene was substituted for a blank background. A white box on one side of the card contains the card number ("American League Player" or "National League Player," each numbered 1 through 25), player's name, personal data, and a career summary. The last year mentioned in the biography will identify the year of issue on cards missing the tab on the bottom. (The tab was a narrow white strip designed to be cut off the card and mailed in with 49 others for a major league cap.) Cards with the tabs intact are worth about 25 percent more. Some collectors feel the tab was designed to be removed and cards without tabs are perfectly acceptable.

FOR

The Red Man cards are a popular issue. The paintings are an attractive alternative to the photos that had become commonplace on other issues by that time—sort of a throwback to baseball cards' earlier days.

AGAINST

Collecting Red Man cards is difficult for the condition-conscious hobbyist who insists on cards with tabs. The recycling of pictures makes the set somewhat unappealing for collectors of superstar cards.

NOTEWORTHY CARDS

The only big names in the set are Willie Mays, Yogi Berra, and Duke Snider.

VALUE

EX-MT CONDITION: Complete set (without tabs), $450; common card, $4.50; stars, $15–$20; Berra, Snider, $25–$40; Mays, $60. 5-YEAR PROJECTION: Above average.

1955 STAHL MEYER

SPECIFICATIONS

SIZE: 3¼ × 4½″. FRONT: Colorized photograph. BACK: Red printing on white cardboard. DISTRIBUTION: New York, single cards inserted in packages of hot dogs.

1955 Stahl Meyer, Phil Rizzuto

HISTORY

It's harder to tell the '55 Stahl Meyer cards from the '54s than it is to tell the '54s from the '53s. The 12-card set for 1955 again pictures four players from each of the three major league teams in the New York area. The '55 and '54 cards used the same player photographs and bright yellow border. The photos were colorized—a popular technique for baseball cards in the early to mid '50s. Below the photo is a box with the player's name and an autograph. To tell the difference between issues, you have to check the card backs. The '55 backs have a drawing of Mickey Mantle in the upper left with an offer for a big league cap and pennant. The bottom half is similar to the '54 set and offers previous season and career stats along with player information. The cards are unnumbered.

FOR

The set features scarce regional cards of popular teams and players.

AGAINST

The cards are too much like the previous set.

NOTEWORTHY CARDS

The checklist for '55 is identical to that for '54, except Willie Mays' card has been replaced by a card of Dusty Rhodes. Today that may seem like an unusual switch, but Rhodes had been the 1954 World Series hero. His pinch-hit home runs and timely hits provided the Giants with wins in the first three games of their four-game sweep of the Indians.

VALUE

EX-MT CONDITION: Complete set, $3,000; common card, $125; stars, $200–$250; Duke Snider, $400; Mickey Mantle, $1,500. 5-YEAR PROJECTION: Average.

1955 RODEO MEATS A'S

SPECIFICATIONS

SIZE: 2½ × 3½″. FRONT: Color photograph. BACK: Black printing on gray cardboard. DISTRIBUTION: Kansas City, in packages of hot dogs and on posters.

HISTORY

The 1955 Rodeo set of Kansas City A's players (their first year after moving from Philadelphia) is one of the largest single-team regional issues in baseball card history. The basic set features virtually the entire team roster as well as manager Lou Boudreau and the coaches. The '55 Rodeo cards were issued in two forms. Wax-coated single cards were packaged with the company's hot dogs. A number of cards were also distributed in poster-form on unwaxed cardboard. Individual cards could then be cut off. The two separate card printings resulted in a number of color variations in the card backgrounds. There are 38 different cards,

1955 Rodeo Meats A's, Lou Boudreau

1955 Rodeo Meats A's, Gus Zernial

but a complete set of '55 Rodeo cards with all variations totals 47. The card front features a portrait or posed-action photo of the player, heavily retouched to accentuate the color. A white strip at the bottom of the card has the player's name, and a Rodeo logo is in the lower left. There is a white border around the photo. Unnumbered card backs carry a scrapbook offer available for 25¢ and a label. The offer lists two cards that were never issued in the set (coach Burleigh Grimes and first baseman Dick Kryhoski). An untrimmed poster is worth about 25 percent more than the individual cards featured on it. The Rodeo Meats A's cards are quite scarce.

FOR
There are some well-known players in this regional set.

AGAINST
The color variations and the high cost of the cards make it difficult to complete.

NOTEWORTHY CARDS
Besides the background color differences, there is another variation: Bobby Shantz's card has his name spelled "Schantz." That error was later corrected.

VALUE
EX-MT CONDITION: Complete set (47 cards), $2,850; common card, $45; Boudreau, Enos Slaughter, "Schantz," $150–$175. 5-YEAR PROJECTION: Below average.

1955 JOHNSTON COOKIE BRAVES

SPECIFICATIONS
SIZE: 2⅞ × 4¹⁄₁₆″. FRONT: Colorized photograph. BACK: Blue and red printing on white cardboard. DISTRIBUTION: Wisconsin, one 6-card panel in packages of cookies.

HISTORY
The third and final Johnston cookie Milwaukee Braves baseball card set was produced in 1955. The 35-card set features the players, manager, coaches, team doctor, trainer, and even the traveling secretary. The '55 Johnstons were distributed in an unusual manner: they were printed in strips of six cards in accordion-style with self-covers. One strip was inserted into each family-size box of Johnston cookies, and each carried an ad that allowed you to get another series for a nickel and a Johnston proof-of-purchase. The card front again features a colorized photo taken at spring training. The variety of poses is much improved over the '54 cards. A box below the photo contains a red Indian logo at left, along with the player's name and facsimile autograph. The card backs are quite similar to the previous two sets: player personal data appears in a pink box at the top, an Indian silhouette at right has the card number (also the

player's uniform number), while a strip across the card carries the team name. A player biography is in the center and stats from the previous two seasons are near the bottom. A Johnston ad appears at the very bottom of the card. There are a total of 36 cards, but Andy Pafko's card (#48) was included in two series. The '55 Johnston cards are larger than the standard size and were printed on uncoated cardboard. Uncut panels of cards are worth about 25 percent more than individual cards. Single cards are most valuable when they are cut on the dotted lines. A surprising number of folders have survived intact. The '55s are the scarcest of the three Johnston sets.

FOR

These excellent cards feature a popular team with lots of stars.

AGAINST

Top condition cards are scarce because of the poor quality of the cardboard and the fact that the cards had to be cut off panels.

NOTEWORTHY CARDS

Hall of Famers Henry Aaron, Warren Spahn, and Eddie Mathews are included in the set.

OUR FAVORITE CARD

The '55 Johnston card of the Braves traveling secretary Duffy Lewis is unique in baseball card history. Lewis was a well-known player from the turn of the century. He was one-third of the famous Boston Red Sox outfield (along with Tris Speaker and Harry Hooper). He played with Boston from 1910 to 1917 and then spent two more years with the Yankees and one with the Senators before retiring from the majors in 1921 with a .284 lifetime average. Collectors in 1955 may not have been aware that Lewis was the only man ever to pinch-hit for Babe Ruth.

VALUE

EX-MT CONDITION: Complete set (neatly cut from folders), $500; common card, $7; Mathews, Spahn, $35; Aaron, $175. 5-YEAR PROJECTION: Below average.

1955 HUNTER'S WIENERS CARDINALS

SPECIFICATIONS

SIZE: 2 × 4¾″. FRONT: Color photograph. BACK: Blank. DISTRIBUTION: St. Louis, two cards on the side panel of packages of hot dogs.

1955 Hunter's Wieners Cardinals, Wally Moon

HISTORY

The last of the Hunter's Wieners baseball cards featured an all-new format. Two photos of the player were included on each card—a posed-action shot and a smaller portrait. A total of 30 cards were produced. A facsimile autograph appears in a white panel below the photos. The player's name and short biographical details appear in white printing on a red background below the autograph. Like the '54 issue, this bottom portion was sometimes cut off to make the card more like the size of then-current Topps and Bowman cards. Because the cards have square corners, they were easier to separate than either of the two earlier issues. The 1955 Hunter's Wieners cards are the scarcest of the company's three issues.

FOR

The new photos include many lesser-known players, much to the delight of team collectors.

AGAINST

Too often, the cards were poorly trimmed.

NOTEWORTHY CARDS

Big-name stars Stan Musial, Vic Raschi, and Red Schoendienst are joined by rookies Ken Boyer and Bill Virdon.

OUR FAVORITE CARD

Typical of many regional issues, the 1955 Hunter's set contains cards that feature the only baseball card appearance of little-known players. "Preacher Jack" Faszholz pitched in just four games for the Cardinals and allowed 16 hits and a walk in 11.2 innings. To his credit, he struck out seven batters. In his own three at-bats, he struck out twice and grounded out. None of this is particularly notable, except that it all happened in 1953—two years before Faszholz appeared in this set. He never pitched another inning in the major leagues. Why he was chosen to appear in the '55 set is a mystery.

VALUE

EX-MT CONDITION: Complete set (neatly cut from package), $3,500; common card, $100; Boyer, Raschi, Schoendienst, Virdon, $175–$200; Musial, $1,500. 5-YEAR PROJECTION: Average.

1955 KAHN'S

SPECIFICATIONS

SIZE: 3¼ × 4″. FRONT: Black-and-white photograph. BACK: Blank. DISTRIBUTION: Cincinnati, given away at an amusement park.

HISTORY

This was the first of a long string of card issues by the Kahn's meat company. An unusual feature marked this 6-card set: all of the players (Cincinnati Reds) are pictured in street clothes rather than baseball uniforms. They are identified by a facsimile autograph on the front. A white panel below the photo contains a Kahn's ad. Cards are unnumbered and the backs are blank. Unlike later Kahn's issues, the '55 cards were given away at a Cincinnati amusement park. This premier Kahn's set is very scarce, but because players are shown out of uniform, it's not as popular or as expensive as might be expected.

FOR

These are rare cards for the team collector.

AGAINST

The players are not in uniform.

NOTEWORTHY CARDS

The six players are Gus Bell, Ted Kluszewski, Roy McMillan, Joe Nuxhall, Wally Post, and Johnny Temple.

VALUE

EX-MT CONDITION: Complete set, $2,100; common card, $300; Kluszewski, $400; Bell, $600. 5-YEAR PROJECTION: Average.

1954 TOPPS

SPECIFICATIONS

SIZE: 2⅝ × 3¾″. FRONT: Colorized and black-and-white photographs. BACK: Green, red, and black printing on white cardboard. DISTRIBUTION: Nationally, in packages with bubblegum.

1954 Topps, Ernie Banks

HISTORY

Topps produced only 250 cards in 1954, but it is one of the company's most attractive and popular issues of the '50s. This was the first time two different pictures of the same player appeared on a single card. The card front combines a color head-and-shoulders portrait of the player with a small black-and-white posed-action shot. The pictures are set against a solid background in one of several bright colors. A color team logo appears in one of the upper corners, along with the player's name, team, and position. The card backs feature the same data as previous years—stats, biography, and short career summary. An interesting feature of the '54 cards is the "Inside Baseball" cartoon that appears at the bottom and features an anecdote about the player. Tigers pitcher Dick Weik's card reads, "Senator owner Clark Griffith got a tip on Weik from a friend! The friend had spotted Weik pitching for a Peoria high school team! Dick signed with the Senators for $4,000—plus a free sight-seeing trip to Washington for his Mom!" Like earlier Topps' sets, the '54 issue has several levels of scarcity. Cards #1-#50 are considered common (there are nine Hall of Famers and at least six potential candidates among them), #76-#250 are somewhat scarce, and #51-#75 are the most scarce. However, the price difference is not that great among the three groups.

FOR

It is one of Topps' most popular sets. It contains no real variations and includes lots of big stars.

AGAINST

There probably isn't a bad word to be said of the '54 Topps.

NOTEWORTHY CARDS

From beginning to end, there are many notable cards in the set. Cards #1 and #250 are of Ted Williams (Topps' way of celebrating their signing Williams to an exclusive five-year baseball card contract). There are a number of significant rookies like Henry Aaron, Ernie Banks, Al Kaline, and Tommy Lasorda (the only major league baseball card issued during his playing career). Another nice feature was the inclusion of more than a dozen managers and coaches—most of them former players. While a few major card sets had issued manager cards in the past, no modern set had ever depicted the coaches. Some of the former players who appeared as coaches in the set never appeared on another baseball card.

OUR FAVORITE CARD

One of the most memorable cards in the set is of Ed & John O'Brien (#139). The O'Briens were the only twin brothers ever to play on the same major league team at the same time. They are pictured together on the card, kneeling with bats on their shoulders. It marked the first time Topps featured more than one player on the same baseball card. The O'Brien twins had appeared in Topps' 1953 set, but on individual cards. They would appear again (separately and together) on Topps cards through 1959.

VALUE

EX-MT CONDITION: Complete set, $5,000; common card, $5–$7; Hall of Famers, $35–$75; Lasorda, $90; Mays, $225; Williams, Kaline, Banks, $300–$350; Aaron, $650. 5-YEAR PROJECTION: Above average.

1954 BOWMAN

SPECIFICATIONS

SIZE: 2½ × 3¾". FRONT: Colorized photograph. BACK: Black and red printing on gray cardboard. DISTRIBUTION: Nationally, in packages with bubblegum.

1954 Bowman, Mickey Mantle

HISTORY

After a popular and successful color set in 1953, Bowman reverted to a less sophisticated technique for its 1954 set. The 224 cards are colorized photographs. A pastel-colored panel in one of the lower corners carries a facsimile autograph or, on some cards, the player's name set in type. A white border surrounds the entire design. The card backs are arranged in a horizontal format. At the top is a red box with a copyright line in the upper left. An outline of a bat contains the player's name, while the card number is contained in a ball at the right. Below the bat is the player's team, position, and personal data. A short biography appears in a gray panel to the left and a corresponding box to the right has previous season and lifetime stats. At the bottom left is a baseball trivia question with the answer in a red box at the bottom right. The '54 Bowman set is best known for having two #66 cards. The common #66 is Jimmy Piersall; the scarce version is Ted Williams. Williams appeared in a Topps set for the first time in '54, and it is believed that his contract with Topps prohibited Bowman from further picturing him on baseball cards. When Topps pressed the issue, Bowman was forced to withdraw the Williams card and issue a new #66. Piersall also appears on another card in the set (#210). While the Ted Williams card is quite expensive, it is not as rare as some sources would have you believe. Bowman used an interesting numbering scheme for this issue: each team is represented by 14 players skip-numbered in increments of 16. For example, Phil Rizzuto of the Yankees is #1 in the set, Tom Gorman (#17) is also a Yankee, etc. The Baltimore Orioles cards are interesting because Bowman artists had to create uniforms for the team, and they came up with a number of variations. The problem was that the Orioles became a major league team in '54 after many years in the A.L. as the St. Louis Browns. When the Bowman set was being produced, nobody knew what the new uniforms would look like. The '54 set is also known for having errors in the stats on a large number of cards. Very few collectors concern themselves with these statistical variations, however, and none of them command a premium.

FOR

The '54 Bowman set is attractive, but it pales in comparison with the '53 and '55 issues.

AGAINST

Not up to the same quality as the '53 and '55 sets, the Bowman issue of 1954 lost the "battle" that year to Topps, which is much more popular among collectors today. The high cost of the Williams card makes completing a set difficult for many collectors.

NOTEWORTHY CARDS

The '54 Bowman set has a few players who do not appear on that year's Topps issue: Pee Wee Reese, Roy Campanella, Robin Roberts, Bob Feller, and Mickey Mantle. There are some variations in the Bowman set that collectors find interesting enough to place a premium on. An updated printing of Vic Raschi's card mentions his trade to St. Louis; the same is true of Dave Philley's card that tells of his trade to Cleveland. The corrected version of Jim Greengrass' card lists his birthplace as "Addison, N.Y.," rather than "Addison, N.J." Memo Luna's card (#222) is different because, rather than a retouched photograph, the card features a poorly done painting of the Cardinals pitcher. Willie Mays' facsimile autograph reads "Willie May."

VALUE

EX-MT CONDITION: Complete set (including Piersall #66), $2,750; common card $5; stars, $10–$15; Hall of Famers, $20–$35; Feller, $45; Campanella, Yogi Berra, Duke Snider, Rizzuto, Piersall #66, $80–$100; Mays, $200; Mantle, $550; Williams, $1,750. 5-YEAR PROJECTION: Above average.

1954 RED MAN

SPECIFICATIONS

SIZE: 3½ × 4″. FRONT: Color painting. BACK: Black printing on gray cardboard. DISTRIBUTION: Nationally, single cards in boxes of chewing tobacco.

1954 Red Man, Del Crandall

HISTORY

In their third year of including baseball cards in boxes of chewing tobacco, the Red Man set of 1954 shows little change from the design of the '52 and '53 issues. The 50 cards in the set are numbered 1 through 25 for each league. There were no cards for managers this year. The players were chosen once again by *The Sporting News* editor, J. Taylor Spink. The basic format is a borderless color painting of the player with a thin white stripe, or "tab" underneath. A collector could redeem 50 tabs for a major league cap of his favorite team. Most collectors prefer cards with the tabs intact, as they were originally issued. The tab on this year's cards listed only the year of issue. Card numbers appear in a white box in one of the upper corners of the card, along with the player's name, personal data, and a career summary. On cards missing tabs, the year of issue can be determined by checking the career summary on the card back. The '54 Red Man backs also carry an ad for the tobacco and details of the free cap offer. The bottom line (above the tab) reads "Red Man 'Chewers'—start a collection for your boys." Cards with tabs are worth about 25 percent more than cards without tabs.

FOR

They are relatively inexpensive cards that were distributed in smaller quantities than the Topps or Bowman issues.

AGAINST

Some of the players in this set appeared on their third consecutive card in the same pose, with only a background change. This makes the issue confusing and not as attractive to superstar collectors as it might otherwise be.

NOTEWORTHY CARDS

Few collectors realize how scarce some of the variation cards in the '54 Red Man set are. These include a trio of A.L. players who were traded and appear in the 1954 set in both their old and new uniforms. The more common of the three cards is Dave Philley, who was traded to the Indians from the A's prior to the beginning of the season. The card depicting him as a member of the A's is the more scarce version. Much harder to find are the cards of George Kell and Sam Mele, both of whom were traded in mid-season. Kell appears in the set as a Red Sox and a White Sox player; Mele appears as an Oriole and a White Sox player. In both cases, the White Sox versions are more scarce. There is also a variation among the N.L. cards: Gus Bell and Enos Slaughter can both be found as card #19. Slaughter, as a St. Louis Cardinal, was the first #19; when he was traded to the Yankees in April 1954, Gus Bell replaced him as #19. The Bell card is the scarcer of the two. Willie Mays returned to the Red Man set in 1954, but Stan Musial was gone. Nevertheless, there is an abundance of Hall of Famers and popular home team heroes in the set.

VALUE

EX-MT CONDITION: Complete set (without tabs, no variations), $500; common card, $5; Hall of Famers, $15–$25; common variation, $10; scarce variation, $20; Mays, $50. 5-YEAR PROJECTION: Above average.

1954 RED HEART

SPECIFICATIONS

SIZE: 2⅝ × 3¾". FRONT: Colorized photograph. BACK: Black printing on gray cardboard. DISTRIBUTION: Nationally, through a mail-in offer.

1954 Red Heart, Mickey Mantle

HISTORY

Not long ago, collectors could still order the 1954 baseball cards issued by the Red Heart dog food company for a couple of dollars. This well-kept secret meant that a large number of cards are available today in top condition. In 1954, Red Heart issued the 33-card set as just one of more than six baseball-related premiums that could be obtained by sending in Red Heart labels and cash. To get a series of 11 baseball cards, you sent in two labels and a dime. Each of the three series has a red, blue, or green background behind the photo of the player. Since far fewer of the red-background cards were sent to collectors in later years, it is assumed that they were printed in smaller quantities. There is no real price difference between the three series. The card front features a colorized photo, but most of the artwork isn't that good, and some of the players' eyes look alien. The player's name is printed inside a colored diamond at the bottom of the photo and the team name appears in the white border at the bottom. The unnumbered card backs are vertical in format and have the player's name, team, and position centered between two baseballs. A short biography appears below that. In the center are personal data and previous season and career stats. At the bottom is a black box with a Red Heart logo and a copyright line for the John Morrell Meat Company. (Though the Red Heart set was a one-year issue, the Morrell name would be seen again on later baseball card issues.)

FOR
It's a scarce, nationally distributed set of the '50s that has luckily been preserved for collectors in decent numbers. This helps to keep the price down.

AGAINST
Some collectors who were left out of the direct-purchase "secret" of a few years ago are hesitant to pay the current price for cards they know were obtained for only a few cents apiece.

NOTEWORTHY CARDS
Stan Musial appears in the red-background series—his only nationally distributed baseball card in 1954. Mickey Mantle is in the blue series, and there are a few other superstars scattered throughout the set. A recent high-quality Red Heart reprint set was issued by an East Coast dealer. Now it's possible to have a reasonable facsimile of the set for less than $10.

VALUE
EX-MT CONDITION: Complete set, $1,000; common card, $15; Hall of Famers, $30–$45; Duke Snider, $65; Musial, $200; Mantle, $375. 5-YEAR PROJECTION: Average.

1954 WILSON'S FRANKS

SPECIFICATIONS
SIZE: 2⅝ × 3¾". FRONT: Colorized photograph. BACK: Black printing on gray cardboard. DISTRIBUTION: Nationally, in packages of hot dogs.

HISTORY
The 20-card Wilson's Franks baseball card set of 1954 is one of the rarest, most expensive, and most popular of the sets issued with hot dogs in the '50s. Unlike most other sets, which concentrated on one or two teams, the Wilson's set featured players from more than a dozen clubs. The cards are quite attractive and feature a colorized player photograph against a solid-color background. The player's name, team, and position appear at the top, and there is a facsimile autograph across the front. A Wilson's Franks package appears above or to the side of the player photo. (These suspended hot dogs sometimes look as if the player is going to hit them with a bat, catch them in an outstretched glove, or get hit in the back of the head.) It is one of the few instances in baseball card history where the product is pictured on the front of the card. Card backs contain the usual player personal data, short career summary, and previous season and career stats. Like most regional card issues of the '50s, the Wilson's cards are unnumbered. While many collectors consider these cards regional, they were distributed nationally (although in limited quantities). The cards were inserted into packages with the hot dogs and are commonly found with grease stains. However, because of their scarcity, most collectors are willing to overlook a little grease.

1954 Wilson's Franks, Nellie Fox

FOR
The cards feature an unusual and attractive design. Collecting this set is a real challenge.

AGAINST
There are many little-known players and managers among the cards in the set. It is hard to find the cards in top condition.

NOTEWORTHY CARDS
The biggest name in the set is Ted Williams, who is joined by fellow Hall of Famers Roy Campanella and Bob Feller.

VALUE
EX-MT CONDITION: Complete set, $3,800; common card, $80; stars, $175–$225; Campanella, Feller, $425; Williams, $1,800. 5-YEAR PROJECTION: Below average.

1954
STAHL MEYER

SPECIFICATIONS
SIZE: 3¼ × 4½″. FRONT: Colorized photograph. BACK: Red printing on white cardboard. DISTRIBUTION: New York, in packages of hot dogs.

1954 Stahl Meyer, Don Newcombe

HISTORY
In its second year of issuing baseball cards, the Stahl Meyer company increased the size of its set to 12 cards. Four players from each of New York's three major league teams were represented. The format was similar to the previous issue except for a yellow border replacing the white one on the front. Card fronts again have colorized photographs and rounded corners. A panel below the picture contains the player's name in print and also a facsimile autograph. Even though some of the same photos were used again, the color of the border makes it easy to tell the two years apart. The card backs are arranged vertically, with the top half offering a baseball kit and the bottom half carrying the player's name, personal data, and previous season and career stats. The backs are unnumbered and have no player biographical info. Overall, the '54 Stahl Meyers are a bit scarcer than the earlier issue.

FOR
These are scarce regional cards of popular players.

AGAINST
Many collectors don't like round corners. The combination of scarce cards and popular players makes the '54 Stahl Meyer cards expensive.

NOTEWORTHY CARDS
The players represented from the Yankees are Hank Bauer, Mickey Mantle, Gil McDougald, and Phil Rizzuto; from the Dodgers: Carl Erskine, Gil Hodges, Don Newcombe, and Duke Snider; from the Giants: Monte Irvin, Whitey Lockman, Willie Mays, and Don Mueller.

VALUE
EX-MT CONDITION: Complete set, $4,000; common card, $125; Irvin, Hodges, Rizzuto, $225–$250; Snider, $500; Mays, $950; Mantle, $1,800. 5-YEAR PROJECTION: Below average.

1954
DAN-DEE
POTATO CHIPS

SPECIFICATIONS
SIZE: 2½ × 3⅝″. FRONT: Colorized photograph. BACK: Blue and red printing on white cardboard. DISTRIBUTION: Regionally, individual cards in bags of potato chips.

1954 Dan-Dee Potato Chips, Bob Feller

HISTORY

The 29-card set from the Dan-Dee potato chip company is one of the more scarce and popular regional issues of the mid '50s. The similarity of these cards to other regional sets of this era indicates that one company may have produced all of them. Players from the Indians, Pirates, Dodgers, Yankees, Giants, and Cardinals are included in this set. The card fronts feature a colorized photograph of the player. Beneath the photo is a box containing the player's name in upper-case letters along with a facsimile autograph. A red Dan-Dee logo is at the left. Unnumbered card backs have a traditional mix of personal data, short biography, and the previous two seasons' stats. An advertisement appears at the bottom. Because the cards were inserted in bags of potato chips, they are sometimes found with grease stains.

FOR

These good-looking cards feature lots of popular stars of the early 1950s.

AGAINST

The same player photos on different regional sets makes the cards less desirable to team or superstar collectors.

NOTEWORTHY CARDS

The Dan-Dee set contains many cards of the 1954 World Champion Cleveland Indians. The Walker Cooper and Paul Smith cards were withdrawn during the promotion: Smith was sent to the minors, and Cooper was dealt to the Cubs in mid-season. Superstars include Bob Feller, Monte Irvin, Bob Lemon, Al Lopez, Mickey Mantle, Duke Snider, and Early Wynn.

VALUE

EX-MT CONDITION: Complete set, $2,800; common card, $35; Hall of Famers, $50–$100; Cooper, $250; Smith, $350; Mantle, $725. 5-YEAR PROJECTION: Below average.

1954 NEW YORK JOURNAL AMERICAN

SPECIFICATIONS

SIZE: 2 × 4". FRONT: Black-and-white photograph. BACK: Black printing on white cardboard. DISTRIBUTION: New York, cards given away with purchase of a daily newspaper.

1954 New York Journal American, Jackie Robinson

HISTORY

The Hearst newspaper chain had a reputation for using innovative ideas to sell newspapers. In 1954 the Hearst papers created a "Lucky Baseball Cards" contest. Newsstand vendors were given baseball cards to be passed out to people buying the New York *Journal American* newspaper. Every card had a serial number printed in red at the bottom. Each day, winning numbers were printed in the paper and $1,000 in cash was given away (as much as $200 for each winning card). Because the cards were really unattractive and "worthless" if they didn't have a winning number, they were often thrown away. Those that survived were usually taken home by the vendors. The 59-card set represents players from all three major league New York teams. Even though those teams are quite popular with collectors and have many superstars, the *Journal American* cards are not popular because of their poor quality. The card front features a black-and-white player photo with a black strip under the picture containing the player's name and team name. The lower half carries an ad for the contest. The unnumbered card backs provide home game schedules for the corresponding team.

FOR

The cards are quite inexpensive considering they are a scarce regional issue.

AGAINST
The cards are really unattractive, and the desirable superstar cards are high priced.

NOTEWORTHY CARDS
All the popular Dodger, Giant, and Yankee stars of the era are included in the set. Erv Palica's card is somewhat scarce because it was withdrawn when he was traded from the Dodgers to the Orioles in mid-season.

VALUE
EX-MT CONDITION: Complete set, $1,000; common card, $6; stars, $15–$25; superstars, $60–$75; Jackie Robinson, $90; Willie Mays, $125; Mickey Mantle, $300. 5-YEAR PROJECTION: Average.

1954 JOHNSTON COOKIE BRAVES

SPECIFICATIONS
SIZE: 2 × 3⅞″. FRONT: Colorized photograph. BACK: Blue and red printing on cream-colored cardboard. DISTRIBUTION: Wisconsin, single cards in packages of cookies.

1954 Johnston Cookie Braves, Andy Pafko

HISTORY
The 35-card Johnston cookie set was the second of three annual issues. The cards include the entire roster of the Milwaukee Braves, the manager, the coaches, and even the team's trainer and doctor. The '54 Johnstons are unusually tall and narrow. Photos were taken at the team's spring-training facility in Bradenton, Florida. Almost all of the cards depict players in front of a chain-link fence with folding chairs in the background. The player's name is printed in a white border beneath the photo. A facsimile autograph appears below that, superimposed on a red Indian chief logo. The card backs are arranged horizontally and contain a short biography, personal data, '52 and '53 season stats, and a Johnston logo. The cards are numbered according to the player's uniform number. The trainer and doctor cards are unnumbered. An offer for a wall-hanging display sheet for the cards appears on the right side. These sheets are rare today and make an interesting addition to the set. The '54 Johnstons are considerably scarcer than the '53 issue.

FOR
This is another great set for Braves collectors, and it features players not seen in other sets.

AGAINST
Most photos have the same boring background. The cards have been reprinted and are now available from many dealers for less than $10.

NOTEWORTHY CARDS
Two cards in this set are much more valuable than the rest. Henry Aaron's card is his rookie card, which makes this issue especially popular with collectors. (It's unusual to see Aaron as #5 as in this set, but that's the uniform number he had for a time before adopting the familiar #44.) Bobby Thomson's card was withdrawn from distribution early in the issue. Thomson broke his ankle in a preseason game and was out for most of the season. Existing uncut sheets indicate that in lieu of the Thomson card the Warren Spahn or Jim Wilson card was double-printed on later press runs. The inclusion of team doctor and trainer cards was very unusual for a major league regional set.

VALUE
EX-MT CONDITION: Complete set, $500; common card, $7; Spahn, Ed Mathews, $35; Thomson, $150; Aaron, $175. 5-YEAR PROJECTION: Below average.

1954 HUNTER'S WIENERS CARDINALS

SPECIFICATIONS

SIZE: 2¼ × 3½″. FRONT: Color photograph. BACK: Blank. DISTRIBUTION: St. Louis, single player and single stat card inserted in packages of hot dogs.

1954 Hunter's Wieners Cardinals, Peanuts Lowery

HISTORY

Although the 30-card Hunter's Wieners set included four more cards than the previous year, only one player card was inserted in packages of hot dogs instead of two. Like the previous issue, the '54 cards have round corners. The photos used for the '54 set were the same ones used in 1953. Instead of the player's name and bio in the white bottom panel, however, there was a line "What's My Name? What's My Record?" printed. An accompanying stat card in the package provided the answers. Since far fewer of the answer cards survived, many collectors are faced with "anonymous" '54 Hunter's cards. You have to know your mid-1950s Cardinals trivia to successfully complete this set. Many cards have been found without the white bottom panel and this greatly reduces the value of the card.

FOR

The expanded 30-card set meant more of the marginal Cardinal players—as well as coaches—were included. This is a bonus for team collectors because some of the players didn't appear on any other baseball cards.

AGAINST

The fact that it takes two individual cards to make a "complete" card creates difficultly in assembling an entire set. The picture cards are scarce and costly.

NOTEWORTHY CARDS

Because he didn't appear in either the Topps or Bowman issue for 1954, Stan Musial's card is highly desirable. Well-known Cardinals in the set include Vic Raschi, Enos Slaughter, and Red Schoendienst. Also appearing is Tom Alston, the first black player on the team.

VALUE

EX-MT CONDITION: Complete set (neatly cut from package), $3,000; common card, $85; Raschi, Schoendienst, $150; Slaughter, $200–$225; Musial, $700. 5-YEAR PROJECTION: Below average.

1954-1955 ESSKAY ORIOLES

SPECIFICATIONS

SIZE: 2¼ × 3½″. FRONT: Color photograph. BACK: Blank. DISTRIBUTION: Baltimore, one 2-card panel printed as part of hot dog packages.

1954-1955 Esskay Orioles, Don Larsen

HISTORY

For the first two years that the Baltimore Orioles were members of the A.L. (following their move from St. Louis), the Esskay meat company printed cards of the players as part of its hot dog packaging. Differentiating between the two issues is difficult because players appearing in both sets are impossible to tell apart. The cards are similar to the Hunter's Wieners St. Louis Cardinals set of the previous year. Card fronts feature a borderless color photo of the player. Beneath the photo is a white strip that has the player's name, position, birth date, home town, and his batting and throwing stats. There is a facsimile autograph in light blue in the background. Cards are unnumbered and the backs are blank. If a player appeared in both '54 and '55 sets, the same photo was used. A detailed checklist or a '54 and/or '55 Orioles roster could help pinpoint the year of issue. A total of 52 different players are represented from both sets, even though 36 cards were issued in 1954 and 27 were issued in 1955. The cards are so rare and expensive that few collectors attempt to complete a set. What's even harder than identifying the year of issue is finding cards in top condition. Because they were printed on the bottom of the hot dog package and had to be separated, many of the Esskay cards are found poorly trimmed. A complete panel of two cards is worth 50 percent more than the individual cards.

FOR

These are valuable cards from an expansion team's first year in a new city.

AGAINST

The cards are too similar to tell apart and that frustrates many who favor collecting complete sets. They're hard to locate, difficult to find in nice condition, and very costly.

NOTEWORTHY CARDS

While many of the players in the 1954-1955 Esskay set are forgettable, at least two—Don Larsen and Bob Turley—went on to greater fame a few years later. It's a great set for team collectors.

VALUE

EX-MT CONDITION: Complete set of 63 cards (neatly cut from package), $5,600; common card, $80–$100; Turley, Larsen, $150. 5-YEAR PROJECTION: Below average.

1953 TOPPS

SPECIFICATIONS

SIZE: 2⅝ × 3¾″. FRONT: Color painting. BACK: Red and black printing on gray cardboard. DISTRIBUTION: Nationally, in packages with bubblegum.

1953 Topps, Satchel Paige

HISTORY

Because of continuing legal battles with Bowman over rights to print players' pictures on gum cards, Topps dramatically cut back the size of its set in 1953 to 280 cards. The players' contracts were so hotly contested that Topps apparently lost six of them after production on the '53 set began. Thus, there are no cards #253, #261, #267, #268, #271, or #275, which makes the set complete at 274 cards. Naturally, the fact that six cards didn't exist didn't hurt Topps' sales of bubblegum packs: collectors had no way of knowing it because there were no checklists. So they kept buying packs hoping to "complete" the 280-card set. The '53 cards are painted portraits of the individual players, usually rendered from team publicity photos. Artists then added stadium backgrounds to the portraits. A color team logo appears at the bottom of the card near a red (A.L.) or black (N.L.) panel, which contains the player's name, team, and position. A white border surrounds the card. The card backs offer brief 1952 and lifetime stats at the bottom, along with biographical details and a short career summary. There is a facsimile autograph in red across the career summary. In '53 Topps initiated a baseball trivia question on the back of its cards ("Dugout Quiz"). It was a device the company would use frequently over the years. The Topps cards exist in three degrees of scarcity: cards #166-#220 are common, #1-#165 are more scarce, and #221-#280 are the scarcest by far. The high numbers contain the cornerstone of the series—Willie Mays (#244).

FOR

The '53 Topps cards are attractive and offer collectors a decent challenge at a much lower cost than the '52 set. The high-number series is scarce enough to keep a collector busy for quite some time.

AGAINST

The fewer number of cards in the set means that many of the game's great stars are absent.

NOTEWORTHY CARDS

The Mays card in the high-number series is in strong demand and short supply. It is scarcer than the more expensive Mickey Mantle card in the same set. Actually, Topps cheated by issuing a 1953 Mays card—he spent the entire season in military service. Because of the scarcity of Mays' card, it was the victim of one of the first modern baseball card counterfeit schemes. The fake card isn't difficult to detect, though. Somebody forgot to tell the printer that the panel at the bottom of the card should be black, not red. The set also features rookie cards of Dodgers Jim Gilliam and Johnny Podres. Jackie Robinson's card (#1) is the hardest to find in Mint condition. Pete Runnels' card (#219) is actually his '52 Senators teammate Don Johnson. Johnson didn't play in the majors in 1953 and didn't have his own baseball card that year either.

OUR FAVORITE CARD

Collectors who want a baseball card of Hall of Fame pitching legend Satchel Paige have little choice but to obtain his 1953 Topps card. Paige appeared on only one other major baseball card issue in his short major league career—a rare series Leaf card from the 1948-1949 issue, which is priced four to five times higher than the Topps card. Paige was the most famous of the Negro Leagues' ballplayers and one of the oldest to successfully make the transition to the major leagues after Jackie Robinson's debut with the Dodgers in 1947. Paige was pitching for the St. Louis Browns when he appeared in the '53 Topps set. For 1952, he was 12-10 with a 3.07 ERA, and he led the A.L. with eight wins and eight losses in relief. Though he often made a game of not revealing his true age, it is generally acknowledged that Paige was 46 years old when he appeared on the '53 Topps card. Paige played part of the following season for the Browns before moving to the minor leagues to coach and instruct pitchers on various teams. In 1965—at age 59—Paige took the major league mound once again as a starting pitcher for the Kansas City A's. He pitched three innings, gave up a hit, and struck out one. Paige was elected to the Hall of Fame on the basis of his long and successful career in the Negro Leagues.

VALUE

EX-MT CONDITION: Complete set, $9,000; common card #1-#165, $10; #166-#220, $8; #221-#280, $32; Hall of Famers, $75–$150; Paige, $250; Robinson, $400; Mays, $1,200; Mantle $1,500. 5-YEAR PROJECTION: Average or above.

1953 BOWMAN COLOR

SPECIFICATIONS

SIZE: 2½ × 3¾″. FRONT: Color photograph. BACK: Red and black printing on cream-colored cardboard. DISTRIBUTION: Nationally, in packages with bubblegum.

1953 Bowman Color, Billy Martin/Phil Rizzuto

HISTORY

Nobody can say that Bowman sat back and let Topps dominate the baseball card market. Bowman responded to the challenge of '52 with a set that is consistently rated as the most popular of modern times in collector polls. To match Topps' larger-format cards, Bowman increased the size of its cards from the previous two years. They brought Joe DiMaggio out of retirement to plug the set by picturing him on the wrapper where he tells kids to "Collect them, trade them, save them." But most important of all, Bowman gave collectors something no other company had: actual color photographs. All previous color cards had been either artists' paintings or colorized photos. Collectors then and now responded to the '53 Bowman Color set in record numbers. Because of the high production cost in those days, Bowman trimmed the number of cards to just 160. However, they managed to retain a good number of stars. The design of the '53 set is straightforward: there is nothing on the front of the card except the gorgeous color photo. (Bowman did not minimize the impact of this baseball card milestone by cluttering the front with type or other design elements.) A black line inside a white border surrounds the photo. The card backs also prove that Bowman recognized the challenge from Topps. For the first time, Bowman included previous season and lifetime stats. An interesting innovation—one that hasn't been copied—was a blank line beneath the two lines of stats labeled "This Year" for the collector to write in the player's current year stats. The rest of the card back contains the usual combination of personal information and a short career summary. The card number appears in a baseball diamond in the upper left. There are three degrees of scarcity in the set: cards #1-#112 are the most common, cards #129-#160 are scarce, and cards #113-#128 are the hardest to find.

FOR

The '53 Bowman Colors have virtually everything going for them, including gorgeous color photos, attractive backs, and a large size.

AGAINST

There are no bad points to this set.

NOTEWORTHY CARDS

While Bowman lost a lot of stars to Topps and others, their set did have the last nationally issued Stan Musial card until 1958. Another innovation Bowman unveiled was the multiplayer card, which was last used in the 19th century. Bowman had two such cards in '53 featuring New York Yankees. One card featured the double-play combination of Phil Rizzuto and Billy Martin. The other card had sluggers Mickey Mantle, Yogi Berra, and Hank Bauer pictured in the dugout. While these two cards were well-received, collectors generally don't attach a high value to multiple player cards. There is a wrong-photo card in the set: Mickey Vernon's card (#159) is actually Floyd Baker. (Baker appears on his own card in the '53 Bowman Black-and-White set.)

OUR FAVORITE CARD

Though he never appeared on another baseball card, the major league career of Jack Daniels has been preserved forever. Known to his teammates as "Sour Mash," the outfielder had a single-season career with the '52 Boston Braves. By the time his '53 Bowman card had been issued, he was back in the minors for good. Daniels was a .187 hitter, but with a great name like that, he deserved at least one baseball card.

VALUE

EX-MT CONDITION: Complete set, $7,000; common card #1-#112, $17; #129-#160, $25; #113-#128, $30; stars, $20–$35; Hall of Famers, $35–$100; Pee Wee Reese, Rizzuto/Martin, $125–$150; Roy Campanella, Martin, Bob Feller, $150–$200; Musial, Whitey Ford, Bauer/Berra/Mantle, $350–$400; Berra, Duke Snider, $400–$425; Mantle, $900. 5-YEAR PROJECTION: Above average.

1953 BOWMAN BLACK-AND-WHITE

SPECIFICATIONS

SIZE: 2½ × 3¾". FRONT: Black-and-white photograph. BACK: Red and black printing on cream-colored cardboard. DISTRIBUTION: Nationally, in packages with bubblegum.

1953 Bowman Black-and-White, Johnny Mize

HISTORY

The 1953 Bowman Black-and-White set was a separate issue from the Bowman Color cards of the same year. They came in a different wrapper and are numbered #1-#64. In format, however, the cards are identical. There is a large photo on the front of the card, surrounded by a black line inside a white border; no other printing or design elements appear. The card backs are also identical, with player information, stats, and a space to write in the '53 season's performance at the bottom. The biggest difference between the two issues (besides the color) is that the 1953 Bowman Black-and-Whites are somewhat scarcer than the color cards. There are no known scarcities or variations in the set.

FOR

While they suffer in comparison with the '53 Bowman Colors, the Black-and-White set is attractive in its own right.

AGAINST

The set is relatively expensive per card for a '50s issue.

NOTEWORTHY CARDS

There are only five Hall of Famers in this set: Casey Stengel, Bob Lemon, Bucky Harris, Johnny Mize, and Hoyt Wilhelm. There are, however, lots of popular stars such as Jimmy Piersall, Ralph Branca, Billy Cox, Andy Pafko, Johnny Sain, and Preacher Roe.

VALUE

EX-MT CONDITION: Complete set, $2,000; common card, $20; stars, $35–$55; Mize, Lemon, Wilhelm, $75–$90; Stengel, $250. 5-YEAR PROJECTION: Average.

1953 RED MAN

SPECIFICATIONS

SIZE: 3½ × 4″. FRONT: Color painting. BACK: Red printing on gray cardboard. DISTRIBUTION: Nationally, one card in each box of chewing tobacco.

HISTORY

Red Man retained the same basic format in 1953 that they had used in their premier issue of 1952. The set again had 52 cards: 25 players from the A.L. and N.L. along with 1952 World Series managers Casey Stengel and Charlie Dreesen. The players for the two squads were chosen by J. Taylor Spink, editor of *The Sporting News.* Spink's selections look impressive to today's hobbyists because the cards contain a high percentage of superstars and Hall of Famers. Card fronts feature a color painting of the player. A white box in the upper corner contains a card number, player data, and a biography. At the bottom, below a dotted line, is a narrow white tab that contains the year, player name, and card number. Once again, the cards are numbered #1-#26 by league. Because the tab indicated the year of issue, it is sometimes hard to differentiate the '53 and '54 Red Man issues without it. (It is possible to tell the year of issue by the mention of the previous season's performance in the write-up.) A person could receive a major league team cap by sending in 50 tabs. Although the caps were quite popular, collectors prefer cards with the tabs intact. A complete card is worth 25 percent more than a card with the tab removed.

1953 Red Man, Johnny Mize

FOR

The 1953 Red Mans are a low-priced, attractive set with lots of superstars.

AGAINST

The cards are hard to find with the tabs intact. Collectors don't like recycled pictures. Cards are not standard size.

NOTEWORTHY CARDS

Ted Williams and Willie Mays were both in the service in 1953, and neither appear in the Red Man set. The biggest name in the set is Stan Musial. Several new players make an appearance.

VALUE

EX-MT CONDITION: Complete set (without tabs), $475; common card, $5; Hall of Famers, $25–$35; Roy Campanella, $40; Musial, $55. 5-YEAR PROJECTION: Above average.

1953-1954 BRIGGS HOT DOGS

SPECIFICATIONS

SIZE: 2¼ × 3½". FRONT: Colorized photograph. BACK: Blank. DISTRIBUTION: Washington, DC, one 2-card panel printed as part of hot dog packages.

1953-1954 Briggs Hot Dogs, Frank Shea

HISTORY

It is generally believed that the 37-card Briggs hot dog set was issued over a period of two years. The unnumbered, blank-backed cards contain 25 Washington Senators and 12 players from the New York Giants, Yankees, and Dodgers. An interesting note is that the pictures of the New York players are the same as those found on the 1954 Dan-Dee potato chip issue and the 1953-1955 Stahl Meyer hot dog issue. The card front features a borderless color picture of the player. On the Senators cards, the player's name, position, birth date, birthplace, and personal data appear in a white panel below the photo along with a blue facsimile autograph. The cards of the New York players have only the player's printed name and a black facsimile autograph in the white box. The Briggs cards were issued in pairs as the bottom of a hot dog package. Complete 2-card panels are worth 25 to 30 percent more than the individual cards.

FOR

The set is in demand by team collectors, especially the Senators, who were the subject of few regional issues.

AGAINST

The use of shared photos with other sets makes the New York players' cards less desirable and less valuable than they would normally be.

NOTEWORTHY CARDS

Among the Senators, Jackie Jensen and Mickey Vernon are the only big names. The New York cards contain lots of popular stars.

VALUE

EX-MT CONDITION: Complete set (neatly cut from panels), $6,000; common card, $100; stars, $175–$250; Duke Snider, $350; Willie Mays, $800; Mickey Mantle, $1,500. 5-YEAR PROJECTION: Below average.

1953 STAHL MEYER

SPECIFICATIONS

SIZE: 3¼ × 4½". FRONT: Colorized photograph. BACK: Red printing on white cardboard. DISTRIBUTION: New York, one card in packages of hot dogs.

HISTORY

Three of the most popular players from each of the New York teams—the Yankees, Dodgers, and Giants—are featured in the baseball card set from the Stahl Meyer meat company in 1953. The round-cornered cards feature a photograph of the player on the front. The colorization process was excellent. Below the photo is a rectangular box with a facsimile autograph and a printed version of his name. A white border surrounds the entire card. The unnumbered card backs are in a horizontal format. On the left is a player biography along with '52 and lifetime batting and fielding stats. The right

1953 Stahl Meyer, Duke Snider

side carries an offer for free tickets to specified New York ball games. In order to win a pair of tickets, you had to mail in a 25-word essay and two of the Stahl Meyer baseball cards.

FOR
The set features scarce, good-looking cards of some of the better-known players of the 1950s.

AGAINST
The combination of scarcity and popular players adds up to high cost.

NOTEWORTHY CARDS
The Yankees in the set are Hank Bauer, Mickey Mantle, and Phil Rizzuto; Dodgers: Roy Campanella, Gil Hodges, and Duke Snider; Giants: Monte Irvin, Whitey Lockman, and Bobby Thomson.

VALUE
EX-MT CONDITION: Complete set, $2,750; Lockman, Bauer, Thomson, $100–$125; Irvin, Rizzuto, Hodges, $200; Campanella, Snider, $450; Mantle, $1,500. 5-YEAR PROJECTION: Below average.

1953 JOHNSTON COOKIE BRAVES

SPECIFICATIONS
SIZE: 2⁹⁄₁₆ × 3⁵⁄₁₆″. FRONT: Colorized photograph. BACK: Blue and red printing on gray cardboard. DISTRIBUTION: Wisconsin, single cards in packages of cookies.

1953 Johnston Cookie Braves, Warren Spahn

HISTORY
One of several companies to welcome the Boston Braves to Milwaukee with a baseball card issue was the Johnston baking company. In 1953 Johnston issued a 25-card set featuring 24 of the Braves players and manager Charlie Grimm. The card fronts feature attractive photographs. In a box below the photo, the player's name is printed along with a facsimile autograph. At the left of the box is a red Indian chief logo. Card backs have the traditional mix of player personal information, stats from the two previous seasons, and a baseball biography taken right out of the Braves' yearbook. The outline of a tomahawk (similar to those on their jerseys that year) have the team name and the card number. The cards were numbered in an unusual manner: card #1 was manager Grimm; cards #2-#12 were the pitchers, in alphabetical order; card #13 was utility player Sibby Sisti; and cards #14-#25 were the fielders, by position. At the bottom of the card back was a Johnston ad. The backs were attractive because of the use of red and blue ink. The 1953 Johnston cards were

inserted individually into each package of cookies and are by far the most common of the three sets issued by the firm.

FOR
It is an attractive, relatively inexpensive regional set of a very popular team.

AGAINST
Nothing negative can be said about the set.

NOTEWORTHY CARDS
Hall of Famers Warren Spahn and Eddie Mathews highlight this set.

VALUE
EX-MT CONDITION: Complete set, $150; common card, $4; stars, $6–$10; Mathews, Spahn, $25–$30. 5-YEAR PROJECTION: Average.

1953 HUNTER'S WIENERS CARDINALS

SPECIFICATIONS
SIZE: 2¼ × 3½″. FRONT: Color photograph. BACK: Blank. DISTRIBUTION: St. Louis, one 2-card panel on each package of hot dogs.

1953 Hunter's Wieners Cardinals, Harvey Haddix

HISTORY
Hunter's Wieners was one of many meat companies that printed baseball cards right on the cardboard used to package hot dogs. The 1953 set was the first of three successive issues by the company, all featuring the St. Louis Cardinals. The round-cornered cards have a color photo of the player. The player's name and brief biographical details appear in a white panel at the bottom with a facsimile autograph printed in light blue. The unnumbered card backs are blank. The '53s are the most common of the three Hunter's issues, but they are still quite scarce—especially in Excellent condition. Cards still attached to the package are more valuable, but are seldom found this way. Like most issues packaged with meat products, the cards picked up grease stains. Also, since the cards were meant to be separated from the bottom of the package, they are often found unevenly cut.

FOR
The cards feature excellent, unique color photos.

AGAINST
The cards are hard to find in neatly trimmed condition.

NOTEWORTHY CARDS
With a price more than ten times that of a common card in the set, Stan Musial is the premier card among the '53 Hunter's.

VALUE
EX-MT CONDITION: Complete set (neatly trimmed from panels), $2,400; common card, $65; Red Schoendienst, $125; Enos Slaughter, $175; Musial, $750. 5-YEAR PROJECTION: Average.

1953 GLENDALE MEATS TIGERS

SPECIFICATIONS
SIZE: 2⅝ × 3¾″. FRONT: Colorized photograph. BACK: Blue and red printing on white cardboard. DISTRIBUTION: Detroit, single cards in packages of hot dogs.

HISTORY
The 20-card Glendale Meats Tigers set was issued in 1953, although some hobbyists insist they were issued in 1954. None of the players traded to the Tigers in late '53 or early '54 are included in the set, and the stats on the card backs only go through '52. The card front features a colorized player photo.

1953 Glendale Meats Tigers, Ned Garver

Below the photo is a white box with his name, facsimile autograph, and a color Tigers logo. The unnumbered card back has personal data and career stats, along with an ad offering prizes to those who mailed in the cards at the end of the year. (That probably explains why surviving cards are so scarce.) The set is popular with Tigers team collectors. Art Houtteman's card is among the scarcest modern baseball cards.

FOR

This hard-to-find, valuable regional issue is great for team collectors.

AGAINST

The rarity of the Houtteman card makes completing a set virtually impossible. The Tigers didn't have many stars in 1953.

NOTEWORTHY CARDS

The only big name in the set is Harvey Kuenn, who appears on his rookie card. The Houtteman card was apparently withdrawn (or never issued) when he was traded in June 1953. To a lesser extent, the Joe Ginsberg and Billy Hoeft cards are also scarcer than the other cards.

VALUE

EX-MT CONDITION: Complete set, $4,100; common card, $95; Kuenn, Hoeft, $200; Ginsberg, $300; Houtteman, $1,800. 5-YEAR PROJECTION: Below average.

1953 MOTHER'S COOKIES

SPECIFICATIONS

SIZE: $2\frac{1}{4} \times 3\frac{1}{2}$". FRONT: Colorized photograph. BACK: Black printing on white cardboard. DISTRIBUTION: West Coast, single cards in packages of cookies.

1953 Mother's Cookies, Stan Hack

HISTORY

The 63-card Pacific Coast League set was the last set to be issued by Mother's Cookies for 30 years. It is very similar to the '52 issue, though most of the players are different. The '53 cards have rounded corners and feature a photo set against a borderless solid-color background. The background color is different for each team. The player's name appears as a facsimile autograph. The team name was printed in the upper right. The card backs carry an offer for an album to house the cards, along with previous season stats for the player and the card number. The '53 set is more common than the '52 set and contains no known variations. The cards were distributed in bags of Mother's and Family cookies. Complete sets are frequently found today.

FOR

They are a nice addition to minor league card sets from the early '50s.

AGAINST

The format is too similar to the '52 issue and the set has few big-name stars. The solid-color background is prone to chipping.

NOTEWORTHY CARDS

George Bamberger, Stan Hack, and Lefty O'Doul are the best-known players in the set.

VALUE

EX-MT CONDITION: Complete set, $400; common card, $6; O'Doul, Bamberger, $13. 5-YEAR PROJECTION: Average.

1952 TOPPS

SPECIFICATIONS

SIZE: 2⅝ × 3¾″. FRONT: Color painting. BACK: Red and/or black printing on gray cardboard. DISTRIBUTION: Nationally, in packages with bubblegum.

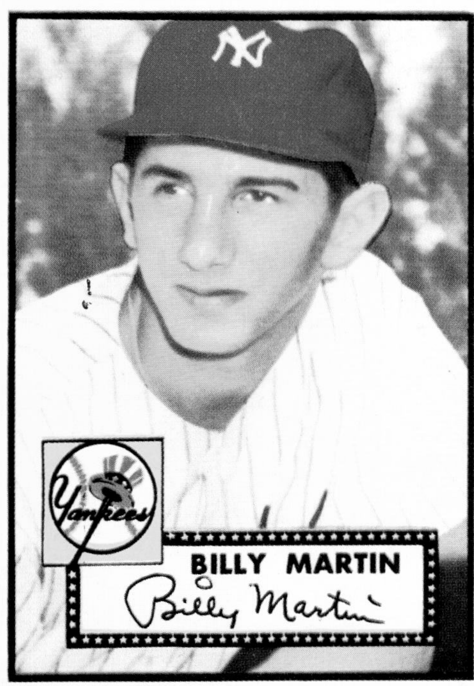

1952 Topps, Billy Martin

HISTORY

When Topps came out with their first major baseball card set in 1952, they went right after Bowman. Collectors still disagree as to which set was better, but no one doubted that Topps was bigger. At 407 cards, Topps outnumbered Bowman by 155 cards. And the cards themselves are bigger as well (2⅝ × 3¾″ versus Bowman's 2$\frac{1}{16}$ × 3⅛″). In the long run, the '52 Topps proved to be more valuable, too. Card fronts feature a color painting of the player framed in a white box with a thin black rule. Toward the bottom of the card, the player's printed name along with a facsimile autograph appear in a white box framed by a black rule with yellow stars in it. A significant innovation was the use of a color team logo on the card front—the first time this was ever done in a major set. Card backs have the player's name, vital information, a short biography, and previous season and lifetime stats. The card number appears in a baseball toward the top of the card. Not all of the cards were issued or distributed equally. The most common of the set are cards #81-#252. Only a bit less common are cards #1-#80. Cards #253-#310 (the semi-high numbers) are scarcer, while cards #311-#407 (the high numbers) are the hardest to find. Cards #253-#407 were printed and issued later in the year after the annual spring rush was over. Most stores did not restock the high-numbered cards; they were issued so late in the summer that collectors were already thinking about football cards. The distribution of the high-numbered cards was very limited—many of the cards were released in Canada. The difficulty of locating these makes collecting a complete 1952 set challenging and very expensive. Because Topps cards were printed on sheets of 100 cards each, a certain number of them were double-printed, which means that some are twice as common as others. The three double-printed cards in the high-number series are Mickey Mantle, Jackie Robinson, and Bobby Thomson. Even today, because of the scarcity of full or partial uncut sheets, most collectors have no idea what cards in a particular year or series were double-printed. Surprisingly, there is little price difference between single- and double-printed cards in a set or series; the value still depends on the condition of the card and the player on it. A color variation exists on the back of the first 80 cards. Those cards can be found with black printing only or with red and black printing. The black-backed cards are scarcer than those with red backs, but few collectors attach any premium to them. The '52 Topps set was so popular with collectors that Topps reprinted them in 1983.

FOR

Most collectors consider the '52 set to be the first real Topps set, and it is widely collected as such. The large-format cards allowed for an attractive design on the front and decent write-ups and stats on the back. Completing a set is challenging enough to keep even the most avid collector searching for a long time. The '52 Topps set has proved to be among the finest investments of all baseball card sets.

AGAINST

For a large number of collectors, completing the set is little more than a fantasy. The high-numbered cards are truly scarce and expensive (especially in top condition). The cards aren't getting any cheaper.

NOTEWORTHY CARDS

Mickey Mantle's card (#311) is the most famous and expensive card in the 1952 Topps set. While it wasn't his first card (he appeared in the 1951 Bowman set), it was his first Topps card and a lot of hobbyists collect nothing but Topps cards. Even though the card was double-printed, it is more than twice as popular as the other cards, and the value continues to climb. There are dozens of other superstars in the '52 set. One major variation in the set: Joe Page's card (#48) was printed with a Johnny Sain back and Sain's card (#49) was printed with a Page back. The cards can also be found with the correct backs. Ben Chapman's card (#391) features a portrait of Sam Chapman.

OUR FAVORITE CARD

Locating a Mint condition card #1 is extremely difficult with cards from the '50s and '60s. In the days before plastic sheets, most collectors rubber-banded their cards, usually in numerical order. The top card tended to receive the most abuse in terms of bent corners and creases. Also, the rubber band had a tendency to dig into the cardboard creating indentations that collectors call "notching." In the '52 Topps set, Andy Pafko's card (#1) is a rare item in Mint condition (four sharp corners, no creases, and no scuffs on the card front).

VALUE

EX-MT CONDITION: Complete set, $38,000; common card, #1-#80, $48; #81-#250, $17; #251-#310, $40; #311-#407, $135; stars, $90–$150; superstars, $200–$250; Pafko, Pee Wee Reese, Hoyt Wilhelm, Bill Dickey, $400–$550; Willie Mays, Robinson, $600–$900; Roy Campanella, $1,100; Eddie Mathews, $1,500; Mantle, $6,500. 5-YEAR PROJECTION: Above average.

1952 BOWMAN

SPECIFICATIONS

SIZE: $2\frac{1}{16} \times 3\frac{1}{8}$". FRONT: Color painting. BACK: Black printing on gray cardboard. DISTRIBUTION: Nationally, in packages with bubblegum.

1952 Bowman, Mickey Mantle

HISTORY

The 1952 Bowman set follows a format similar to the 1951 issue. Players on the card fronts are depicted in paintings made from photographs. Unlike the '51 set, none of the paintings are repeats from previous years. For that reason, the '52 set has greater collector appeal than the earlier issues. The only other difference is that the player's name on the '52 cards appears as a facsimile autograph rather than in print. The card backs are also quite similar to the '51s. The player's name and vital data appear at the top and there is a short career biography at center. The card number appears in three lines of type reading, "No. xx in 1952 SERIES/ BASEBALL/PICTURE CARDS." Beneath that is an offer for a major league baseball cap available for 50¢ and five gum wrappers. A copyright line is at the bottom. (An interesting note: there is a registered trademark symbol next to the word "BASEBALL" on the backs of the cards. That little symbol figured prominently in the early "Card Wars" between Bowman and its new competitor, Topps. Bowman went to court contending that they alone had the legal right to use the word "baseball" in conjunction with bubblegum cards. The court disagreed and Topps was allowed to advertise its product as "baseball cards" also.) The number of 1952 Bowman cards was cut from the previous year's 324 to 252. Like many sets from the '50s and '60s, the high-numbered cards (#217-#252) are scarcer than the rest of the cards, and more expensive.

FOR

The '52 Bowman issue is an appealing set of well-done, all-new paintings. There are no confusing variations.

AGAINST
There's nothing bad to be said about this set.

NOTEWORTHY CARDS
Ted Williams and Jackie Robinson are notably absent from the set. Williams appeared that year in the Red Man tobacco card issue, and Robinson appeared in the '52 Topps set. This was the last year Bowman had virtually uncontested use of players' pictures in their card sets. From '53 to '55, they would have to fight with Topps for exclusive rights to the big-name stars.

OUR FAVORITE CARD
One of baseball's greatest nicknames is preserved in the autograph on card #20 in the 1952 Bowman set. Willie Jones' signature is reproduced on the card as "Puddin Head Jones." Jones' card is one of the handful of horizontal cards in the set.

VALUE
EX-MT CONDITION: Complete set, \$6,350; common card, #1-#216, \$10; #217-#252, \$16; minor stars, \$15–\$20; Hall of Famers, \$25–\$50; Roy Campanella, Duke Snider, Casey Stengel, Frank Crosetti, \$85–\$100; Stan Musial, \$300; Yogi Berra, \$375; Willie Mays, \$600; Mickey Mantle, \$1,200. 5-YEAR PROJECTION: Above average.

1952 Red Man, Stan Musial

1952 RED MAN

SPECIFICATIONS
SIZE: 3½ × 4". FRONT: Color painting. BACK: Green printing on gray cardboard. DISTRIBUTION: Nationally, one card in packages of chewing tobacco.

HISTORY
After more than 40 years had passed since tobacco products used baseball cards as premiums, the Red Man chewing tobacco company began using them in 1952. Each cellophane-wrapped box of Red Man contained one of 52 "All-Star" cards. There were 25 players for each league, plus cards for the 1951 World Series managers, Casey Stengel and Leo Durocher. According to the wording on the back of the card, the players for the set were selected by J. Taylor Spink, editor of *The Sporting News.* The card front features a borderless color painting of the player with either a blank background or a stadium background. Some cards feature portraits that were used on previous issues with only the color of the background being changed. In one of the upper corners, the player's name appears in red in a white box, along with a couple of lines of personal data and a career summary. A white tab at the bottom has the card number along with the year of issue. On cards without tabs, the player's write-up on the previous season is helpful in determining the year of issue. The Red Man cards are numbered #1-#26 by league. Card backs have Red Man advertising and details of a baseball cap offer. One of the most prominent features on the Red Man cards (and one that greatly affects their value) is the white tab at the bottom of the card beneath the player's picture. The tab was designed to be cut off and mailed in to receive "a big league style baseball cap" of your favorite team. Fifty tabs had to be collected for each cap, and the majority of Red Man cards today are without the tab. Complete cards are worth about 25 percent more than cards without the tab. Though the Red Man cards are sometimes considered a regional set, they were issued nationwide.

FOR
Because of the variety of teams represented and the high percentage of big-name stars, the Red Man set is one of the more popular of the 1950s. The portraits are well-done and a nice change from the usual photos found on cards of the era. Considering their scarcity in comparison to Topps or Bowman cards of '52, they are quite inexpensive.

AGAINST

So few '52 Red Mans exist with the tabs intact that collecting a complete set in this form is too challenging for most collectors, even though the cost is not that high. Use of the same pictures for successive issues makes the cards unpopular with some collectors.

NOTEWORTHY CARDS

Ted Williams' best 1952 baseball card is in the Red Man set; he didn't appear in Topps' or Bowman's set that year, and his card in the Berk Ross set is unattractive. In comparison with later Red Man issues, the 1952 set is somewhat lean on superstars, but does include more than a dozen Hall of Famers.

VALUE

EX-MT CONDITION: Complete set (without tabs), \$500; common card, \$4.50; stars, \$8–\$12; Hall of Famers, \$15–\$35; Willie Mays, Stan Musial, \$50; Williams, \$75. 5-YEAR PROJECTION: Above average.

1952 WHEATIES

SPECIFICATIONS

SIZE: 2 × 2¾″. FRONT: Blue line drawing. BACK: Blank. DISTRIBUTION: Nationally, eight or ten cards printed on backs of cereal boxes.

1952 Wheaties, Bob Lemon

HISTORY

The 30 athletes in the 1952 Wheaties set include 10 baseball players. All 30 appear in both portrait and action cards. The round-cornered cards have a white border surrounding a blue line drawing on an orange background. The player's name, team, and position appear at the bottom. The unnumbered card backs are blank. Though Wheaties had been issuing sports card sets on the backs of cereal boxes since 1935, this 60-card set is the only widely collected Wheaties issue.

FOR

These are inexpensive cards for the superstar collector.

AGAINST

The line drawings make the cards seem antiquated. Collectors generally don't like sets in which baseball players are mixed with other athletes.

NOTEWORTHY CARDS

Hall of Famers in the set are Yogi Berra, Roy Campanella, Bob Feller, George Kell, Ralph Kiner, Bob Lemon, Stan Musial, and Ted Williams. The other two baseball players are Preacher Roe and Phil Rizzuto. There are many well-known football players and women athletes among the rest of the cards.

VALUE

EX-MT CONDITION: Complete set of 20 baseball player cards (neatly cut from box), \$400; common card, \$7; Hall of Famers, \$12–\$25; Williams, Musial, \$35–\$45. 5-YEAR PROJECTION: Average.

1952 BERK ROSS

SPECIFICATIONS

SIZE: 2 × 3″. FRONT: Tinted photograph. BACK: Black printing on white cardboard. DISTRIBUTION: Nationally, two cards packaged in a small box.

1952 Berk Ross, Johnny Mize

HISTORY

In its second and final year of baseball card production, Berk Ross continued to emulate the Bowman sets. Nothing else was changed from their 1951 issue except they included only baseball players this year. The 72-card set features 71 different players: there are two cards of Phil Rizzuto—one bunting, one swinging. Card backs are almost identical to the previous year's effort and have a few lines of type with the player's name, team, position, personal info, and previous season stats. The set is unnumbered. In comparing the 1952 Berk Ross cards with the Bowman cards of the same year, they finish a poor second. While some of the same photos of players were used in both companies' sets, the Berk Ross tinting method resulted in drab-looking cards.

FOR

The Berk Ross set has more of 1952's superstars than either Bowman or Topps. There is an abundance of players from the 1951 World Champion New York Yankees.

AGAINST

The cards are unattractive and there is little demand for them, even for the superstars.

NOTEWORTHY CARDS

Even though he retired after the 1951 season, Joe DiMaggio appears in the '52 Berk Ross set as one of many New York Yankees. Also in the set are second-year cards of Mickey Mantle and Willie Mays. Stan Musial appears again, and there are cards of Ted Williams and Jackie Robinson. There are two error cards in the set: Ewell Blackwell's card has a Nellie Fox back; and Fox's card has a Blackwell back.

VALUE

EX-MT CONDITION: Complete set, $2,400; common card, $9; stars, $25–$50; Musial, Robinson, $150; Mays, Williams, $250; DiMaggio, $450; Mantle, $700. 5-YEAR PROJECTION: Average.

1952 NUM NUM INDIANS

SPECIFICATIONS

SIZE: 3½ × 4½″. FRONT: Black-and-white photograph. BACK: Black printing on white cardboard. DISTRIBUTION: Cleveland, in packages of potato chips and also team-issued.

HISTORY

Two versions of this set were issued in 1952. Cards with a one-inch tab at the bottom were issued in packages of Num Num potato chips. Cards without the tab were issued directly by the team. The card fronts have a black-and-white player photo with a white border. The card backs have a card number along with the player's life story. The tabs also had a card number. When a collector acquired a set of 20 cards, they could be redeemed for an official American League ball autographed by their favorite Indians player. The tab was separated from the rest of the card by a dotted line. Complete cards are worth about 25 percent more than cards without the tab.

FOR

This reasonably priced regional issue is great for team collectors.

AGAINST

The set was issued in an unpopular size.

NOTEWORTHY CARDS

The heart of the Indians team that took the A.L. pennant in 1954 is present in this set including Hall of Fame pitchers Bob Feller, Bob Lemon, and Early Wynn. Bob Kennedy's card (#16) is much scarcer than the rest because it was withdrawn when he left the team to spend most of the season in the service.

VALUE

EX-MT CONDITION: Complete set (without tabs), $600; common card, $15; Hall of Famers, $40–$60; Kennedy, $250. 5-YEAR PROJECTION: Below average.

1952 FROSTADE

SPECIFICATIONS

SIZE: 2 × 2½″. FRONT: Black-and-white photograph. BACK: Red printing on white cardboard. DISTRIBUTION: Canada, in packages of soft drink mix.

HISTORY

One of the few regional baseball card sets issued in Canada, the 1952 Frostade set contains 100 cards and features players of Canada's three teams in the Triple-A International League: the Montreal Royals, Ottawa Athletics, and Toronto Maple Leafs. The set includes many players who were major leaguers. An unusual aspect of the set is that it features 22

1952 Frostade, Walt Moryn

playing tips cards and a card of the Toronto stadium. The card front has a black-and-white photo surrounded by a black line inside a white border. The unnumbered card backs, printed in red, have a few facts about the player, a mail-in offer for various toys, and a Frostade ad.

FOR

The set is challenging to complete for a minor league set.

AGAINST

The cards are hard to find in the U.S. Many collectors only want cards of players in major-league uniforms.

NOTEWORTHY CARDS

The most popular card belongs to Dodger manager Tommy Lasorda: he was a pitcher for Montreal in the Dodgers' organization. Other big names include Walter Alston, Jim Gilliam, Jim Pendleton, Gino Cimoli, and Johnny Podres.

VALUE

EX-MT CONDITION: Complete set, $750; common card, $6; minor stars, $8–$12; Alston, Lasorda, $25.
5-YEAR PROJECTION: Average.

1952 MOTHER'S COOKIES

SPECIFICATIONS

SIZE: 2¼ × 3½". FRONT: Colorized photograph.
BACK: Black printing on white cardboard.
DISTRIBUTION: West Coast, single cards in packages of cookies.

1952 Mother's Cookies, Stan Hack

HISTORY

The Mother's Cookies Pacific Coast League 64-card issue of 1952 included all the teams in the league. The cards were packaged in bags of cookies and are often found with grease stains. The round-cornered cards feature borderless, colorized photographs. (Borderless cards from this era tend to be prone to chipping.) The background on the card is color-coded to a specific team. The player's name appears in small type at the upper left, and his team is in the upper right. The card backs feature a number at the top and a few lines of player data.

FOR

These are attractive cards that feature many players who were in the major leagues. Some of them don't appear on any other baseball card issue.

AGAINST

Collectors don't like round-cornered cards.

NOTEWORTHY CARDS

Several cards in the set are scarce, probably because they were withdrawn when the players were traded or demoted. The cards of Joe Erautt and Buddy Peterson are the scarcest. Some well-known players appear in the set as managers including Frank O'Doul, Mel Ott, and Stan Hack. Chuck Connors' card (#4) is the most sought-after card in the set. Connors, who went on to greater fame as a TV star, was a first baseman for the Los Angeles Angels. He played briefly with the Cubs and the Dodgers in the major leagues before leaving baseball for Hollywood.

VALUE
EX-MT CONDITION: Complete set, $1,100; common card, $10–$12; stars, $15–$25; Ott, $65; Peterson, Erautt, $100; Connors, $120. 5-YEAR PROJECTION: Average.

1951 BOWMAN

SPECIFICATIONS
SIZE: $2\frac{1}{16} \times 3\frac{1}{8}''$. FRONT: Color painting. BACK: Red and blue printing on gray cardboard. DISTRIBUTION: Nationally, in packages with bubblegum.

1951 Bowman, Willie Mays

HISTORY
Bowman's 324-card 1951 set was their largest issue up to that date. Bowman also made the individual cards larger, moving to a size that would be used for two years. Some of the player paintings that had appeared in the previous set were used in an enlarged version for this year. The only other change for '51 was the addition of the player's name in white in a black box. The card backs are vertical in format and feature the basic lineup of player personal data, a short biography, card number, and Bowman copyright line. Bowman continued to print its cards in 36-card sheets. The final 72 cards (#253-#324) are scarcer than the first 252. Bowman became the first company of the postwar era to issue a card for every major league manager as part of its regular set.

FOR
This set is a popular starting point for many collectors; it was the first of Bowman's larger-format sets. The paintings are attractive and the set is not too difficult to complete.

AGAINST
There are too many recycled pictures from the 1950 set.

NOTEWORTHY CARDS
The rookie cards of Mickey Mantle and Willie Mays appear in the high-number series. Whitey Ford's rookie card is the first card in the set. George Kell's card back reads "No. 46 in the 1950 SERIES," rather than 1951. White Sox manager Paul Richards' card is unusual because it features a caricature instead of a painting.

VALUE
EX-MT CONDITION: Complete set, $12,500; common card, #1-#252, $10; #253-#324, $33; stars, $25–$60; Hall of Famers, $125–$150; Yogi Berra, $250; Ted Williams, $350; Ford, $700; Mays, $1,200; Mantle, $5,200. 5-YEAR PROJECTION: Above average.

1951 TOPPS RED BACKS

SPECIFICATIONS
SIZE: $2 \times 2\frac{5}{8}''$. FRONT: Black-and-white photograph. BACK: Red printing on white cardboard. DISTRIBUTION: Nationally, in 2-card panels.

1951 Topps Red Backs, Maurice McDermott

HISTORY
The most common of Topps' five baseball card issues for 1951, the 52-card Red Backs were designed to be used to play a game of baseball. In addition to a player photo set in a baseball diamond in the center of the card, the front of each round-cornered card featured the player's name, a short write-up, and a card number. Also appearing in diagonal corners were such baseball terms as "OUT," "WALK," "BALL," or "DOUBLE."

Card backs contain no information; only a design featuring crossed bats, a baseball diamond, four baseballs with the word "official" in them, and a few pennants at the top and bottom. The cards were meant to be shuffled, stacked, and turned over one at a time to simulate a baseball game. Topps most likely issued these cards to avoid a court fight with Bowman, who at that time held the exclusive right to market current baseball players' cards with bubblegum. (The two companies' legal battles continued until 1955 when Topps bought out Bowman.) The Red Backs were presumably packaged with the Connie Mack All-Star and Major League All-Star card sets of 1951. They were issued in panels of two cards, perforated for easy separation. A large supply of cards—complete in the original boxes—was discovered in a Philadelphia warehouse several years ago. Cards, wrappers, and boxes are currently available in top condition at reasonable prices. The similar Topps Blue Backs were found mixed in with the Red Backs in this supply, indicating that the two had been circulated at about the same time.

FOR

The cards are currently available at reasonable prices.

AGAINST

It's a good thing they were produced by Topps; collectors aren't generally interested in game-style baseball cards.

NOTEWORTHY CARDS

The big names include Yogi Berra, Bob Feller, Warren Spahn, Gil Hodges, and Duke Snider. Gus Zernial's card (#36) exists with either a Philadelphia or Chicago designation—he was traded to the Athletics from the White Sox at the beginning of the season. Tommy Holmes' card (#52) can be found with either a Boston (Braves) or Hartford designation—after a nine-year major league career with Boston, he opened the '51 season as a player/manager with the Braves' Hartford minor league team in the Eastern League. On June 20, 1951, Holmes was recalled to Boston to fill in as an outfielder.

VALUE

EX-MT CONDITION: Complete set, $400; common card, $3–$4; stars, $5–$15; Hall of Famers, $15–$20; Zernial, $16; Holmes, Feller, $20; Snider, $30; Berra, $35. 5-YEAR PROJECTION: Average.

1951 TOPPS BLUE BACKS

SPECIFICATIONS

SIZE: 2 × 2⅝″. FRONT: Black-and-white photograph. BACK: Blue printing on white cardboard. DISTRIBUTION: Nationally, in 2-card panels.

1951 Topps Blue Backs, Johnny Mize

HISTORY

Identical in design, set size (52 cards), and game format to the Topps Red Backs of the same year, the '51 Blue Backs are much scarcer and quite challenging to complete. The large supply of Red Backs discovered in a warehouse a few years ago contained only a small number of Blue Backs packaged in what appeared to be leftover Red Backs wrappers. The two sets were originally issued differently. Both types of cards were sold two to a pack; however, the wrapper for the Blue Backs stated "Baseball Candy" while the Red Backs wrapper made no mention of gum or candy. Like the Reds, the Blues have various baseball terms printed on the front allowing a simulated game to be played. Because the cards were printed on thick cardboard and have rounded corners, they have held up quite well over the years and are often found in top condition.

FOR

They represent good value for the money in terms of scarcity, but that means demand for the issue will someday increase.

AGAINST

They're not very attractive, they're a peculiar size, and collectors don't generally care for game cards.

NOTEWORTHY CARDS

There are some big-name stars in the Blue Backs set, most notably Hall of Famers Johnny Mize, Enos Slaughter, and Bobby Doerr.

VALUE

EX-MT CONDITION: Complete set, $1,100; common card, $16–$18; stars, $25–$35; Doerr, Slaughter, Mize, $40–$50. 5-YEAR PROJECTION: Average.

1951 TOPPS CONNIE MACK ALL-STARS

SPECIFICATIONS

SIZE: 2¹⁄₁₆ × 5¼″. FRONT: Black-and-white photograph. BACK: Red printing on white cardboard. DISTRIBUTION: Nationally, presumably in packages with 1951 Topps Red Backs.

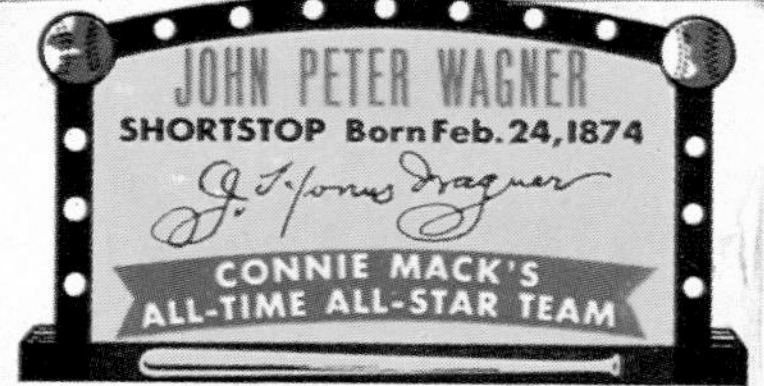

1951 Topps Connie Mack All-Stars, Honus Wagner

HISTORY

The 11-card 1951 Connie Mack All-Stars set features Hall of Famers in a black-and-white action pose set against a red background. The plaque at bottom of the card is in red, white, blue, yellow, and black and contains the player's name, position, facsimile autograph, year of birth and (when applicable) death, and a banner reading "Connie Mack's All-Time All-Star Team." The cards are unnumbered. It is not yet known how these cards were originally sold. The wax wrappers state "Baseball Trading Card Candy." The candy may have been bubblegum or a piece of caramel. It is known that these large die-cut cards were packaged with an uncut pair of Topps Red Backs in 1951. (It is quite likely that they were also packaged alone, one card to a pack.) Despite the fact that collectors usually stay away from cards depicting retired players, the Connie Mack All-Stars are a scarce and popular issue. These cards are quite similar to the "Batter Up" cards of 1934-1936. The cards were die-cut so that most of the red background could be removed and the card could be folded to create a stand-up figure. Collectors prefer cards with the background intact. Complete cards are worth about twice as much as cards without the background.

FOR

These attractive cards of baseball's greats are quite scarce.

AGAINST

The players are not contemporary. It is hard to complete a set in nice condition.

NOTEWORTHY CARDS

All of the players are Hall of Famers: Grover Alexander, Mickey Cochrane, Eddie Collins, Jimmy Collins, Lou Gehrig, Walter Johnson, Connie Mack, Christy Mathewson, Babe Ruth, Tris Speaker, and Honus Wagner.

VALUE

EX-MT CONDITION: Complete set (with background intact), $3,450; common card, $100–$125; Johnson, Alexander, $330–$400; Gehrig, $750; Ruth, $950. 5-YEAR PROJECTION: Average.

1951 TOPPS MAJOR LEAGUE ALL-STARS

SPECIFICATIONS

SIZE: 2¹⁄₁₆ × 5¼″. FRONT: Black-and-white photograph. BACK: Blue printing on white cardboard. DISTRIBUTION: Nationally, presumably in packages with candy or gum.

1951 Topps Major League All-Stars, Ralph Kiner

HISTORY

This 11-card set is often referred to as Major League All-Stars to differentiate it from the similar Connie Mack All-Stars of the same year. The method of distribution of the set is unclear, although it has been assumed that the cards were issued at the same time as the Connie Mack All-Stars in the same type of wrapper. Like the Connie Macks, the unnumbered All-Stars cards were die-cut so the card could be folded and made to stand up. The card front features a black-and-white photograph of a current all-star. At the bottom of the card is a plaque in red, white, blue, yellow, and black with the player's biographical sketch. While the Major League All-Stars set officially consists of 11 cards, only eight of them were actually issued. It is likely that ongoing legal battles with Bowman over players' contracts resulted in withholding the cards of Jim Konstanty, Robin Roberts, and Eddie Stanky. The cards of these players are among the rarest of legitimate baseball card issues (fewer than 5 each are known to exist). The rest of the set is also quite scarce. Collectors prefer unfolded cards with the background intact. Complete cards are worth about twice as much as those without the background.

FOR

These are truly scarce cards depicting star players in an attractive format.

AGAINST

They are hard to find in nice condition.

NOTEWORTHY CARDS

Of the eight regularly issued cards, four are Hall of Famers: Yogi Berra, George Kell, Ralph Kiner, and Bob Lemon. Phil Rizzuto, Hoot Evers, Larry Doby, and Walt Dropo are the other four.

VALUE

EX-MT CONDITION: Complete set of eight cards (with background intact), $2,900; common card, $150; Dropo, $250; Kell, Kiner, Lemon, Rizzuto, $400; Berra, $600; Roberts, Konstanty, Stanky, $5,000. 5-YEAR PROJECTION: Average.

1951 TOPPS TEAM CARDS

SPECIFICATIONS

SIZE: 5¼ × 2¹⁄₁₆″. FRONT: Black-and-white photograph. BACK: Red printing on white cardboard. DISTRIBUTION: Nationally, presumably in packs with 1951 Connie Mack All-Stars and Major League All-Stars.

HISTORY

As was the case with Topps' four other baseball card issues of 1951, there is some question as to how this set was distributed. The Team Cards are the same size as the Connie Mack All-Stars and the Major League All-Stars. Also, they were packaged in the same wax wrappers as the All-Star cards. Whether they were included in packages with the All-Stars and/or Red Backs is not known. The Team Cards depict nine of the 16 major league teams of the day: the Boston Red Sox, Brooklyn Dodgers,

1951 Topps Team Cards, Brooklyn Dodgers

Chicago White Sox, Cincinnati Reds, New York Giants, Philadelphia Athletics, Philadelphia Phillies, St. Louis Cardinals, and Washington Senators. The card front features an entire team photo surrounded by a yellow border. The team name appears in white type in a black box. The unnumbered card back identifies the players on the front. Two versions of each card are known to exist: with and without the date "1950" in the black box on the front. Neither variety is more scarce than the other and demand for the two is about equal. The cards are quite hard to find and remain among the more popular of the '51 Topps issues. After this set it would be another five years before Topps again produced team cards.

FOR

This set was innovative for the early '50s. The large format works well when picturing entire teams.

AGAINST

The set is incomplete because it doesn't include all 16 teams.

VALUE

EX-MT CONDITION: Complete set, $1,200; Phillies, Senators, Reds, Athletics, $120; Dodgers, White Sox, Giants, $150; Cardinals, Red Sox, $200. 5-YEAR PROJECTION: Below average.

1951 BERK ROSS

SPECIFICATIONS

SIZE: 2 1/16 × 2 1/2". FRONT: Tinted photograph. BACK: Black printing on white cardboard. DISTRIBUTION: Nationally, one 2-card panel packaged in a small box.

HISTORY

Berk Ross relied on the success of Bowman baseball cards for its "Hit Parade of Champions" set in 1951. The cards are the same size as the 1948-1950 Bowmans and they use a number of the photographs that Bowman paintings were based on. The card fronts are devoid of any printing. The similarity ends there, however, for the Berk Ross cards are of poor quality. The photographs are heavily retouched and the tinting method produced drab-looking cards. The card backs contain the player's name and a few biographical and career details. The 72 cards are numbered in four groups of 18 (#1-1 to #1-18, #2-1 to #2-18, #3-1 to #3-18, and #4-1 to #4-18). An innovation was the inclusion of many different sports stars in the set. While 40 of the 72 cards were baseball players; football and basketball players, boxers, golfers, and a few women athletes also appear. The two cards in each box were perforated for easy separation. Collectors generally don't care whether the cards are still attached, but complete 2-card panels are worth about 10 percent more. The Berk Ross cards never achieved any great acclaim, and they are not particularly popular with collectors.

1951 Berk Ross, Yogi Berra

FOR

The cards are available for a low cost.

AGAINST

Mixing of sports in a card set is unpopular. The cards are unattractive.

NOTEWORTHY CARDS

Berk Ross scored quite a coup in 1951 by featuring a Joe DiMaggio card in his last season; it was DiMaggio's first card since the 1948 Leaf set. Stan Musial appeared in only two baseball card sets in 1951—Wheaties and Berk Ross. The set also features a good number of the 1950 Philadelphia Phillies "Whiz Kids," who took the N.L. pennant the previous year. The nonbaseball players in the set include Bob Cousy, Ben Hogan, Sugar Ray Robinson, Dick Button, and Jesse Owens.

VALUE

EX-MT CONDITION: Complete set, $300; common card (nonbaseball), $2.50; common card (baseball), $4.50; stars, $10–$15; Musial, $35; DiMaggio, $65. 5-YEAR PROJECTION: Below average.

1950 BOWMAN

SPECIFICATIONS

SIZE: $2\frac{1}{16} \times 2\frac{1}{2}$". FRONT: Color painting. BACK: Red and black printing on cream-colored cardboard. DISTRIBUTION: Nationally, in packages with bubblegum.

1950 Bowman, Casey Stengel

HISTORY

By increasing the number of cards to 252, Bowman was able to print the entire 1950 set in seven sheets of 36 cards each without having to reprint cards from earlier series. Although the '50 Bowmans maintained the same dimensions of the '48 and '49 sets, there was a major change in the design. Working from black-and-white photographs, artists created color portraits of each player. The result was a far more pleasing product than the heavily retouched photos used in 1949. Every card in the 1950 set is a work of art. The horizontal card backs contain a five-star circular Bowman logo with the words "Picture Card Collectors Club" in the upper right. In the upper left is the player's name, position, and team. Personal data appears below along with a brief player write-up. The card number is at the bottom. Cards #181-#252 can be found with or without a Bowman copyright, but collectors do not value one version over the other. Like most card sets of the '50s, '60s, and '70s, the 1950 Bowmans were not printed in equal quantities. However, the scarce cards in this set are not the high-numbered cards, but rather #1-#72. Unfortunately for today's collectors, most of the big-name stars in the '50 Bowman set appear in the first 72 cards. The beauty of this set helped Bowman develop the collector loyalty they would soon need to face competition from Topps.

FOR

This set was one of the most attractive, least complicated, and least expensive of Bowman's early issues.

AGAINST

It's hard to say anything bad about this set.

NOTEWORTHY CARDS

Ted Williams joined the Bowman lineup for 1950. Hall of Famer Luke Appling appears on his last card as an active player. Bowman started a trend by featuring cards of selected nonplaying managers that included Hall of Famer Casey Stengel, Leo Durocher, and Frank Frisch. An unusual aspect and one of the few drawbacks is that there are no noteworthy rookie cards.

VALUE

EX-MT CONDITION: Complete set, $5,875; common card, #73-#252, $9; #1-#72, $20; stars, $20–$35; Hall of Famers, $30–$50; Pee Wee Reese, Bob Feller, $95; Mel Parnell, Duke Snider, Roy Campanella, $150–$175; Yogi Berra, $225; Williams, Jackie Robinson, $350. 5-YEAR PROJECTION: Above average.

1950 DRAKE'S

SPECIFICATIONS

SIZE: 2½ × 2½". FRONT: Black-and-white photograph. BACK: Black printing on gray cardboard. DISTRIBUTION: New York, inserted in packages of bakery products.

1950 Drake's, Warren Spahn

HISTORY

The popularity of the television was used by Drake's in their 1950 design. The 36-card set features a black-and-white photo of the player in a round-cornered white frame (as if being viewed on a TV screen). A white strip at the top of the black border reads "TV Baseball Series." The card back features the usual player data, career summary, card number, and a Drake's ad. This regional set is among the scarcer issues of the early '50s. It was Drake's only baseball card issue until 1981 when they began their annual "Big Hitters" series. In 1955, Bowman would adapt a similar style for its color card set; but in 1950, the Drake's issue must have seemed quite clever.

FOR

The innovative set features many stars of the era.

AGAINST

The black-and-white cards seem outdated in an era when virtually every regional set was using color.

NOTEWORTHY CARDS

The 36 players in the set are mainly from New York and Boston teams and include many popular stars of the day like Roy Campanella, Duke Snider, Warren Spahn, Pee Wee Reese, and Yogi Berra.

VALUE

EX-MT CONDITION: Complete set, $2,000; common card, $35; Hall of Famers, $100–$125; Berra, Snider, Campanella, $200–$250. 5-YEAR PROJECTION: Below average.

1950 REMAR BAKING COMPANY

SPECIFICATIONS

SIZE: 2 × 3". FRONT: Black-and-white photograph. BACK: Blue printing on white cardboard. DISTRIBUTION: Oakland, with purchases of bread.

1950 Remar Baking Company, George Bamberger

HISTORY

The 27-card 1950 set was the last issue from the Remar Baking Company. The set features the Pacific Coast League Oakland Oaks. The cards follow the same format and, in some cases, use the same pictures as the 1949 set. The only way to differentiate between issues is to check the stats on the card backs. The card fronts feature a black-and-white photograph in a white border with the player's name and position listed below. The card backs carry previous season's stats, player data, and ads for the bakery and a local radio station. Unlike the '49 issue, the '50 Remar cards were equally distributed and contain no known scarcities.

FOR
It is an easy set for the regional collector to complete.

AGAINST
It is too easily confused with the 1949 set.

NOTEWORTHY CARDS
There are no real big names in the 1950 Remar set, although Cookie Lavagetto, George Bamberger, Chuck Dressen, and Billy Herman would become major league managers.

VALUE
EX-MT CONDITION: Complete set, $100; common card, $2–$3; stars, $5–$10. 5-YEAR PROJECTION: Below average.

1950-1956 CALLAHAN HALL OF FAME

SPECIFICATIONS
SIZE: 1¾ × 2½″. FRONT: Black-and-white drawing. BACK: Black printing on white cardboard. DISTRIBUTION: Cooperstown, New York, sold in sets at the Baseball Hall of Fame.

HISTORY
This 82-card set was issued over a period of seven years by the Baseball Hall of Fame. The initial group of more than 60 cards was distributed in 1950. Every year, when new baseball figures were elected, cards were produced to update the set. Besides the enshrined players, managers, and executives, the set included cards of then-baseball commissioner Happy Chandler, and interior and exterior drawings of the Hall of Fame building. The card front features a black-and-white glossy line drawing of the player in a simple black frame with a white border. The unnumbered card back contains a detailed baseball biography of the player. Several biographical variations are known to exist. These cards were discontinued in favor of new sets of postcards, which the Hall of Fame has been selling at its souvenir shop.

FOR
The fact that they were issued by the Hall of Fame makes them more desirable than most "old-timers" baseball card issues. The black-and-white drawings are excellent.

AGAINST
Their small size is a negative. They are complete only through the mid-1950s.

NOTEWORTHY CARDS
Mickey Cochrane's card can be found with his name spelled correctly and also spelled "Cochran."

VALUE
EX-MT CONDITION: Complete set, $300; common card, $1–$5; superstars, $5–$8; "Cochran," $10; Ty Cobb, Lou Gehrig, $20; Joe DiMaggio, Babe Ruth, $50. 5-YEAR PROJECTION: Below average.

1950 WORLD WIDE GUM

SPECIFICATIONS
SIZE: 3¼ × 2½″. FRONT: Blue-and-white photograph. BACK: Blank. DISTRIBUTION: Canada, in packages with bubblegum.

HISTORY
The Canadian-issued World Wide Gum cards of 1950 are the last legacy of the Goudey Gum company. (World Wide was the brand name under which Goudey cards had been issued in Canada in the '30s.) The 48-card set consists of players from the International League and includes many future and former major leaguers. The card fronts are horizontal with a blue-and-white photo of the player at the left. At the right is a column of type with the player's name and team. Below that (in English and French) are the player's position, personal data, and career summary. The card number is at the bottom along with the words "Big League Stars."

FOR
It's an interesting multi-team minor league set.

AGAINST
The cards are not particularly attractive.

NOTEWORTHY CARDS
Minor league pitcher Tommy Lasorda appears in the set. The most popular card belongs to Lasorda's teammate, Chuck Connors. Connors is best remembered for his part in the TV series *The Rifleman.*

VALUE
EX-MT CONDITION: Complete set, $850; common card, $15; minor stars, $20–$25; Lasorda, $75; Connors, $100. 5-YEAR PROJECTION: Below average.

1949 TO 1940

1948 Bowman, Johnny Mize

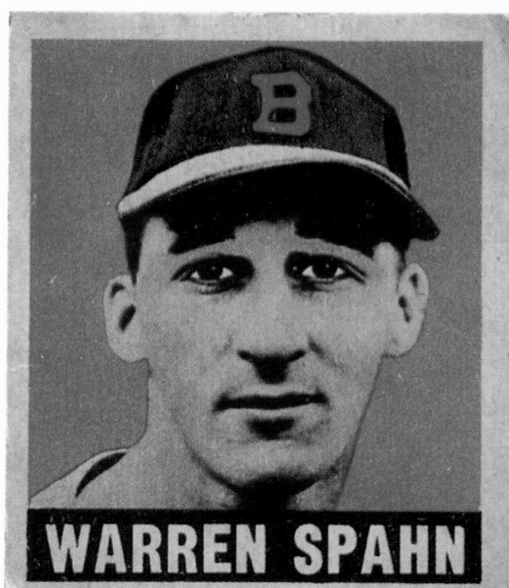

1948 Leaf, Warren Spahn

1941 Play Ball, Joe DiMaggio

1949 BOWMAN

SPECIFICATIONS

SIZE: 2 1/16 × 2½″. FRONT: Colorized photograph. BACK: Red and blue printing on cream-colored cardboard. DISTRIBUTION: Nationally, in packages with bubblegum.

1949 Bowman, Satchel Paige

HISTORY

After its premier issue of 48 cards in 1948, Bowman really hit its stride in '49 with one of the largest baseball card issues up to that time—240 cards. The 1949 Bowmans retained the nearly square format of the previous year, but the black-and-white photos were colorized and set against a solid-color background instead of a stadium background. Most low-number cards (#1-#108) have backgrounds in bright colors like red, blue, and orange; the high-number cards (#109-#240) are in pastel colors. The high numbers include the player's name on the card front in a thin white strip toward the bottom of the card; most low-number cards do not (those that do are from a second printing). All 240 cards feature the same basic information on back: a card number, a few personal facts about the player, a short career write-up, and a premium offer. Cards #1-#108 (as well as a handful of the later cards) have the player's name in printed form, while most cards #109-#240 have a facsimile autograph. The 1949 Bowman set was produced in seven series of 36 cards each, and the last three series (#145-#240) are much more scarce than the other four. In addition to the 96 "new" cards in the last three series, the company reprinted a dozen cards from the earlier series with some changes. Cards #4, #78, #83, #85, #88, and #98 were printed in the later series with the names on the front of the card, while cards #109, #124, #126, #127, #132, and #143 had the name on the back changed from a facsimile autograph to a printed name. Since these 12 cards can be found in early-series versions, they are not as valuable as the rest of the high numbers since most hobbyists do not collect the variations.

FOR

The 1949 Bowman set has historical value because it was the first large-scale baseball card issue of modern times. It includes many players of the 1940s who don't appear in other sets.

AGAINST

The colorization doesn't look that great. The 96 high numbers make assembling a complete set expensive. The varieties can be confusing.

NOTEWORTHY CARDS

Virtually all of the major stars of the day appear in the 1949 Bowman set, with the exception of Joe DiMaggio and Ted Williams, who were apparently under exclusive contract with the Leaf gum company. The rookie cards of Hall of Fame hurler Robin Roberts and outfielder Duke Snider appear in the set. One wrong-photo card is of special interest. Norman "Babe" Young's card (#240) shows a head-and-shoulders portrait of a New York Yankees player. The photo is actually Bobby Young, who was a St. Louis Cardinals rookie in 1948, but spent the 1949 season in the minors. Since Babe Young's middle name was Robert, the mistake is understandable. What is hard to fathom is why the player is in a Yankees uniform, since neither player ever played for that team.

OUR FAVORITE CARD

Within a few days after the cards were issued in 1949, many collectors had managed to acquire most of the first 71 cards of the set. But no matter how many packs of gum you bought, or how many flips you won, you could never seem to find card #4. (In the days before checklist cards nobody even knew which player they were looking for.) Later in the summer, card #4 finally showed up, and nobody was very excited to find out it was Gerry Priddy, the second baseman of the St. Louis Browns. Later it was found by examining uncut 36-card sheets that the place that should have held card #4 was held by card #73, Billy Cox, and card #4 wasn't printed until later. It seems that Bowman didn't want it to be too easy to complete the first run of 72 cards, so they deliberately withheld #4.

VALUE

EX-MT CONDITION: Complete set, $11,000; common card, #1-#144, $10; #141-#240, $45–$50; stars, $25–$45; Roberts, Johnny Mize, Larry Doby, $75–$80; Yogi Berra, Bob Lemon, $125–$150; Richie Ashburn, Roy Campanella, Stan Musial, $300; Jackie Robinson, $400; Snider, $700–$750; Satchel Paige, $900. 5-YEAR PROJECTION: Average.

1949, 1951 ROYAL DESSERT

SPECIFICATIONS

SIZE: 3½ × 2½″. FRONT: Black-and-white photograph. BACK: Blank. DISTRIBUTION: Nationally, on the back of boxes of pudding and gelatin desserts.

1949, 1951 Royal Dessert, Andy Pafko

HISTORY

The baseball player and movie star cards issued on the backs of Royal pudding and gelatin dessert boxes were the predecessors of the Jell-O cards of the early '60s. The Royal dessert sets included 24 ballplayers, along with popular movie stars. The card features a black-and-white photo on the left with a facsimile autograph. There is a red strip at the top with the card number. A player biography is at the top right, and in the lower right is an ad for an album to house the cards. Some cards have been found with an advertising message on the back; these were distributed as promotional items for the set. The Royal cards were issued in two years, 1949 and 1951. The '51 set notes team changes for a couple of the players who were traded during that period. The biographies on the right side of the card were also updated in '51 and give a clue to the year of issue.

FOR

It was a forerunner of the more popular Jell-O cards of the 1960s.

AGAINST

The cards are of poor quality and are quite scarce.

NOTEWORTHY CARDS

The Hall of Famers in the set are Stan Musial, Pee Wee Reese, George Kell, Warren Spahn, and Luke Appling.

VALUE

EX-MT CONDITION: Complete set (neatly cut from box), $700; common card, $10–$12; Hall of Famers, $20–$40; Musial, $100. 5-YEAR PROJECTION: Average.

1949 BOWMAN PACIFIC COAST LEAGUE

SPECIFICATIONS

SIZE: $2\frac{1}{16} \times 2\frac{1}{2}$″. FRONT: Colorized photograph. BACK: Red and blue printing on cream-colored cardboard. DISTRIBUTION: West Coast, single cards in packages with bubblegum; uncut sheets sold in stores.

1949 Bowman Pacific Coast League, Maurice Van Robays

HISTORY

One of the scarcest modern baseball card issues is the 36-card 1949 Bowman Pacific Coast League set. In the years before the Dodgers and Giants moved from New York to California, the Pacific Coast League was a virtual third major league, populated with players who were on their way to the majors, on their way down from the majors, or who did not want to leave the West Coast to play ball in the East. The Bowman Pacific Coast League set is identical in format to the regular 1949 Bowman set. Colorized photographs were set against a bright, solid-color background, surrounded by a white border. There is no name or other printing on the front of the card. Backs are also quite similar to the regular Bowman set, except the card number at the top is preceded by "PCL." The player's name, position, and team appear below the card number, along with personal data and a short career summary. Nearly the entire bottom half of the card is taken up with one of several premium offers, which could be obtained for a few cents and gum wrappers. The 1949 Bowman PCL cards were sold in penny packages with bubblegum, but the complete set in uncut sheet form could also be bought at dimestores. Many of the surviving cards have ragged borders from being cut off the sheets. Strangely, not a single example of an uncut sheet is known to have survived—further proof of the rarity of this popular set.

FOR

This scarce issue features many players not found in other sets. It is the ultimate modern set for collectors of minor league cards.

AGAINST

The colorization wasn't very well done and looks heavy-handed.

NOTEWORTHY CARDS

Many of the players in the '49 Bowman set played in the majors, but there are no real stars.

VALUE

EX-MT CONDITION: Complete set, $5,000; common card, $150. 5-YEAR PROJECTION: Below average.

1949 REMAR BAKING COMPANY

SPECIFICATIONS

SIZE: 2×3″. FRONT: Black-and-white photograph. BACK: Blue printing on white cardboard. DISTRIBUTION: Oakland, single cards with purchases of bread.

HISTORY

After a one-year hiatus, Remar was back in 1949 with a 32-card set of the Oakland Oaks of the Triple-A Pacific Coast League. The '49 set is similar to the '47 issue, but the photo on the card front is surrounded by a white border. The player's name and position are printed below the photo, but the card number from '47 is gone. The card backs were changed a little for '49. Vital stats and 1948 season performance figures replaced the player biography, while the ads for a local radio station and Sunbeam bread remained.

1949 Remar Baking Company, Chuck Dressen

FOR

This scarce, popular set includes some good players from the PCL.

AGAINST

Uneven distribution resulted in scarce cards, which makes it difficult to complete a set.

NOTEWORTHY CARDS

Twelve cards are scarcer than the rest. Billy Martin and Jackie Jensen appear in the set.

VALUE

EX-MT CONDITION: Complete set, $175; common card, $3–$4; scarce card, $10; Jensen, $15; Martin, $30. 5-YEAR PROJECTION: Below average.

1949 SOMMER & KAUFMANN SAN FRANCISCO SEALS

SPECIFICATIONS

SIZE: 2×3″. FRONT: Black-and-white photograph. BACK: Black printing on white cardboard. DISTRIBUTION: San Francisco, in clothing stores.

1949 Sommer & Kaufmann San Francisco Seals, Bert Singleton

HISTORY

Almost identical to the 1948 issue, the '49 set issued by Sommer & Kaufmann clothing stores includes 28 cards of the San Francisco Seals of the Triple-A Pacific Coast League. The best way to tell the two sets apart is to examine the backs. The 1948 cards have the words "BOYS' SHOP" above the Sommer & Kaufmann logo; the 1949 set does not. The card front features a borderless black-and-white photo of the player taken at Seals Stadium. Below the photo is a white strip with the player's name, position, and card number. Besides the store ad, the card back includes a short biography of the player. The 1949 Sommer & Kaufmann set is quite scarce.

FOR

It is another good-looking regional PCL set of the 1940s.

AGAINST

The cards are easily confused with the 1948 issue.

NOTEWORTHY CARDS

The set features two well-known players of the 1930s: Lefty O'Doul, who managed the Seals in 1949; and Arky Vaughan, who was playing in the minors after a distinguished 14-year major league career.

VALUE

EX-MT CONDITION: Complete set, $600; common card, $15–$20; Vaughan, O'Doul, $35. 5-YEAR PROJECTION: Below average.

1948 BOWMAN

SPECIFICATIONS

SIZE: 2 1/16 × 2 1/2". FRONT: Black-and-white photograph. BACK: Black printing on gray cardboard. DISTRIBUTION: Nationally, one card in packages with bubblegum.

1948 Bowman, Yogi Berra

HISTORY

The Philadelphia-based Bowman company entered the baseball card market in 1948 with a 48-card set. Within a year, Bowman had achieved such dominance that it had the national baseball card market all to itself. A determined program of signing players to contracts to appear on its cards left potential competitors with little subject matter for a competing issue. The '48 Bowman set, though, was a modest beginning. The company chose a small, squarish format for its cards, along the lines of the Goudey issues of the 1930s and the competing Leaf gum issue of 1948. Unlike those cards, though, which used artists' drawings or colorized photos, the '48 Bowmans featured a black-and-white photo of the player, with no printing or other design elements. The photo was bordered in white. The backs of the 1948 Bowmans have the card number, player's name, position, and team at top, followed by personal data and a short baseball biography. The bottom third of the card is an ad for Bowman's "Blony" brand gum. Because the early Bowman baseball cards were printed in sheets of 36 cards, and the 1948 issue consists of 48 cards, there is a group of 12 cards that were short-printed and are scarcer today than the other 36. This premier Bowman issue is a major baseball card milestone. Many collectors consider it a perfect point at which to begin their collections since the set features many of the players who would go on to greatness in the '50s and '60s, before entering the Hall of Fame.

FOR

Bowman's rookie year cards have a simple, appealing design using unretouched ballpark photos. The set, with the 12 scarce cards, is challenging, but not all that expensive.

AGAINST

The black-and-white design on a 1948 baseball card issue is a throwback to cards of the 1920s.

NOTEWORTHY CARDS

For a set of only 48 cards, there is a remarkably high percentage of Hall of Famers in the set. There are seven of them—Ralph Kiner, Johnny Mize, Bob Feller, Yogi Berra, Warren Spahn, Stan Musial, and Enos Slaughter—and two more who probably will someday be elected—Phil Rizzuto and Marty Marion. The 12 short-printed cards in the set are: Pete Reiser (#7), Rizzuto (#8), Willard Marshall (#13), Jack Lohrke (#16), Buddy Kerr (#20), Floyd Bevins (#22), Dutch Leonard (#24), Frank Shea (#26), Emil Verban (#28), Joe Page (#29), Whitey Lockman (#30), and Sheldon Jones (#34).

OUR FAVORITE CARD

The 1948 Bowman set contains the first baseball card of Emil Verban. It's one of the dozen short-printed cards in the set. Emil Verban is not exactly a household name in the world of baseball, though in seven major league seasons the second baseman accumulated a respectable lifetime .272 average, and a .412 average in the 1944 World Series. No, Emil Verban is a symbol of futility. The official organization for long-suffering Chicago Cubs fans is called "The Emil Verban Society," and numbers among its members former President Ronald Reagan. Verban played for the Cubs from mid-1947 to mid-1950 and is representative of the suffering of fans who have been waiting since 1945 for a pennant.

VALUE

EX-MT CONDITION: Complete set, $1,900; common card, $10–$20; short-printed cards, $30; stars, $35–$50; Spahn, Feller, $80; Rizzuto, $125; Berra, $200–$225; Musial, $350. 5-YEAR PROJECTION: Above average.

1948-1949 LEAF

SPECIFICATIONS

SIZE: 2⅜ × 2⅞″. FRONT: Colorized photograph. BACK: Black printing on gray cardboard. DISTRIBUTION: Nationally, in packages with bubblegum.

1948-1949 Leaf, Stan Musial

HISTORY

The premier Leaf baseball card issue was unusual in that it was issued in late 1948 and early 1949, rather than in the spring as has become traditional with baseball cards. Because Babe Ruth, who died in August 1948, is the only noncoaching, noncontemporary player in the set, it is assumed that the 1948-1949 Leafs were released sometime after his death. Some of the cards carry a 1948 copyright date, others have a 1949 copyright. The set was the first baseball card issue of the post-WWII era to use color, though by today's standards the color is rather drab. Black-and-white photographs of the players were colorized and set against solid-color backgrounds. A colored strip at the bottom of the photo has the player's name in white letters. Leaf chose the nearly square format that Goudey gum cards had made popular in the 1930s. Except for the inclusion of the name on the bottom of the card, the 1948-1949 Leaf cards closely resemble those issued later in 1949 by Bowman. (In its later series, Bowman also added the player's name to the front of its cards.) Card backs have the player's name and card number at the top, and also include a brief biography of the player and one of three premium offers. For ten gum wrappers, the collector could get a 5 × 7″ photo; for five wrappers and a dime, a felt pennant; and five wrappers and a quarter got the collector a 32-page album. While the set contained only 98 cards, it was skip-numbered to #168. The premium offer on the back of some cards states that the album, "Can display 168 different Baseball cards." By not issuing 70 cards, Leaf kept collectors looking for nonexistent cards to complete their collections; this was in the days before checklists. There are two degrees of scarcity within the 1948-1949 Leaf set: exactly half of the cards are considerably scarcer than the rest. A detailed checklist is necessary to tell which is which. In general, the Leaf cards are scarcer than the contemporary Bowman issue.

FOR

It is a challenging set for collectors of modern-era cards, with many big stars who did not appear in Bowman's sets of 1948 and 1949.

AGAINST

The cards are not very attractive. The 49 scarce cards are hard to find and very expensive.

NOTEWORTHY CARDS

Leaf was able to give collectors something Bowman, its larger and ultimately more successful competitor, could not: baseball cards of Joe DiMaggio, Ted Williams, and Jackie Robinson. These are just three of the superstars who appear in the Leaf issue. Two big names among the scarce-series cards are Satchel Paige and Bob Feller. Two variation cards appear in the Leaf set: Gene Hermanski's card (#102) can be found with his name spelled "Hermansk", and Cliff Aberson's card (#136) can be found with long blue jersey sleeves painted on or with short sleeves.

OUR FAVORITE CARD

Often, when the story of the hobby's most famous baseball card (the T-206 cigarette card of Honus Wagner) is told, the reason cited for the withdrawal and subsequent rarity of the card is Wagner's "opposition to tobacco use." Actually, it was only smoking that Wagner was opposed to, not chewing, as well as not being paid royalties for use of his picture by the cigarette company. In the 1948-1949 Leaf set, Wagner, then a coach for the Pittsburgh Pirates, is shown on card #70 stuffing his jaw with chewing tobacco.

VALUE

EX-MT CONDITION: Complete set, $13,500; common series, $13–$14; scarce series, $180; Hall of Famers, $50–$75; Wagner, $135; "Hermansk," $150; Stan Musial, Robinson, $175–$200; Dom DiMaggio, Larry Doby, Williams, $225–$250; George Kell, Enos Slaughter, $375–$400; Joe DiMaggio, Feller, $600–$650; Ruth, $800; Paige, $1,000. 5-YEAR PROJECTION: Average.

1948 SWELL SPORTS THRILLS

SPECIFICATIONS

SIZE: 2½ × 3″. FRONT: Black-and-white photograph. BACK: Black printing on gray cardboard. DISTRIBUTION: Nationally, one card in packages with bubblegum.

1948 Swell Sports Thrills, Pee Wee Reese

HISTORY

One of the few baseball card sets depicting game-action photographs rather than posed portraits, the Sports Thrills set was one of two issued in 1948 by the Philadelphia Chewing Gum Corporation in packages of its Swell brand bubblegum. The 20-card set features a news photo of a baseball highlight on the front, while the back recounts the details in story form. The set mixed current players with former players and leaned heavily on the Brooklyn Dodgers. Many of the highlights are drawn from World Series or All-Star Games, like Ted Williams' game-winning three-run homer in the ninth inning of the '41 All-Star Game, and Al Gionfriddo's catch in the '47 World Series which robbed Joe DiMaggio of a three-run homer and caused a seventh game to be played. Others recall baseball feats like Lou Gehrig's four homers in a game and Johnny Vander Meer's back-to-back no-hitters. Although the set is not a popular collectible, many superstar collectors try to obtain a card of their favorite player.

FOR
The set is an interesting change from single player cards and can spice up a superstar collection. The cards are much scarcer than their prices would indicate.

AGAINST
Some collectors have an aversion to cards that don't show a simple portrait shot of the featured player.

NOTEWORTHY CARDS
Many of the plays depicted in the Sports Thrills set involve stars like Williams, Babe Ruth, Gehrig, Jackie Robinson, Pee Wee Reese, and others. Other cards in the set depict some of baseball's best-remembered moments, which are certainly worth seeing again.

OUR FAVORITE CARD
Card #12 in the set supposedly depicts Ruth's famous "called shot" home run in the 1932 World Series when he pointed to the spot in the stands where he would land the next pitch. The fact is, no photograph exists of that famous bit of baseball folklore. Many of the Chicago Cubs on the field that day—as well as some of Ruth's own teammates—deny that he ever made such a gesture. Indeed, most agree that if Cubs pitcher Charlie Root (a notorious "purpose" pitcher) had thought Ruth was challenging him, the Babe would have taken the next pitch in the ear. Photos of Babe pointing like the one on the Sports Thrills card are after-the-fact shots recreated for the photographers.

VALUE
EX-MT CONDITION: Complete set, $500; common card, $12; superstars, $25–$35; Ruth, Gehrig, Williams, $90–$135. 5-YEAR PROJECTION: Below average.

1948 BABE RUTH STORY

SPECIFICATIONS
SIZE: 2 × 2½". FRONT: Black-and-white photograph. BACK: Black printing on gray cardboard. DISTRIBUTION: Nationally (?), one card in packages with bubblegum.

1948 Babe Ruth Story

HISTORY
This 28-card set was an unabashed attempt to cash in on the August 1948 death of Babe Ruth, and the subsequent movie *The Babe Ruth Story* starring William Bendix and released in 1949. The set is one of only two baseball card issues produced by Philadelphia Chewing Gum Corporation, which is better known for its football card issues of the early '60s. Some of the cards are scenes from the movie, while some feature the actors with baseball players (including Babe Ruth) on the movie set. Cards #1-#16 are about twice as common as cards #17-#28. Unfortunately, only one of the common cards (#1) pictures the real Babe Ruth. The rest of the cards picturing Ruth (and other baseball players) are in the scarce high-number series. The card back has an advertisement for the movie, a cast of characters, and a story describing the action shown.

FOR
The set includes Babe's last contemporary cards.

AGAINST
Most of the cards show an actor portraying a baseball player. Almost all of the cards of real players are in the scarce high-number series.

NOTEWORTHY CARDS
Besides the cards featuring Babe Ruth (#1, #25, #26, #27, and #28), Hall of Famers Ted Lyons, Bucky Harris, and Lefty Gomez, along with Charlie Grimm, are also pictured in the set.

VALUE
EX-MT CONDITION: Complete set, $600; common card, #2-#16, $8; #17-#28, $24; real player cards, $30–$40; Ruth cards, $35–$75. 5-YEAR PROJECTION: Below average.

1948 SIGNAL OIL

SPECIFICATIONS

SIZE: 2⅜ × 3½″. FRONT: Colorized photograph. BACK: Black or blue printing on white cardboard. DISTRIBUTION: Oakland, at gas stations.

1948 Signal Oil, Cookie Lavagetto

HISTORY

Unlike their 1947 issue, the 24-card 1948 Signal Oil set includes members of the Triple-A Pacific Coast League Oakland Oaks. The card front features a borderless colorized player photograph. There is no other printing on the front. The card back has the player's name and position, along with a short baseball biography and ads for Signal and a local radio station.

FOR

One of the more attractive 1940s PCL regional issues.

AGAINST

Many collectors aren't interested in minor league cards.

NOTEWORTHY CARDS

The most noteworthy cards are of Billy Martin and his mentor Casey Stengel. Also included are Merrill Coombs, Cookie Lavagetto, and Ernie Lombardi. There is a card of the team's radio announcer, Bud Foster.

VALUE

EX-MT CONDITION: Complete set, $325; common card, $10; Martin, $50; Stengel, $60. 5-YEAR PROJECTION: Below average.

1948 SMITH'S CLOTHING

SPECIFICATIONS

SIZE: 2 × 3″. FRONT: Black-and-white photograph. BACK: Black printing on white cardboard. DISTRIBUTION: Oakland, at clothing stores.

CHARLES (Casey) STENGEL
Oaks Manager 20

1948 Smith's Clothing, Casey Stengel

HISTORY

The 1948 Smith's set is considerably more collectible than their premier issue of '47. The 25-card 1948 set again features the Oakland Oaks of the Triple-A Pacific Coast League. The format closely follows that of the 1947 set. A borderless black-and-white player photograph appears on the card front. Beneath the photo is a white strip containing the player's name, position, and card number. The card back has a short write-up of the player, along with an ad for the clothing store. Although the store's picture and logo are different from the ones used in '47, the easiest way to differentiate between the two issues is the "Union-made" logo on the back of the '48 cards in the lower left. This set was printed on much heavier cardboard than the previous issue.

FOR

It is one of the more collectible and least expensive of the popular PCL sets of the late 1940s.

AGAINST

The format is too similar to other issues on the West Coast during the same time.

NOTEWORTHY CARDS

While there are several former and future major leaguers in the set, the only especially valuable cards are those of Oaks manager Casey Stengel and Billy Martin.

VALUE

EX-MT CONDITION: Complete set, $275; common card, $10; Martin, $35; Stengel, $50. 5-YEAR PROJECTION: Below average.

1948 SOMMER & KAUFMANN SAN FRANCISCO SEALS

SPECIFICATIONS

SIZE: 2 × 3″. FRONT: Black-and-white photograph. BACK: Black printing on white cardboard. DISTRIBUTION: San Francisco, at clothing stores.

1948 Sommer & Kaufmann San Francisco Seals, Lefty O'Doul

HISTORY

The Sommer & Kaufmann set is just one of several baseball card sets issued in the late '40s by California clothing stores. This 32-card set features the San Francisco Seals of the Pacific Coast League. The card front features a borderless black-and-white player photo taken at Seals stadium. His name and position are centered in a white strip below the photo, and a card number appears in the lower right. The card back has a short career write-up along with an ad for the store.

FOR

This is a challenging set for the PCL collector.

AGAINST

The cards are hard to find in most parts of the country.

NOTEWORTHY CARDS

Manager Lefty O'Doul and outfielder Gene Woodling are the best-known names in the set.

VALUE

EX-MT CONDITION: Complete set, $600; common card, $20; Woodling, $30; O'Doul, $40. 5-YEAR PROJECTION: Below average.

1947 BLUE TINTS

SPECIFICATIONS

SIZE: 2 × $2\frac{5}{8}$″. FRONT: Tinted photograph. BACK: Blank. DISTRIBUTION: Nationally, sold in strips.

1947 Blue Tints, Joe DiMaggio

HISTORY

Strip cards were produced as far back as 1910 and were most popular in the '20s. They came in strips of 10 or 12 cards which were usually cut apart. Strip cards are not popular with collectors because they were cheaply made, with poor drawings on thin cardboard. The Blue Tints were one of the first major post-WWII sets. The distribution of this set is unknown, but they are fairly popular today because of the number of superstars who appear in the set. The card front features a blue-tinted photograph on a dark blue background. The player's name and team are printed on the front, and a card number is at the lower right. The backs are blank.

FOR

It is one of the earliest postwar issues, which gives it historical significance.

AGAINST

The Blue Tints were cheaply made and have a shoddy appearance.

NOTEWORTHY CARDS

What Lou Gehrig was doing in the '47 Blue Tint set is hard to say; he had played his last game in 1939 and died in 1941. The set includes the last contemporary cards of Hank Greenberg and Mel Ott. There is a rookie card of Jackie Robinson. The Leo Durocher card can be found with him as a Dodger or as a Giant. Ott's card can be found either with or without the team name.

VALUE

EX-MT CONDITION: Complete set, $400; common card, $5; Hall of Famers, $8–$15; Ott, $30; Robinson, Ted Williams, $50–$60; Joe DiMaggio, Gehrig, $80. 5-YEAR PROJECTION: Below average.

1947 HOMOGENIZED BREAD

SPECIFICATIONS

SIZE: 2¼ × 3½". FRONT: Black-and-white photograph. BACK: Blank or movie star photograph. DISTRIBUTION: Nationally, in loaves bread.

HISTORY

This 48-card set has two unusual features: it includes 44 baseball players and four boxers (including Joe Louis and Jake LaMotta), and some of the cards have a movie star photo on the back. The set has historical significance because it was one of the first major card issues after WWII and immediately preceded the first Bowman bubblegum cards of 1948. The set offers rookie cards of Gil Hodges, Bobby Thomson, Yogi Berra, and Jackie

1947 Homogenized Bread, Gil Hodges

Robinson. Many stars from the prewar era also appear including Ted Williams, Joe DiMaggio, Stan Musial, and Pee Wee Reese. The card front features a round-cornered black-and-white player photograph with a facsimile autograph. The cards contain no stats or biographical write-ups. Although the cards are much scarcer than the Bowman issues that followed them, they are not in great demand.

FOR

These attractive cards feature lots of superstars.

AGAINST

Most collectors don't like round-cornered cards or sets that mix other sports figures with baseball players.

NOTEWORTHY CARDS

There's a high percentage of Hall of Famers among the 44 players in this set.

VALUE

EX-MT CONDITION: Complete set, $350; common card, $4–$5; Hall of Famers, $10–$15; Musial, Robinson, Williams, $30–$40; DiMaggio, $60–$75. 5-YEAR PROJECTION: Below average.

1947 TIP TOP

SPECIFICATIONS

SIZE: 2¼ × 3″. FRONT: Black-and-white photograph. BACK: Black printing on white cardboard. DISTRIBUTION: Regionally, in loaves of bread.

1947 Tip Top Bread, Enos Slaughter

HISTORY

Although the 1947 Tip Top bread set is complete at 163 cards, it is composed of 11 separate regional issues that share a common design. A statement on the card back indicates that there were varying numbers of cards issued in each city. The entire unnumbered card back is an ad for the bakery. The card front features a borderless black-and-white player photo with a white strip below containing his name, position, city, and league. The common teams are the New York Yankees, Dodgers, and Giants; the St. Louis Cardinals and Browns; and the Pittsburgh Pirates. Somewhat more scarce are the Boston Red Sox and Braves; the Chicago Cubs and White Sox; and the Detroit Tigers. The set was supposed to include 164 cards, but one of the New York Giants cards was never issued. The Tip Top set is significant because it includes many players who were never depicted on another baseball card—they were picked up during the talent-lean WWII years and then quickly replaced when the war was over.

FOR

Many of the players are not depicted on any other card, which makes the set popular with team collectors.

AGAINST

The cards are really quite scarce and expensive.

NOTEWORTHY CARDS

There are many rookie players in the set as well as older players who were making their final baseball card appearances. Among the significant rookie cards in the set are Yogi Berra and Joe Garagiola. One rookie that was overlooked was Jackie Robinson. Another major figure missing is Stan Musial.

OUR FAVORITE CARD

John Beradino, who portrays Dr. Steve Hardy on TV's *General Hospital,* was a former major league infielder. He played on the St. Louis Browns (under his real name, John Berardino) from 1939 to 1942 and again in 1946-47. Then he played for different teams including the Indians and Pirates until 1952. He compiled a lifetime .249 average in 912 games spanning 11 seasons. Berardino appears in the '51 Bowman and '52 Topps set as well. His TV star status raised the value of his card to two to three times that of a common card.

VALUE

EX-MT CONDITION: Complete set, $7,500; common card, $20; scarce card, $60; stars, $65–$80. 5-YEAR PROJECTION: Below average.

1947 BOND BREAD JACKIE ROBINSON

SPECIFICATIONS

SIZE: 2¼ × 3½″. FRONT: Black-and-white photograph. BACK: Black printing on white cardboard. DISTRIBUTION: New York, in loaves of bread.

HISTORY

One of the few successful "one-player" issues, the 1947 Bond Bread set features Jackie Robinson, then in his rookie year for the Brooklyn Dodgers. The set includes 13 cards of the major leagues' first black ballplayer in a variety of portrait and posed-action photos. The card front has a round-cornered photo surrounded by a white border. Some of the pictures are horizontal and some are vertical. One card, which has a facsimile autograph and is more common than the rest, shows a closeup of Robinson as if he were ready to catch a ball. On

1947 Bond Bread Jackie Robinson

other cards, the autograph is on the back. Unnumbered card backs have Bond logos and pictures, or drawings of Robinson. All backs contain an endorsement of Bond bread by Robinson. Because they feature one of baseball's greatest players and were issued in small numbers, 1947 Bond cards are scarce and expensive.

FOR
This rare and valuable issue is a set of rookie cards devoted to one great player.

AGAINST
The cards are scarce, and assembling a complete set is an expensive proposition.

NOTEWORTHY CARDS
Because they feature Jackie Robinson, they're all special.

VALUE
EX-MT CONDITION: Complete set, $3,500; autographed front, $175; all others, $300. 5-YEAR PROJECTION: Below average.

1947 REMAR BAKING COMPANY

SPECIFICATIONS
SIZE: 2 × 3″. FRONT: Black-and-white photograph. BACK: Blue printing on white cardboard. DISTRIBUTION: Oakland, with purchases of bread.

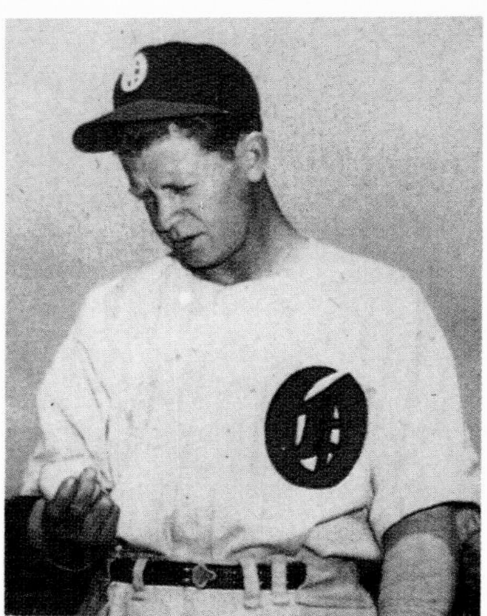

1947 Remar Baking Company, Henry Pippen

HISTORY
The 25-card Remar set of 1947 featured the Oakland Oaks of the Pacific Coast League. The cards were given away at stores with purchases of bread. The cards are identical to the '46 set and many of the player photos are the same, but the card numbers are different. The card front features a borderless black-and-white photo with the player's name and position in a white strip underneath. The card backs are printed in blue and feature a short biography of the player, a radio station ad, and a picture of a loaf of Sunbeam bread.

FOR
This is an attractive issue for the team or minor league collector.

AGAINST
The design is too similar to the 1946 set.

NOTEWORTHY CARDS
The only famous name in the 1947 Remar set is manager Casey Stengel.

VALUE
EX-MT CONDITION: Complete set, $150; common card, $3–$5; Stengel, $40. 5-YEAR PROJECTION: Below average.

FOR
The cards have the distinction of having been drawn by a former major league player.

AGAINST
Most collectors prefer photographs over drawings, and there is also a bias against postcard-size issues. A few scarce cards make assembling a complete set quite difficult.

NOTEWORTHY CARDS
The cards of Woody Williams (Hollywood) and Charlie Ripple (Sacramento) are much scarcer than the rest. Many of the players are former or future major leaguers including Vince DiMaggio and Casey Stengel.

1947 SIGNAL OIL

SPECIFICATIONS
SIZE: 5½ × 3½". FRONT: Black-and-white drawing. BACK: Black printing on white cardboard. DISTRIBUTION: West Coast, at gas stations.

1947 Signal Oil, Dario Lodigiani

HISTORY
Though it is one of the more unusual Pacific Coast League sets of the late '40s, the 1947 Signal Oil 89-card set is not particularly popular. The cards are horizontal in format and feature line drawings of the players from five of the six teams in the league. Besides the portrait, there are a couple of player cartoons and a Signal logo. The drawings are the work of Al Demaree, a former major league pitcher. The left side of the unnumbered card back includes personal data, a few player facts, and a summary of his baseball experience. On the right are Signal and local radio station ads. The '47 Signal cards were only distributed in each team's hometown. The Sacramento and Seattle cards are harder to find than the others. Because of cards being withdrawn when players left the teams, there are also some scarcities.

VALUE
EX-MT CONDITION: Complete set, $800; common card, $5; Seattle or Sacramento card, $15; DiMaggio, $30; Stengel, $60; Ripple, $90; Williams, $150. 5-YEAR PROJECTION: Below average.

1947 SMITH'S CLOTHING

SPECIFICATIONS
SIZE: 2 × 3". FRONT: Black-and-white photograph. BACK: Black printing on white cardboard. DISTRIBUTION: Oakland, at clothing stores.

1947 Smith's Clothing, Casey Stengel

HISTORY

One of the more challenging Pacific Coast League regional issues of the late '40s is this 25-card set of Oakland Oaks players issued by Smith's clothing stores. The format of the Smith's cards is very similar to the Remar Bread and Sommer & Kaufmann issues of the late '40s. The cards were issued over a period of a few weeks. The card front features a borderless black-and-white photo of the player. In a wide white strip at the bottom of the card are the player's name, position, and card number. Card backs have a short write-up of the player's career and a large ad for the clothing store, complete with picture. The 1947 Smith's set is printed on very thin cardboard and the cards are easily creased.

FOR

Minor league collectors can find cards of players not issued anywhere else.

AGAINST

The format is too similar to other issues of the era, and the cardboard is too thin.

NOTEWORTHY CARDS

The only popular card in the set is that of manager Casey Stengel. Max Marshall's card is quite elusive and expensive. His card was presumably withdrawn when he left the team. To a lesser extent, the cards of Paul Gillespie, Damon Hayes, and Joe Faria are also scarce.

VALUE

EX-MT CONDITION: Complete set, $300; common card, $6–$8; Gillespie, Faria, $12–$15; Hayes, Stengel, $35; Marshall, $150. 5-YEAR PROJECTION: Below average.

1947 SUNBEAM BREAD

SPECIFICATIONS

SIZE: 2 × 3″. FRONT: Black-and-white photograph. BACK: Blue, red, and yellow printing on white cardboard. DISTRIBUTION: Sacramento, cards given away with purchases of bread.

1947 Sunbeam Bread, Johnny Rizzo

HISTORY

The 26-card 1947 Sunbeam set features the Sacramento Solons of the Pacific Coast League. The card fronts are virtually identical to the previous year: a black-and-white photo above a white strip with the name, year, and position of the player, along with a photo credit. No player info or card number appears on the back, just a color picture of a loaf of bread.

FOR

This is a scarce minor league issue.

AGAINST

There are no big-name players in the set.

NOTEWORTHY CARDS

There are no famous players or scarcities in the set.

VALUE
EX-MT CONDITION: Complete set, $140; common card, $6–$8. 5-YEAR PROJECTION: Below average.

1946 REMAR BAKING COMPANY

SPECIFICATIONS
SIZE: 2 × 3″. FRONT: Black-and-white photograph. BACK: Red and black printing on white cardboard. DISTRIBUTION: Oakland, with purchases of bread.

1946 Remar Baking Company, Casey Stengel

HISTORY
Remar used an unusual method of distribution for its card sets in 1946 through 1950. The cards were given to grocers, who generally placed them on a shelf next to the bread, free for the taking. This created some problems with uneven distribution. The set includes 23 cards of the Oakland Oaks of the Pacific Coast League. The card front features a borderless black-and-white photo with a white strip below containing the player's name and position. Eighteen of the cards have a card number. Card backs have a brief player write-up, a picture of a loaf of Remar bread, and an ad for a local radio station.

FOR
Team and minor league collectors like this issue.

AGAINST
Many collectors don't like minor league cards.

NOTEWORTHY CARDS
Manager Casey Stengel appears in the set. The unnumbered Bill Raimondi card is quite scarce.

VALUE
EX-MT CONDITION: Complete set, $175; common card, $7–$8; Raimondi, $30; Stengel, $35. 5-YEAR PROJECTION: Below average.

1946 SUNBEAM BREAD

SPECIFICATIONS
SIZE: 2 × 3″. FRONT: Black-and-white photograph. BACK: Red, blue, and yellow printing on white cardboard. DISTRIBUTION: Sacramento, with purchases of bread.

1946 Sunbeam Bread, Jess Landrum

HISTORY
A product of the same bakery that produced the 1946-1950 Remar cards, this 21-card Sunbeam set features the Sacramento Solons of the Pacific Coast League. Card fronts have a borderless black-and-white photo with a white panel below containing the player's name and position, the year, and a photo credit. Colorful card backs have a short, snappy write-up of the player, a picture of a loaf of bread, and an ad for a local radio station. The cards are unnumbered. Like the Remar cards, the Sunbeam cards were apparently distributed to grocers, who then handed them out to customers or left them on the shelves for the taking.

FOR
It is a good set for minor league collectors. The set is quite scarce, but not too expensive.

AGAINST
There are no big-name players in the set.

NOTEWORTHY CARDS
Few players in the 1946 Sunbeam set ever made it in the major leagues. Gerry Staley is the best-known of the lot.

VALUE
EX-MT CONDITION: Complete set, $175; common card, $8–$10. 5-YEAR PROJECTION: Below average.

1941 PLAY BALL

SPECIFICATIONS
SIZE: 2½ × 3⅛". FRONT: Tinted photograph. BACK: Black printing on white cardboard. DISTRIBUTION: Nationally, one card in packages with bubblegum.

1941 Play Ball, Charlie Gehringer

HISTORY
The 1941 Play Ball set was the last baseball card set issued by Philadelphia's Gum, Inc. The commencement of WWII, which cut off paper and gum-base supplies, cut the issue short at just 72 cards. The '41 Play Balls are quite similar to the company's 1939 and 1940 issues, except that color was added to the black-and-white photos. Many of the same photos were used from the previous year. The card front features a player photo with a colored frame inside a white border. A white banner below the photo contains the player's name, and often his nickname is given. Card backs are almost identical to the 1939 and 1940 issues, with a card number and personal data at the top, a player biography at center, and a Play Ball/Gum, Inc. ad at the bottom. The ad reads, "Play Ball Sports Hall of Fame. Watch for other famous sports stars, famous fighters, tennis players, football heroes, etc. in this series." Those cards were never issued. For its day, the color wasn't bad, and this has contributed to the popularity of the set. Cards #49-#72 are considered somewhat scarcer than the lower numbers. In addition to the regular cards, the 1941 Play Balls can also be found in sheets printed on thin paper.

FOR
These cards are colorful, easy to collect, and feature many stars.

AGAINST
There's really nothing to criticize about the 1941 Play Balls. The price per card may seem high, but they are quite scarce. It should be remembered that many of the cards, like other prewar sets, were turned in during war-time scrap paper drives.

NOTEWORTHY CARDS
All of the big stars of the prewar years are included with the exception of Bob Feller. The set contains the rookie card of Pee Wee Reese and is the only issue to contain cards of all three DiMaggio brothers—Joe, Dom, and Vince.

VALUE
EX-MT CONDITION: Complete set, $4,900; common card, #1-#48, $19; #49-#72, $28; Hall of Famers, $50–$100; Reese, $250; Ted Williams, $550; Joe DiMaggio, $1,000. 5-YEAR PROJECTION: Above average.

1941 GOUDEY

SPECIFICATIONS
SIZE: 2⅜ × 2⅞". FRONT: Black-and-white photograph. BACK: Blank. DISTRIBUTION: Nationally, in packages with bubblegum.

HISTORY
The 1941 set of 33 cards was the final issue for the Goudey Gum Company. The intervention of WWII halted virtually all baseball card production; the

1941 Goudey, George Case

paper and gum-base were needed for the war effort. The 1941 Goudey set includes 33 different players, and each player can be found with four different backgrounds—yellow, blue, green, and red. The card front features a black-and-white portrait photo set against the colored background with the player's name, team, and position in a panel underneath. A card number appears in the lower left, although some cards are found without the number. A white baseball in an upper corner has a "Big League Gum" logo. The card backs are blank. The '41 Goudey cards are scarce, but not very expensive.

FOR

It is the last of the historic Goudey issues. The format is appealing.

AGAINST

The cards seem incomplete without something on the back.

NOTEWORTHY CARDS

Several players made their only baseball card appearance in the '41 Goudey set; by the time the war was over, they were out of major league baseball. This makes the cards very attractive to team collectors. The only big names in the set are Carl Hubbell and Mel Ott. Cards #21-#25 are considered scarcer than the rest.

VALUE

EX-MT CONDITION: Complete set of 33 players (any background), $2,000; common card, #1-#20, #26-#33, $27; #21-#25, $150; Hubbell, Ott, $100–$125. 5-YEAR PROJECTION: Below average.

1941 DOUBLE PLAY

SPECIFICATIONS

SIZE: $2\frac{1}{2} \times 3\frac{1}{8}$". FRONT: Sepia-tone photograph. BACK: Blank. DISTRIBUTION: Nationally, one card in packages with bubblegum.

DIXIE WALKER
BROOKLYN DODGERS. Born Sept. 24, 1910. Bats left. Throws right. Height 6 ft. Weight 175 lbs. Batted .308.
No. 21 Double Play

DUCKY MEDWICK
BROOKLYN DODGERS. Left fielder. Born Nov. 24, 1911. Bats and throws right. Height 5 ft. 10 in. Weight 180 lbs. Batted .304.
No. 22 Double Play

1941 Double Play, Dixie Walker/Ducky Medwick

HISTORY

One of the less-appreciated prewar sets is Gum Products' 1941 Double Play issue. Each of the 75 cards features photos of two players from the same team. The sepia-toned photos are a mix of portrait and action shots. Cards #81/#82 through #99/#100 are action shots of players who also appear on portrait cards. The action cards are arranged vertically so the player photos are tall and thin, cards with portrait photos are horizontal. The player's name, personal data, and previous season's batting average or won-loss record are printed under each player's photo, along with a separate card number. The card backs are blank. The two-player layout of the cards encourages cutting them in half, which reduces the card's value. Few collectors are interested in individual cards. Cards #101/#102 through #149/#150 are considered scarcer than the rest.

FOR

The cards have an interesting format and feature lesser-known players to entice the team collector.

AGAINST

It is hard to find cards in nice condition.

NOTEWORTHY CARDS

Most of the stars of prewar baseball are represented in the set; many appearing on both portrait and action cards. Pee Wee Reese's rookie card appears in this set.

VALUE

EX-MT CONDITION: Complete set (uncut), $2,100; common card, #1/#2 through #99/#100, $15; #101/#102 through #149/#150, $18; Hall of Famers, $30–$50; Joe Cronin/Jimmie Foxx, Lefty Gomez/Phil Rizzuto, $100; Ted Williams, $200; Joe DiMaggio, $250. 5-YEAR PROJECTION: Below average.

1940 PLAY BALL

SPECIFICATIONS

SIZE: $2\frac{1}{2} \times 3\frac{1}{8}$″. FRONT: Black-and-white photograph. BACK: Black printing on gray cardboard. DISTRIBUTION: Nationally, one card in packages with bubblegum.

1940 Play Ball, Joe DiMaggio

HISTORY

In its second year of baseball card production, Gum, Inc. increased the size of its set to 240 cards. Besides current players, the 1940 set also included many cards of old-timers, making it one of the earliest sets to include past players. The cards are quite similar in design to the company's '39 issue, the biggest change being that the 1940 photos are framed with lines. Below the black-and-white player photo is a banner with the player's name (often with his nickname in quotes), along with a pair of baseballs, a bat, glove, and catcher's mask. Card backs are virtually identical to the '39 cards. A card number appears in the upper left. At the top is the player's personal data, with a well-written baseball biography underneath. At the bottom of the card is an ad for Gum, Inc., which describes the cards as "A pictorial news record of America's favorite sport." A 1940 copyright line appears in the lower left. The high numbers (#181-#240) are considerably harder to find than the low numbers.

FOR

This is a well-designed set chronicling baseball in the pre-WWII era. Many of the players never appeared on another baseball card.

AGAINST

The relatively expensive high-number cards make completing a set too costly for most collectors. Mixing current players with old-timers has never been popular with collectors.

NOTEWORTHY CARDS

The set includes all of the big stars of the day—most notably Joe DiMaggio (#1) and Ted Williams. Some of the nicknames are well worth the price of the card: "Stormy" Weatherly, "Soup" Campbell, "Bad News" Hale, and "Twinkletoes" Selkirk.

VALUE

EX-MT CONDITION: Complete set, $8,700; common card, #1-#180, $10; #181-#240, $33; Hall of Famers, $50–$150; Joe Jackson, $500; Williams, $600; DiMaggio, $1,000. 5-YEAR PROJECTION: Average.

1939 TO 1930

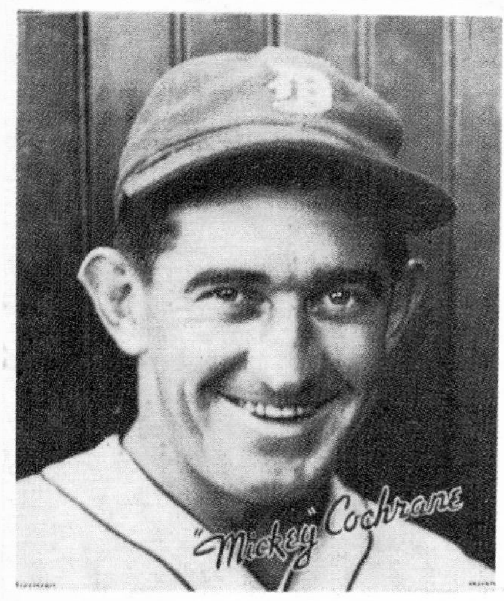

1936 Goudey, Mickey Cochrane

1934 Goudey, Luke Appling

1935 Batter-Up, Jimmie Foxx

1939 PLAY BALL

SPECIFICATIONS

SIZE: 2½ × 3⅛". FRONT: Black-and-white photograph. BACK: Black printing on gray cardboard. DISTRIBUTION: Nationally, one card in packages with bubblegum.

1939 Play Ball, Carl Hubbell

HISTORY

This baseball card set produced by Gum, Inc., is a popular starting point for collectors. After the first bubblegum card sets of the 1933-1936 era, the Depression virtually ended card production until this Play Ball set came out in 1939. One of the reasons for this set's popularity is that many of the players went on to continue their baseball careers after WWII, forming the mainstay of baseball card sets in the late 1940s. Chief among these are Joe DiMaggio and Ted Williams. The '39 Play Ball set is straightforward in design. The card front features a plain black-and-white photograph surrounded by a white border. There is no other printing on the front of the card. The card backs have a number in the upper left. The player's name, team, position, and vital data appears at the top. His career write-up is in the middle. The bottom carries a copyright for Play Ball and a notation stating, "This is one of a series of 250 pictures of leading baseball players. Save to get them all." However, the set doesn't contain 250 cards. Only cards #1-#162 are known to exist and card #126 was apparently never printed. Shortages of paper and gum base were probably responsible for the set stopping at 161 cards. The cards can sometimes be found with the words "Sample Card" stamped on the back. There are two levels of scarcity in the set: cards #1-#115 are more common than cards #116-#162.

FOR

This set is a popular starting point for modern baseball card collectors. The cards feature a simple format and good photos of the players of the day, many of whom don't appear in other card sets.

AGAINST

There are no negative factors in the 1939 Play Ball set.

NOTEWORTHY CARDS

Williams' rookie card and one of the more common cards of DiMaggio highlight this issue.

VALUE

EX-MT CONDITION: Complete set, $5,000; common card, #1-#115, $7; #116-#162, $50; Hall of Famers, $50–$150; Williams, $550; DiMaggio, $650. 5-YEAR PROJECTION: Average.

1938 GOUDEY HEADS-UP

SPECIFICATIONS

SIZE: 2⅜ × 2⅞". FRONT: Tinted black-and-white photographs and color drawings. BACK: Black printing on white cardboard. DISTRIBUTION: Nationally, one card in packages with bubblegum.

1938 Goudey Heads-Up, Joe DiMaggio

HISTORY

It's hard to say what the Goudey company had in mind when they created this 48-card set in 1938. The set contains two different versions of the same card for 24 players. The first version, numbered on the back from #241-#264, features a photograph of the player's head and cap, onto which a caricature body has been drawn. Cards #265-#288 feature the same photo/drawing, but have a cartoon added in each corner of the card. The player's name and team appear on the front in a colored strip at the bottom. The card backs contain a brief career summary, personal data, a card number, and a Goudey ad at the bottom. Card backs of the first group state, "This is one of a series of 288 Baseball Stars"; backs of the second group claim there are 312 cards in the set. Whether Goudey meant this issue to be an extension of its premier 240-card set of 1933 is unknown. In any case, the total comes to 288 cards for both years. The '38 Goudey set is commonly known as Heads-Up, and is not as popular as the company's '33 and '34 issues, though the cards are quite valuable. The second group of cards is considered the scarcer of the two.

FOR

It is an unusual set that offers a large percentage of major stars of the late '30s.

AGAINST

Having two versions of each card seems pointless.

NOTEWORTHY CARDS

Of the 24 different players in the set, seven are Hall of Famers. The '38 Goudey set is the first major issue to feature cards of Joe DiMaggio and Bob Feller.

VALUE

EX-MT CONDITION: Complete set, $7,000; common card, #241-#264, $45–$50; #265-#288, $60; Charlie Gehringer, Hank Greenberg, Joe Medwick, $200–$250; Jimmie Foxx, Feller, $300–$350; DiMaggio, $1,100. 5-YEAR PROJECTION: Below average.

1936 GOUDEY

SPECIFICATIONS

SIZE: 2⅜ × 2⅞". FRONT: Black-and-white photograph. BACK: Game card. DISTRIBUTION: Nationally, one card with packages of bubblegum.

1936 Goudey, Chuck Klein

HISTORY

One of the less popular Goudey issues, the 25-card set of 1936 differs from its predecessors in that it features black-and-white player photographs rather than color drawings. The only other element on the card front is a facsimile autograph. Card backs contain a short biographical write-up and a pair of baseball terms that could be used to simulate a baseball game. Because the set was unpopular, the cards are quite scarce today compared with earlier Goudey issues.

FOR

The set provides nice photos of better-known players of the mid-1930s.

AGAINST

Game cards have never attracted much interest. Playing games with baseball cards is detrimental to the card's value.

NOTEWORTHY CARDS

Almost a third of the 1936 Goudeys are Hall of Famers: Mickey Cochrane, Kiki Cuyler, Rick Ferrell, Lefty Gomez, Hank Greenberg, Bucky Harris, Chuck Klein, and Paul Waner.

VALUE

EX-MT CONDITION: Complete set, $1,000; common card, $25; Hall of Famers, $60-$100. 5-YEAR PROJECTION: Below average.

1935 GOUDEY 4-IN-1

SPECIFICATIONS

SIZE: 2⅜ × 2⅞″. FRONT: Color painting. BACK: Black-and-white photograph. DISTRIBUTION: Nationally, one card in packages with bubblegum.

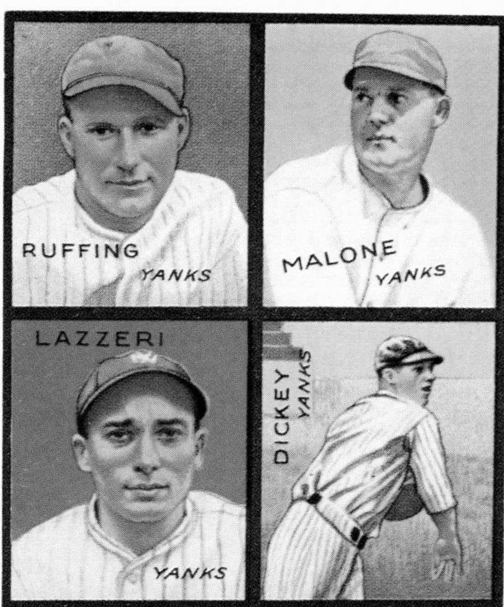

1935 Goudey 4-in-1, Ruffing/Malone/Lazzeri/Dickey

HISTORY

The format of Goudey's third major baseball card set was a departure from anything done before, and it set the stage for many similar test issues from Topps in later years. Each of the '35 Goudey "4-in-1s" features four different players' pictures on the card front. The pictures are surrounded and separated by a red (sometimes blue) border. All of the players on any given card are teammates. The pictures are generally the same ones used on the previous two sets in reduced size and set against a plain background. The player's last name and team nickname appear in his part of the card. Card backs make up one portion of a large "puzzle" that could be assembled by gathering cards with the same "Picture" number. There are nine different back puzzles. Individual puzzles of Chuck Klein, Frank Frisch, Mickey Cochrane, Joe Cronin, Jimmy Foxx, and Al Simmons require six different card backs. Team pictures of either the Tigers, Senators, or Indians require 12 different card backs. In all, a complete set by back and front combination would contain 114 cards. Most collectors, however, prefer to assemble just the 36 different card fronts. The cards with blue borders are scarce, but they're not necessary to complete a set.

FOR

The idea was innovative and would be copied in later years.

AGAINST

The set is too confusing. Many collectors don't like baseball cards with more than one player apiece.

NOTEWORTHY CARDS

Babe Ruth returned to the Goudey set in '35—his last year as a player—appearing with three of his new Braves teammates.

VALUE

EX-MT CONDITION: Complete set (36 different fronts), $2,800; common card, $30; Frank Frisch/Dizzy Dean/Ernie Orsatti/Tex Carleton, $125; Ruth/Marty McManus/Ed Brandt/Rabbit Maranville, $650. 5-YEAR PROJECTION: Below average.

1934 GOUDEY

SPECIFICATIONS

SIZE: 2⅜ × 2⅞″. FRONT: Color painting. BACK: Green printing on white cardboard. DISTRIBUTION: Nationally, one card in packages with bubblegum.

1934 Goudey, Mickey Cochrane

HISTORY

In its second year of baseball card production, Goudey cut its set from 240 cards to 96. Popular Yankees star Lou Gehrig was used to help promote the 1934 set. The wrappers of the Big League Chewing Gum brand identified the cards as the

"Lou Gehrig Series," and 84 of the 96 cards have a small photo of Gehrig at the bottom left with the words, "Lou Gehrig says...." What Gehrig says appears on the back of the card in the form of a write-up on the pictured player, giving the impression that it had been penned by Gehrig. Card fronts feature a color painting of the player set against a solid-color background. On the background are silhouettes of a baseball diamond and a couple of players in action. The player's name appears at the top of the card. Card backs also include card number and the notation "1934 Series," the player's name and team, and a Goudey ad. On 12 of the cards in the scarcer high-number series (#73-#96), the photo and saying were changed to "Chuck Klein says...." Klein had led the N.L. in 1933 in hits, doubles, home runs, RBIs, and batting and slugging averages. There are three levels of scarcity: cards #1-#48 are the most common, cards #49-#72 are somewhat scarce, and cards #73-#96 are quite scarce. Because the '34 Goudeys were printed on heavy cardboard, they have held up pretty well over the years. As with the '33 set, many of the star cards in this issue have been reproduced, usually on thinner and glossier cardboard. Most are clearly marked as reprints.

FOR

It's a popular set that is challenging enough for serious collectors.

AGAINST

The scarce and expensive high-number cards put the '34 Goudey set beyond the reach of many collectors.

NOTEWORTHY CARDS

Lou Gehrig has two cards in the '34 Goudey set. Surprisingly and inexplicably, there is no Babe Ruth card. Many other Hall of Famers are present, though, along with lots of players who are obscure enough to be of interest only to the team collector.

VALUE

EX-MT CONDITION: Complete set, $9,500; common card, #1-#48, $30; #49-#72, $40; #73-#96, $125; Hall of Famers, $50–$200; Hank Greenberg, $125; Kiki Cuyler, $250; Dizzy Dean, Jimmie Foxx, $350; Gehrig, $1,500–$1,750. 5-YEAR PROJECTION: Above average.

1934-1936 BATTER-UP

SPECIFICATIONS

SIZE: 2⅜ × 3¼″ and 2⅜ × 3″. FRONT: Black-and-white or tinted photograph. BACK: Blank. DISTRIBUTION: Nationally, one card in packages with bubblegum.

1934-1936 Batter-Up, Lloyd Waner

HISTORY

A second issue by the National Chicle company in the mid-1930s was, the 192-card Batter-Up series–distributed over the same three-year span as the Diamond Stars issue. The Batter-Up cards were the first die-cut baseball cards of the bubblegum card era. (Topps based its similar 1951 and 1964 sets on this issue). The Batter-Up card fronts feature a full-length photograph of a player with a natural background. The cards were die-cut around the player, which allows the background to be folded over to make the player "stand up" in an action pose. A white box to the left or right of the player has the words "Batter-Up," and the player's last name, team, and position. On cards #1-#80, the card number is printed outside the box; on cards #81-#192, the card number is printed inside the box. Another difference between the two series is that the low-number cards are 3¼″ long, while the high-number cards are only 3″ long. The high numbers are also considerably scarcer. Each of the 192 cards in the set can be found as either a black-and-white or a tinted photograph in colors of blue, green, brown, sepia, red, or purple. Collectors usually assemble sets without regard to the tint. The card backs are blank. Some players appear on more than one card. Like all die-cut baseball cards, the Batter-Ups are more desirable when they remain intact. Those cards that have been folded over are less desirable, and cards that have the background removed are in little demand.

FOR

The cards feature actual photographs of the players.

AGAINST

It is hard to find cards in unfolded condition. Most of the big-name players appear in the scarcer, more expensive high-number series.

NOTEWORTHY CARDS

The Batter-Up set features three multiplayer cards: Earl Webb and Wally Moses, Jim Bottomley and "Poison" Ivy Andrews, and Ted Lyons and Frankie Hayes. Most of the big-name players are included, though there are no cards of Babe Ruth or Lou Gehrig.

VALUE

EX-MT CONDITION: Complete set (unfolded), \$12,000; common card, #1-#80, \$25; #81-#192, \$60; Hall of Famers (low numbers), \$60–\$100; Hall of Famers (high numbers), \$125–\$250. 5-YEAR PROJECTION: Below average.

1934-1936 DIAMOND STARS

SPECIFICATIONS

SIZE: 2⅜ × 2⅞". FRONT: Color drawing. BACK: Green or blue printing on white cardboard. DISTRIBUTION: Nationally, one card in packages with bubblegum.

1934-1936 Diamond Stars, Travis Jackson

HISTORY

While the Diamond Stars issue produced by the National Chicle company does not fit neatly into the standard definition of a "set," it remains a popular favorite among '30s sets. Over the three-year period from 1934 to 1936, 108 different card fronts were issued (96 different players, with the final 12 cards being repeats of players who had been on earlier cards). However, because many cards were issued in two or three of those years with different backs, 168 combinations are known to exist. The card front features a color drawing of the player—often set against a stadium or baseball diamond background, but sometimes posed in front of a multicolored background. The only writing that appears is the player's name. A white border frames the card. The card backs have either green (1934 and 1935) or blue (1935 and 1936) printing and contain a card number at top, a baseball playing tip by *Boston American* sportswriter Austen Lake, a three- or four-line write-up, and a National Chicle copyright line. There is also a note stating the card is "one of 240 major league players with playing tips." Considering that a 12-card blank-backed proof sheet for unissued cards was recently discovered (and a reprint set made from it), it appears that National Chicle intended to continue the issue to 240 cards, but was probably prohibited from doing so because of the Depression. The cards that were reissued in 1935 or 1936 were updated by changing the player's stats, though the copyright line remained 1934. Luckily for collectors, the Diamond Stars were issued in a somewhat logical fashion. Cards #1-#24 comprise the original 1934 set. All 24 were reissued in 1935, along with cards #25-#84. Of the 1935 issue, cards #25-#72 are found with backs printed only in green, while cards #73-#84 can be found with either green or blue printing on back. The '36 issue (with blue printing on the backs) included some of the cards from the #1-#31 sequence, all of #73-#84, and the final run #85-#108. These high-numbered cards (#97-#108) were apparently printed in smaller quantities than the rest of the set and are quite scarce today. Despite the confusing combination of fronts and backs, the set is usually considered complete at 108 cards, without regard to the back variations.

FOR

These attractive cards of the 1930s are surprisingly low-priced. The thick cardboard on which they were printed has helped them retain their value.

AGAINST

The confusion over the back variations makes the set less popular than it would otherwise be.

NOTEWORTHY CARDS

While the 1934 Diamond Stars set has many Hall of Famers and well-known favorites of the '30s, it lacks the two biggest names of that era—Babe Ruth (then at the end of his career) and Lou Gehrig (in his prime).

VALUE

EX-MT CONDITION: Complete set (108 cards), \$6,500; common card, #1-#84, \$30; #85-#96, \$50; #97-#108, \$150; Hall of Famers (low numbers), \$60–\$90; Rogers Hornsby, Jimmie Foxx, \$150; Hall of Famers (high numbers), \$200–\$350. 5-YEAR PROJECTION: Average, or a bit above.

1933 GOUDEY

SPECIFICATIONS

SIZE: 2⅜ × 2⅞". FRONT: Color painting. BACK: Green printing on white cardboard. DISTRIBUTION: Nationally, one card in packages with bubblegum.

1933 Goudey, Babe Ruth

HISTORY

For many collectors, the 240-card baseball card set produced by Goudey in 1933 marks the beginning of the modern baseball card era. The '33 set was the first major bubblegum card set and was a prototype of the cards being produced today. The card front features a color painting of the player—either full-length, partial length, or a portrait—set against a solid-color background with a white border. There is a red strip at the bottom with an ad for "Big League Chewing Gum." The player's name appears in one of the upper corners. The card backs have a number at the top, followed by the player's name and team, and a baseball biography. A Goudey ad appears at the bottom, with a reference to "Indian Gum" (another Goudey brand, which featured similar cards with American Indians on them). While there are 240 cards in the set, several of the better-known players appear on more than one card—there are four of Babe Ruth. Napoleon Lajoie's card (#106) was not issued at all in 1933. This set, as well as issues that followed from Goudey, was printed on very sturdy cardboard. They can often be found in surprisingly good shape. Many of the cards in the '33 set have been reprinted since the mid-1970s. The reprints (usually featuring superstars of the era) are not all marked as reprints. They can usually be distinguished by the thinner, whiter cardboard and glossy surface.

FOR

This was a historically important baseball card set. With the exception of the Lajoie card, the set is not too hard to complete, though it can be expensive. Since the '33 Goudeys came along ten years after the last batch of major baseball card sets, there are many players who make their first and/or only appearance in this issue, which makes it popular with team collectors.

AGAINST

The extreme scarcity of the Lajoie card makes completing this set an impossibility for most collectors.

NOTEWORTHY CARDS

The set is a grand mix of stars from baseball's middle years. Many of the stars of the '20s are included in their later years—often as managers. Young players of 1933—many of whom would remain active into the '40s and '50s—are included. Besides the Hall of Famers, there are plenty of good players in the set.

OUR FAVORITE CARD

The Goudey card backs indicated that there were 240 cards. Try as they might, the collectors in 1933 could only find 239. Nap Lajoie's card (#106) was not issued at all in 1933. Spurred by complaints, Goudey issued the card the following year. But it was available only to those who wrote the company and voiced their displeasure about not finding the card in the gum packs. An uncut sheet of 1934 Goudey cards—including the '33 Lajoie card—is one of the great treasures of the baseball card hobby.

VALUE

EX-MT CONDITION: Complete set (without #106), $18,000; common card, $35; Hall of Famers, $50–$150; Dizzy Dean, $350; Gehrig, $900; Ruth, $2,500; Lajoie, $9,000. 5-YEAR PROJECTION: Above average.

1933 DELONG

SPECIFICATIONS

SIZE: 2 × 3″. FRONT: Black-and-white photograph and color drawing. BACK: Black printing on white cardboard. DISTRIBUTION: Nationally, one card in packages with bubblegum.

1933 Delong, Chick Hafey

HISTORY

The Delong Gum Company produced just one 24-card baseball card set. The 1933 cards have an unusual design that combines a black-and-white photograph of the player with a color drawing of a stadium scene. The player photo is superimposed over the ballpark, which makes him look like a giant. A single stadium scene is used for the background on all the cards, and its vivid colors make the '33 set quite eye-catching. A yellow, blue, or red strip at the bottom of the card contains the player's name and team in a contrasting color. There is a white border around the entire card. The card back has a playing tip aimed at youngsters, and a Delong ad. There is a card number in the upper left and, on some cards, a small drawing to illustrate the playing tip. The write-ups carry the byline of Austen Lake, baseball editor of the *Boston Transcript* newspaper. The cards were distributed in packages of "Play Ball" gum, a brand name that would reappear often in connection with baseball cards.

FOR

The set is historically important because—along with the 1933 Goudey issue—it was one of the first bubblegum baseball card sets. Their unusually attractive design and scarcity have made them popular collectibles.

AGAINST

The only negative factor is that the cards are quite expensive.

NOTEWORTHY CARDS

For a set of only 24 cards, the Delongs include a lot of Hall of Famers, notably Lou Gehrig.

VALUE

EX-MT CONDITION: Complete set, $6,000; common card, $125; stars, $200; superstars, $225–$250; Jimmie Foxx, $450; Gehrig, $1,750. 5-YEAR PROJECTION: Average, or a bit above.

1933 SPORT KINGS

SPECIFICATIONS

SIZE: $2\frac{3}{8} \times 2\frac{7}{8}$″. FRONT: Color painting. BACK: Black printing on white cardboard. DISTRIBUTION: Nationally, one card in packages with bubblegum.

1933 Sports Kings, Babe Ruth

HISTORY

While only three of the 48 cards in the Sport Kings set are baseball players, the set is popular and includes a large number of famous athletes. The set is one of the few 20th century card issues to include women athletes. The card front features a color painting of the athlete with a solid-color background. Silhouettes below the picture depict the sport for which the athlete is known. A strip at the bottom contains the athlete's name. A red banner at the top of the card has the brand-name "Sport Kings Gum." The card back is quite similar in format to the regular-issue 1933 Goudey baseball cards. There is a card number at the top along with the athlete's name, the sport(s) for which he or she is known, a biography, and a Goudey ad. The Sport Kings set features baseball, football, basketball, hockey, swimming, aviation, riding, wrestling, and dogsledding.

FOR

An interesting set for the collector whose focus goes beyond baseball cards.

AGAINST

Most collectors don't like to mix sports in a card set.

NOTEWORTHY CARDS

The three baseball players in the set are Babe Ruth, Ty Cobb, and Carl Hubbell. Other notable athletes in the issue include Red Grange, Jim Thorpe, and Knute Rockne (football); Jack Dempsey and Gene Tunney (boxing); Bobby Jones, Gene Sarazen, and Walter Hagen (golf); Babe Didrikson (track); and Olympic swimming star Johnny Weissmuller in the days before he became famous as Tarzan in the movies.

VALUE

EX-MT CONDITION: Complete set, $4,500; common card, $20–$40; Dempsey, Grange, $150; Hubbell, Weissmuller, Didrikson, Thorpe, $175–$225; Rockne, $350–$400; Cobb, $750; Ruth, $1,000.
5-YEAR PROJECTION: Below average.

1933 GEORGE C. MILLER

SPECIFICATIONS

SIZE: 2½ × 3″. FRONT: Color painting. BACK: Black printing on white cardboard. DISTRIBUTION: Nationally, one card in packages with candy.

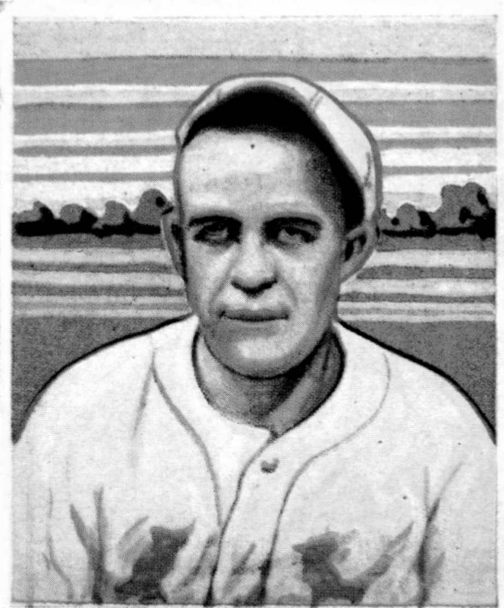

1933 George C. Miller, Jim Bottomley

HISTORY

Issued nearly ten years after the last major candy card set, the George C. Miller company cards of 1933 are contemporaries of the more common Goudey set. The 32-card set includes two players from each of the 16 major league teams. The card front features a painted color portrait set against a natural background of field, trees, and sky. The overall impression is visually appealing. There is no writing on the front of the cards. The card back offers a few biographical details and stats along with a set checklist. Also included on the back is an offer to redeem complete 32-card sets for the choice of a "fielder's mitt, regulation American or National League baseball, or one Grandstand Seat to any American or National League Game (except World's Series) at any Park." The offer continued that the "pictures" (cards) would be returned "cancelled" with the prize. Canceling the cards required removing the bottom strip, which contained the redemption offer. This accounts for the many damaged Miller cards today. Canceled cards are worth only 10 percent of the complete card's value. Apparently, the "Poison" Ivy Andrews card was not distributed in the same quantity as the other 31 cards and it is quite scarce. All of these cards are among the scarcest of the Depression-era issues.

FOR

These are attractive cards with a unique format. The set represents a challenge for the serious collector willing to spend money.

AGAINST
The cards are too expensive for most collectors.

NOTEWORTHY CARDS
This is another set with a high percentage of Hall of Famers. They include Earl Averill, Jim Bottomley, Joe Cronin, Dizzy Dean, Bill Dickey, Jimmie Foxx, Frank Frisch, Charlie Gehringer, Goose Goslin, Lefty Grove, Chick Hafey, Chuck Klein, Rabbit Maranville, Mel Ott, Red Ruffing, Al Simmons, Bill Terry, Lloyd Waner, and Paul Waner.

VALUE
EX-MT CONDITION: Complete set, $11,000; common card, $250; Hall of Famers, $350–$450; Dean, $750; Andrews, $1,500. 5-YEAR PROJECTION: Below average.

1933 TATTOO ORBIT

SPECIFICATIONS
SIZE: 2 × 2¼″. FRONT: Tinted photograph. BACK: Black printing on white cardboard. DISTRIBUTION: Nationally, one card in packages with bubblegum.

1933 Tattoo Orbit, Jesse Haines

HISTORY
You really have to know your baseball cards to recognize this 60-card set at first glance. There is nothing on the cards to identify the issuer. The cards were produced by the Orbit Gum Company, which inserted them into packages of their Tattoo brand gum. Each small, almost square, card features a tinted photograph. The photo is separated from the colorful, stylized ballpark background by a black line. The red, yellow, and green background draws the eye away from the rather drab photos. A wide white border surrounds the design. There is no other printing on the front. The unnumbered card back is extremely simple and features only the player's name, team, position, birth date, height, and weight. While the Tattoo Orbit cards are really quite scarce, they are not that expensive; lack of collector interest keeps the prices low. Like many sets of this era, these cards were reprinted in recent years, though reprints are usually marked as such.

FOR
It is a reasonably priced set for the collector who desires cards of the '30s. They have an unusual format and are really quite attractive.

AGAINST
The card backs are quite plain, with none of the stats and biography that most collectors like.

NOTEWORTHY CARDS
Four of the cards are scarcer than the rest. The cards of Ivy Andrews and Rogers Hornsby (who was traded from the Cardinals to the Browns in mid-season) are considered hard to find, but less so than those of Bump Hadley and George Blaeholder.

VALUE
EX-MT CONDITION: Complete set, $2,400; common card, $25; Hall of Famers, $30–$40; Jimmie Foxx, $100; Blaeholder, Hadley, $125; Dizzy Dean, Hornsby, $150–$200. 5-YEAR PROJECTION: Below average.

1932 U.S. CARAMEL

SPECIFICATIONS
SIZE: 2½ × 3″. FRONT: Black-and-white photograph. BACK: Black printing on white cardboard. DISTRIBUTION: Nationally, in packages with caramels.

HISTORY
In 1932 the U.S. Caramel company produced one of the last—and one of the rarest—of the caramel card sets that had been a baseball card staple since the late 1800s. The card market was about to become dominated by bubblegum companies, and this 31-card issue of famous athletes was the last of a dying breed. There are 26 baseball players, three boxers, and two golfers in the set. These cards are similar to the 1914-1915 Cracker Jack set in appearance. The card front features a black-and-

1932 U.S. Caramel, Mickey Cochrane

1932 U.S. Caramel, Lefty Grove

white photograph set against a red background with a white border. The player's name appears in white above the picture. On the card back are the player's name, position, team, league, and career summary. A card number appears in the upper left. The bottom contains a mail-in offer allowing the collector to receive a baseball for one set of cards or a baseball glove for three sets (cards would be returned along with the prize). For many years it was believed that card #16 (picturing Joe Kuhel) was never issued, which made "completing" a set impossible. Recently, an East Coast dealer discovered the card, but it pictures Freddy Linstrom. Because this was the only #16 found, it appears that it was the only one printed. The Linstrom card was a historic find. It was estimated when it was found that the card was worth more than $100,000.

FOR

The set is historically important because it was one of the last caramel sets.

AGAINST

The inclusion of nonbaseball players and the absence of card #16 detract from the collectibility of this set.

NOTEWORTHY CARDS

The baseball players in the '32 U.S. Caramel set are virtually all Hall of Famers and include Babe Ruth, Lou Gehrig, and Ty Cobb (even though Cobb had been retired since 1928). The golfers in the set are Gene Sarazen and Bobby Jones; the boxers are Jack Dempsey, Gene Tunney, and Jack Sharkey.

VALUE

EX-MT CONDITION: Complete set (without #16), $10,000; common card (nonbaseball), $100; common card (baseball), $175; Dempsey, Tunney, $175; superstars, $400–$450; Cobb, $1,300; Gehrig, $1,400; Ruth, $1,500. 5-YEAR PROJECTION: Below average.

1929 TO 1920

1922 American Caramels, Eddie Collins

1922 American Caramels, Ty Cobb

1922 (E-120) AMERICAN CARAMELS

SPECIFICATIONS

SIZE: 2 × 3½″. FRONT: Sepia or blue/green tinted photograph. BACK: Brown or blue/green printing on white cardboard. DISTRIBUTION: Nationally, in packages with caramels.

1922 (E-120) American Caramels, Eddie Collins

HISTORY

This is probably the most popularly collected candy card issue of the '20s. In spite of its limited use of color, it is also one of the more attractive sets. With no real variations, this 240-card set presents a reasonable collecting challenge. The 1922 American Caramels issue is almost universally known by its catalog number—E-120—assigned by Jefferson Burdick in his early reference work, *The American Card Catalog.* (This designation is used here because it will help avoid confusion with another set issued by American Caramels at the same time.) The card front features a player photograph (generally a posed shot) in an elaborate oval frame. The frame contains drawings of baseball players and/or equipment in the corners. In the wide border at the bottom, the player's full name is printed, along with his position, team, and league. The cards of N.L. players are printed in blue/green; the A.L. players' cards are printed in sepia. The printing on the unnumbered card back matches the front. Backs contain the city name and league at the top, and the team nickname, manager's name, and a checklist of the 15 players who appear for that team in the set. An ad at the bottom carries an offer for an album to house the set. There are 15 players for each of the 16 teams represented. The photographs were also used in a black-and-white blank-backed strip card set and a pair of Canadian issues (each containing 120 cards) advertising Neilson's chocolate bars. These cards are printed on thin cardboard and can usually be found with creases.

FOR

The set is one of the few large-size caramel card issues of the '20s that can be reasonably completed.

AGAINST

Some of the pictures appeared on other caramel sets, and the entire design was repeated on others. This lack of exclusivity diminishes demand for the E-120 set.

NOTEWORTHY CARDS

All of the big stars of the early '20s appear in the set and include Babe Ruth and Ty Cobb. Cobb's name is spelled "Cob" on the front.

VALUE

EX-MT CONDITION: Complete set, $3,500; common card, $15–$18; Hall of Famers, $25–$30; Rogers Hornsby, Walter Johnson, $75; Cobb, $125; Ruth, $250. 5-YEAR PROJECTION: Average.

1922 (E-121) AMERICAN CARAMELS

SPECIFICATIONS

SIZE: 2 × 3½″. FRONT: Black-and-white photograph. BACK: Black printing on white cardboard. DISTRIBUTION: Nationally, in packages with caramels.

1922 (E-121) American Caramels, Ty Cobb

HISTORY

The caramel card set known to collectors as E-121 (a catalog designation assigned by Jefferson Burdick in *The American Card Catalog*) is one of the most commonly encountered, yet least understood, candy sets of the early '20s. For instance, it's not known why the American Caramel company chose to issue a second set of cards in the same year as its E-120 set. It also remains a mystery as to how many cards make up a complete set. Some E-121 cards have printing on the back stating, "This set consists of pictures of eighty of the leading Base Ball Stars...," while others are found with backs indicating a 120-card set. The card front features a black-and-white photo framed by a thin black line in a wide white border. The player's name, position, team, and league appear in the bottom of the border. Many of the pictures were used in other card sets of that era. The unnumbered card back has an American Caramel ad. Many error, variation, and correction cards are found in the set. In fact, there are more than 220 E-121 cards known to exist. Besides the E-121s with American Caramel advertising on the backs, cards can also be found blank-backed or with backs containing other advertisements (most often for Holsum Bread). Collectors usually try to assemble a set of E-121s on the basis of the front photographs, regardless of the backs.

FOR

This is a challenging set for the collector who wants to delve into an early '20s issue.

AGAINST

The difficulty of completing a set leaves many collectors frustrated. There is nothing unique about a set that features photos that were repeated on other card sets.

NOTEWORTHY CARDS

All the big stars appear. Many of the biggest names—including Ty Cobb, Babe Ruth, and Walter Johnson—have several different poses in the set.

VALUE

EX-MT CONDITION: Complete set, (value unknown); common card, \$10–\$15; Hall of Famers, \$20–\$40; Rogers Hornsby, Tris Speaker, Johnson, \$50–\$60; Cobb, \$150; Ruth, \$175. 5-YEAR PROJECTION: Average.

1919 TO 1910

1912 Brown Background, Roger Bresnahan

1911 Gold Border, Rube Marquard

1914, 1915 Cracker Jack, Honus Wagner

1916 SPORTING NEWS

SPECIFICATIONS

SIZE: $1\frac{5}{8} \times 3$″. FRONT: Black-and-white photograph. BACK: Black printing on white cardboard. DISTRIBUTION: Nationally, through a mail-in offer.

1916 Sporting News, Ty Cobb

1916 Sporting News, Nap Lajoie

HISTORY

Published in St. Louis, *The Sporting News* called itself "The Baseball Paper of the World" on the backs of its two sets of baseball cards issued in 1916. They are virtually identical, the only differences being the inclusion of some different players, a few team changes, and a new card number. Many of the pictures on the Sporting News 200-card set are quite familiar to collectors; they are the same ones used in the popular 1922 American Caramels sets and many other regional issues of the day. This reduced the popularity and collectibility of the Sporting News issue. The card front features a full-length, black-and-white posed or action photo of the player surrounded by a wide white border. At the bottom is the player's full name, position and team, and a card number. The cards are numbered alphabetically. The card backs have a *Sporting News* ad.

FOR

The set features an early use of actual player photographs.

AGAINST

Reuse of the pictures in other card sets limits the popularity of this issue. The fact that two sets were issued within a year's time with only minor changes creates confusion among collectors. The same player's picture can be found with two different card numbers.

NOTEWORTHY CARDS

Lots of the major stars of the day are featured in the Sporting News set. It is one of the few contemporary sets to have cards of both Ty Cobb and Babe Ruth.

VALUE

EX-MT CONDITION: Complete set (200 cards), \$2,750; common card, \$10–\$15; Hall of Famers, \$20–\$40; Honus Wagner, Walter Johnson, Nap Lajoie, Joe Jackson, \$50–\$75; Cobb, \$250; Ruth, \$300. 5-YEAR PROJECTION: Average.

1916 COLLINS-McCARTHY

SPECIFICATIONS

SIZE: $2 \times 3\frac{1}{4}$″. FRONT: Black-and-white photograph. BACK: Black printing on white cardboard. DISTRIBUTION: Northern California, in packages with candy.

1916 Collins-McCarthy, Casey Stengel

HISTORY

This 200-card set was one of the few regional issues of the early 20th century. The Collins-McCarthy "Hall of Fame" set (as they're called on the card backs) was identical in design to several other regionally issued sets of the same year. Each of the cards, regardless of the advertising on the back, carries the statement, "This is one of a series of 200 action pictures of Major League Baseball Players, comprising Baseball's Hall of Fame." Naturally, not all of the players in the set have been enshrined in Cooperstown. (The Hall of Fame wasn't even established until 1936.) The card front features a black-and-white posed-action photo surrounded by a thin black line. Beneath the photo are the player's name, position and team, and the card number. Presumably, one printing company supplied blank-backed cards to all the different issuers. Advertisements were then printed on the backs by the issuers or by the printing company. This "Hall of Fame" series was Collins-McCarthy's only major league baseball card issue. The company is well-known today for being the producer of the 1911 to 1939 Zeenut card sets.

FOR

If you want to collect a "generic" baseball card set from the early 1900s, the Collins-McCarthy set is the natural choice. It is a quality issue that can be completed fairly easily.

AGAINST

There's really nothing unique about the Collins-McCarthy cards except for the advertising on the back.

NOTEWORTHY CARDS

There are many true Hall of Famers in this set, notably Babe Ruth and Casey Stengel. Ruth is pictured as a Boston Red Sox pitcher. Some fans may not recall that Ruth began his career as a lefthander before moving on to New York to become the famous Yankee home run king. He had two seasons in which he won more than 20 games and in 1916 led the A.L. with a 1.75 ERA in 40 starts. Stengel (the "Old Perfesser") is pictured as an outfielder for the Brooklyn Dodgers. Before he went on to become one of the finest and most popular managers in baseball, he had a 14-year playing career and compiled a lifetime batting average of .284.

VALUE

EX-MT CONDITION: Complete set, $4,000; common card, $15–$20; Hall of Famers, $40–$75; Cobb, $250; Ruth, $350. 5-YEAR PROJECTION: Average.

1914, 1915 CRACKER JACK

SPECIFICATIONS

SIZE: 2¼ × 3". FRONT: Color lithograph. BACK: Black printing on heavy white paper. DISTRIBUTION: Nationally, in packages of Cracker Jack (1914 and 1915) and through a mail-in offer (1915).

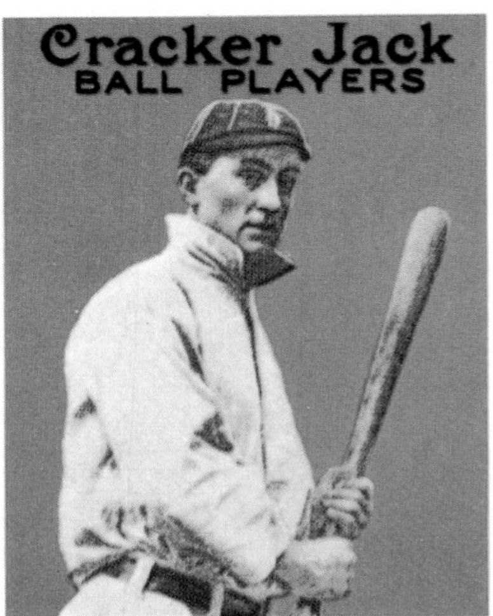

1914, 1915 Cracker Jack, Ty Cobb

HISTORY

Probably the most popular of the many pre-1920 candy card sets are those issued by Cracker Jack in 1914 and 1915. The sets are similar; the easiest way to differentiate the two is to look at the card backs. The 1914 set mentions 144 cards; the 1915 set mentions 176 cards. The latter included several new players, players that had been traded, and a few different player poses. The card fronts were identical for both years and feature a color lithograph of the player set against a bright red background. The words "Cracker Jack Ball Players" appear in black at the top. At the bottom in a white border are the player's last name, team, and league. The card backs have a number at the top followed by a brief player write-up. At the bottom is an ad for Cracker Jack. The ad on the 1914 cards mentions that either 10 million or 15 million cards were printed, while the ad on the 1915 cards carries an offer for the entire set and an album to house the cards. The 1914 cards were inserted in packages of Cracker Jack and are often found with food stains. The 1915 cards (also inserted in packages) could be obtained by mailing in "100 Cracker Jack Coupons, or 1 Coupon and 25¢." The album was offered for "50 Coupons, or 1

Coupon and 10¢." Part of the sets' popularity was that they included players from the Federal League as well as the American and National Leagues. The 144 players who appeared in the 1914 set also appeared in the 1915 set with the same card number. The cards were printed on heavy paper, not cardboard, which makes them susceptible to damage.

FOR
These colorful cards detail an important historical era in baseball. It is one of the few sets in which Federal League players can be found.

AGAINST
The cards are hard to find in good condition. The similarity of the two sets makes collecting both of them redundant.

NOTEWORTHY CARDS
All of the big stars and managers of the decade are in the set and it includes more than a dozen Hall of Famers.

VALUE
EX-MT CONDITION: Complete set (1914), $13,500; complete set (1915), $11,500; common card, $55; Hall of Famers, $100–$450; Walter Johnson, Christy Mathewson, $500–$600; Joe Jackson, $1,200; Ty Cobb, $1,500–$1,800. 5-YEAR PROJECTION: Above average.

1914-1915 (T-213, T-214, T-215) AMERICAN TOBACCO COMPANY

SPECIFICATIONS
SIZE: 1½ × 2⅝″. FRONT: Color drawing. BACK: Black or red printing on white cardboard. DISTRIBUTION: Nationally, in packages of cigarettes.

HISTORY
Several years after first issuing its famous T-206 set, the American Tobacco Company reissued many of the cards under three new brand names: Coupon, Red Cross, and Victory. While the same pictures are used in all of the sets, there are some variations in team designations, particularly in comparison with the T-206 issue. Players from the short-lived Federal League are included in the set. The card front features a color drawing of the player in a white frame. Beneath the frame, the

1914-1915 American Tobacco Company, Chief Meyers

1914-1915 American Tobacco Company, Rube Marquard

player's last name, team, and (sometimes) league are printed in blue or brown. The card backs have an ad for the brand of tobacco in which the card was packaged. Because of their similarity to the T-206 set, the American Tobacco cards of 1914-1915 are not popularly collected. However, because of their scarcity, they are considerably more expensive, and the cards of the star players of the day are two to five times as valuable as the common cards. The cards are unnumbered and checklists are known to be inaccurate. There are currently some 190 cards known to exist; the Victory card backs indicate there were 90 in that set, and the Red Cross set advertises 100.

FOR
The set represents a real test for the tobacco card collector. One of the very few issues to chronicle the brief era of the Federal League.

AGAINST
The set is too similar to the T-206 issue, and more expensive.

NOTEWORTHY CARDS
Many of the same Hall of Famer's that are in the T-206 set are also present in this issue, including the most popular card, Ty Cobb.

VALUE
EX-MT CONDITION: Complete set, (unknown); common card, Coupon, $12–$20; Red Cross, $25–$35; Victory, $50–$60; Hall of Famers, (2-3 times common price); Cobb, (6 times common price). 5-YEAR PROJECTION: Below average.

1914-1915 (T-216) PEOPLES TOBACCO COMPANY

SPECIFICATIONS

SIZE: 1½ × 2⅝". FRONT: Color drawing. BACK: Black printing on white cardboard. DISTRIBUTION: Southern U.S., in packages of cigarettes.

1914-1915
Peoples Tobacco Company,
Ty Cobb

1914-1915
Peoples Tobacco Company,
Joe Tinker

HISTORY

Among the lesser-known early 20th century tobacco cards are those issued by the Peoples Tobacco Company through their three brands of cigarettes: Kotton (most common), Mino (scarce), and Virginia Extra (scarcest). An interesting feature is the ad on the card backs stating that the company is "Not in a Trust," a reference to the American Tobacco Company conglomerate that controlled virtually the entire cigarette industry at that time. Also, the pictures on the cards are the same as those used on several other caramel card sets of the day. The card front features a color drawing of the player surrounded by a white border. Beneath the picture are the player's last name, position, team, and league. The unnumbered card backs carry an ad for the brand of cigarette in which they were packaged. The set is quite scarce, and most collectors attempt to find one version of each of the 101 known cards, regardless of the ad on the back.

FOR

The pictures are different from the ones on the American Tobacco Company cards.

AGAINST

The set is too similar to the contemporary caramel card issues to elicit much collector interest.

NOTEWORTHY CARDS

Honus Wagner appears in two different poses. Most of the Hall of Famers of the day are included.

VALUE

EX-MT CONDITION: Complete set, (unknown); common card, \$20–\$25; Hall of Famers, \$50–\$75; Ty Cobb, Wagner, \$90–\$100. 5-YEAR PROJECTION: Below average.

1912 (T-207) BROWN BACKGROUND

SPECIFICATIONS

SIZE: 1½ × 2⅝". FRONT: Color lithograph. BACK: Black printing on white cardboard. DISTRIBUTION: Nationally, in packages of cigarettes.

1912 T-207
Brown Background,
Joe Tinker

1912 T-207
Brown Background,
John Lewis

HISTORY

The 200-card T-207 set, the T-205 "Gold Border," and the T-206 "White Border" are the "Big 3" cigarette card sets from the period between 1910 and 1920. It is the least popular of the trio for a number of reasons: it is the scarcest, it's not that attractive, there are few big-name stars in the set, and it has a large number of high-value cards, including some of the classic rarities of the hobby. Like the T-205 and T-206 sets, the T-207s take their number from *The American Card Catalog,* authored by hobbyist Jefferson Burdick. The card front features a color lithograph of a player (portrait or action) set against a dark brown background. The player pictures are drab, with little color except for uniform details. Below the picture is a white strip with the player's last name, team, and league. A tan border surrounds the design. The set doesn't have the same visual appeal as the more colorful T-205 and T-206 cards. The unnumbered card back contains the player's full name, a biography, and a cigarette ad. The T-207 set was issued by the American Tobacco Company in packages of several of their brands of cigarettes: Recruit (by far the most common), Broadleaf, Cycle, Napoleon, Red Cross, and Coupon. While the card back includes an ad for one of these brands, no Coupon ads have ever been discovered. The large number of obscure players in the issue makes it a bonanza for team collectors. Many of the players who are found in the Brown Background set are not featured in other card sets. Although 200 cards were issued, seven major variation cards are generally collected to make a set complete at 207.

FOR

The set provides a real challenge for the serious baseball card collector interested in the period from 1910 to 1920.

AGAINST

The set includes many obscure players. The color is drab.

NOTEWORTHY CARDS

The big names in the set are Tris Speaker and Walter Johnson. The set does contain three of the classic rarities of the era: John Lewis (Boston-Nat.), Ward Miller (Chicago-Nat.), and Louis Lowdermilk (St. Louis-Nat.). There are other Lewis and Miller cards in the set, so collectors have to be sure of the team to know if they have the scarce card. Because of the number of scarce cards and the major variations, a detailed checklist is needed before seriously pursuing them. The Heinie Wagner and Bill Carrigan cards can be found with the correct card backs and with switched card backs.

VALUE

EX-MT CONDITION: Complete set, $16,000; common card, $30–$35; Hall of Famers, $100–$300; Johnson, $350; Speaker, $400–$500; Miller, Lewis, Lowdermilk, $1,500. 5-YEAR PROJECTION: Average.

1912 (T-202) HASSAN TRIPLE FOLDERS

SPECIFICATIONS

SIZE: 5¼ × 2¼″. FRONT: Color lithograph, black-and-white engraving. BACK: Red or black printing. DISTRIBUTION: Nationally, in packages of cigarettes.

HISTORY

Hassan cigarettes took the concept of multiplayer cards a step further than Mecca's Double Folder cards of 1911. The Hassan set actually contains a panel of three baseball cards. The center card features a black-and-white engraving of a baseball action scene or a posed-action shot of a player. At the sides are individual cards of two different players. (Interestingly enough, the two end cards are almost exact duplicates of the T-205 Gold Border cards issued in 1911.) The individual cards feature color portrait lithographs with colorful borders. The Hassan cards are called Triple Folders because the two end cards can be folded over the center card and stored this way—sort of like a booklet. Generally, the two player cards have nothing in common with the action scene in the center. There are 74 different center cards known to exist with some having different end cards. The total number of different panel combinations is 134. (More combinations may yet be discovered.) The center card back contains a write-up on the action depicted on the front, while the end-card backs have a biography of the player. Each of the unnumbered backs carries a Hassan ad at the bottom. Card values depend upon the scene in the center and the quality of the players on the ends.

FOR

It was certainly one of the most innovative baseball card designs ever created.

AGAINST

The many combinations are confusing to most collectors. The similarity of the end cards to the T-205 Gold Borders is also a negative factor.

NOTEWORTHY CARDS

Some of the most famous baseball photos of the early 1900s are reproduced on the center panels. The set includes many Hall of Famers. The card with the center panel, "Birmingham Gets a Home Run," is quite a bit scarcer than the rest of the set.

1912 Hassan Triple Folders, Hugh Jennings/Ty Cobb

VALUE

EX-MT CONDITION: Complete set, $12,500; common card, $65; Hall of Famers, $90–$150; "Birmingham" center panel, $250; Cobb (end panel), $400–$500; Cobb (center panel), $500–$650. 5-YEAR PROJECTION: Average.

FOR

The set is an attractive, scarce baseball card issue from the West Coast.

1912 Home Run Kisses

1912 HOME RUN KISSES

SPECIFICATIONS

SIZE: 2¼ × 4¼″. FRONT: Sepia-tone photograph. BACK: Black printing on buff cardboard. DISTRIBUTION: Northern California, in packages with candy.

HISTORY

In the years they issued baseball cards, the Collins-McCarthy company usually inserted the same cards in all of their major candy products: Zeenuts, Home Run Kisses, and Ruf-Neks. However, in 1912 (the company's second year of card production), a separate set was produced for inclusion with Home Run Kisses. The 90-card set comprises the six teams in the Pacific Coast League. The card fronts feature a posed-action player photo against a blank background. The name of the candy product and the player's last name and team appear on the side. The card is surrounded by an ornate picture-frame border. Some card backs have a message offering a premium list; most have a small logo of the photographer, "Bardell Sepia, San Francisco."

AGAINST

It's a hard set to complete, and quite expensive.

NOTEWORTHY CARDS

The PCL enjoyed a unique status for most of its history as the best of the minor leagues. There are few big-name players in the set, but there is at least one Hall of Famer—Dave Bancroft of Portland. He became a premier shortstop in the National League and played from 1915 to 1930.

VALUE

EX-MT CONDITION: Complete set, $2,500; common card, $30–$35; Bancroft, $80. 5-YEAR PROJECTION: Below average.

1912 EASTERN LEAGUE

SPECIFICATIONS

SIZE: 1½ × 2¾″. FRONT: Black-and-white photograph. BACK: Black printing on white cardboard. DISTRIBUTION: Canada, Northeastern U.S., in packages of cigarettes.

1912 Eastern League

1912 Eastern League

HISTORY

This 90-card minor league set of Eastern League players is one of the lesser-known cigarette card issues of the 1910-1920 period. The area of distribution is still unknown. The set is generally cataloged under Canadian card issues and the cards are most often found in Canada. The Eastern League was the predecessor of the International League. The players in this set represent two Canadian and six U.S. teams. The cards are well-designed and attractive. The card front features an oval black-and-white player portrait printed on an engraving of a baseball bat that gives the appearance of a wooden plaque. A baseball glove appears in the upper left and a baseball is in the lower right. An oval at the bottom contains the player's last name. The card back repeats the player's last name, has a brief career summary, and includes a card number at the bottom. Because it is considered a Canadian set (even though there are more U.S. teams represented), it is not widely collected in the States.

FOR

This set has an attractive and unusual design.

AGAINST

The Canadian and minor league status of the issue limits its popularity.

NOTEWORTHY CARDS

While most of the players in the set were career minor leaguers, some did make it to the majors. This is one of very few issues that include Hall of Famers Joe Kelley and Iron Man McGinnity, both at the end of their careers.

VALUE

EX-MT CONDITION: Complete set, $2,000; common card, $20; McGinnity, Kelley, $50. 5-YEAR PROJECTION: Below average.

1911-1912 (T-205) GOLD BORDER

SPECIFICATIONS

SIZE: 1½ × 2⅝″. FRONT: Color lithograph. BACK: Black or red printing on white cardboard. DISTRIBUTION: Nationally, in packages of cigarettes.

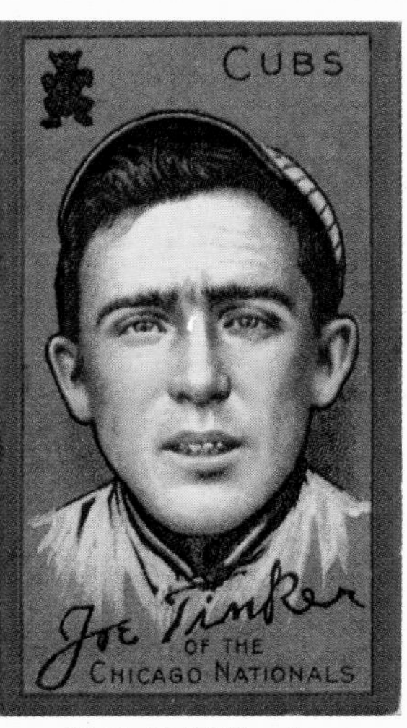

1911 Gold Border, Joe Tinker

1911 Gold Border, Christy Mathewson

HISTORY

The more than 200 cards known as the T-205 or "Gold Border" set includes three distinctively different groups of cards, and the American Tobacco Company may have intended them as separate issues. Nonetheless, collectors consider them as component parts of the same set. Indeed, all of the cards share the distinctive gold border that gives the set its name. In *The American Card Catalog*, Jefferson Burdick assigned the number T-205 to the set, which often leads collectors to assume it was issued before the T-206 (White Border) set. In fact, the Gold Borders were first issued in 1911, about the time the last T-206 cards were produced, and were issued well into 1912. The Gold Borders came with many of the same cigarette brands that the White Borders had been packaged with, and can be found with ads for the following brands: American Beauty, Broadleaf, Cycle, Drum, Hassan, Honest Long Cut, Piedmont, Polar Bear, Sovereign, and Sweet Caporal. As with most tobacco card sets, a complete T-205 set is determined by the card front, with no regard for which ad appears on the back. The T-205s are among the most striking cards of the era. Framed by the distinctive gold border is a color lithograph of the player—generally a portrait, though the set includes a few action poses. The three groups have slightly different designs. On American League cards the player is pictured inside a stylized baseball diamond with the player's last name and team in a banner below. At the bottom are a pair of baseball bats, a ball, a glove, and a catcher's mask. In the upper corners are a team logo and nickname. National League cards have a head-and-shoulders portrait of the player set against a plain background. At the bottom are the team name and a facsimile autograph (the first on a major baseball card set). In the upper corners are a team logo and nickname. While N.L and A.L. cards comprise the vast majority of the set, there are also 12 players from the Eastern League (now known as the International League). Those cards have an action picture or a three-quarter-length portrait of the player in an elaborate frame of columns and other decorations. The player's last name and the city for which he played are printed in a white strip toward the bottom. Shields in the upper corners have the first letter of the team's city. The major league card backs have the player's full name at the top of the card—another first for baseball cards, as previous sets had included only the last name—followed by a short career summary and stats for the 1908 to 1910 seasons. Minor league backs are similar, but have no seasonal stats. All of the Gold Border card backs are unnumbered and have an ad at the bottom for the cigarette brand the card was issued with. Many of the backs also have a line that reads, "Base Ball Series 400 Designs," but only 200 different players are represented. Many collectors who specialize in T-205s consider eight or nine of the variations necessary for a complete set. Although the cards are contemporary with the T-206s, they are not as popularly collected. One advantage of the T-205 set is that it contains no ultra-expensive rarities, making it a set collectors can reasonably hope to complete—though not without some challenge and expense.

FOR

The design is striking. Because of the large number of surviving cards, complete sets are attainable even now, as long as the collector isn't too fussy about condition.

AGAINST

The three different designs within the set do not fit most modern collectors' idea of what a "set" should be. Condition-conscious collectors avoid the set because the gold borders tended to chip and the thin cardboard was easily creased.

NOTEWORTHY CARDS

The T-205 Gold Borders include many valuable star cards—Ty Cobb, Walter Johnson, Cy Young, Christy Mathewson, and others. There are also some fairly scarce cards that command a decent price, as do some of the variation cards. Serious collectors will need a detailed checklist in order to pursue them. The minor league cards are considerably scarcer than the major leaguers, and this group contains a card of Hall of Fame third baseman Jimmy Collins. He played in the majors from 1895 to 1908. When the T-205s were issued he was a playing manager for Providence—at the age of 41.

VALUE

EX-MT CONDITION: Complete set, $15,000; common card, $40; minor leaguer, $125; Hall of Famers, $100–$250; Collins, $250; Johnson, $400; Cobb, $1,000. 5-YEAR PROJECTION: Average, or a bit below.

1911 (T-3) TURKEY RED

SPECIFICATIONS

SIZE: 5¾ × 8″. FRONT: Color lithograph. BACK: Black or red printing on white cardboard. DISTRIBUTION: Nationally, available through a mail-in offer with cigarette coupons.

1911 Turkey Red, Nap Lajoie

HISTORY

The Turkey Red set is the most popularly collected cabinet-size baseball card issue of the early 20th century. The term "cabinet-size" denotes a large card, generally on very heavy cardboard with a wide mat around it. Many early baseball card issues offered cabinet-size cards as a premium for wrappers or coupons. The Turkey Red series consists of 100 baseball players and 25 boxers. Some of the unnumbered card backs contain a list that categorizes the cards by numbers. Other card backs carry an ad for Turkey Red cigarettes. These cards could be obtained by mailing in coupons found in Turkey Red, Fez, and Old Mill brand cigarettes. Considering that the cost of the necessary coupons totaled $1 (a considerable sum in 1911), it is surprising that a large number of cards have survived. The Turkey Red issue is the only baseball cabinet set that collectors can reasonably hope to complete. The card front features a large, extremely well-done, colorful lithograph of the player in an action pose. There is a wide gray frame around the picture and a yellow plaque at the bottom with the player's last name and team designation. Besides the individual player cards, there are several cards featuring two players in action. The baseball player cards in the set were reprinted in a 1983 special collectors' edition. The reprints are in the modern 2½ × 3½″ size rather than the 5¾ × 8″ size of the originals.

FOR

One of the most gorgeous sets of the period, it includes many stars and is popular with type collectors. Because of the large size and heavy cardboard, the cards have held up well.

AGAINST

Due to the amount of cards and the high cost of commons, assembling a complete set may be prohibitively expensive. Most collectors do not like mixing sports in a card set.

NOTEWORTHY CARDS

Many Hall of Famers are included among the baseball player cards, including Ty Cobb, Walter Johnson, and Christy Mathewson.

VALUE

EX-MT CONDITION: Complete set (100 cards), \$21,300; common card, \$150; Hall of Famers, \$300–\$600; Johnson, \$950; Cobb, \$2,800. 5-YEAR PROJECTION: Average, or a bit above.

1911 (T-201) MECCA DOUBLE FOLDERS

SPECIFICATIONS

SIZE: 2¼ × 4¹¹⁄₁₆″. FRONT: Color lithograph. BACK: Red printing on white cardboard. DISTRIBUTION: Nationally, in packages of cigarettes.

HISTORY

This 50-card set featuring 100 baseball players was probably the most innovative baseball card issue up until that time. Each folding card pictured two players: when unfolded, the card depicted a full-length picture of the player in a stadium setting, with his last name and team in black script in the upper left. When the top of the card was folded down, the body of a second player appeared over the legs of the first, creating a second player picture—again with the player's name and team in the upper left in black script lettering. The card backs were printed in red with a Mecca cigarette ad at the bottom and another innovation—player statistics—at the top. Mecca called these cards the "Base Ball Folder Series," and judging from the number of surviving cards, they must have been quite popular in their day. The idea was so good that Topps used it in 1955 for their "Double Headers" set. The unnumbered cards include both major and minor league players.

1911 Mecca Double Folders, Sam Crawford

FOR

It was an innovative card set. It was one of the first sets to list player stats.

AGAINST

The player lithographs are a little crude, but considering that the players had to share legs, it's understandable.

NOTEWORTHY CARDS

Many Hall of Famers, including Ty Cobb, appear in the set. The card of White Sox teammates Patsy Dougherty and Harry Lord is scarcer than the rest.

VALUE
EX-MT CONDITION: Complete set, $2,000; common card, $20–$25; stars, $75–$150; Dougherty/Lord, $250; Cobb/Sam Crawford, $400. 5-YEAR PROJECTION: Below average.

1911 SPORTING LIFE

SPECIFICATIONS
SIZE: 1½ × 2⅝". FRONT: Color lithograph. BACK: Blue printing on white cardboard. DISTRIBUTION: Nationally, through a mail-in offer.

Tinker, Chicago Nationals

1911 Sporting Life, Joe Tinker

Hans Wagner, Pitts. Nationals

1911 Sporting Life, Honus Wagner

HISTORY
The Philadelphia-based weekly newspaper, *Sporting Life*, was an important source of major and minor league baseball information as far back as the 1880s. For many years it competed with *The Sporting News*, which eventually won the battle and is still being published. In 1911 *Sporting Life* jumped on the baseball card bandwagon with an issue that would eventually include 288 different cards. The cards were released in twenty-four 12-card series that could be obtained by sending in postage stamps and a coupon from the paper. Each individual series was mailed in an envelope that carried the series number (the cards themselves are not numbered). With the exception of nine players in the later series, all of the cards depict major leaguers. Many of the portraits used are identical to those on the T-206 White Border set. The cards are interesting in that the players are pictured without their caps, set against a plain pastel background. The white border around the portrait is wider than on the T-206s. The player's last name, team, and league are printed at the bottom of the card. The card back contains one of three different ads for the newspaper. The *Sporting Life* set is much scarcer than the T-206s. They aren't much more expensive though, because there are in much less demand.

FOR
This interesting set provides real portraits of the top players of 1911.

AGAINST
The set is too expensive per card to be attractive to most collectors. The pictures on most of the cards can also be found on other tobacco or candy card sets of the era.

NOTEWORTHY CARDS
The *Sporting Life* set has all of the major stars of the day. There are only a few collectible variations in the issue. The McConnell and McQuillan cards can be found with different team names. Series 19 through 24 are scarcer than the first 18 series.

VALUE
EX-MT CONDITION: Complete set, $5,000; common card, $15–$20; Hall of Famers, $30–$75; Walter Johnson, Honus Wagner, $125; Cobb, $180. 5-YEAR PROJECTION: Average.

1911-1939 ZEENUTS

HISTORY
The Zeenut series was one of the longest-running and most successful baseball card issues of all time. The cards were produced by the Collins-McCarthy company (which also produced the 1912 Home Run Kisses and 1916 "Hall of Fame" card sets). They were inserted in boxes of their three major candy products—Home Run Kisses, Ruf-Neks, and Zeenut. (Zeenut competed with Cracker Jack.) Their 28-year run of continuous baseball card production was a hobby record until 1979, when Topps began their 29th year as a card producer. For virtually all of 1911-1939, Zeenut had a monopoly on West Coast issues of Pacific Coast League players. The first two Zeenut sets, 1911 and 1912, are sometimes found with a rubber-stamped premium offer on the back. From 1913 until 1937, all Zeenut cards were issued with a coupon at the bottom that could be redeemed for "valuable premiums" such as sports equipment, cameras, and toys. For this reason, Zeenut cards are seldom found with the coupon attached, and are always

1911 Zeenuts

priced without it. Cards with tabs are worth about 25 percent more. Cards with the coupon torn off are worth less than cards that had the coupon cut off neatly. However, condition is generally not a major factor for collectors of Zeenut cards—they are scarce in any condition. The problem of the coupon was eliminated in 1938 when the company began packaging a separate coupon along with the baseball card. The lack of coupons on most cards makes checklisting—or even identifying cards by year of issue—difficult and sometimes impossible. On some cards, the year of issue is printed on the front. Some have only the last two digits of the year. Other Zeenut cards have no date at all, except on the coupon, and that is usually missing. Some cards are not even identified as Zeenuts, though most of the early issues have the words "Zeenut Series" on the front. The 1913 cards state "P.C. League Season 1913." But from 1931 on, the cards are identified only as "Coast League." Complete checklists are nonexistent. Diligent collectors have discovered about 3,700 different cards, with more being discovered every year. A few early premium lists from the company name the players in each year's set, but whether all of them were actually released is unknown. A 1921 flier, for instance, lists 180 cards, but collectors have found only 168 of them so far. All of the Zeenut card issues are summarized here. All of the sizes given are for complete cards with the coupon; cards missing the coupon will be about a half-inch shorter.

SPECIFICATIONS

1911—SIZE: 2⅛ × 4″; Some players' cards have been found with varying photo sizes. FRONT: Sepia-tone photograph on dark brown background, white border. BACK: Blank.

1912—SIZE: 2⅛ × 4″. FRONT: Sepia-tone photograph on dark brown background, no border. BACK: Blank.

1913—SIZE: 2 × 3¼″. FRONT: Sepia-tone photograph on light yellow background. BACK: Blank.

1914—SIZE: 2 × 4″. FRONT: Black-and-white photograph on dark background. BACK: Blank.

1915—SIZE: 2 × 3¾″. FRONT: Black-and-white photograph on white background. BACK: Blank. NOTE: Only two players known from Vernon team.

1916—SIZE: 2 × 3½″. FRONT: Black-and-white photograph on blue background. BACK: Blank. NOTE: Some cards found with 1916 date, some without.

1917—SIZE: 1¾ × 3½″. FRONT: Black-and-white photograph on white background. BACK: Blank.

1918—SIZE: 1¾ × 3½″. FRONT: Black-and-white photograph, white background, red border around card above coupon. BACK: Blank.

1919—SIZE: 1¾ × 3½″. FRONT: Black-and-white photograph on gray background. BACK: Blank.

1920—SIZE: 1¾ × 3¾″. FRONT: Black-and-white photograph against grandstand background. BACK: Blank.

1921-1923—SIZE: 1¾ × 3½″. FRONT: Black-and-white photograph on white background. BACK: Blank.

1924-1931—SIZE: 1¾ × 3½″. FRONT: Black-and-white stadium photograph. BACK: Blank. NOTE: Some 1927 Zeenut cards have a "27" designation near the player's name; on others it appears in a white circle at the top.

1932—SIZE: 1¾ × 3½″. FRONT: Black-and-white photograph on white background. BACK: Blank. NOTE: For the only time in the series, the words "Coast League," the player's last name, and the team name were typeset, rather than hand-lettered, on the printing negative.

1933-1936—SIZE: 1¾ × 3½″. FRONT: Black-and-white (1933-1936) or sepia-tone (some 1933) stadium photograph. BACK: Blank. NOTE:

Identifying year of issue is difficult in this era. Cards were issued in identical style: a borderless photo with the player and team information in a round-cornered box toward the bottom of the card. Determining year of card issue—on cards without the coupon—is impossible because player pictures were repeated from one year to the next.

1937-1938—SIZE: 1¾ × 3½″. FRONT: Black-and-white stadium photograph. BACK: Blank. NOTE: The final two years of Zeenut cards are quite similar to the 1933-1936 series, but the black box with player data has square corners. Again, because the same pictures were used of players appearing in both sets, it is difficult to distinguish the actual year of issue.

DISTRIBUTION: It has been assumed that the Zeenut cards were issued within a relatively small area in Northern California, centered around the San Francisco-Oakland area.

FOR

Collectors who want the ultimate baseball card challenge love the Zeenut series. However, for most collectors a few type cards is a sufficient sampling. The Zeenut series does fill some very important historical voids—most of the 1920s, for example, when other baseball card issues were virtually nonexistent. The set has much to offer collectors who enjoy researching the early days of minor league baseball. There are a lot of players in these sets who cannot be found anywhere else; the problem is that since only last names are given many of them have never been satisfactorily identified.

AGAINST

Too little is known about the range of the Zeenut series to contemplate building a complete set. Indeed, the high cost of nearly 4,000 different cards would tax most hobbyists' resources beyond the limit. The cards are not particularly attractive.

NOTEWORTHY CARDS

Because for most of its history the Pacific Coast League represented the highest level of minor league play, its teams often included a good mix of young players on their way up, players whose major careers were through, and career minor league ballplayers. There are dozens of cards featuring players like Hall of Famer Joe Cronin and longtime Pacific Coast League manager Lefty O'Doul, but the most sought-after cards in the series are those of Joe DiMaggio and his brothers Vince and Dom. A peculiarity of the DiMaggio cards is that all of them spell the family name as "DeMaggio."

VALUE

EX-MT CONDITION (without coupon), 1911-1919, $7–$14; 1920s, 1930s, $3–$5; Joe DiMaggio, $350. 5-YEAR PROJECTION: Average.

1910-1920 GENERIC CARAMEL CARDS

SPECIFICATIONS

SIZE: 1½ × 2¾″. FRONT: Color lithograph. BACK: Many variations. DISTRIBUTION: Nationally, in different brands of candy.

HISTORY

More than two dozen sets of baseball cards—representing both major and minor leagues—were issued with various brands of caramels and other candy between 1910 and 1920. Caramel cards are not as widely collected as cigarette cards, mainly because many caramel sets share the same player pictures. Apparently, one printing company supplied the same "generic" set of baseball cards to several different candy companies. The backs of some of the cards carry advertisements for specific brands of candy; others carry checklists or simple statements like, "This card is one of a set of 50 baseball players. Prominent members of National and American Leagues." The card front generally features a color lithograph of the player surrounded by a white border. Beneath the picture are the player's last name, position, and team. Collectors who wish to specialize in the caramel cards of this period will need detailed checklists of the many different sets.

FOR

Fortunately for specimen-card collectors, the generic caramel cards are fairly inexpensive considering their age. Sets can usually be collected without too much trouble or expense, though some research is necessary.

AGAINST

The use of shared pictures on many of the sets makes the issues confusing for collectors. The lithographs are generally not as detailed as those on cigarette cards of the same era, which is one reason why the tobacco cards are more expensive.

NOTEWORTHY CARDS

Most of the major stars of the era are represented in the caramel sets.

VALUE
EX-MT CONDITION: Common card, $10–$20; Hall of Famers, $30–$60; Honus Wagner, $150–$200; Ty Cobb, $400–$500. 5-YEAR PROJECTION: Below average.

1910 OLD MILL

SPECIFICATIONS
SIZE: 1½ × 2⅝″. FRONT: Black-and-white photograph. BACK: Black printing on white cardboard. DISTRIBUTION: Southeastern U.S., in packages of cigarettes.

1910 Old Mill

1910 Old Mill

HISTORY
Commonly called "Red Borders" by collectors, the Old Mill cigarette card issue of 1910 is the largest, but least known, tobacco card set of the early 1900s. Currently, more than 600 cards are known to exist and more are discovered every year. The Old Mill set comprises eight minor leagues from the Southeastern United States. There is a different series for each league and that is designated on the card back. The number of cards in the different series varies greatly—fewer than 20 in some, and at least 120 in others. The card front features a black-and-white photo of the player in a distinctive red border. The player's last name and team are printed in black at the bottom. The card back features an ad for Old Mill cigarettes.

FOR
The set is a wide-open field for baseball card researchers. They are challenging enough to keep a collector busy for years.

AGAINST
Complete checklists are currently unavailable. The leagues and players represented are obscure.

NOTEWORTHY CARDS
The best-known card in the Old Mill set is the premier card of Casey Stengel, who was then playing for Maysville in the Blue Grass League.

VALUE
EX-MT CONDITION: Complete set, (value unknown); common card, $5–$10; Stengel, $175. 5-YEAR PROJECTION: Below average.

1910 RED SUN

SPECIFICATIONS
SIZE: 1½ × 2⅝″. FRONT: Black-and-white photograph. BACK: Red printing on white cardboard. DISTRIBUTION: Southeastern U.S., in packages of cigarettes.

HISTORY
Collectors looking for challenging, but not impossible, early minor league tobacco card sets should consider the 1910 Red Sun issue. Commonly known as "Green Borders," the set was produced by a New Orleans cigarette company that was part of the American Tobacco Company. The Red Sun cards have a distinctive green border around a glossy black-and-white player photo, with the player's last name and team name printed in black at the bottom. The unnumbered card back has a flashy red advertisement for the cigarette the cards were packaged in. The Green Border set contains 75 cards (indicated on the back), and features players from the Southern Association.

FOR
It is a challenging set for specialists.

AGAINST
The cards are scarce and expensive, and feature obscure players. Many of the photos crack or peel, so top-grade cards are scarce.

NOTEWORTHY CARDS
None of the players represented are stars.

VALUE
EX-MT CONDITION: Complete set, (value unknown); common card, $24–$30. 5-YEAR PROJECTION: Below average.

1909 TO 1900

1909-1911 White Border, Joe Tinker

1909-1911 White Border, Honus Wagner

1908-1910 American Caramel Company, Sam Crawford

1909-1911 (T-206) WHITE BORDER

SPECIFICATIONS

SIZE: $1\frac{1}{2} \times 2\frac{5}{8}$". FRONT: Color lithograph. BACK: Black, blue, or red printing on white cardboard. DISTRIBUTION: Nationally, in packages of cigarettes.

1909-1911 White Border, Ty Cobb

1909-1911 White Border, Hugh Duffy

HISTORY

Throughout most of the hobby's history, this has been the single most popularly collected baseball card set. It is also one of the most difficult and expensive sets to complete because it contains the famous "King of Baseball Cards"—the rare and expensive Honus Wagner card. To assemble a complete set of the T-206s, a collector will have to pay around $80,000 for the Wagner card alone, plus another $10,000 or so for the other scarce cards in the set. Even without the rarities, the T-206s are challenging enough to keep a collector busy for many years. The giant American Tobacco Company issued the T-206 cards with 16 of its cigarette brands over a three-year period beginning in 1909. The T-206 designation comes from *The American Card Catalog,* first published by hobby pioneer Jefferson Burdick in the 1930s. The cards are also referred to as "White Borders," but since there are many white-bordered tobacco cards from that era, the name T-206 is less confusing. The card front features a well-done color lithograph of the player—either a portrait or action picture—with a white border. At the bottom of the card, printed in black, are the player's last name, the team's city, and (in the case of two-team cities: Boston, Philadelphia, New York, and Chicago) the league designation. The pictures give modern collectors a fascinating look at what baseball was like in the early 1900s. The players are set against a variety of backdrops: some have solid-color backgrounds, others have simulated field or stadium backgrounds. Many players appear on more than one card in the set. The dimensions of the card became the standard for baseball cards for many years. All card backs carry an advertisement for the brand of cigarette in which they were packaged. Some backs indicate "Base Ball Series/150 Subjects," "350 Subjects," or, on some of the later issues, "350-460 Subjects." It is estimated that there are as many as 7,500 different front/back combinations, but collectors generally agree that the set is complete at 523 cards, including major variations. It is important for collectors to know what combination of varieties comprise a complete set, and various checklists are available. The most common brand by far is Piedmont, followed by (in ascending order of rarity) Sweet Caporal, Polar Bear, Old Mill (not to be confused with the "Red Borders"), Sovereign, American Beauty, El Principle de Gales, Cycle, Tolstoi, Hindu, Broadleaf, Carolina Brights, Lenox, Uzit, Drum, and Ty Cobb. The Ty Cobbs (all of which picture Cobb with a red background) are extremely scarce. Only about six are known to exist, which makes them far rarer than the Wagner card; however, they are currently much less expensive. Some front/back combinations may actually be scarcer than the Wagner card, but will never be as valuable. The most popular method of collecting T-206s is by assembling a set of one card of each front design, regardless of the brand on the back. Some hobbyists attempt to collect all of the cards of a specific brand. Polar Bear cards are often collected this way because of their distinctive white lettering on a dark blue background. The players, coaches, and managers in the T-206 set include major and minor leaguers. Major league cards were issued first, in 1909. The minor league cards came out with the reissues of 1910 and 1911. The late issues account for many of the scarce and valuable variations. Besides adding new players every year, the company also updated cards by changing team names and uniforms, often creating a new picture to reflect a trade. Some of the more popular players were issued in several poses. In general, the minor league players (American Association and Eastern League) are scarcer than the major leaguers, though not in as great demand. The "Southern League" players (Southern Association, South Atlantic, Texas, and Virginia leagues) are the scarcest of all. Including variations, the T-206 set includes a total of 389 major league players and 134 minor leaguers—a formidable undertaking for any collector.

FOR

The T-206 White Borders represent the ultimate challenge for baseball card collectors. The set is rich in history and rarities, yet it can be collected in part by even novice collectors. T-206 commons can be surprisingly inexpensive for an early 1900s issue.

AGAINST

The futility of collecting a "complete" T-206 set is a deterent for many collectors. It requires a great deal of research, as a definitive history of the set has yet to be written. The many checklists available conflict in some details. The prohibitively high cost of several of the cards is also a drawback.

NOTEWORTHY CARDS

The T-206 set is full of major stars and Hall of Famers of the period, and each commands a premium. Many of the variety cards are also quite valuable (a detailed checklist is needed). Some of the more valuable varieties include the error card of Sherwood Magee, which spells his name "Magie" (worth $6,000 in top condition), and the "traded" cards of Demmitt "St. L. Amer." and O'Hara "St. L. Nat'l." (worth about $1,500 each). Also rare is Elberfeld's Washington portrait pose (as opposed to his fielding pose), a $700 card. The second most valuable card is that of Philadelphia Athletics pitcher Eddie Plank. The scarcity of the Plank card is believed to have been caused by a damaged printing plate ruining most of the cards in production. Whatever the reason, the Plank card is very scarce, and usually commands a price of $8,000 or more in top condition.

OUR FAVORITE CARD

Naturally, everybody's favorite baseball card is the one worth $80,000—especially if you happen to stumble across it in grandpa's attic. The Honus Wagner card is the most famous baseball card in the hobby. While there are many cards that are far rarer than the Wagner card, it is because the Wagner card appears in the popular T-206 set that it is in such demand. There are no variations of this card in the set. The card features a bareheaded portrait of the great Pittsburgh (spelled "Pittsburg" on the card) shortstop, set against an orange background. Some 40 to 50 cards are known to exist, but there are literally thousands of reprints and reproductions, so collectors had better know what to look for when they encounter a supposedly genuine Honus Wagner T-206. Collectors who find a T-206 Wagner card should also be aware that there is another player named Wagner in the set—Boston Red Sox shortstop Heinie Wagner, who appears in portrait and batting poses. The Wagner "Boston Amer." card has probably dashed more dreams of instant wealth than any other baseball card. The story behind famous card is that Wagner demanded that the tobacco company cease using his picture to advertise their cigarettes; he was opposed to smoking and felt that his picture on the card would encourage youngsters to smoke. But there is some evidence to suggest that Wagner's demand was partly due to the fact that he had not been paid for the use of his picture.

VALUE

EX-MT CONDITION: Complete set, $100,000; major leaguer, $25–$30; American Assn. or Eastern League player, $20–$25; Southern League player, $75; Hall of Famers, $100–$300; Cobb, $600–$900; Wagner, $80,000. 5-YEAR PROJECTION: Average.

1909 (T-204) RAMLY

SPECIFICATIONS

SIZE: 2 × 2½". FRONT: Black-and-white photograph BACK: Black printing on white cardboard. DISTRIBUTION: Nationally, in packages of cigarettes.

1909 Ramly, Joe Tinker

HISTORY

Probably the most ornate and unusual cigarette cards of the early 1900s were the cards issued with the Ramly and T.T.T. brands of Turkish cigarettes in 1909. The cards are so scarce that nobody distinguishes between the two different backs when building a collection. Since the Ramlys are more common, collectors generally use that name. Actually, few collectors even try to complete a set: the cards are so rare and in such demand that even common players in top grade command a huge price. So far, 121 different Ramly cards are known to exist, but others may be discovered in the future. The thing that makes the Ramly cards so attractive is the unusual frame around the oval portrait of the player—an ornate network of gold vines and flowers embossed (raised) against an ivory background. The player's last name, position, team, and league appear in a panel under the photo. The combination of the black-and-white photo, gold frame, and slick ivory paper makes the cards unique and quite striking. The card backs carry only the cigarette brand and the address of the tobacco factory. Like many baseball card sets of this era, the Ramly set contains several misspelled names, but that doesn't seem to detract from their collectibility.

FOR

One of the most attractive early baseball card sets, the Ramlys are genuinely scarce and challenging to collect.

AGAINST

The Ramly set is too expensive for most collectors. It lacks some of the top stars of the era, such as Ty Cobb and Honus Wagner.

NOTEWORTHY CARDS

While there are no cards of Cobb or Wagner in the Ramly set, the issue includes other Hall of Famers. Because the commons are so expensive, star cards don't command as great a premium as would normally be the case.

VALUE

EX-MT CONDITION: Complete set, $13,000; common card, $100; Hall of Famers, $200–$300; Walter Johnson, $650. 5-YEAR PROJECTION: Below average.

1909-1911 OBAK

SPECIFICATIONS

SIZE: 1½ × 2⅝″. FRONT: Color drawing. BACK: Blue (1909 and 1910) or red (1911) printing on white cardboard. DISTRIBUTION: Western U.S., in packages of cigarettes.

HISTORY

The three sets of Obak cigarette cards issued between 1909 and 1911 are closely related to the more popular T-206 set. They were, in fact produced by the Western branch of the American Tobacco Company, which issued the T-206 and most other cigarette cards of the era. Although the three Obak sets are easy to tell apart, they are usually collected together. All sets are similar in format: a color drawing of the player appears on

1909-1911 Obak

the front of the card surrounded by a white border, with the player's last name, team, and league (on 1910 and 1911 cards) printed in black letters at the bottom. Card backs include only an Obak advertisement in 1909 and 1910; the 1911 cards include stats and a short biography. The year of issue can be determined by the style of card back: 1909 cards have the word "Obak" on a slant with a bullet inside the "O"; 1910 cards have the word "Obak" in straight block letters; and 1911 cards have backs printed in red, rather than blue. The 1909 cards feature players of the Pacific Coast League only, while the 1910 and 1911 sets also include players from the Northwest League. The 1909 issue is the scarcest, followed by the 1911. The three Obak issues include a total of 426 cards.

FOR

It is an interesting series for the researcher.

AGAINST

The cards are scarce in most parts of the country.

NOTEWORTHY CARDS

When these cards were released the PCL was the best of the minor leagues, with many former and future major league players. Some of these players never appeared on a major league card, which makes their cards desirable for team collectors.

VALUE

EX-MT CONDITION: Complete set, $3,100; common card, 1909, $15–$20; 1910, $6–$8; 1911, $8–$10. 5-YEAR PROJECTION: Average.

1909-1911 BASE BALL CARAMELS

SPECIFICATIONS

SIZE: 1½ × 2¾". FRONT: Color lithograph. BACK: Black printing on white cardboard. DISTRIBUTION: Nationally, in packages of caramels.

Tinker, s.s. Chicago Nat'l

1909-1911 Base Ball Caramels, Joe Tinker

HISTORY

Perhaps the most collectible of the caramel card issues are the "Base Ball Caramels" series issued by the American Caramel company beginning in 1909. Unlike the 1908 American Caramel set (which has different players represented by the same "generic" picture), these cards have color lithographs of the players. Although some card backs indicate that there are "100 Subjects" in the "Base Ball Series," there are actually more players and several pose variations, bringing the number of different cards to at least 120. The basic set was apparently issued through 1911, and some of the variations reflect traded players. The Base Ball Caramels cards are quite similar in design to the tobacco cards of the era. The front features a color portrait or action lithograph of the player, surrounded by a white border. At the bottom, printed in black, are the player's last name, an abbreviation for his position, and his team designation. The card backs have a pair of crossed baseball bats in the center. Above them are a ball and the words "Base Ball," with a catcher's mitt and the word "Caramels" below. At the top of the card is the statement "Base Ball Series/100 Subjects," and at the bottom is "Mfg By/American Caramel Co./Phila., Pa." As with most pre-1920 caramel sets, the cards are unnumbered. Obtaining a complete set with all the rarities and variations can be difficult and expensive.

FOR

It's a good starting point for collectors who want to specialize in caramel cards of the early 20th century.

AGAINST

The many scarce cards make the set too challenging for most collectors.

NOTEWORTHY CARDS

Many of the game's early greats appear in the Base Ball Caramels set and include Ty Cobb, Honus Wagner, Nap Lajoie, Joe Jackson, and Cy Young. The scarce cards in the set are very valuable. The serious collector will need a detailed checklist.

VALUE

EX-MT CONDITION: Complete set, $3,750; common card, $10–$12; Hall of Famers, $40–$125; Graham, $200; Sweeney (Boston), $250; Mitchell (Cincinnati), $450. 5-YEAR PROJECTION: Average.

1909-1910 CONTENTNEA

SPECIFICATIONS

SIZE: 1½ × 2⅝". FRONT: Color drawing or black-and-white photograph. BACK: Black printing on white cardboard. DISTRIBUTION: Mid-Atlantic states, in packages of cigarettes.

BOOLES, RALEIGH

1909-1910 Contentnea

ARMSTRONG, WILSON

1909-1910 Contentnea

HISTORY

Two distinctive sets of baseball cards were issued in packages of Contentnea brand cigarettes in 1909 and 1910. Sixteen of the cards are in the style of most other cigarette cards of the era, and feature a color drawing of the player with his last name and team printed in blue in the bottom border. The card back contains a cigarette ad and a notice that the set contains players from the Virginia and Eastern Carolina Leagues and the Carolina Association. The rest of the Contentnea cards are unusual in that they feature black-and-white photos. The team name and the player's last name are printed in the white border at the bottom of the card. The backs of the photo cards are similar to the cards with drawings, but have the notation "Photo Series" at the top. Because of the small number of drawn cards, it is believed that the two sets were issued together. There are currently some 225 Contentnea photo cards known to exist, with new discoveries still being made.

FOR
The set is a real gold-mine for researchers and specialists.

AGAINST
The cards are scarce and picture obscure players, and there is little demand for them.

NOTEWORTHY CARDS
Because so little research has been done on the cards, it's hard to tell if there are any famous big-leaguers in the set.

VALUE
EX-MT CONDITION: Complete set, (value unknown); common card, \$15–\$20. 5-YEAR PROJECTION: Below average.

1908-1910 (E-91) AMERICAN CARAMEL COMPANY

SPECIFICATIONS
SIZE: $1\frac{1}{2} \times 2\frac{3}{4}$". FRONT: Color drawing. BACK: Black printing on white cardboard. DISTRIBUTION: Nationally, in packages of caramels.

HISTORY
One of the most common caramel card sets of the early 20th century, this particular issue of "Base Ball Caramels" cards is not a collector favorite. The problem lies in the use of "generic" pictures in the three different series that make up the set. A picture issued in 1908 with one player's name would be issued again in 1910 and identified as

1908-1910 American Caramel Company, Mordecai Brown

1908-1910 American Caramel Company, Sam Crawford

another player. The set began in 1908 with 33 cards supposedly representing players of the Philadelphia Athletics, New York Giants, and Chicago Cubs. In 1910, the same cards were reissued, often with different players named, and supposedly including players from the Pittsburgh, Washington, and Boston (Red Sox) teams. In all, 75 different players are named in the set, but there are only 33 different pictures.

FOR
The cards are inexpensive examples of early candy card issues.

AGAINST
Few collectors are interested in cards that do not actually picture the player named.

NOTEWORTHY CARDS
There are lots of famous names in the set, but since the pictures aren't necessarily of the player named, star cards don't command as much of a premium as they do in other issues.

VALUE
EX-MT CONDITION: Complete set, \$600; common card, \$5; superstars, \$12–\$15. 5-YEAR PROJECTION: Below average.

19th CENTURY

1895 Mayo Cut Plug,
Jimmy Ryan

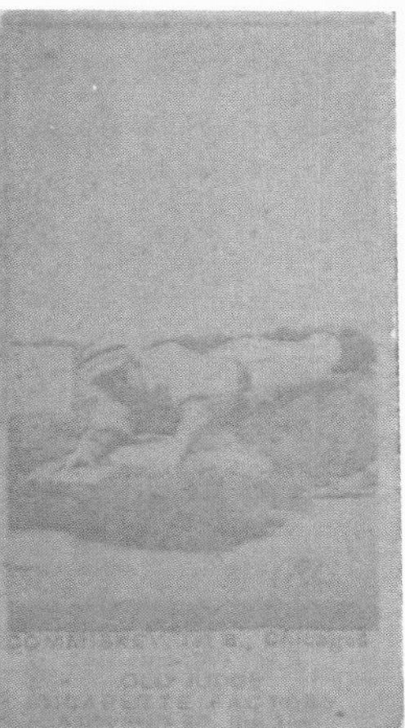

1890 Old Judge,
Charles Comiskey

1888 Goodwin Champions,
Dan Brouthers

1895 (N-300) MAYO CUT PLUG

SPECIFICATIONS

SIZE: 1⅝ × 2⅞". FRONT: Sepia-tone or black-and-white photograph. BACK: Blank. DISTRIBUTION: Nationally, in packages of chewing/smoking tobacco.

1895 Mayo Cut Plug, Bill Dahlen

1895 Mayo Cut Plug, Jimmy Ryan

HISTORY

The formation of the American Tobacco company in 1890 ended the first great era in baseball card history. Allen & Ginter, W. Duke & Sons, Goodwin & Co., William S. Kimball—all baseball card issuers—and Kinney Brothers merged to form the new company. Since American Tobacco had virtually no competition, there was no longer any need to issue cards as incentives. Why the Richmond, Virginia, firm of P.H. Mayo & Brother chose to do so in 1895 is a mystery. Whatever the reason, collectors are glad the cards were produced because they fill a gap in the history of major baseball card sets that would have extended until 1908. Several of the players in the 1895 Mayo set never appear on any other cards. When the Mayo cards were distributed in 1895, the only league in existence was the 12-team National League. (The American League was formed in 1901.) Forty players from all 12 teams appear in the 48-card set. Perhaps the most visually striking of the 19th century tobacco cards, the 1895 Mayos feature a sepia-tone or black-and-white photograph on a black background. Card backs are also black. It's interesting to note that on 12 of the cards, the player is pictured in his street clothes. Several variations are known to exist: some cards were reissued with new team names on the jerseys, and misspelled names were corrected.

FOR

The only major baseball card set of the 1890s, it offers collectors a chance to complete a set of 19th century cards at a fairly reasonable price. Some players are not available in any other sets.

AGAINST

The variations make it difficult to complete a set. The 12 Hall of Famers in the set are expensive.

NOTEWORTHY CARDS

More significant than the Hall of Famers are the eight players in the set who were not featured anywhere else: Charles Abbey, James Bannon, Ed Cartwright, Tom Corcoran, Bill Joyce, Tom Kinslow, Bill Murphy, and Otis Stocksdale.

VALUE

EX-MT CONDITION: Complete set, $7,250; common card, $125; Hall of Famers, $200–$400; Cap Anson, $600. 5-YEAR PROJECTION: Below average.

1890 (N-172) OLD JUDGE

SPECIFICATIONS

SIZE: 1½ × 2½". FRONT: Sepia-tone photograph. BACK: Blank. DISTRIBUTION: Nationally, in packages of cigarettes.

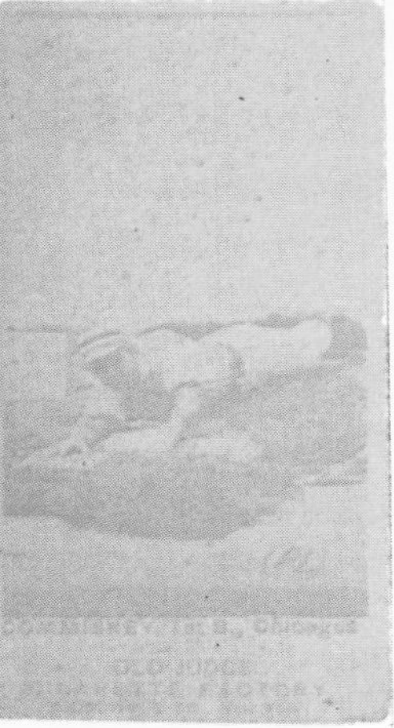

1890 Old Judge, Charles Comiskey

HISTORY

The last series of the long-running N-172 set were issued in 1890. Once again, the 1890 cards were mostly updates of earlier issues. They reflect the formation of another new league—the Players League—which had an interesting, though brief, history. Irked at the reserve clause that automatically tied a player to his team for the following season each time he signed a contract, a large number of N.L. players (led by John "Monte" Ward of the Giants) rebelled in 1890 and formed the Players League as an outgrowth of their "The Brotherhood of Professional Ball Players" union. They went into competition with the National League and formed teams in seven of the eight N.L. cities (the N.L. had another team in Cincinnati; the Players League had a team in Buffalo). The Players League lasted only one year—there weren't enough interested fans, and the high salaries they offered National Leaguers to join proved disastrous to management. In 1891 the players were allowed to return to their former N.L. teams. Old Judge attempted to keep abreast of the changing world of baseball and made the necessary team changes in the card captions. All Old Judge cards feature a sepia-tone player photo and have the words "Goodwin & Co., New York" (or "N.Y.") printed at the bottom. The 1890s can sometimes be distinguished by the initials N.L. or P.L., which are found in the caption or penned on the negative. (See the 1887 Old Judge listing for more information on these cards.)

FOR
These cards document an important year in baseball history—the beginning of a movement that would lead to the free agency.

AGAINST
The quality of the 1890 Old Judges is poor compared with earlier issues. Low-grade photo processing seems to have been used, as the cards are more prone to fading.

NOTEWORTHY CARDS
The notable cards are those featuring members of the Players League. A checklist is needed.

VALUE
EX-MT CONDITION: Complete set, (value unknown); common card, \$30–\$50; Hall of Famers, \$75–\$250. 5-YEAR PROJECTION: Below average.

1889 (N-172) OLD JUDGE

SPECIFICATIONS
SIZE: 1½ × 2½″. FRONT: Sepia-tone photograph. BACK: Blank. DISTRIBUTION: Nationally, in packages of cigarettes.

1889 Old Judge, Charles 'Kid' Nichols

HISTORY
In 1889 Old Judge released more updated cards in its long-running N-172 series. While there are a few new players represented, most of the cards are merely new poses or changes in team and/or league captions. The 1889 cards can sometimes be distinguished from the earlier issues by the wording at the bottom, "OLD JUDGE CIGARETTE FACTORY"; earlier issues do not have the word "FACTORY." The free and easy movement of players between teams and leagues continued to create problems for Goodwin & Company in keeping their cigarette cards current. Three teams had to be added to the American Association roster (St. Joseph, Sioux City, and Denver), and three teams had to be dropped (Chicago, St. Louis, and Columbus). Cleveland replaced Detroit in the National League, and because of team changes by players who had been on earlier Old Judge cards, the company decided to issue a few cards for teams in the International League, Atlantic Association, and Tri-State League. Finally, players were added from the California League teams (Oakland, Sacramento, and two San Francisco teams). Only one pose each of 17 different California League players is currently known to exist, and these cards are often collected as a subset. (See the 1887 Old Judge listing for more information on this series.)

FOR
The addition of new teams and wider distribution of the 1889 Old Judge cards gives collectors a reason to acquire a type card, if nothing else. Completing the California League subset is an attainable, though challenging and expensive, goal.

AGAINST

Because of the obscurity and short life of many of the teams, far fewer of these cards were saved compared with the National League cards.

NOTEWORTHY CARDS

At least three Hall of Famers who were not represented in the earlier issues are found in the 1889 Old Judge set. The Charles "Kid" Nichols' cards are the most difficult to find, though five different poses exist (he pitched for Omaha that season). Amos Rusie also appears in the set; he went on to a 10-year major league career that led to his induction in the Hall of Fame. Perhaps the most interesting card is of Clark Griffith, best-known as the founder of the Washington Senators. (His nephew, Calvin, is the current general manager of the Minnesota Twins—formerly the Senators.) Griffith, who appears with Milwaukee, was a pitcher from 1891 to 1914. He compiled a lifetime 240-140 record.

VALUE

EX-MT CONDITION: Complete set, (value unknown); common card, \$30–\$60; two-player card, \$50–\$90; California League player, \$75; Hall of Famers, \$75–\$250. 5-YEAR PROJECTION: Below average.

1889 HESS MAJOR LEAGUE

SPECIFICATIONS

SIZE: 1½ × 2¾". FRONT: Sepia-tone photograph. BACK: Blank. DISTRIBUTION: Nationally, in packages of cigarettes.

1889 Hess Major League, Arthur Whitney

HISTORY

This major league set proved more popular with collectors than Hess' previous California League issue. The 21 cards known to exist feature 16 New York Giants cards and a handful of players from the rival New York Metropolitans and St. Louis Browns of the American Association, and from the National League Detroit team. All of the Giants appear in a portrait with an oval frame. Most of the other players are in poses identical to those found in the contemporary Old Judge set. It is not known which brands of cigarettes the cards were packaged with; the ad at the bottom states, "S.F. HESS & CO.'S CIGARETTES." It is reasonable to assume that they were distributed in the Eastern U.S. in packages of the Creole brand.

FOR

It is a good set for New York Giants team collectors; most of the portraits are unique.

AGAINST

Nobody knows the total number of cards in the set; the high cost per card discourages trying to complete a set.

NOTEWORTHY CARDS

The 1889 Hess set contains four Giants teammates who are now in the Hall of Fame: Roger Connor, Buck Ewing, John M. Ward, and Mickey Welch. It seems likely that cards will someday be discovered for fellow Hall of Famers Jim O'Rourke and Tim Keefe—also teammates on that famous 1889 New York club.

OUR FAVORITE CARD

Although he is best-remembered as a coach for the New York Giants in later years, Walter "Arlie" Latham is pictured in the 1889 Hess issue as a St. Louis Browns third baseman. Latham had an unusual 17-season major league career that spanned nearly 30 years, beginning with Buffalo in 1880 and ending with the Giants in 1909. He played in four games that year—after a 10-year layoff—at the age of 50. It sounds incredible, but the 50-year-old Latham stole a base in one of those games. In 1887, the first time records were kept on stolen bases, Latham had 129. The following year, he led the league with 109.

VALUE

EX-MT CONDITION: Complete set, (unknown); common card, \$250–\$350; Hall of Famers, \$500. 5-YEAR PROJECTION: Below average.

1888 OLD JUDGE (N-172)

SPECIFICATIONS

SIZE: 1½ × 2½″. FRONT: Sepia-tone photograph. BACK: Blank. DISTRIBUTION: Nationally, in packages of cigarettes.

1888 Old Judge, Hugh Duffy

HISTORY

Three more series were released by Goodwin between 1888 and 1890, mostly in order to update the first three series released. There are no card numbers, and the "OLD JUDGE Cigarettes" caption which had appeared above the player's head was also dropped. Added for 1888 were the rest of the American Association teams, the Western Association, and more players from the National League. Numerous team changes are also reflected. Many photos were merely retouched or given new captions, but there are some new photos as well. All Old Judge cards feature a sepia-tone player photo and have the words "Goodwin & Co., New York" (or "N.Y.") at the bottom of the card. (For more information on the N-172 series, see the 1887 Old Judge listing.)

FOR

The additional teams and players represented make these cards desirable. Many Hall of Famers are included, as well as players who would later become famous as managers or owners. The prices are reasonable, considering that the cards are more than 100 years old.

AGAINST

Since no one knows how many cards are in the set, completing a set is impossible, even for the few who could afford it.

NOTEWORTHY CARDS

Evangelist Billy Sunday appears in the set near the end of an eight-year major league career in which he was known as one of the National League's premier base-stealers. John Tener's mediocre pitching career was also about over when he appeared on the Old Judge cards. He went on to become a congressman and later the governor of Pennsylvania. Also of special interest are the two-player cards, usually featuring players from different teams in a posed "action shot," with one tagging the other out. The set includes a few umpires and team owners, and even the boys who served as mascots for Chicago and New York.

OUR FAVORITE CARD

Baseball was a rough game around the turn of the century. No one seemed to mind that deaf-mute William Ellsworth Hoy was universally known as "Dummy." Hoy was an outfielder in the major leagues from 1888 to 1902 until he retired at the age of 40 after having played for six teams in the N.L., A.L., Players League, and the American Association. In his first year in the majors, Hoy led the N.L. with an incredible 82 stolen bases for Washington. Hoy left the game of baseball with a legacy that remains to this day: it is believed that as an accommodation to Hoy, who couldn't hear the umpire's calls, the umps began throwing up their right arms to indicate a ball and their left arms for a strike so Hoy would know how to position himself in the outfield. Hoy appears in five different poses in the Old Judge set. He was never in any other issue.

VALUE

EX-MT CONDITION: Complete set, (value unknown); common card, \$30–\$60; two-player card, \$50–\$90; Hall of Famers, \$75–\$250. 5-YEAR PROJECTION: Below average.

1888 (N-162) GOODWIN CHAMPIONS

SPECIFICATIONS

SIZE: 1½ × 2⅝″. FRONT: Color lithograph. BACK: Checklist. DISTRIBUTION: Nationally, in packages of cigarettes.

1888 Goodwin Champions, Cap Anson

1888 Goodwin Champions, Jack Glasscock

HISTORY

Issued in direct competition with Allen & Ginter's "The World's Champions" cards, this 50-card "Champions" series by Goodwin & Co. was distributed in Old Judge and Gypsy cigarettes. Eight baseball players are included, along with well-known names of the day in categories such as Bicyclist, Billiards, Broadswordsman, Chess, Football, High Jumper, Jockey, Lawn Tennis, Marksman, Oarsman, Pedestrian, Pugilist, Runner, Strongest Man in the World, Wild West Hunter, and Wrestler. Some of the same athletes appear in both the Goodwin and Allen & Ginter sets, notably Buffalo Bill Cody, John L. Sullivan and, among the ballplayers, Cap Anson, Bob Caruthers, Jack Glasscock, Tim Keefe, and Mike Kelly. Seven of the eight N.L. teams are represented, with only the last-place Washington team omitted. The eighth card is of star Brooklyn (American Association) pitcher "Parisian Bob" Caruthers. The cards feature extremely attractive lithographs with a thick cardboard backing. The production quality is better than the Allen & Ginter series. All of the baseball players are depicted in portraits, with the exception of Glasscock who is shown in a fielding position.

FOR

As one of many Old Judge issues, the Goodwin Champions are popular with type collectors. The quality of the color lithography is a major strong point. The baseball player cards in the set are not exceptionally rare—just expensive.

AGAINST

The cost is high and the demand for 19th century baseball cards is low.

NOTEWORTHY CARDS

Four of the eight baseball players in the Goodwin Champions set are now enshrined in the Hall of Fame: Anson, Kelly, Brouthers, and Keefe.

VALUE

EX-MT CONDITION: Complete set, $2,400; common card, $125; Brouthers, Keefe, $225; Kelly, $300; Anson, $500. 5-YEAR PROJECTION: Below average.

1888 (N-29, N-43) ALLEN & GINTER

SPECIFICATIONS

SIZE: 1½ × 2¾" and 2⅞ × 3¼". FRONT: Color lithograph. BACK: Checklist. DISTRIBUTION: Nationally, in packages of cigarettes.

1888 Allen & Ginter, John Morrill

1888 Allen & Ginter, Buck Ewing

HISTORY

Following their initial success in 1887, the Allen & Ginter company came out with a second series of "The World's Champions" cards in 1888, this time in two different sizes. The smaller cards (N-29) were included in 10-cigarette packages, while the backs of the larger cards (N-43) indicate, "One packed in every box of 20 Richmond Straight Cut No. 1 Cigarettes." Both sizes featured the same athletes, but an attractive background design corresponding to the sport was added to the N-43s. The sports featured in 1888 include "Cyclists, Base Ball Players, All Around Athletes, High Jumper,

Pole Vaulter, Lawn Tennis Players, Wrestlers, Skaters, Pedestrians (Walkers, Runners and Go-as-you-Please), Weight Lifter, Hammer Thrower, Club Swinger, Pugilists, Oarsmen, and Swimmers." With the exception of wrestler Theobaud Bauer, the subjects in the set are entirely different from those in the 1887 issue. Because so many sports were added, the number of baseball players was cut from ten to six—all from the National League. Instead of having an Allen & Ginter ad on the card front as in 1887, the 1888 cards feature the player's team and position beneath his name.

FOR

The attractive design of these cards captures the flavor of the national pastime in the late 1880s.

AGAINST

Considerably scarcer than the 1887 set, the smaller N-29 cards are quite expensive, and the N-43s are even more costly. The players depicted are not as well-known as the 1887 players.

NOTEWORTHY CARDS

Of the six baseball players in the 1888 set, only New York Nationals catcher William "Buck" Ewing is a Hall of Famer. Jimmy Ryan, Chicago "centre fielder," must have seemed like a good choice back in 1888; he led the N.L. that season with 182 hits, 33 doubles, and 16 home runs. There are three misspellings among the six players: Jas. G. Fogarty's middle initial appears as an "H", Boston first baseman John Morrill's name is spelled "Morrell", and Detroit pitcher Chas. H. Getzein's name appears "Getzin." There are some great nicknames too: "Honest John" Morrill, "Pretzels" Getzein, and "Doggie" Miller—who was also known as "Foghorn" and "Calliope."

VALUE

EX-MT CONDITION: Complete set, $2,400; common baseball card, $300; common large card, $330; Ewing (small card), $600; Ewing (large card), $630. 5-YEAR PROJECTION: Below average.

1888 (N-184) KIMBALL CHAMPIONS

SPECIFICATIONS

SIZE: 1½ × 2¾". FRONT: Color lithograph. BACK: Checklist. DISTRIBUTION: Nationally, in packages of cigarettes.

1888 Kimball Champions, James "Tip" O'Neill

1888 Kimball Champions, Blondin

HISTORY

In much the same style as the Goodwin and Allen & Ginter sets of 1888, the W.S. Kimball & Company firm produced a 50-card set titled "Champions of Games and Sports." Only four of the cards are of baseball players; the rest represent a much wider range of athletes than either of the competitors. Some of the more interesting categories include "Checker Player, Colored Jockey, Six Days Roller Skater, Female Boxer of World, Hand Ball Player, and Cannon Ball Catcher!" Like the Goodwin and Allen & Ginter cards, the Kimballs feature a color lithograph portrait of the player and a small "action" scene. Like many tobacco issues of the day, the Kimball set offered an album to house the cards that could be obtained by mailing in coupons found in the cigarette packages. Collectors should be aware that the paper pages of the album contained the same lithographs as the cards themselves, and these paper lithographs could easily be cut out of the album and pasted onto a common nonbaseball card. This could turn a low-priced "swimmer" card into an expensive baseball card.

FOR

The quality of production is excellent. The small size of baseball players' subset make it attainable for collectors.

AGAINST

The high cost per card and the lack of big names among the baseball players make the subset less desirable.

NOTEWORTHY CARDS

Undoubtedly the best-known of the ballplayers in the series is James "Tip" O'Neill (misspelled "O'Neil" on the card). He was certainly baseball's champion when the cards were issued in 1888. In 1887, playing for the World Champion St. Louis Browns of the American Association, O'Neill led the league in hits, doubles, triples, home runs, home run percentage, runs, batting average, and slugging average. His .435 batting average of that year remains the major league baseball record. Actually, that .435 is a modern adjustment; walks and getting hit by a pitch were counted as hits in 1887, and O'Neill was originally credited with a .492 average.

OUR FAVORITE CARD

The most interesting cards in the set are not necessarily the baseball players. Consider, for instance, the card of the world champion tightrope walker, Blondin. Born Jean-Francois Gravelet in Paris in 1824, Blondin made his fortune crossing a 1,100-foot-long tightrope suspended 160 feet above Niagara Falls. After his first crossing in 1859, he repeated the feat many times, often with a new twist: blindfolded, tied in a sack, pushing a wheelbarrow, carrying a man on his back, on stilts, etc. The great acrobat performed until he was 72. He died in London a year later.

VALUE

EX-MT CONDITION: Complete set, $1,000; common card (baseball), $200; O'Neill, $225. 5-YEAR PROJECTION: Below average.

1888 (E-223) G&B CHEWING GUM

SPECIFICATIONS

SIZE: 1 × 2⅛″. FRONT: Sepia-tone photograph or line drawing. BACK: Blank. DISTRIBUTION: Nationally, in packages with chewing gum.

HISTORY

These small cards produced by the obscure G&B company are historically significant because they were the first widely distributed baseball cards to be inserted into a product other than cigarettes or chewing tobacco. A total of 56 different designs representing 46 players are currently known, and more will surely be discovered. While the words "AMERICAN LEAGUE" appear on some of the cards, the teams and players depicted are actually

1888 G&B Chewing Gum, Tom Burns

1888 G&B Chewing Gum, Cap Anson

members of the American Association. The cards with a "NATIONAL LEAGUE" designation sometimes have the words "CHEWING GUM" printed in the bottom panel. Little is known about this set, but the G&B set was probably linked in some way to the August Beck Yum Yum tobacco cards of the same year.

FOR

The set has the historical significance of being the first gum cards.

AGAINST

The lack of information about the set makes collecting these cards difficult.

NOTEWORTHY CARDS

The set includes the top players and Hall of Famers of the late 1880s.

VALUE

EX-MT CONDITION: Complete set, (value unknown); common card, drawing, $150; common card, photograph, $225; Hall of Famers, drawing, $325; Hall of Famers, photograph, $425; Anson, photograph, $500. 5-YEAR PROJECTION: Below average.

1888 YUM YUM

SPECIFICATIONS

SIZE: 1⅜ × 2¾″. FRONT: Sepia-tone photograph or line drawing. BACK: Blank. DISTRIBUTION: Nationally, in packages of tobacco.

1888 Yum Yum, Jimmy Ryan

1888 Yum Yum, Silver Flint

HISTORY

One of the rarest 19th century tobacco card issues, this 36-card set features 31 different players. The cards are found either as photographs or full-length line drawings that seem to have been rendered from contemporary Old Judge cards. All eight N.L. teams, along with the Brooklyn club of the American Association, are represented. Because the set was distributed by August Beck & Company of Chicago, there are six players (in seven poses) representing the White Stockings. All Chicago players are pictured in street clothes rather than in baseball uniforms.

FOR

The set features unique photos of well-known players of the day.

AGAINST

The extreme rarity and high price tag makes collecting a complete set almost impossible.

NOTEWORTHY CARDS

Hall of Famers in the set are Dan Brouthers, John Clarkson, Buck Ewing, Pud Galvin, Jim O'Rourke, and Mickey Welch.

OUR FAVORITE CARD

Pictured in his street clothes, Billy Sunday looks more like the famous evangelist he was to become than the ballplayer he was. Sunday was an N.L. outfielder for eight years with Chicago, Pittsburgh, and Philadelphia. He took a modest .248 lifetime batting average with him when he left the playing field for the pulpit in 1890. Sunday was personally responsible for "converting" a fair number of baseball players. Less well-known is that he took under his wing and supported financially many former ballplayers who were down on their luck.

VALUE

EX-MT CONDITION: Complete set, (value unknown); common card, drawing, $300; common card, photograph, $325; Hall of Famers, drawing, $375; Hall of Famers, photograph, $475. 5-YEAR PROJECTION: Below average.

1888 HESS CALIFORNIA LEAGUE

SPECIFICATIONS

SIZE: 1½ × 2⅞″. FRONT: Color lithograph or sepia-tone photograph. BACK: Blank. DISTRIBUTION: California, in packages of cigarettes.

1888 Hess California League

1888 Hess California League

HISTORY

In 1888 the S.F. Hess Tobacco company became the first of many baseball card producers to create a set for the California market. Far removed from major league baseball, which would not venture further west than St. Louis for another 67 years, the California League became the Golden State's substitute. Later, in 1903, the California League became the Pacific Coast League. For much of its history the league was on a virtual par with the major leagues back east. Until the Giants and the Dodgers moved west in 1958, there was continual agitation to designate the Pacific Coast League as a third major league. Certainly Hess' inclusion of California League player cards in its Creole brand cigarettes helped boost sales on the West Coast. Two separate issues of Creole cards exist: one pictures the players in sepia-tone photographs; the other depicts them in color lithographs—often rendered from the same photos. Both types are extremely rare. Just 40 lithograph cards and 16 photograph cards are known to exist. All four California League teams are represented: the Greenwood & Morans of Oakland, San Francisco's Haverlys and Pioneers, and the Stocktons.

FOR

The set has historical significance as the first of dozens of Pacific Coast League sets. The photograph cards give collectors an interesting glimpse of how the sport looked more than a century ago.

AGAINST

It is a minor league set with no big-name stars. The high cost per card and unknown set size make it too challenging for most collectors.

NOTEWORTHY CARDS

The Creole set contains a lithograph card of umpire J. Smith. It is one of very few baseball card sets to feature the umps.

VALUE

EX-MT CONDITION: Complete set, (value unknown); common card, $300–$350. 5-YEAR PROJECTION: Below average.

1887 (N-172) OLD JUDGE

SPECIFICATIONS

SIZE: 1½ × 2½". FRONT: Sepia-tone photograph. BACK: Blank. DISTRIBUTION: Nationally, in packages of cigarettes.

1887 Old Judge, Mike 'King' Kelly

1887 Old Judge, Connie Mack

HISTORY

Produced by Goodwin & Company, a large New York tobacco firm, to promote their "Old Judge" and "Gypsy Queen" cigarettes, this enormous set is probably the best-known baseball card issue of the 19th century. The cards are actual photographs of the players glued to a stiff cardboard backing. Thus, they served a dual purpose for Goodwin: besides being a sales incentive, the stiff cardboard made the package more rigid, protecting the cigarettes. The cards were released in six series between 1887 and 1890, and the entire set comprises at least 2,400 different cards (more are being discovered every year). The exact date of each series is unknown, and there were a great many printings and reprintings, making it extremely difficult to date the cards by year of issue. Many cards have a copyright date, but this refers only to the photograph, many of which were reused again and again in later series. All of the cards feature a sepia-tone player photo and have the words "Goodwin & Co., New York" (or "N.Y.") at the bottom of the card, along with the player's last name and team. The backs are blank. Most of the photos were shot in the Brooklyn studio of photographer Joseph Hall, who provided the photographs for many 19th-century baseball card sets. The old-fashioned backdrop cloths and props such as suspended baseballs give the cards a quaint charm. It is believed that three printings were made in 1887. Included were players from the eight National League teams and three American Association teams (St. Louis, Brooklyn, and New York). The best way to distinguish 1887 cards is to look for the words "OLD JUDGE Cigarettes," which appear in a band in an upper corner or across the top of the card. Most of the cards have a number, either penned on the negative in the upper-right corner or as part of the caption below the photo. The Old Judge set contains several distinct subsets that are often collected separately. One such subset known as the "script series" has the players' names handwritten instead of in type. Another subset is the "Spotted Ties." These cards are unnumbered and feature photos of the New York Metropolitans wearing dress shirts and sporting polka-dot ties. Another popular subset is a group of 13 "Browns Champions 1886" cards. These unnumbered cards feature the members of the A.A. pennant winning team wearing distinctive striped caps and laced-up jerseys. It is believed that the rare Gypsy Queen cards (only 100 different cards are known) were also issued in 1887. These cards are quite similar to the Old Judges (they have slightly different borders and advertising) but because of their rarity they are three times as valuable. There are many ways to collect Old Judge cards. Many hobbyists collect the subsets; others try to collect one card of each known player. It would be virtually impossible to collect every pose of each player.

FOR
This is an attractive, popular baseball card set. The subsets provide reasonable, though expensive, collecting goals. Because of their stiff cardboard backing, these cards have held up quite well.

AGAINST
The lack of a definitive checklist reduces the collectibility of the Old Judge series. New cards are being discovered every year, and a "complete" set is an impossible goal. There is surprisingly little collector interest in turn-of-the-century baseball cards. The cards often fade or turn pink from exposure to light.

NOTEWORTHY CARDS
There are ten different 1887 Old Judge cards depicting Mike "King" Kelly, the premier player of the day. He was purchased by Boston from Chicago in February 1887 for the unprecedented price of $10,000, and each card in the set carries the notation "$10,000 Kelly." Kelly appears in both a Chicago uniform and a Boston uniform. Also of special interest is the card of St. Louis Browns owner Chris Von Der Ahe in the Browns subset. He is credited with being the first person to serve hot dogs at a baseball game. Another noteworthy St. Louis Brown member is manager Charles Comiskey, the "Old Roman," whose name is immortalized in Chicago's A.L. ball park.

OUR FAVORITE CARD
Today when a rookie ballplayer makes it big in the major leagues, he is referred to as a "phenom." An Old Judge card partially explains why. One of the cards is of pitcher John Smith, also known as "Phenomenal Smith." When the 1887 Old Judges were issued, Smith had only been in the major leagues for three years and compiled a 4-9 record—hardly phenomenal. Playing in the majors through 1891, he retired with a mediocre record of 57-78. If the card was issued in late 1887, it is possible that the nickname referred to Smith's total of 55 pitching decisions that year; he had a 25-30 record with the Baltimore Orioles of the American Association. Wherever the name came from, it lives on today as part of "baseballese."

VALUE
EX-MT CONDITION: Complete set, (value unknown); common card, $30–$60; Von Der Ahe, Smith, $150; "Spotted Ties," $225; Kelly, Comiskey, $200; Cap Anson, Harry Wright, $300. 5-YEAR PROJECTION: Below average.

1887 (N-28) ALLEN & GINTER

SPECIFICATIONS
SIZE: 1½ × 2¾". FRONT: Color lithograph. BACK: Checklist. DISTRIBUTION: Nationally, in packages of cigarettes.

1887 Allen & Ginter, Cap Anson

1887 Allen & Ginter, Charles Comiskey

HISTORY
This set is believed to be the first nationally distributed baseball card issue. Entitled "The World's Champions," it included 50 subjects—10 of which were contemporary baseball heroes. As checklisted on the back of each card, the remaining 40 "Champions" represented the finest "Oarsmen, Wrestlers, Pugilists, Rifle Shooters, Billiard Players, and Pool Players" of the late 1880s. Noteworthy among the nonballplayers are boxer John L. Sullivan, and sharpshooters Annie Oakley and the "Hon. W.F. Cody," better known as Buffalo Bill. Collectors should note that the Jack Dempsey listed among the boxers is not the "Manassa Mauler." (The 1920s champion wasn't even born until 1895.) The ten baseball players in the set include eight National Leaguers and two American Association players. Both of the A.A. players (Charles Comiskey and Bob Caruthers) were from the 1886 World Champion St. Louis Browns. Collectors should be aware that paper "cards" can be found with no back printing; these have been cut from an advertising poster and are worth only a fraction as much as actual cards.

FOR

If a collector wants to own just one 19th century baseball card, it should be an Allen & Ginter. No card better captures—by means of the uniforms and poses depicted—the spirit of baseball in the 19th century. The color lithography on a borderless white background (state of the art in its day) adds to the flavor of the set. Though not cheap, the complete set of ten baseball players is a reasonable goal for collectors.

AGAINST

Modern collectors seem to have passed these cards by; there are few 19th century baseball card collectors.

NOTEWORTHY CARDS

Of the ten baseball players in the 1887 Allen & Ginter set, six have been enshrined in the Hall of Fame: Adrian "Cap" Anson, John Clarkson, Charles Comiskey, Timothy Keefe, Mike Kelly, and John "Monte" Ward. The other four, with the possible exception of Detroit backup catcher Charles W. Bennett, were also major stars of the day.

VALUE

EX-MT CONDITION: Complete set, $2,800; common baseball card, $125; Hall of Famers, $250–$300; Kelly, $350; Anson, $600. 5-YEAR PROJECTION: Below average.

1887 (N-284) BUCHNER GOLD COIN

SPECIFICATIONS

SIZE: 1¾ × 3″. FRONT: Color lithograph. BACK: Blue or black advertisement. DISTRIBUTION: Nationally, in packages of chewing tobacco.

HISTORY

With 143 cards depicting 118 different players, this is the second largest baseball card set of the 19th century. The cards were inserted in packages of D. Buchner & Company's Gold Coin chewing tobacco. The baseball players in the issue are really just a subset of a larger issue, which, according to the wording on the backs of some of the cards, featured "The portraits of all the leading base-ball players, police inspectors and captains, jockeys, actors & chiefs of fire departments in the country in full uniform and costume." The baseball players in the set include members of all eight N.L. teams, Brooklyn and St. Louis from the American Association, and Milwaukee and La Crosse of the Northwestern League. The issue is somewhat confusing in that it was apparently distributed in three different printings, possibly over the span of more than one year. The first printing contains the body of the set, 76 cards; a later issue features 14 members of the St. Louis Browns; while the third group of 53 cards features 27 new players and 26 "updated" players (there are a few position changes and minor changes in the captions). As with other sets that feature player variation cards, most collectors are content to acquire one card per player. There are many misspelled player names in the set, as well as errors in the player's position. The most notable feature of the set is the use of "generic" drawings: most "centre fielders" in the set share the same picture of a player standing with hands cupped and outstretched to catch a fly ball. The only difference between the various center fielders is the color of the uniform. A mustache will occasionally be added to a player's face for the sake of accuracy. This practice was especially prevalent in the 76 cards in the first printing. The 14 cards in the St. Louis subset all have unique poses (with the exception of Browns President Chris Von Der Ahe's card, which is based on a photograph), but the drawings on the cards bear no resemblance to the actual players. There are more new poses in the third 53-card subset, and a few of them seem to actually portray the named player.

1887 Buchner Gold Coin, James "Tip" O'Neill

FOR

The Buchner Gold Coin cards offer a nostalgic look at baseball in the days when it was played bare-handed—some of the players are even wearing spats!

AGAINST
The generic player lithographs are the biggest drawback of the Buchner set. Collectors want real pictures of the players on their cards.

NOTEWORTHY CARDS
The cards "picturing" Charles Comiskey, King Kelly, Chris Von Der Ahe, and Cap Anson carry the highest premium.

VALUE
EX-MT CONDITION: Complete set, $9,000; common card, $50–$60; Hall of Famers, $75–$125; Comiskey, Kelly, Von Der Ahe, $150–$175; Anson, $250. 5-YEAR PROJECTION: Below average.

1887 (N-690-2) FOUR BASE HITS

SPECIFICATIONS
SIZE: 2¼ × 3⅞". FRONT: Sepia-tone photograph. BACK: Blank. DISTRIBUTION: Nationally, in packages of cigars.

1887 Four Base Hits, Tom Daly (Billy Sunday)

HISTORY
Among the rarest and most desirable of 19th century baseball cards, these relatively large cards are also one of the most obscure. It is not yet known how many cards make up a complete set. Because of similarities in size, the double-entendre use of the word "bat" for a tobacco product, and a couple of shared photographs, many believe the cards were produced by the Charles Gross & Company firm, which also issued their Kalamazoo Bats cards that same year. However, other collectors attribute the issue to the firm of August Beck because of shared photos and similarities of design and typography between the Four Base Hits cards and Beck's 1888 Yum Yum cards. Regardless of who issued them, the Four Base Hits cards are scarce and valuable. Nine different player cards are currently known to exist.

FOR
The extreme rarity and the high production quality make these cards appealing. The cards are closer to today's standard size and modern collectors feel they are more like real baseball cards.

AGAINST
The high cost per card and the lack of information as to what constitutes a complete set make these cards less desirable.

NOTEWORTHY CARDS
One of the first major errors can be found in the Four Base Hits set. It is a type of error that continues to plague card companies today—the use of the wrong player's photo. Chicago White Stockings catcher Tom Daly's card (spelled "Daily" on the front) actually features teammate Billy Sunday.

VALUE
EX-MT CONDITION: Complete set, (value unknown); common card, $500; Mickey Welch, $750; Kelly, $800. 5-YEAR PROJECTION: Below average.

1887 (N-690) KALAMAZOO BATS

SPECIFICATIONS
SIZE: 2¼ × 4." FRONT: Sepia-tone photograph. BACK: Blank or with list of available premiums. DISTRIBUTION: Presumably New York and Philadelphia, in packages of cigarettes.

HISTORY
While most of the 50 known Kalamazoo Bats player cards (the brand name gets double mileage from an 1880s nickname for a particular style of hand-rolled cigarette) can positively be identified as an 1887 issue, there is some evidence that others were

1887 Kalamazoo Bats, Joe Mulvey

issued in 1886 and 1888. Elmer Foster and Larry Corcoran, pictured as New York Metropolitans (American Association), were only with the team in 1886. Lee Gibson, shown in the set as a Philadelphia Athletics (American Association) catcher, played in only one game in the major leagues in 1888. There is even one "mystery player" in the set, a fellow named Gallagher. Nobody by that name played for Philly, or anywhere else in the major leagues, at that time. There is a lot more to be learned about this rare and popular set issued by the tobacco firm of Charles Gross & Company. In addition to the New York Metropolitans and Philadelphia Athletics, their N.L. counterparts—the New York Giants and Philadelphia Phillies—are also included. The player photographs are interesting. The Mets and the Giants are featured in portrait shots with the Giants wearing uniforms, ties, and hats; the Mets are without hats. The two Philadelphia teams were photographed in full-length, posed-action shots. The Athletics were photographed in a studio with an artificial backdrop. The Phillies were photographed in their home stadium (the old Baker Bowl), a unique setting for 19th century baseball cards. Besides individual player cards, there are a number of multiplayer cards and a subset of six team photo cards—the two Philadelphia teams, Baltimore, Detroit, Boston, and Pittsburg (as it was spelled in those days). For collectors of extremely rare items, there are also cabinet-size cards, believed to be production proof cards, in player and team formats. Most of the card backs are blank, but some carry an offer to redeem cards for premiums. The offer ranges from a 25-cent "plain Meerschaum cigar tube" for 50 cards, to "A very fine silk umbrella, with gold mounted handle. Value five dollars." for 400 cards. These premium offers probably account for the scarcity of surviving cards.

FOR

The larger size of the cards makes them more attractive to modern-day collectors. The photos, especially those taken in the Philadelphia stadium, are significant baseball artifacts.

AGAINST

The high cost and great rarity of the cards, especially the team and cabinet issues, make it virtually impossible to assemble a complete set.

NOTEWORTHY CARDS

The Kalamazoo Bats is one of only two baseball card sets to feature Harry Wright, shown as the Phillies manager seated in the dugout. The British-born Wright was a true baseball pioneer. His career began as a catcher with the Boston Red Stockings of the National Association in 1871. When the National League was formed in 1876, Wright became manager of the Boston team and managed in the majors through 1893. Also worth mentioning is Harry Stow (who played under the name Harry Stovey but appears as Stow in the set), one of just three sets in which he is featured. If ever an old-time player was unjustly passed over by the Hall of Fame, it's Harry Stovey. In his 14-year major league career he compiled a .301 lifetime average and led the league twice in hits, six times in home runs, and once or twice in most other offensive categories. He even had a .404 batting average in 1884. Other Hall of Famers found in the Kalamazoo Bats set but seldom seen in other baseball card issues, are Athletics catcher Wilbert Robinson, who went on to fame as manager of the "Daffiness Boys" Brooklyn Dodgers of the 1920s; "Orator Jim" O'Rourke, the Giants third baseman whose 19-season career spanned the period 1876 to 1904 and included a lifetime .310 average; and Roger Connor, the Giants third baseman who compiled a .318 average over 18 seasons (1880 to 1897) in the majors and whose 233 triples are fifth on the all-time list.

VALUE

EX-MT CONDITION: Complete set, (value unknown); common card, $250; Connor, O'Rourke, Robinson, $400–$500; Wright, $700; team card, $750. 5-YEAR PROJECTION: Below average.

1887 (N-370) LONE JACK

SPECIFICATIONS

SIZE: 1½ × 2½". FRONT: Sepia-tone photograph. BACK: Blank. DISTRIBUTION: Regionally, in packages of cigarettes.

1887 Lone Jack, Bill Gleason

HISTORY

One of the scarcest 19th century baseball card sets, the 13-card Lone Jack issue was produced by the small tobacco company of the same name. The Lone Jack cards are one of many sets of the era that depict players from the 1886 World Champion St. Louis Browns. While many baseball fans and collectors do not trace the history of the World Series beyond the first meeting between N.L. and A.L. pennant winners in 1904, there was a championship series played between the winners of the National League and American Association as far back as 1884. The 1886 contest marked the first time an American Association team had defeated the National League (Chicago White Stockings) in the postseason series. The photos that appear on the Lone Jack cards are the same photos found on Old Judge's "Brown's Champions" cards of the same year. It is evident that Lone Jack acquired the photos from the Joseph Hall studio in Brooklyn. The words "LONE JACK" were written on the negative to the left of the player portrait, and appear in white on the cards; "Cigarettes" appears on the right. The player's last name (misspelled about 50 percent of the time) is in black lettering at the bottom edge of the picture. A common, but unproven, tale often heard in collector circles is that the unusual name of the issuer stems from the fact that the tobacco company was once won on a bluff in a high-stakes poker game—the gutsy gambler holding nothing in his hand but a "lone jack."

FOR

The cards are truly scarce, but not that expensive.

AGAINST

The collector can find a nearly identical card in the Old Judge series for a fraction of the price.

NOTEWORTHY CARDS

Hall of Famer Charlie Comiskey (spelled "Commisky") and Browns' president Chris Von Der Ahe are in the set.

VALUE

EX-MT CONDITION: Complete set, (value unknown); common card, $325–$350; Comiskey, $600. 5-YEAR PROJECTION: Below average.

HALL OF FAME

A popular baseball card collecting specialty is assembling a set of cards of members of the National Baseball Hall of Fame. While not all Hall of Famers were depicted on baseball cards contemporary with their playing careers, all have since been immortalized either on retrospective card issues or in the official postcards sold by the Hall of Fame. For the benefit of collectors, here is the list of players honored along with the year of their enshrinement and their principal playing position.

PLAYER	YEAR	POSITION
Henry Aaron	1982	OF
Grover Cleveland Alexander	1938	RHP
Walter Alston	1983	Manager
Cap Anson	1939	1B
Luis Aparicio	1984	SS
Luke Appling	1964	SS
Earl Averill	1975	OF
Frank "Home Run" Baker	1955	3B
Dave Bancroft	1971	SS
Ernie Banks	1977	1B
Edward Barrow	1953	Executive
Jake Beckley	1971	1B
James "Cool Papa" Bell	1974	OF/Negro Leagues
Johnny Bench	1989	C
Charles "Chief" Bender	1953	RHP
Yogi Berra	1972	C
Jim Bottomley	1974	1B
Lou Boudreau	1970	SS
Roger Bresnahan	1945	C
Lou Brock	1985	OF
Dennis "Dan" Brouthers	1945	1B
Mordecai Brown	1949	RHP
Morgan Bulkeley	1937	Executive
Jesse Burkett	1946	OF
Roy Campanella	1969	C
Max Carey	1961	OF
Alexander Cartwright	1938	Executive
Henry Chadwick	1938	Executive
Frank Chance	1946	1B
Albert "Happy" Chandler	1982	Executive
Oscar Charleston	1976	OF/Negro Leagues
Jack Chesbro	1946	RHP
Fred Clarke	1945	OF
John Clarkson	1963	RHP
Roberto Clemente	1973	OF
Ty Cobb	1936	OF
Mickey Cochrane	1947	C
Eddie Collins	1939	2B
Jimmy Collins	1945	3B
Earle Combs	1970	OF
Charles Comiskey	1939	Manager
John "Jocko" Conlan	1974	Umpire
Thomas Connolly	1953	Umpire
Roger Connor	1976	1B
Stan Coveleski	1969	RHP
Sam Crawford	1957	OF
Joe Cronin	1956	SS
William "Candy" Cummings	1939	RHP
Kiki Cuyler	1968	OF
Ray Dandridge	1987	3B/Negro Leagues
Dizzy Dean	1953	RHP
Ed Delahanty	1945	OF
Bill Dickey	1954	C
Martin DiHigo	1977	P/Negro Leagues
Joe DiMaggio	1955	OF
Bobby Doerr	1986	2B
Don Drysdale	1984	RHP
Hugh Duffy	1945	OF
William Evans	1973	Umpire/Executive
Johnny Evers	1939	2B
William "Buck" Ewing	1946	C
Red Faber	1964	RHP
Bob Feller	1962	RHP
Rick Ferrell	1984	C
Elmer Flick	1963	OF
Whitey Ford	1974	LHP
Rube Foster	1981	Executive
Jimmie Foxx	1951	1B
Ford C. Frick	1970	Executive
Frankie Frisch	1947	2B
James "Pud" Galvin	1965	RHP
Lou Gehrig	1939	1B
Charlie Gehringer	1949	2B
Bob Gibson	1981	RHP
Josh Gibson	1972	C/Negro Leagues
Warren Giles	1979	Executive
Vernon "Lefty" Gomez	1972	LHP
Goose Goslin	1968	OF
Hank Greenberg	1956	1B
Clark C. Griffith	1946	Manager
Burleigh Grimes	1964	RHP
Robert "Lefty" Grove	1947	LHP
Chick Hafey	1971	OF
Jesse "Pop" Haines	1970	RHP
Billy Hamilton	1961	OF
William Harridge	1972	Executive
Stanley "Bucky" Harris	1975	Manager
Gabby Hartnett	1955	C
Harry Heilmann	1952	OF
Billy Herman	1975	2B
Harry Hooper	1971	OF
Rogers Hornsby	1942	2B

Waite Hoyt	1969	RHP
Cal Hubbard	1976	Umpire
Carl Hubbell	1947	LHP
Miller Huggins	1964	Manager
Catfish Hunter	1987	RHP
Monte Irvin	1973	OF/Negro Leagues
Travis Jackson	1982	SS
Hughie Jennings	1945	SS
Byron "Ban" Johnson	1937	Executive
Walter Johnson	1936	RHP
William "Judy" Johnson	1975	3B/Negro Leagues
Adrian "Addie" Joss	1978	RHP
Al Kaline	1980	OF
Tim Keefe	1964	RHP
Willie Keeler	1939	OF
George Kell	1983	3B
Joe Kelley	1971	OF
George Kelly	1973	1B
Michael "King" Kelly	1945	C
Harmon Killebrew	1984	1B
Ralph Kiner	1975	OF
Chuck Klein	1980	OF
William Klem	1953	Umpire
Sandy Koufax	1972	LHP
Napoleon Lajoie	1937	2B
Judge Kenesaw Landis	1944	Executive
Bob Lemon	1976	RHP
Walter "Buck" Leonard	1972	1B/Negro Leagues
Fred Lindstrom	1976	3B
John "Pop" Lloyd	1977	SS/Negro Leagues
Ernie Lombardi	1986	C
Al Lopez	1977	Manager
Ted Lyons	1955	RHP
Connie Mack	1937	Manager
Mickey Mantle	1974	OF
Henry "Heinie" Manush	1964	OF
Walter "Rabbit" Maranville	1954	SS
Juan Marichal	1983	RHP
Rube Marquard	1971	LHP
Eddie Mathews	1978	3B
Christy Mathewson	1936	RHP
Willie Mays	1979	OF
Joe McCarthy	1957	Manager
Tommy McCarthy	1946	OF
Willie McCovey	1986	1B
Joe McGinnity	1946	RHP
John J. McGraw	1937	Manager
Bill McKechnie	1962	Manager
Leland "Larry" McPhail	1978	Executive
Joe Medwick	1968	OF
Johnny Mize	1981	1B
Stan Musial	1969	OF
Charles "Kid" Nichols	1949	RHP
Jim O'Rourke	1945	OF
Mel Ott	1951	OF
Satchel Paige	1971	RHP/Negro Leagues
Herb Pennock	1948	LHP
Eddie Plank	1946	LHP
Charles "Old Hoss" Radbourn	1939	RHP
Pee Wee Reese	1984	SS
Edgar "Sam" Rice	1963	OF
Branch Rickey	1967	Executive
Eppa Rixey	1963	LHP
Robin Roberts	1976	RHP
Brooks Robinson	1983	3B
Frank Robinson	1982	OF
Jackie Robinson	1962	2B
Wilbert Robinson	1945	Manager
Edd Roush	1962	OF
Charles "Red" Ruffing	1967	RHP
Amos Rusie	1977	RHP
Babe Ruth	1936	OF
Theodore "Ray" Schalk	1955	C
Red Schoendienst	1989	2B
Joe Sewell	1977	SS
Al Simmons	1953	OF
George Sisler	1939	1B
Enos Slaughter	1985	OF
Duke Snider	1980	OF
Warren Spahn	1973	LHP
Al Spalding	1939	RHP
Tris Speaker	1937	OF
Willie Stargell	1988	1B
Casey Stengel	1966	Manager
Bill Terry	1954	1B
Sam Thompson	1974	OF
Joe Tinker	1946	SS
Pie Traynor	1948	3B
Dazzy Vance	1955	RHP
Arky Vaughn	1985	SS
Rube Waddell	1946	LHP
Honus Wagner	1936	SS
Bobby Wallace	1953	SS
Ed Walsh	1946	RHP
Lloyd Waner	1967	OF
Paul Waner	1952	OF
Monte Ward	1964	SS
George M. Weiss	1971	Executive
Mickey Welch	1973	RHP
Zach Wheat	1959	OF
Hoyt Wilhelm	1985	RHP
Billy Williams	1987	OF
Ted Williams	1966	OF
Hack Wilson	1979	OF
George Wright	1937	Manager
Harry Wright	1953	Manager
Early Wynn	1972	RHP
Carl Yastrzemski	1989	OF
Tom Yawkey	1980	Executive
Cy Young	1937	RHP
Ross Youngs	1972	OF

INDEX